UNILATERAL SANCTIONS IN INTERNATIONAL LAW

This book explores whether there are any rules in international law applicable to unilateral sanctions and if so, what they are.

The first study of this kind devoted to the examination of unilateral sanctions, the book examines both the legality of unilateral sanctions and the limitations within which they should operate. In doing so, it includes an analysis of State practice, the provisions of various international legal instruments dealing with such sanctions and their impact on other areas of international law such as freedom of navigation, aviation and transit, and the principles of international trade, investment and regional economic integration.

Unilateral Sanctions in International Law

Edited by
Surya P Subedi

QC (Hon), OBE, DCL, DPhil (Oxford)

Professor of International Law, University of Leeds, United Kingdom

Member, Institut de Droit International

Barrister, Three Stone Chambers, Lincoln's Inn, London

Formerly UN Special Rapporteur for Human Rights in Cambodia

• HART •

OXFORD • LONDON • NEW YORK • NEW DELHI • SYDNEY

HART PUBLISHING

Bloomsbury Publishing Plc

Kemp House, Chawley Park, Cumnor Hill, Oxford, OX2 9PH, UK

1385 Broadway, New York, NY 10018, USA

29 Earlsfort Terrace, Dublin 2, Ireland

HART PUBLISHING, the Hart/Stag logo, BLOOMSBURY and the Diana logo are trademarks of Bloomsbury Publishing Plc

First published in Great Britain 2021

A catalogue record for this book is available from the British Library.

Library of Congress Cataloging-in-Publication data

Names: Subedi, Surya P., 1958- editor.

Title: Unilateral sanctions in international law / edited by Surya P Subedi, QC (Hon), OBE, DCL, DPhil (Oxford), Professor of International Law, University of Leeds, United Kingdom Member, Institut de Droit International Barrister, Three Stone Chambers, Lincoln's Inn, London Formerly UN Special Rapporteur for Human Rights in Cambodia.

Description: Oxford, UK ; New York, NY : Hart Publishing, an imprint of Bloomsbury Publishing, 2021. | Includes bibliographical references and index.

Identifiers: LCCN 2021011506 (print) | LCCN 2021011507 (ebook) | ISBN 9781509948383 (hardback) | ISBN 9781509948420 (paperback) | ISBN 9781509948406 (pdf) | ISBN 9781509948390 (Epub)

Subjects: LCSH: Sanctions (International law)

Classification: LCC KZ6373 .U53 2021 (print) | LCC KZ6373 (ebook) | DDC 341.5/82—dc23

LC record available at https://lccn.loc.gov/2021011506

LC ebook record available at https://lccn.loc.gov/2021011507

ISBN: HB: 978-1-50994-838-3
ePDF: 978-1-50994-840-6
ePub: 978-1-50994-839-0

Typeset by Compuscript Ltd, Shannon

PREFACE

In *Right V. Might*,[1] the celebrated international lawyer Professor Louis Henkin and his fellow lawyers examine the question as to whether international law permits the use of military force to promote democracy and human rights. This was published in 1989, in the wake of a decade of conflicts in several countries around the globe. Today, the ostensible use of force to promote democracy and human rights is no longer as common as it was during the old Cold War period. The use of unilateral economic or financial force or other forms of unilateral coercive measures, commonly known as 'sanctions', have now become the preferred foreign policy tool of many states, with the number of sanctions ever increasing in recent decades.

While the use of armed force as such is prohibited in international law and UN sanctions are permitted under the Charter of the UN, the lawfulness of unilateral sanctions, imposed by one state or a group of states on another state without the authorisation of the UN Security Council, has remained a contested issue in international law. Unilateral sanctions have been used at will by states, mainly by those with the ability to exert political, military and economic power, for a variety of objectives ranging from the pursuance of narrow national political or economic interests to the promotion of the global good such as the protection of human rights, the prevention of terrorism and the proliferation of nuclear weapons.

Unilateral sanctions are used supposedly as an 'emergency button' pushed to address promptly a major impending or ongoing crisis such as violations of human rights, the commission of crimes against humanity, or the commission of other internationally wrongful acts by a state, when no other alternative measures seem available or adequate to address the situation. However, due to the lack of clarity of the rules governing the conditions in which this 'emergency button' could be pushed, and of the rules governing the consequences of any improper use of it, unilateral sanctions currently mostly operate in a legal vacuum, and differing interpretations of different rules of international law have been invoked to justify both the support of and the opposition to such sanctions.

Throughout my career, I have been advocating fairness in international affairs, so the ambivalence of the lawfulness of unilateral sanctions in international law attracted my curiosity. In collaboration with a group of scholars from around the globe, I decided to conduct an inquiry into international law as it applies to the use of economic or financial force or unilateral sanctions. I also was intrigued and concerned by the violations

[1] Louis Henkin et al, *Right V. Might: International Law and the Use of Force* (Council on Foreign Relations Press, New York, 1989).

of human rights and of the principles of humanitarian law caused by the use of the very sanctions purportedly designed to protect human rights. Therefore, I conceived, designed and developed the project some three years ago with a view to publishing a book that provides a comprehensive treatment of the institution of unilateral sanctions, and contains an authoritative statement on the subject matter. This volume is the product of that endeavour. This project has been a labour of love for me for the past three years and I hope it fills an important gap in the international legal literature and adds clarity to the law applicable to unilateral sanctions.

This book is the first study of this kind devoted to the examination of unilateral sanctions. It investigates the status of unilateral sanctions, the use of economic or financial force and other forms of unilateral coercive measures in international law – reflecting the approach of the *Right V. Might* book in relation to the use of armed force some 30 years ago – as well as the issues raised by the use of unilateral sanctions are similar. It examines whether unilateral sanctions are lawful in international law and, even if they are, what the limitations are within which they should operate. This volume includes an analysis of state practice, the provisions of various international legal instruments dealing with such sanctions and the impact of them on other areas of international law such as freedom of navigation, aviation and transit, the enjoyment of human rights, the protection of the environment, and on the principles of international trade, investment and regional economic integration.

This study finds that unilateral sanctions, or economic or financial force, or other forms of unilateral coercive measures, as opposed to 'smart' or targeted sanctions of limited scope, would be unlawful, unless they met the procedural and substantive requirements stipulated in international law. It identifies and consolidates these requirements scattered across different areas of international law, including the additional rules of customary international law that have emerged out of the recent practice of states and that increase the limitations on the use of unilateral sanctions. This study establishes that there is now a positive prohibition in customary international law on uses of financial and economic force if such measures do not meet these requirements. It also concludes that those unilateral sanctions that undermine the sovereignty of third states are unlawful under international law.

I would like to thank each esteemed contributor to this volume, which is the work of scholars, both senior and early career, representing the global south and the global north, developed and developing countries, Eastern and Western countries. I thank them for their contribution and for putting up with my queries and comments at various stages of writing their chapters. I feel honoured and privileged to have had such a wonderful group of colleagues and friends working with me on this project. I would like to thank particularly Dr Ali Abusedra, a long-term friend and colleague of mine, for sharing his valuable ideas with me throughout the gestation period of this book.

I also wish to thank from the bottom of my heart Mevrouw Usha, who has been an amazing source of support in so many ways throughout the whole project. Furthermore, my sincere thanks are due to the ever so efficient team at Hart Publishing, Oxford, and especially Ms Roberta Bassi, for their enthusiasm in publishing this book and for their superb assistance throughout the production of this volume. Finally, my thanks also go to the different external reviewers of the manuscript for their helpful comments at various stages of progress of this book.

Surya P Subedi
London
30 November 2020

TABLE OF CONTENTS

BIOGRAPHICAL NOTES OF CONTRIBUTORS

Ali Abusedra

Ali Abusedra completed his LLM in International Law and PhD in International Economic Law at the University of Hull, and is currently working as a Visiting Research Fellow at Hull. He has provided legal services to governments in many countries, including Dubai, Abu Dhabi, Ajman, and Qatar. He was twice appointed chairman of the Libyan Investment Authority, but returned to law practice on both occasions. He has provided consultancy services to states on dispute before the International Court of Justice and various international arbitration tribunals.

Louisa Ashley

Louisa Ashley is Head of Law (Postgraduate) at Leeds Law School, Leeds Beckett University, with a professional background in legal practice and devised theatre. Louisa has published on topics related to international human rights, legal pluralism and equality law in academic journals and edited book collections. She is a solicitor of the Supreme Court of England and Wales (non-practising) who trained and then practised as an employment lawyer at a large corporate law firm in Leeds. Before becoming a lawyer, she was one of the founding members of UK-based award-winning Unlimited Theatre. She is a qualified coach and mentor and is also a poet who enjoys performing her poetry at festivals, events and open mic nights.

Abhinayan Basu Bal

Abhinayan Basu Bal is a Senior Lecturer at the School of Business, Economics and Law in Gothenburg, Sweden. He lectures and researches in commercial and maritime laws. His research endeavours have been funded by the European Union, various national governments and industry associations. Since 2013, he is the accredited Swedish observer to the United Nations Commission on International Trade Law, Working Group IV on Electronic Commerce. He has published monographs, chapters in books, and articles in peer-reviewed journals.

Nicolette Butler

Nicolette Butler is a Senior Lecturer at the University of Manchester, England. She has published various works within the field of international economic law and won a number of grants to carry out associated research. She is the Principal Investigator on an ESRC Impact Accelerator project, which examines the relationship between investment and human rights. She is also a Scientific Advisor on matters relating to trade/investment and health for a Brussels-based NGO. She holds an LLM and PhD from the University of Leeds. Prior to joining the University of Manchester in 2013, she taught at the Universities of Leeds and Sunderland.

Joy Gordon

Joy Gordon is the Ignacio Ellacuría, SJ Professor of Social Ethics at Loyola University Chicago, where she holds a joint appointment in the Philosophy Department and the School of Law. She works in the fields of human rights, international law and ethical issues in international relations, with a focus on legal and ethical aspects of economic sanctions. Her works include *Invisible War: The United States and the Iraq Sanctions* (Harvard University Press, 2010). She has also published articles in *Ethics and International Affairs*, *Georgetown Journal of International Law*, *Le Monde Diplomatique*, *Philosophy and Public Policy Quarterly*, *Yale Journal of International Affairs*, *Global Governance*, *Harvard International Law Journal*, *Philosophy and Social Criticism*, *Foreign Policy*, *Chicago Journal of International Law*, and *Yale Human Rights and Development Law Journal*.

Nick Grief

Nick Grief is Emeritus Professor of Law at the University of Kent and practises at the Bar from Doughty Street Chambers, London, where he is an Associate Tenant. Probably best known for his work on the illegality of nuclear weapons, he also has a keen interest in air and space law and its intersection with human rights. In 2018 he cofounded the Airspace Tribunal to examine the case for and against a proposed new human right to live without physical or psychological threat from above.

Md Toriqul Islam

Md Toriqul Islam is Assistant Professor at the Department of Law and Justice of Bangladesh University of Business and Technology. He has been an enlisted lawyer at Dhaka Judge Court since 2008. The main areas of his research are public international law, international humanitarian law, privacy and data protection law, law and technology, constitutional law and human rights law. He has published articles in various national and international law journals. He is currently undertaking research for a PhD at the Faculty of Law, University of Malaya, Malaysia.

Abu Bakar Munir

Abu Bakar Munir is an expert and consultant on cyber law and data protection law. He was previously a Professor of Law at the Faculty of Law, University of Malaya, and is currently an Adjunct Professor of Law at the Faculty of Law, University of Indonesia, a Research Consultant at Eversheds Harry Elias LLP, and an Adviser and Expert Council Member of the Pandya Astagina Institute. He is also the Legal Adviser and Data Protection Consultant to Straits Interactive Private Ltd, Senior Adviser to Schinder Law Firm, and a member of the Asian Privacy Scholars Network (APSN), Australia. He is the author of several books, including *Cyberlaw: Policies and Challenges* (1999), *Privacy and Data Protection* (2002) and *Information and Communication Technology Law: State, Internet and Information* (2010).

Amrisha Pandey

Amrisha Pandey is enrolled as a lawyer in the Indian Bar Council with a lifetime membership. She completed her graduation BA/LLB (Hons) in 2011 from India. She holds an LLM in International Environmental Law (2012) from the University of Nottingham and a PhD from the University of Leeds; the topic of her PhD research was 'Regulation of Freshwater and the Access to Right to Water in India' (March 2015 – February 2019). She is currently working with the Government of India on an environmental conservation project and has published articles on international environmental law and watercourses law in leading international law journals.

Trisha Rajput

Trisha Rajput is an Assistant Professor at the School of Business, Economics and Law, University of Gothenburg where she lectures to both law and management students on international trade law. Her work on single window interoperability has been presented at United Nations Commission on International Trade Law in Vienna. Funding from the EU, national governments and industry bodies has supported some of her research endeavours. During the last two years, she worked on a cross-disciplinary project on supply chain finance funded by Swedish innovation agency Vinnova. She holds a doctorate in law and a master's degree in European and International Business Law from the University of Leeds. She took her bachelor's degree in Law in India and was admitted to the Bar Council of India in 2005.

Surya P Subedi

Surya P Subedi holds a DPhil and DCL from the University of Oxford. He is Professor of International Law at the University of Leeds and barrister at Three Stone Chambers, Lincoln's Inn, London. He was made a QC (Hon) in 2017. He was elected to the *Institut de Droit International* in 2011. He has worked at a senior level within the UN system of human rights and has advised governments in several countries on international legal matters. He also has acted as a counsel in cases before the International Court of Justice and the International Centre for Settlement of Investment Disputes. He has published extensively in all major areas of international law, has edited a good number of scholarly books and peer-reviewed journals throughout his academic career spanning some 30 years.

James Watson

James Watson works in Brussels as the Secretary General of Eurogas, the association representing the European gas sector. Prior to this, he was the Chief Executive Officer of Solar Power Europe, the European solar industry association. He has worked in Brussels for over 12 years, specialising in energy, environment and trade policy. Prior to that, he worked for the Commonwealth Secretariat on a European Commission project on trade and sustainable development based in Ethiopia. He holds a PhD in International Trade and Environmental Law from the University of Leeds and is currently a Visiting Professor at the Vrije Universiteit Brussel. He has published contributions to, and a book on, international environmental law, energy, international trade law and international trade negotiations.

Nigel D White

Nigel D White is Professor of Public International Law at the University of Nottingham, formerly Professor of International Law at the University of Sheffield. He is sole author of *The United Nations and the Maintenance of International Peace and Security* (1990), *Keeping the Peace* (1997), *The UN System: Toward International Justice* (2002), *The Law of International Organisations*, 3rd edn (2017), *Democracy Goes to War* (2009) and *The Cuban Embargo Under International Law* (2015). He is co-author and co-editor of a number of other books in the area of international law and has published over 100 essays and articles in the area. He has been a visiting Professor at the Universities of Utrecht, Uppsala, the Australian National University and Kobe University. He has been a co-editor of the *Journal of Conflict and Security Law* (Oxford University Press) since its foundation in 1995.

Introduction

SURYA P SUBEDI

The use of unilateral economic or financial force or other forms of unilateral coercive measures, commonly known as sanctions, have become the preferred foreign policy tool of many states, with an ever-increasing number of sanctions in recent decades. While the use of armed force as such is prohibited in international law, and UN sanctions are permitted under the Charter of the UN, the lawfulness of unilateral sanctions, imposed by one state (or a group of states) on another state without the authorisation of the UN Security Council, has remained a contested issue in international law.

In this study, unilateral sanctions are defined as measures that fall short of the use of force but are more serious than retorsive measures and are above and beyond the scope of countermeasures. Generally speaking, unilateral sanctions are high-intensity coercive economic, financial or other kind of measures taken against a target state to express displeasure of its conduct in a particular area, or to deter it from committing an internationally wrongful act by removing certain economic facilities or instruments from it, or to retaliate against a prior breach of international law committed by it.

Unilateral sanctions are designed to limit or deprive altogether the economic and financial freedom of the target state through various economic or financial instruments. They could also be designed to restrict the freedom of navigation, aviation and transit, the right to communications, etc. This study is designed to examine the status in international law of these kinds of unilateral sanctions taken by states without the authorisation of the UN Security Council. It should be stated at the outset that there is a thin line between high-intensity unilateral sanctions and low-intensity measures of retorsive character, including those measures commonly known as 'smart' or targeted sanctions. It depends partly on the intention of the state imposing sanctions, the gravity of the measures taken and their impact on the target state and its people. A case-by-case analysis is required to draw a clear distinction between high-intensity unilateral sanctions and low-intensity sanctions of retorsive character, since there is no judicial or other international mechanism to adjudicate upon the matter. This means that the state or group of states imposing unilateral sanctions of dubious character against another state are presupposing a prior determination that the alleged act in question by the target state was illegal. This is not a satisfactory state of affairs.

In defining the term 'unilateral sanctions' many scholars have used the definition of economic sanctions provided by Lowenfeld since most of the unilateral sanctions are economic sanctions:

> '[M]easures of an economic – as contrasted with diplomatic or military – character taken by states to express disapproval of the acts of the target state or to induce that state to change some policy or practice or even its governmental structure'.[1]

Such sanctions generally include the following measures: economic and financial sanctions, asset freezes, trade sanctions, arms embargoes, commodity interdictions, diplomatic sanctions, and travel bans, etc.[2] However, the term 'unilateral sanctions' connotes measures broader than merely economic measures and could include non-economic measures too. The UN Special Rapporteur on the Negative Impact of the Unilateral Coercive Measures on the Enjoyment of Human Rights, Jazairy, notes

> the accelerating expansion of new and different forms, types and terms used to identify unilateral means of pressure (unilateral coercive measures, sanctions, unilateral sanctions, bilateral sanctions, international sanctions, autonomous sanctions, sectoral or territorial sanctions, etc.), and the need to identify the actors involved (targeting and targeted States, source States, etc.).[3]

Therefore, the term 'unilateral sanctions' could be defined as follows: Measures of exercising pressures short of the threat or use of armed force directed against a target state or entity, which are taken by an individual state or a group of states, measures which are not authorised by the United Nations and which seek to limit or deprive altogether the freedom that other states enjoy as sovereign states under international law. Alongside economic and financial sanctions, restrictions on the freedom of navigation, aviation and transit and on the right to communications would also come within the ambit of unilateral sanctions.

International law includes a set of rules that apply to situations where a state breaches a rule of international law. In serious cases of commission of an internationally wrongful act, or of an act that constitutes a threat or breach of international peace and security, the UN Security Council is empowered to take forcible and non-forcible measures against the wrongdoing state. In cases of an armed attack occurring against a state, that state can use force in self-defence. In less serious cases of commission of internationally wrongful acts, individual states or a group of states are entitled to resort to countermeasures themselves. This legal course of action is regulated by general international law as outlined in international legal instruments such as the Draft Articles on State Responsibility adopted by the International Law Commission (ILC). In cases of minor breaches of international law or misdemeanours, states can take retorsive measures, including 'smart' or targeted sanctions, which would be permissible under international law as an attribute to state sovereignty. Generally speaking, they are low-intensity measures taken by one state or by a group of states against another state, or a private

[1] AF Lowenfeld, *International Economic Law* (Oxford University Press, 2002) 698.

[2] R Gordon, M Smyth and T Cornell, *Sanctions Law* (Hart Publishing, 2019) 17–20.

[3] OHCHR, 'Call for submissions: UCM-Study on the notion, characteristics, legal status and targets of unilateral sanctions', available at www.ohchr.org/EN/Issues/UCM/Pages/Call-for-submissions-UCM-Study.aspx.

organisation, or an individual of another country, for an alleged violation of international law, including human rights, or for supporting or financing or abetting terrorism, or for other delinquent behaviour against the established norms of international law, international relations or diplomacy. Such sanctions range from tit-for-tat measures to cyber sanctions, diplomatic boycott, and severance of diplomatic or consular relations.

However, there is no clear body of law that regulates unilateral sanctions. Unilateral sanctions have been used at will by states, mainly by those with the ability to exert political, military and economic power, for a variety of objectives ranging from the pursuance of narrow national political or economic interests to the promotion of the global good such as the protection of human rights and the prevention of terrorism and proliferation of nuclear weapons. Unilateral sanctions are used supposedly as an 'emergency button' pushed to address promptly a major impending or ongoing crisis such as violations of human rights, or the commission of crimes against humanity, or the commission of other internationally wrongful acts by a state, when no other alternative measures seem available or adequate to address the situation. However, due to the lack of clarity of the rules governing the conditions in which this emergency button could be pushed and of the rules governing the consequences of any improper use of it, unilateral sanctions currently mostly operate in a legal vacuum, and differing interpretations of different rules of international law have been invoked to justify both the support of and the opposition to such sanctions.

Although the ILC, through its Draft Articles on State Responsibility,[4] recommends some rules on the employment and scope of non-forcible countermeasures, no clear rules have been codified or developed to regulate unilateral sanctions. The general consensus is that rules to this effect are developing through state practice, but there is no unanimity on the content of such rules. While some states and scholars regard non-retorsive unilateral sanctions to be lawful, others regard them to be unlawful. Those states that have sought to justify the lawfulness of unilateral sanctions have done so by treating them as countermeasures permitted under international law, or as part of the exercise of their rights as sovereign states.

However, there are competing, equally powerful rules of international law such as those relating to the principle of non-intervention, the right of self-determination of states, the protection of human rights in the target state as well as the rules on proportionality and necessity, that impose limitations on the rights of states to resort to such sanctions. For this reason, the legality of unilateral sanctions has been contested both in scholarly literature and in state practice and has been denounced in the resolutions of various international organisations, including the UN General Assembly and the Human Rights Council. Furthermore, the difficulty also lies in drawing a line between permissible low-intensity unilateral sanctions of limited scope and more comprehensive and high-intensity unilateral sanctions. There is no defined threshold to distinguish the two. It depends on a case-by-case analysis of each and every kind of sanction and their impact on the target state.

Generally speaking, unilateral sanctions should have no place in the realm of the rules-based intentional order in this increasingly globalised and interdependent

[4] ILC, 'Draft Articles on Responsibility of States for Internationally Wrongful Acts, with commentaries 2001' 128, available at legal.un.org/ilc/texts/instruments/english/commentaries/9_6_2001.pdf.

world, where states are bound by a network of treaties designed to promote peaceful resolution of disputes and cooperation and coexistence among states. A plethora of treaties relating to international trade, commerce, investment, economic cooperation, regional economic integration and the protection of human rights bring states together as members of the international community. The Charter of the UN requires states to settle their disputes thorough peaceful means and the Security Council has the powers to take any forcible and non-forcible measures against a state which poses a threat to or is in breach of international peace and security. Still, unilateral sanctions exist as extraordinary measures taken in response to extraordinary events. They have been described by some commentators as 'an option for when words aren't good enough, but war is too much'.[5]

In the absence of rules regulating unilateral sanctions, states and scholars have sought support for such sanctions either in the concept of countermeasures in international law or on the principle of sovereignty of states. Unilateral sanctions are currently primed to fulfil the purpose of emergency buttons to alert to a major impending or ongoing crisis such as massive violations of human rights or the commission of crimes against humanity or the commission of a major internationally wrongful act by a state, and to set in place emergency measures to alleviate the crises, when no other alternative measures are available or adequate to address the situation. Yet in international law there is a lack of clarity of the rules governing the legal conditions which call forth the implementation of unilateral sanctions, and of the rules governing the legal consequences of any improper use of unilateral sanctions.

Even when unilateral sanctions are claimed to be permissible measures as countermeasures, the two questions arising are to what extent countermeasures themselves are permissible under contemporary international law, and whether all unilateral sanctions can be classified as countermeasures. The opinion is divided on the rules on countermeasures themselves and there is no legally binding instrument defining the nature and scope of countermeasures either. International courts and tribunals, as well as most scholars, seem to regard the recommendations of the rules on countermeasures, developed by the ILC through its Draft Articles on State Responsibility and adopted in 2001, as authoritative statement of the law on countermeasures.

More recent state practice, however, appears to differ on many counts from the rules recommended by the Commission by putting further limitations on the rights of states to resort to countermeasures against an internationally wrongful act. Thus, there is room to question the continuous validity of some of the recommendations of the ILC made in 2001, which are based on the state practice up until that time, and so may no longer be entirely applicable to a world which is vastly different, due not only to the consequences of 9/11, but also to the enormous political and economic changes that have taken place since the turn of the millennium.

With regard to the invocation of the principle of state sovereignty, human rights and the protection of the integrity of the international legal order to justify unilateral economic sanctions, it should be borne in mind that there are other equally powerful competing rules of international law such as those relating to the principle of non-intervention, the

[5] 'Sanctions: Financial Carpet-bombing' *The Economist*, 30 November 2019, 42.

right of self-determination of states, the protection of human rights in the target state, as well as the rules on proportionality and necessity that impose limitations on the sovereign rights of states to resort to unilateral sanctions. The corollary of state sovereignty is that if something is not prohibited by international law it is permissible, as sovereign states retain the power to respond to a wrongful act carried out by another state.

However, the tendency of some powerful states has been to act as self-appointed police of the world and impose unilateral sanctions on other states, but in doing so they themselves often end up violating the very norms, including human rights, which they profess to uphold. Currently, the recourse to sanctions is left largely to the mercy of political considerations and power games. This is because these kinds of sanctions are currently operating in a legal vacuum since there is no international treaty governing them. During his speech at the UN General Assembly in September 2019, the then Malaysian Prime Minister, Dr Mahathir Mohamad, made the following stark statement: 'We are also seeing sanctions being applied to countries. We do not know under what laws sanctions are applied ... If we want to have sanctions, let us have a law to govern them'.[6] Therefore, this study is an attempt to bring clarity to the law and suggest measures to fill the gap in the law on the subject matter.

I. Challenges Posed to the International Legal Order by Unilateral Sanctions

While unilateral sanctions have become a frequently used foreign policy tool, the absence of clarity in the law governing unilateral sanctions and their extraterritorial reach pose a challenge to the aim of developing and maintaining a rules-based international legal order. Most unilateral sanctions are imposed as a reaction to an alleged illegal act, which means that the state or group of states imposing sanctions against another state are taking it upon themselves to judge the alleged act as illegal. According to what legal body is this judgement reached? What are the consequences if that presupposition turns out to be wrong? Thus, in imposing unilateral sanctions against another state the targeting states are themselves risking committing an international wrongful act against the target state. Some unilateral economic and financial sanctions are imposed as anticipatory measures to deter states from violating norms such as the nuclear non-proliferation regime, or from supporting or financing terrorism. Is there a provision in international law for the legality of such anticipatory economic and financial sanctions?

II. Increase in the Use of Unilateral Sanctions

Unilateral sanctions are expected to be employed only in exceptional circumstances, but their use has become very frequent in recent years. A survey by the UN demonstrated that a total of 38 states and territories had been subjected to some degree of

[6] 'Dr M's full speech text at the 74th UNGA' *New Strait Times*, 28 September 2019, available at www.nst.com.my/news/nation/2019/09/525269/dr-ms-full-speech-text-74th-unga.

unilateral sanctions during the period 2000–15.[7] This increase is partly caused by the inability of the UN Security Council to take decisions on different cases of crisis around the globe, which in turn is caused by the veto power wielded by some of the five permanent members of the Council. Jazairy explains that when the Council was unable to take such measures against the wrongdoer, or when its procedures were too lengthy to do so, states decided to consider other options at their disposal and often opted for unilateral coercive measures to address the situation. Thus, it was to be expected that unilateral coercive economic measures would be adopted to remedy such deficiencies.[8] Among the more recent examples of unilateral sanctions are the ones against Iran and Qatar: Iran has been subjected to US economic sanctions[9] and Qatar[10] to unilateral sanctions led by a group of Arab countries.

III. Changing Character of Unilateral Sanctions

The legality of unilateral sanctions has traditionally been considered in the context of First World and Second World, East and West relations, North and South relations, or developed and developing countries.[11] Now, some developing countries have also started to resort to unilateral sanctions against one another. Two examples are the UAE–Saudi Arabia-led unilateral sanctions against the State of Qatar in 2017, and the sanctions imposed by the League of Arab States against Syria in an unprecedented move by the League against an Arab state.[12] Therefore, this study seeks to examine the lawfulness of unilateral sanctions with reference not only to the sanctions imposed by developed states on developing states, but also with reference to new cases of sanctions imposed by a developing country or a group of developing countries against another developing country.

[7] UN Doc A/70/152 of 16 July 2015, 4–5.

[8] UN Doc A/HRC/30/45, of 10 August 2015, para 59.

[9] Iran instituted proceedings at the International Court of Justice on 16 July 2018 under a bilateral treaty against the US challenging its unilateral sanctions against Iran: 'Iran institutes proceedings against the United States with regard to a dispute concerning alleged violations of the Treaty of Amity, Economic Relations, and Consular Rights between Iran and the United States, and requests the Court to indicate provisional measures', press release of the ICJ: No 2018/34 of 17 July 2018. See also J Klingler, B Barnes and T Sepehri Far, 'Is the U.S. in Breach of the ICC's Provisional Measures Order in Alleged Violations of the 1965 Treaty of Amity' (2020) 24 *ASIL Insights*.

[10] The State of Qatar instituted proceedings against the United Arab Emirates (UAE) at the ICJ with regard to alleged violations of the International Convention on the Elimination of All Forms of Racial Discrimination (CERD) of 21 December 1965. The alleged violations were part of a package of economic and other measures taken by the UAE together with Bahrain, Egypt and Saudi Arabia against Qatar on 5 June 2017. Qatar complained that some of these measures taken by the UAE against Qatar and the Qatari people violated UAE's obligations under the CERD. Press Release of the ICJ: No 2018/26 of 11 June 2018.

[11] Report of the UN Secretary-General, 'Unilateral economic measures as a means of political and economic coercion against developing countries', UN Docs A/70/152 of 16 July 2015 and A/68/218 of 29 July 2013.

[12] Report of the Secretary-General, 'Unilateral economic sanctions as a means of political and economic coercion against developing countries', UN Doc A/72/307 of 9 August 2017, 20–21.

IV. Legal Response to Unilateral Sanctions

Both Iran and Qatar have turned to the International Court of Justice to challenge some of the unilateral economic measures taken against them.[13] Qatar has also turned to the Dispute Settlement Body of the WTO for support against the measures taken by the UAE during the economic blockade of Qatar.[14] Even a private entity, whether natural or juridical, within a country affected by unlawful unilateral sanctions can take legal action under some bilateral or regional investment treaties against the targeting state and seek compensation. Qatar Airways chose this strategy by instituting proceedings under various investment treaties against[15] four Arab States – Bahrain, Egypt, Saudi Arabia and the UAE – which imposed coercive economic measures against Qatar in June 2017.

Owing to the proliferation of unilateral sanctions and the legal challenges mounted against such sanctions, there is an increasing amount of interest in the legal status of sanctions amongst policy and decision-makers, judges, lawyers, diplomats and scholars of both international law and international relations, which further necessitates the need to bring clarity to this area. However, no comprehensive study has yet been carried out that investigates the legality and ramifications of unilateral sanctions in international law and the remedies available to states subjected to illegal economic sanctions.[16]

V. The Rationale for this Study

Although states have long been resorting to unilateral sanctions to further their political and economic objectives, no international treaty on the regulation of such sanctions is in existence and therefore their legality in customary international law is contested. Cameron states that the legal regulation of the use of sanctions is 'one of the most unclear areas of international law'.[17] This is true to an even greater degree for unilateral sanctions. White and Abass also state that the issue of enforcement of international obligations 'by means of non-forcible measures is one of the least developed areas of international law'.[18]

[13] See for the ramifications of the US sanctions on Iran, MJ Menkes, 'The Legality of US Investment Sanctions against Iran before the ICJ: A Watershed Moment for the Essential Security Interests and Necessity Exceptions' (2018) 56 *The Canadian Yearbook of International Law*.

[14] See for a brief account of the cases referred to various international dispute settlement mechanisms, CD Gaver, 'Lingering Gulf Dispute Gives Rise to Multi-Forum Legal Proceedings' (2020) 24 *ASIL Insight*.

[15] V Djanic, 'Qatar Airways Lodges Treaty-based Arbitration Cases against Four Middle Eastern Countries' *Investment Arbitration Reporter*, 22 July 2020, available at www.iareporter.com/articles/qatar-airways-lodges-treaty-based-arbitration-cases-against-four-middle-eastern-states. See also 'Qatar Airways seeks $5bn in compensation' *Gulf Times*, 23 July 2020, 1.

[16] A Tzanakopoulos, 'State reactions to illegal sanctions' in M Happold and P Eden (eds), *Economic Sanctions and International Law* (Hart Publishing, 2016) 67–87.

[17] CE Cameron, 'Developing a standard for politically related state economic sanction' (1991) 13 *Michigan Journal of International Law* 218, 253.

[18] ND White and A Abass, 'Countermeasures and Sanctions' in MD Evans (ed), *International Law*, 5th edn (Oxford University Press, 2018) 521, 521.

The legality of sanctions is indeed a complex topic: 'a topic where law meets politics, while touching upon almost all areas of the law: public international law, private international law, even private law and public law,'[19] say Forlati and Sicilianos. It is not only a topic in which law meets politics or economics, but an area in which various competing principles of international law collide. For instance, every state has the right to take measures in exercise of its sovereign rights to protect its legitimate interests against the commission of an internationally wrongful act by another state, but if the measures it takes exceed the limits of the law, such measures themselves constitute a violation of other equally important principles of international law, such as the prohibition on the interference in the affairs of other states. States can take certain measures against another state's violations of human rights, but such measures must not result inadvertently in the violations of human rights in the target country. Kelsen states that a sanction is supposed to be used as a reaction to illegality,[20] but states have been using unilateral sanctions for all sorts of political and economic purposes for a long time, and some of these sanctions have been anticipatory sanctions designed to deter the target state from violating international norms.

There is neither clarity in the law on unilateral sanctions nor a compulsory legal mechanism to settle disputes associated with such sanctions. If a state regards the unilateral sanctions imposed on it as unlawful, it would be entitled to resort to its own retaliatory unilateral sanctions against the state which had targeted it with sanctions.[21] The Russian Federation, for example, resorted to retaliatory unilateral sanctions against those Western countries who had imposed unilateral sanctions on it.

The precise legal regulation of unilateral sanctions is said to be subject to development through state practice, but state practice and the opinion of publicists remain divided on the legality of such sanctions and the framework within which they should operate. To ascertain the legality of particular unilateral sanctions, a case-by-case analysis of each would be required. Bowett wrote in 1972 that 'The inevitable conclusion is that it will require a great deal of practice, of "case law", to give the concept of illegal economic coercion substance and definition'.[22] He thus hoped that 'more concrete norms governing the limits of permissible economic coercion will emerge in the same way as the norm or norms on military coercion'.[23] However, the question remains whether we now have reached the stage where state practice or case law can provide substance and definition to the concept of illegal coercion.

[19] L Picchio Forlati and L-A Sicilianos, *Economic Sanctions in International Law* (Brill/Nijhoff, 2004) xxxv.

[20] H Kelsen, *The Law of the United Nations: A Critical Analysis of its Fundamental Problems* (Praeger, 1950) 706.

[21] See Art 42 of the ILC's Draft Articles on State Responsibility. It reads as follows: 'Article 42. Invocation of responsibility by an injured State: A State is entitled as an injured State to invoke the responsibility of another State if the obligation breached is owed to: (a) that State individually; or (b) a group of States including that State, or the international community as a whole, and the breach of the obligation: (i) specially affects that State; or (ii) is of such a character as radically to change the position of all the other States to which the obligation is owed with respect to the further performance of the obligation.' See ILC, 'Draft articles on Responsibility of States for Internationally Wrongful Acts, with commentaries 2001, 112, available at legal.un.org/ilc/texts/instruments/english/commentaries/9_6_2001.pdf.

[22] DW Bowett, 'Economic Coercion and Reprisals by States' (1972) 18 *Virginia Journal of International Law* 1, 4.

[23] ibid, 12.

Therefore, this study is designed to identify the gaps that exist in the law and bring clarity to the law by means of an analysis of relevant treaties, state practice, the decisions of international courts and tribunals, and the resolutions of international organisations, including the UN General Assembly and the Human Rights Council. The claim of the legality of unilateral or autonomous sanctions is mainly based on the notion of countermeasures in international law. Therefore, this study will examine the status of countermeasures in international law to the extent relevant to unilateral sanctions, relying on the work of the ILC on State Responsibility and its Draft Articles on the Responsibility of States for Internationally Wrongful Acts.[24]

VI. Scope of this Study

The main question that this study addresses is whether unilateral sanctions are lawful in international law and, if they are lawful, within which limitations they must operate. In doing so, this study examines an assortment of hard and soft law principles that are pivotal in determining the status of sanctions in international law. It scrutinises state practice to ascertain the legality or illegality of unilateral sanctions. The objective is to enquire whether the state practice on unilateral sanctions has crystallised into rules of customary international law and if so, what is the resulting law on unilateral sanctions.

This study does not cover political aggression such as propaganda against the target state. Although unilateral sanctions are often motivated by political objectives, and any study on sanctions could be considered to cover 'political and economic sanctions', as both are often intertwined, this study does not cover political or diplomatic sanctions. Political sanctions do not produce the degree of detrimental impact on the target state that economic sanctions do. Therefore, political sanctions do not raise the same amount of legal issues and urgency in international law as unilateral sanctions of economic nature do.

Much of the existing body of literature on the status of coercive measures in international law deals with the legality of economic sanctions in general, or with UN imposed sanctions, or with a selection of country examples of economic sanctions. This study, on the other hand, goes beyond the existing literature to examine in a comprehensive manner the status of unilateral sanctions in international law with reference to more recent examples of unilateral sanctions, and the implications of such measures on other international treaties and on the wider regional and international legal order. The focus is the legal status of unilateral sanctions or, in the words of Reisman, the different forms of 'intense unilateral violence'[25] of largely economic and financial nature and their ramifications in international law.

[24] Mainly Arts 49–54 of the ILC's Draft Articles. *Yearbook of the International Law Commission* (2001) Vol 2.

[25] WM Reisman, 'Sanctions in International Law' (2009) 4 *Intercultural Human Rights Law Review* (Yale Law School Leal Scholarship Repository) 9, 11.

This study does not include analyses of the following aspects of unilateral sanctions which have already been studied extensively: the effectiveness of unilateral sanctions;[26] a state's economic, moral and political justification of their use; the merits of unilateral sanctions; their utility, their positive and negative impact; their *modus operandi*; and the parameters of UN sanctions and those of other institutional sanctions.[27]

When surveying the status of unilateral sanctions under international law, this study does not confuse the distinction between *lex ferenda* and *lex lata*. On the basis of an analysis of the impact of unilateral sanctions on different areas of international law presented throughout this study by various scholars, and an analysis of the extant and evolving principles of international law derived from the sources of international law as stipulated in Article 38 of the Statute of the International Court of Justice, in its concluding chapter this study articulates the law on the application and operation of unilateral sanctions at present.

VII. Sanctions Imposed by the EU and Other Regional Organisations

The sanctions imposed by the EU and other regional organisation of states such as the African Union or the Organization of American States, are a class of their own. If sanctions are imposed on a Member State of the organisation, they are not regarded as unilateral sanctions under the constituent instruments of the relevant organisation, whereas sanctions imposed on non-member states of the organisation concerned would be classified as unilateral sanctions. For this reason, this study does not focus on the EU sanctions, or the sanctions of other regional organisations imposed on a member of the same organisation.

VIII. UN Sanctions

Since the objective of this book is to produce a comprehensive and authoritative study on the status of unilateral sanctions in international law, it does not devote much space to the collective measures taken by the UN Security Council or the so-called 'UN sanctions' as they are permitted under Articles 41 and 42 of the Charter of the United Nations. Furthermore, a considerable amount of literature is already available on UN sanctions[28]

[26] See generally, WM Reisman and DL Stevick, 'The Applicability of International Law Standards to United Nations Sanctions Programmes' (1998) 9 *European Journal of International Law* 86; AZ Marossi and MR Bassett (eds), *Economic Sanctions under International Law: Unilateralism, Multilateralism, Legitimacy, and Consequences* (TMC Asser Press, 2015); ME O'Connell, 'Debating the Law of Sanctions' (2002) 13 *European Journal of International Law* 63; A Pellet and A Miron, 'Sanctions' in R Wolfrum (ed) *The Max Planck Encyclopaedia of Public International Law*, Vol IX (Oxford University Press, 2012) 105.

[27] See generally on the macroeconomic effects of economic sanctions, CES Warburton, 'The International Law and Economics of Coercive Diplomacy: Macroeconomic Effects and Empirical Findings' (2016) 16 *Applied Economics and International Development* 35.

[28] See generally, V Gowlland-Debbas (ed), *United Nations Sanctions and International Law* (Kluwer, 2001); N Ronzitti (ed), *Coercive Diplomacy, Sanctions and International Law* (Brill/Nijhoff, 2016); L Picchio Forlati

and various study groups[29] are further investigating the status, effectiveness and lawfulness of them. This study examines the legal status of unilateral sanctions imposed by a state or a group of states against another state; it also examines sanctions, imposed outside of the UN framework, as well as secondary sanctions associated with them, and the ramifications of these kinds of sanctions for the wider international legal order.

IX. Parallel Sanctions

The term 'parallel sanctions' denotes sanctions that comprise either UN sanctions as well as unilateral sanctions, or UN sanctions as well as sanctions imposed by regional organisations such as the EU or the African Union, or unilateral sanctions imposed by an individual state or a group of states as well as by the EU or any other regional organisations. A detailed examination of parallel sanctions, or the ramifications of such sanctions in their entirety, is beyond the scope of this work and a considerable body of literature on parallel sanctions is already available.

X. Retorsions and 'Smart' or Targeted Sanctions

This study does not focus on the retorsive measures or other low-intensity sanctions of limited scope which are commonly known as 'smart' or 'targeted' sanctions, since they are ordinarily permitted activities in international relations.[30] Smart or

and L-A Sicilianos, *Economic Sanctions in International Law* (Brill/Martinus Nijhoff, 2004); MP Doxey, *Economic Sanctions and International Enforcement* (The Royal Institute of International Affairs, 1980); AZ Marossi and MR Bassett (eds), *Economic Sanctions under International Law* (Springer/The T.M.C. Asser Press, 2015); M Happold and P Eden (eds), *Economic Sanctions and International Law* (Hart Publishing, 2016); LC Brown-John, *Multilateral Sanctions in International Law: A Comparative Analysis* (Praeger, 1975); JM Farral, *United Nations Sanctions and the Rule of Law* (Cambridge University Press, 2007); E Zoller, *Peacetime Unilateral Remedies: An Analysis of Countermeasures* (Transnational, 1984); O Elagab, *The Legality of Non-forcible Countermeasures in International Law* (Oxford University Press, 1988); L van den Herik (ed), *Research Handbook on UN Sanctions and International Law* (Edward Elgar, 2017); BE Carter, *International Economic Sanctions: Improving the Haphazard US Legal Regime* (Cambridge University Press, 1989); M Dawidowicz, *Third-Party Countermeasures in International Law* (Cambridge University Press, 2017); R Gordon, M Smyth and T Cornell, *Sanctions Law* (Hart Publishing, 2019); M Asada (e.), *Economic Sanctions in International Law and Practice* (Routledge, 2019).

[29] For instance, the International Law Association has established a Study Group on UN Sanctions and International Law. See www.ila-hq.org/index.php/study-groups?study-groupsID=73.

[30] The terms 'smart' or 'targeted' sanctions denote 'unfriendly' conduct carried out by a state within the scope of exercising the sovereign powers inherent in a state. Examples of smart or targeted sanctions include severance of diplomatic relations, declaring a diplomat *persona non grata*, stopping overseas development assistance, denying recognition of a new government that has come to power through a military coup or other undemocratic means, stopping trading with or investing in the target state, terminating or suspending or limiting diplomatic relations, or recalling ambassadors or suspending the operation of treaties within the limits prescribed in the treaties themselves or in the Vienna Convention on the Law of Treaties, restricting or impeding trade, provided that they do not result in the violation of obligations under the WTO law, imposing visa bans or freezing assets of the associated with the government that has violated human rights or committed other internationally wrongful acts or blacklisting of individuals alleged to have violated human rights or engaged in economic or financial misconduct such as money laundering.

targeted sanctions are taken not only against individuals in the government or associated with the government that violates human rights, but are also often imposed against individuals and business organisations known to be engaged in activities such as violations of human rights, money laundering, and cyber attacks. Since smart or targeted sanctions are used very frequently, numbering in thousands, a separate study is required to do justice to the legal nuances associated with them. Furthermore, the individuals affected by such sanctions can challenge the measures taken by a government before the judiciary in the targeting country or before regional and international human rights institutions which have the powers to determine the lawfulness of such sanctions.

XI. Countermeasures and Unilateral Sanctions

This study does not specifically focus on the nature and scope of countermeasures since such measures are ordinarily permitted activities in international relations within narrowly defined conditions. Countermeasures are a recognised institution in international law. They can be legally implemented against a state in response to its breach of international obligations, provided that a number of substantive and procedural requirements are met. In contrast, unilateral sanctions are not a recognised institution in international law, albeit commonplace in international relations. The lawfulness of unilateral sanctions depends on their permissibility under customary international law, bilateral treaty arrangements and obligations under multilateral treaties applicable to the states in question.

Finally, this book is not about unilateral sanctions in their entirety, nor about all legal issues arising from such sanctions. The aim of this study is to bring clarity to the law on unilateral sanctions on the basis of a representative sample of case studies covering different areas of international law ranging from the law of the sea, the law of trade and investment, the freedom of aviation and communications, human rights law, to environmental protection. This volume presents a diverse range of case studies and informed conclusions are drawn from them as to the status of unilateral sanctions in international law. This enables the editor of the volume to make some policy recommendations pertinent to the regime of unilateral sanctions.

XII. Organisation of the Study

In this book scholars and practitioners in international law discuss different aspects of unilateral sanctions in international law. Each case study in this volume is based on the analysis of the relevant literature, international legal instruments (eg, treaties, charters, conventions) and judgments of international courts and tribunals and resolutions of international organisations including the UN General Assembly and the Human Rights Council. Combined, the chapters cover the wide-ranging impact of unilateral sanctions on several areas of public international law. Since unilateral sanctions impinge on so many areas of international law, this volume analyses the lawfulness of unilateral sanctions by means of case studies from a representative selection of areas of international law. In doing so, we look at the impact of unilateral sanctions on other areas of international law such as the protection of human rights of the people in the state subjected to unilateral sanctions, the protection of the environment, the freedom of navigation or aviation, the freedom of transit and the right to communications. The objective is to draw helpful conclusions from the analyses presented of both state practice and treaty law on the current status of unilateral sanctions in international law and the limits placed on these sanctions by rules pertaining to different areas of international law. The book is comprised of an introductory chapter and the following main chapters:

Chapter one, by the editor of this volume, Professor Surya P Subedi of the University of Leeds, discusses the legal status of non-retorsive unilateral sanctions. It examines the lack of a distinct set of rules of international law that govern the implementation of unilateral sanctions, and it discusses the international legal issues currently arising from the use of such sanctions. This chapter examines the contemporary practice of states as well as the soft and hard law instruments provision for unilateral sanctions, with a view to deducing the rules of international law that regulate unilateral sanctions. In the process, it analyses the nature and scope of unilateral measures and their status in international law with special reference to the principles of the sovereignty of states, prohibition on the use of force, non-intervention, and protection of human rights as based on both treaty law and the contemporary norms of customary international law. Thereby, this chapter lays the theoretical groundwork for the entire volume.

Chapter two, by Professor Nigel White of the University of Nottingham, examines the issues associated with unilateral sanctions in a wider context under the title 'Shades of Grey: Autonomous Sanctions in the International Legal Order'. The chapter addresses the legal framework applicable to sanctions by exploring the understanding and nature of sanctions to show that their dominant purpose has been to respond to threats, or to breaches of international peace and as such are clearly within the competence of international organisations, but not individual states. Having outlined both the conceptual and legal framework for understanding sanctions, the chapter considers sanctions imposed against states and non-state actors and explores whether the move towards targeted sanctions is a form of response to violations of international law, and possibly one that can lawfully be taken by individual states autonomously or unilaterally. The chapter finishes by considering that, in contrast to countermeasures and other unilateral measures, collective sanctions are inherently lawful, but can only be legally justified as measures adopted out of necessity to prevent major ruptures to peace and international law.

Chapter three, by Professor Joy Gordon of the Philosophy Department and School of Law of Loyola University, Chicago, examines how the state imposing sanctions holds a monopoly on a critical market or, in some other regard, holds a singular role in the global economy, and how unilateral sanctions may in effect function as though they were global. Hence, it also examines how extraterritorial as well as secondary sanctions have the consequence of expanding the scope of the sanction's regime well beyond the sanctioner's own nationals. This chapter also assesses the implications of unilateral sanctions where the sanctions regulations are vague or unpredictably enforced, and where the penalties are severe, such as exclusion from the US market or banking system and the impact of asset freezes. After laying out the broad theoretical framework, this chapter discusses how these various issues can be seen to work in the context of current US sanctions against Cuba, Venezuela and Iran.

Chapter four, by Professor Nick Grief of the University of Kent, explores the implications of unilateral sanctions for the freedom of aviation with special reference to the US sanctions on Iran and the sanctions against Qatar by four Arab states. This chapter discusses the implications for the freedom of aviation under international law (in particular the Chicago Convention 1944 and related treaties) when a state or a group of states imposes unilateral sanctions against another state, and the remedies available to the state subjected to such sanctions. It is not concerned with sanctions imposed within the UN framework under Chapter VII of the UN Charter, or with flight bans imposed for safety reasons or because of military tension.

Chapter five, by Dr Ali Abusedra of the University of Hull, explores the impact of unilateral sanctions on regional economic integration treaties, with special reference to the Charter of the Gulf Cooperation Council and other treaties concerning economic cooperation among the Gulf countries. There are a number of regional economic integration and cooperation agreements that have been concluded between states around the globe. Many of these treaties create regional economic and political organisations to foster close cooperation between the states which are parties to the constituent agreements of such organisations. However, what happens to the obligations under these treaties when one Member State, or a group of states, decides to impose unilateral sanctions against another member of the organisation, a member they accuse of a breach of its obligations under international law? What impact do such sanctions have on the integrity of such regional economic and political cooperation organisations? These are the questions that this chapter examines with particular reference to the GCC treaties.

Chapter six, by Dr Nicolette Butler of the University of Manchester, examines the impact of unilateral sanctions on bilateral and international investment treaties. International investment takes places when a national of one state invests in, or engages in, business activities in a different state. International investors are entitled to various protections under international law. The most basic protections available to investors and their property are collectively recognised as customary international law principles. Individual investors may also enjoy additional protections by virtue of an extensive network of almost 3,000 bilateral investment treaties and treaties with investment provisions. The implementation of unilateral sanctions impacts the target state and its foreign investors. The issue of the effect of unilateral sanctions on foreign investors of the target states has historically not attracted much scholarly attention. This chapter seeks to fill a gap in the literature by analysing the effects of unilateral sanctions on foreign investors and the foreign investment regime more generally. Can the imposition of unilateral sanctions cause breaches of investor protection obligations? What remedies are available to aggrieved foreign investors? This chapter examines these issues and considers whether the target state is eligible to invoke any defences (eg necessity) in response to any action brought by foreign investors.

Chapter seven, by Dr James Watson, Secretary General of Eurogas, Brussels, titled 'The World Trade Organisation and Unilateral Economic Sanctions: Prohibited but Possible?', assesses the implications of unilateral sanctions on the World Trade Organization (WTO). It explores the use of unilateral sanctions in the context of international trade law, as governed by the WTO. Given that a number of WTO members have employed, or are employing, unilateral sanctions on trade counterparts, it is no surprise that the WTO dispute settlement system, advanced as it is, has been called on to assess the validity of unilateral sanctions in international trade law. This chapter looks at the evolution of the law in the WTO in relation to unilateral sanctions and their use by members, focusing on the interpretations of the dispute panels and appellate body, including recent cases involving Qatar and Russia. The chapter argues that despite the existence of exceptions from the basic principles of the WTO in Article XX and Article XXI, which could foresee the allowance of unilateral sanctions for various reasons, it would be very difficult to imagine the dispute settlement organs of the WTO reaching a conclusion that such measures could be avoided. In principle, the WTO supports the free movement of goods and services and has a history of carefully considering any measures that do not uphold these basic fundamental principles of international trade law.

Chapter eight, by Dr Trisha Rajput of the University of Gothenburg, assesses the implications of unilateral sanctions on the right of communication of the individuals in the target states under the rules of the Universal Postal Union (UPU). Although academic discussion on the interplay of sanction and postal communication is limited, the consideration of the interplay between sanctions and postal communication is timely and important given the reimposition of sanctions on Iran by the Trump administration. The purpose of this chapter is to consider the interplay of sanctions with rules of the UPU that guarantees postal communication and state responsibility. More specifically, it considers whether sanctions that impact the right of communications under the UPU regime can be justified.

Chapter nine, by Dr Louisa Ashley, Head of School of Law at Leeds Beckett University, examines the impact of unilateral sanctions on the regime of international humanitarian law and human rights under the title 'Unilateral Coercive Measures: Towards International Humanitarian Law and International Human Rights'. Whilst the use of sanctions is increasingly favoured by states as an alternative to the use of force, the impact of such measures on the humanitarian capacity of the target state can be devastating and result in associated gross human rights violations. This chapter examines the applicability of principles of international humanitarian law (IHL) to unilateral sanctions regimes with case studies of particular sanctions regimes. It explores the argument that IHL offers an apt framework for governance of unilateral sanctions regimes, particularly where those regimes operate as a form of 'decentralised economic warfare'. It does so by assessing the consequences of sanctions and their concomitant legal limits in the context of IHL principles including necessity, distinction, proportionality and precaution, with reference to unilateral sanctions regimes in force against specific target states, for example, Venezuela, Cuba, Iran and Qatar.

Chapter ten, by Dr Abhinayan Basu Bal of the University of Gothenburg, examines some of the law of the sea issues arising from the imposition of unilateral sanctions and certain maritime actions, such as blockade and interdiction to enforce such sanctions on passing ships. It examines the situation when the right of innocent passage and possibly transit passage could be suspended, even temporarily, by the state imposing unilateral sanctions for vessels trading with the targeted state, and elucidates the notion of maritime lawfare, investigating what is permissible and what is not, and what are the possible grey areas that could be exploited by the state imposing sanctions. In doing so, it examines as a case study of Gibraltar's act as a coastal state to detain *Grace 1* in 2018 by questioning whether the detention of the vessel is legally tenable from the vantage point of international maritime law.

Chapter eleven, by Dr Amrisha Pandey of Bhopal University and currently working with the Government of India on an environmental conservation project, is entitled 'Can Unilateral Sanctions and International Environmental Obligations of States Coexist?' It examines the impact of unilateral sanctions on the environment, with a focus on the impact of sanctions on the environment of the sanctioned country, and the manner in which unilateral sanctions interfere with the international obligations arising from environmental treaties and conventions. It furthermore discusses the legality of unilateral sanctions in the context of environmental disasters and associated problems caused by these sanctions in both the sanctioned country and the sanctioning country.

Chapter twelve, by Dr Ali Abusedra of the University of Hull, Professor Abu Bakar Munir of the University of Malay, and Md Toriqul Islam, Assistant Professor of Bangladesh University of Business and Technology, examines the use of cyber means to enforce unilateral coercive measures in international law. In doing so, it assesses the legal issues arising from the use of cyberwar in the implementation of unilateral sanctions. It looks at the use of cyberwar as part of unilateral sanctions against the target state, and assesses the lawfulness of the cyber sanctions regime with reference to a number of cyber sanctions regimes which were developed and employed by states with the technological capacity to do so.

Finally, the concluding chapter draws on the major findings of the research conducted in this study on the status of unilateral sanctions in international law to outline the conventional and the contemporary rules of customary international law applicable to unilateral sanctions. The representative case studies included in this volume enable the editor of the volume not only to state the current law on the subject matter, but also to make some policy recommendations, including the adoption of a declaration by the UN General Assembly, pertinent to the regime of unilateral sanctions. Accordingly, a draft of a potential declaration by the UN General Assembly on the use of unilateral sanctions is included in Appendix 1 of this volume.

XIII. Hope for the Future

Any unlawful unilateral sanctions are liable to undermine the whole international legal order built around the Charter of the UN and the norms of international human rights and humanitarian law. Clarity in the law is needed to build and sustain orderly international relations between states, and this study aims to contribute to that endeavour. Therefore, it can be hoped that a study of this nature becomes a catalyst for action by the UN or the International Law Commission for the development of a treaty, a set of draft articles or a resolution by the General Assembly outlining the rules applicable to unilateral sanctions. This study can also assist in the work of other learned assemblies of international lawyers such as the *Institut de Droit International*[31] and the International Law Association[32] and of the UN Special Rapporteur on the Negative Impact of the Unilateral Coercive Measures on the Enjoyment of Human Rights.[33]

It can also be hoped that this volume will serve as a prime source of reference for scholars, diplomats, judges and arbitrators of national and international courts and tribunals who are called upon to adjudicate on issues arising from unilateral sanctions. The volume should also be useful for decision- and policy-makers, law practitioners, government lawyers and in-house lawyers who work for business organisations, especially those linked to countries affected by unilateral sanctions, including multinational enterprises around the globe.

[31] Professor Alain Pellet proposed during the Tallinn Session of 2015 of the *Institut de Droit International* that it should study the topic and come up with Articles on the legal status of unilateral sanctions; 'Memorandum from Mr Alain Pellet' of 26 August 2015 proposing the creation of a new Commission on Unilateral Sanctions and International Law: *Annuaire de l'Institut de Droit International - Session de Tallinn*, Vol 76, 723–36.

[32] The International Law Association has already established a Study Group on UN Sanctions and International Law. See www.ila-hq.org/index.php/study-groups?study-groupsID=73. It could also investigate other non-UN related sanctions in the future to complete its studies on different regime of sanctions in international law generally.

[33] The UN Special Rapporteur on the Negative Impact of the Unilateral Coercive Measures on the Enjoyment of Human Rights has issued a call for submissions on Unilateral Coercive Measures-Study on the notion, characteristics, legal status and targets of unilateral sanctions. See OHCHR (n 3).

1

The Status of Unilateral Sanctions in International Law

SURYA P SUBEDI

I. Introduction

Unilateral sanctions have become part of life in international relations. But there is no comprehensive treaty regulating the activities of states in this area. That said, there is an assortment of hard and soft law instruments in international law as well as the extant and emerging rules of customary international law, all seeking to fill this legal vacuum. However, no focused and comprehensive analysis of the nature and scope of unilateral sanctions and of the principles of international law that would be applicable to such sanctions has yet been conducted. It is in this context that this chapter seeks to examine the nature and scope of unilateral sanctions, contemporary practice of states in this area and the provisions of both soft and hard law instruments as well as the rules of customary international law concerning unilateral sanctions, with a view to deducing and identifying the rules of international law regulating such sanctions. In doing so, it will analyse the status of unilateral sanctions in international law with special reference to the principles of the sovereignty of states, prohibition on the use of force, non-intervention, and protection of human rights based on both treaty law and the contemporary norms of customary international law.

II. The Nature and Scope of Unilateral Sanctions

In the long history of international law, the term 'sanctions' is a relatively recent phenomenon. As stated by the International Law Commission (ILC) in its commentaries to the Draft Articles on State Responsibility,[1] until recently the more usual terminology was that of 'legitimate reprisals' or, more generally, measures of 'self-protection' or 'self-help'. The term 'sanctions' has generally been used for collective measures such

[1] ILC, 'Draft articles on Responsibility of States for Internationally Wrongful Acts, with commentaries 2001' 128, available at legal.un.org/ilc/texts/instruments/english/commentaries/9_6_2001.pdf.

as those taken by the UN Security Council under Chapter VII of the Charter of the UN – despite the fact that the Charter uses the term 'measures', not 'sanctions'. The term 'countermeasures' has been favoured over the term 'sanctions' to signify measures taken in response to a prior breach of international law mainly since the *Air Service Agreement* arbitration and it was adopted by the ILC for the purposes of the Draft Articles on State Responsibility.

However, the term 'sanctions'[2] itself has been used by various writers synonymously with a host of other terms such as economic blockade,[3] boycott,[4] embargo,[5] countermeasures,[6] retorsion,[7] reprisals,[8] economic warfare,[9] economic coercion,[10] economic force or economic aggression,[11] economic weapon[12] and a tool for 'financial carpet bombing'.[13] Furthermore, the terms 'smart' or 'targeted' sanctions have also been used to signify low-intensity unilateral sanctions of limited scope.

Not only scholars but some states too have characterised the employment of unilateral sanctions as 'economic war' and the statement of the Foreign Minister of Iran in

[2] See for a comprehensive treatment of the operation of unilateral sanctions and especially the sanctions applied by the US in the conduct of its foreign relations: A Lowenfeld, *International Economic Law* (Oxford University Press, 2002) Pt VII, chs 22 and 23; BE Carter, *International Economic Sanctions: Improving the Haphazard US Legal Regime* (Cambridge University Press, 1989).

[3] W Heintschel von Heinegg, 'Blockade' in *Max Planck Encyclopaedia of Public International Law* (Oxford University Press, 2015); MG Fraunces, 'The International Law of Blockade: New Guiding Principles in Contemporary State Practice' (1992) 101 *The Yale Law Journal* 893.

[4] H Lauterpacht, 'Boycott in International Relations' (1933) 14 *British Yearbook of International Law* 125; CL Bouve, 'The National Boycott as an International Delinquency' (1934) 28 *AJIL* 19; YZ Blum, 'Economic Boycotts in International Law' (1977) 12 *Texas International Law Journal* 5.

[5] JP Chamberlain, 'Embargo as a sanction of international law' (1933) 27 *Proceedings of the American Society of International Law at Its Annual Meeting (1921–1969)* 66–78.

[6] O Elagab, *The Legality of Non-forcible Countermeasures in International Law* (Oxford University Press, 1988). DJ Bederman, 'Counterintuiting Countermeasures' (2002) 96 *AJIL* 817; D Alland, 'The Definition of Countermeasures' in J Crawford, A Pellet, S Olleson, and K Parlett (eds), *The Law of International Responsibility* (Oxford University Press, 2010) 1127–36; ND White and A Abass, 'Countermeasures and Sanctions' in MD Evans (ed), *International Law*, 5th edn (Oxford University Press, 2018) 521–47; J Crawford, 'Countermeasures as Interim Measures' (1994) 5 *EJIL* 65; E. Zoller, *Peacetime Unilateral Remedies: An Analysis of Countermeasures* (Transnational, 1984).

[7] T Giegerich, 'Retorsion' in R Wolfrum (ed), *Max Planck Encyclopaedia of Public International Law*, vol VIII (Oxford University Press, 2012) 976; T Ruys, 'Sanction, Retorsions and Countermeasures: Concepts and International Legal Framework' in L van den Herik (ed), *Research Handbook on UN Sanctions and International Law* (Edward Elgar, 2017) 19; A Tzanakopoulos, 'The Right to Be Free from Economic Coercion' (2015) 4 *Cambridge Journal of International and Comparative Law* 616, 626–27.

[8] Tzanakopoulos is of the view that 'Reprisals are still around in the guise of countermeasures and countermeasures are predominantly economic in nature'. A Tzanakopoulos, 'The Right to Be Free from Economic Coercion' (2015) 4 *Cambridge Journal of International and Comparative Law* 616. See also on reprisals, ND White and A Abass, 'Countermeasures and Sanctions' in MD Evans (ed), *International Law*, 5th edn (Oxford University Press, 2018) 521–47; KJ Partsch, 'Reprisals' in R Bernhardt (ed), *Encyclopaedia of Public International Law* (Elsevier, 2000).

[9] AV Lowe and A Tzanakopoulos, 'Economic Warfare' in R Wolfrum (ed), *Max Planck Encyclopaedia of Public International Law* (Oxford University Press, 2012).

[10] C Parry, 'Defining Economic Coercion in International Law' in 12 *Texas International Law Journal* (1977) 1; BE Carter, 'Economic Coercion' in R Wolfrum (ed), *Max Planck Encyclopaedia of Public International Law* (Oxford University Press, 2009).

[11] M Domb, 'Defining Economic Aggression in International Law: The Possibility of Regional Action by the Organization of American States' (1978) 11 *Cornell International Law Journal* 85.

[12] L Picchio Forlati and L-A Sicilianos, *Economic Sanctions in International Law* (Brill/Nijhoff, 2004) xxxv.

[13] 'Sanctions: Financial Carpet-bombing' *The Economist* (30 November 2019) 41.

response to the US sanctions against his country in June 2019 is an example.[14] He termed the US unilateral sanctions as 'economic terrorism'.[15] Turkish President Erdogan also stated that Turkey would not accept 'the use of economic sanctions as weapons' by the US against his country. He made these remarks in response to the use of unilateral sanctions by the US in 2018.[16] A commentator states that successive US governments have weaponised America's economic might.[17] Cameron says that the developing or Second World states prefer the term 'economic sanctions' and that he prefers the term 'economic diplomacy' to signify unilateral economic coercion or economic sanctions.[18] In the words of a commentator, sanctions are 'an option for when words aren't good enough, but war is too much'.[19] As opposed to the collective sanctions employed by the UN, other forms of sanctions, and especially unilateral economic sanctions, are a kind of means of 'private justice' (in the words of Pellet),[20] or a sort of 'safety valve' (in the words of Cameron),[21] whereby a state or a group of states decides to impose sanctions on the target state for an alleged prior violation of a rule of international law or to deter a state from violating international norms.

There is no universally agreed definition of the term 'sanctions' itself, let alone the definition of 'unilateral sanctions' in international law. There is a thin line between low-intensity unilateral sanctions of retorsive character and high-intensity unilateral sanctions. A case-by-case analysis will have to be conducted to draw a clear distinction between the high-intensity unilateral sanctions and low-intensity unilateral sanctions of retorsive character, since there is no judicial or other international mechanism to adjudicate upon the matter. However, generally speaking, the term 'sanctions' means any measure taken by the targeting state against the target state to require it to adhere to international law or to punish it for a breach of international law. But in reality, sanctions have been used by states for a variety of purposes. As stated by Ruys, 'sanctions can serve a variety of purposes, namely: (i) to coerce or change behaviour; (ii) to constrain access to resources needed to engage in certain activities; or (iii) to signal and stigmatize'.[22] He goes on to state that

> it is clear that sanctions adopted by individual States – such as the notorious US sanctions imposed on Cuba pursuant to the Helms-Burton Act – often serve foreign-policy purposes

[14] 'Iran tells US that ending "economic war" is only way to reduce tensions' *The Guardian* (11 June 2019) 28; 'Iran warns over "economic war" waged through US sanctions' *Gulf Times* (11 June 2019) 3.

[15] The statement of the Iranian Foreign Minister Javad Zarif, as quoted in 'Trump orders tougher sanctions on Iran' *The Financial Times* (19 September 2019) 4.

[16] 'Turkey cannot remain silent over use of sanctions as weapons: Erdogan' *Gulf Time* (26 September 2018) 3.

[17] P Stephens, 'Sanctions are Trump's new way of war' *The Financial Times* (18 October 2019) 11.

[18] CE Cameron, 'Developing a standard for politically related state economic sanction' (1991) 13 *Michigan Journal of International Law* 218, 218. However, it should be noted that the term 'economic diplomacy' has a more positive meaning in contemporary diplomatic vocabulary and implies diplomatic initiatives of governments to promote economic development or expansion of trade and investment with other countries.

[19] 'Sanctions' *The Economist* (2019) 42.

[20] Memorandum from Mr Alain Pellet of 26 August 2015 proposing the creation of a new Commission on Unilateral Sanctions and International Law: Annuaire de l'Institut de Droit International – Session de Tallinn, Vol 76, 723–736.

[21] Cameron, 'Developing a standard' (1991) 253.

[22] Ruys, 'Sanctions, retorsions and countermeasures' (2017) 22–23.

> of the State(s) concerned, without necessarily constituting a reaction to a prior breach of international law.[23]

Szasz provides the following broad definition of 'sanctions': 'all means of exercising pressures short of the threat or use of military force directly against a target state or entity'.[24] Farer states that sanctions constitute 'efforts to project influence across frontiers by denying or conditioning access to a country's resources, raw materials, semi- or finished products, capital, technology, services or consumers'.[25] According to Jazairy, the UN Special Rapporteur on the negative impact of unilateral coercive measures on the enjoyment of human rights,

> unilateral coercive measures are measures including, but not limited to, economic and political ones, imposed by States or groups of States to coerce another State in order to obtain from it the subordination of the exercise of its sovereign rights with a view to securing some specific change in its policy.[26]

However, in defining the term 'sanctions' many scholars have adopted the definition of 'economic sanctions' provided by Lowenfeld, who defines economic coercion as

> measures of an economic – as contrasted with diplomatic or military – character taken by states to express disapproval of the acts of the target state or to induce that state to change some policy or practice or even its governmental structure.[27]

Economic sanctions can include any of the following measures: financial sanctions, asset freezes, trade sanctions, arms embargoes, commodity interdictions, diplomatic sanctions and travel bans, etc.[28] However, the term 'unilateral sanctions' connotes measures broader than merely economic measures and could include non-economic measures too. Therefore, the term 'unilateral sanctions' could be defined as follows: measures of exercising pressures short of the threat or use of military force directed against a target state or entity, which are taken by an individual state or a group of states, which are not authorised by the United Nations and which seek to limit or deprive altogether the freedom that other states enjoy as sovereign states under international law. Not only economic and financial sanctions would come within the ambit of unilateral sanctions, but also restrictions on the freedom of navigation, aviation and transit and on the right to communications.

Some of the most comprehensive unilateral sanctions in recent times have been the US sanctions against Cuba, Syria, the Russian Federation, Iran and North Korea and the comprehensive unilateral sanctions imposed on Qatar by four other Arab states in 2017. The US-imposed sanctions seem to include a wide range of measures ranging from the economic, banking and other financial restrictions, a ban on the sale of

[23] ibid, 23. See the Cuban Liberty and Democratic Solidarity (LIBERTAD) Act 1996, 22 USC §§ 6021–6091.

[24] P Szasz, 'The Law of Economic Sanctions' in MN Schmitt and LC Green (ed), *The Law of Armed Conflict: Into the Next Millennium* (International Law Studies, Vol 71, Naval War College, 1998) 455–491, 455.

[25] TJ Farer, 'Political and economic coercion in contemporary international law' (1985) 79 *American Journal of International Law* 405, 408.

[26] UN Doc A/HRC/30/45 of 10 August 2015, para 13.

[27] AF Lowenfeld, *International Economic Law* (Oxford University Press, 2002) 698.

[28] R Gordon, M Smyth and T Cornell, *Sanctions Law* (Hart Publishing, 2019) 17–20.

weapons and technology to a restriction on travel to these countries by US citizens.[29] These measures also affect other countries and their citizens, including US citizens themselves, who are not allowed to visit the target country as tourists. The extraterritorial scope of such measures ensures that all matters pertaining to the target country, especially international banking transactions, are targeted by US authorities, even in third countries.[30]

A series of comprehensive sanctions by the US against the Russian Federation between 2014 and 2016, in the aftermath of its action in Crimea and Sevastopol, included freezing the assets of a number of Russian and Ukrainian officials in connection with the situation in Ukraine, restrictions on the sale of military and dual use products to Russia, and imposing an export licensing regime on goods designed for a number of oil projects in Russia related to deep water, shale and Arctic oil exploration. These wide-ranging sanctions have considerable impact on the economy of the target country. For instance, the Russian Minister of Finance, Anton Siluanov, estimated that Russia was losing around US$ 40 billion per year because of these sanctions, and a further US$ 90 to 100 billion per year on account of the drop in the oil price. Presidential adviser Sergey Glazyev believes that the cost of the damage wrought on the Russian financial industry by the sanctions against Russia was US$ 250 billion over two years, bearing in mind that Russian borrowers had already been compelled to pay back about US$ 200 billion.[31]

Some of the most comprehensive sanctions with far reaching implications were the sanctions against Syria by the US, EU and the League of Arab States. They included measures ranging from an export ban on arms and related material and on equipment, an import ban on crude oil and petroleum products from Syria, a ban on investment in the Syrian oil industry and in companies engaged in the construction of new power plants for electricity production in Syria, prohibition from participating in the construction of new power plants, including related technical or financial assistance, a ban on exports to Syria of key equipment and technology for the oil and gas industry, the freezing of the assets of the Central Bank of Syria within the EU, an export ban on equipment, technology or software primarily intended for monitoring or interception

[29] According to a report submitted by Cuba to the UN, 'There are just four aspects of the blockade that the President of the United States cannot act upon since they require action by Congress to be eliminated or changed, since they are regulated by law: 1. The prohibition on United States subsidiaries in third countries from doing business with Cuba (Torricelli Act) 2. The prohibition on carrying out transactions with United States properties that were nationalized in Cuba (Helms-Burton Act) 3. Preventing United States citizens from travelling to Cuba as tourists (Trade Sanctions Reform and Export Enhancement Act of 2000) 4. The prohibition on financing for sales of United States agricultural products to Cuba (Trade Sanctions Reform and Export Enhancement Act of 2000)'. 'Unilateral sanctions as a means of political and economic coercion against developing countries', Report of the Secretary-General, UN Doc A/72/307 of 9 August 2017.

[30] UN Doc A/72/307 of 9 August 2017 (ibid). By virtue of sanctions, the target countries would be unable to freely export and import products and services to or from the US; they cannot have direct banking relations with the US and receive US investment in so many sectors of the economy. Large fines against US and other foreign banks that can be imposed by the Office of Foreign Assets Control and other US federal and state institutions can create a negative environment that is liable to lead to systematic denial of banking and financial services to the banks, companies, and citizens of the target country. The US measures are applied rigorously by US Government agencies, especially by the Departments of the Treasury and Commerce, and in particular by the Office of Foreign Assets Control.

[31] UN Doc A/72/307 (n 29) 12–14.

of the Internet or telephone communications, and the prohibition from trading Syrian public or public guaranteed bonds to or from the Government of Syria or its public bodies and Syrian financial institutions.[32]

III. The Practice of Imposing Unilateral Sanctions

States have long been resorting to the use of coercive diplomacy or non-forcible measures, including unilateral sanctions, as an instrument to further their political and economic objectives.[33] A survey by the UN demonstrated that a total of 38 states and territories had been subjected to some degree of unilateral sanctions during the period 2000–15.[34] As stated in a UK Government's White Paper, 'Sanctions are a key foreign policy tool' which are designed to communicate a clear political signal and can be used 'to constrain or help effect a change in behaviour'.[35] Although the unilateral sanctions are expected to be used only as an exceptional measure, their use has become so common that it is seen as legal whether authorised by the UN Security Council or not. Indeed, the 1990s has been referred to as the 'sanctions decade' for the unprecedented high number of unilateral sanctions employed by states[36] during that time. The trend continued in the following decade. Although the number of comprehensive and high-intensity unilateral sanctions has declined slightly in the recent past, the number of low-intensity unilateral sanctions of limited scope commonly known as 'smart' or targeted sanctions is on the increase.[37]

According to a report, the US sanctions list runs to 1,300 pages, detailing some 8,755 of them, thereby exceeding the number of sanctions imposed by the EU, the UK Treasury or the UN[38] by more than four times. Responding to Iran's decision to institute proceedings against the US at the ICJ, alleging that the US unilateral sanctions violated the 1955 Treaty of Amity, Economic Relations, and Consular Rights between the US and Iran, US Secretary of State Mike Pompeo issued a statement saying that Iran's lawsuit was an 'attempt to interfere with the sovereign rights of the United States to take lawful actions, including re-imposition of sanctions, which are necessary to protect our national security'.[39] Similarly, the UAE stated in response to Qatar's intervention at the Human Rights Council in a statement issued together with other countries that the UAE will 'continue to exercise their sovereign rights' to boycott the Government of Qatar, guaranteed by international law.[40]

[32] ibid, 18–21.

[33] P Wallensteen, 'A Century of Economic Sanctions: A Field Revisited', Uppsala Peace Research Papers No 1 (Department of Peace and Conflict Research, Uppsala University, Sweden, 2000) 1–23.

[34] UN Doc A/70/152 of 16 July 2015, 4–5.

[35] 'The Future Relationship between the UK and the EU', White Paper, CM 9593 (July 2019) 65.

[36] D Cortright and GA Lopez, *The Sanctions Decade, Assessing United Nations Strategies in the 1990s* (Lynne Rienner, 2000).

[37] UN Doc A/70/152 (n 34) 4–5.

[38] C Philp, 'Sanctions are Trump's foreign policy tool' *The Times* (16 October 2019).

[39] BBC News, 'Iran urges UN court to halt US reimposed nuclear sanctions', 28 August 2018, available at www.bbc.co.uk/news/world-middle-east-45320362.

[40] 'Arab Quartet responds to Qatar's remarks at the UN Human Rights Council' *Al Arabia English* (28 February 2019) 2.

Rejecting the possibility of illegality of US sanctions imposed on other states, one leading US commentator stated that 'the suggestion that economic sanctions are unlawful unless approved by the Security Council (or by a regional organization such as the OAS) is obsolete'. He added that 'sanctions have become sufficiently common – and often better than the alternatives – to have become tolerated (not to say accepted) as a tool of foreign relations'.[41] Since the US imposes sanctions on so many states, entities and individuals, it is not surprising for the US to regard unilateral sanctions as sufficiently common. However, other states may view the use of such sanctions very differently, and the status of unilateral sanction in international law has yet to be clarified.

Those states that have imposed unilateral sanctions on other states have often sought support for their measures in the principle of sovereignty. In doing so, they have invoked national security or control of terrorism, or the protection and preservation of the sanctity of international treaties relating to nuclear non-proliferation, or the prevention and abolition of chemical weapons, or the protection of human rights. It was held in the *Lotus* case that 'restrictions upon the independence of States cannot … be presumed' and states possess 'a wide measure of discretion which is only limited in certain cases by prohibitive rules'.[42]

According to the principle of sovereignty, states are considered to be free to exercise any sovereign rights that are not forbidden either by a treaty or by a rule of customary international law. Thus, in the absence of a treaty or a rule of customary international law prohibiting the use of unilateral sanctions, states would seem to be free to employ such sanctions against other states as a tool of their foreign policy. This inference seems also to be supported by the rulings of the ICJ in the *Nicaragua* case.[43]

However, the difficulty with the invocation of sovereignty is that the target state can also invoke the same principle of sovereignty to argue that the unilateral sanctions undermine the target state's sovereignty and the principles of sovereign equality and non-interference in internal affairs of other states. For instance, in its response to certain unilateral sanctions of limited character imposed by the US against some high-level Cambodian authorities for violating human rights, the Cambodian Government claimed that the US sanctions had violated Cambodia's sovereignty.[44]

It should be submitted that the principle of sovereignty is not an absolute principle. It is constrained by a number of other competing and equally powerful principles of international law. A number of treaties and rules of customary international law impose limitations on the use of unilateral sanctions. As a UN study states: 'A potential unlawfulness of general economic sanctions can have various sources. International humanitarian law as well as human rights treaties may contain limitations on the imposition of economic sanctions'.[45]

[41] As cited in A Lowenfeld, 'Unilateral versus Collective Sanctions: An American Perception' in V Gowland-Debbas (ed), *United Nations Sanctions and International Law* (Kluwer, 2001) 95.

[42] Case of the *SS Lotus (France v Turkey)*, 1927 PCIJ (Series A), No 10.

[43] *Military and Paramilitary Activities in and against Nicaragua (Nicaragua v United States of America)*, Merits, Judgment of 27 June 1986, ICJ Reports 1986, 14, para 276.

[44] 'US sanctions Cambodia PM's top bodyguard' *Gulf Times* (14 June 2018) 17.

[45] 'Thematic study of the Office of the United Nations High Commissioner for Human Rights on the impact of unilateral coercive measures on the enjoyment of human rights, including recommendations on actions aimed at ending such measures', UN Doc A/HRC/19/33 of 11 January 2012, para 7.

The imposition of unilateral sanctions by stronger states or groups of states against weaker ones is not new.[46] According to Hufbauer and Schott, the history of sanctions goes back to at least 432 BC, when the Greek statesman and general Pericles issued the so-called 'Megarian decree' in response to the abduction of three Aspaisan women.[47] There are records that indicate that already in Ancient Greece in 492 BC, the city-state of Aegina seized Athenian ships and held their passengers hostage in response to Athens holding Aeginians captive. Likewise, during the Crusades in the Middle Ages, religious leaders and church councils in Europe practised unilateral coercive measures by prohibiting the export of ships, weapons and ammunitions to the Saracens, as Arabs or Muslims were referred to in those days.

Such measures, which were traditionally known as reprisals, are known these days as unilateral sanctions. Powerful states used to exercise 'gun-boat' diplomacy until war was renounced. The blockade of Germany after the cessation of World War I in order to coerce Germany to stand down from its opposition to certain leonine clauses of the Treaty of Versailles is a modern example. The General Treaty for Renunciation of War concluded in 1928 outlawed war, but not sanctions, as a means of settling disputes between states. The Charter of the UN goes one step further and not only prohibits the use of force, but also enjoins states to settle their disputes with other states through peaceful means.

Instances of the use of unilateral coercive measures in the post-World War II period are the ones applied at the initiative of Western countries against the Soviet Union in 1949 through the Coordinating Committee for Multilateral Export Controls and against China in 1951 through the China Committee. As stated by Jazairy:

> Except for the cases of Southern Rhodesia and South Africa under apartheid, most recent unilateral coercive measures before 1975 were implemented in the context of the East-West ideological rivalry. Then came the Final Act of the Conference on Security and Cooperation in Europe, which, in its principle VI, expressed the resolve of the signatories to put an end to autonomous policies of coercive measures.'[48]

In the absence of a clear prohibition, the use of non-forcible measures, including unilateral sanctions, has become a preferred foreign policy instrument of different governments around the globe in recent times. For instance, the UK Government implemented about 30 UN, EU and unilateral sanctions regimes in 2018, dealing with a range of situations of international concern from sanctions against Russia in response to its annexation of Crimea, to sanctions against Al Qaida and Da'esh.[49] In order to regulate these sanctions regimes, The Sanctions and Anti-Money Laundering Act 2018 was enacted.[50] This law gives the UK Government wide powers to implement all sorts of sanctions, including financial sanctions, trade sanctions and immigration sanctions in response to a variety of situations including violations of human rights in other countries[51] in the manner

[46] UN Doc A/HRC/30/45 (n 26) paras 23–26 (footnotes omitted).

[47] K Rogoff, 'Economic sanctions have a long and chequered history' *The Guardian* (5 January 2015).

[48] UN Doc A/HRC/30/45 of 10 August 2015 (n 26) para 27.

[49] CM 9593 65 (n 35).

[50] The law is available at www.legislation.gov.uk/ukpga/2018/13/pdfs/ukpga_20180013_en.pdf.

[51] Section 1 of the Act confers broad powers on the Secretary of State and the Treasury ('an appropriate Minister') to impose sanctions regulations considered 'appropriate' for the purposes of compliance with a

similar to the US 'Magnitsky' provisions.[52] Indeed, in announcing the UK's support for the targeted sanctions of the EU against the Maduro regime of Venezuela for grave human rights violations in September 2019, the UK Government stated that 'the UK will deliver its own Magnitsky human rights sanctions … against human rights abuses anywhere in the world'.[53]

Forcible measures that require another state to change their behaviour have been regulated by international law since 1928, first through the General Agreement on the Renunciation of the Use of Force and then through the prohibition on the use of force through the Charter of the UN in 1945. However, no specific international treaty has ever been concluded to regulate the use of non-forcible measures including unilateral sanctions. Consequently, states acting unilaterally or in concert with a group of like-minded states have been employing at will sanctions against other states for an alleged prior violation of a rule of international law or bilateral agreements, and sometimes to deter a state from violating international norms. Sanctions have also been employed to convey disapproval of the target state's demeanour, or to protest against it, or to require the target state to conduct itself within a certain political, economic or legal framework.[54]

IV. Lawfulness of Unilateral Sanctions

There is no generally agreed definition of the term 'unilateral sanctions'. According to the UN Human Rights Council Advisory Committee, the core elements of the definition of unilateral coercive measures is as follows:

> [T]he use of economic, trade or other measures taken by a State, group of States or international organizations acting autonomously to compel a change of policy of another State or to pressure individuals, groups or entities in targeted States to influence a course of action without the authorization of the Security Council.[55]

UN obligation, for the purposes of compliance with any other international obligation or for a purpose that would: further the prevention of terrorism, in the UK or elsewhere; be in the interests of national security; be in the interests of international peace and security; further a foreign policy objective of the government of the UK; promote the resolution of armed conflicts or the protection of civilians in conflict zones; provide accountability for or be a deterrent to gross violations of human rights, or otherwise promote compliance with international human rights law, or respect for human rights; promote compliance with international humanitarian law; contribute to multilateral efforts to prevent the spread and use of weapons and materials of mass destruction; or promote respect for democracy, the rule of law and good governance. See a comment on this new UK law at www.shearman.com/perspectives/2018/06/sanctions-and-anti-money-laundering-act.

[52] The Global Magnitsky Human Rights and Accountability Act 2016 (formally known as the Russia and Moldova Jackson–Vanik Repeal and Sergei Magnitsky Rule of Law Accountability Act) gives powers to the US Government to impose unilateral sanctions on those who it sees as human rights offenders, freezing their assets, and ban them from entering the US: see S 284 – 114th Congress (2015–2016).

[53] 'UK welcomes new sanctions against Maduro regime', Press Release of the British Foreign & Commonwealth Office (27 September 2019), available at www.gov.uk/government/news/uk-welcomes-new-sanctions-against-maduro-regime.

[54] DW Bowett, 'Economic Coercion and Reprisals by States' (1972) 18 *Virginia Journal of International Law* 1.

[55] OHCHR Technical Mission to the State of Qatar, 'Report on the impact of the Gulf Crisis on human rights' (2017) 61.

In the absence of a treaty, or even a soft law instrument providing guidance, and in view of the divided opinion of states and publicists, those unilateral sanctions which are not authorised by the UN or by a regional organisation such as the EU, seem to operate in a legal vacuum; and this 'grey area' of international law[56] appears to be getting greyer as the world witnesses a trend towards unilateralism, nationalism and protectionism.

After analysing state practice on this topic until 1991 and citing a statement of the International Court of Justice in its judgment in the *Nicaragua v US* case in 1986[57] and a judgment of a US Federal Court of Appeals in *Banco Nacional de Cuba v Sabbatino*[58] Cameron concluded that 'no current customary international law prohibition of the use of economic diplomacy [his preferred term for economic sanctions] exists'.[59] Not only scholarly opinion, but also state practice, is divided on the legality or the ramifications of such unilateral coercive measures.[60]

Bowett identifies three conditions under which unilateral sanctions would be illegal: those in violation of (i) specific treaty commitments; (ii) general principles of international law; and (iii) the principle of non-intervention.[61] However, the difficulty with the second criterion is that it is not yet settled in international law what constitutes general principles of international law applicable to unilateral sanctions. With regard to the third criterion, the difficulty is that it is not an absolute principle; it is a qualified principle and its precise definition is contested by different groupings of states and has been interpreted differently at different times. Therefore, it is not easy to draw a line between legality and illegality of unilateral sanctions. Bowett goes on to state that 'it will be necessary to characterize unlawful economic measures by their intent rather than their effect'.[62] However, establishing the intent of one state to cause economic harm to another state is as hard as establishing *mens rea* of the accused in criminal cases before national criminal courts.

Although it has also been argued by some scholars that the principle of the prohibition of the use of force enshrined in Article 2(4) of the Charter of the UN encompasses not only military force against the territorial integrity of another state, but also coercive measures against the political independence (and, by implication, economic independence too) of another state, opinion remains divided. The legislative history of the Charter of the UN suggests that Article 2(4) was designed to outlaw the use of force, meaning

[56] In the words of Hofer, 'legal doctrine generally finds that the limitations of economic coercion are a grey area of international law'. A Hofer, 'The Developed/Developing Divide on Unilateral Coercive Measures: Legitimate Enforcement or Illegitimate Intervention' (2017) 16 *Chinese Journal of International Law* 175, 175.

[57] The ICJ stated in its decision on US activity in Nicaragua, '[a] State is not bound to continue particular trade relations longer than it sees fit to do so, in the absence of a treaty commitment or other specific obligation'. *Military and Paramilitary Activities in and Against Nicaragua (Nicaragua v US)* ICJ Reports (1986) 14, 138.

[58] *Banco Nacional de Cuba v Sabbatino*: 307 F.2d 845, 866 (2d Cir.1966).

[59] Cameron (n 18) 248.

[60] See generally, BE Carter, 'Economic Sanctions' in *Max Planck Encyclopedia of Public International Law* (Oxford University Press, 2011); GC Hufbauer, JJ Schott, KA Elliott and B Oegg, *Economic Sanctions Reconsidered*, 3rd edn (Peterson Inst of International Economics, 2009); MP Doxey *Economic Sanctions and International Enforcement* (Palgrave Macmillan, 1980); Picchio Forlati and Sicilianos, *Economic Sanctions* (2004); Carter, 'International Economic Sanctions' (1987). See generally on unilateral acts of states in international law: P Saganek, *Unilateral Acts of States in Public International Law* (Brill/Nijhoff, 2015).

[61] Bowett, 'Economic Coercion' (1972) 2–3.

[62] ibid, 5.

military force rather than the use of other non-forcible measures including coercive economic measures. Having said this, there have been a number of further international legal developments since the adoption of the UN Charter, all designed either to flesh out the provisions of the Charter or to contribute to the progressive development and/or codification of international law either through hard law or soft law instruments, that have sought to impose limitations on the right of states to employ unilateral sanctions.

According to the UN General Assembly Declaration on the Inadmissibility of Intervention in the Domestic Affairs of States and Protection of Their Independence and Sovereignty (1965):

> No state may use or encourage the use of economic, political or any other type of measures to coerce another state in order to obtain from it the subordination of the exercise of its sovereign rights or to secure from it advantages of any kind.[63]

The 1970 Declaration of Friendly Relations Among States and the 1973 Charter of Economic Rights and Duties of States contain similar provisions. The 1970 Declaration reads as follows:

> No State may use or encourage the use of economic, political or any other type of measures to coerce another State in order to obtain from it the subordination of the exercise of its sovereign rights and to secure from it advantages of any kind.[64]

By putting these instruments together, one could argue that in international law not only the use of force against the territorial integrity and political independence of another state in the traditional sense of the term is prohibited, but also unilateral sanctions against the political and economic independence of another state are prohibited.[65] According to Domb:

> Any unilateral act by a state directed against another state or group of states which is *intended* to and which *does in fact* deprive such state or states of *essential* resources or which *seriously* impairs its normal economic activities, thereby threatening the state's sovereign right to make its own political decisions, is an act of economic aggression. [emphasis in original but footnotes omitted][66]

As stated by Blum, even if unilateral sanctions do not amount to a use of force prohibited under Article 2(4) of the Charter of the UN,

> most of them certainly constitute a violation of the rule of non-intervention into the domestic matters of another sovereign state, with a view to influencing their foreign or domestic policy

[63] UN GA Resolution 2131 (XX), para 2.

[64] Resolution 2625 (XXV) of Declaration on Principles of International Law concerning Friendly Relations and Cooperation among States in accordance with the Charter of the United Nations.

[65] See, eg, the views of the Secretary-General of the Asian-African Legal Consultative Organization: R Mohamad, 'Unilateral Sanctions in International Law: A Quest for Legality' in AZ Marossi and MR Bassett (eds), *Economic Sanctions under International Law* (Springer/TMC Asser Press, 2015) 71–82; Report of the Special Rapporteur on the negative impact of unilateral coercive measures on the enjoyment of human rights, UN Doc A/HRC/36/44 of 26 July 2017; T Boumedra, 'Economic Coercion under International Law' (1990) 2 *African Society of International and Comparative Law Proceedings of the Second Annual Conference* 81.

[66] M Domb, 'Defining Economic Aggression in International Law: The Possibility of Regional Action by the Organization of American States' (1978) 11 *Cornell International Law Journal* 85, 99.

> in an unjustifiable manner. They are also unquestionably incompatible with the duty of states, under Article 2(3) of the Charter, to settle international disputes by peaceful means.[67]

Relying on these principles and other treaty provisions, Henderson has argued that the US unilateral economic sanctions such as those against Nicaragua are unlawful.[68] His analysis would also apply to most of the unilateral sanctions of similar nature in operation today.

Of course, not all unilateral sanctions are unlawful since some of them and especially those of a retorsive character known commonly as 'smart' or targeted sanctions would be permissible under international law. Indeed, 'international law would not pass judgment on economic policies not intended to impair the sovereignty of other nations, even if these policies otherwise forced the affected state into direst of circumstances'.[69] Measures such as declaring a diplomat *persona non grata*, stopping overseas development assistance, denying recognition of a new government that has come to power through a military coup or other undemocratic means, stopping trade with or investment in the target state, terminating or suspending diplomatic relations, or recalling ambassadors in situations provided for in the Vienna Convention on Diplomatic Relations or imposing visa restrictions on certain individuals engaged in the violation of human rights or money laundering or cyber attacks all are permitted activities. States do frequently take measures affecting diplomatic or consular privileges, and they are permissible, but these measures must not prejudice the inviolability of diplomatic or consular personnel or of premises, archives and documents.

However, the difficulty lies in drawing a line between permissible low-intensity unilateral sanctions of limited scope and more comprehensive and high-intensity unilateral sanctions. There is no defined threshold to distinguish the two. It depends on a case-by-case analysis of each and every kind of sanction and their impact on the target state. As stated by Hofer, some sanctions 'qualify as retorsions – defined as unfriendly yet lawful acts'[70] or as lawful countermeasures if they meet the conditions for such measures. The ILC has observed that: 'Countermeasures are a feature of a decentralized system by which injured States may seek to vindicate their rights and to restore the legal relationship with the responsible State which has been ruptured by the internationally

[67] YZ Blum, 'Economic Boycotts in International Law' (1977) 12 *Texas International Law Journal* 5, 15.

[68] Henderson states that 'the application of such measures violates a number of specific treaty commitments as well as customary international law. By implementing an extensive trade embargo against Nicaragua, the United States has breached its obligation under the U.N. Charter to settle its disputes in a peaceful manner. The sanctions also violate provisions of the General Agreement on Tariffs and Trade, the OAS Charter, and the bilateral FCN Treaty between Nicaragua and the United States. Furthermore, customary international law, as evidenced by U.N. resolutions and the principle of non-intervention, does not permit the use of economic sanctions designed to coerce the independent will of another state. The Reagan Administration's trade embargo exceeds the boundaries of permissible influence, becoming instead an illicit intervention into the sovereign affairs of Nicaragua'. JC Henderson, 'Legality of Economic Sanctions Under International Law: The Case of Nicaragua' (1986) 43 *Washington and Lee Law Review* 167, 196 (footnotes omitted).

[69] Comment by the Editors of the University of Pennsylvania Law Review, 'The Use of Nonviolent Coercion: A Study in Legality under Article 2(4) of the Charter of the United Nations' (1974) 122 *University of Pennsylvania Law Review* 983, 1010.

[70] A Hofer, 'The "Curiouser and Curiouser" Legal Nature of Non-UN Sanctions: The Case of the US Sanctions against Russia' (2018) 23 *Journal of Conflict & Security Law* (2018) 1, 2.

wrongful act'.[71] However, the ILC added that: 'A fundamental prerequisite for any lawful countermeasure is the existence of an internationally wrongful act which injured the State taking the countermeasure'.[72]

Tzanakopoulos argues that a 'countermeasure is, by definition, an unlawful act in the first instance' if the state taking countermeasures has not met the prerequisites under international law[73] such as those outlined in Articles 49–53 of the ILC's Draft Articles on State Responsibility.[74] Ronzitti maintains that 'States, individually or in coalition among themselves, are not entitled to adopt sanctions independently from a Resolution of the SC [Security Council]. They may only adopt restrictive measures in the form of countermeasures to react against an international wrong committed by the target State'.[75]

Happold is of the view that if unilateral sanctions do not breach any existing treaty provisions, whether bilateral or multilateral, or a rule of customary international law, then they are lawful.[76] Indeed, a number of treaties do permit states to take economic action against other states under narrowly defined conditions. For instance, GATT article XXI, paragraphs (b)(iii) and (c), do allow a state 'to take any action' that it considers necessary for the protection of its essential security interests or in time of war or other emergency in international relations. Similarly, GATT Article VI allows states to impose countervailing duties against the distortion of international trade by another state and Article XIX allows states to take emergency measures under narrowly defined conditions.

With regard to the legality of unilateral sanctions Judge Koroma has observed that it depends on the motive and modus operandi of such sanctions:

> For some, unilateral sanctions are intended to implement rights and obligations: in other words, coercive measures are taken for rights to be observed and obligations undertaken respected. For others, sanctions are intended to rectify a deviant behaviour or conduct. Unilateral sanctions have also been purportedly imposed as a reaction to an illegal act. However, the imposition of sanctions in response to an illegal act, by definition, presupposes a prior determination that the act in question was, indeed, illegal. Accordingly, for sanctions to be legal they must be in accordance with certain criteria under international law. It is therefore open to question whether the State imposing the sanction should be the one making the determination that there has been a breach of an international obligation or a violation of international law.[77]

[71] Report of the International Law Commission on the work of its Fifty-Third Session (23 April–1 June, and 2 July–10 August 2001), UN Doc A/56/10, Ch II 304.

[72] ILC Commentary on Article 49 of the Draft Articles on State Responsibility 'Object and limits of countermeasures' (ibid, 309).

[73] A Tzanakopoulos, 'State reactions to illegal sanctions' in M Happold and P Eden (eds), *Economic Sanctions and International Law* (Hart Publishing, 2016) 69.

[74] J Crawford, *The International Law Commission's Articles on State Responsibility: Introduction, Text and Commentaries* (Cambridge University Press, 2002); Crawford, Pellet, Olleson and Parlett, *International Responsibility* (2010).

[75] N Ronzitti (ed), *Coercive Diplomacy, Sanctions and International Law* (Brill/Nijhoff, 2016) 31.

[76] M Happold, 'Economic Sanction and International Law: An Introduction' in M Happold and P Eden (eds), *Economic Sanctions and International Law* (Hart Publishing, 2016) 3.

[77] AG Koroma, 'Foreword' in AZ Marossi and MR Bassett (eds), *Economic Sanctions under International Law: Unilateralism, Multilateralism, Legitimacy, and Consequences* (TMC Asser Press and Springer, 2015) xvi.

This is the crux of the matter. He goes on to add that the reasons, purposes or justifications of unilateral sanctions vary:

> It is in that context that we can see a potential danger that a State acting unilaterally, singly, may make an incorrect determination that there has been a violation by the target State of international law or an international obligation when no such violation or breach, objectively determined, had in fact taken place. There is also the danger of unilateral sanctions being imposed for reasons other than those publicly offered. In other words, a reason is offered that is meant to bring the target State in conformity with international law and its international obligations when, in fact, there is a different agenda.[78]

As stated by Tzanakopoulos 'a unilateral reaction to illegality, i.e., a countermeasure, may itself constitute an illegality'[79] if the measure does not meet the prerequisites prescribed in international law. One could go further and argue that unilateral sanctions are unlawful by definition since they are the instruments employed to bypass the requirement to settle international disputes by peaceful means since all members of the UN have a duty to refer any dispute with other states to a mechanism for peaceful settlement of disputes stipulated in Articles 2(3) and 33 of the Charter of the UN. It could also be argued that unilateral sanctions undermine the authority of the Security Council under the Charter of the UN which has granted the Security Council the powers to impose sanctions against a state which has breached or poses a threat to international peace and security by committing an internationally wrongful act against another state. It is partly in this context that various UN General Assembly resolutions and other soft law instruments produced by other UN agencies or other international organisations have sought to regard unilateral sanctions as illegal measures under international law.[80] However, in the absence of a binding international treaty regulating unilateral sanctions and without identifying or establishing the existence or formulation of a rule of customary international law regulating unilateral sanctions it is difficult to regard such sanctions unlawful.

V. Divided Scholarly Opinion

The opinion of publicists has been shifting with different twists and turns in international relations and different authors have expressed their differing views on the legality of not only unilateral sanctions but also the sanctions imposed by the UN. A line of division on scholarly opinion is also recognisable along the developed and the developing countries' positions.[81] Those scholars sympathetic to the position of

[78] ibid.

[79] Tzanakopoulos, 'State reactions to illegal sanctions' (2016) 69.

[80] Examples are Resolution 2625 (XXV) (n 64); Declaration and the Programme of Action on the Establishment of a New International Economic Order, 1974; Charter of Economic Rights and Duties of States, 1974; Ministerial Declaration on General Agreement on Tariffs and Trade at their thirty-eighth session, 1982, para 7(iii); Resolution 152 (VI) of the United Nations Conference on Trade and Development, 'Rejection of Coercive Economic Measures'.

[81] See for an excellent analysis of the developed/developing country perspectives on these issues: Hofer, 'The Developed/Developing Divide' (2017).

developing countries which have traditionally been on the receiving end of unilateral sanctions by developed countries, have regarded such sanctions illegal under international law by relying on a wider interpretation of the term 'force' in Article 2(4) to include high intensity coercive measures and on the provisions of Articles 2(3), 2(7) and 33 and a number of UN General Assembly resolutions such as the 1970 Declaration of Friendly Relations Among States and the 1973 Charter of Economic Rights and Duties of States.[82]

However, those scholars sympathetic to the position or actions taken by the developed countries have sought to justify the legality of such sanctions on a narrow interpretation of the provisions in Article 2(4) and the dismissal of the legal weight to be accorded to the UN General Assembly resolutions.[83] But there are other scholars, such as Hofer, who adopt a more balanced view in passing judgment on the lawfulness and desirability of unilateral sanctions.[84] Although she states that the UN General Assembly resolutions 'are generally political in nature and adopted by a heavily divided vote, thus lacking legal authority'[85] and goes on to add that the Charter of Economic Rights and Duties of States 'does not have normative value',[86] she makes the point that many of the resolutions of the UN General Assembly resolutions on unilateral sanctions 'illustrate tension between the aspirations of developing countries to restrict the use of economic coercion, even when their alleged aim is to enforce compliance with essential international norms, and the continuing practice of developed States'.[87] On the whole, she is critical of the adoption of sanctions and concludes that sanctions should be foregone completely.[88]

It is interesting to note that around the time of the Arab Oil Embargo in the early 1970s a considerable amount of literature was published in the developed world which argues that such measures are illegal under international law.[89] As stated by Ruys, it was the US which in 1948 was critical of the secondary boycott of Israel implemented by the Arab League. However, it is the US itself which 'has become the leading proponent of measures that have an extraterritorial reach'.[90] When the US and the EU began imposing their own sanctions on a number of developing countries for alleged violations of the nuclear non-proliferation regime or violations of human rights or 'supporting' or 'financing' terrorism, many scholars in the developed world sought to justify the use of unilateral sanctions.

[82] See, eg, the views of the Secretary-General of the Asian-African Legal Consultative Organization: Mohamad, 'Unilateral Sanctions in International Law' (2015); UN Doc A/HRC/36/44 (n 65); Boumedra, 'Economic Coercion under International Law' (1990) 2 *African Society of International and Comparative Law Proceedings of the Second Annual Conference* 81.

[83] See for instance Cameron (n 18) 218–54; Happold, 'Economic Sanction and International Law' (2016) 1–12.

[84] Hofer (n 56).

[85] ibid, 184.

[86] ibid, 185.

[87] ibid, 196.

[88] See also Hofer, 'The "Curiouser and Curiouser" Legal Nature of Non-UN Sanctions' (2018); A Hofer, 'Negotiating International Public Policy through the Adoption and Contestation of Sanctions' (2017) (Special Issue 2) *Revue Belge de Droit International* 440–73.

[89] For instance, see JJ Paust and AP Blaustin, 'The Arab Oil Weapon – A Threat to International Peace' (1974) 68 *AJIL* 410.

[90] Ruys (n 7) 29.

VI. Division Along First World and Third World Approaches

Traditionally, unilateral sanctions have been used by First World states against Second or Third World states. Therefore, the legality of unilateral sanctions has traditionally been considered in the context of the developed and developing countries or East–West or North–South relations.[91] First World states have denied the illegality of unilateral sanctions, regarding them as an exercise of sovereign rights or economic diplomacy in the conduct of their foreign affairs that are perfectly permissible under international law. Second World or Third World states, which have often been on the receiving end of unilateral sanctions, have asserted that certain economic measures of high intensity constitute 'economic coercion' which are contrary to international law.

However, with the imposition of very wide-ranging unilateral sanctions by the four developing Arab countries Bahrain, Egypt, Saudi Arabia and the United Arab Emirates against Qatar, another developing Arab country, in June 2017 and a comprehensive set of sanctions imposed by the League of Arab States against Syria, an Arab state,[92] the traditional divide between developed and developing countries on the legality of unilateral sanctions has somewhat been rendered obsolete. States seem not to be aligning themselves along the traditional alliances but conducting themselves on the basis of their own national interests, whether economic, political or military or they are keeping quiet on such matters if it is politically convenient to do so.

VII. Justification of Unilateral Sanctions as Countermeasures

Although common in practice, the implementation of unilateral sanctions is not a recognised institution in international law. According to the ILC's Draft Articles on State Responsibility, wrongfulness could be precluded in the following circumstances: consent, self-defence, countermeasures, *force majeure*, distress and necessity. Unilateral sanctions do not figure in the circumstances that could preclude wrongfulness. Hence, if we go by the approach taken by the ILC, any imposition of unilateral sanctions that does not fall within the scope of permissible countermeasures would be unlawful. Therefore, those states which impose unilateral sanctions against other states seek to justify their action by relying on the institution of countermeasures.

However, the difficulty is that the notion of countermeasures itself is contested and not all unilateral sanctions are countermeasures and most of the unilateral sanctions go beyond the scope of the permissible level of countermeasures. In international law, countermeasures generally mean non-performance of international obligations by one state in response to internationally wrongful acts committed by another state. A general meaning of the very term 'countermeasure' should mean taking measures similar to

[91] See UN Doc A/70/152 (n 34) and A/68/218 of 29 July 2013; Happold (n 76) 5.
[92] UN Doc A/72/307 (n 29) 20–21.

those taken by the state alleged to have committed an internationally wrongful act in the first place, albeit non-reciprocal countermeasures would also be admissible under certain narrowly defined conditions if the reciprocal measures are not viable, adequate or effective. In common parlance, a countermeasure is some kind of 'tit for tat'. However, there have been attempts to accord a wider meaning to the term countermeasures in recent years.

Although the term countermeasures was used in other prior legal studies and in the award of a tribunal in the *Air Services Agreement* case in 1978,[93] the notion of countermeasures was institutionalised in various reports of the rapporteurs of the ILC on state responsibility and it found its expression in the Draft Articles on State Responsibility adopted by the ILC and presented to the UN General Assembly in 2001. Since then the Draft Articles have been influential in the decisions of international courts and tribunals since some of the Draft Articles have been regarded either as declaratory of existing rules of customary international law or part of progressive development of international law. Indeed, the fact that the UN General Assembly Resolution 56/83 of 12 December 2001 annexed the text of the ILC's Draft Articles and commended them to governments add to their legal weight. That is not to say that the Draft Articles are binding or the final words on countermeasures. The ILC's Draft Articles on countermeasures are merely recommendations to the UN General Assembly formulated on the basis of the evidence of state practice available at the time.

As stated by the ILC in its Commentary to the Draft Articles on State Responsibility, 'Judicial decisions, State practice and doctrine confirm the proposition that countermeasures meeting certain substantive and procedural conditions may be legitimate'.[94] The ICJ has held that that countermeasures might justify an otherwise unlawful conduct 'taken in response to a previous international wrongful act of another State and … directed against that State',[95] provided certain conditions are met. The Court went on to add that the purpose of the countermeasures 'must be to induce the wrongdoing state to comply with its obligations under international law, and that the measures must therefore be reversible'.[96] According to the ILC, these conditions include: the requirement of proportionality, the temporary or reversible character of countermeasures and the status of certain fundamental obligations such as those arising from the principles of *jus cogens* character which may not be subject to countermeasures. As stated in the ILC's Commentaries to the Draft Articles on State Responsibility, 'A fundamental prerequisite for any lawful countermeasure is the existence of an internationally wrongful act which injured the State taking the countermeasure'.[97]

[93] The case concerning *Air Services Agreement of 27 March 1946 between the USA and France*, RIAA, vol 18 458 (para 81).

[94] ILC (n 1) 75.

[95] *Gabčíkovo-Nagymaros Project (Hungary-Slovakia)*, Judgment, ICJ Reports 1997, 55 (para 83). The ILC referred to other cases in which similar recognition of the legitimacy of measures of this kind in certain cases can be found. They include, in particular, the *Naulilaa*, *Cysne* and *Air Service Agreement* cases. ILC (n 1) 75.

[96] *Gabčíkovo-Nagymaros Project (Hungary-Slovakia)* (ibid) 56 (para 85).

[97] ILC (n 1) 130. In stipulating this condition, the ILC referred to the opinion of the ICJ in the *Gabčíkovo Nagymaros Project* in which the Court had held that 'In order to be justifiable, a countermeasure must meet certain conditions … In the first place it must be taken in response to a previous international wrongful act of another State and must be directed against that State'.

Thus, although states are permitted to resort to countermeasures under narrowly defined conditions, it can be invoked only in exceptional circumstances. As stated by Jazairy, the UN Rapporteur on the negative impact of unilateral coercive measures on the enjoyment of human rights, there are limitations to the exercise of countermeasures. Such measures would be 'wrongful if they affected obligations for the protection of fundamental human rights; obligations of a humanitarian character prohibiting reprisals; or other obligations under peremptory norms of general international law'.[98] Of course, the ILC Draft Articles on State Responsibility admit the notion of countermeasures under narrowly defined conditions, but it is not clear whether the views of the ILC expressed in 2001 are still valid in their entirety in the contemporary world. At the time the ILC relied heavily on state practice to admit the notion of countermeasures, but the state practice has changed considerably since then. It is submitted that international law and especially customary international law are organic or dynamic and continue to evolve with time. If so, one has to ask whether the views or recommendations of the ILC made in 2001 are still valid.

When developing these Draft Articles, the ILC was relying on state practice, and especially the state practice of the second half of the twentieth century which was dominated by the Cold War rivalry between the two superpowers of the time, ie the US and the then USSR. According to Burke, the Draft Articles 'are subordinate to the UN Charter'.[99] He goes on to add that the

> Draft Articles are not law and are the product of the ILC, a commission that drafts model legislation. With the single exception that the Draft Articles partially embody customary law of State responsibility, the Draft Articles may be used as guidelines, but nothing more.[100]

Azaria states that, 'Neither the ILC nor the UNGA has suggested that the ASR [the Draft Articles of the ILC on State Responsibility] in their entirety reflect existing custom'.[101]

With the ILC relying on limited state practice in formulating its Draft Articles in State Responsibility, some Draft Articles reflect custom, others represent progressive development of the law. The ILC's own commentaries state that these Draft Articles 'seek to formulate, by way of codification and progressive development, the basic rules of international law concerning the responsibility of States for their internationally wrongful acts'.[102] Even if the ILC's Draft Articles are regarded as declaratory or codification of the rules of customary international law on countermeasures, the fact of the matter is that the rules of customary international law themselves are not static and are liable to change through subsequent state practice. In our rapidly changing world, various developments have been taking place in state practice since the adoption of the Draft Articles in 2001. Therefore, when ascertaining the status and scope of countermeasures in international law today, one will have to take into account the developments in state practice that have taken place during the intervening years.

[98] UN Doc A/HRC/30/45 (n 26) para 38.

[99] JJA Burke, 'Economic Sanctions Against the Russian Federation Are Illegal under Public International Law' (2015) 3 *Russian Law Journal* 126, 129.

[100] ibid, 136.

[101] D Azaria, *Treaties on Transit of Energy via Pipelines and Countermeasures* (Oxford University Press, 2015) 16.

[102] ILC (n 1) 31.

VIII. Unilateral Sanctions in Customary International Law

Since there is no international treaty regulating unilateral sanctions, first, it needs to be established whether there exists a rule of customary international law that regulates such sanctions. For this purpose, it is crucial to examine state practice and assess the existence of *opinio juris* in such practice. As state practice is also divided on the legality of such coercive measures, it is necessary to examine whether the state practice of some states to resort to the use of unilateral sanctions, or the state practice of other states who oppose such sanctions, has given rise to the crystallisation of a rule of customary international law to this effect.

A survey of recent state practice demonstrates that an overwhelming majority of states oppose the use of unilateral sanctions as a tool to achieve foreign policy objectives by a state. For instance, a near unanimous vote was cast in the UN General Assembly[103] in favour of a resolution entitled 'Necessity of ending the economic, commercial and financial embargo imposed against Cuba' on 1 November 2018. An overwhelming majority of states (189) voted for this resolution, with two abstentions (Ukraine and Moldova) and two against (US and Israel) out of the total UN membership of 193.[104] The position of the US and Israel in their opposition of such a resolution has not been consistent either. For instance, the US and Israel had not opposed such a resolution in 2016 in the General Assembly. The 2016 resolution was adopted with 191 votes in favour, none against and two abstentions (US and Israel).

It may be debatable whether such state practice was coupled with *opinio juris* to meet the requirements for the formation of a customary rule of international law. The existence of the legal conviction or the psychological element of *opinio juris*, however, could be discerned from the repeated stand taken by an overwhelming majority of states against unilateral coercive measures within the UN and other international fora, as well as from the content of such resolutions themselves, from the statements made by delegates in the General Assembly during the debate on the resolutions, and from the responses from states to a request for information by the Secretary-General of the UN on the implementation of the resolutions concerned. For instance, in its resolution 72/4, entitled 'Necessity of ending the economic, commercial and financial embargo imposed by the United States of America against Cuba', the Secretary-General had been asked to report on the implementation of the resolution *in the light of the purposes and principles of the Charter of the United Nations and international law* and to submit it to the Assembly.

When the Secretary-General wrote to states for information to this effect, an overwhelming majority of states responded stating, inter alia, that they opposed the use of unilateral sanctions by one state against another, adding that such sanctions were against the principles of international law.[105] In adopting the resolution on this subject matter on 1 November 2018, the General Assembly referred to the principles of the

[103] UN Press release GA/12086 of 1 November 2018 with a summary of the statements made by states, available at www.un.org/press/en/2018/ga12086.doc.htm.

[104] A/RES/73/8.

[105] UN Doc A/73/85 of 29 August 2018: Report of the Secretary General on 'Necessity of ending the economic, commercial and financial embargo imposed by the United States of America against Cuba'.

sovereign equality of States, non-intervention and non-interference in their internal affairs and freedom of international trade and navigation, which are also enshrined in many international legal instruments.[106] This indicates the existence of *opinio juris* or legal conviction on the part of the states that voted for the resolution, that the unilateral sanctions imposed by the US against Cuba were not consistent with the existing norms of international law.

Another exercise that would strengthen this view is the response from a vast majority of states to the request of the UN Secretary-General for information about their compliance with a UN General Assembly resolution on the US against sanctions against Cuba in 2012. A total of 145 states responded and a vast majority of them opposed the US sanctions and deemed them to be inconsistent with international law, including the Charter of the UN.[107] The UN has collected similar information not only in relation to a particular state, but also in relation to a general theme of unilateral economic measures as a means of political and economic coercion. A good number of states stated in their response to the UN Secretary-General's request that they regarded such sanctions to be inconsistent with the principles of international law, including the Charter of the UN.[108] Such statements are powerful examples of state practice coupled with *opinio juris*.

There are other examples of state practice outside of the UN which endorse the practice within the UN. For instance, in a joint declaration on the Promotion of International Law issued in June 2016, both China and Russia stated that unilateral sanctions or non-UN sanctions were excluded under the 'generally recognised principles and rules of international law'.[109] Earlier in April 2016, China, India and Russia had issued a similar declaration stating that unilateral sanctions or non-UN sanctions were against the principles of sovereign equality of states and non-intervention.[110] Therefore, a resolution supported by an overwhelming majority of states rejecting the use of unilateral sanctions as a tool to achieve foreign policy objectives by a state has been passed in the UN General Assembly year after year. This demonstrates that such state practice appears to meet the test of consistency, uniformity and generality required for a state practice to crystallise into a rule of customary international law to this effect.

IX. Legal Weight of Developed and Developing Country Practice

There is a tendency to regard the state practice that opposes unilateral sanctions as the practice of developing countries or Third World countries and attach less weight to them. However, the traditional divide between the practice of developed and developing

[106] A/RES 73/8.

[107] UN Doc A/67/118 of 16 August 2012.

[108] See for instance comments of states in their response to the UN Secretary-General: UN Doc A/68/218 (n 91) and UN Doc A/70/152 (n 34).

[109] As cited by Hofer (n 56) 176.

[110] As cited in ibid.

countries is no longer valid since states are aligning themselves these days along the issues of the day that serve their national interests. States have aligned themselves within many international organisations such as the WTO with any group that serves their national interest.[111] It also is no longer valid to consider any view as a view of 'Third World' countries. After the collapse of the USSR and the end of Communism in Europe, it is no longer appropriate to regard the former Warsaw Pact countries as part of the Second World. Many of the former Second World states have entered the ranks of the First World countries by joining regional institutions such as the EU.

The ideological divide that existed between the Western and Eastern countries during the old Cold War no longer exists. Likewise, communism in the real sense of the word or as an ideology is no longer in practice in China or Vietnam. These countries have embraced capitalism, joined the WTO, recognised private property and prospered. It is only for reasons of history and of practical expediency that these countries are still ruled by communist parties. China, Vietnam, Singapore and South Korea are no longer 'Third World' countries in the traditional sense of this term. China is already the second largest world economy and poised to become the largest economy by 2030. South Korea announced in 2019 that it no longer expects the WTO to treat it as a developing country.[112] The Asian, African and Latin American countries are at the forefront of making and shaping the mainstream international law in the areas of human rights, environmental protection and regulation of international trade, commerce and investment.[113] Therefore, it is an insult to treat the practice of many states in Asia, Africa and Latin America as the practice of 'Third World' countries.

The attempt to denigrate certain norms as 'Third World' norms is based on the traditional Euro-centric approach to state practice and the formation of the rules of customary international law. However, the world has moved on, and the values and principles championed by the non-European or non-Western countries have become part of mainstream international law. The Principles of *Panchasheel* is an example. It is the developing, or the so-called 'Third World' countries, that are now shaping the rules of international law on human rights and environmental protection. Informed by the Hindu/Buddhist philosophies of tolerance, peaceful coexistence and non-violence, and adopted and practised by India, China and many members of the Non-Aligned Movement, particularly Asian and African members, these principles of Eastern origin have been regarded as important principles of international law, as equally pertinent as any other principles included in the core international law-making treaties.[114] Thus, the practice of non-Western states, evidenced through the voting for and against a

[111] See SP Subedi, 'The Notion of Free Trade and the First Ten Years of the World Trade Organization: How Level is the "Level Playing Field"?' (2006) 53 *Netherlands International Law Review* 273–96.

[112] 'South Korea gives up WTO developing country status' *The Financial Times* (26 October 2019) 8.

[113] See generally C Cai, 'New Powers and International Law in the 21st Century' (2013) 24 *European Journal of International Law* 755.

[114] See generally, CH Alexandrowicz, 'The Afro-Asian World and the Law of Nations' (1968) 123 *Recueil des Cours* 121; CH Alexandrowicz, 'Kautilyan Principles and the Law of Nations' (1965) 41 *British Yearbook of International Law* 301; SP Subedi, 'Are the Principles of Human Rights "Western" Ideas? An Analysis of the Claim of the "Asian" Concept of Human Rights from the Perspectives of Hinduism' (1999) 30 *California Western International Law Journal* 45; M Ritter, 'Human Rights: The Universalist Controversy. A Response

resolution in the UN General Assembly or through other declarations and diplomatic exchanges, are capable of contributing to the formation of a rule of customary international law or modification of the existing rules as much as the practice of Western states or any other states.

As noted by Chimni, customary international law has traditionally revealed 'the foundational role of the interests of European States, European legal consciousness, and European social and political theories in the making of modern international law'.[115] But this should no longer be the case in this multipolar and trans-civilisational world in which the power is gradually shifting from the West to the East.[116] Therefore, the practice of non-Western states, whether 'Third World' or the former Second World nations, whether within or outside of the UN, should be given equal weight in deciding whether a body of state practice has given rise to the formulation of a rule of customary international law. Accordingly, the General Assembly resolutions characterising unilateral sanctions as not consistent with the Charter of the UN and other rules of international law and hence as unlawful, should be regarded as contributing to the formation of a new rule of customary international law, or as modifying the existing rules, if such practice meets the other requirements for custom such as generality, consistency, and uniformity as well as *opinio juris*.

Chimni is right in observing that 'A postmodern doctrine would treat qualifying resolutions of international organisations – those that are the outcome of extended negotiations, broad consensus, clear articulation and subsequent affirmations – as prima facie yielding rules of CIL [customary international law]'.[117] This indeed is the case with the General Assembly resolutions declaring that those unlawful unilateral sanctions that are not consistent with the Charter of the UN and other rules of international law, should be regarded as capable of creating a new rule or modifying an existing rule of customary international law on the subject. Law, whether municipal or international, is and should be an expression of popular will. It is this popular will that provides legitimacy to any law. In any democratic society, whether national or international, it is the popular will that makes or changes the law. Thus, if the popular will of the international community is to regard certain unilateral sanctions as unlawful then they should be treated as such.

X. The Jurisprudence

The ICJ held in its advisory opinion in the case concerning *Legal Consequences of the Separation of the Chagos Archipelago from Mauritius in 1965*, that when customary international law matters were at issue, the Court would be willing to consider the evolution

to the "Are the Principles of Human Rights 'Western' Ideas? An Analysis of the Claim of the 'Asian' Concept of Human Rights from the Perspectives of Hinduism", by Surya P. Subedi' (1999) 30 *California Western International Law Journal* 71.

[115] BS Chimni, 'Customary international law: A Third World Perspective' (2018) 112 *AJIL* (2018) 1, 12.

[116] See generally SP Subedi, 'The Universality of Human Rights and the UN Human Rights Agenda: The Impact of the Shift of Power to the East and the Resurgence of the BRICS' (2015) 55 *Indian Journal of International Law* 177.

[117] Chimni, 'Customary international law' (2018) 41.

of the law on self-determination since the adoption of the Charter of the UN and a General Assembly resolution on the subject matter.[118] The Court stated that: 'Indeed, State practice and *opinio juris*, i.e. the acceptance of that practice as law (Article 38 of the Statute of the Court), are consolidated and confirmed gradually over time'. It went on to add that it 'may also rely on legal instruments which postdate the period in question, when those instruments confirm or interpret pre-existing rules or principles'.[119] Thus, by implication, the ICJ would be willing to look into the evolution of the law on unilateral sanctions or countermeasures that has taken place after the ILC's recommendation of the Draft Articles on State Responsibility in 2001. Referring to its earlier decision in the *North Sea Continental Shelf* case, the ICJ went on to state that 'Custom is constituted through "general practice accepted as law" (Article 38 of the Statute of the Court)' and that 'both elements, namely general practice and *opinio juris*, which are constitutive of international custom, are closely linked'.[120]

In the *North Sea Continental Shelf* case itself the Court had held that:

> Not only must the acts concerned amount to a settled practice, but they must also be such, or be carried out in such a way, as to be evidence of a belief that this practice is rendered obligatory by the existence of a rule of law requiring it. The need for such a belief, i.e., the existence of a subjective element, is implicit in the very notion of the *opinio juris sive necessitatis*. The States concerned must therefore feel that they are conforming to what amounts to a legal obligation. The frequency, or even habitual character of the acts is not in itself enough.[121]

What is needed for state practice to crystalise into custom is generality, consistency and uniformity of the practice in question and it should be coupled with *opnio juris*. Not only the evidence of such state practice but also the emergence of an *opinio juris* could be inferred from the manner in which states conduct themselves in the adoption of a UN General Assembly resolution and in other multilateral or bilateral fora. In its Advisory Opinion on the *Legality of the Threat or Use of Nuclear Weapons* the Court noted that:

> General Assembly resolutions, even if they are not binding, may sometimes have normative value. They can, in certain circumstances, provide evidence important for establishing the existence of a rule or the emergence of an *opinio juris*. To establish whether this is true of a given General Assembly resolution, it is necessary to look at its content and the conditions of its adoption; it is also necessary to see whether an *opinio juris* exists as to its normative character.[122]

Accordingly, with reference to the General Assembly Resolution 1514 (XV) containing the Declaration on the Granting of Independence to Colonial Countries and Peoples, the Court held in the case concerning *Legal Consequences of the Separation of the Chagos Archipelago from Mauritius in 1965* that:

> although resolution 1514 (XV) is formally a recommendation, it has a declaratory character with regard to the right to self-determination as a customary norm, in view of its content and

[118] *Legal Consequences of the Separation of the Chagos Archipelago from Mauritius in 1965*, advisory opinion of the International Court of Justice of 25 February 2019 (General List No.169), para 142.

[119] ibid, para 143.

[120] ibid, para 149.

[121] *North Sea Continental Shelf*, Judgment, ICJ Reports (1969) 44, para 77.

[122] *Legality of the Threat or Use of Nuclear Weapons*, Advisory Opinion, ICJ. Reports 1996 (I) 254–55, para 70.

> the conditions of its adoption. The resolution was adopted by 89 votes with 9 abstentions. None of the States participating in the vote contested the existence of the right of peoples to self-determination. Certain States justified their abstention on the basis of the time required for the implementation of such a right.[123]

The Court is seeking to establish a normative character of a General Assembly resolution, in order for the resolution to be able to contribute to the formation of custom. Therefore, the resolutions of normative character of the UN General Assembly pronouncing that unilateral sanctions which are not consistent with the Charter of the UN are in fact unlawful, deem capable of contributing to the formation of custom on the law governing unilateral sanctions. Accordingly, the law governing the unilateral sanctions today seems to be the one which has been pronounced through the UN General Assembly resolutions and resolutions of other international organisations such as the UN Human Rights Council and the Non-Aligned Movement on the subject matter. This conclusion seems to be supported by the combined effect of the normative character of the UN General Assembly resolutions and those of the UN Human Rights Council on the unlawfulness of the use of unilateral sanctions. This is especially so with regard to those unilateral sanctions with extraterritorial application, which have been characterised as not being consistent with the Charter of the UN and human rights obligations of states; and an overwhelming majority of states seems to support such a view. As demonstrated in the preceding paragraphs, the UN General Assembly has consistently called upon states that impose unilateral sanctions not consistent with international law, including the Charter of the UN, to stop adopting, maintaining or implementing such sanctions.

XI. Unilateral Sanctions with Extraterritorial Reach

Even if the legal status of other forms of unilateral sanctions was debatable, the one on unilateral sanctions with territorial reach seems near universal: an overwhelming majority of states deems them unlawful. For instance, in a resolution on human rights and unilateral coercive measures the UN General Assembly placed a special emphasis on rejecting unilateral economic measures with extraterritorial reach when calling upon states to refrain from adopting or implementing any unilateral measure not in accordance with international law and the Charter of the United Nations. The General Assembly states that it:

> Rejects unilateral coercive measures with all their extraterritorial effects as tools for political or economic pressure against any country, in particular against developing countries, because of their negative effects on the realization of all the human rights of vast sectors of their populations, in particular children, women and the elderly.[124]

Likewise, the Member States of the Asian–African Legal Consultative Organisation (AALCO) have expressed their view that unilateral sanctions imposed against

[123] *Legal Consequences of the Separation of the Chagos Archipelago from Mauritius in 1965* (n 118) para 152.
[124] UN Doc A/RES/51/103 of 12 December 1996.

third states violate various principles of international law.[125] Article 20 of the Charter of the Organisation of the American States provides that: 'No State may use or encourage the use of coercive measures of an economic or political character in order to force the sovereign will of another State and obtain from it advantages of any kind'.[126] In the final document of the sixteenth summit of the Heads of State and Government of the Non-Aligned Movement, held in Tehran in August 2012, the Member States of the Movement decided to refrain from recognising, adopting or implementing extraterritorial or unilateral coercive measures or laws.[127] Another example of state practice against the use of unilateral sanctions is a resolution of the UN Human Rights Council of 23 March 2018 titled 'Human rights and unilateral coercive measures'. In it the Council called upon all states

> to stop adopting, maintaining or implementing unilateral coercive measures not in accordance with international law, international humanitarian law, the Charter of the United Nations and the norms and principles governing peaceful relations among States, in particular those of a coercive nature with extraterritorial effects, which create obstacles to trade relations among States, thus impeding the full realization of the rights set forth in the Universal Declaration of Human Rights and other international human rights instruments, in particular the right of individuals and peoples to development.[128]

The Council urged all states to refrain from imposing unilateral coercive measures and to remove measures stating that they are contrary to the Charter and norms and principles governing peaceful relations among states at all levels. The Council went to add that it

> strongly objects to the extraterritorial nature of those measures which, in addition, threaten the sovereignty of States, and in this context calls upon all Member States neither to recognize these measures nor to apply them, and to take effective administrative or legislative measures, as appropriate, to counteract the extraterritorial application or effects of unilateral coercive measures" and expressed its "grave concern that any unilateral coercive measure imposed necessarily runs counter to some provisions of the International Bill of Human Rights or peremptory norms and other provisions of customary law, and entails adverse consequences for the enjoyment of human rights by innocent people.[129]

This resolution was adopted by a recorded vote (28 to 15, with three abstentions).[130] Resolutions of this nature cannot be dismissed as mere political statements of a political body, since they are adopted as statements of states on the legal status of unilateral

[125] Mohamad (n 65) 72; and the AALCO sources cited at 76, fn 21.

[126] Art 20 of the Charter of the Organization of American States of 1967, available at www.oas.org/en/sla/dil/docs/inter_american_treaties_A-41_charter_OAS.pdf.

[127] As cited in UN Doc A/HRC/RES/24/14 of 8 October 2013.

[128] UN Doc A/HRC/RES/37/21 of 13 April 2018, para 1, available at documents-dds-ny.un.org/doc/UNDOC/LTD/G18/067/36/PDF/G1806736.pdf?OpenElement.

[129] ibid, paras 2–6.

[130] The voting was as follows. In favour: Angola, Burundi, Chile, China, Côte d'Ivoire, Cuba, Democratic Republic of the Congo, Ecuador, Egypt, Ethiopia, Iraq, Kenya, Kyrgyzstan, Mongolia, Nepal, Nigeria, Pakistan, Peru, Philippines, Qatar, Rwanda, Saudi Arabia, Senegal, South Africa, Togo, Tunisia, United Arab Emirates, Venezuela (Bolivarian Republic of) Against: Australia, Belgium, Croatia, Georgia, Germany, Hungary, Japan, Republic of Korea, Slovakia, Slovenia, Spain, Switzerland, Ukraine, United Kingdom of Great Britain and Northern Ireland, United States of America. Abstaining: Afghanistan, Brazil, Mexico.

sanctions, touching on pertinent principles of international law, framed within international law and couched in a legal language. Of course, the resolutions of the UN Human Rights Council as such are not legally binding instruments but they represent the views of states on an international legal issue and thus constitute state practice and demonstrate the legal conviction (*opinio juris*) of states. Given its content, this resolution has the characteristics of a soft-law instrument. What is more, this resolution was built on the report of the Special Rapporteur on the negative impact of unilateral coercive measures on the enjoyment of human rights.[131]

Along with this resolution, a number of other resolutions of the UN General Assembly, other UN studies and reports,[132] as well as the Vienna Declaration and Programme of Action adopted by the World Conference on Human Rights in 1993 have called upon states to

> refrain from any unilateral measure not in accordance with international law and the Charter of the United Nations that creates obstacles to trade relations among States and impede the full realization of the human rights set forth in the Universal Declaration of Human Rights and in international human rights instruments, in particular the rights of everyone to a standard of living adequate for their health and well-being, including food and medical care, housing and the necessary social services.[133]

There is other evidence of state practice of this nature against the imposition of unilateral sanctions with extraterritorial reach. For instance, France, Germany and the UK distanced themselves from the unilateral sanctions imposed by the US against Iran to preserve the Iran nuclear deal, ie, the Joint Comprehensive Plan of Action (JCPoA) endorsed by the UN Security Council Resolution 2231. In January 2019, they created an Instrument for Supporting Trade Exchanges (INSTEX SAS), a Special Purpose Vehicle aimed at facilitating legitimate trade between European economic operators and Iran.[134] These three European powers went further and issued a joint statement together with the High Representative of the European Union on 4 May 2019 stating that they 'take note with regret and concern of the decision by the United States not to extend waivers with regards to trade in oil with Iran'. They added: 'The lifting of nuclear-related sanctions is an essential part of the JCPoA … We deeply regret the re-imposition of sanctions by the United States following their withdrawal from the JCPoA'.[135]

This was not the first instance of European states distancing themselves from the extraterritorial application of US domestic law. For instance, in 1996 the EU adopted

[131] A/HRC/36/44 (n 65).

[132] See for a summary of these resolutions, reports and studies: 'Human rights and unilateral coercive measure', available at www.ohchr.org/EN/NewsEvents/Seminars/Pages/WorkshopCoerciveMeasures.aspx.

[133] The Vienna Declaration and Programme of Action adopted by the World Conference on Human Rights, 1993: A/CONF 157/23, para 31.

[134] 'New mechanism to facilitate trade with Iran: joint statement', available at www.gov.uk/government/news/joint-statement-on-the-new-mechanism-to-facilitate-trade-with-iran; 'European States launch Iran trade channel to counter curbs' *The Financial Times* (1 February 2019).

[135] 'Statement by the High Representative of the European Union and the Foreign Ministers of France, Germany and the United Kingdom' 4 May 2019, available at www.gov.uk/government/news/statement-by-the-high-representative-of-the-european-union-and-the-foreign-ministers-of-france-germany-and-the-united-kingdom.

instruments of EU law designed to counter the purported extraterritorial effects of US sanctions regimes, which the EU sees as unlawful.[136] The provisions state:

> A third country has enacted certain laws, regulations, and other legislative instruments which purport to regulate activities of natural and legal persons under the jurisdiction of the [European Union] Member State; ... by their extra-territorial application such laws, regulations and other legislative instruments violate international law.[137]

State practice of this nature is capable of giving rise to the formation of a new rule of customary international law that rejects the use of unilateral sanctions against the principles of international law, or that modifies the existing rule to support the use of unilateral sanctions by one state or a group of states against another state against the principles of international law. Such a strong trend in state practice also narrows down the scope of the provisions on countermeasures included in the Draft Articles on State Responsibility adopted by the ILC.

In its advisory opinion in the case concerning *Legal Consequences of the Separation of the Chagos Archipelago from Mauritius in 1965*, the ICJ was willing to attach weight to the UN General Assembly resolutions on matters in which the Assembly had 'a long and consistent record'.[138] This is certainly the case with regard to the General Assembly resolutions on the unlawfulness of the unilateral sanctions not consistent with the Charter of the UN. Therefore, it can be submitted that there is now a rule of customary international law that renders unlawful unilateral sanctions with extraterritorial reach.

A considerable weight of scholarly opinion also holds the view that although the General Assembly resolutions as such are not binding, they can serve as evidence of state practice and *opinio juris*. Brownlie states, 'when they are concerned with general norms of international law, then acceptance by a majority vote constitutes *evidence* of the opinion of governments in the widest forum for the expression of such opinions'. He adds:

> Even when they are framed as general principles, resolutions of this kind provide a basis for the progressive development of the law and the speedy consolidation of customary rules ... In general each individual resolution must be assessed in the light of all the circumstances and also by reference to other evidence of the opinions of States on the point in issue.[139]

Indeed, as analysed in the preceding paragraphs, the views of states expressed in the relevant resolutions of the UN General Assembly and Human Rights Council are supported by other evidence of the opinions of states on the unlawfulness of unilateral sanctions, especially those with extraterritorial application.

The rules concerning the persistent and subsequent objector would mean that those states that have opposed the resolutions of the UN General Assembly or the Human Rights Council may not be bound either by the resolutions themselves or the customary international law emerging out of such resolutions. But the fact is that these resolutions are founded on the provisions of the Charter of the UN, other rules of international

[136] UN Doc A/HRC/36/44 (n 65) para 21.
[137] As cited by Idriss Jazairy in ibid.
[138] *Legal Consequences of the Separation of the Chagos Archipelago from Mauritius in 1965* (n 118) para 87.
[139] I Brownlie, *Principles of Public International Law*, 7th edn (Oxford University Press, 2008) 15.

law, including the principles of *jus cogens* character such as the principles of self-determination and non-discrimination, human rights and humanitarian law treaties and those resolutions of the UN General Assembly which enjoyed universal or near universal acceptance by states. As stated by the ICJ in the *Nicaragua v USA* case:

> It is not to be expected that in the practice of States the application of the rules in question should have been perfect, in the sense that States should have refrained, with complete consistency, from the use of force or from intervention in each other's internal affairs. The Court does not consider that, for a rule to be established as customary, the corresponding practice must be in absolutely rigorous conformity with the rule. In order to deduce the existence of customary rules, the Court deems it sufficient that the conduct of States should, in general, be consistent with such rules, and that instances of State conduct inconsistent with a given rule should generally have been treated as breaches of that rule, not as indications of the recognition of a new rule.[140]

The Court also made it clear that the practice of states in contravention of the existing rules and principles of international law do not constitute custom. The Court held that:

> If a State acts in a way prima facie incompatible with a recognized rule, but defends its conduct by appealing to exceptions or justifications contained within the rule itself, then whether or not the State's conduct is in fact justifiable on that basis, the significance of that attitude is to confirm rather than to weaken the rule.[141]

Thus, the practice of those states that impose unilateral sanctions on other states that are not consistent with the Charter of the UN and other rules of international law does not constitute custom, even if they invoke the principle of sovereignty of states to justify their actions.

The state practice on the lawfulness of unilateral sanctions appear to meet the tests of consistency, uniformity and generality required to constitute custom on the subject matter, since this state practice seems also to indicate the existence of an *opinio juris* on this issue. For instance, the UN Human Rights Council states in its resolution on Human Rights and Unilateral Coercive Measures that 'unilateral coercive measures and legislation are contrary to international law, international humanitarian law, the Charter and the norms and principles governing peaceful relations among States' and goes on to call upon states 'to stop adopting, maintaining or implementing unilateral coercive measures not in accordance with international law, international humanitarian law, the Charter of the United Nations and the norms and principles governing peaceful relations among States'.[142] The UN Human Rights Council was in effect seeking to confirm the normative character of various UN General Assembly resolutions dating back to the 1970 Declaration on Friendly Relations Among States,[143] in declaring the unlawfulness of unilateral sanctions, especially those with extraterritorial application not consistent with international law, international humanitarian law, and the Charter of the United Nations.

[140] *Military and Paramilitary Activities in und against Nicaragua (Nicaragua v United States of America)* (n 57) para 186.
[141] ibid.
[142] UN Doc A/HRC/37/21 of 19 March 2018 preambular para 6 and operative para 1 respectively.
[143] Resolution 2625 (XXV) (n 64).

The 1970 Declaration states that:

> No State may use or encourage the use of economic political or any other type of measures to coerce another State in order to obtain from it the subordination of the exercise of its sovereign rights and to secure from it advantages of any kind.[144]

It should be noted that the 1970 Declaration is widely accepted as the authoritative interpretation of the Charter of the UN. Similar language was used in another landmark resolution of the General Assembly in 1974. In Resolution 3281 (XXIX) containing the Charter of Economic Rights and Duties of States of 12 December 1974, the UN General Assembly declared that 'No State may use or encourage the use of economic, political or any other type of measures to coerce another State in order to obtain from it the subordination of the exercise of its sovereign rights'. An *ad hoc* group of experts convened by the UN Secretariat in 1997 on 'economic measures as a means of political and economic coercion against developing countries' concluded, under the heading 'basic legal norms', that

> the basic principles of international law … as set out in the Charter of the United Nations, elaborated in a number of international legal instruments and backed by declarations adopted by international conferences, proscribe … the imposition of coercive economic measures as instruments of intervention in matters that are essentially Within the domestic jurisdiction of any State.[145]

This statement sums up the status of unilateral sanctions in international law. Similarly, the Doha Mandate adopted at the UNCTAD's Thirteenth Session held in 2012 in Doha, Qatar, strongly urged states

> to refrain from promulgating and applying any unilateral economic, financial or trade measures not in accordance with international law and the Charter of the United Nations that impedes the full achievement of economic and social development, particularly in developing countries, and that affects commercial interests.[146]

Unilateral sanctions generally prohibit only the targeting state's government, business organisations and citizens from doing business with the targeted state. Extraterritorial sanctions, also known as secondary sanctions, on the other hand seek to restrict the economic activity of governments, companies and nationals of third countries. This is one reason why the unilateral sanctions with extraterritorial reach have been regarded as a violation of the sovereignty of third states. The practice of extraterritorial sanctions appears to undermine the extraterritorial and universal character of human rights obligations. Commentators have observed that 'States are considered to assume certain extraterritorial obligations under human rights instruments to which they are parties'.[147] After analysing the position of the ICJ in the *Case Concerning Application of*

[144] ibid.
[145] UN Doc A/52/459 of 1997.
[146] UN Doc TD/L.427 of 26 April 2012, para 25.
[147] The Report of the UN Special Rapporteur on the negative impact of unilateral coercive measures on the enjoyment of human rights of 29 August 2017: UN Doc A/HRC/72/370, para 34. See also M Milanovic, *Extraterritorial Application of Human Rights Treaties* (Oxford University Press, 2011); and G Grisel, *Application extraterritoriale du droit international des droits de l'homme* (Helbing Lichtenhahn/LGDJ/Bruylant, 2010).

the International Convention on the Elimination of All Forms of Racial Discrimination (Georgia v Russian Federation),[148] the UN Special Rapporteur comments on the negative impact of unilateral coercive measures on the enjoyment of human rights that

> the Court seemed to operate on a presumption that human rights treaties applied to extra-territorial acts of the State unless treaty provisions contained a specific territorial limitation; and ... the broad language [in the decision of the Court] suggests that, in the eyes of the Court at least, this approach is not limited to the International Convention on the Elimination of All Forms of Racial Discrimination, but applies to human rights treaties in general ... Such an approach has been labelled a 'cause and effect' approach, whereby 'persons fall within a State's jurisdiction when a State through lawful or unlawful exercises of power causes human rights violations extraterritorially.[149]

Indeed, all Members of the UN have pledged themselves to respect human rights internationally through the Charter of the UN, the Universal Declaration of Human Rights, the 2005 World Outcome Document[150] and other international human rights treaties of near universal character. The UN Special Rapporteur on the negative impact of unilateral coercive measures on the enjoyment of human rights goes on to add that:

> It seems difficult to deny, in that respect, that international sanctions come within the category of situations where States can influence situations located abroad, and actually do influence situations abroad to the extent that they affect the enjoyment of human rights by populations (or segments of the population) of the target State ... In the light of the growing recognition of the existence of extraterritorial obligations of States under human rights instruments, it is reasonable to assume that in the case of international sanctions that have extraterritorial effects by their very nature, a State imposing them should incur liability for human rights violations, even if it does not exercise formal 'jurisdiction' or 'control' over the population or the territory targeted.[151]

This view is shared by Skogly who states that:

> The violation of the human rights of individuals by a State outside its jurisdiction would imply that the State has committed an internationally wrongful act and should not be able to do so with impunity ... If the protection from human rights treaties is dependent upon States acting within their jurisdiction, the danger is that extra-jurisdiction acts can be carried out without responsibility being triggered.[152]

If the unilateral sanctions imposed by one UN Member against another Member result in the violation of human rights of the people residing in the target State, then the targeting state would be in breach of its international obligations to respect human rights internationally. Although strictly speaking the obligation of states to protect most human rights[153] is limited to the people residing within their own territories, the duty

[148] *Application of the International Convention on the Elimination of All Forms of Racial Discrimination (Georgia v Russian Federation)*, Preliminary Objections, Judgment, ICJ Reports (2011) 70.
[149] UN Doc A/HRC/72/370 (n 147) paras 41 and 42 (footnote omitted).
[150] A/RES/60/1 of 24 October 2005.
[151] A/HRC/36/44 (n 65) paras 44 and 45.
[152] SI Skogly, 'Extraterritoriality: universal human rights without universal obligations?' in S Joseph and A McBeth (eds), *Research Handbook on International Human Rights Law* (Edward Elgar, 2010) 93, as cited in UN Doc A/HRC/72/370 (n 147) para 43.
[153] But the economic, social and cultural rights have no such territorial limitation and the duty of the states party to the 1966 Covenant on Economic, Social and Cultural Rights to protect such rights seem to apply internationally.

to respect human rights applies vis-à-vis the people residing anywhere and everywhere. As stated by Jazairy:

> Applying a strict requirement of jurisdiction for victims of human rights violations caused by the extraterritorial actions of a foreign State (especially economic sanctions) would result in a protection gap. This would amount to a paradoxical situation in which victims residing abroad would indeed be deprived of the treaty protection merely because they were not, legally speaking, within the jurisdiction of the foreign State that implemented sanctions affecting them.[154]

The Special Rapporteur has highlighted the harmful consequences of the practice of extraterritorial sanctions, that is, sanctions regimes that purport to apply to foreign states and their economic and financial sectors, as well as persons, acting outside the sanctioning country.[155] This is especially so 'when they conduct business with individuals, groups, regimes or countries that are the target of the primary sanctions regime'.[156] For instance, the US has commonly applied its domestic sanctions law to foreign persons and institutions and such laws are liable to undermine in many situations the human rights of the people in the target state.

Such extraterritorial application of the domestic law of a given state is also liable to undermine the sovereignty of the target state and commonly accepted rules governing the jurisdiction of the target state under international law. Thus, unilateral sanctions with extraterritorial application can be deemed to be unlawful under public international law. According to Jazairy, unilateral sanctions with extraterritorial application of the domestic laws of the target state 'cannot generally be justified as legitimate countermeasures under the law of State responsibility'.[157] He goes on to add that: 'The assumption that extraterritorial sanctions are unlawful is shared by a vast number of countries' and cites the annual UN General Assembly resolutions condemning the extraterritorial reach of the embargo imposed on Cuba by the US and the 1996 EU blocking statute under which EU companies are prohibited from complying with extraterritorial sanctions imposed by the US.[158] As stated by Jazairy, it also is 'highly questionable that any State should take upon itself to impose sanctions that apply worldwide "without borders", without any justifiable right to exercise universal jurisdiction, which is in the purview solely of the Security Council'.[159] Accordingly, he concludes that:

> To the extent that States are bound by human rights obligations when applying sanctions, it is submitted that extraterritorial sanctions may attract the international responsibility of the sanctioning State, not only in relation to its own sanctions, but also in relation to sanctions applied by third countries on the targeted State with a view to complying with extraterritorial measures enacted by the primary sanctioning State.[160]

[154] A/HRC/36/44 (n 65) para 49.
[155] A/HRC/36/44 (n 65) para 52.
[156] Ruys (n 7) 28, as cited in A/HRC/36/44 (n 65) para 52.
[157] A/HRC/36/44 (n 65) para 24.
[158] ibid, para 25.
[159] Report of the Special Rapporteur on the negative impact of unilateral coercive measures on the enjoyment of human rights, A/72/370 of 29 August 2017, para 55.
[160] ibid, para 56.

The pressure brought upon by the state which is imposing unilateral sanctions on third states to apply its measures against the target state subjected to unilateral sanctions, has generated a number of questions in international law. A recent case in point are the US sanctions applied against Iran for its alleged refusal not to develop nuclear energy for non-peaceful purposes. The rest of the world and especially the European powers, as well as China and Russia, have resisted the pressure of the US to apply its sanctions against Iran.[161] These resisting states seem to be concerned about the attempt by the US to apply extraterritorially its regime of sanctions which are based solely on the US's distinct domestic legislation such as the Magnitsky Act of 2012.[162] This is because such an extraterritorial application of a national regime of sanctions creates its own challenges to the rules governing the jurisdiction of states under international law.

In sum, unilateral sanctions that go beyond the scope of countermeasures are not a recognised institution in international law. This is especially so with regard to the sanctions that have an extraterritorial character and result in the harm to the civilian population in the target State. Sachs states that 'Such sanctions are tantamount to war, in violation of the United Nations Charter. And, because they are aimed at the civilian population, they constitute, or at least should constitute a crime against humanity'.[163] One may not go as far as Sachs has in regarding unilateral sanctions aimed at the civilian population as a crime against humanity; they certainly are unlawful if they operate beyond the framework outlined by the ILC for countermeasures and against the contemporary rules of customary international law. Thus, any continuous use of unilateral sanctions not consistent with international law by a state may constitute a wrongful act entailing the international responsibility of that state and thereby opening the door to the possibility of compensation or reparation for the victims of the use of such unilateral sanctions. This position may have been *de lege ferenda* until the end of the twentieth century, but the world has changed since then, and the new evidence of state practice has made it *lex lata*.

XII. Unilateral Sanctions and Human Rights

Unilateral sanctions not sanctioned by the UN are basically measures of self-help by states and the very notion of self-help runs counter to the idea of an international legal order based on the principles enshrined in the Charter of the UN, like the protection and promotion of human rights. By resorting to such unilateral coercive measures, states run the risk of breaching specific terms of international treaties such as the International Convention on the Elimination of All Forms of Racial Discrimination of 1965 (CERD). For instance, following the economic blockade of Qatar by a group of Arab countries in 2017, which Gordon, Smyth and Cornell, describe as 'the imposition of draconian sanctions',[164] Qatar filed a case against the United Arab Emirates (UAE),

[161] See, eg, 'Britain seeks advice to get around [US] sanctions on Iran' *The Times* (28 August 2018) 2.

[162] The full name of this Act is 'Russia and Moldova Jackson-Vanik Repeal and Sergei Magnitsky Rule of Law Accountability Act of 2012'

[163] J Sachs, 'Europe must oppose Trump' *Gulf Times* (20 August 2019) 14.

[164] R Gordon, M Smyth and T Cornell, *Sanctions Law* (Hart Publishing, 2019) 16.

before the ICJ in June 2018 alleging violation of certain provisions of the CERD[165] and the Court issued provisional orders against the UAE on 23 July 2018.[166]

As stated by the UN Special Rapporteur on the negative impact of unilateral coercive measures on the enjoyment of human rights, Jazairy says,

> any unilateral coercive measure imposed on a country necessarily runs counter to some provisions of the International Bill of Human Rights or peremptory norms and other provisions of customary law. Such measures entail, to different degrees, adverse consequences on the enjoyment of the human rights of innocent people.[167]

Citing the 1966 Covenants on Civil and Political Rights and on Economic, Social and Cultural Rights, he goes on to add that the use of unilateral sanctions runs counter to the principle of self-determination which 'is also a recognized principle of customary international law that even economic measures not otherwise prohibited become unlawful if they coerce a State to take action in an area in which it has the right to decide freely'.[168]

One could go further and submit that the principle of self-determination is a norm of *jus cogens* character and the unilateral sanctions not consistent with the Charter of the UN may result in the violation of this cardinal principle of international law. As stated by the ICJ in the *East Timor* case, 'The principle of self-determination … is one of the essential principles of contemporary international law', which gives rise to an obligation to the international community as a whole to permit and respect its exercise.[169]

The same applies to the prohibition against racial discrimination since it too is regarded as a peremptory norm of international law.[170] Thus, according to the ILC's Draft Articles on State Responsibility, the violations of the principles of racial discrimination and self-determination by the use of unilateral sanctions that are not consistent with the Charter of the UN may amount to a 'serious breach of obligations' under the peremptory norms of international law.

Indeed, in the *Kadi I* case[171] the EU Court of First Instance espoused that even the sanctions imposed by the UN Security Council, let alone unilateral sanctions, could not take precedence over peremptory norms of international law. Non-performance of international obligations by one state in response to an internationally wrongful act committed by another state is one thing, but proactive unilateral coercive measures are

[165] ICJ Press Release No 2018/26, 'The State of Qatar institutes proceedings against the United Arab Emirates and request the Court to indicate provisional measures', 11 June 2018.

[166] ICJ Press Release No 2018/36, 'The Court indicates provisional measures to protect certain rights claimed by Qatar and orders the Parties to refrain from any action which might aggravate or extend the dispute', 23 July 2018.

[167] UN Doc A/HRC/30/45 (n 26) para 18.

[168] ibid, para 34. In support of his arguments he also cites the provisions in para 31 of the Vienna Declaration of 1993 which called upon all states 'to refrain from any unilateral measure not in accordance with international law and the Charter of the United Nations that create obstacles to trade relations among States and impedes the full realization of the human rights set forth in the Universal Declaration of Human Rights and international human rights instruments in particular the right of everyone to a standard of living adequate for their health and wellbeing including food and medical care, housing and the necessary social services'.

[169] As cited in ILC (n 1) 113.

[170] See ILC (n 1) 112.

[171] Case C-402/05, *Yassin Abdullah Kadi and Al Barakaat International Foundation v Council of the European Union and Commission of the European Communities* [2008] ECR I-6351 (*Kadi I*).

quite another. Even non-performance of international obligations has to be proportionate to the injury caused and consistent with the provisions in the Vienna Convention on the Law of Treaties.

There are a number of principles of international law in general and international human rights law in particular that will come into the equation when considering the legality of unilateral sanctions. One of them is the principles of non-discrimination. The basic principles of non-discrimination are well established in customary international law. The starting point is the UN Charter, which states that the UN shall 'promote universal respect for and observance of human rights and fundamental freedoms for all without distinction as to race, sex or religion' and confirms that all UN Member States have pledged themselves to take action for the achievement of that goal.

In the *South West Africa* case, the ICJ noted that the

> distinctions, exclusions, restrictions and limitations exclusively based on the grounds of race, colour, descent or national or ethnic origin which constitute a denial of fundamental human rights is a flagrant violation of the purposes and principles of the [UN] Charter.[172]

The principle of non-discrimination is also regarded as a peremptory norm of international law (so-called '*jus cogens*'). Peremptory norms are fundamental norms which safeguard the overriding interests and values of the international community as a whole as distinct from the interests of individual states.[173]

The Inter-American Court of Human Rights (IACtHR) held in its Advisory Opinion on Juridical Condition and Rights of Undocumented Migrants that *jus cogens* encompasses the basic principle of humanity and non-discrimination.[174] The IACtHR found that states have the duty to respect and secure respect of human rights in the light of the general and basic principle of equality and non-discrimination. Any discriminatory treatment in relation to the protection and exercise of such rights triggers the international responsibility of the states. The IACtHR further determined that the principles of equal protection before the law and non-discrimination belong to *jus cogens*, 'because the whole legal structure of national and international public order rests on it and it is a fundamental principle that permeates all laws'.

The IACtHR went on, noting that:

> Nowadays, no legal act that is in conflict with this fundamental principle is acceptable, and discriminatory treatment of any person, owing to gender, race, colour, language, religion or belief, political or other opinion, national, ethnic or social origin, nationality, age, economic situation, property, civil status, birth or any other status is unacceptable.

Article 1 of the Universal Declaration of Human Rights 1948 states[175] that all 'human beings are born equal in dignity and in rights' and Article 2 confirms that everyone is entitled to all the rights and freedoms set out in the Declaration 'without distinction

[172] *Legal Consequences for States of the Continued Presence of South Africa in Namibia* (South West Africa) notwithstanding Security Council Resolution 276 (1970), Advisory Opinion, ICJ Reports 1972, para 131.

[173] A Orakhleshvili, *Peremptory Norms in International Law* (Oxford University Press, 2006) 46 and 50. The concept of *jus cogens* was accepted by the ILC and incorporated in Art 53 of the Vienna Convention on the Law of the Treaties, as a base of invalidity and termination of treaties.

[174] *Juridical Condition and Rights of the Undocumented Migrants*, Advisory Opinion OC-18/03, 17 September 2003, IACtHR (Series A) No 18 (2003), paras 97–101 and 110.

[175] UN General Assembly, Universal Declaration of Human Rights, 1948, 217 A (III).

of any kind'.[176] In applying these principles, the ICJ has held that states have specific obligations towards the international community as a whole to protect from racial discrimination.[177]

The core principles of non-discrimination are also contained in numerous regional instruments as well as multilateral conventions adopted under the auspices of the UN.[178] Thus, the state imposing unilateral sanctions against the target state would be violating the principle of non-discrimination, a peremptory norm (*jus cogens*) of international law, if the sanctions imposed would hurt the people in the target country unfairly and violate their human rights. Since many of these UN conventions on human rights have been ratified by an overwhelming majority of states, many of their provisions can be regarded as rules of customary international binding on all states except for those which are subsequent and persistent objectors. For instance, the UN Convention on the Elimination of All Forms of Racial Discrimination (CERD) has been ratified by 177 states, making it one of the most significant and near universally accepted treaties in the world.

Unilateral sanctions have a significant impact upon the human rights of persons both within the target state and in the state imposing such sanctions. It is not only the nationals of the target state, but also those of other nationalities residing within that country such as migrant workers, and the nationals of the state imposing sanctions residing in the target state, which would be affected by such sanctions. All of them can experience violations of their right to freedom of movement as well as a range of other repercussions upon their civil, economic, social and cultural rights. Such sanctions have the potential to disrupt their lives significantly simply because they belong to one of the nationalities involved in the dispute. When Bahrain, Egypt, Saudi Arabia and the UAE imposed economic blockades on Qatar in June 2017, the UN High Commissioner for Human Rights sent a technical mission in November 2017 to Qatar in order to examine the situation. Its report highlighted the concerns relating to the situation of human rights of the different category of people within Qatar.[179] The wide ramifications of unilateral sanctions for the persons in the target state was highlighted in the report. The observations of the technical mission on the consequences of these sanctions were expressed in paragraphs 60–62 as follows:

> The team found that the unilateral measures, consisting of severe restrictions of movement, termination and disruption of trade, financial and investment flows, as well as suspension of social and cultural exchanges imposed on the State of Qatar, had immediately translated into

[176] 'Everyone is entitled to all the rights and freedoms set forth in this Declaration, without distinction of any kind, such as race, colour, sex, language, religion, political or other opinion, national or social origin, property, birth or other status. Furthermore, no distinction shall be made on the basis of the political, jurisdictional or international status of the country or territory to which a person belongs, whether it be independent, trust, non-self-governing or under any other limitation of sovereignty.'

[177] *Barcelona Traction, Light and Power Company Limited (Belgium v Spain)* Second Phase, Judgment, ICJ Report 1970, paras 33 and 34.

[178] Such as the American Convention on Human Rights, the Arab Charter on Human Rights and the European Convention on Human Rights, the International Covenant on Civil and Political Rights 1966, UN Treaty Series, 999 (ICCPR); and International Covenant on Economic, Social, and Cultural Rights 1966, UN Treaty Series, 993 (ICESCR).

[179] OHCHR Technical Mission to the State of Qatar, 17–24 November 2017, Report on the impact of the Gulf Crisis on human rights, December 2017.

> actions applying to nationals and residents of Qatar … Many of these measures have a potentially durable effect on the enjoyment of the human rights and fundamental freedoms of those affected. As there is no evidence of any legal decisions motivating these various measures, and due to the lack of any legal recourse for most individuals concerned, these measures can be considered as arbitrary.[180]
>
> The majority of the measures were broad and non-targeted, making no distinction between the Government of Qatar and its population … Moreover, measures targeting individuals on the basis of their Qatari nationality or their links with Qatar can be qualified as non-disproportionate and discriminatory.[181]
>
> The considerable economic impact of the crisis takes over the dimension of an economic warfare, with significant financial losses for the State, companies and individuals, and the confidence of investors being eroded.[182]

As can be deduced from the above-mentioned report of the technical mission of the UN High Commissioner, unilateral economic measures can result in the violation of a number of rights and freedoms such as the freedom of movement and separation of families, the rights relating to nationality and residence, the right to education, the right to health, economic rights, and the right to property.

Similarly, several mandate-holders of the special procedures of the Human Rights Council also echoed the report of the technical mission of the UN High Commissioner for Human Rights:

> Serious concerns are expressed at the numerous rights being infringed, including the right to movement and residence, family reunification, education, work, freedom of expression, health, freedom of religious practice, and the right to private property, without discrimination on any basis.[183]

Indeed, as stated in General Comment No 8 (1997) by the Committee on Economic, Social and Cultural Rights established under the 1966 Covenant on Economic, Social and Cultural Rights,

> the provisions of the Covenant, virtually all of which are also reflected in a range of other human rights treaties as well as the Universal Declaration of Human Rights, cannot be considered to be inoperative, or in any way inapplicable, solely because a decision has been taken that considerations of international peace and security warrant the imposition of sanctions. Just as the international community insists that any targeted State must respect the civil and political rights of its citizens, so too must that State and the international community itself do everything possible to protect at least the core content of the economic, social and cultural rights of the affected peoples of that State.[184]

[180] ibid, para 60.

[181] ibid, para 61.

[182] ibid, para 62.

[183] Communication to Government of the United Arab Emirates, Mandates of the Special Rapporteur on the promotion and protection of the right to freedom of opinion and expression; the Special Rapporteur on the right of everyone to the enjoyment of the highest attainable standard of physical and mental health; the Special Rapporteur on the human rights of migrants; the Special Rapporteur on contemporary forms of racism, racial discrimination, xenophobia and related intolerance; the Special Rapporteur on the promotion and protection of human rights while countering terrorism; and the Special Rapporteur on the right to education, 18 August 2017.

[184] UN Doc E/C.12/1997/8 of 12 December 1997.

This statement of the Committee on Economic, Social and Cultural Rights applies to other UN human rights treaties too. Therefore, what can be submitted is that it is not permissible under international law in general and under international human rights law in particular to use unilateral sanctions that result in the violation of human rights. As stated by the ILC in its commentaries to the Draft Article on State Responsibility, Draft Article 28 (which provides that the international responsibility of a state which is entailed by an internationally wrongful act involving legal consequences) does not exclude the possibility that an internationally wrongful act may involve legal consequences in the relations between the state responsible for that act and persons or entities other than states. 'Thus, State responsibility extends, for example, to human rights violations and other breaches of international law where the primary beneficiary of the obligation breached is not a State'.[185]

If the state imposing unilateral sanctions is a party to the International Covenant on Civil and Political Rights and the International Covenant on Economic, Social and Cultural Rights, it has an obligation to respect the human rights of the people in the target state. For instance, Article 2(1) of the International Covenant on Economic, Social and Cultural Rights requires a state party

> to take steps, individually and through international assistance and cooperation, especially economic and technical, to the maximum of its available resources, with a view to achieving progressively the full realization of the rights recognized in the present Covenant by all appropriate means, including particularly the adoption of legislative measures.

Similarly, Article 2(2) requires states parties 'to guarantee that the rights enunciated in the present Covenant will be exercised without discrimination of any kind as to race, colour, sex, language, religion, political or other opinion, national or social origin, property, birth or other status'.

Given the provisions in Articles 1(3), 55 and 56 of the Charter of the UN, the universal character of the rights and freedoms enshrined in the Universal Declaration of Human Rights and its endorsement as a legally binding instrument through a UN General Assembly resolution in 2005 and the near universal acceptance of the 1966 Covenants on Political and Civil Rights and on Economic, Social and Cultural Rights, it can be argued that the rights and freedoms guaranteed in these instruments have an extraterritorial scope whereby all states are under an obligation to respect human rights anywhere and everywhere. Indeed, the Special Rapporteur on the negative impact of unilateral coercive measures on the enjoyment of human rights of the Human Rights Council has stated that

> there are strong and convergent legal arguments pointing to the existence of extraterritorial State obligations under the Covenant that may cover situations of imposition of international sanctions … It seems difficult to deny that sanctions come within the category of situations where States can influence situations located abroad.[186]

[185] ILC (n 1) 87.
[186] UN Doc A/HRC/36/44 (n 65) para 33.

XIII. Protection of Human Rights as *Erga Omnes* Obligations and Unilateral Sanctions

There is a tendency on the part of some states to invoke the obligation to protect human rights as obligations of *erga omnes* character in support of unilateral sanctions relying on the principles of countermeasures under which any state other than an injured state could be entitled to resort to countermeasures to protect human rights and uphold the integrity of the international legal order. According to Article 48 of the ILC's Draft Articles on State Responsibility, 'any State other than an injured State is entitled to invoke the responsibility of another State … if … the obligation breached is owed to the international community as a whole'.[187] This article complements the rule contained in Article 42 which expounds the invocation of the responsibility by states, other than the injured state, to act in the collective interest. The ILC's Commentaries to the Draft Articles make it clear that:

> A State which is entitled to invoke responsibility under article 48 is acting not in its individual capacity by reason of having suffered injury, but in its capacity as a member of a group of States to which the obligation is owed, or indeed as a member of the international community as a whole.[188]

It goes on to add:

> Article 48 is based on the idea that in case of breaches of specific obligations protecting the collective interests of a group of States or the interests of the international community as a whole, responsibility may be invoked by States which are not themselves injured in the sense of article 42.[189]

Kawasaki argues that 'human rights obligations are aimed at protecting collective or "extra-State" interests. Thus, they are in themselves owed not to a single State but to all other States'.[190] In support of his arguments he cites the General Comment 31 of 2004 of

[187] Art 48 reads as follows: 'Invocation of responsibility by a State other than an injured State 1. Any State other than an injured State is entitled to invoke the responsibility of another State in accordance with paragraph 2 if: (a) the obligation breached is owed to a group of States including that State, and is established for the protection of a collective interest of the group; or (b) the obligation breached is owed to the international community as a whole. 2. Any State entitled to invoke responsibility under paragraph 1 may claim from the responsible State: (a) cessation of the internationally wrongful act, and assurances and guarantees of non-repetition in accordance with article 30; and (b) performance of the obligation of reparation in accordance with the preceding articles, in the interest of the injured State or of the beneficiaries of the obligation breached. 3. The requirements for the invocation of responsibility by an injured State under articles 43, 44 and 45 apply to an invocation of responsibility by a State entitled to do so under paragraph 1'. ILC (n 1) 126.

[188] ILC (n 1) 126.

[189] Art 42 reads as follows: 'Invocation of responsibility by an injured State: A State is entitled as an injured State to invoke the responsibility of another State if the obligation breached is owed to: (a) that State individually; or (b) a group of States including that State, or the international community as a whole, and the breach of the obligation: (i) specially affects that State; or (ii) is of such a character as radically to change the position of all the other States to which the obligation is owed with respect to the further performance of the obligation'. ILC (n 1) 117.

[190] K Kawasaki, as cited by Chiara Franco in a report of the Italian think-tank Istituto Affari Internazionali on 'Coercive Diplomacy, Sanctions and International Law' (2015) 17. See 'Coercive diplomacy, sanctions and international law', available at www.iai.it/en/pubblicazioni/coercive-diplomacy-sanctions-and-international-law.

the Human Rights Committee[191] operating under the 1966 International Covenant on Civil and Political Rights, which states that

> every State Party has a legal interest in the performance by every other State Party of its obligations … the Committee commends to States Parties the view that violations of Covenant rights by any State Party deserve their attention. To draw attention to possible breaches of Covenant obligations by other States Parties and to call on them to comply with their Covenant obligations should, far from being regarded as an unfriendly act, be considered as a reflection of legitimate community interest.

It is one of these reasons that leads Kawasaki to conclude that: 'This follows from the fact that the "rules concerning the basic rights of the human person" are *erga omnes* obligations'.[192] If states have an obligation *erga omnes* in international law to resort to unilateral sanctions or countermeasures by invoking state responsibility of the delinquent state, they also have an obligation to ensure that such measures do not violate the human rights of the people in the target country. It is a balancing act that states are required to perform by international law. Countermeasures or unilateral sanctions are not a tool that can easily be invoked by any state other than an injured state. They are a tool to be used only in exceptional cases and under narrowly defined conditions. As stated in a UN study,

> countermeasures must not affect the prohibition on the use of force, obligations for the protection of fundamental human rights, obligations of a humanitarian character prohibiting reprisals and other obligations under peremptory norms of general international law. They also must be proportional. The proportionality of the countermeasure is a crucial element in assessing the legality of a specific measure.[193]

XIV. Conclusions

As seen from the analysis in this chapter, there is now a new rule of customary international law emerging out of the more recent practice of states which renders high intensity unilateral sanctions unlawful, even if they are claimed to be countermeasures. Equally, measures claimed to be unilateral sanctions or countermeasures are not permissible under international law if they undermine third parties. The more recent practice of states has the effect of creating additional rules of customary international

[191] The Human Rights Committee stated 'While article 2 [of the ICCPR] is couched in terms of the obligations of State Parties towards individuals as the right-holders under the Covenant, every State Party has a legal interest in the performance by every other State Party of its obligations. This follows from the fact that the "rules concerning the basic rights of the human person" are *erga omnes* obligations and that, as indicated in the fourth preambular paragraph of the Covenant, there is a United Nations Charter obligation to promote universal respect for, and observance of, human rights and fundamental freedoms. Furthermore, the contractual dimension of the treaty involves any State Party to a treaty being obligated to every other State Party to comply with its undertakings under the treaty'. UN Doc CCPR/C/21/Rev.1/Add. 13 of 26 May 2004, para 2.

[192] Kyoji Kawasaki, as cited by Chiara Franco in 'Coercive Diplomacy' (2015) 17–18.

[193] 'Thematic study of the Office of the United Nations High Commissioner for Human Rights on the impact of unilateral coercive measures on the enjoyment of human rights, including recommendations on actions aimed at ending such measures', UN Doc A/HRC/19/33 (n 45) para 23 (footnotes omitted).

law on countermeasures that in turn limit the scope of unilateral sanctions. Of course, many states continue to impose unilateral sanctions on other states, and this too is evidence of state practice. However, not any state practice against the established norms of international law can lead to the formation of a rule of customary international law.

Referring to the more recent state practice and the resolutions of various regional and global international organisations rejecting the use of economic sanctions, Dupont states that 'This convergence of views has given the impression that an emergent norm of customary international law prohibiting the use of economic sanctions might be in the process of crystallizing within the international community'.[194] He then concludes that

> there is probably a minima a quasi-consensus of the international community, giving rise to a new norm of customary law, that at least those economic sanctions regimes which do not incorporate (and ensure) minimal regard vi-a-vis basic human rights … as well as the requirements of proportionality and discrimination in terms of the intended targets, and appropriate humanitarian exemptions, are certainly unlawful under international law.[195]

One of the main justifications for unilateral sanctions is based on the freedom of action of states under the principle of sovereignty of states. But such freedom of action cannot be invoked if a certain activity is prohibited by a treaty or a rule of customary international law. As stated above, since additional rules of customary international law have emerged out of the more recent practice of states prohibiting unilateral sanctions, these new rules of customary international law have limited the freedom of action of states founded on the principle of sovereignty of states to impose unilateral sanctions on other states.

International law in existence today does not regard as unlawful every kind of unilateral sanctions such as 'smart' or targeted sanctions of limited scope or 'cyber sanctions' in response either to a prior illegal act or to deter a potential illegal act by individuals in the government or associated with the government that violates human rights or commits other internationally wrongful acts. Cameron writes that states must be able to take certain economic actions against one another as a sort of safety valve[196] and contemporary international law does permit this to a certain extent. The same is the case with countermeasures which are permissible under narrowly defined conditions. But the endeavour inside and outside of the UN has been to set the framework within which non-retorsive unilateral sanctions have to operate. According to this framework, non-retorsive unilateral sanctions that affect third states, and those which exceed the limitations for unilateral sanctions contained in customary international law, would be unlawful.

As seen throughout this study, the international community has moved towards a restrictive customary international law regulation of unilateral sanctions and countermeasures since the adoption of the Draft Articles on State Responsibility by the International Law Commission in 2001. There are now many authoritative documents

[194] P-E Dupont, 'Human rights implications of sanctions' in M Asada (ed), *Economic Sanctions in International Law & Practice* (Routledge, 2019) 37.

[195] ibid 37–38.

[196] Cameron (n 18) 253.

which impose restrictions on the use of unilateral sanctions. Enough evidence now exists in the practice of an overwhelming majority of states needed for the formation of a rule of customary international law to this effect. Such practice contains more than statements of general character in the Charter of the UN and in other international legal instruments. The state practice in favour of such restrictions is of such magnitude that it meets the tests of consistency, uniformity and generality and the requirement of *opinio juris* that is capable of elevating the restrictions on the use of such sanctions from *lex ferenda* to *lex lata*.

To conclude, the ground rules for unilateral sanctions that are founded on treaty law concerning different areas of state activity, and on the contemporary rules of customary international law that have come into existence through modern practice, suggest that comprehensive unilateral sanctions – as opposed to 'smart' or targeted sanctions of limited scope – would be unlawful, unless they meet the procedural and substantive requirements stipulated in international law, including those requirements stipulated for countermeasures in the ILC's Draft Articles on State Responsibility. The analysis presented in this chapter establishes that there is now a positive prohibition in customary international law on the use of financial and economic force by states if such use does not meet these requirements. It also indicates that unilateral sanctions that undermine the sovereignty of third states or violate human rights in the target states are unlawful under international law.

2

Shades of Grey: Autonomous Sanctions in the International Legal Order

NIGEL D WHITE*

I. Introduction

In 2018, the UK Parliament adopted the Sanctions and Anti-Money Laundering Act, which came into force upon the UK's withdrawal from the EU. This legislation embodies a right to impose 'autonomous sanctions' against other states and non-state actors on the basis that the UK will no longer be able to benefit from the EU's collective sanctioning competence. With this piece of domestic legislation, the spotlight is again on the nature and purposes of sanctions in international law. The issue for this chapter is whether such autonomous sanctions operate in a grey area of international law, where the legality of such is unclear, in effect where practice by states might create rights. Alternatively, are a limited number of states claiming a right to impose autonomous sanctions illegally abrogating to themselves powers that can only belong to organisations as a result of an act of collective empowerment by Member States? The chapter addresses the legal framework applicable to sanctions by first of all exploring the understanding and nature of sanctions to show that the dominant purpose has been to respond to threats to or breaches of international peace and, as such, sanctions are clearly within the competence of international organisations, not so individual states. Having outlined both conceptual and legal frameworks within which to understanding sanctions, the chapter considers sanctions imposed against states and non-state actors and explores whether the move towards targeted sanctions is a form of response to violations of international law, and possibly one that can lawfully be taken by individual states autonomously or unilaterally. The chapter finishes by considering that, in contrast to countermeasures and other unilateral measures, collective sanctions are inherently lawful, but can only be legally justified as measures adopted out of necessity to prevent major ruptures to peace and international law. In contrast, beyond the regime of bilateral and, more contentiously, collective countermeasures, autonomous

* This chapter is partly based on ideas in an article entitled 'Autonomous and Collective Sanctions in the International Legal Order' (2017) XXVII *Italian Yearbook of International Law* 3.

or unilateral sanctions are inherently unlawful. The assertion of such a right by a handful of states does not change this calculus, although there is the prospect that other economically powerful states may follow suit.

II. The Growth of Autonomous Sanctions

Sanctions are embedded in international relations, but their status in international law is often controversial and they are seen as operating in a grey area between clearly lawful UN collective sanctions and clearly lawful countermeasures taken within a bilateral inter-state relationship. In this context, it is worth considering the UK Government's response to its consultation of 2017 on the 'future legal framework for imposing and implementing sanctions', which would follow from the UK's withdrawal from the EU, and consequent inability to help shape, or rely on, the EU's sanctioning powers. The UK Government stated that the

> UK needs to be able to impose and implement sanctions in order to comply with our obligations under the … UN Charter and to support our wider foreign policy and national goals. Many of our current sanctions regimes are established via powers in the European Communities Act 1972 (ECA) so we will need new legal powers to replace those once the ECA is repealed.[1]

In the White Paper of April 2017, which shaped the consultation, the Government stated that 'when the UK withdraws from the EU we will need new legal powers that are compliant with our domestic legal system'; these powers 'will enable us to preserve and update UN sanctions, and to impose autonomous UK sanctions in coordination with our allies and partners'.[2]

The idea that powers belonging to the EU as an international organisation with separate legal personality could be straightforwardly claimed by the UK as a non-EU Member State, in the form of what in 2018 became the Sanctions and Anti-Money Laundering Act does not withstand scrutiny unless there is a separate international, and not merely national, legal basis for such 'autonomous' or unilateral sanctioning powers. It is interesting that in justifying the move the UK did not feel the need to claim an international legal basis for autonomous sanctions when the doctrine of countermeasures might have provided an obvious, though problematic, legal basis. The UK's failure to put forward an international legal basis might be due to the fact that it views autonomous sanctions as something much broader than temporary and proportionate non-forcible measures taken in response to a violation of international law (countermeasures). It certainly suggested this by depicting sanctions as 'an important foreign policy and

[1] HM Government, 'Public consultation on the United Kingdom's future legal framework for imposing and implementing sanctions: Government response', August 2017, para I.1, available at assets.publishing.service.gov.uk/government/uploads/system/uploads/attachment_data/file/635101/consultation-uk-future-legal-framework-sanctions-government-response.pdf.

[2] HM Government, 'Public consultation on the United Kingdom's future legal framework for imposing and implementing sanctions', April 2017, 7, available at assets.publishing.service.gov.uk/government/uploads/system/uploads/attachment_data/file/609986/Public_consultation_on_the_UK_s_future_legal_framework_for_imposing_and_implementing_sanctions__Print_pdf_version_.pdf.

national security tool', which 'can be used to coerce a change in behaviour, to constrain behaviour by limiting access to resources, or to communicate a clear political message'.[3]

In the Sanctions and Anti-Money Laundering Act 2018, s 1(1), an appropriate minister

> may make sanctions regulations where that Minister considers it appropriate to make the regulations: (a) for the purposes of compliance with a UN obligation, (b) for the purposes of compliance with any other international obligation, or (c) for the purposes within subsection (2).

Section 1(2) broadens the purposes of autonomous sanctions to:

> (a) further the prevention of terrorism in the UK or elsewhere, (b) be in the interests of national security, (c) be in the interests of international peace and security, (d) further a foreign policy objective of the government of the United Kingdom, (e) promote the resolution of armed conflicts or the protection of civilians in conflict zones, (f) provide accountability for or be a deterrent to gross violations of human rights, or otherwise promote (i) compliance with international human rights law, or (ii) respects for human rights, (g) promote compliance with international humanitarian law, (h) contribute to multilateral efforts to prevent the spread and use of weapons and materials of mass destruction, or (f) promote respect for democracy, the rule of law and good governance.[4]

It follows from this expansive list that the UK Government views sanctions as distinct from countermeasures and other non-forcible measures of self-help by linking sanctions to its foreign policy and security and not just as responses to violations of the UK's international legal rights by another state, or in fulfilment of its obligations arising under the UN Charter (something already provided for in the United Nations Act of 1946).[5] In introducing the Autonomous Sanctions Bill for a second reading to the Australian Parliament in 2010, the Australian Minister of Foreign Affairs explained that 'they are called "autonomous" sanctions to distinguish them from sanctions applied under international obligations arising from United Nations Security Council (UNSC) decisions'. The purpose of the Bill, which was to become the Autonomous Sanctions Act 2011, is

> to strengthen Australia's autonomous sanctions regime by allowing greater flexibility in the range of measures Australia can implement, beyond those achievable under existing instruments, thus ensuring that Australia's autonomous sanctions can match the scope and extent of measures implemented by like-minded states,

pointing to the US, Canada, New Zealand and the EU.[6]

There is considerable US practice on sanctions some of which will feature in this chapter. The UK's regime has only just come into force, while Australia's was introduced

[3] ibid, 6.

[4] Sanctions and Anti-Money Laundering Act 2018, available at www.legislation.gov.uk/ukpga/2018/13/contents/enacted.

[5] For UK practice under the 2018 Act, imposing targeted sanctions against individuals and entities in Russia, Saudi Arabia, Myanmar, North Korea and Belarus, see www.gov.uk/government/publications/the-uk-sanctions-list.

[6] A Chapman and S Kealey, 'Australian Practice in International Law 2010' (2013) 31 *Australian Yearbook of International Law* 219, 279.

in 2011. In New Zealand an Autonomous Sanctions Bill was introduced in 2017, but is not yet law. The purpose of the Bill

> is to enable New Zealand to impose and enforce sanctions autonomously, so as to assist in maintaining of restoring peace and security in response either to a threat to peace and security in the Asia-Pacific region or a breach of international peace and security.

The latter situation is further specified to be one where the UN Security Council has not acted under Article 41 of the Charter, or has so acted 'but the action is insufficient to maintain or restore international peace and security'.[7] In addition to sanctions imposed pursuant to a UN Security Council decision, Canadian domestic legislation allows Canada to impose sanctions autonomously by the adoption of regulations under the Special Economic Measures Act of 1992. According to the Government, 'Canada uses autonomous sanctions as a discretionary tool of foreign policy to influence behaviour, with the object of addressing international peace and security concerns, human rights violations, and corruption'.[8]

The issue for this chapter is whether such autonomous sanctions operate in a grey area of international law, where the legality of such is unclear, in effect where growing practice might create rights. Alternatively, are the handful of states claiming a right to impose autonomous sanctions illegally abrogating to themselves powers belonging to organisations that have such competence only by reason of an act of collective empowerment by Member States?

III. International Law and Sanctions

Sanctions were defined by the Royal Institute of International Affairs in 1938 as 'measures taken in support of law' that 'are applied with and by the general authority, not by any individual'.[9] This definition went further and stated that 'with the substitution of the word "state" for the word "individual" this is true … of the sanctions of international, as well as national, law'.[10] The key feature is that sanctions are imposed by a central authority, a feature that is given even greater emphasis in this definition than the events that trigger the sanctions themselves. However, such centralisation is contradicted by the fact that the UK has joined longstanding practitioners – the US,[11] along with other states, principally Australia and Canada[12] – to claim that non-forcible measures taken by individual states without any authorisation from the UN or regional organisation can constitute lawful 'autonomous sanctions'. This, as shall be seen, is a term which is used in a broader sense than 'countermeasures', which are responses to breaches of a

[7] Sections 3 and 8 Autonomous Sanctions Bill 2017, available at www.legislation.govt.nz/bill/government/2017/0259/latest/DLM7248306.html?src=qs.

[8] www.international.gc.ca/world-monde/international_relations-relations_internationales/sanctions/faq.aspx?lang=eng.

[9] JP Grant and JC Barker, *Parry and Grant Encyclopaedic Dictionary of International Law*, 3rd edn (Oxford University Press, 2009) 539.

[10] ibid.

[11] LF Damrosch, 'Enforcing International Law through Non-Forcible Measures' (1997) 269 *RCADI* 99–101; AF Lowenfeld, 'Unilateral versus Collective Sanctions: An American's Perception' in V Gowlland-Debbas (ed), *United Nations Sanctions and International Law* (Nijhoff, 2001) 95.

[12] Chapman and Kealey, 'Australian Practice' (2013).

state's international rights by other states in the form of temporary and proportionate counter-breaches. It is also a term that overlaps with but remains distinct from acts of retorsion, which are acts of 'discourtesy or unfriendliness', which are not inconsistent with the initiating state's existing obligations, and are not necessarily taken in response to breaches by the target state, though they often will be.[13] Taken as a whole, non-forcible measures are a disputed aspect of international law even though there is a great deal of practice by states as well as international organisations. While it is clear that states have the right to impose certain non-forcible measures in international law, the grey area occupied by broader claims by states to take autonomous sanctions needs exploration, particularly when states claim the right to impose 'sanctions' akin to those within the competence of the UN Security Council.

There remains profound disagreement on the nature of sanctions in international law, especially over whether they should be imposed centrally or can be left to states.[14] However, it is true to say that modern international law, especially in the period after the Cold War, has not only witnessed an increased institutional sanctions usage but also a clarification of the law concerning unilateral non-forcible measures. There is a growing understanding of the distinction between collective sanctions and unilateral countermeasures: the former being deployed for the 'public' enforcement of community based norms, while the latter are used for the 'private' enforcement of bilateral norms. Unilateral victim state responses to breaches of legal duties owed to it by another state are seen as non-forcible reprisals or, to use the modern term, countermeasures; whereas sanctions are a collective power given by groups of states to international organisations, namely the UN and regional organisations. In this vein, Abi-Saab defined sanctions as 'coercive measures taken in execution of a decision of a competent social organ, i.e. an organ legally empowered to act in the name of the society or community that is governed by the legal system'. Sanctions are distinct from 'coercive measures taken individually by States or group of States outside a determination and a decision by a legally competent social organ'. Such reprisals, countermeasures and acts of retorsion 'are manifestations of "self-help" or "private justice", and their legality is confined to the very narrow limits within which "remnants" of "self-help" are still admitted in contemporary international law'.[15]

Despite the post-1945 proliferation of international organisations, the ILC's Articles on the Responsibility of States for Internationally Wrongful Acts of 2001 did not include sanctions in its system of secondary rules, only countermeasures as a bilateral means of law enforcement in a decentralised system,[16] whereby an injured state 'may seek to vindicate their rights and to restore the legal relationship' with the responsible state, a relationship that 'has been ruptured by' an unlawful act.[17] As noted by Alland,

[13] T Ruys, 'Sanctions, Retorsions and Countermeasures' in L Van den Herik (ed), *Research Handbook on UN Sanctions and International Law* (Edward Elgar, 2017) 24.

[14] For views that states have the right to impose sanction see, for example, JL Brierly, 'Sanctions' (1932) *Transactions of the Grotius Society* 68; JL Kunz, 'Sanctions in International Law' (1960) 54 *American Journal of International Law* 324.

[15] G Abi-Saab, 'The Concept of Sanction in International Law' in Gowlland-Debbas, *United Nations Sanctions* (2001) 38.

[16] Articles on Responsibility of States for Internationally Wrongful Acts (ARSIWA) 2001, Arts 49–54.

[17] J Crawford, *The International Law Commission's Articles on State Responsibility* (Cambridge University Press, 2002) 281.

'countermeasures are a mechanism of private justice', which produce 'contradictions inherent in a self-assessed (i.e. auto-interpreted or auto-appreciated) decentralized policing of an international *ordre public*'.[18] Provost is even more explicit in depicting the weaknesses of such a system: 'the right of states unilaterally to assess a breach by another state and to validate what would otherwise be an illegal act has the potential of significantly destabilizing international relations'.[19] The depiction of states' use of countermeasures as a form of policing, albeit of a potentially destabilising kind, of an international *ordre public* is blurring countermeasures, which are an auto-interpretive mechanism of law enforcement of bilateral rights and duties, with sanctions which are a collective response to threats to the public order, peace and stability of states.

It is worthwhile hypothesising about why the ILC did not include the notion of sanctions within its secondary rules on state responsibility. It is suggested that sanctions were beyond the ILC's remit given their more fundamental role as measures for preserving peace and security, and not just as secondary responses to breaches of the primary rules of international law.[20] The distinction between 'public' sanctions and 'private' countermeasures is relatively straightforward to draw when considering the paradigmatic instances of each. However, the concept of countermeasures as depicted by the ILC is very narrow and does not capture the range of state practice on unilateral non-forcible measures and other forms of economic coercion.[21] Bederman suggests that 'the central conceptual mission' of the ILC's Articles on countermeasures was 'the search for a polite international society'.[22] He contends further that the Articles on countermeasures represent a 'profound impulse toward social engineering for international relations … imagining a time in international life when unilateral and horizontal means of enforcement through robust self-help will be a thing of the past'.[23] The narrow clarity of the ILC's Articles on countermeasures leaves a great deal of practice on non-forcible forms of coercion seemingly unregulated by international law.[24]

Despite Hart's view that international law epitomises a diffused reactive legal system,[25] the evidence is that there has been greater centralisation of sanctions in the international legal order than the pure customary system depicted by Hart, and that sanctions adopted by those centralised organs are both lawful and legitimate. Moreover, such sanctions are arguably the only clear forms of lawful non-forcible measures designed to enforce community norms. Private justice is left in the hands of states that want to respond to a breach of a bilateral legal relationship with another state; these responses are seen as acts of self-help, not autonomous sanctions. The problem is that there is a grey area in between collective sanctions and unilateral countermeasures, where states make a range of claims to be able to take non-forcible measures, which

[18] J Alland, 'The Definition of Countermeasures' in J Crawford, A Pellet and S Olleson (eds), *The Law of International Responsibility* (Oxford University Press, 2010) 1223–35.

[19] R Provost, *State Responsibility in International Law* (Dartmouth, 2002) xv.

[20] Crawford, *Articles on State Responsibility* (2002) 168, 282, preferring the term 'measures' to 'sanctions'.

[21] OY Elagab, *The Legality of Non-Forcible Counter-Measures in International Law* (Oxford University Press, 1988) 212–13.

[22] D Bederman, 'Counterintuiting Countermeasures' (2002) 96 *American Journal of International Law* 819.

[23] ibid, 831.

[24] Ruys, 'Sanctions' (2017) 24.

[25] HLA Hart, *The Concept of Law*, 3rd edn (Oxford University Press, 2012) 213.

are either depicted as 'collective countermeasures', or 'autonomous (unilateral) sanctions' taken by states in response to what each participating state perceives as breaches of community norms or, indeed, threats to their national interests. The use of the term 'collective' in connection with 'countermeasures' should not disguise the fact that such measures are not institutional and may well be adopted by each sanctioning state independently of any other. In fact, the term 'autonomous sanctions' more fairly embodies the type of power being claimed by states as a right exercised independently from any international organisation. It is also marginally more accurate than 'unilateral sanctions', as measures are often imposed by a number of like-minded states.

IV. Enforcing International Peace or International Law?

According to Kelsen 'law is, by its very nature, a coercive order'.[26] For Kelsen, sanctions are integral to law in that law specifies the proscribed behaviour and also the response to such behaviour.[27] Kelsen was clear that the same conception applies to a legal order providing for collective security when he wrote that 'a social order guaranteeing collective security is by its very nature a legal order, and a legal order is a system of norms providing for sanctions'.[28] While this appears to be more difficult to sustain at the international level, where the sanction element of any law is often unspecified or unused, Kelsen's analysis of sanctions is a normative one meaning that sanctions ought to be imposed, not that they will be.

Even in theories such as Hart's, in which sanctions are not viewed as primary rules themselves, they remain as a form of punishment or response to breaches of those rules, responses that become more centralised as the legal system develops from a primitive set of primary rules.[29] In Hart's words: 'most systems have, after some delay, seen the advantages of further centralization of social pressure; and have partially prohibited the use of physical punishments or violent self-help by private individuals'. Instead, legal systems have 'supplemented the primary rules of obligation by further secondary rules, specifying … the penalties for violation', including an 'exclusive power' conferred on officials of the system to impose penalties. Hart states that 'these secondary rules provide the centralized official "sanctions" of the system'.[30]

The issue of whether sanctions are primary rules of international law or secondary rules of responsibility where they would sit alongside countermeasures remains under-analysed, but certainly for Kelsen a sanction is part of the law not simply a consequence of its breach. Furthermore, according to Kelsen, and implicitly for most commentators, sanctions are 'coercive reactions against an actual violation of the law', or alternatively against suspected or expected violations.[31] This formulation allows for

[26] H Kelsen, *The Law of the United Nations* (Praeger, 1950) 706.
[27] H Kelsen, 'The Pure Theory of Law, Its Method and Fundamental Concepts' (1934) 50 *Law Quarterly Review* 484–85.
[28] H Kelsen, *Collective Security under International Law* (Naval War College, 1957) 101.
[29] Hart, *Concept of Law* (2012) 91–99.
[30] ibid, 97–98.
[31] Kelsen, *Collective Security* (1957) 102.

some anticipatory sanctions, but the triggers remain actual or potential violations of the law. In contrast, it is clear that in the international legal order, especially in its collective security component, 'sanctions' are not confined to actual or potential violations of international law, rather the primary triggers are actual or threatened ruptures of the peace. In this way, they reinforce the basic preconditions necessary for any legal order to exist. Kelsen accepts that legal systems generally recognise the legitimacy of coercive measures that have no relation to actual or potential violations of the law but, nevertheless, remain necessary to maintain or restore peace and security.

However, the examples given by Kelsen show that this is the exception rather than the rule within national legal orders. His examples of when sanctions may be imposed for reasons of necessity include the forcible destruction of buildings to prevent the spread of fire, or the forcible internment of people suffering infectious diseases in order to prevent an epidemic from spreading.[32] Arguably, in the international order, these sorts of exceptions are the norm so that sanctions are imposed by the UN Security Council to address threats to the peace,[33] whether or not those threats entails actual or possible violations of the law.[34] A different way of looking at it would be to see sanctions being directed at shoring up the basic conditions of peace and security necessary for a legal order to survive, thereby making sanctions part of the legal order. Kelsen does not go quite this far, but accepts that 'by declaring the conduct of a state to be a threat to, or breach of, the peace, the Security Council may create new law', imposing an 'obligation to refrain from this conduct'.[35]

For Gowlland-Debbas, however, sanctions are an aspect of the 'creation of international institutional responses to violations of … core norms'. She argues that although Chapter VII measures imposed by the Security Council were not intended to be restricted to cases of non-compliance with international law, the practice of the Council has moved considerably towards using its powers to address the responsibility of states for breaches of core norms of international law.[36] In a sense this anticipates the arguments for a Responsibility to Protect in international law emerging in 2001 with the proposition that when a state has failed to protect its population from the commission of core crimes then a responsibility lies with the Security Council to take measures, a proposition that remains *de lege fereda*.[37]

It is argued in this chapter that sanctions against states remain primarily designed to tackle threats to, or breaches of, international peace and security, and only secondarily to respond to breaches of international law. However, the development of sanctions against non-state actors is indicative of a trend towards punishment for violations of the law, given that this development has occurred within a broader context of a move towards addressing individual responsibility for core crimes. Nonetheless, although

[32] ibid.

[33] Charter of the United Nations, 24 October 1945, 1 UNTS XVI, Art 39.

[34] Kunz, 'Sanctions' (1960) 329.

[35] Kelsen, *Law of the United Nations* (1950) 736.

[36] V Gowlland-Debbas, 'UN Sanctions and International Law: An Overview' in Gowlland-Debbas (n 11) 7–9; V Gowlland-Debbas, 'Security Council Enforcement Action and Issues of State Responsibility' (1994) 43 *International and Comparative Law Quarterly* 55.

[37] C Focarelli, 'The Responsibility to Protect Doctrine and Humanitarian Intervention: Too Many Ambiguities for a Working Doctrine' (2008) 13 *Journal of Conflict & Security Law* 191.

sanctions against non-state actors remain a mixture of enforcing peace and law, their primary purpose is the former.[38] While decisions about international peace and security are clearly those belonging to the central collective security organs of the international community, could it be argued that decisions taken to enforce legal obligations could be taken by other international legal persons, namely states? Furthermore, the brief review of actual and proposed national autonomous sanctions regimes enacted by the US, Australia, Canada, the UK and New Zealand indicates wider purposes than simply to enforce international laws; they extend to taking measures in responses to threats to international peace and security as well as national security.

V. Where Does Sanctioning Competence Lie?

Thus far, the understanding of sanctions is of non-forcible measures imposed by centralised authorities in response to breaches of peace, security and increasingly law, while countermeasures and other acts of non-forcible self-help are imposed by a state in responses to breaches of law suffered at the hands of another state. Collective countermeasures blur this distinction to some extent in that they represent non-forcible attempts by non-victim states to enforce self-defined community norms outside of the institutional collective security regime and the bilateral mechanisms of normal countermeasures.[39] Autonomous sanctions, in the sense used by those states indicated in section II of this chapter, further try to bridge the gap between sanctions imposed by international organisations and bilateral or collective countermeasures taken by states in response to breaches of fundamental international laws.

In theory, sanctions imposed by organisations and countermeasures imposed by states are distinct.[40] However, if a collective right to take countermeasures is recognised, whereby states are permitted to take measures against a state in breach of obligations owed *erga omnes* ie to the whole international community, the line between countermeasures and sanctions appears less clear. Nevertheless, the concepts of collective sanctions and collective countermeasures are not the same, given that countermeasures, whether unilateral or collective, are rights of states to respond to violations of international law. Countermeasures signify the temporary non-fulfilment of obligations owed by the victim state(s) to the responsible state; while sanctions are powers exercised by competent organisations that can go above and beyond suspending any existing obligations of states and, moreover, are not currently conceived primarily as punishments for violations of international law but responses to threats to international public order. It follows that a sanctions regime could, like proportionate countermeasures, merely lead to the suspension of trade and arms agreements with a state; but it could go further and terminate those agreements and outlaw any further agreements on trade, arms or other

[38] ND White, 'Sanctions against Non-State Actors' in N Ronzitti (ed), *Coercive Diplomacy, Sanctions and International Law* (Nijhoff, 2016) 135–38.

[39] E Katselli-Proukaki, *The Problem of Enforcement in International Law: Countermeasures, the Non-Injured State and the Idea of International Community* (Routledge, 2010) 90–209; M. Dawidowicz, *Third Party Countermeasures in International Law* (Cambridge University Press, 2017) 3–5.

[40] E Zoller, *Peacetime Unilateral Remedies: An Analysis of Countermeasures* (Transnational, 1984) 106.

areas such as technology and finance and, furthermore, could oblige all member states to adopt such measures.

The type of sanctions just described can be lawfully applied by a few international actors, namely the UN Security Council under Chapter VII of the UN Charter, and regional organisations as identified under Chapter VIII of the UN Charter and empowered by their own constituent treaties. As such, sanctions are clearly the result of a significant attribution of powers by the member states acting collectively to those organisations. The limited range of institutional actors with sanctioning competence is not only due to the hierarchy contained in the UN Charter, whereby regional organisations are limited in their enforcement powers by the authority of the UN Security Council, but also by the obligation on Member States to give priority to obligations arising from the UN Charter over those arising from other treaties including regional ones.[41]

This explains which organisations have competence, but it does not explain why states do not have such. Certainly an examination of the growing practice of a group of Western states (in section II of this chapter) seems to be based on a clear legal belief that they have the right to adopt and enforce sanctions of the type within the competence of the UN Security Council, especially when that organ fails to act or adopts what those states perceive to be inadequate measures. This introduces the familiar problem of auto-interpretation by these states: they decide whether there is a threat to the peace and whether or not the Security Council has adequately addressed such. Certainly, individual states do not possess the power to impose collective sanctions. That lack of sanctioning power is because only the UN and competent regional organisations have the power to impose collective measures that bind all Member States to impose non-forcible measures against a target state or non-state actor. No single state has the power to bind other states to act in this way, although they may try to enmesh other states and actors by including an extraterritorial element in unilateral non-forcible measures imposed on a target state. For instance, under the US Helms-Burton Act 1996 penalties for breach of the Cuban embargo (emplaced under Presidential Executive Order since 1962)[42] (eg by importing into the US any goods of Cuban origin, in whole or in part) were increased.[43] Specifically, Title III of the Act granted US citizens a remedy in domestic courts against anyone 'trafficking' in property that was US-owned before its seizure by the Cuban Government in the early 1960s. This was one of the so-called extraterritorial effects of Helms-Burton objected to by the UK and EU amongst others as a breach of international laws limiting jurisdiction.[44]

Such over-reach is not an issue for most competent international organisations. Member States have not simply given the organisation in question the right to take

[41] UN Charter, Arts 53 and 103.

[42] Proclamation 3347 – Embargo on All Trade with Cuba, 3 February 1962, in which the President, acting under the Foreign Assistance Act 1961, prohibited 'the importation into the United States of all goods of Cuban origin and all goods imported from or through Cuba'.

[43] Cuban Liberty and Democratic Solidarity (Libertad) Act of 1996 (Helms-Burton Act), 110 Stat 785, Section 110(a).

[44] UK Protection of Trading Interests Acts 1980, applied by The Extraterritorial US Legislation (Sanctions against Cuba, Iran and Libya) (Protection of Trading Interests) Order 1996, SI 1996/3171, to trade with Cuba; Council Regulation (EC) Regulation 2271/96, 22 November 1996. Both remain in force, though there has been little enforcement.

measures that each of them has individually, but have collectively given the organisation a power to take measures against a target state that will require each member to adjust its diplomatic, financial, economic or sporting relations with the targeted state or non-state actor. No state has the power or right to ensure collective sanctions are taken under international law, although they have the right to take individual non-forcible counter-measures in response to violations of their rights by other states.[45] States attempting to take coordinated autonomous sanctions against a target state or non-state actors to protect their security are purporting to act in the absence of effective centralised sanctions and thereby are acting contrary to the existing legal framework governing sanctions imposed for peace and security. Such states are in effect trying to seize back powers from organisations disregarding the fact that such powers were granted to the organisation by a collective decision of Member States and, therefore, could only be taken back by a collective decision of Member States. However, if a group of like-minded states impose non-forcible measures in response to breaches of international legal obligations owed *erga omnes*, then they have a stronger claim to legality on the basis of the doctrine of collective countermeasures. Thus, for example, it might be possible legally to justify some of the provisions of the UK's Autonomous Sanctions and Anti-Money Laundering Act of 2018, which allow for the enforcement of human rights law, or humanitarian law, for example, but not for such measures designed to secure international peace and security or national security.

The UN Security Council is expressly empowered to impose non-forcible measures, including the 'complete or partial interruption of economic relations and of rail, sea, air, postal, telegraphic, radio, and other means of communication, and the severance of diplomatic relations', in response to threats to the peace, breaches of the peace and acts of aggression.[46] This power is granted to the organisation, specifically the Security Council, by the founding states to use against a Member State and to oblige other members to so act,[47] although the almost universal nature of the UN has meant that the Council tends to impose the obligations created by its non-forcible measures on all states, an extension that could be said to develop the obligation on the UN to ensure that non-Member States act in accordance with the UN's principles 'as far as may be necessary for the maintenance of international peace and security'.[48] Nonetheless, this falls short of imposing obligation on non-Member States meaning that the UN's extension of its sanctions' obligations to 'all states' is problematic, as non-Member States have not consented to the adoption of such measures. Arguments that the UN Charter is the constitution of the international community may help overcome this limitation, but they have not been fully developed or explained.[49]

Examples of regional organisations with sanctioning competence include the Organisation of American States (OAS) which, in response to any 'fact or situation

[45] But see FL Morrison, 'The Role of Regional Organizations in the Enforcement of International Law' in J Delbruck (ed), *The Allocation of Law Enforcement Authority in the International System* (Duncker & Humblot, 1995) 46–47, where he states that organisations cannot possess more powers than Member States.

[46] UN Charter, Arts 39 and 41.

[47] ibid, Art 25.

[48] ibid, Art 2(6).

[49] B Fassbender, *The United Nations Charter as the Constitution of the International Community* (Nijhoff, 2009) 78.

that might endanger the peace of America',[50] is empowered through its Organ of Consultation to take the following non-forcible measures against Member States: 'recall of chiefs of diplomatic missions; breaking of diplomatic relations; breaking of consular relations; partial or complete interruption of economic relations or of rail, sea, air, postal, telegraphic, telephonic, and radiotelephonic or radiotelegraphic communications'.[51] The African Union (AU), which replaced the Organisation of African Unity (OAU) in 2000, provides that

> any Member State that fails to comply with the decisions and policies of the Union may be subjected to … sanctions, such as the denial of transport and communications links with other Member States, and other measures of a political and economic nature to be determined by the Assembly.[52]

The EU's sanctioning competence, however, is external-facing and targeted at non-Member States although measures only bind EU Member States.[53] Given that these external measures do not bind the target state only EU Member States, the lack of consent (to be bound) by the target state is not a legally insurmountable problem. However, assuming that a collective sanctioning power belongs to an organisation for the purpose of controlling its membership, then the legal basis claimed for the EU's external measures must be that they are a form of collective countermeasures.[54] If the EU's external non-forcible measures extend beyond the doctrine of countermeasures the legal ground becomes more unstable in that they would represent steps towards claiming autonomous external sanctioning powers by a regional organisation.

Chapter VIII of the UN Charter governs relations between the UN and regional organisations. Under this framework regional organisations have autonomy in matters of peace and security 'as are appropriate for regional action', as long as they act consistently with the purposes and principles of the UN Charter. As regards 'enforcement action' by organisations for the purposes of collective or regional security, Article 53 of the Charter empowers the Security Council to utilise regional organisations for enforcement action taken under its authority, but clearly stipulates that 'no enforcement action shall be taken' by regional organisations 'without the authorization' of the UN Security Council. The ambiguity in the meaning of 'enforcement action' is whether it covers both economic and military measures.[55]

Placing sanctions in the hands of central organs of a legal order is certainly the norm in modern domestic legal orders, but this has not been fully realised in the international legal order. For a start, sanctions are primarily adopted in response to threats to international public order, not breaches of international law.[56] Furthermore, while the use of

[50] Charter of the Organisation of American States, 30 April 1948, entered into force 13 December 1951, Art 29.

[51] Inter-American Treaty of Reciprocal Assistance (Rio Treaty), 2 September 1947, Art 8.

[52] Constitutive Act of the African Union, 1 July 2000, Art 23(2).

[53] Treaty on European Union, 7 February 1992, Art 29; Treaty on the Functioning of the European Union, 13 December 2007, Art 215. See M Gestri, 'Sanctions Imposed by the European Union: Legal and Institutional Aspects' in Ronzitti, *Coercive Diplomacy* (2016) 100.

[54] Gestri, 'Sanctions Imposed by the European Union' (2016) 99.

[55] C Walter, 'Article 53' in B Simma (ed), *The Charter of the United Nations: A Commentary*, 3rd edn (Oxford University Press, 2012) 1481.

[56] N Tsagourias and ND White, *Collective Security: Theory, Law and Practice* (Cambridge University Press, 2013) 224.

military force by states is ruled out by the UN Charter except in the exercise of the right of self-defence or under the authority of the Security Council,[57] there is no equivalent clear prohibition on states deploying autonomous non-forcible measures.[58] It follows that while many domestic legal orders have ruled out self-help, this has not happened in the international legal order at least in the case of non-forcible measures. Nonetheless, the supremacy of the Security Council should not be underestimated, given that it is empowered to adopt sanctions that oblige Member States to take such measures against the target state, group or individuals in order to address threats to the peace.[59] Finally, there is the aforementioned requirement that regional enforcement action needs authorisation from the Security Council.[60] The intention was to create supranational competence in the Security Council to oblige all Member States (thereby having almost universal effect) to take non-forcible enforcement action, a competence not possessed by any other organisation or actor,[61] although regional organisations have carved out an autonomy to impose sanctions on their own membership by dint of consent (in the treaty) and practice. The EU's extra-regional application of sanctions is exceptional in this regard and can either be put down to a form of collective countermeasures or, most controversially, as a form of autonomous sanctions if they extend beyond the limitations upon countermeasures.

Gestri states that with over 30 sanctions programmes in place, often imposed autonomously from the UN Security Council, the EU has become a 'key player in the sanctions game' and, despite its claim to always act in full conformity with international law, the

> EU can be regarded as a trailblazer by the advocates of the controversial doctrine of collective countermeasures in reaction to *erga omnes* obligations, having on numerous occasions adopted sanctions without being individually affected by the breach of international law allegedly committed by the target state.[62]

Furthermore, Gestri points to the pulling power of the EU on third states to bring their conduct towards the target state into line with the EU's,[63] and the broadening jurisdictional scope of EU sanctions in spite of its criticisms of the extraterritorial extension of sanction regimes by the US.[64] Collective countermeasures taken in response to violations of fundamental international laws remain controversial but, on a spectrum of legality, a reasonable argument can be made in their favour. In contrast, if sanctions going beyond countermeasures were to be imposed by the EU, it would become an even more controversial trailblazer for an autonomous external sanctioning power for regional organisations. Furthermore, such a development might be pointed to by states such as the US, the UK, Australia and Canada as evidence of a more general right to impose autonomous sanctions by states for the purposes of securing international peace and security.

Institutional powers and practice on sanctions are difficult to reconcile with orthodox views of international law, where the state is the principal actor on the

[57] UN Charter, Arts 2(4), 42, 51 and 53.
[58] Elagab, *Non-Forcible Counter-Measures* (1988).
[59] UN Charter, Arts 25, 39 and 41.
[60] ibid, Art 53.
[61] C Schreuer, 'Comments' in Delbruck, *Allocation of Law Enforcement Authority* (1995) 82.
[62] Gestri (n 53) 99.
[63] ibid.
[64] ibid, 79.

international stage with the most complete set of international rights and duties. Consequently, there have been attempts to rationalise the sanctioning power of organisations by characterising it as the collective application of rights belonging to states.[65] However, when the founding states adopted the UN Charter in 1945, they collectively placed sanctioning power in the hands of a separate corporate entity – the UN Security Council. Arguments for autonomous sanctioning power remaining in the hands of states have greater compatibility with the legal order that existed before the adoption of the UN Charter, when self-help dominated. Indeed, sanctions under the League of Nations were largely auto-interpretive. Article 16 of the Covenant defined the event upon which sanctions were to become applicable, namely 'resort to war by a member state in disregard of its covenants', triggering obligations which then fell due from the other members.[66] Each member of the League had to decide for themselves whether the event had happened and the obligation was due. Such a system led to varying responses from members and, irrespective of the League's poor performance, it did allow for sanctions to be imposed by members when, under the UN system a veto by one permanent member blocks collective measures. In the UN system, dissatisfaction with the inability of the Security Council consistently to tackle threats to the peace has increasingly led to states taking unilateral non-forcible measures outside the UN system.[67] While the triggers for sanctions under the Covenant were relatively precisely defined, they are opaque under the Charter (especially the trigger of 'threat to the peace' in Article 39), and does little to ensure that the Security Council will make a determination or that its determination is just. Nonetheless, the choice to centralise sanctioning power in the hands of the Security Council was made in 1945, placing a clear insurmountable legal obstacle in the way of those advocates of unilateral or autonomous sanctions.

VI. Targeted Sanctions: Towards Decentralised Law Enforcement?

Whether viewed as integral to law or a consequence of law's breach, collective sanctions are not unlawful per se, unlike countermeasures by states, the wrongfulness of which is only precluded if they are taken in response to a prior breach of international law.[68] So far, it has been shown that collective sanctions in the international legal order are imposed in response to, or to prevent, threats to or breaches of the peace which, at least in orthodox thinking, are not concepts embodied in law. However, given that sanctions

[65] F Dopagne, 'Sanctions and Countermeasures by International Organizations' in R. Collins and ND White (eds), *International Organizations and the Idea of Autonomy: Institutional Independence in the International Legal Order* (Routledge, 2011) 178.

[66] JL Brierly, 'The Covenant and the Charter' (1946) 23 *British Yearbook of International Law* 87.

[67] On the UN General Assembly's competence to recommend sanctions see ND White, 'The Relationship Between the UN Security Council and General Assembly in Matters of International Peace and Security' in M Weller (ed), *The Oxford Handbook of the Use of Force in International Law* (Oxford University Press, 2015) 308.

[68] ARSIWA, Art 22.

are imposed to protect extra-legal values that ensure basic conditions of stability in the international order, it can be contended that they are primordially lawful actions. This section explores the move from general to targeted sanctions in order to ascertain whether a change in target has been accompanied by a change in purpose, namely from enforcing peace to enforcing law. Furthermore, if there is such a move, does this signify that states can have an autonomous role as enforcers of international law? Underdeveloped legal systems often depend upon diffused law enforcement and, moreover, those laws are created by states to govern their relations and, therefore, arguably they have *locus standi* to enforce them. Furthermore, unlike concepts of international peace and security that are predicated on achieving inter-subjective community consensus, clear breaches of laws are in theory at least objectively verifiable and, therefore, less susceptible to unilateral manipulation. Furthermore, enforcement of fundamental international laws by states taking collective countermeasures has gained significant traction in international law.[69]

The rare instances of UN collective sanctions imposed during the Cold War had the appearance of community responses to violations of basic international laws respecting human rights and self-determination specifically by white racist regimes against the black majorities in Rhodesia and South Africa. However, a close reading of the applicable resolutions indicates that the measures were taken to tackle threats to international peace and security. The Security Council was careful to base its determinations of threats to the peace on a combination of the nature of the regimes, and the impact that those regimes' policies had on peace for the region, with evidence that internal violent struggles for freedom were spreading to neighbouring countries. This is clearly encapsulated in Resolution 418 (1977) imposing a mandatory arms embargo against South Africa in 1977, when the Security Council, 'having regard to the policies and acts of the South African Government', determined that 'the acquisition by South Africa of arms and related *materiel*' constituted 'a threat to the maintenance of international peace and security'. Other resolutions adopted the typology of simply determining that the situation in Southern Rhodesia was a threat to international peace and security,[70] thereby not linking the determination to anything other than peace and security.

The more recent turn to targeted sanctions imposed against non-state actors and regime elites are often explained as humane responses to concerns about the devastating effects of general sanctions imposed on Iraq to force it to withdraw from Kuwait following its aggressive occupation of that country in 1990,[71] and instead to target those individual violators of international standards and law.[72] In fact, targeted sanctions were first imposed in the early 1990s against non-state actors who were in control of territory. In other words, the rationale was similar to those sanctions imposed against states in terms of imposing measures against a territory and those groups exercising control over it in order to force them towards peace.

[69] Katselli-Proukaki, *The Problem of Enforcement in International Law* (2010) n 39.

[70] UN Doc S/RES/232 (1966).

[71] UN Doc S/RES/661 (1990).

[72] Report of the Secretary-General's High-Level Panel on Threats, Challenges and Change, A More Secure World: Our Shared Responsibility, UN Doc A/59/565 (2004) para 179.

The early post-Cold War instances of sanctions against non-state actors were imposed against those holding power but who had not attained full status as state actors. Measures in the 1990s were imposed against rebel groups with de facto belligerent status (eg UNITA in Angola and the Bosnian Serbs), or against de facto governments (eg the Taliban in Afghanistan). The measures against UNITA rebels were designed to force that armed group to accept the Peace Accords that it had previously signed but had breached through its continued military actions in Angola, thereby constituting a threat to international peace and security.[73] UN collective sanctions taken against the Bosnian Serbs in the 1990s, the party to the conflict seen as acting most often in violation of international humanitarian law,[74] remain measures aimed at restoring peace and security. While certain other non-forcible measures were taken on the basis that the violations of international law themselves constituted threats to the peace, particularly the creation of the ICTY,[75] non-forcible sanctions were imposed upon the Bosnian Serb leadership for refusing to settle peacefully and for continued fighting. In other words, they were designed to tackle the threat to the peace caused by the Bosnian Serbs' continued aggression and failure to accept various peace plans.[76] Furthermore, the non-forcible measures taken by the UN Security Council to tackle violations of international law (viz the establishment of the ICTY) were not targeted at the Bosnian Serbs leadership per se but at individual violators of international criminal law (including individuals from other armed groups as well as emerging states). That aspect of the threat arising from the violence in Bosnia and consisting of violations of international law was addressed by the creation of an international criminal tribunal with powers of punishment, while the continuing conflict and refusal by the Bosnian Serbs to settle peacefully were addressed by a variety of non-forcible and forcible measures imposed by the Security Council.

Even historically the first UN sanctions regime was imposed against the illegitimate white racist regime in Rhodesia in the late 1960s, a de facto government, though the measures imposed were not targeted and had a wider impact on the population.[77] The first generation of smart sanctions against non-state actors in the 1990s were pragmatically driven measures against those in control of territories even though they had not achieved recognition as legitimate leaders of states. A clear departure from measures analogous to sanctions against states was only taken with the extension of the Taliban sanctions regime, imposed in 1999, to Al-Qaida in 2000, which removed the link between Al-Qaida and the territory of Afghanistan,[78] followed in 2011 by the complete separation of the two regimes.[79]

A contrast can be made with EU sanctions which, because of the narrower consensus necessary to take decisions to impose measures and broader agreement on the

[73] UN Doc S/RES/864 (1993).

[74] Final Report of the Commission of Experts Established Pursuant to Security Council Resolution 780 (1992), UN Doc S/1994/674.

[75] UN Doc S/RES/827 (1993). See also Appeals Chamber, *Prosecutor v Tadic*, Case No IT-94-1-IT, Judgment of 10 August 1995, para 19.

[76] UN Doc S/RES/942 (1994).

[77] UN Doc S/RES 232 (1966).

[78] UN Doc S/RES/1267 (1999); UN Doc S/RES/1333 (2000).

[79] UN Doc S/RES/1988 (2011); UN Doc S/RES/1989 (2011).

values to be protected or promoted, show a faster and deeper trend towards sanctions directed at regime elites (for example, in Zimbabwe and Russia),[80] and to a lesser extent non-state actors such as terrorist groups.[81] For instance, targeted EU sanctions were initially imposed in 2002 by the Council against individuals in Zimbabwe on the basis of its assessment that the 'Government of Zimbabwe continues to engage in serious violations of human rights and of the freedom of opinion, of association and of peaceful assembly'. It decided that 'for as long as the violations occur the Council deems it necessary to introduce restrictive measures against the Government of Zimbabwe and those who bear a wide responsibility for such violations'.[82]

The EU's measures are framed as a response to violations of international human rights standards occurring in Zimbabwe and, therefore, fit the prescription for collective countermeasures. In contrast, in the case of measures imposed by the US on Zimbabwe, in an Executive Order of 2003, the President

> determined that the actions and policies of certain members of the Government of Zimbabwe and other persons to undermine Zimbabwe's democratic processes or institutions contributing to the deliberate breakdown in the rule of law in Zimbabwe, to politically motivated violence and intimidation in that country, and to political and economic instability in the southern African region, constitute an unusual and extraordinary threat to the foreign policy of the United States

and declared 'a national emergency to deal with that threat'.[83] The formula of an executive Presidential Order, which finds a threat to the foreign policy and national security of the US and declaring a national emergency to deal with the threat, has been used on a number of occasions by the US to tackle a variety of perceived threats by imposing targeted autonomous sanctions against individuals and other non-state actors.[84] Less frequently, more normative based determinations of violations of human rights have been used by Congress to pass legislation imposing targeted sanctions.[85] The Presidential executive power to impose sanctions, derived from the International Emergency Economic Powers Act (IEEPA) originally adopted in 1977,[86] has been criticised on the

[80] See, for example, EU targeted sanctions against regime individuals in Zimbabwe (Council Decision 2011/101/CFSP of 15 February 2011, OJ L42/6), and Syria (Council Decision 2013/255/CFSP of 1 June 2013, OJ L147/14). Targeted sanctions were imposed against certain Russian individuals responsible for actions, which undermined or threatened the territorial integrity, sovereignty and independence of Ukraine following intervention in Ukraine (Council Decision 2014/145/CFSP of 17 March 2014, OJ L78/16).

[81] Measures against Al Qaida in Common Position 2002/402/CFSP of 29 May 2002, OJ L139/4; measures against individuals and entities associated with Al Qaida in Council Regulation (EC) No 881/2000 of 29 May 2002, OJ L139/9. See also Common Position 2001/931/CFSP of 28 December 2001, OJ L344/93; Council Regulation (EC) No 2580/2001 of 28 December 2001, OJ L344/70, freezing funds and economic resources of certain persons, groups and entities with a view to combating terrorism.

[82] Restrictive measures against Zimbabwe in Common Position 2002/145/CFSP of 21 February 2002, OJ L 50/1.

[83] Executive Order 13288 – Blocking Property of Persons Undermining Democratic Processes or Institutions in Zimbabwe, 10 March 2003, 68 FR 11457.

[84] See for example: Executive Order 13611 – Blocking Property of Persons Threatening the Peace, Security, or Stability of Yemen, 16 May 2012, 77 FR 29533; Executive Order 13338 – Blocking Property of Certain Persons and Prohibiting the Export of Certain Goods to Syria, 13 May 2004, 69 FR 26751; Executive Order 13067 – Blocking Sudanese Government Property and Prohibiting Transactions With Sudan, 5 November 1997, 62 FR 59989.

[85] Venezuela Defense of Human Rights and Civil Society Act of 2014, 128 Stat 3011, S 2142.

[86] 50 USC 35 (1982), Sections 1701–02.

grounds that 'experience with IEEPA raises concerns that it may be used casually for spurious national emergencies'.[87] The language of the Presidential executive order on Zimbabwe also demonstrates that executive security powers are being invoked to tackle threats arising out of denial of democratic rights.

The autonomous sanctioning right claimed by the US is not just problematic under US constitutional law but, as the above analysis shows, is also unsupported in international law. Understandings of what constitutes international threats to the peace can only be made by a competent organ of the international community based on intersubjective agreement. Those decisions are inherently ones for competent international organisations making collective judgments that the peace of their members is threatened. While states and regional organisations (when acting externally) have a legal basis for enforcing community norms, such as serious violations of human rights or international humanitarian law, they have no legal basis to make determinations of whether a situation in a particular country, or by non-state actors, is a threat to international peace. Declaring that the situation in another country is a threat to the sanctioning state's national security might seem to remove the need for collective decision-making at the international level. However, this constitutes a wholly subjective judgment enabling a state to take coercive measures on the international stage solely on the basis of a political judgment by the executive of one state.

In the case of sanctions imposed on Iran on the basis that its nuclear programme was not being developed solely for peaceful purposes, the Security Council imposed sanctions on the basis that this constituted a threat to international peace and security.[88] The US imposed sanctions against Iran that not only fulfilled its obligations deriving from the Security Council's decisions, but also going beyond those measures. Under the Joint Comprehensive Plan of Action, or Iran nuclear deal of 2015 with the P5 plus Germany and the EU, Iran agreed to restrict its nuclear activities and permit more stringent IAEA inspections. In December 2015, the IAEA Board of Governors voted to end its 10-year-long investigation into the possible military dimension of Iran's nuclear programme. Security Council sanctions would 'snap-back' if Iran violated the agreement. This positive diplomatic development centred around the P5, showed that it is possible for the Security Council to cooperate to address a threat to international peace caused by a proliferation of nuclear weapons.[89] However, this was undermined by the US withdrawal from the treaty in May 2018, and its reimposition of unilateral sanctions against Iran in November 2018 – 'the toughest U.S. sanctions ever imposed on Iran', targeting 'critical sectors of Iran's economy, such as the energy, shipping and shipbuilding, and financial sectors'.[90] President Trump's Executive Order of August 2018 stated that the purpose of reimposing sanctions was

> to advance the goal of applying financial pressure on the Iranian regime in pursuit of a comprehensive and lasting solution to the full range of the threats posed by Iran, including Iran's

[87] BE Carter, 'International Economic Sanctions: Improving the Haphazard U.S. Legal Regime' (1987) 75 *California Law Review* 1238.

[88] Commencing with UN Doc S/RES/1737 (2006).

[89] UN Doc S/RES/2231 (2015).

[90] See US OFAC at home.treasury.gov/policy-issues/financial-sanctions/sanctions-programs-and-country-information.

> proliferation and development of missiles and other asymmetric and conventional weapons capabilities, its network and campaign of regional aggression, its support for terrorist groups, and the malign activities of the Islamic Revolutionary Guard Corps and its surrogates.[91]

In response to a request for provisional measures brought by Iran against the US on the basis of alleged violations of the Treaty of Amity of 1955 between the two states, the International Court of Justice considered that the US, 'in accordance with its obligations under the 1955 Treaty, must remove, by means of its choosing, any impediments arising from the measures' announced by the US 'to the free exportation to the territory of Iran of goods required for humanitarian needs', such as medicines, foodstuffs, and goods and services required for the safety of civil aviation.[92] The case may produce clarity on the legality of autonomous sanctions if it proceeds to the merits.

The trend in UN Security Council targeted sanctions practice is to move towards widening the concept of 'threat to the peace' to enable action to be taken to tackle the threat including measures directed at deterring or stopping the violence by non-state actors, with specific focus on those responsible for violations of human rights law and humanitarian law. Assets freezes, travel bans and other targeted measures have been imposed on individuals and groups either because they undermine the peace process or otherwise threaten the peace, but also if they threaten the human security of civilians, manifested in the commission of violations of international law. This is a reflection of a move towards not only securing peace within the state but also in establishing the security of individuals within it. Thus, although appearing to be a form of punishment for breaches of the law, they remain measures aimed at restoring peace and security, but at the local level as well as state level. As well as the example mentioned above, whereby sanctions were taken on this basis against armed groups in the CAR, other examples can be found in Cote D'Ivoire,[93] Lebanon[94] and Sudan.[95] However, in other instances, targeted measures are more narrowly directed at those regime elites and non-state actors who have threatened the peace: for example in Guinea-Bissau,[96] Iran,[97] North Korea,[98] Liberia,[99] Sierra Leone,[100] Somalia,[101] Eritrea,[102] South Sudan[103] and Yemen.[104]

This review of UN, EU and US practice indicates a predominant trend towards targeted sanctions, but also that for the UN and US a primary concern is to tackle peace and security and only indirectly violations of international law. Targeted UN sanctions have a clear constitutional basis in the UN Charter. US sanctions are legally problematic

[91] 'Reimposing Certain Sanctions with Respect to Iran', Executive Order 13846, 6 August 2018, 83 FR, 152.
[92] *Alleged Violations of the 1955 Treaty of Amity, Economic Relations and Consular Rights (Islamic Republic of Iran v United States of America)* Request for the Indication of Provisional Measures (2018) ICJ Rep 623, para 98.
[93] For example, UN Doc S/RES/1572 (2004) para 9.
[94] For example, UN Doc S/RES/1636 (2005) para 3.
[95] For example, UN Doc S/RES/1591 (2005) para 3(c).
[96] UN Doc S/RES/2048 (2012) para 6.
[97] For example, UN Doc S/RES/1737 (2006) paras 10–12.
[98] For example, UN Doc S/RES/1718 (2006) para 8(c).
[99] For example, UN Doc S/RES/1343 (2001) paras. 2 and 5–7.
[100] For example, UN Doc S/RES/1132 (1997) para 5.
[101] For example, UN Doc S/RES/1844 (2008) paras 1 and 3.
[102] For example, UN Doc S/RES/1907 (2009) para 14.
[103] UN Doc S/RES/2206 (2015) para 6.
[104] For example, UN Doc S/RES/2140 (2014).

as they extend beyond unilateral or 'collective' countermeasures or other forms of non-forcible measures of self-help and, thereby, constitute coercive measures in violation of the international legal principle of non-intervention.[105] The EU's move towards targeted sanctions against regime elites and non-state actors is largely premised on the enforcement of community norms and are, therefore, more readily justifiable as collective countermeasures, although that doctrine remains disputed in international law.[106]

VII. The Inherent Illegality of Autonomous Sanctions

Countermeasures are unlawful if they are not taken in response to actual breaches of international law, or if they are permanent or disproportionate, making them inherently destabilising because such judgements are unlikely to be made by an independent court, rather they are made by states themselves. Countermeasures and other forms of self-help may therefore be met by counter-countermeasures, as with Russia's response to the measures imposed on it by EU and other states for its intervention in Ukraine.[107] Although there is clear justification for imposing collective countermeasures against Russia for its breach of community norms prohibiting aggression on the assumption that collective countermeasures are accepted as lawful, in other instances acts of self-help are clearly either spurious or disproportionate, thereby rendering them unlawful acts of coercion. A recent example of this involved Gulf States imposing an embargo on Qatar in June 2017 for allegedly supporting terrorism, including the demand that Qatar close the Al-Jazeera media network as well as desist in its support for Hamas, the Muslim Brotherhood and Hezbollah, and end its relations with Turkey and Iran. These non-forcible measures of self-help taken by Saudi Arabia, the UAE, Bahrain and Egypt demonstrate the weaknesses of self-declared victim states acting as judge, jury and executioner.[108]

Unilateral non-forcible measures of coercion are unlawful unless taken under a secondary rule of international law as countermeasures in response to a violation of a primary rule. On this basis there is no unilateral form of autonomous sanctioning power belonging to states. Collective sanctions are not inherently unlawful and, indeed,

[105] Embodied, for example, in the Declaration on Principles of International Law concerning Friendly Relations and Cooperation among States in accordance with the Charter of the United Nations, UN Doc A/RES/25/2625 (1970): 'No State may use or encourage the use of economic, political or any other type of measures to coerce another State in order to obtain from it the subordination of the exercise of its sovereign rights and to secure from it advantages of any kind'. See also Declaration on the Inadmissibility of Intervention in the Domestic Affairs of States and the Protection of their Independence and Sovereignty, UN Doc A/RES/20/2131 (1965) para 2.

[106] The ILC's Articles did not clearly accept their legality in 2001: see ARSIWA, Art 54.

[107] K Krause, 'Western Economic and Political Sanctions as Instruments of Strategic Competition with Russia – Opportunities and Risks' in Ronzitti (n 38) 270.

[108] Although aspects of the dispute are being considered by the Council of the ICAO, resulting in an appeal to the International Court of Justice, which upheld the jurisdiction of the Council of the ICAO in *Appeal Relating to the Jurisdiction of the ICAO Council under Article 84 of the Convention on Civil Aviation (Bahrain, Egypt, Saudi Arabia and United Arab Emirates v Qatar)* (2020) ICJ Rep, 14 July 2020. See also the case brought to the ICJ by Qatar against the UAE in *Application of the International Convention on the Elimination of All Forms if Racial Discrimination (Qatar v United Arab Emirates)*, Provisional Measures (2019) ICJ Rep 361.

Kelsen's view is that they are an integral part of a legal system so that a law consists of a proscription of behaviour and a punishment for misbehaviour. Furthermore, accepting the proposition discussed at the outset of this article, namely that sanctions are imposed by central authorities, the judgement on imposition is taken away from individual states and belongs to political organs of international organisations consisting of states but acting in a corporate manner, voting by majority, qualified majority or unanimity, depending upon the voting rules specified in the constituent treaty.

The inherent legality of sanctions imposed by competent organisations does not immunise decisions to impose them from international law. Sanctions can often be seen to be the cause of violations of international law. The devastating impact of sanctions against Iraq was well-known and recorded. The Security Council responded by adopting the 'oil-for-food' Resolution 706 (1991). Despite the mitigating effects of the mismanaged and corrupted oil-for-food programme, the devastating impact of UN sanctions on the people of Iraq cannot be over-stated. Furthermore, despite the significant impact on the human rights of the peoples of Iraq, it has been argued that human rights *laws* are inapplicable to those sanctions given that, even if they bind the UN as an intergovernmental organisation possessing international legal personality as a matter of customary law, there was no intention by the Security Council to violate those rights.[109] On the understanding that the Security Council did not intend to violate the rights of the Iraqi people, and, furthermore, that it is necessary to show intent to establish that it had violated international law in this regard,[110] it still should have foreseen the possibility and, therefore at the very least, it had obligations of due diligence to do all in its power to prevent human rights violations that are likely to result from its actions.[111]

The violative nature of unilateral sanctions that go beyond temporary and proportionate countermeasures is shown by the US embargo of Cuba first imposed 1962 in response to Cuba's nationalisation of US property and businesses. This was tightened considerably with the fall of the Soviet Union and the withdrawal of its support for Cuba in 1991 (meaning an immediate loss of 75–80 per cent of Cuban trade),[112] by its incorporation in legislation in the form of the Torricelli and Helms-Burton Acts of 1992 and 1996 respectively.[113] The hardening of the embargo had dramatic effects on the health of the Cuban population. The Government of the United States took cruel advantage of the removal of Soviet support to try to force regime change by a starving population. The effect on life expectancy, the reduction in weight of the average Cuban and the impact on newborn babies were all detailed in a report by the independent and respected American Association for World Health (AAWH) in 1997.[114] For a period of five-to-10 years after the demise of the Soviet Union, when the Cuban population was

[109] ME O'Connell, 'Debating the Law of Sanctions' (2002) 13 *European Journal of International Law* 73.

[110] I Brownlie, *System of the Law of Nations: State Responsibility Part I* (Oxford University Press, 1983) 40.

[111] International Law Association, Final Report of Committee on Accountability of International Organizations (2004) 15.

[112] J Gordon, 'Economic Sanctions as Negative Development' (2016) 28 *Journal of International Development* 474.

[113] WM LeoGrande, 'Enemies Evermore: US Policy Towards Cuba After Helms-Burton' (1997) 29 *Journal of Latin American Studies* 211.

[114] AAWH, 'Denial of Food and Medicine: The Impact of the US Embargo on Health and Nutrition in Cuba' (1997).

especially vulnerable, the US legislature chose to continue, indeed intensify, its sanctions against Cuba. That demonstrated sufficient intent to cause deliberate harm and damage to Cuba and to its people, over and above the US exercising its freedom to choose trade partners. Finishing off a weakened Cuban government would inevitably impact upon an even weaker Cuban population, a population who were not comforted by the stated purposes of the Helms-Burton Act, namely to: 'assist the Cuban people in regaining their freedom and prosperity'; ensure free and fair elections; protect the US from Cuban terrorism; address the 'theft' of US-owned property; and respond to Cuba's violation of human rights.[115]

One of the unaddressed aspects of when an organisation or a state can be held legally responsible for violations of international law is causation – did the wrongful act (in the UN's continuation of sanctions against Iraq in the period 1991–2003, or by the continuation and tightening of the US embargo against Cuba in the period 1992–96) cause damage to the Iraqi and Cuban peoples?[116] The decisions to continue the embargoes were clearly attributable to the UN and the US, but did the resulting measures cause the losses suffered by the Iraqi and Cuban populations? The evidence drawn from independent bodies[117] clearly points to violations of the socio-economic rights of thousands of individuals in Iraq and Cuba as a result of the measures imposed as a result of decisions by the UN and US respectively.[118] This was foreseeable damage inflicted on Iraq and Cuba – more specifically the populations of those countries – and was not sufficiently mitigated by any of humanitarian exceptions built into the embargoes.[119]

The fact that organisations and states imposing sanctions try to mitigate the effects of such measures on the ordinary people of the target state is indicative that they realise that such powers and rights should be exercised in ways that minimise human rights' violations. For instance, in the decision that imposed a comprehensive embargo against Iraq, the Security Council created an exception for payments and shipments of humanitarian foodstuffs and medical supplies.[120] However, this did not mean that Iraq bought or distributed such supplies to its weakening citizens – hence the advent of the oil-for-food programme some years later. Although the intention behind the humanitarian exception in sanctions resolutions is to reduce the impact of sanctions on the population, the evidence is that the powerful elites in the target country will take control of the supplies, and that such exceptions will encourage a black market in goods from which elites benefit, thereby strengthening their wealth and position and blunting the positive effects of humanitarian exceptions.

[115] Helms-Burton Act 1996 (n 43).

[116] B Stern, 'The Elements of an Internationally Wrongful Act' in Crawford, Pellet and Olleson, *International Responsibility* (2010) 193.

[117] See also UN Human Rights Council, Report Submitted by the Personal Representative of the High Commissioner for Human Rights on the Situation of Human Rights in Cuba, 26 January 2007, UN Doc A/HRC/4/12, para 7.

[118] J Gordon, *Invisible War: The United States and the Iraq Sanctions* (Harvard University Press, 2010) 86–102; Gordon, 'Economic Sanctions' (2016) 474.

[119] For example, the prohibition of ships trading with Cuba from docking in the US meant that mixed cargoes containing medical supplies, for instance, would not be exported to Cuba: see Cuban Government's statement in UN Secretary General's Report, UN Doc A/71/91 (2016).

[120] UN Doc S/RES/661 (1991).

In striving to achieve security aims, the UN's general sanctions against countries as a whole have proved too damaging to human rights and, thereby, have not achieved both peace and human rights. In what could perhaps be a developing duty of due diligence to ensure that human rights of the population are not violated, the Council has tried a number of routes including humanitarian exceptions and oil-for-food, but none have sufficiently mitigated the adverse effects of sanctions on the population. The use of lawfully imposed collective sanctions against a whole state seemed to have come to a natural and ugly end in 2003 when Saddam's regime was toppled. It is somewhat ironic that the main example of unlawful unilateral economic sanctions, the US embargo imposed and enforced against Cuba, continues despite overwhelming recognition of its illegality by the UN General Assembly.[121]

While new-style targeted sanctions have raised their own human rights concerns in terms of due process, rights to property, privacy and freedom of movement, they are quantitatively far fewer human rights violations when compared with the effects of punitive sanctions imposed against a state and, therefore, against the population of a state. Nonetheless, there is no doubt that effectively implemented targeted sanctions can have a profound effect on the lives of those targeted and their families. In an important national judgment – the *Ahmed* case decided by the UK Supreme Court in 2010 – the Court was highly critical of the targeted sanctions regime in terms of its effects of such measures on the lives of individuals. Lord Hope described the impact of the executive orders on targeted individuals and their families as making them effectively 'prisoners of the state'.[122]

As with general sanctions, there is an ongoing debate about the violative nature of targeted sanctions, especially of due process norms. However, the issue has not been resolved in favour of such measures causing clear rights violations since the listing of individuals can be conceived as an executive or administrative process on the basis of perceived security threats, rather than a judicial one equivalent to a criminal conviction for breaches of core crimes, even though the listing results in set of coercive measures, arguably de facto punishment, of those listed. Nevertheless, this has not stopped targeted individuals from alleging rights violations before domestic[123] and regional courts,[124] and in individual complaints to the Human Rights Committee.[125] While the temporary freezing of an individual's assets could be seen as a preventive

[121] For example, UN Doc A/RES/72/4 (2017) adopted by 191 votes to two (US and Israel). For the argument that unilateral embargoes may be lawful acts of retorsion see Ruys (n 13) 26–27. See statement by the International Court of Justice in *Military and Paramilitary Activities in and Against Nicaragua (Nicaragua v United States of America)*, Judgment of 27 June 1986, (1986) ICJ Rep 14, para 245. Without offering reasons, the Court found that a US trade embargo imposed on Nicaragua did not breach the customary international law principle of non-intervention.

[122] *Her Majesty's Treasury v Mohammed Jabar Ahmed and Others* [2010] UKSC 2 [4].

[123] For example, *Abdelrazik v Canada (Minister of Foreign Affairs)* [2010] 1 FCR 267.

[124] Joined Cases C-402/05 P and C-415/05 P, *Yassin Abdullah Kadi and Al Barakaat International Foundation v Council and Commission*, ECR, 2008, I-06351, para 334; European Court of Human Rights, *Nada v Switzerland*, Application No 10593/08, Judgment of 12 September 2012; European Court of Human Rights, *Case of Al-Dulimi and Montana Management Inc v Switzerland*, Application No 5809/08, Judgment of 21 June 2016.

[125] *Nabil Sayadi and Patricia Vinck v Belgium*, Communication No 1472/2006, 29 December 2008, 16 IHHR 427.

administrative measure and not, therefore, subject to full due process protections, the fact that there is a degree of permanence in a number of listings means that there should be avenues for challenging such decisions. Temporary preventive targeted sanctions imposed by the UN Security Council in response to specific threats might enable states to modify their human rights obligations to the extent of suspending any conflict with their obligations arising under the UN Charter.[126] However, targeted sanctions imposed by states pursuant to the legislative resolutions of the Security Council, principally Resolution 1373 (2001),[127] do not fit the model of executive decisions necessitating the temporary trumping of human rights obligations. Furthermore, obligations arising from sanctions imposed by states unilaterally cannot claim to have primacy over human rights obligations owed by states.

Thus, sanctions decided by a competent international organisation are inherently lawful, but their imposition is still judged by applicable international laws. The move towards targeted sanctions is an attempt to mitigate human rights violations, and organisations can benefit from a temporary human rights override if necessary for peace and security. Autonomous sanctions imposed by states, in contrast, are inherently unlawful, and can only be excused if they are response to breach of fundamental international laws and follow the proscriptions on countermeasures. Their application may also breach human rights laws and they cannot benefit from any human rights override.

VIII. Conclusion

Sanctions have changed over the decades: they have become more humane, they have become more common, but they remain somewhat outside the international legal order in the sense that they are largely imposed to enforce peace not law. Given the centrality of sanctions to any legal system, there are clearly significant adjustments to be made to place sanctions within the parameters of international law, ensuring that they do not themselves violate fundamental norms. This is not to forget the Security Council's primary responsibility for peace and security or to argue that it should be solely an executive enforcer of international law. International law is not developed sufficiently to do that, nor is the UN itself based on a separation of powers. Furthermore, the shift towards enforcement of international law by organisations and states has strengthened the argument for recognising collective countermeasures. However, claims to be able to undertake autonomous or unilateral sanctions to secure international peace and security, or to protect national security, are in violation of the existing legal regime governing sanctions. Autonomous sanctions imposed unilaterally by states should not be seen as a form of growing state practice and *opinio juris* in a 'grey area' situated somewhere between clearly lawful collective sanctions and clearly lawful unilateral countermeasures, Rather, the analysis in this chapter, has sought to demonstrate that they are unlawful claims by a handful of like-minded states desirous to combine their economic power not simply to enforce community norms, but to protect and enforce their conceptions of peace and security.

[126] UN Charter, Art 103.
[127] UN Doc S/RES/1373 (2001).

Collective sanctions imposed by legitimate centralised institutions, either universal or regional, are not only inherently lawful but are of a different order to the secondary rules of responsibility that permit states to apply what would otherwise be inherently unlawful measures in response to breaches of their international rights by other states, a right that can easily be abused and become unbridled economic coercion as the enduring embargo of Cuba by the US demonstrates. It follows that there is no autonomous right belonging to states to impose sanctions beyond the limited forms of non-forcible self-help recognised primarily in the doctrine of countermeasures, despite extensive US practice and the recent development of domestic legislation and some practice by a handful of other states.

Collective countermeasures, as responses to breaches of core international crimes, are understandable responses to such egregious behaviour and, as such, can be categorised as 'public' responses to assaults on the international legal order, rather than the normal form of 'private' countermeasures imposed in a strictly bilateral relationship. However, given the inherent weaknesses in unilateral and subjective judgements made by states as to when to impose such non-forcible measures, they can only ever be an unstable and, therefore, temporary stepping stone toward collective, centrally imposed, sanctions. Collective countermeasures operate to some extent in the grey area between lawful collective sanctions and strictly bilateral countermeasures. In contrast, autonomous sanctions that purport to enforce a combination of law and security matters, based solely on the perception of the states taking such measures, do not exploit a gap in the law. Rather autonomous sanctions are breaches of the laws prohibiting coercive intervention as well as representing a challenge to the legal structures established in 1945 that placed sanctioning competence, for better or for worse, within an international institutional framework based on collective perceptions that 'peace' and 'security' are being threatened. There is little doubt that the collective sanctioning process has many weaknesses, but replacing such a collective process with unilateral determinations often based on executive decision-making by the government of a state declaring a state of emergency or threat to its security, opens up the possibility of a world riven by economic warfare.

3

Unilateral Sanctions: Creating Chaos at Bargain Rates

JOY GORDON

I. Introduction

There is a widely held view that sanctions imposed by an international organisation or a coalition of countries are much more likely to have a significant impact than unilateral measures:

> It is well known that the widest possible implementation of economic sanctions is a precondition to their effectiveness … Quite simply, the more States that implement a specific thread of economic sanctions, the smaller the potential for the State target to circumvent the measures by turning to other partners and markets. As a result, single-State sanctions should be weaker than sanctions imposed by a group of States.[1]

It would seem that unilateral sanctions are necessarily limited in both their scope and impact: when a single country denies the target country access to a single market, that seems very different from multilateral sanctions, or sanctions imposed by a body of global governance. The economic consequences will be less; and unilateral sanctions lack the legitimacy and moral force of multilateral or collective measures, so other states and private actors will be less inclined to abide by them.

But, in fact, it makes little sense to speak in generalities in this regard. The effectiveness of unilateral sanctions, or at least the damage done, depends entirely on who the sanctioner is, and the extent of its powers and international influence; and who the target is, and the depth of its vulnerabilities. Indeed, when the country imposing the sanctions holds a monopoly on a critical market, or in some other context holds a singular role in the global economy, unilateral sanctions may in effect function as though they were global.

A country imposing unilateral measures may also employ extraterritorial sanctions, expanding the scope of the sanctions regime beyond the sanctioner's own nationals.

[1] C Beaucillon, 'Practice Makes Perfect, Eventually? Unilateral State Sanctions and the Extraterritorial Effects of National Legislation,' in N Ronzitti (ed), *Coercive Diplomacy, Sanctions and International Law* (Brill Nijhoff, 2016) 104.

In addition, where the sanctions regulations are vague or unpredictably enforced, and where the penalties are severe – such as exclusion from a major market or banking system – private actors may then withdraw from the target country altogether, foregoing even those transactions that are permitted, such as the delivery of humanitarian goods. These decisions are not based directly on legal considerations, but rather on risk assessment that exceeds the explicit legal prohibitions.

There can be a broad impact even in the case of asset freezes. On their face, it seems that asset freezes would only affect individual persons and companies, and the term 'asset freezes' suggests only that these entities would be denied access to their personal or corporate assets. In fact, these financial blacklists may prohibit all transactions, both personal and official. Consequently, when government officials, such as a minister of health or agriculture, are blacklisted they cannot engage in any transactions relative to their work, such as purchasing medicines or agricultural inputs. When multiple key government officials are blacklisted, the government may effectively be paralysed.

Although many of these measures are described as 'targeted sanctions', ostensibly impacting only individuals or specific companies, or specific goods such as weapons, in fact the results in many cases are macroeconomic in scope, broadly affecting the target country's imports and exports, access to the international banking system, access to fuel, and access to goods needed for the country's infrastructure; or compromising the capacity of the state to perform its core functions.

All of these features of unilateral sanctions are particularly evident in the case of measures imposed by the United States.

This chapter will discuss some of the most significant ways in which unilateral sanctions may reach well beyond the sanctioner's own nationals; may effectively function as though they were global measures; and consequently may cause broad economic and humanitarian harm to the target country, and in particular its most vulnerable populations.

II. The Asymmetry of Unilateral Sanctions

Unilateral sanctions have, to some extent, been used by large and wealthy nations against each other. During the Cold War, for example, the US imposed a grain embargo against the Soviet Union in 1980, in addition to ongoing export restrictions on strategic goods. In the post-Cold War era, there have been some exchanges of sanctions among the great powers. In the 1990s, the US imposed sanctions against Russian companies for arms and technology transfers, as well as imposing secondary sanctions against Russian individuals or companies for doing business with Iran, North Korea, Syria and other countries. The Clinton administration sanctioned Russian companies for their involvement with Iran's nuclear and missile program; and under the George W Bush administration, US sanctions pressured Russia to reduce arms sales to Iran.[2]

[2] A Weiss and R Nephew (2016) 'The Role of Sanctions in U.S.–Russian Relations,' Carnegie Endowment for International Peace, available at carnegieendowment.org/2016/07/11/role-of-sanctions-in-u.s.-russian-relations-pub-64056.

During the Korean War, the US imposed an embargo on China, which continued until 1969, when the Nixon administration lifted most restrictions on trade. After the massacre at Tiananmen Square in 1989, the first Bush administration suspended some trade with China regarding arms and commercial goods, but kept China's most-favoured-nation status. More recently, the US has sanctioned China on various grounds. Congress adopted legislation penalising Chinese officials for human rights violations against the Uighurs.[3] The Trump administration blacklisted Huawei, the Chinese telecom giant, and filed criminal charges against the company, claiming technology theft; and prohibited trade with dozens of other Chinese companies. As part of the US' 'maximum pressure' campaign against Iran, the US also imposed secondary sanctions on Chinese oil companies for doing business with Iran.

But it is unlikely that sanctions imposed on a powerful and wealthy country, particularly one with a diversified economy, could have a devastating impact. In the case of Cold War measures, one commentator noted that 'It is doubtful whether these cases yielded positive results, not least because it is difficult to hamper the military capabilities of a major power by inflicting marginal degrees of economic deprivation'.[4]

When sanctions are directed at powerful countries, there is also a risk of retribution. When the US, EU, and others imposed sanctions against Russia following Russia's military intervention in Ukraine, Russia responded by banning food imports from the US, EU, Norway, Canada and Australia, triggering losses to those countries in the billions of dollars. Even if there is not deliberate retribution, sanctions against a country with an economy of global significance can be costly to the sanctioner. In regard to China, one commentator noted that:

> Since a great share of Chinese goods enter the US market as intermediate inputs, directly affecting the production of US firms, it is estimated that a 10% increase in tariffs on Chinese imports would cause a million job losses in the United States. This is all due to the production fragmentation between China and the United States, making the use of sanctions self-defeating ...[5]

In recent years, the Trump administration increased tariffs on China, with far-reaching economic consequences for the US.

There may be a few cases where a smaller country with strategic resources, alone or with allies, will seek to impose sanctions to impede a larger country's access to those resources. This occurred most notably during the Arab oil embargo of 1973.[6] But for the most part, it would simply be economically self-destructive for a small or mid-sized country to sanction a country with greater wealth or resources.

So it is unsurprising that unilateral sanctions are overwhelmingly a tool of large and wealthy nations against countries whose economies are far smaller. Reviewing 174 sanctions cases, the third edition of the seminal study *Economic Sanctions Reconsidered* (ESR3) notes that the countries that had imposed sanctions most frequently were the

[3] US Congress, 'Uyghur Human Rights Policy Act of 2020' Public Law 116-145, 1.

[4] G Hufbauer, G Clyde, JJ Schott, KA Elliott and B Oegg, *Economic Sanctions Reconsidered*, 3rd edn (Peterson Institute for International Economics, 2009) 11.

[5] D Kim, 'Coercive Assets? Foreign Direct Investment and the Use of Economic Sanctions' (2013) 39 *International Interactions* 113.

[6] Hufbauer, Clyde, Schott, Elliott and Oegg, *Economic Sanctions Reconsidered* (2009) 90.

US, the UK, the EU/EC and the Russia/Soviet Union.[7] At the same time, the countries targeted by sanctions tend to have economies that are far smaller. In the sanctions episodes over the last century,

> [t]he sender's GNP is more than 10 times greater than the target's GNP in 80 percent of cases, and in half the cases, the ratio is greater than 100 times. These lopsided ratios reflect, on one hand, the prominence of the United States, the United Kingdom, the former Soviet Union, and recently the United Nations and the European Union as senders and, on the other hand, the small size of the countries they usually try to influence with economic sanctions.[8]

Furthermore, in the latter part of the twentieth century, the disparity grew considerably: the sanctioner-to-target ratio before 1985 was 45:1, and between 1985 and 2000 this ratio was 453:1.[9]

The target countries not only have far smaller economies, but frequently are also economically underdeveloped. A country in the developing world would be particularly vulnerable to sanctions:

> If the sanctioned country has the ability to produce the embargoed products but does not do so because it is cheaper to import them, the target will produce those goods once the sanctions succeed in raising the price of imports above the cost of domestic production. If, however, the sanctioned nation does not have the technological ability to produce the embargoed products, it will be forced to turn to an alternate supplier. Therefore, we should expect economic sanctions to be most effective against underdeveloped nations that cannot supply the embargoed goods domestically under any conditions.[10]

It is not surprising that sanctions are such an attractive tool of foreign policy to countries with great wealth. Where sanctions are directed against small countries, or countries whose economies are particularly vulnerable, there is little economic cost to the sanctioner, and there is little risk of retribution in kind. A sanctioner that wields considerable economic power globally can create economic chaos at bargain rates. According to ESR3, in most cases, imposing sanctions was nothing more than a 'trivial dislocation'[11] for the sanctioner's economy, impacting less than two per cent of the sanctioner's GNP in over two-thirds of the cases.[12]

While sanctioners overwhelmingly consist of OECD countries, among the sanctioning states the US holds a singular role. In the second half of the twentieth century, the US 'had a near monopoly on the aggressive use of the economic instrument to achieve its objectives'.[13] ESR3 notes that in 204 sanctions episodes from the end of World War I up through 2000, the US was a sanctioner in 140 of these situations,[14] and has been a sanctioner with comparable frequency since 2000.[15] The US has imposed sanctions on more occasions than all other sanctioners combined.[16] This includes not only nations

[7] ibid, 17.
[8] ibid, 89.
[9] ibid, 105.
[10] Z Selden, *Economic Sanctions as Instruments of American Foreign Policy* (Praeger, 1999) 17.
[11] Hufbauer, Clyde, Schott, Elliott and Oegg (n 4) 111.
[12] ibid, 109.
[13] J Scharfen, *The Dismal Battlefield: Mobilizing for Economic Conflict* (Naval Institute Press, 1995) 48–49.
[14] Hufbauer, Clyde, Schott, Elliott and Oegg (n 4) 94–96.
[15] ibid, 'Post-2000 cases' database.
[16] ibid, 17.

but also international bodies, such as the UN Security Council and the Arab League. In cases involving financial sanctions, the role of the US is even more striking. The US participated in 80 per cent of the financial sanctions regimes (unaccompanied by trade sanctions).[17] In stand-alone cases of financial sanctions prior to 1990, the US was the sole sanctioner in 25 of 31 cases.[18]

In the last three decades, the lopsided use of sanctions by the US has been even more pronounced, and the relative economic impact has been even greater. Since the end of the Cold War, the US has in many regards taken on a singular role within the global economy, such that unilateral measures, when they are imposed by the US, may function as though they are global. Meanwhile, in the last two decades, the use of sanctions by the US has expanded in every regard. US sanctions are more far reaching than they have ever been, directly targeting an unprecedented number of states, individuals, and companies; and indirectly shaping the decisions of entire global industries. While purporting to be 'smart', affecting only wrongdoers or weapons proliferation, US sanctions in fact routinely target the most fundamental functions of a country's economy and society: imports, exports, infrastructure, industry, fuel, access to shipping, access to the international banking network, and technology. These measures, in turn, can trigger or contribute to macroeconomic shocks, such as unemployment or hyperinflation, and may cause or contribute to shortages of critical consumer goods, including food, and can then trigger or increase population displacement. The enforcement of US sanctions has also become increasingly rigorous, and increasingly burdensome and costly for banks, shipping companies, insurers, manufacturers and others. The draconian enforcement practices have, in turn, played a significant role in the 'chilling effect' of sanctions, undermining commerce and banking transactions with the target country in a manner that extends well beyond the formal prohibitions of the sanctions.

III. Extraterritorial and Secondary Measures

Unilateral sanctions can extend well beyond the sanctioner's own nationals when the sanctions are extraterritorial or secondary measures. Secondary sanctions punish third-party countries or their nationals for doing business with the target of the sanctions. Secondary sanctions are often extraterritorial. Extraterritorial measures impose restrictions on third-country companies doing business with the target country, even though those companies would not generally be subject to the sanctioner's jurisdiction. This may occur where the sanctioner prohibits third countries from buying goods from the target country, or investing in its enterprises, or selling technology to it.

Extraterritorial measures have long been contentious under international law, and are often viewed as a violation of the sovereign right of third countries to trade with whomever they choose. During the Cold War, the impact of extraterritorial measures was limited; as with sanctions in general, if the US interfered in the target country's

[17] ibid, 96.
[18] ibid, 97.

trade with third parties in the West, the target country could simply trade with the Eastern bloc. And there was little to be gained by then imposing secondary sanctions on the Eastern bloc countries for trading with the target country. But the 1990s saw the emergence of multiple rounds of legislation authorising extraterritorial sanctions regimes, notably the Iran and Libya Sanctions Act (ILSA), and the Torricelli Act and the Helms-Burton Act, both targeting Cuba. The international community responded with anger. Canada,[19] Mexico[20] and the EU[21] passed 'clawback legislation', authorising litigation to recover any losses suffered as a result of the US's extraterritorial laws. The EU brought an action against the US before the World Trade Organization (WTO), and the US agreed to suspend the most controversial measures, although the legislation remained in force.[22]

The measures adopted by EU, Canada and others also prohibited their own nationals from complying with the US's extraterritorial laws.[23] This created an untenable situation for banks, manufacturers, and others engaged in international commerce: on one hand, if they conducted business with Cuba or other countries targeted by the US, they risked severe penalties, including possible exclusion from the US market. On the other hand, if they did not do business with these countries, in order to comply with US law, they were then in violation of their national laws.

Under the Trump administration, we saw a resurgence of extraterritorial measures, once again triggering vocal opposition not only from the targeted countries, but from US allies and trading partners. This occurred, for example, in the case of Iran. In 2015, under the Joint Comprehensive Plan of Action (JCPOA), Iran agreed to reduce its nuclear capacities, and UN sanctions would be lifted, along with some of the sanctions imposed by the other parties to the agreement: the five permanent members of the Security Council, along with Germany and the EU. Accordingly, the EU and most of the other countries resumed trade with Iran. However, starting in 2017, the US reimposed extensive sanctions on Iran, including measures that would impact foreign companies doing business with Iran. The EU updated its blocking legislation, prohibiting EU nationals from complying with extraterritorial measures, such as those of the US. But European companies then found themselves in a difficult position. For example, under the JCPOA, commercial air travel to Iran was to resume. But a number of European airlines, including British Airways, Air France and KLM, suspended flights to Iran, presumably to avoid the draconian penalties imposed by the US, or the loss of access to the US market; though they could not acknowledge this, for fear of being subject to penalties under the EU's blocking legislation.[24]

[19] J Roy, *Cuba, the United States, and the Helms-Burton Doctrine: International Reactions* (University Press of Florida, 2000) 88.

[20] ibid, 93.

[21] ibid, 120.

[22] M Albright (1998) 'Statement on U.S.–E.U. Understanding on Expropriated Property' (18 May 1998).

[23] Council Regulation (EC) No 2271/96 Protecting against the Effects of the Extra Territorial Application of Legislation Adopted by a Third Country, and Actions Based Thereon or Resulting Therefrom [1996] OJ L309/1.

[24] R Gladstone and Z Wichter, 'British Airways and Air France to Suspend Iran Service' *New York Times*, 23 August 2018.

IV. When Unilateral Measures are Global: The Case of Cuba

Unilateral sanctions may function as though they were global measures in many different contexts. This may happen where a single country provides a critical market for which there is no comparable substitute, or otherwise serves a unique role in the international commercial landscape. It may happen as well where a company or industry of global reach is based in the sanctioning country, such that national laws constrain an international industry. It may also arise where a country holds great influence within an international institution, by virtue of the voting structure or a specific institutional arrangement. In particular, there are a number of ways in which US measures function as global measures.

This can be seen in the international financial institutions (IFIs) where the US holds disproportionate influence due to weighted voting. In the International Bank for Reconstruction and Development, the US holds 15.78 per cent of the voting power.[25] In the International Finance Corporation of the World Bank, the US holds 20.99 per cent of the voting power.[26] In the IMF, the US holds 16.51 per cent of the voting power.[27] In these and several other IFIs, the US voting power is far greater than that of any other country; overriding the US vote would be impossible unless efforts were undertaken by a coalition of the US's own allies who hold significant voting shares; Japan, China, Germany, France, and the UK each have voting power of roughly 4–6 per cent in these institutions. At the same time, in these IFIs, dozens of countries, overwhelmingly those in the developing world, hold voting power of 0.10 per cent or less, making it flatly impossible that even several dozen of them could ever override the US. Thus, a unilateral decision by the US could effectively block a target country from access to these global financial institutions.

In addition, while denying access to the US market may indeed be only unilateral, that exclusion is of extraordinary significance, given that the US has the largest economy in the world, with an annual GDP of over $20 trillion, constituting nearly one-quarter of the global GDP. Furthermore, in many regards, US companies hold major roles in global infrastructure. For example, the US ranks third in the world in the number of ships owned by its companies.[28] The US company SSA Marine is one of the largest terminal operators in the world.[29] And additionally, in some cases, US products may serve as the industry standard globally; for example, Microsoft Windows has nearly 90 per cent of the global market share in desktop/laptop operating systems.[30] Other products, such as certain pharmaceuticals, are produced only by US companies.

Thus, denial of access to the US market has far greater impact than the loss of a market in a small or mid-sized economy. A unilateral measure by the US may disrupt a company's access to international shipping routes; may prevent a country from using

[25] World Bank, 'International Bank for Reconstruction and Development: Subscriptions and Voting Power of Member Countries' (2020) (as of 16 June 2020).

[26] ibid.

[27] International Monetary Fund (2020), 'IMF Members' Quotas and Voting Power, and IMF Board of Governors' (2020) (as of 22 June 2020).

[28] United Nations Conference on Trade and Development, 'Review of Maritime Transport 2019' (2019) 39.

[29] ibid, 51.

[30] Net Market Share, 'Operating System Market Share' (2020) (as of May 2020).

the IMF or World Bank to restructure its loans or to fund development projects; or may deny a country access to specific medical equipment, computer software, or other technology that is only produced in the US.

All of these are apparent in the case of the US's unilateral sanctions against Cuba. To begin with, the US would be Cuba's natural and closest market for many of its key exports, such as coffee, tobacco, lobsters and aquaculture.[31] In some cases, there are goods that are manufactured only in the US, such that a prohibition on trade with Cuba may as well be global. Much of Cuba's infrastructure that was built in the first half of the twentieth century relied on equipment manufactured by US companies. For example, many of the key components of Cuba's water treatment system were manufactured by the US company Wallace & Tiernan. After the US tightened the embargo in the 1990s, Cuba could no longer purchase the parts for its chlorination system manufactured by that company. According to the AAWH, 'that single embargo-related prohibition jeopardizes safe drinking water of every city in Cuba with over 100,000 inhabitants – a total of four million people'.[32] US companies produce state-of-the-art agricultural inputs, such as highly effective pesticides, which are of great urgency given Cuba's tenuous food security, and these are unavailable to Cuba.[33] Cuba's Institute of Oncology and Radiology was blocked from purchasing a PET/CT scanner for which the only manufacturers were US companies.[34]

US sanctions against Cuba are also extraterritorial in many regards as well. The US not only prohibits US companies from trading with Cuba, but also extends the prohibition to foreign subsidiaries of US companies as well. The US considers them to be US nationals for purposes of sanctions laws, even though this runs counter to international commercial law, under which they are nationals of the countries where they are incorporated. As a result, the scope of the US sanctions is expanded considerably whenever a US company acquires a or merges with a foreign corporation. For example, a Swedish company, Pharmacia, sold medical equipment and pharmaceuticals to Cuba for decades until it merged with the US company Upjohn, and all sales to Cuba were then prohibited.[35]

Cuba's access to the international banking system is also profoundly disrupted by the US's unilateral restrictions. In part, this is because the majority of the world's funds are held in US financial institutions, and the majority of the world's financial transactions go through US financial institutions. The scope of US sanctions is expanded considerably because the US considers that it has the right to restrict who may use US dollars, regardless of their nationality or the nationality of the parties to the transaction. Consequently, any foreign bank that provides an account in US dollars, or facilitates a transaction in US dollars with a person or entity that is sanctioned by the US, is, in the

[31] United Nations Secretary-General, 'Necessity of Ending the Economic, Commercial and Financial Embargo Imposed by the United States of America against Cuba' (A/68/116, 2013).

[32] American Association for World Health (1997), 'Denial of Food and Medicine: The Impact of the U.S. Embargo on Health and Nutrition in Cuba: Executive Summary' 20.

[33] United Nations Secretary-General (A/58/287, 2003) 82.

[34] Amnesty International, 'The US Embargo against Cuba: Its Impact on Economic and Social Rights' (Amnesty International, 2009) 18.

[35] V Hidalgo and M Martinez, 'Is the U.S. Economic Embargo on Cuba Morally Defensible?' (2000) 3 *Logos: A Journal of Catholic Thought and Culture*, 109–10.

eyes of the US, in violation of US law. The US Treasury Department has been extremely aggressive about enforcing these restrictions against foreign banks. The Obama administration dramatically increased the scope and severity of the Treasury Department's enforcement measures, imposing penalties on the order of half a billion dollars on Credit Suisse Bank, the Dutch bank ING, and others, for transactions involving Cuba and other countries.[36] HSBC was fined in total $2 billion for sanctions and other violations. The French bank BNP Paribas was fined a total of $9 billion by the Treasury Department and US banking regulators, and was temporarily suspended from access to the US Federal Reserve system. In the face of these measures, it was not surprising when many Canadian and European banks severed ties with Cuba – including Barclays, the Bank of Nova Scotia, Credit Suisse, Deutsche Bank, Royal Bank of Canada and HSBC – rather than risk the harsh US penalties.[37]

In addition, Cuba's imports and exports in general are affected by US unilateral measures concerning shipping. US sanctions prohibit ships of any nationality from docking at a US port if it has entered a Cuban port within 180 days. But many cargo ships carrying goods to or from Cuba would normally also have cargo destined for the US. In the face of these restrictions, contracts are sometimes cancelled due to lack of transport, as was the case with a New Zealand company that was under contract to sell powdered milk to Cuba.[38] Alternatively, Cuba has to pay for a ship to carry, for example, goods from Spain, and then pay for the ship to return empty, doubling Cuba's cargo costs. Even then, Cuba has difficulty finding carriers willing to provide these services.

The US measures against Cuba are also extraterritorial in other regards. The Helms-Burton law of 1996 provides that no goods from any country may be exported to the US if they contain even trace amounts of any materials from Cuba.[39] Cuba's leading exports are sugar and nickel. Consequently, a candy manufacturer in, say, Brazil, must ensure that the candy containing Cuban sugar is only sold to countries other than the US; an arrangement that is logistically untenable. Often the only commercially feasible option is simply not to buy any Cuban sugar at all. The same is true of nickel, which is used in the production of stainless steel. As a result, the US measures are extraterritorial in the extreme: any country that wishes to sell goods to the US – or produce any materials, such as stainless steel, that may eventually be used in goods that make their way to the US – must either go to great lengths to segregate its products made with Cuban raw materials, which would be a logistical nightmare, or find themselves involuntarily boycotting all Cuban imports.

Finally, the weighted voting structure of IFIs effectively ensures that a unilateral policy of the US functions as a global denial of access to the most significant capital markets. In the case of Cuba, the Helms-Burton Act of 1996 requires the US representatives to the boards of major IFIs – including the International Monetary Fund, the World Bank, the International Bank for Reconstruction and Development, and the

[36] Latin American and the Caribbean Economic System (2010), 'Follow-up Report on the Application of the Helms Burton Law, 2009–2010' (Permanent Secretariat of SELA) 6.

[37] US Government Accountability Office, 'Economic Sanctions: Agencies Face Competing Priorities in Enforcing the U.S. Embargo on Cuba' (2007) 54 fn 110.

[38] Hidalgo and Martinez, 'U.S. Economic Embargo on Cuba' (2000) 108.

[39] Cuban Liberty and Democratic Solidarity (Libertad) Act of 1996 (Helms-Burton Act), 104–114, US Code 22 §6021, Sec 110(a)).

Inter-American Development Bank – to oppose any efforts to grant Cuba admission to these organisations or extend financial assistance.[40] In the unlikely event that the US were outvoted, and one of these institutions approved a loan or other assistance to Cuba, the Helms-Burton law requires the US to withhold its contributions to that institution in a corresponding amount,[41] penalising the institution severely in the event that it provides Cuba with financial services.

V. Financial Sanctions

Many view the introduction of targeted financial sanctions as a powerful yet precise development in the evolution of economic sanctions. Whereas commodity sanctions, or sectoral sanctions, could trigger macroeconomic shocks, there was no concern that this could happen when sanctions were imposed on individual persons, companies or foundations. It seemed that these lists of Specially Designated Nationals (SDNs) offered an ideal means to cut off funding for terrorists, dictators, and so forth, without any 'collateral damage'. In some cases that has been true. But, in practice, even unilateral listings have not been nearly as narrow in their impact as many would claim.

This occurs most directly when the SDN is a government official, a government body or a national company, because US financial sanctions do not simply freeze ill-gotten assets, but rather prohibit all transactions with a listed entity. Where the SDN is a national shipping company, all of the country's exports and imports may be impacted. Where the SDN is a government body that manages an enterprise that generates foreign exchange, the country's capacity to pay for needed imports will be compromised. Where the SDN is a government body that builds or maintains the infrastructure for electricity generation, transportation or telecommunication, that will impact industry, agriculture, food security, and the health and well-being of the population. When Sectoral Sanctions Identifications (SSI) lists were formulated, it seemed that they would bring greater precision to the process, since SSIs do not prohibit all dealings with the blacklisted entity, but rather preclude particular types of transactions. The SSI listing may, for example, prohibit energy exports or the extension of credit. But that hardly means that only 'bad actors' will be affected. On the contrary, where sanctions impede a country's transactions related to energy production or energy imports, the impact on every aspect of a modern economy will be vast, regardless of whether that occurs by an SDN or a 'narrower' SSI listing. When sanctions in one form or another interfere in the country's major sources of revenue – regardless of whether that occurs by interfering in shipping or penalising those who engage in commercial or financial transactions – the result will be substantial economic disruption.

While the *impact* of a sanctions regime may go well beyond the individual who is blacklisted, the *scope* of a sanctions regime can also be expanded exponentially through other mechanisms. One of the most extreme forms of this is the Foreign Sanctions Evaders (FSE) list, used in the US's sanctions against Iran and Syria. Under US law,

[40] ibid, Sec 104(a)(1).
[41] ibid, Sec 104.

'US persons' already include a broad swathe of foreign companies, on the reasoning that they are subsidiaries of US companies, or interact with the US financial system.[42] But the category of 'foreign sanctions evaders' extends the reach of US sanctions to a much broader range of foreign persons or entities. These 'evasions' of US sanctions are not limited to facilitating weapons purchases or hiding illicit assets. Even where US sanctions are over-broad in the extreme, interfering in the ordinary and necessary economic activities of the target country, a foreign company that facilitates normal commercial activity is then itself subject to being blacklisted. Once this happens, then 'US persons' in turn are prohibited from engaging in 'all transactions or dealings, whether direct or indirect' with the 'foreign sanctions evader'. So, for example, the US maintains that Swiss shipping company Bluemarine SA and the Dutch company Staroil[43] assisted Syria in circumventing US sanctions. Consequently, a European bank could in turn be penalised for processing a transaction in US dollars for these 'foreign sanctions evaders'. In effect, US sanctions are not only extraterritorial, but may penalise a foreign company for doing business with a foreign company that, in turn, does business with a country the US has sanctioned. Thus, the scope of the US sanctions is expanded exponentially.

The magnified impact of targeted financial sanctions can be seen in the case of Venezuela. In 2015, the Obama administration declared that the Maduro Government's human rights violations constituted a threat to the national security of the US, and on that basis ordered the imposition of sanctions on both current and former officials of the Venezuelan Government.[44] Over the course of the Obama and Trump administrations, the US blacklisted Venezuela's president, Nicolás Maduro, the former vice-president, Tareck El Aissami, and the current vice-president, Delcy Rodriguez. The US blacklisted Rocco Albisinni Serrano, the president of CENCOEX, the government agency that sets the foreign exchange rate, as well as Bernal Rosales, the Minister for Agriculture, and Alejandro Antonio Fleming Cabrera, the vice minister for Europe of Venezuela's Ministry of Foreign Affairs.[45] The US blacklisted Carlos Alberto Rotondaro Cova, the former head of Venezuela's agency charged with providing medicines to patients with chronic conditions, as well as William Antonio Contreras, the head of the agency for socioeconomic rights.[46] The director of the country's central bank was also blacklisted.[47]

If the sanctions only affected the personal accounts of these individuals, with their putative ill-gotten gains, the sanctions might have little impact on the state or the economy as a whole. But the sanctions restrict *all* transactions with listed individuals,

[42] Office of Foreign Assets Control, 'List of Foreign Sanctions Evaders Sanctioned Pursuant to Executive Order 13608 (US Department of the Treasury, 2020).

[43] ibid.

[44] 'Executive Order 13692 of March 8, 2015, Blocking Property and Suspending Entry of Certain Persons Contributing to the Situation in Venezuela' *Federal Register* 80, no 40.

[45] US Department of the Treasury (2017), 'Treasury Sanctions 13 Current and Former Senior Officials of the Government of Venezuela' news release, 26 July 2017; J Fernandez, AM Smith, CT Timura and JA Lee, 'The Outlook for 2018 U.S. Economic and Trade Sanctions against Venezuela' (Gibson Dunn, 2018), 10.

[46] US Department of the Treasury, 'Treasury sanctions four current or former Venezuelan officials' press release, 19 March 2018.

[47] C Seelke, 'Venezuela: Overview of U.S. Sanctions' Congressional Research Service, 2 June 2020, 1.

making it prohibitively difficult for Venezuelan officials to, say, purchase medicines and agricultural inputs, or engage in diplomatic or financial negotiations with their international counterparts. Thus, sanctions that seem to address only individuals in fact can do much to paralyse the state in its core functions.

At the same time, the SDN lists served to cripple Venezuela's revenues from oil exports, by targeting Venezuela's national oil company, Petróleos de Venezuela, SA (PdVSA). Nearly all of the country's export revenue comes from oil sales.[48] Thus, while PdVSA may be an 'individual' company, it holds a critical role in the Venezuelan economy. As one analyst noted:

> Cutting off the government's access to dollars will leave the economy without the hard currency needed to pay for imports of food and medicine. Starving the Venezuelan economy of its foreign currency earnings risks turning the country's current humanitarian crisis into a full-blown humanitarian catastrophe.[49]

This indeed came to pass.

Targeted financial sanctions have greatly impacted Venezuela's economy in other ways. One of the most damaging set of sanctions intervened in Venezuela's access to credit. As Venezuela scrambled to avoid defaulting on its debt, the US added new sanctions prohibiting any 'US person' from extending credit to Venezuela if it would come due in more than 30 days. A 'US person', in turn, extended well beyond US nationals. For purposes of the sanctions restrictions, the Treasury Department considered 'US persons' to include foreign subsidiaries of US companies, even if those subsidiaries were incorporated in foreign countries, and did business exclusively in foreign countries. Thus, not only were US banks and creditors prohibited from restructuring Venezuela's debt, but a substantial sector of the international financial community was also subject to severe penalties by the US for doing so. In 2019, the reach of the sanctions on Venezuela was extended still further, as additional regulations authorised financial sanctions on even non-'US persons' who assisted or supported the Maduro Government.[50]

VI. The 'Chilling Effect'

While the explicit unilateral prohibitions on trade may be extensive, for the reasons discussed above, there is an additional impact that occurs when the sanctions regulations are vague and the requirements for compliance are not clear, or are not feasible, and at the same time, the stakes are very high, where banks and corporations may be subject to penalties in the billions of dollars, or may lose access to a major market or financial system. Under these conditions, it is not surprising that companies would be deeply averse to the risk of doing any business with anyone who might have even a remote relationship to a country or an entity that has been sanctioned. As a result, it is common to see private actors, including banks, shipping companies, insurers and

[48] F Rodríguez, 'Why More Sanctions Won't Help Venezuela' 12 January 2018, available at foreignpolicy.com/2018/01/12/why-more-sanctions-wont-help-venezuela.

[49] ibid,

[50] Seelke, 'Venezuela' (2020) 2.

manufacturers, go to great lengths to avoid any possible connection, however attenuated, given how high the stakes are.

The first component – the ambiguous requirements for compliance – can be seen in the due diligence standard. Under Treasury Department regulations, companies are expected to do far more than simply checking potential customers or transactions against the SDN list. They are also expected to exercise due diligence in ways that are not fully explicit in the regulations. Companies are required to engage in risk assessments on many levels: (1) risks posed by third parties, such as customers, suppliers and intermediaries; (2) risks posed by products and services; and (3) risks based on geographic locations of operations and third parties.[51] But while companies are expected to take extensive measures to reduce their risks of inadvertently violating US sanctions, it is not entirely clear exactly what those measures must consist of. Risk-based compliance 'is tailored to a company's current business model'. Indeed, a company that seeks to apply a standardised set of procedures may find itself subject to even harsher treatment:

> Recent OFAC enforcement actions show that a one-size-fits-all paper program, which fails to account for individualized business models, customer bases, and geographic operations, will not result in mitigation credit should potential violations arise under those programs, and may even be an aggravating factor.[52]

In addition, complying with US sanctions regulations may force a company into violating the laws of other jurisdictions; or may make demands that are commercially untenable. At one point, a US State Department official 'sent emails to the captain of an Iranian tanker that was suspected to be en route to Syria, asking him to steer the tanker to a country that would impound it on behalf of Washington'.[53] In May 2020, the Trump administration issued guidance for the global shipping industry, calling for insurance companies to share data on their clients with the US Government, but these practices would conflict with European privacy laws. The US also called for marine insurers to constantly monitor the locations of vessels they insure, which would be commercially and logistically untenable. The US Government also called on the insurance industry to investigate suspected sanctions violations involving the ships, even though insurance companies are ill-equipped (and deeply reluctant) to take on responsibility for enforcing US laws.

At the same time, the stakes are extremely high. In 2014, Deutsche Forfait (DF), a financial services company that purchases receivables, was accused by the US Treasury Department's Office of Foreign Assets Control of engaging in commercial transactions with Iran, and the German company was then blacklisted. Once it had been placed on the SDN list, it was blocked from engaging in any US dollar-denominated transactions, and much of its business was suspended. Eight months later, DF was removed from the SDN list, apparently vindicated, without paying a penalty. DF's chief financial officer

[51] US Department of the Treasury, 'A Framework for OFAC Compliance Commitments' (2019).

[52] M Mancuso and A Cotterill, 'What OFAC Means by a Risk-Based Approach to Compliance' 26 May 2020, available at www.kirkland.com/publications/article/2020/05/what-ofac-means-by-risk_based-approach-compliance.

[53] J Saul, H Pamuk and T Gardner, 'U.S. Sanctions Advisory Raises Hurdles for Global Maritime Industry' *Reuters*, 27 May 2020, available at www.reuters.com/article/us-usa-sanctions-maritime/u-s-sanctions-advisory-raises-hurdles-for-global-maritime-industry-idUSKBN2332LG.

noted that the company was blacklisted for a far shorter period than usual – only eight months, whereas the average time an entity spends on the SDN list is over two years.[54] Even so, the blacklisting was profoundly damaging; the company 'was forced into an extensive restructuring and was at one stage placed into liquidation proceedings'.[55]

BNP Paribas, France's largest bank, did not fare so well. In 2014, it agreed to pay penalties of $8.9 billion for violating US sanctions against Cuba, Iran and Sudan. However, 'the transactions in question were not illegal under French or EU law. Nor did they fall foul of France's obligations under the World Trade Organization or the United Nations; no agreements between France and the US were violated'.[56] The US claimed jurisdiction over these transactions because they were denominated in US dollars and passed through the US financial system. However questionable this claim may be, foreign banks – certainly all major Western banks – have little choice but to comply. In addition to the enormous monetary penalty, BNP Paribas was temporarily suspended from clearing certain transactions through the US Federal Reserve, a penalty that sent a chill through the international banking community: for any major Western bank, to be denied access to the US banking system, making it unable to clear US dollar transactions, is known as the 'death penalty'.

Given the vagueness and untenability of the due diligence requirements, and the very high risks, it is not surprising to see how extensive and thoroughgoing the chilling effect has become. Private actors are reluctant to engage in even those transactions that are exempt from sanctions, such as humanitarian shipments or transactions. In the case of Syria, for example, humanitarian aid is not only threatened by the intensity of the armed conflict, but is then compromised as well by the sanctions put in place by the US, the EU and others.

To begin with, humanitarian organisations depend upon financial transfers to support projects such as providing potable water, producing or distributing food, and building shelter facilities, which in turn may require hiring local employees.[57] Financial transfers, in either euros or dollars, are problematic in part because of the collapse of much of Syria's banking system, but also because various countries have imposed sanctions on Syria's largest state-owned banks, as well as the Central Bank of Syria.[58] Commercial or humanitarian actors must navigate a labyrinth of sanctions programs, varying in their scope and particulars, including those imposed by the US, the EU, Japan, Canada, Australia, Switzerland, Norway, Turkey and the Arab League. The US sanctions are the most extensive in their scope, including not only broad financial

[54] DF Deutsche Forfait AG (2014), 'DF Deutsche Forfait AG Removed from OFAC Sanctions List without Having to Pay a Fine,' news release, 17 October 2014, available at www.dfag.de/wp-content/uploads/2014/10/14OCT17_PM-OFAC-Delisting_final_EN.pdf.

[55] V Damyanova (2018), 'Deutsche Forfait Issues 2018 Profit Warning as US Sanctions Hit Iran Business', *S&P Global Market Intelligence* (20 June 2018), available at www.spglobal.com/marketintelligence/en/news-insights/trending/z0clllym05wfauvjvqvj9w2.

[56] International Bar Association (2015), 'BNP Paribas Sanctions Case Highlights US Power over International Deals' (20 February 2015), available at www.ibanet.org/Article/NewDetail.aspx?ArticleUid=c88b73a0-ca06-46ac-83e6-00757f7fffcc.

[57] J Walker, 'Risk Management Principles Guide for Sending Humanitarian Funds into Syria and Similar High-Risk Jurisdictions' (May 2020) 9.

[58] ibid, 11.

measures but also a blanket prohibition on US exports, which in turn includes not only goods produced in the US, but also goods produced abroad, where US components make up 10 per cent or more of the item.[59]

Unsurprisingly, both financial institutions and manufacturers are wary of engaging in any transactions with Syria. If goods or funds were to end up in the hands of persons or companies that are blacklisted, the penalties could be severe; and even with considerable effort, in a volatile and unpredictable setting such as Syria, it would be difficult to ensure that no goods or funds are diverted.

The result is a 'chilling effect' in which financial institutions and other companies will go far beyond what is required, in order to minimise any risk of violation. In addition, 'even where goods and finance may be possible, the legal costs associated with undertaking due diligence and acquiring a license may in some instances be higher than the value of the goods and services'.[60] But while the risk assessment by banks and exporters may be quite reasonable, given their commercial interests and the conditions under which they are operating, the outcome is that the humanitarian situation is worsened catastrophically. Idriss Jazairy, the UN's Rapporteur on Unilateral Coercive Measures, noted that

> the lack of clarity around humanitarian exemptions have led risk-adverse banks, insurance and shipping companies, and sellers of humanitarian goods from engaging with anyone related to Syria. The 'chilling effect' resulting from over-compliance with sanctions is forcing humanitarian and economic actors to find irregular payment mechanisms which increase costs, add delays, decrease transparency and in some cases make it impossible for businesses to continue.[61]

VII. Economic Rights and the Right to Development

Many have noted that sanctions may compromise the economic rights of the target country's population to survival and wellbeing, and may also compromise the right of the target country to economic development. Whereas sanctions imposed in the name of global governance may carry presumptive legitimacy, the same cannot be said of unilateral measures, which may be used solely to further the economic and political interests of the sanctioner. The UN Human Rights Council, the General Assembly and the UN Special Rapporteur on Unilateral Coercive Measures have all raised the concern that unilateral sanctions may well conflict with human rights; and that this may be the case even where the sanctioner purports to be defending human rights. There have been numerous international instruments that also express this concern. The Vienna

[59] ibid.

[60] ibid, 26.

[61] United Nations Human Rights Office of the High Commissioner (2018), 'UN Expert Says Unilateral Coercive Measures Exacerbate Humanitarian Crisis in Syria,' news release, 17 May 2018, available at www.ohchr.org/EN/NewsEvents/Pages/DisplayNews.aspx?NewsID=23096&LangID=E.

Declaration, adopted by the World Conference on Human Rights in 1993, called upon states to

> refrain from any unilateral measure not in accordance with international law and the Charter of the United Nations that creates obstacles to trade relations among States and impede the full realization of the human rights set forth in the Universal Declaration of Human Rights and in international human rights instruments, in particular the rights of everyone to a standard of living adequate for their health and well-being, including food and medical care, housing and the necessary social services.[62]

Certainly there is support for the position that, whatever their justification, unilateral sanctions must themselves comport with international human rights law. General Comment 8 of the Committee on Economic, Social and Cultural Rights, which was adopted in 1997, notes with concern that:

> Economic sanctions are being imposed with increasing frequency, both internationally, regionally and unilaterally … such sanctions … often cause significant disruption in the distribution of food, pharmaceuticals and sanitation supplies, jeopardize the quality of food and the availability of clean drinking water, severely interfere with the functioning of basic health and education systems, and undermine the right to work.[63]

In 2000, the UN Human Rights Commission released a report which found that 'A sanctions regime imposed unilaterally … must meet all the requirements for such sanctions inherent in the Charter, including conformity with the principles of justice and international law'.[64] And in 2012, the UN High Commissioner for Human Rights proposed that all sanctions regimes

> must be imposed no longer than necessary, be proportional and be subject to appropriate human rights safeguards, including human rights impact assessments and monitoring conducted by independent experts. In particular, the positive impact that sanctions imposed with the objective of protecting human rights can be reasonably expected to have must outweigh the negative impact, taking into account the views of the population suffering under the human rights violations that gave rise to the sanctions and the impact on the most vulnerable parts of society.[65]

In 1986, the General Assembly's 'Declaration of the Right to Development' asserted that:

> The right to development is an inalienable human right by virtue of which every human person and all peoples are entitled to participate in, contribute to, and enjoy economic, social, cultural and political development, in which all human rights and fundamental freedoms can be fully realized.[66]

[62] United Nations General Assembly (1993), 'Vienna Declaration and Programme of Action,' A/CONF.157/23.

[63] United Nations Committee on Economic Social and Cultural Rights: Economic and Social Council (1997), 'Implementation of the International Covenant on Economic Social and Cultural Rights General Comment No. 8 (1997) the Relationship between Economic Sanctions and Respect for Economic Social and Cultural Rights', E/C.12/1997/8, 1–2.

[64] United Nations Commission on Human Rights: Sub-Commission on the Promotion and Protection of Human Rights, 'The Adverse Consequences of Economic Sanctions on the Enjoyment of Human Rights: Working Paper Prepared by Mr. Marc Bossuyt' (2000) E /Cn.4/Sub.2/2000/33, 11.

[65] United Nations General Assembly (2012), 'Thematic Study of the Office of the United Nations High Commissioner for Human Rights on the Impact of Unilateral Coercive Measures on the Enjoyment of Human Rights, Including Recommendations on Actions Aimed at Ending Such Measures' A/HRC/19/33, 11 January 2012, 11.

[66] 'Declaration on the Right to Development' (1986), A/RES/41/128, 4 December 1986, Art 1(1).

However, unilateral sanctions may run counter to the right to development, particularly since sanctions for the most part are imposed on countries in the developing world. While unilateral sanctions sometimes do indeed only impact terrorists or dictators, or affect only the proliferation of weapons, in many cases unilateral sanctions, directly or indirectly, interfere in a developing country's access to fuel, impede its access to the international banking system, compromise its imports and exports in a variety of ways, block its access to technology, and impede or prevent foreign investment. All of these compromise the target country's level of economic and social development, and its capacity for growth, in contravention of the international community's commitment to development.

When unilateral sanctions worsen impoverishment or affect the target country's infrastructure they would certainly run afoul of the Millennium Development Goals, articulated in 2000, which included the eradication of extreme poverty, achieving universal primary education, reducing child mortality, and combating HIV/AIDS, malaria and other diseases.[67] But unilateral sanctions of the sort we commonly see also run counter to the Sustainable Development Goals (SDGs). The SDGs, adopted by the UN General Assembly in 2015, included enhancing access to science and technology,[68] capacity-building in developing countries,[69] promoting an open, non-discriminatory and equitable multilateral trading system,[70] significantly increasing the exports of developing countries, 'with a view to doubling the least developed countries' share of global exports by 2020'.[71] The Agenda for Sustainable Development notes that:

> International trade is an engine for inclusive economic growth and poverty reduction, and contributes to the promotion of sustainable development … We attach great importance to providing trade-related capacity-building for developing countries, including African countries, least developed countries, landlocked developing countries, small island developing States and middle-income countries …[72]

Insofar as sanctions interfere in, among other things, foreign investment, the acquisition of sophisticated technology, or increased energy production, it would seem that the sanctions would clearly run counter to the SDGs and other international instruments that affirm the right to economic development.

In the case of Cuba, this is apparent in several regards. For example, Cuba invested heavily in higher education, educating software engineers, doctors and healthcare professionals; and also invested in the development of the sciences, particularly those related to medicine and biotechnology. All of these were integral to Cuba's vision of its social and economic development. However, US sanctions law specifically prohibits the export of any item that might be used in Cuba's biotech production.[73] As a result, items related to medicine and healthcare have been prohibited, even when they are produced

[67] United Nations 'The Millennium Development Goals Report: Summary' (2015) 3–5.

[68] United Nations General Assembly (2015), 'Transforming Our World: The 2030 Agenda for Sustainable Development' A/RES/70/1, 25 September 2015, Goal 17.6.

[69] ibid, Goal 17.9.

[70] ibid, Goal 17.10.

[71] ibid, Goal 17.11.

[72] ibid, para 68.

[73] Cuban Democracy Act, 102–484, Title 22, sec 6004(c)(4).

only by US companies and could not be obtained elsewhere. This occurred, for example, when the US company Applied Biosystems was prohibited from selling a genetic analyser, which is essential for researching genetic disorders such as hereditary breast cancer, to Cuba's National Centre for Medical Genetics.[74]

In addition, Cuba is well positioned to develop the field of software engineering. Cuba's system of higher education is well developed, producing a large number of university graduates with computer skills. However, the sanctions prevent Cuba from purchasing the equipment and software needed to train software engineers and support the growth of the field. US companies such as Apple and Hewlett Packard are prohibited from selling their products to Cubans; but in addition, even Japanese companies, such as Toshiba, cannot sell their products to Cuba, when those use components produced in the US, such as Intel processors.[75]

VIII. Conclusion

We might say that there is a dark irony that characterises the landscape of unilateral sanctions. On one hand, many commentators continue to repeat the truism that unilateral measures are weak: they have little effect, and little success, and do little harm. That might have been the case during the Cold War, or the occasional exchanges among the US, China and Russia, where countries with relative parity impose measures on each other that may amount to little more than inconvenience or symbolism. But the reality is that almost all of the sanctions of the post-Cold War era have been characterised by a deep asymmetry; unilateral sanctions are predominantly imposed by countries of tremendous wealth and global influence, upon mid-sized countries with significant economic vulnerabilities, or small countries in the developing world. While the justifications are often moralistic in tone, the outcome can be unconscionable: triggering or worsening food shortages and health crises; worsening or contributing to power outages; the collapse of transportation systems; widespread unemployment; and refugee crises. This disparity between the common view of unilateral sanctions and the reality is rooted in large part in the fact that unilateral sanctions are overwhelmingly a tool of the US; and the US, in turn, can make or break entire global industries, along with the economic health of entire regions. It hardly matters that the extraterritorial sanctions regimes imposed by the US run counter to international law. For any airline, bank, shipping company, insurer, exporter, oil producer – in fact, any actor in the international business domain – there really is little choice. As Deutsche Forfait, as well as BNP Paribas and PB Tankers, learned, the penalties will be so severe that they cannot be seen as a cost of doing business, but rather as threatening the destruction of the enterprise.

The story of unilateral sanctions, particularly financial blacklisting, as akin to surgical strikes, likewise seems to suffer from a certain absurdity. It is not just that there are sometimes 'unintentional consequences' that inadvertently result from blacklisting a

[74] United Nations Secretary-General (n 31) 31–32.
[75] ibid, 34.

country's oil industry, shipping lines, and banks. When a state is bankrupted and paralysed, or a country's fuel imports are cut in half, or all of the ordinary transactions necessary to operate a country's economy must somehow take place without access to any major bank in the US or Europe, the consequences are quite certain, quite foreseeable and quite indecent. Whatever the justification may be – we are punishing or chastising or coercing political leaders who are corrupt or incompetent or tyrannical – the imposition of unilateral sanctions by the US, and occasionally others, with little restraint, and with no accountability, does nothing to make the world less chaotic, less violent, or less desperate.

4

The Implications of Unilateral Sanctions for the Freedom of Aviation

NICK GRIEF

I. Introduction and Scope

This chapter discusses the implications for the freedom of aviation under international law (in particular the Chicago Convention 1944 and related treaties) when a state or a group of states imposes sanctions against another state, and the remedies available to the state subjected to such sanctions. It is not concerned with sanctions imposed within the UN framework under Chapter VII of the UN Charter[1] or with flight bans imposed for safety reasons[2] or because of military tension.[3]

Whether economic sanctions are permissible in international law in the absence of a UN Security Council resolution depends on all the circumstances.[4] They have to be compatible with the sanctioning state's international obligations. Of course, that can be controversial. On 16 September 1998 in response to the humanitarian crisis in Kosovo, for example, the Foreign Secretary stated that all flights to the UK by Yugoslav carriers would be banned with immediate effect pursuant to European Community legislation which provided for the freezing of Yugoslav funds and an immediate flight ban.[5] For the UK and other states including France and Germany, this implied the non-performance of their bilateral aviation agreements with the (former) Federal Republic of Yugoslavia (FRY).[6] The UK Government considered delaying implementation of the flight ban until after the expiry of the 12-month notice period provided for in Article 17

[1] Action with respect to threats to the peace, breaches of the peace, and acts of aggression.

[2] See, eg, the EU Air Safety List: ec.europa.eu/transport/modes/air/safety/air-ban_en.

[3] A recent example being the closure by Pakistan's Civil Aviation Authority of the country's airspace on 27 February 2019 following an aerial engagement with India over Kashmir, as a result of which international flights had to be re-routed: www.caapakistan.com.pk/upload/Notams/A0200-19.TXT.

[4] See United Kingdom Materials on International Law (hereafter UKMIL) 1996, (1996) 67 *BYIL* 833.

[5] Especially Council Regulation (EC) No 1901/98. The prohibition was given effect in UK law by the Yugoslavia (Prohibition of Flights) Regulations 1998: UKMIL 1999, (1999) 70 *BYIL* 555.

[6] Commentary on Art 54 of the Articles on the Responsibility of States for Internationally Wrongful Acts 2001 (hereafter ARSIWA), para 3: *Yearbook of the International Law Commission* (hereafter *YBILC*), 2001, Vol II, Pt 2, 138, available at legal.un.org/ilc/texts/instruments/english/commentaries/9_6_2001.pdf.

of the UK–Yugoslavia Air Services Agreement of 1959.[7] However, the Foreign Secretary explained that although the latter, being a pre-accession Agreement, was not overridden by the Community legislation,[8]

> given the worsening humanitarian situation on the ground in Kosovo and in particular the reports of serious human rights abuses committed by the FRY and Serbian security forces [he had] concluded that, on moral and political grounds, Milosevic had forfeited the right to the 12 months' notice which would normally apply under the terms of the ASA.[9]

More recently there have been several instances of states threatening or introducing overflight restrictions, or imposing sanctions having implications for aviation. In August 2014, for example, it was reported that Russia was considering a Siberian overflight ban in response to EU sanctions following Russia's annexation of Crimea and its actions in Ukraine.[10] In June 2017, Bahrain, Egypt, Saudi Arabia and the UAE imposed airspace restrictions on aircraft registered in Qatar as part of a general diplomatic and economic blockade in response to Qatar's alleged support for terrorism.[11] Furthermore, in May 2018 President Trump announced that the US would withdraw from the Joint Comprehensive Plan of Action (JCPOA), leading to the reinstatement of US sanctions against Iran with serious implications for civil aviation.[12] Each of those situations is considered below, with particular emphasis on the restrictions affecting Qatar-registered aircraft. Whereas 'sanctions' was the word used by President Trump, 'countermeasures' is the term used by Bahrain, Egypt, Saudi Arabia and the UAE in respect of their airspace restrictions. The use of that term in that context is supported by the International Law Commission's commentary on Article 22 of ARSIWA, 'Countermeasures in respect of an internationally wrongful act'.[13] As we shall see, however, there is reason to doubt the legality of those restrictions.[14]

[7] United Kingdom *Treaty Series* No 10 (1960).

[8] Since Art 234 of the EC Treaty provided that a pre-accession agreement between a Member State and a third country was not affected by the EC Treaty or legislation based upon it. See now Art 351 of the Treaty on the Functioning of the European Union.

[9] UKMIL 1999 (n 5). The FRY protested that the measures were 'unlawful, unilateral and an example of the policy of discrimination': see Commentary on ARSIWA Art 54 (n 6) 139, citing M Weller, *The Crisis in Kosovo 1989–1999* (Documents & Analysis Publishing, 1999) 227. The UK Government subsequently justified NATO's intervention in Kosovo on the grounds of overwhelming humanitarian necessity. See *Hansard*, HC, 23 March 1999, col 161. The Foreign Affairs Committee concluded that 'NATO's military action, if of dubious legality in the current state of international law, was justified on moral grounds'. See Select Committee on Foreign Affairs, Session 1999–2000, Fourth Report, para 138, available at publications.parliament.uk/pa/cm199900/cmselect/cmfaff/28/2802.htm.

[10] www.helsinkitimes.fi/finland/finland-news/domestic/11454-siberian-overflight-ban-would-be-a-blow-to-finnair.html.

[11] They accuse Qatar of violating the 2013 and 2014 Riyadh Agreements: see below.

[12] White House briefing, 8 May 2018, available at www.whitehouse.gov/briefings-statements/remarks-president-trump-joint-comprehensive-plan-action.

[13] Above (n 6) 75, para 3.

[14] Regarding terminology, Carpanelli calls unilateral sanctions 'autonomous sanctions'. See E Carpanelli, 'To Overfly, or not to Overfly …? Autonomous Sanctions in International Civil Aviation amidst the Recent "Gulf Crisis" – Part II' (25 September 2017), available at grojil.org/2017/09/25/to-overfly-or-not-to-overfly-autonomous-sanctions-in-international-civil-aviation-amidst-the-recent-gulf-crisis-pt2.

II. Legal Framework

In order to establish this chapter's legal context and inform discussion of the three case studies, key instruments, provisions and principles will be outlined in this section, beginning with the Chicago Convention 1944 and the UN Convention on the Law of the Sea 1982.

A. The Chicago Convention and the UN Convention on the Law of the Sea

Article 1 of the Chicago Convention[15] declares 'The contracting States recognise that every State has complete and exclusive sovereignty over the airspace above its territory'.[16] Article 2 provides 'For the purposes of this Convention the territory of a State shall be deemed to be the land areas and territorial waters adjacent thereto under the sovereignty, suzerainty, protection or mandate of such State'. Those provisions represent 'firmly established and longstanding tenets of customary international law'.[17] They are also reflected in the UN Convention on the Law of the Sea (UNCLOS),[18] Article 2(2) of which provides 'This sovereignty [of the coastal State over its land territory and territorial sea] extends to the airspace over the territorial sea'. In contrast, Article 87(1) of UNCLOS declares that the high seas are open to all states and that freedom of the high seas comprises the freedom of overflight.[19] That status is also reflected in Article 12 of the Chicago Convention (Rules of the air), which provides 'Over the high seas, the rules in force shall be those established under this Convention'. Article 12 underlines the international status of the airspace over the high seas since it means that compliance with the rules of the air established by ICAO and set out in Annex 2[20] to the Convention is mandatory in that airspace. This is designed to prevent regulatory variations which might endanger international aviation.[21] The horizontal limit of a coastal state's sovereignty over the airspace above its territory normally extends to the outer limit of its territorial sea, which can be up to 12 nautical miles from the baselines from which the territorial sea is measured.[22] With regard to vertical delimitation, although there

[15] Convention on International Civil Aviation (Chicago, 7 December 1944, ICAO Doc 7300). The Convention entered into force on 4 April 1947 and is virtually universal. Dominica became ICAO's 193rd Member State following its adherence to the Convention on 13 April 2019.

[16] Airspace begins immediately above the surface of the earth. See UKMIL 1998, (1998) 69 *BYIL* 550.

[17] *Military and Paramilitary Activities in and against Nicaragua (Nicaragua v United States of America), Merits, Judgment*, ICJ Reports 1986, 14, para 212.

[18] Montego Bay, 10 December 1982, 1833 UNTS 3.

[19] See in particular Art 87(1)(b). The freedom of overflight also prevails in the airspace of the exclusive economic zone: ibid, Art 58(1).

[20] 10th edn, July 2005.

[21] See further N Grief, *Public International Law in the Airspace of the High Seas* (Martinus Nijhoff, 1994) 61–63.

[22] UNCLOS, Art 3.

is no sovereignty in outer space[23] and various approaches to delimitation have been proposed,[24] the boundary between airspace and outer space has not yet been agreed. For practical purposes, the upper limit of airspace is at least as high as an aircraft can fly.[25]

B. Flight Information Regions

As ICAO explains,

> The world's airspace is divided into a series of contiguous flight information regions (FIRs) within which air traffic services are provided. In some cases, the flight information regions cover large oceanic areas with relatively low air traffic density, within which only flight information service and alerting service are provided.[26]

Each FIR is managed by a controlling authority responsible for ensuring that air traffic services are provided to the aircraft flying within it.[27] The term 'flight information region' is defined in Annex 11 to the Chicago Convention[28] as 'An airspace of defined dimensions within which flight information service[29] and alerting service[30] are provided'.[31] Schubert observes that 'States are required to establish FIRs in those portions of their airspace where FIS and ALRS will be provided'.[32] For smaller countries airspace is typically encompassed within a single FIR, whereas for larger ones it may be subdivided into a number of regional FIRs.[33] Schubert explains that the delineation of FIR limits

> is a relatively rigid process, conducted in accordance with ICAO guidelines; but States are free to delineate the FIRs over their territory. Annex 11 foresees that FIRs should be delineated to meet operational and technical needs rather than to reflect national boundaries.[34]

[23] Under Art II of the Outer Space Treaty 1967 and customary international law, outer space is not subject to national appropriation by claim of sovereignty, by means of use or occupation, or by any other means.

[24] See Shawcross and Beaumont, *Air Law* (LexisNexis, 2018), Vol 1, Div V, para 102.

[25] Taking a functional approach to delimitation, the launching of a satellite or other space object is deemed to be an outer space activity and the flight of aircraft is considered to be an activity in airspace. See UKMIL 1998, Part Twelve: II.A (1998) 69 *BYIL* 550–51.

[26] ICAO, *The Convention on International Civil Aviation, Annexes 1 to 18*, Annex 11, 'Air Traffic Services', available at www.icao.int/safety/AirNavigation/NationalityMarks/annexes_booklet_en.pdf.

[27] The Civil Aviation Authority (CAA) is the controlling authority for the UK. NATS (formerly National Air Traffic Services) provides air traffic services for it. See www.nats.aero/ae-home/introduction-to-airspace.

[28] 13th edn (July 2001). Entitled 'Air Traffic Services', Annex 11 'pertains to the establishment of airspace, units and services necessary to promote a safe, orderly and expeditious flow of air traffic': ibid, Foreword.

[29] 'FIS': 'A service provided for the purpose of giving advice and information useful for the safe and efficient conduct of flights'.

[30] 'ALRS': 'A service provided to notify appropriate organisations regarding aircraft in need of search and rescue aid, and assist such organisations as required'.

[31] Footnotes added. For all definitions see Annex 11, Ch 1.

[32] F Schubert, 'Air Navigation' in PS Dempsey and RS Jakhu (eds), *Routledge Handbook of Public Aviation Law* (Routledge, 2017) 106. See further Annex 11, para 2.5.2.1.

[33] YPR Bhalotra, *Gaborone flight information region requirements for meteorological service* (Department of Meteorological Services, Gaborone, 1990). For example, UK airspace is divided into three FIRs: London, Scottish and Shanwick Oceanic. The London FIR covers England and Wales. The Scottish FIR covers Scotland and Northern Ireland. The Shanwick Oceanic FIR covers 700,000 square miles over the North East Atlantic: www.nats.aero/ae-home/introduction-to-airspace.

[34] Schubert, 'Air Navigation' (2017). See further Annex 11 to the Chicago Convention, Chapter 2.10. FIRs are sometimes divided vertically, the upper portion being referred to as an upper flight information region or UIR.

NATS Airspace Explorer[35] notes that 'Airspace over the ocean is typically divided into two or more FIRs and delegated to controlling authorities within countries that border it.[36] For the purpose of this chapter and to inform discussion of the Saudi-led restrictions affecting Qatar-registered aircraft, it is important to recognise that whilst a landlocked state's airspace is necessarily all sovereign, the FIR(s) of coastal states can include areas of non-sovereign, international airspace in respect of which they provide air traffic services on behalf of ICAO. Only the airspace above a state's land and, if coastal, sea territory is subject to its sovereignty, however.

Under Article 28 of the Chicago Convention, each contracting state is responsible for providing, in its territory, facilities, services and procedures to facilitate international air navigation. The regional air navigation plan may include services to be provided in portions of airspace over the high seas, together with associated facilities and procedures. A state accepting responsibility for providing such services over the high seas may apply ICAO's provisions there in a manner consistent with that adopted for airspace under its jurisdiction.[37] In their FIRs beyond their own territorial limits, therefore, coastal states provide flight information and alerting services on behalf of ICAO for the benefit of all, effectively exercising stewardship of a common resource: the airspace there is international and the freedom of aviation applies, but the freedom must be regulated so that it can be exercised safely by everyone entitled to enjoy it.[38] While the coastal state may apply ICAO's provisions in the maritime airspace beyond its territorial limits in a manner consistent with that adopted for its own sovereign airspace, the international airspace within a coastal state's FIR is not that state's to appropriate and control as if it were its sovereign airspace, especially as FIR delineation reflects operational and technical needs rather than national boundaries.

The emphasis on operational needs and efficiency of service accounts for certain anomalies. In particular, as Figure 4.1 shows, Qatar lies entirely within the Bahrain FIR.[39] Macheras explains the background:

> When Bahrain and Qatar gained their independence from the UK in 1971, there wasn't any change to the FIR shapes in the Gulf region, which had previously been determined based on where military radars had initially been installed. These radars were positioned from a military efficiency perspective, without taking into account a future of thriving Gulf airline carriers.[40]

[35] A flight tracking and airspace education app developed by NATS in partnership with FlightAware.

[36] www.nats.aero/ae-home/introduction-to-airspace.

[37] ICAO Doc 7754, European Region Air Navigation Plan, Vol 1, Basic ANP, 2nd edn (2010), Introduction, para 9, available at gis.icao.int/ANPDOWNLOAD/EUR/Doc.7754.Vol.01.alltext.pdf. See also Annex 11 to the Chicago Convention, Ch 2.1.2.

[38] In September 2020, following the interception of two Russian military aircraft by RAF Typhoons in international airspace over the North Sea, an RAF spokesperson explained: 'The two aircraft approached the UK's Flight Information Region or FIR. This airspace is managed by NATS, the National Air Traffic Services for the UK, where aircraft operating within it should follow instructions from Air Traffic Controllers. These aircraft were not talking to NATS controllers, and while this is international airspace, this behaviour creates a hazard for other air users including civilian airliners'. See K McIntosh, 'Leuchars-based RAF fighter jets intercept Russian aircraft for third time in six days' *The Courier*, 17 September 2020, available at www.thecourier.co.uk/fp/news/local/fife/1587973/leuchars-based-raf-fighter-jets-intercept-russian-aircraft-for-third-time-in-six-days.

[39] Figure 4.1 shows the approximate FIR boundaries. For the relevant ICAO chart, see ICAO Viewer: gis.icao.int/icaoviewernew/#/51.1678/26.8148/6.

[40] A Macheras, 'Gulf crisis: how Bahrain was trusted with vast airspace, before the blockade', 7 September 2018, available at aviationanalyst.co.uk/2018/09/07/gulf-crisis-how-bahrain-was-trusted-with-vast-airspace-before-the-blockade. For more on the history of FIRs in the Middle East, including a 1946 map showing the Middle East Air Traffic Control Scheme, see www.wdl.org/en/item/13042.

Figure 4.1 FIR boundaries in the Persian Gulf region

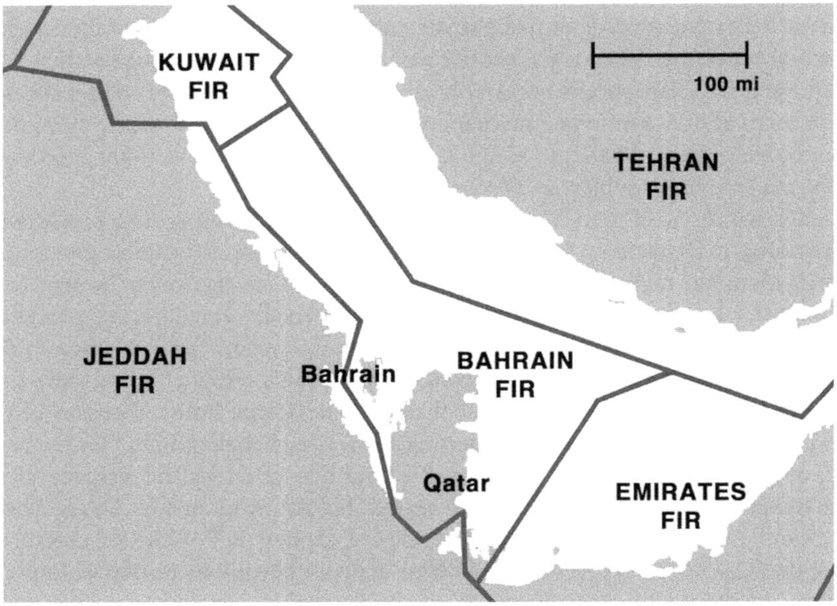

Macheras further explains that airspace distribution in the Gulf was maintained for administrative convenience:

> Back in the 1970s, it was determined that equally distributing FIR areas (airspace) to each state would require flight crew to speak to four different air traffic controllers within the space of around 15–20 minutes. While there are some areas of the world where this occurs, the Gulf states didn't see the need for a redistribution, given the hassle it would present to airline flight crew.[41]

The implications of this will be considered in more detail when discussing the Saudi-led airspace restrictions on Qatar-registered aircraft, which have prompted Qatar to ask ICAO for its own FIR[42] 'to enable broader operational control of its airspace'.[43]

C. Other Key Provisions of the Chicago Convention

For the purposes of this chapter, other key provisions of the Chicago Convention include Article 6 (Scheduled air services), Article 9 (Prohibited areas), Article 22 (Facilitation of formalities) and Article 84 (Settlement of disputes). Article 6 provides

[41] Macheras, 'Gulf crisis' (2018).

[42] 'ICAO directive a big victory for Qatar' *Gulf Times* (1 August 2017), available at www.gulf-times.com/story/558593/ICAO-directive-a-big-victory-for-Qatar.

[43] Kennedys, 'The Middle East crisis: implications for the aviation industry' (12 June 2017), available at www.kennedyslaw.com/thought-leadership/article/the-middle-east-crisis-implications-for-the-aviation-industry.

'No scheduled international air service[44] may be operated over or into the territory of a contracting State, except with the special permission or other authorization of that State, and in accordance with the terms of such permission or authorization'. With regard to scheduled international air services, therefore, special permission or other authorisation of the state concerned is required to fly over or into its territory and the terms of such permission or authorisation must be respected.[45] Shawcross and Beaumont explain:

> As between the states belonging to the 'Chicago system' (which now covers most of the world), rights resulting in 'permission or authorization' for scheduled services may be granted by one or more of the following methods –
>
> (a) By the 'Two Freedoms' Agreement made at the Chicago Conference;
> (b) By the 'Five Freedoms' Agreement made at the Chicago Conference;
> (c) By bilateral treaties between the states concerned.[46]

Article 9(a) of the Convention provides:

> Each contracting State may, for reasons of military necessity or public safety, restrict or prohibit uniformly the aircraft of other States from flying over certain areas of its territory, provided that no distinction in this respect is made between the aircraft of the State whose territory is involved, engaged in international scheduled airline services, and the aircraft of the other contracting States likewise engaged.[47]

Similarly, under Article 9(b) each contracting State reserves the right,

> in exceptional circumstances or during a period of emergency, in the interest of public safety, and with immediate effect, to restrict or prohibit flying over the whole or any part of its territory, on condition that such restriction or prohibition shall be applicable without distinction of nationality to aircraft of all other States.[48]

[44] Art 96 of the Convention defines 'air service' as 'any scheduled air service performed by aircraft for the public transport of passengers, mail or cargo' and 'international air service' as 'an air service which passes through the airspace over the territory of more than one State'.

[45] *cf* Art 5 whereby each contracting state agrees that all aircraft of the other contracting states, not engaged in scheduled international air services, shall have the right, subject to observing the Convention, to make flights into or across its territory and to make stops for non-traffic purposes without the need to obtain prior permission, and subject to the right of the state flown over to require landing.

[46] Shawcross and Beaumont, *Air Law* (2018) Vol 1, Div V, para 201 (footnotes omitted). For more details of those agreements and bilateral treaties, see below.

[47] Art 9(a) adds that prohibited areas shall be of reasonable extent and location so as not to interfere unnecessarily with air navigation and that descriptions of such prohibited areas as well as any alterations therein shall be communicated as soon as possible to the other contracting states and to ICAO.

[48] A recent example being the closure of Pakistan's airspace in February 2019: see n 3 above. It was presumably Art 9(b) that the FRY had in mind when it described the flight ban imposed on it in September 1998 as 'unlawful, unilateral and an example of the policy of discrimination'. As the Pakistan airspace closure illustrates, airspace restrictions are communicated through NOTAMS (Notices to Airmen) which are defined in Annex 11 as 'A notice containing information concerning the establishment, condition or change of any aeronautical facility, service, procedure or hazard, the timely knowledge of which is essential to personnel concerned with flight operations'. Under Art 9(c) of the Convention, each contracting state may require any aircraft entering the areas contemplated in subparagraphs (a) or (b) to land as soon as practicable at some designated airport within its territory. Art 3 *bis* of the Convention, on aerial interception and the use of weapons against civil aircraft in flight, is mentioned below in the context of the airspace restrictions affecting Qatar-registered aircraft.

Article 22 provides that each contracting state agrees to adopt all practicable measures to facilitate and expedite air navigation between the territories of contracting states.

With regard to the settlement of disputes, Article 84 of the Convention gives the ICAO Council an important quasi-judicial function.[49] Contained in Chapter XVIII entitled 'Disputes and Default', it provides:

> If any disagreement between two or more contracting States relating to the interpretation or application of this Convention and its Annexes cannot be settled by negotiation, it shall, on the application of any State concerned in the disagreement, be decided by the Council ... Any contracting State may, subject to Article 85,[50] appeal from the decision of the Council to an ad hoc arbitral tribunal agreed upon with the other parties to the dispute or to the Permanent Court of International Justice.[51] Any such appeal shall be notified to the Council within sixty days of receipt of notification of the decision of the Council.[52]

Another relevant provision is Article 54. Under the heading 'Mandatory functions of the Council', it provides 'The Council shall ... *n)* Consider any matter relating to the Convention which any contracting State refers to it'.[53] Weber notes that compared with Article 84, the settlement of disputes under Article 54(n) often has the advantage of greater flexibility and less publicity for the parties.[54] Although both provisions feature in discussion of the restrictions on Qatar-registered aircraft, we should bear in mind Dempsey's cautionary observation about the difficulty of using the ICAO Council – 'a political body comprised of governmental representatives appointed for their technical, administrative or diplomatic skills, or indeed, their political relationships in their home country, rather than their legal abilities' – as an adjudicatory tribunal.[55]

[49] The term 'quasi-judicial' is preferred because, as Shawcross and Beaumont (n 24) state, although the Council decides legal issues and in doing so acts very much like a court, it is not truly a judicial body: Vol 1, Div II, paras 12–13; *cf* L Weber, 'The Chicago Convention' in Dempsey and Jakhu, *Routledge Handbook* (2017) 27. In the recent *Appeal relating to the Jurisdiction of the ICAO Council under Article 84 of the Convention on International Civil Aviation*, the ICJ observed that the Council is 'composed of delegated representatives of the contracting States elected by the Assembly, rather than of individuals acting independently in their personal capacity as is characteristic of a judicial body', and that although the Council has been given the function of settling disputes between two or more contracting States concerning the interpretation or application of the Convention, this 'does not transform the Council into a judicial institution in the proper sense of that term': below, n 144, para 60. See further the separate opinion of Judge *Ad Hoc* Berman, ibid.

[50] Art 85 provides for an arbitration procedure.

[51] Art 37 of the Statute of the International Court of Justice effects a transfer of jurisdiction from the PCIJ to the ICJ: 'Whenever a treaty or convention in force provides for reference of a matter ... to the Permanent Court of International Justice, the matter shall, as between the parties to the present Statute, be referred to the International Court of Justice.'

[52] Proceedings before the Council under Art 84 are governed by the Rules of Procedure for the Settlement of Differences, ICAO Doc 7782. See further Shawcross and Beaumont (n 24) Vol 1, Division II, para 13. Art 88 of the Convention provides that the ICAO Assembly shall suspend the voting rights of any contracting state found in default under Chapter XVIII.

[53] Proceedings under Art 54(n) are governed by the Rules of Procedure for the Council, ICAO Doc 7559.

[54] Weber, 'The Chicago Convention' (2017) 29.

[55] PS Dempsey, 'Flights of Fancy and Fights of Fury: Arbitration and Adjudication of Commercial and Political Disputes in International Aviation' (2004) 32 *Georgia Journal of International and Comparative Law* 231, 302.

D. The Freedoms of the Air and the Freedom of Overflight

In the context of the Chicago Convention, the Freedoms of the Air are a series of reciprocal treaty rights and obligations agreed under a regime whose cornerstone is the fundamental principle that every state has complete and exclusive sovereignty over the airspace above its land and sea territory. The term 'Freedoms of the Air' is therefore something of a misnomer. As Shawcross and Beaumont explain:

> In international aviation, the concept of sovereignty is the keystone upon which virtually all air law is built,[56] since any flight in international aviation requires the prior consent of the state overflown, which is usually granted by treaty.[57]

Although there are nine Freedoms of the Air, 'ICAO characterizes all "freedoms" beyond the Fifth as "so-called" because only the first five "freedoms" have been officially recognized as such by international treaty'.[58] Those five freedoms granted by each contracting state to the other contracting states in respect of scheduled international air services are:

(1) the privilege to fly across its territory without landing;
(2) the privilege to land for non-traffic purposes;
(3) the privilege to put down passengers, mail and cargo taken on in the territory of the State whose nationality the aircraft possesses;
(4) the privilege to take on passengers, mail and cargo destined for the territory of the state whose nationality the aircraft possesses; and
(5) the privilege to take on passengers, mail and cargo destined for the territory of any other contracting state and the privilege to put down passengers, mail and cargo coming from any such territory.[59]

The Freedoms of the Air in the Chicago context should not be confused with the freedom of overflight in the airspace of the high seas under UNCLOS and customary international law.[60] Such freedom reflects the international status of that airspace. An arguable corollary is that the customary rule that ships on the high seas are in principle subject to the exclusive jurisdiction of their flag state[61] applies by analogy in the superjacent airspace, making aircraft overflying the high seas in principle subject to the exclusive jurisdiction of the state in which they are registered.[62] That analogy is contested, however.[63] Certainly, analogies with the law of the sea do not always work.

[56] See RY Jennings, 'International Civil Aviation and the Law' (1945) 22 *BYIL* 191, 208.

[57] Shawcross and Beaumont (n 24) Vol 1, Div 1, para 38 (footnote in the original).

[58] ICAO, 'Freedoms of the Air', available at www.icao.int/Pages/freedomsAir.aspx, citing as its source the *Manual on the Regulation of International Air Transport* (Doc 9626, Part 4).

[59] The first and second freedoms are contained in the Two Freedoms Agreement 1944, also known as the Transit Agreement or IASTA: see below. All five freedoms are articulated in the International Air Transport Agreement 1944, also known as the Five Freedoms or Transport Agreement. The latter entered into force on 8 February 1945 but only has 11 parties. For the other freedoms, see ICAO, 'Freedoms of the Air' (ibid) n 58.

[60] See Grief, *Public International Law* (1994) 77–78.

[61] *Lotus* case, PCIJ, Series A, No 10, 25. UNCLOS, Art 92(1).

[62] See Grief (n 21) 77–78.

[63] See, eg, Case C-366/10, *Air Transport Association of America and Others v Secretary of State for Energy and Climate Change* [2011] ECR I-13833, at para 106, where the Court of Justice of the European Union held

In particular, whereas ships of all states have the right of innocent passage through the territorial sea subject to certain conditions,[64] there is no equivalent right of innocent passage for aircraft in the airspace above the territorial sea:

> While maritime law has traditionally sought to guarantee states and vessels the freedom of the seas and presumed a right of innocent passage, aviation law does not guarantee such a right. States have the ultimate legal right to regulate and control their airspace as they see fit … Denying permission outright is therefore legally unproblematic.[65] Powers derived from the Chicago Convention grant states exclusive jurisdiction and sovereignty over their airspace. However, denying permission in view of various bilateral and multilateral transit agreements is somewhat more controversial.[66]

Some of the legal implications of those other agreements will now be considered.

E. The International Air Services Transit Agreement 1944

In terms of the Freedoms of the Air, the most important multilateral treaty besides the Chicago Convention itself is the International Air Services Transit Agreement 1944 (IASTA), also known as the Two Freedoms Agreement and the Transit Agreement.[67] Article I, Section 1, enshrines the first two Freedoms of the Air:

> Each contracting State grants to the other contracting States the following freedoms of the air in respect of scheduled international air services:
>
> (1) the privilege to fly across its territory, without landing;
> (2) the privilege to land for non-traffic purposes.
>
> …[68]

As Carpanelli observes, 'consent to be bound by IASTA satisfies, *vis-à-vis* the other Contracting States, the "special permission" requirement imposed by Article 6' of the Chicago Convention.[69] There is overflight as of right, without any need for further permission.[70]

that there was 'insufficient evidence' that the principle applicable to ships on the high seas applied by analogy to aircraft in the airspace above.

[64] UNCLOS, Arts 17–26.

[65] But note that all aircraft enjoy the right of unimpeded transit passage over straits used for international navigation between one part of the high seas or an EEZ and another part of the high seas or an EEZ, subject to complying with certain duties: ibid, Arts 37–39.

[66] E Omanovic, 'Effective Embargo Enforcement: Overflight Denial and Control', EU Non-Proliferation Consortium, Non-Proliferation Papers No 26, February 2013, 4–5, available at www.nonproliferation.eu/effective-embargo-enforcement-overflight-denial-and-control.

[67] IASTA entered into force on 30 January 1945 and has 133 parties. States that are not parties to it include Russia and Saudi Arabia.

[68] Art 96(d) of the Chicago Convention defines 'non-traffic purposes' as 'any purpose other than taking on or discharging passengers, cargo or mail'. However, with regard to Art 5 the ICAO Council has stated, inter alia, that a stop for non-traffic purposes 'should not be regarded as a traffic stop by reason of the temporary unloading of passengers, mail or goods in transit, if the stop is made for reasons of technical necessity or convenience of operation of the flight'. See Shawcross and Beaumont (n 24) Vol 1, Div V, para 202, fn 4.

[69] E Carpanelli, 'To Overfly, or not to Overfly …? Autonomous Sanctions in International Civil Aviation amidst the Recent "Gulf Crisis" – Part I' (22 September 2017), available at grojil.org/2017/09/22/to-overfly-or-not-to-overfly-autonomous-sanctions-in-international-civil-aviation-amidst-the-recent-gulf-crisis.

[70] This was confirmed by the ICAO Council in 1951. It ruled that the Chicago Convention, in particular Art 6, does not override Art 1, Section 1, of IASTA and that each state party to the latter grants the privileges

The Agreement's dispute settlement provisions are also relevant, especially Article II, Section 2:

> If any disagreement between two or more contracting States relating to the interpretation or application of this Agreement cannot be settled by negotiation, the provisions of Chapter XVIII of the [Chicago] Convention shall be applicable in the same manner as provided therein with reference to any disagreement relating to the interpretation or application of the above-mentioned Convention.

Thus, IASTA provides for an appeal to the ICJ by reference to Article 84 of the Chicago Convention, one of the provisions of Chapter XVIII. The ICJ acknowledged its role in the 'good functioning' of ICAO in *India v Pakistan – Appeal Relating to the Jurisdiction of the ICAO Council*.[71] The Court noted that although the case had been presented to it in the guise of an ordinary dispute between states, it was the act of a third entity (the Council of ICAO) which one of the parties was impugning and the other defending. It continued:

> the appeal to the Court contemplated by the Chicago Convention and the Transit Agreement must be regarded as an element of the general regime established in respect of ICAO. In thus providing for judicial recourse by way of appeal to the Court against decisions of the Council concerning interpretation and application … the Chicago Treaties gave member States, and through them the Council, the possibility of ensuring a certain measure of supervision by the Court over those decisions. To this extent, these Treaties enlist the support of the Court for the good functioning of the Organization, and therefore the first reassurance for the Council lies in the knowledge that means exist for determining whether a decision as to its own competence is in conformity or not with the provisions of the treaties governing its action.[72]

F. Bilateral Air Services Agreements

Bilateral air services agreements (ASAs) have been described as 'the very foundation of scheduled international air services'.[73] Shawcross and Beaumont explain their importance:

> As between states which are parties to the Chicago Convention, but are not parties to the Two Freedoms or Five Freedoms Agreements, the method of granting the 'permission or authorisation' required for scheduled services by the Convention is by a bilateral treaty. This method is also used as between states which are parties to the Two Freedoms Agreement, and wish to make a mutual grant of additional rights, although not prepared to accept the full Five

of transit and landing for non-traffic purposes (subject to other provisions of the Agreement) to the other states parties with respect to their scheduled international services. See Shawcross and Beaumont (n 24) Vol 1, Div V, para 202, fn 5.

[71] ICJ Reports 1972, 46. This case is considered further in relation to the ICJ's recent judgments concerning the ICAO Council's jurisdiction regarding the airspace restrictions on Qatar-registered aircraft, below.

[72] ibid, para 26.

[73] UK representative Anthony Aust speaking on 21 October 1985 at the Third ICAO Conference in Montreal, UKMIL 1985, (1985) 56 *BYIL* 504. Addressing the subject of unilateral measures which affect international air transport, Mr Aust concluded by asking the Conference to reaffirm 'the vital principle that all Member States must ensure that their laws … are applied in such a way that there is no conflict with their obligations under air services agreements': ibid, 505, 507.

> Freedoms Agreement. As between states which are not all parties to the Chicago Convention, apart from temporary or informal arrangements, a bilateral treaty is at present the only practicable method of granting rights of either scheduled or non-scheduled flight.[74]

For States like Russia and Saudi Arabia which are parties to the Chicago Convention but not to IASTA, therefore, bilateral treaties satisfy the requirements of Article 6 of the former as far as overflight and traffic rights are concerned. An example is the Agreement between Qatar and Saudi Arabia on air transport services between and beyond their respective territories.[75] Similarly, states which are parties to IASTA need to conclude bilateral treaties with other states in order to confer and enjoy more extensive rights.

In the light of that overview of the legal framework, the three case studies will now be considered.

III. Russia's Threat to Close its Airspace to EU and US Airlines

In a blog concerning Russia's threat to close its airspace to EU and US airlines after sanctions were imposed on it in August 2014 following its military intervention in Ukraine, Szambelan explained why Russia had the right to introduce an overflight ban and why it was unlikely to do so:

> Unlike the USA and all the EU countries, Russia has never signed the International Air Services Transit Agreement (IASTA), through which 130 countries mutually granted each other access to their airspace for the use of commercial aviation. Other governments, including Russia, preferred to maintain more control over who enters its airspace and has solved the matter of access by signing separate agreements with countries individually. Therefore, banning EU carriers from flying over Siberia would not breach any international laws [... Nevertheless,] restricting airspace access would cost the Russian side at least as much as it would cost the EU. As for all other services in the aviation sector, there are fees collected by each nation for the right to cross its airspace. The airlines have to pay for using the [air] traffic control services of the country they travel through, usually around $50 per 100 nautical miles. In Russia, the exact prices per plane are kept secret, but the total annual toll is known to exceed $170m. Collected by Aeroflot, it is a persistent flow of state aid to the national airline carrier. Given that the airline yielded a $230m profit in 2013, according to its financial statements, the overflight ban would likely result in putting Russia's biggest airline close to the break-even point.[76]

In fact, it seems that Russia was imposing overflight fees rather than charging for the use of its air navigation services. The latter is consistent with the Chicago Convention, the

[74] Shawcross and Beaumont (n 24) Vol 1, Div V, para 201 (footnotes omitted). Such agreements must be registered with the ICAO Council and are contained in an online database: see Arts 81–83 of the Convention and www.icao.int/sustainability/Pages/Doc9511.aspx.

[75] Jeddah, 14 May 2001, 2340 *UNTS* 333.

[76] P Szambelan, 'Why Russia will not close its sky to EU airlines (and why it might)', *European Public Affairs.eu* (22 September 2014), available at www.europeanpublicaffairs.eu/author/patryk-szambelan.

former is not. Article 15 allows contracting states to impose charges for the use of air navigation facilities as long as they are not higher than those payable by their national aircraft engaged in similar scheduled international air services.[77] ICAO's policies on charges state:[78]

> As a general principle, where air navigation services are provided for international use, the State may require the users of such services to pay the portion of costs properly allocable to them ... The allocation of the costs of air navigation services among aeronautical users should be carried out in an equitable manner ... States should ensure that systems used for charging for air navigation services be established in accordance with the following principles.[79]

Significantly, Article 15 provides that no fees, dues or other charges shall be imposed by any contracting state in respect solely of the right of transit over its territory of any aircraft of a contracting state. In 2006 the EU and Russia agreed in principle to abolish the overflight charges that EU air carriers had to pay to fly over Siberia to destinations in Asia.[80] It was estimated that these payments came to around €320 million per year, most of it going to Aeroflot. The European Commission was concerned that the payments, 'anchored in the obligation for airlines to conclude a commercial agreement with Aeroflot set out in a bilateral agreement between member states and Russia',[81] were in breach of EU law[82] and the Chicago Convention. The agreement was finalised in 2011, the intention being that from 1 January 2014 Siberian overflight charges would be cost-related, transparent and non-discriminatory.[83] However, Russia continued to enforce the overflight charges when the EU included aviation in its Emissions Trading System (ETS) in 2012.[84] It still appears to be doing so. In March 2018, the House of Commons' European Scrutiny Committee noted that although IASTA provides transit

[77] Art 15(b).

[78] ICAO Doc 9082, 'ICAO's Policies on Charges for Airports and Air Navigation Services', 9th edn (2012), available at www.icao.int/publications/Documents/9082_9ed_en.pdf.

[79] ibid, Sections III-1, III-5 and III-6.

[80] This was 'a relic of the Cold War, when Russian airspace was out of bounds and Russia excluded Siberia in return for a fee'. See 'Overflight Fees Bring EU Lawsuits', *The Moscow Times* (27 January 2011), available at: www.themoscowtimes.com/2011/01/27/overflight-fees-bring-eu-lawsuits-a4565.

[81] J Leijonhielm, 'The Russian System Concerning Air Traffic Security and Incidents' in T Hellenberg, P Visuri and L Nicander (eds), *Securing Air Traffic* (Aleksanteri Institute, University of Helsinki, 2011) 175, 182.

[82] On the grounds that airlines should not be forced to conclude agreements with a competitor and because the bilateral ASAs between individual Member States and Russia did not treat all EU carriers equally as required by the EU's 'freedom of establishment' provisions as interpreted by the European Court of Justice in its 'Open Skies' judgments in 2002. See European Commission, Press Release, 'Air transport: Commission launches infringement procedures against six Member States over agreements with Russia on equal treatment of EU airlines and Siberian overflights' (14 March 2011), available at europa.eu/rapid/press-release_IP-11-298_en.htm.

[83] And enabling the EU to support Russia's accession to the WTO. See European Commission, Press Release, 'Air transport: Commission welcomes agreement on Siberian overflights' (1 December 2011), available at europa.eu/rapid/press-release_IP-11-1490_en.htm.

[84] Council of the European Union, information note from the Commission on EU-Russia Transport Relations (25 October 2012), available at register.consilium.europa.eu/doc/srv?l=EN&f=ST%2014838%20 2012%20INIT. As a result of ICAO initiatives to reduce aviation carbon emissions, the EU has limited the scope of the ETS for aviation to intra-European Economic Area flights until 2023: see Regulation (EU) 2017/2392 amending Directive 2003/87/EC (the ETS Directive), [2017] OJ L350/7.

rights, including overflight on an unrestricted basis, 'some countries (eg Russia) have not signed up to the agreement and charge significant fees to use their airspace'.[85]

Szambelan points out that in addition to the direct financial consequences for Aeroflot, an overflight ban could have been circumvented:

> For example, the German [airline] Lufthansa could easily use its codeshare agreement with All Nippon Airlines, allowing the Japanese airline to become the operating carrier of the flights that currently connect Frankfurt with Tokyo, Osaka and Nagoya, whilst using the aircraft belonging to the German national carrier. Ensuring the effectiveness of the overflight ban would require Russia to put itself in isolation not only from the West, but also from the East. Should this scenario become real, Russia would have to also close its airspace to the Asian partners of the EU airlines in the next potential step. This would mean opening a new front of antagonised countries ... All of the above renders the overflight ban as a reckless step with no chances of success.[86]

In short, it was clearly in Russia's interests not to introduce a Siberia overflight ban in response to EU sanctions. Doing so would have been costly and possibly futile.

IV. US Sanctions against Iran: Implications for the Safety of Civil Aviation

Pursuant to his decision in May 2018 to withdraw from the JCPOA,[87] President Trump reimposed certain sanctions with respect to Iran following wind-down periods of 90 or 180 days depending on the activity involved.[88] Accordingly, on 5 November 2018 the US fully reimposed the sanctions that had been lifted or waived under the JCPOA.[89] Under that Agreement, besides removing Iran Air from the SDN[90] list, the US had allowed the following:

> 1. the sale of commercial aircraft and related parts and services to Iran by licensing the export, re-export, sale, lease, or transfer to Iran of commercial passenger aircraft exclusively for civil aviation end use,

[85] House of Commons, European Scrutiny, Documents considered by the Committee on 7 March 2018, ICAO, Summary and Committee's conclusions, para 4.14, available at publications.parliament.uk/pa/cm201719/cmselect/cmeuleg/301-xvii/30107.htm.

[86] Szambelan, 'Why Russia will not close its sky' (2014).

[87] An agreement between the P5+1 (Germany), the EU and Iran under which, in exchange for the lifting of UN Security Council sanctions as well as multilateral and national sanctions relating to Iran's nuclear programme, Iran guaranteed the exclusively peaceful nature of its nuclear programme. The JCPOA was agreed at Vienna on 14 July 2015, came into effect on 18 October 2015 and was implemented from 16 January 2016. It was endorsed by Security Council Resolution 2231 (2015). See Arms Control Association, 'The Joint Comprehensive Plan of Action (JCPOA) at a Glance', available at www.armscontrol.org/factsheets/JCPOA-at-a-glance.

[88] Executive Order 13846 of 6 August 2018, available at www.federalregister.gov/documents/2018/08/07/2018-17068/reimposing-certain-sanctions-with-respect-to-iran.

[89] The EU has continued to support the JCPOA, establishing a mechanism called the Instrument in Support of Trade Exchanges (INSTEX) to facilitate trade with Iran. See Arms Control Association, 25 February 2019, 'The P4+1 and Iran Nuclear Deal Alert', available at www.armscontrol.org/blog/2019-02-25/p41-iran-nuclear-deal-alert-feb-25-2019.

[90] Specially Designated Nationals and Blocked Persons.

2. the export, re-export, sale, lease, or transfer to Iran of spare parts and components for commercial passenger aircraft, and
3. the provision of associated services including warranty, maintenance, repair services, and safety-related inspections for all the foregoing, provided that licensed items and services were used exclusively for commercial passenger aviation.[91]

Iran's commercial passenger aircraft fleet is one of the oldest in the world and this licensing policy was 'intended to make it less difficult for Iran to purchase commercial passenger aircraft and parts, even where that transaction had a US nexus'.[92] With the reinstatement of sanctions, Iran Air and 67 aircraft operated by it went back onto the SDN List.[93] FAQs posted by the Office of Foreign Assets Control (OFAC) on the US Treasury Department website confirm that payments or the facilitation of payments to Iran's civil aviation authorities for overflights of Iran or landing in Iran by aircraft owned by a non-US person and registered outside the US are not subject to sanctions under US law 'Provided that the relevant transactions do not involve the U.S. financial system or persons on the Specially Designated Nationals and Blocked Persons List (SDN List)'.[94] However,

> U.S. persons and U.S.-owned or -controlled foreign entities cannot participate in transactions related to the payment of overflight or landing fees to the Iranian Government, nor can such transactions transit the U.S. financial system, unless the transactions fall within the scope of [certain exemptions].[95]

On 16 July 2018, Iran instituted proceedings against the USA in the ICJ[96] alleging that the sanctions violate the bilateral Treaty of Amity, Economic Relations and Consular Rights 1955.[97] It also requested the indication of provisional measures.[98] On 3 October 2018 the Court unanimously ordered the US, inter alia,

> [T]o remove, by means of its choosing, any impediments arising from the measures announced on 8 May 2018 to the free exportation to the territory of the Islamic Republic of Iran of … (iii) spare parts, equipment and associated services (including warranty, maintenance, repair services and inspections) necessary for the safety of civil aviation.[99]

[91] OFAC Sanctions Attorney, Price Benowitz LLP, 'JCPOA Impact on Civil Aviation', in 'Iran Sanctions: Civil Aviation', available at ofaclawyer.net/economic-sanctions-programs/iran/civil-aviation.

[92] HFW Briefing, 'Iran Sanctions: Aerospace Focus' (May 2018), available at www.hfw.com/Iran-sanctions-Aerospace-focus-May-2018.

[93] US Department of the Treasury, Press Release, 5 November 2018, 'U.S. Government fully re-imposes sanctions on the Iranian regime as part of unprecedented U.S. economic pressure campaign', 'Aviation', available at home.treasury.gov/news/press-releases/sm541.

[94] FAQ 417, 5 November 2018: www.treasury.gov/resource-center/faqs/Sanctions/Pages/faq_iran.aspx#417. HFW pointed out that the relisting of IranAir and other Iranian government-owned airlines on the SDN List would 'have the effect of prohibiting code-sharing and similar arrangements with those Iranian carriers': www.hfw.com/Iran-sanctions-Aerospace-focus-May-2018.

[95] FAQ 417 (ibid).

[96] www.icj-cij.org/public/files/case-related/175/175-20180716-APP-01-00-EN.pdf.

[97] Tehran, 15 August 1955, 284 UNTS 93. The Treaty entered into force on 16 June 1957. Art XXI(2) provides: 'Any dispute between the High Contracting Parties as to the interpretation or application of the present Treaty, not satisfactorily adjusted by diplomacy, shall be submitted to the International Court of Justice, unless the High Contracting Parties agree to settlement by some other pacific means'.

[98] www.icj-cij.org/public/files/case-related/175/175-20180716-REQ-01-00-EN.pdf.

[99] *Alleged Violations of the 1955 Treaty of Amity, Economic Relations, and Consular Rights (Islamic Republic of Iran v United States of America), Provisional Measures, Order of 3 October 2018*, ICJ Reports 2018, 623,

Regarding the risk of irreparable prejudice and urgency,[100] the Court was satisfied that

> the measures adopted by the United States have the potential to endanger civil aviation safety in Iran and the lives of its users to the extent that they prevent Iranian airlines from acquiring spare parts and other necessary equipment, as well as from accessing associated services (including warranty, maintenance, repair services and safety-related inspections) necessary for civil aircraft.[101]

Iran had argued that the sanctions had left its commercial airlines and civil passengers with 'an ageing fleet [and] limited access to maintenance information, services and spare parts';[102] and that

> by preventing Iranian airlines from renewing their already old airline fleets, purchasing spare parts and other necessary equipment and services, training pilots to international standards or using foreign airport services, the lives of Iranian passengers and crew, and other customers of Iranian airlines will be placed in danger.[103]

This was noted by Macheras, who also reported how a new Norwegian Air Boeing 737 MAX 8 airliner was stranded in Iran for 10 weeks after making an emergency landing at Shiraz International Airport on 14 December 2018 while flying from Dubai to Oslo. The passengers were able to continue their journey to Norway the following day on a different aircraft but the spare parts and licences needed for the Boeing's engine repair were hit by the US sanctions.[104] The airliner finally left Shiraz on 22 February 2019.[105]

The US had argued, inter alia, that the sanctions could not be challenged in the ICJ as they were covered by provisions in the 1955 Treaty allowing it to take measures to address matters of national security.[106] The Court did not determine the validity of that contention at this stage of the proceedings, limiting its assessment to the plausibility of the rights invoked by Iran and the real and imminent risk of irreparable prejudice. It emphasised that its decision on provisional measures did not prejudge the question of its jurisdiction to deal with the merits of the case or any questions relating to the admissibility of the Application or to the merits themselves.[107] In response to the Order, US Secretary of State Mike Pompeo announced that the USA would withdraw from the Treaty.[108]

para 102, point 1, available at www.icj-cij.org/public/files/case-related/175/175-20181003-ORD-01-00-EN.pdf. The Court also unanimously ordered the USA 'to ensure that licences and necessary authorizations are granted and that payments and other transfers of funds are not subject to any restriction in so far as they relate to the goods and services referred to in point (1)'; and both Parties 'to refrain from any action which might aggravate or extend the dispute before the Court or make it more difficult to resolve': ibid, points 2 and 3. According to *UN News*, this was the first time that international judges had ruled on a case of 'economic warfare': news.un.org/en/story/2018/10/1022142.

[100] Two of the conditions governing the indication of provisional measures: Order of 3 October 2018 (ibid), paras 77 and 78.

[101] bid, para 91.

[102] ibid, para 81.

[103] ibid. See also paras 32 and 33 of Iran's Application instituting proceedings (n 96).

[104] A Macheras, 'Norwegian Air's ongoing nightmare in Iran', *Aviation Analyst* (10 January 2019), available at aviationanalyst.co.uk/2019/01/10/norwegian-airs-ongoing-nightmare-in-iran.

[105] L Karagiannopoulos, 'Iran-stranded Boeing airliner took off and expected in Sweden – Norwegian Air', *Reuters*, Aerospace & Defense (22 February 2019), available at www.reuters.com/article/norweg-air-shut-iran/iran-stranded-boeing-airliner-took-off-and-expected-in-sweden-norwegian-air-idUSL5N20H6OL.

[106] Treaty of Amity, Economic Relations, and Consular Rights 1955 (n 97), Art XX(1).

[107] Order of 3 October 2018 (n 99) para 101.

[108] *UN News*, 3 October 2018, available at news.un.org/en/story/2018/10/1022142. Nevertheless, the case continues. On 3 February 2021, the Court found that it had jurisdiction to entertain Iran's Application and that the Application was admissible: www.icj-cij.org/public/files/case-related/175/175-20210203-JUD-01-00-EN.pdf.

V. The Saudi-Led Airspace Restrictions Affecting Qatar-Registered Aircraft

On 5 June 2017 Bahrain, Egypt, Saudi Arabia and the UAE severed diplomatic ties with Qatar and imposed a land, air and sea blockade on it. They accused Qatar of breaching the Riyadh Agreements[109] and supporting terrorism, charges which Qatar strongly denied.[110] The restrictions have had serious implications for the freedom of aviation: 18 air corridors were immediately reduced to two. *Flightradar24* explained:

> Beginning at 0000 UTC on 6 June 2017 Qatari flights were not permitted to fly through Saudi Arabia's airspace. Many of Qatar Airways' flights to southern Europe and Africa pass through Saudi Arabia. It was reported that flights to Europe would most likely be rerouted through Iran and Turkey, and that flights to Africa may route via Iran and Oman and then south.[111]

Similarly, besides banning flights between Qatar and Bahrain, Bahrain restricted the routes available to Qatar-registered aircraft through the Bahrain FIR within which Qatar lies.[112] Qatar-registered aircraft inbound to Qatar had to enter the Bahrain FIR via waypoint MIDSI at the Tehran FIR boundary and follow route UR659. Aircraft departing from Qatar had to use route UT430 and leave the Bahrain FIR via waypoint RAGAS at the Tehran FIR boundary.[113] Five days later, however, Bahrain eased the routing restrictions, allowing Qatar-registered aircraft access to all routes in the FIR except for certain airways.[114]

The implications for aviation were noted in the UK Parliament. Concluding a House of Lords debate on 'Gulf Countries and Qatar' on 11 July 2017, Baroness Goldie stated:

> It is the case that air and sea routes for people and goods in and out of Qatar have been rerouted through Oman and Iran where no direct route is available. That has meant that travel around the region has increased in time and cost, both of which will have impacts on businesses that operate regionally. However, businesses are adopting alternative supply and flight routes for the time being, while the blockade continues, but the UK is supportive of Kuwait's mediation efforts and we hope these will lead to a swift de-escalation of the situation.[115]

[109] Under the Riyadh Agreements of 2013 and 2014, Qatar is committed to, inter alia, avoiding interfering in the internal affairs of other Gulf States, not supporting the Muslim Brotherhood or opposition groups in Yemen and preventing Al-Jazeera (which is based in Qatar) from being used to challenge the Egyptian Government. The secret Agreements were leaked in July 2017. Qatar alleged that the leak was intended to weaken mediation efforts in the region. See J Sciutto and J Herb, 'Exclusive: The secret documents that help explain the Qatar crisis', *CNN Politics* (11 July 2017), available at edition.cnn.com/2017/07/10/politics/secret-documents-qatar-crisis-gulf-saudi/index.html.

[110] On 23 June 2017 the Saudi side presented Qatar with 13 demands. For those demands and more on the crisis, see B Smith, 'Qatar Crisis', House of Commons Library, Briefing Paper No CPB 8030 (30 June 2017), available at researchbriefings.files.parliament.uk/documents/CBP-8030/CBP-8030.pdf.

[111] I Petchenik, 'Flight Ban for Qatar Flights in UAE, Saudi Arabia, Bahrain, and Egypt', *flightradar24* (5 June 2017), available at www.flightradar24.com/blog/flight-ban-for-qatar-flights-in-uae-saudi-arabia-bahrain-and-egypt. This includes the relevant NOTAMS issued by Bahrain, Egypt, Saudi Arabia and the UAE. UTC stands for Universal Time Coordinated, which shares the same current time as Greenwich Mean Time (GMT).

[112] See Figure 4.1.

[113] NOTAM A0208/17. See Petchenik, 'Flight Ban for Qatar Flights' (2017). In order to manage the additional traffic, the Iranian authorities issued a NOTAM identifying routes available to aircraft to and from Qatar transiting the Tehran FIR: ibid. See also Kennedys, 'The Middle East crisis' (2017).

[114] Petchenik (n 111) 'Update', 11 June 2017.

[115] *Hansard*, HL, Vol 783, col 1229 (11 July 2017), available at hansard.parliament.uk/Lords/2017-07-11/debates/659B9371-6EE3-4EC5-9B52-E90475F9997C/GulfCountriesAndQatar?highlight=qatar#contribution-06404516-ABE2-4AB9-AC1F-CA4EDE229D7B.

On 8 June 2017 Qatar requested that a special session of the ICAO Council be convened under Article 54(n) of the Chicago Convention[116] to consider the 'matter of the actions of the Arab Republic of Egypt, the Kingdom of Bahrain, the Kingdom of Saudi Arabia and the United Arab Emirates to close their airspace to aircraft registered in the State of Qatar'.[117] The Council held an extraordinary meeting to consider Qatar's request on 31 July 2017. Its Chairman declared that ICAO's priority was to focus on the safety and security of international civil aviation[118] and that the 'overarching political issues [were] to be addressed' in 'appropriate fora'.[119] For technical rather than political reasons, the Council approved a joint working paper presented by the Saudi-led quartet

> which included actions taken in cooperation with the ICAO regional office in Cairo to promote safety over international waters in the Middle East region [and the] opening of nine additional air routes to relieve the pressure on current routes over international waters.[120]

The Council urged 'all Member States of ICAO to abide by the spirit of the Chicago Convention and to cooperate to ensure the safety, security, efficiency and sustainability of international civil aviation'.[121] Tension increased on 20 August 2017, however, when Qatar filed a complaint with ICAO over a Saudi television news channel's report simulating the shooting down of a Qatar Airways plane, calling this 'a clear and serious violation of international treaties and conventions, particularly the 1944 Chicago Convention, the international air traffic service agreement and international air law'.[122]

The following month, attention switched to the UN General Assembly where representatives of Qatar and the other states concerned made statements during the

[116] See above.

[117] See para 10 of the Joint Application of Bahrain, Egypt, Saudi Arabia and the UAE instituting proceedings against Qatar in the ICJ, *Appeal relating to the Jurisdiction of the ICAO Council under Article 84 of the Convention on International Civil Aviation*, available at www.icj-cij.org/public/files/case-related/173/173-20180704-APP-01-00-EN.pdf.

[118] Art 44 of the Convention provides that ICAO's aims and objectives 'are to develop the principles and techniques of international air navigation and to foster the planning and development of international air transport so as to: a) Insure the safe and orderly growth of international civil aviation throughout the world; … d) Meet the needs of the peoples of the world for safe, regular, efficient and economical air transport; … f) Insure that the rights of contracting States are fully respected and that every contracting State has a fair opportunity to operate international airlines'.

[119] Joint Application (n 117) para 11. By 'appropriate fora' the Council presumably meant the Gulf Cooperation Council in particular. In a debate on 'UK Relations with Qatar' in May 2018, the Minister for the Middle East stated 'Gulf Co-operation Council unity matters to the United Kingdom. It supports regional stability and security, which is why, since last June, the UK Government at all levels have continued to support Kuwait's mediation efforts. We work closely with international partners, including the US, to support the GCC to find a resolution … We believe a solution is most likely to be found from within the GCC'. See *Hansard*, HC, 23 May 2018, Vol 641, col 412WH, available at hansard.parliament.uk/Commons/2018-05-23/debates/29B21BEA-EF33-43BE-B26E-D60BADF6D0DA/UKRelationsWithQatar?highlight=qatar#contribution-09E0E919-0CF4-4B0C-B445-7FE267B47066. See further n 190.

[120] S Murdock, 'How the airspace corridors came to be established – the penumbra of ICAO' *JDA Journal* (8 August 2017), available at jdasolutions.aero/blog/airspace-corridors/#_blank. The article highlights conflicting accounts of the Council meeting but concludes that 'ICAO's authority is more accurately explained' in the *Saudi Gazette* version cited here.

[121] ibid.

[122] 'Qatar files complaint with ICAO over Al Arabiya report', *Al Jazeera* (19 August 2017), available at www.aljazeera.com/news/2017/08/19/qatar-files-complaint-with-icao-over-al-arabiya-report. Qatar Airways

Assembly's annual general debate. The Amir of Qatar spoke defiantly against the blockade imposed on his country:

> I stand here while my country and my people are subjected to a continuing and unjust blockade imposed since June 5th by neighbouring countries … Qatar is currently managing successfully its living, economy, development plans, and its outreach to the outside world, thanks to sea and air routes that these countries have no control over.[123]

For his part, Saudi Arabia's Minister for Foreign Affairs explained that 'The position taken by the four States was meant to demand that Qatar follow the principles of international law in fighting terrorism'.[124]

A. Proceedings before the ICAO Council

On 30 October 2017 Qatar submitted two Applications to the Council, one pursuant to Article 84 of the Chicago Convention (Application (A)) and the other pursuant to Article II, Section 2, of IASTA (Application (B)). The former alleged various violations of the Convention. In particular, that:

> On 5 June 2017, the Governments of [Bahrain, Egypt, Saudi Arabia and the UAE] announced, with immediate effect and without any previous negotiation or warning, that Qatar-registered aircraft are not permitted to fly to or from the airports within their territories and would be banned not only from their respective national air spaces, but also from their Flight Information Regions (FIRs) extending beyond their national airspace even over the high seas.[125]

The latter alleged violations of IASTA. In particular, that:

> On 5 June 2017, the Governments of [Bahrain, Egypt and the UAE] announced, with immediate effect and without any previous negotiation or warning, that Qatar-registered aircraft are not permitted to fly to or from the airports within their territories and are banned from their respective national air spaces.[126]

subsequently sued Al Arabiya and others in the English High Court arguing that the video simulation constituted malicious falsehood and an interference with its business. The defendants disputed the Court's jurisdiction, but on 6 November 2020 the Court dismissed their challenge. See *Qatar Airways Group QCSC v Middle East News FZ LLC, Middle East News UK Limited, MBC FZ LLC and Al Arabiya News Channel FZ LLC* [2020] EWHC 2975 (QB). Paras 48–61 of the judgment outline relevant aspects of international aviation law, including Art 3 *bis* of the Chicago Convention, inserted after the shooting down of a Korean airliner by Soviet military aircraft in 1983, which provides: '(a) The contracting States recognize that every State must refrain from resorting to the use of weapons against civil aircraft in flight and that, in case of interception, the lives of persons on board and the safety of aircraft must not be endangered. This provision shall not be interpreted as modifying in any way the rights and obligations of States set forth in the Charter of the United Nations'.

[123] Address by His Highness Sheikh Tamim bin Hamad Al-Thani, Amir of the State of Qatar, at the General Debate of the 72nd session of the United Nations General Assembly, New York (19 September 2017), available at gadebate.un.org/sites/default/files/gastatements/72/qa_en.pdf.

[124] Statement by Adel Ahmed Al-Jubeir on 23 September 2017 as reported by *UN News*, available at news.un.org/en/story/2017/09/566832-un-assembly-saudi-arabia-pledges-press-ahead-combat-against-terrorism-extremism.

[125] Joint Application (n 117) para 14.

[126] See para 15 of the Joint Application of Bahrain, Egypt and the UAE instituting proceedings against Qatar in the ICJ, *Appeal relating to the Jurisdiction of the ICAO Council under Article II, Section 2, of the 1944 International Air Services Transit Agreement*, available at www.icj-cij.org/public/files/case-related/174/174-20180704-APP-01-00-EN.pdf.

On 19 March 2018 the Respondents raised Preliminary Objections in respect of each Application, contesting the jurisdiction of the Council to adjudicate the claims or, in the alternative, their admissibility.[127] In respect of Application (A), Bahrain, Egypt, Saudi Arabia and the UAE argued that the dispute would require the Council

> to determine issues that [fell] outside its jurisdiction [since] to rule on the lawfulness of the countermeasures adopted by the Applicants, including certain airspace restrictions, the Council would be required to rule on Qatar's compliance with critical obligations under international law entirely unrelated to, and outwith, the Chicago Convention.[128]

They also contended, inter alia, that

> Qatar had not complied with the necessary precondition to the existence of jurisdiction of the Council, contained in Article 84 of the Chicago Convention, of first attempting to resolve the disagreement regarding the airspace restrictions … through negotiations prior to submitting its claims to the Council.[129]

Qatar filed its response to the Preliminary Objections on 30 April 2018. On 28 May, in accordance with Article 28 of the Rules for the Settlement of Differences,[130] and despite Qatar's protests, the Council permitted the Respondents to file a Rejoinder.[131] Meanwhile, when addressing the European Parliament's Committee on Transport and Tourism on 15 May, Qatar Airways Group's Chief Executive strongly criticised ICAO for not taking appropriate measures against 'the extraordinary illegal blockade'. HE Mr Akbar Al Baker asserted that 'The extreme violations were carried out without provocation and without a mandate from the UN Security Council or any other international body'.[132] He continued:

> The clear intention of the blockading states was to endanger the economy of the State of Qatar by threatening the livelihood of residents, but the State of Qatar and Qatar Airways responded to protect the nation, the people, the economy and the airline's customers.
>
> With 18 air corridors immediately reduced to just two corridors, elaborate measures were necessary to assure safe operations into and out of Qatar. In the middle of the holy month of Ramadan, the normal flow of goods and basic supplies such as medicine, food and water, was dangerously interrupted.[133]

The ICAO Council heard oral argument on 26 June 2018 and then proceeded to vote on the Preliminary Objections.[134] Those concerning Application (A) were rejected by 23 votes to four, with six abstentions. Those relating to Application (B) were rejected

[127] In accordance with Art 5(3) of the ICAO Rules, the proceedings on the merits were suspended pending the Council's decisions on the Preliminary Objections.

[128] Joint Application (n 117) para 19(i).

[129] ibid, para 19(ii). The Preliminary Objections of Bahrain, Egypt and the UAE in respect of Application (B) were the same but referred to IASTA.

[130] ICAO Doc 7782.

[131] The Rejoinder was filed on 12 June 2018.

[132] *Aviator* (15 May 2018), available at newsroom.aviator.aero/qatar-airways-group-chief-executive-h-e-mr-akbar-al-baker-addresses-the-parliament-of-the-european-union-on-illegal-blockade-and-increasing-eu-investment.

[133] ibid.

[134] Art 52 of the Chicago Convention provides 'Decisions by the Council shall require approval by a majority of its members'.

by 18 votes to two, with five abstentions. In each case, the Council adopted its 'Decision … on the Preliminary Objection' on 29 June 2018.[135]

B. Appeals to the ICJ[136]

Following the rejection of their Preliminary Objections, the Respondents invoked the supervisory jurisdiction of the ICJ. On 4 July 2018, pursuant to Article 84 of the Chicago Convention in conjunction with Articles 36(1) and 37 of the Statute of the Court,[137] Bahrain, Egypt, Saudi Arabia and the UAE filed a Joint Application appealing against the Council's decision on their Preliminary Objections concerning Application (A).[138] On the same day, pursuant to Article II, Section 2, of IASTA in conjunction with Articles 36(1) and 37 of the Statute, Bahrain, Egypt and the UAE submitted a Joint Application appealing against the Council's decision relating to Application (B).[139] Both asserted that in 2013 and 2014, Member States of the Gulf Cooperation Council had concluded the Riyadh Agreements under which Qatar had 'committed to cease supporting, financing or harbouring persons or groups presenting a danger to national security, in particular terrorist groups'.[140] They continued:

> When subsequently Qatar failed to abide by the commitments it had undertaken (and reaffirmed) in the Riyadh Agreements, as well as its other relevant obligations under international law, and after repeated calls upon Qatar to honour its obligations were of no avail, the Applicants adopted a range of measures on 5 June 2017 with the aim of inducing compliance by Qatar. The measures adopted included the airspace restrictions forming the subject of Qatar's Application to the ICAO Council. These measures were intended to be and in fact constitute a legitimate, justified, and proportionate response to Qatar's breaches of its international obligations and are lawful countermeasures authorized by general international law.[141]

The Applicants advanced three grounds of appeal. Under the first, they argued that the decisions of the ICAO Council were 'manifestly flawed and in violation of fundamental principles of due process and the right to be heard'. Under the second and third grounds, they claimed that 'the ICAO Council [had] erred in fact and in law'.[142] They requested

[135] See the two Joint Applications (n 117 paras 24–25 and n 126 paras 25–26). In both cases the respondents complained that despite their oral intervention to clarify that there were two separate Preliminary Objections, the Council Decision had referred to a single 'Preliminary Objection' and not given any reasons for the rejection.

[136] Besides the two cases discussed here, on 11 June 2018 Qatar instituted proceedings against the UAE in the ICJ alleging violations of the International Convention on the Elimination of All Forms of Racial Discrimination 1965. On 4 February 2021, however, by 11 votes to six, the Court upheld the UAE's first preliminary objection and found that it had no jurisdiction to entertain Qatar's Application: www.icj-cij.org/public/files/case-related/172/172-20210204-JUD-01-00-EN.pdf. Qatar also challenged the embargo at the WTO. See J Fahner, 'Qatar under Siege: Chances for an Article XXI Case?' *EJIL: Talk!* (9 January 2018), available at www.ejiltalk.org/qatar-under-siege-chances-for-an-article-xxi-case.

[137] Art 36(1) provides 'The jurisdiction of the Court comprises all cases which the parties refer to it and all matters specially provided for in the Charter of the United Nations or in treaties or conventions in force'. Art 37 effects a transfer of jurisdiction from the PCIJ to the ICJ.

[138] n 117.

[139] n 126.

[140] Joint Applications (n 117 para 8 and n 126 para 9).

[141] ibid, paras 9 and 10 respectively.

[142] ibid, paras 28–31 and 29–32 respectively.

the Court to adjudge and declare that the decisions reflected 'a manifest failure to act judicially … and a manifest lack of due process'; that the Council was 'not competent to adjudicate upon the disagreement'; and that the decisions of the Council were 'null and void and without effect'.[143]

C. Some Reflections on the Outcome of the Appeals

The ICJ gave judgment in the two cases on 14 July 2020.[144] It unanimously rejected the appeals from the decisions of the ICAO Council and, by 15 votes to one, held that the Council had jurisdiction to entertain Qatar's application and that the latter was admissible. It is instructive to consider this outcome in the light of the ICJ's judgment in *India v Pakistan* nearly 50 years earlier, the first appeal to be submitted to the Court against a decision of the ICAO Council.[145]

In February 1971, following a hijacking incident involving the diversion of an Indian aircraft to Pakistan, India suspended overflights of its territory by Pakistan's civil aircraft. Pakistan took the view that this was in breach of the Chicago Convention and IASTA and complained to the ICAO Council. India raised preliminary objections to the Council's jurisdiction, but these were rejected and India appealed to the ICJ. During the written and oral proceedings, Pakistan contended, inter alia, that the Court was not competent to hear the appeal. The Court emphasised that its sole function was to determine 'the purely jurisdictional issue' referred to it, namely the competence of the Council to hear and determine the case submitted by Pakistan.[146] In its judgment of 18 August 1972, the ICJ found that it was competent to hear India's appeal. It further decided that the Council was competent to deal with both the Application and the Complaint of which it had been seised by Pakistan, and accordingly dismissed India's appeal.[147] Certain key aspects of the recent cases will now be considered briefly with reference to that judgment.

The scope of the jurisdictional clauses: Although Qatar expressly recognised the appellants' right to appeal the Council's decision on jurisdiction,[148] the Court noted that Article 84 does not specify whether only final decisions of the Council on the merits of disputes are subject to appeal.[149] It held that it had settled that issue in *India v Pakistan*.[150]

[143] ibid, paras 32–33 respectively.

[144] *Appeal relating to the Jurisdiction of the ICAO Council under Article 84 of the Convention on International Civil Aviation (Bahrain, Egypt, Saudi Arabia and United Arab Emirates v Qatar)*, available at www.icj-cij.org/public/files/case-related/173/173-20200714-JUD-01-00-EN.pdf; *Appeal relating to the Jurisdiction of the ICAO Council under Article II, Section 2, of the 1944 International Air Services Transit Agreement (Bahrain, Egypt and United Arab Emirates v Qatar)*, available at www.icj-cij.org/public/files/case-related/174/174-20200714-JUD-01-00-EN.pdf.

[145] ICJ Reports 1972 (n 71).

[146] ibid, para 11.

[147] By 14 votes to two. The dispute was eventually settled through direct negotiations. See Weber (n 49) 29. See further M Papadaki, 'Compromissory Clauses as the Gatekeepers of the Law to be "Used" in the ICJ and the PCIJ' (2014) 5 *Journal of International Dispute Settlement* 560, 582–83.

[148] n 144, para 32 of both judgments.

[149] ibid, para 30.

[150] ibid.

Rejecting Pakistan's objection that the clauses 'only allow of an appeal to the Court from a decision of the Council on the merits of the dispute referred to it, and not from a decision concerning the Council's jurisdiction to entertain the reference',[151] the Court had explained that 'it would be contrary to accepted standards of the good administration of justice to allow an international organ to examine and discuss the merits of a dispute when its competence to do so was not only undermined but actively challenged'.[152] It had concluded that 'from the standpoint of the supervision by the Court of the validity of the Council's acts, there is no ground for distinguishing between supervision as to jurisdiction, and supervision as to merits'.[153] Accordingly, the Court was satisfied that it had jurisdiction to entertain the recent appeals.[154]

The meaning of 'disagreement ... relating to the interpretation or application of [the] Convention', and whether the dispute would require the Council to determine issues falling outside its jurisdiction: In *India v Pakistan*, noting that specific provisions of the Treaties (especially Article 5 of the Chicago Convention and Article I, Section 1, of IASTA) were cited by Pakistan as having been infringed by India's denial of overflight rights, the Court concluded that there was a 'disagreement' relating to the application of the Treaties. The case presented by Pakistan to the ICAO Council 'was essentially a charge of breaches of the Treaties, and in order to determine these, the Council would inevitably be obliged to interpret and apply the Treaties, and thus to deal with matters unquestionably within its jurisdiction'.[155] The same was true of Qatar's complaints to the Council. For example, in its memorial Qatar had identified several provisions of the Chicago Convention with which, in its view, the measures taken by the appellants were not in conformity.[156] The Court added that the fact that this disagreement between the parties about the interpretation or application of the Convention had arisen in a broader political context did not deprive the ICAO Council of jurisdiction.[157]

The Court also rejected the argument that since the appellants had characterised the restrictions imposed on Qatar-registered aircraft as lawful countermeasures, the Council had no jurisdiction to hear Qatar's claims.[158] It further held that 'the integrity of the Council's dispute settlement function would not be affected if the Council examined issues outside matters of civil aviation for the exclusive purpose of deciding a dispute which falls within its jurisdiction under Article 84'.[159] The appellants had argued that in order to rule on the lawfulness of their airspace restrictions as countermeasures, the Council would have to rule on Qatar's compliance with obligations under international law entirely unrelated to, and outwith, the Chicago Convention and IASTA.[160] The Court had been faced with a similar argument in *India v Pakistan*. India had contended

[151] ICJ Reports 1972 (n 71) para 14.
[152] ibid, para 18(e).
[153] ibid, para 26.
[154] n 144, para 33 of both judgments.
[155] ICJ Reports 1972 (n 71) para 36.
[156] In particular Arts 2, 3*bis*, 4, 5, 6, 9, 37 and 89: n 144, para 47 of the first judgment.
[157] ibid, para 48 of both judgments.
[158] ibid, para 49. For further discussion of whether the Gulf airspace restrictions constitute countermeasures, see below.
[159] ibid, para 61 of the first judgment. In the same paragraph of the second judgment, the Court referred to Art II, Section 2, of IASTA. *cf* the Declaration of Judge Gevorgian.
[160] See paras 19(1) and 20(1) of the Joint Applications (nn 117 and 126 respectively).

that in suspending overflights by Pakistan, it was not invoking a right afforded by the Treaties but acting outside them on the basis of a general principle of international law, and therefore 'the Council, whose jurisdiction was derived from the Treaties, and which was entitled to deal only with matters arising under them, must be incompetent'.[161] The Court firmly rejected that argument:

> The point is not that these contentions are necessarily wrong but that their validity has not yet been determined. Since therefore the Parties are in disagreement as to whether the Treaties ever were (validly) suspended or replaced by something else; ... and as to whether India's action in relation to Pakistan overflights was such as not to involve the Treaties, but to be justifiable *aliter et aliunde*: – these very questions are in issue before the Council, and no conclusions as to jurisdiction can be drawn from them, at least at this stage, so as to exclude *ipso facto* and *a priori* the competence of the Council.[162]

The Court was, and clearly remains, unwilling to countenance 'a wholesale nullification of the practical value of jurisdictional clauses'.[163]

The implications of the alleged procedural irregularities: Here too the 1972 judgment favoured Qatar. India had argued that regardless of the correctness in law of the Council's decision assuming jurisdiction, it was vitiated by various procedural irregularities and should therefore be declared null and void. The contention was that but for those alleged irregularities, the result before the Council would or might have been different. Consequently, if the Court endorsed India's view as to the existence of these procedural irregularities, it should refrain from pronouncing on the question of the Council's jurisdiction, declare the latter's decision null and void, and send the case back to it for re-decision under a correct procedure.[164] However, the Court did not deem it necessary or even appropriate to go into this matter, noting that its task was to give a ruling as to whether the Council had jurisdiction in the case. This was 'an objective question of law, the answer to which cannot depend on what occurred before the Council'.[165] Since the Court had held that the Council did have jurisdiction, then, if there were in fact procedural irregularities, the position would be that the Council had reached the right conclusion in the wrong way. Nevertheless it would have reached the right conclusion. If, on the other hand, the Court had held that there was no jurisdiction, then, even in the absence of any irregularities, the Council's decision to assume it would have been reversed.[166]

In the recent cases, the appellants alleged that there had been a manifest lack of due process before the ICAO Council and that the Council lacked jurisdiction because Qatar had failed to meet the negotiation precondition in Article 84. Regarding the first of those claims, the Court recalled its 1972 judgment in which it had declared that it 'had no need to examine whether a decision of the Council that was legally correct should nevertheless be annulled because of procedural irregularities'.[167] In any event,

[161] ICJ Reports 1972 (n 71) para 31.
[162] ibid.
[163] ibid, para 32.
[164] ibid, para 44.
[165] ibid, para 45.
[166] ibid.
[167] n 144, para 122 of the first judgment and para 123 of the second.

the Court considered that 'the procedures followed by the Council did not prejudice in any fundamental way the requirements of a just procedure'.[168] As for the second claim, the Court held that Qatar had made a genuine attempt within ICAO to settle by negotiation its disagreement with the appellants concerning the interpretation and application of the Chicago Convention and of IASTA; and that, when it filed its applications before the Council, there was no reasonable probability of a negotiated settlement.[169]

In the light of its judgment in *India v Pakistan*, it was always likely that the Court would decide that it was competent to hear the recent appeals and that the ICAO Council was competent to deal with the complaints brought by Qatar. Whether the Council would be able to resolve such a politically charged dispute remains to be seen, however.[170]

D. Do the Airspace Restrictions Constitute Countermeasures?

On the face of it, the airspace restrictions imposed on Qatar-registered aircraft are incompatible with the Chicago Convention and IASTA, as well as with UNCLOS and customary international law. The 'permission or authorisation' required by such aircraft to overfly the other states' territories under Article 6 of the Chicago Convention is satisfied by the fact that Qatar, Bahrain, Egypt and the UAE are all parties to IASTA,[171] and Qatar and Saudi Arabia have a bilateral ASA.[172] The restrictions violate Article 1, Section 1(1) of IASTA and cannot be based on Article 9 of the Chicago Convention since they do not meet its requirements.[173] They also appear to breach the Agreement between Qatar and Saudi Arabia.[174] Insofar as they apply to international airspace, moreover, the restrictions constitute an unreasonable interference with the freedom of overflight under UNCLOS and customary international law,[175] even though this was eventually mitigated by the action taken in cooperation with ICAO's regional office in Cairo to promote safety and relieve pressure on routes over international waters.[176]

[168] ibid, paras 123 and 124 respectively. *cf* para 18 of the separate opinion of Judge *Ad Hoc* Berman, who regretted that the Court had not subjected to 'more nuanced attention' the 'cavalier approach' to due process considerations in its 1972 judgment.

[169] ibid, paras 92 and 96, and paras 93 and 97 respectively. The ICJ also found that the Council had not erred in rejecting the claim that Qatar's application was inadmissible for failing to comply with Art 2(g) of the ICAO Rules for the Settlement of Differences: ibid, paras 103–05 and paras 104–06 respectively.

[170] See n 190. A week after the ICJ delivered its judgments, Qatar Airways announced that it would seek at least $5bn in compensation from Bahrain, Egypt, Saudi Arabia and the UAE for the airspace restrictions, which had necessitated longer, costlier routes. See *Middle East Eye* (22 July 2020), available at www.middleeasteye.net/news/qatar-blockade-airways-seeks-compensation-airspace-closure.

[171] See Shawcross and Beaumont (n 24) Vol 2, Appendix A. None of those States has invoked Art III of IASTA which provides for denunciation of the Agreement on one year's notice.

[172] n 75.

[173] See above. In particular, they discriminate against Qatar-registered aircraft.

[174] Carpanelli observes that no restriction or exception is envisaged in that Agreement, which subjects its termination to one year's written notice by either of the contracting States: 'To Overfly, or not to Overfly …?' Part I (2017).

[175] See above. Bahrain, Egypt, Qatar and Saudi Arabia are all parties to UNCLOS. Although the UAE is only a signatory, it is bound by the equivalent customary rules.

[176] See above, text at n 120.

Furthermore, there do not appear to be any grounds for asserting a material breach by Qatar of its Chicago Convention, IASTA or ASA obligations, which would have entitled Saudi Arabia and the other states to terminate those treaties or suspend their operation.[177]

However, Saudi Arabia and its partners have sought to justify the restrictions as countermeasures in response to what they see as Qatar's breach of the Riyadh Agreements. As the ILC explains, 'Countermeasures are a feature of a decentralized system by which injured States may seek to vindicate their rights and to restore the legal relationship with the responsible State which has been ruptured by the internationally wrongful act'.[178] The object is to induce compliance. In this regard, it will be recalled that in his statement to the UN General Assembly in September 2017, Saudi Arabia's Minister for Foreign Affairs said that 'the position taken by the four States was meant to demand that Qatar follow the principles of international law in fighting terrorism'.[179] Nevertheless, the restrictions imposed on Qatar-registered aircraft raise several issues under the law on countermeasures, particularly in terms of proportionality which is the focus here.

Assuming for the sake of argument that Qatar has violated the Riyadh Agreements, it would appear that Saudi Arabia and its partners can each claim to have been 'injured' by the breach. Referring to Article 42(a) of ARSIWA, which provides that a state is entitled as an injured state to invoke the responsibility of another state if the obligation breached is owed to that state individually, Carpanelli observes:

> As to States parties to the Riyadh Agreements, no problem seems to arise in the event that evidence was submitted stating that Qatar had interfered with their internal affairs, as, in that case, the breach would relate to an obligation owed to them 'individually'.[180]

In any event, though, the legality of the Saudi-led response is called into question when proportionality is considered. Article 51 of ARSIWA provides 'Countermeasures must be commensurate with the injury suffered, taking into account the gravity of the internationally wrongful act and the rights in question'. That principle was emphasised by the ICJ in the *Gabčíkovo-Nagymaros Project* case.[181] However, judging proportionality is not an exact science. In the *Air Services Agreement* case,[182] an arbitral tribunal had to consider whether a US countermeasure which suspended Air France flights to Los Angeles was in proportion to France's refusal to allow a change of gauge (ie a change of aircraft while retaining the same flight number) on Pan Am flights from the west coast of the US to Paris via London.[183] After holding by a majority that a change of gauge in

[177] See Art 60 of the Vienna Convention on the Law of Treaties 1969, 1155 UNTS 331; and Carpanelli, 'To Overfly, or not to Overfly …?' Part II (2017).

[178] Commentary on ARSIWA, Pt 3, Ch II, 'Countermeasures', para 1, *YBILC*, 2001, Vol II, 128. For an extensive critique of countermeasures, see Judge Cançado Trindade's separate opinion in the recent *Appeals relating to the Jurisdiction of the ICAO Council* (n 144).

[179] Above, n 124.

[180] Carpanelli (n 14). Art 46 of ARSIWA provides that where several states are injured by the same internationally wrongful act, each injured state may separately invoke the responsibility of the state which has committed that act.

[181] *Hungary v Slovakia*, ICJ Reports 1997, 7, paras 83–85.

[182] *Case Concerning the Air Services Agreement of 27 March 1946 (United States v France)*, International Law Reports, Vol 54, 304.

[183] The French authorities rejected the proposed change of aircraft in London from a Boeing 747 to a smaller Boeing 727 on the grounds that it was inconsistent with the 1946 ASA between the USA and France.

London was permitted as long as a continuous service was maintained and the change did not mean a separate service,[184] the tribunal unanimously held that the US measures satisfied the principle of proportionality:

> It has been observed, generally, that judging the 'proportionality' of counter-measures is not an easy task and can at best be accomplished by approximation. In the Tribunal's view, it is essential, in a dispute between States, to take into account not only the injuries suffered by the companies concerned but also the importance of the questions of principle arising from the alleged breach. The Tribunal thinks that it will not suffice, in the present case, to compare the losses suffered by Pan Am on account of the suspension of the projected services with the losses which the French companies would have suffered as a result of the counter-measures; it will also be necessary to take into account the importance of the positions of principle which were taken when the French authorities prohibited changes of gauge in third countries. If the importance of the issue is viewed within the framework of the general air transport policy adopted by the United States Government and implemented by the conclusion of a large number of international agreements with countries other than France, the measures taken by the United States do not appear to be clearly disproportionate when compared to those taken by France. Neither Party has provided the Tribunal with evidence that would be sufficient to affirm or reject the existence of proportionality in these terms, and the Tribunal must be satisfied with a very approximative appreciation.[185]

Given the questions of principle at stake, there is reason to doubt the proportionality of the Saudi-led response to Qatar's alleged breach of the Riyadh Agreements. In the first place, as Carpanelli observes,

> it may be difficult for *multilateral* countermeasures to be proportionate ... This consideration appears particularly true in the case at hand, where the closure of airspace is only one of a set of measures taken against Qatar and where its contextual implementation by a plurality of States has translated into a sort of 'air blockade'.[186]

What must also be taken into account, however, is the fact that the freedom of aviation for Qatar-registered aircraft in international airspace has been significantly curtailed by the unilateral usurpation of a shared resource. As explained above, FIR delineation reflects operational and technical needs rather than national boundaries, and the international airspace within a coastal state's FIR is not that state's to appropriate and control as if it were its own sovereign airspace. To the extent that they apply beyond the limits of sovereign airspace, therefore, the unilateral, discriminatory restrictions imposed by Saudi Arabia and its partners are incompatible with their obligations of stewardship of that international airspace implied by Article 12 of the Chicago Convention and Article 87(1)(b) of UNCLOS and its customary equivalent.[187] There are clear parallels with the *Gabčíkovo-Nagymaros Project* case, where the ICJ held that

> Czechoslovakia, *by unilaterally assuming control of a shared resource* and thereby depriving Hungary of its right to an equitable and reasonable share of the natural resources of the

[184] n 182, paras 43–65.
[185] ibid, para 83.
[186] Carpanelli (n 14) citing A Tzanakopoulos, 'State Reactions to Illegal Sanctions' in M Happold and P Eden (eds), *Economic Sanctions and International Law* (Hart Publishing, 2016) 71.
[187] Stewardship of international airspace within FIRs is also implied by Arts 1 and 2 of the Chicago Convention which determine the horizontal extent of national sovereignty.

> Danube – with the continuing effects of the diversion of these waters on the ecology of the riparian area of the Szigetköz – had failed to respect the proportionality which is required by international law.[188]

Although the mitigation measures taken after some two months, namely the allocation of emergency corridors to Qatar-registered aircraft and the action in cooperation with ICAO's regional office in Cairo to promote safety and relieve pressure on routes over international waters, will have gone some way towards remedying breaches of the stewardship obligations and of the proportionality principle, those breaches should not have occurred in the first place.

VI. Conclusion

This chapter has considered the implications for the freedom of aviation under international law when a state or a group of states imposes sanctions against another state, and the remedies available to the latter. It has outlined the legal framework of the freedom of aviation and the Freedoms of the Air with particular reference to the Chicago Convention, UNCLOS, IASTA and bilateral Air Services Agreements. In so doing it has illustrated some of the implications of a horizontal, decentralised international legal system.[189] The EU saw Russia's conduct in Ukraine as an illegal act and imposed sanctions, whereas Russia regarded the EU's sanctions as an illegal act and threatened countermeasures. If Russia had introduced overflight restrictions, they would have been costly and probably futile. Similarly, Qatar views the Saudi-led airspace restrictions as a breach of international law, whereas its Gulf neighbours regard them as countermeasures justified by what they see as Qatar's violation of the Riyadh Agreements. Despite their eventual mitigation, those restrictions have had serious implications for the freedom of aviation in the Gulf. Thanks to the dispute settlement provisions of the Chicago Convention and IASTA, however, there has been intervention by ICAO and, exercising its important supervisory role, the ICJ. This underlines the importance of the jurisdictional clauses in those treaties. Notwithstanding any limitations the Council may have as an adjudicatory tribunal, we should not underestimate the operational contributions which it and ICAO's Cairo office have made towards restoring the freedom of aviation over the region's international waters.

In that regard, whether or not a Qatari FIR is established to resolve the FIR delimitation anomaly in the Gulf and give Qatar broader operational control of the maritime airspace adjacent to its territory,[190] there is a fundamental principle at stake. Where a

[188] n 181, para 85 (emphasis added). The Court cited the PCIJ's judgment in the *River Oder* case, PCIJ, Series A, No 23 (1929). See n 191.

[189] R Higgins, *Problems & Process: International Law and How We Use It* (Oxford University Press, 2004) 1.

[190] On 3 September 2020, Bahrain announced that it would allow all flights to and from the UAE, including Israel flights, to use Bahrain's airspace. See 'New Bahrain policy to allow flights between Israel and UAE to cross its airspace' *Reuters* (3 September 2020), available at www.reuters.com/article/us-israel-emirates-bahrain-flights/new-bahrain-policy-to-allow-flights-between-israel-and-uae-to-cross-its-airspace-idUSKBN25U304. The announcement followed a similar one by Saudi Arabia and came 12 days before Bahrain and the UAE signed agreements normalising their relations with Israel. The restrictions for Qatar-registered aircraft remained in place. However, on 4 January 2021 Saudi Arabia agreed to reopen its land and sea borders and

coastal state provides air traffic services in an FIR over international waters on behalf of ICAO for the benefit of the international community, it is exercising stewardship of a shared resource. Subject only to genuine safety considerations, the community of interest in that airspace forms the basis of a common legal right.[191] No state can treat that international airspace, which like the high seas is *res communis omnium*,[192] as if it were under its 'complete and exclusive sovereignty'. In the absence of circumstances justifying the right of self-defence under Article 51 of the UN Charter, therefore, it is submitted that UN Security Council authorisation is required for the imposition of overflight restrictions in such airspace.[193] But it seems fitting to end by emphasising an even more important principle. The inconvenience to Qatar-registered aircraft as a result of the Saudi-led airspace restrictions is overshadowed by the risks caused by US sanctions to the safety of civil aviation in Iran and the lives of its users.[194] The freedom of aviation means little if safety is compromised.

airspace to Qatar ahead of a GCC summit at which the five states agreed to set aside their differences. See 'Qatar crisis: Saudi Arabia and allies restore diplomatic ties with emirate' *BBC* (5 January 2021), available at www.bbc.co.uk/news/world-middle-east-55538792.

[191] *cf* the following passage from the PCIJ's judgment with regard to navigation on the River Oder (n 188), which the ICJ cited in the *Gabčíkovo-Nagymaros Project* case (n 181): 'This community of interest in a navigable river becomes the basis of a common legal right, the essential features of which are the perfect equality of all riparian States in the user of the whole course of the river and the exclusion of any preferential privilege of any one riparian State in relation to the others'.

[192] Belonging to everyone. See J Kish, *The Law of International Spaces* (Sijthoff, 1973) 61–62 and 66–67.

[193] Under Ch VII of the UN Charter, if the Security Council has determined the existence of any threat to the peace, breach of the peace or act of aggression, the non-military measures it may authorise include 'complete or partial interruption of economic relations and of rail, sea, *air*, postal, telegraphic, radio and other means of communication, and the severance of diplomatic relations' (Art 41, emphasis added).

[194] *cf* the US Secretary of State's assertion that the renewed sanctions would not hurt ordinary Iranian people. See E Pilkington, 'Mike Pompeo insists US sanctions will not hurt ordinary people' *The Guardian* (4 November 2018), available at www.theguardian.com/world/2018/nov/04/pompeo-trump-us-sanctions-oil-iran-iranian-people.

5

The Impact of Unilateral Sanctions on Regional Integration Treaties with Special Reference to the Gulf Cooperation Council

ALI ABUSEDRA

I. Introduction

The purpose of this chapter is to consider the effects of unilateral sanctions on regional economic integration treaties, with special reference to the Charter of the Gulf Cooperation Council (GCC) and other treaties concerning economic cooperation among the Gulf countries. There are several regional economic integration and cooperation agreements that have been concluded between states globally. Many of these treaties create regional economic and political organisations to foster close cooperation between the states which are parties to the constituent agreements of such organisations. Examples are the European Union (EU), the North American Free Trade Agreement (NAFTA), the Association of Southeast Asian Nations (ASEAN) and the Gulf Cooperation Council (GCC). However, what happens to the obligations under these treaties when one Member State, or group of states, decide to impose unilateral sanctions against another member of the organisation for an alleged breach of its obligations under international law? What impact do such sanctions have on the integrity of such regional economic and political cooperation organisations themselves? These are the questions that this chapter seeks to examine, with particular reference to the GCC treaties. As will be discussed, the GCC has generally been considered a success story for economic integration among its participating Arab countries. However, recent political developments have resulted in the existence of the GCC as a body which fosters economic integration now being called into question.

In 2017, three Member States of the GCC, namely Saudi Arabia, Bahrain and the United Arab Emirates, as well as Egypt, imposed unilateral sanctions on Qatar, bringing diplomatic and economic ties to a halt, while also enforcing a blockade of land, sea and air spaces against Qatar. This the first instance that a group of Gulf countries have implemented unilateral sanctions against a fellow GCC country. The justification for these actions were founded on allegations by the sanctioning countries that Qatar was a supporter of terrorism, as demonstrated by their purported violation of a series of agreements in 2013 and 2014, known as the 'Riyadh Agreements'.[1] In this regard, the effects of the sanctions imposed on Qatar and whether the measures are justifiable in international law will also be discussed in this chapter. The chapter will begin by examining the historical background leading to the establishment of the GCC and the various treaties concluded by the GCC countries to promote closer economic cooperation among them. It will then consider the events leading to sanctions being imposed on Qatar and discuss the legality of such sanctions under international law and the law on regional economic cooperation among the GCC countries. In conclusion, this chapter will suggest that unilateral sanctions against another country tends to undermine the principle of sovereign equality of states and can create a situation where human rights may be at risk of being violated due adverse consequences arising from the sanctioning mechanisms. It will further suggest that unilateral sanctions also have the effect of posing a threat to regional norms of cooperation, peaceful existence and integration in situations where countries agree to become part of a system which facilitates such practice.

II. Background to the Gulf Cooperation Council

The GCC is an international organisation established in 1981 between six Gulf countries, namely Bahrain,[2] the United Arab Emirates (UAE), Kuwait, Oman, Qatar and the Kingdom of Saudi Arabia. According to the GCC Supreme Council, the organisation was established to foster and manage cooperation between GCC Member States, and to serve their common interests.[3] From 1820 to 1971, the British held hegemony over the Persian Gulf, with Onley suggesting that the relationship was largely mutually beneficial.[4] British military protection and dispute arbitration proved to be beneficial for Sheikhs and tribal leaders, as external threats and disputes were a common occurrence. Consequently, Britain held de facto responsibility for decision-making on strategic issues, while benefiting from the receipt of substantial royalties from trade. Most of the GCC Member States acquired independence in 1971 following the departure of the British from the Persian Gulf, with each country establishing their unique state institutions. For instance, Saudi Arabia was established on strong religious foundations, with the political decision-making process being inseparable from the application of religious doctrines intended to govern its citizens, while Kuwait has implemented a liberal

[1] Appeal Relating to the Jurisdiction of the ICAO Council Under Article 84 of the Convention on International Civil Aviation (*Bahrain, Egypt, Saudi Arabia, and United Arab Emirates v Qatar*) [The Riyadh Agreements], Available online at www.icj-cij.org/en/case/173.

[2] Now the Kingdom of Bahrain.

[3] The Supreme Council, First Meeting (1981).

[4] J Onley, 'Britain and the Gulf Shaikhdoms, 1820–1971: The Politics of Protection' (2009) CIRS Occasional Papers No 4.

trade policy, particularly in the oil sector, although labour relation rules, and access to citizenship for non-natives prove to be rigid.[5]

The creation of the GCC was driven by the unprecedented developments which proved a threat to regional security, such as the Iranian Revolution of 1979, the Soviet invasion of Afghanistan, which also took place in 1979, and the Iran–Iraq war of the 1980s.[6] As a consequence, the founding Member States acknowledged that cooperation was in the best interest of their collective national security.[7] It has been argued that these events forced Member States 'to create the GCC too abruptly, leaving it with an unclear purpose (Is it an economic organization or a security organization or both?) and with processes that lacked efficacy in matters of co-operation and dispute settlement'"[8] Following inconclusive talks and differing visions on the form that a regional organisation should adopt, the GCC came into being within a matter of months in early 1981, being formally launched in Abu Dhabi at a summit on 25 May 1981. Although the main reason for Gulf integration was the creation of a security community, it was evident from an early stage that economic and technical collaboration were also areas of consideration. Cooperation in the area of security has been evident in the establishment of the Peninsula Shield Force (PSF) in 1984; the Joint Defence Agreement in December 2000, with a Joint Defence Council and a Military Committee responsible for oversight; and a Unified Military Command in 2013. By means of these series of security and defence agreements, the GCC was also able to establish a security community among its Member States which aided in building a comprehensive regional security structure. The founding Charter of the GCC states that it was formed to strengthen relations among its Member States and to promote cooperation among their citizens.[9] Linked to this intention was the basic objectives listed in Article 4 of the GCC Charter, which are, to deepen and strengthen existing relations and effect coordination, integration and interconnection between Member States in all fields in order to achieve unity between them.[10] Article 9 of the GCC Charter addresses governance and institution building through the establishment of the main GCC governing bodies. These included the highest decision-making body known as the Supreme Council; an ad hoc Commission for Settlement of Dispute; a Ministerial Council, and the Secretariat General. Article 10 addresses the decision-making and voting process for the Supreme Council, whereby each of the six members are granted one vote. This article also provides that Supreme Council resolutions are to be unanimous in substantive matters, whereas procedural matters are decided by majority vote.

From its inception, the states comprising the GCC have entered into several common joint projects and agreements. For example, economic agreements include the

[5] Turki Al-hamad, 'Will the Gulf Monarchies Work Together?' [1997] 4 Middle East Quarterly 47–53.

[6] AM Altamimi, 'An Appraisal of the Gulf Cooperation Council's Mechanisms for Co-operation and the Settlement of Disputes' (2020) *Asian Journal of International Law* 1, 4.

[7] ibid.

[8] ibid.

[9] 1288 UNTS 151.

[10] ibid.

1981 Unified Economic Agreement, the 2001 Economic Agreement, the Custom Union Agreement in 2003 and the Common Market Agreement in 2008. It was also the intention of the GCC to implement a monetary union and single currency by 2010, but this was delayed. The GCC Common Market established a single market with the freedom of movement of goods, capital and people, while the Customs Union (CU) 'provided an appropriate platform for collective free trade negotiations and strategic dialogues with global partners'.[11] Furthermore, the GCC initiated common infrastructure projects such as a power grid connectivity system and a common rail network. Both individually and collectively, GCC states have been successful in maintaining broad ranging economic, defence and security cooperation with international partners, such as the US, the EU, NATO, China and India. These agreements have been helpful in facilitating global economic cooperation and integration, while assisting with the strengthening of security frameworks. The GCC has also had measured levels of success in acting collectively at regional and international levels, such as at the United Nations (UN), the Arab League, and the Organisation of Islamic Cooperation (OIC). The GCC has therefore demonstrated its ability to strengthen integration and represent Member States in the international arena, despite internal delays and occasional disagreements.

One of the main aims of the GCC Charter is the promotion of economic growth in the region by means of greater integration of the six economies. GCC Member States are among some of the most prosperous economies in the world, having gained their wealth from oil and gas exports. Member States display per capita incomes which are comparable to advanced industrialised countries, although they face several challenges owing to their heavy reliance on a non-renewable fossil fuel.[12] These include the prospect of future shortfalls in income as a result of diminishing oil reserves and increasing competition from alternative energy sources; risks associated with poor diversification resulting from a historical dependence on the oil industry; and a comparatively high unemployment rate, mostly concentrated amongst the younger population, particularly women.[13] The six-member countries have operated with very similar economic and social structures, which, if diversified, do not need to depend on nominal exchange rates during times of systemic shocks and can therefore increase welfare by engaging in a monetary union.[14] There is also cultural and traditional unity amongst the members of the GCC. Cooperation among GCC members is facilitated by their link to a common Arabic cultural religion, heritage, ethnicity and language. The countries share similar societal structures that allow social and economic integration across borders. The GCC's unity has been important for not only ensuring outward economic growth and regional stability, but also securing internal assurances and partnerships. GCC unity essentially contributes towards regional unity and its members' internal political stability, self-defence and economic growth. GCC unity also ensures that members can depend

[11] A Baabood, 'The Future of the GCC Amid the Gulf Divide' in A Krieg (ed), *Security and Defense Structures in Arab Gulf States: The Anatomy of a Crisis* (Palgrave Macmillan, 2019) 164.

[12] D Chadee, B Roxas and T Rogmans, *Prospects and Challenges of Free Trade Agreements: Markets – Unlocking Business Opportunities in the Gulf Cooperation Council (GCC)* (Palgrave, 2015), 94.

[13] ibid.

[14] S Pattanaik, 'How closely the GCC approximates an optimum currency area?' [2007] 22 *Journal of Economic Integration* 573–97.

on the organisation to safeguard their interests in the face of international pressure. Harmony within the GCC would therefore facilitate members being able to assist each other in resolving systemic issues and defend members from negative influence that can affect the integrity of a member.

Approximately 40 rules have been established with the intention to standardise the economic rules and regulations of GCC Member States, with some of these instruments being binding, although the majority of them are guiding. From this, certain GCC institutions have been established such as the Gulf Investment Corporation, the Commercial Arbitration Centre, the Standardization Authority and the Patent Office. The main aim behind the establishment of the GCC CU was to liberalise trade among its Member States and therefore allow the free movement of goods, whether national or foreign, without any tariff or non-tariff barriers.[15] Notwithstanding the delay in its launch, 'the GCC CU is, from a legal perspective, one of the most sophisticated CUs anywhere'.[16] According to Puig and Al-Haddab, this sophistication 'is due to the fact that most of its rules and principles were agreed many years earlier and so now have the benefit of maturity'.[17] The RTA mechanisms established within the GCC appears to have encouraged intra-regional trade amongst Member States, with one study indicating that the annual growth of such trade has exceeded 20 per cent.[18]

III. The Growth of Free Trade Agreements and Economic Integration in the GCC

In order to understand the impact of the unilateral sanctions placed on Qatar in the context of the GCC and the effects on its agreements which address regional economic cooperation, it is necessary to consider the function of Regional Trade Agreements (RTAs). Developments over the past two decades have indicated an increase in the conclusion of RTAs.[19] As Puig and Al-Haddab explain:

> Some RTAs are multilateral in form and so involve several countries, but most take a strictly bilateral form. Most RTAs function within a single region while others function across several regions. Some RTAs entail complete economic integration while others merely establish a preferential trade area. Individual features aside, RTAs are, undeniably, a prominent phenomenon of the current multilateral trading system.[20]

The purpose of RTAs, whether in in the form of a Customs Union (CU) or a Free Trade Area (FTA), tends to be directed at removing trade barriers among parties. The establishment of a regional common market is often the outcome of the conclusion

[15] G Vilatta Puig and B Al-Haddab, 'The Constitutionalisation of Free Trade in the Gulf Cooperation Council' [2011] 25 *Arab Law Quarterly*, 311–24, 316.

[16] ibid.

[17] ibid, 316.

[18] The Cooperation Council for the Arab States of the Gulf – Secretariat General, The Cooperation Council for the Arab States in its Third Decade: Integration and Unity (GCC Secretariat General Information Centre, 2009).

[19] Puig and Al-Haddab, 'The Constitutionalisation of Free Trade' [2011] 312.

[20] ibid.

of RTAs. In this regard, the GCC 'is one of the oldest and most dynamic RTAs worldwide'.[21] Its origins are rooted in a movement to liberalise intra-regional trade in the Arabian Peninsula from the early 1980s, following which it evolved into a CU in 2003 with a Common External Tariff.[22]

RTAs are therefore indicative of economic integration, which in itself comprises several stages. According to Bhala, the process commences with the formation of a FTA, which is essentially 'an arrangement between two or more countries removing all, or substantially all, barriers to trade between or among them'.[23] The second stage of economic integration is often signaled by members agreeing to remove most, or all barriers to internal trade. Members of the CU would also agree to a Common External Tariff (CET) by which a harmonised system is established with the purpose of setting out trade barriers on the same categories of products, thereby creating unified customs laws and procedures.[24] The third stage is the establishment of a common market where Member States provide a guarantee of the free movement of goods, labour, capital and services across the market, with the imposition of a CET on imports from other states.[25] The fourth stage is usually defined by the establishment of a monetary union, and the agreement to institute a central monetary authority which serves the function of formulating and determining the monetary policies of member states.[26] The fifth and final stage of economic integration is 'an economic union where members unite trade in goods and services, adopt a CET, and guarantee the free movement of capital and labour"[27] while also agreeing to harmonise domestic policies and act as a single entity externally.

Early steps towards economic integration were taken by GCC states from the early 1980s when barriers to free movement of capital, goods, labour and nationals were removed, and national preferential treatment was granted to corporations and individuals. Common external tariffs were imposed in 2003 under the umbrella of a CU with Article 1 of the Economic Agreement stating that the CU sets the framework for trade between the GCC Member States. Under this provision, the GCC CU is required to embrace a CET, common customs regulations and procedures, as well as a single-entry point for the collection of customs duties. Furthermore, there exists the requirement to eliminate all tariff and non-tariff barriers as well as reassess laws on agricultural and veterinarian quarantine and laws on prohibited and restricted goods. In addition, all goods produced in any Member State are to be given the same treatment as national goods. At its meeting in Bahrain in 2000, the Supreme Council of the GCC agreed to pursue working plan and a timetable to establish a single currency, and by the end of 2002 the currencies of the GCC states had been pegged to the US dollar.

The existing policies which address economic integration and harmonisation within the GCC economies have been included in the GCC Charter, the Unified Economic

[21] ibid.
[22] ibid.
[23] R Bhala, *International Trade Law: Interdisciplinary Theory and Practice*, 3rd edn (LexisNexis, 2008).
[24] Puig and Al-Haddab (n 15) 314.
[25] ibid.
[26] ibid.
[27] ibid.

Agreement and at the 2001 Muscat Heads of States Summit. The GCC Charter places emphasis on the strengthening of relations and collective coordination, extending to similar regulations in economic, commercial and financial affairs, as well as in tourism, education, and cultural, social and administrative affairs, as well as the establishment of joint ventures. The 1981 Unified Economic Agreement also stresses these objectives, 'as well as advocating free trade, freedom of movement, work and residence and better treatment for GCC nationals in ownership, inheritance, and exercise of economic activities and co-ordination of monetary policies'.[28] The outcome of the Muscat GCC Summit in 2001, in its statement 'Economic Agreement between the States of the Co-operation Council', further included some measures of common external tariffs; a single entry point principle; Customs Union implementation by January 2003; harmonisation of all product standards; national treatment of GCC capital/investment/employment/ ownership of real estate and equity, and complete integration/harmonization of regulation of financial markets.[29]

Certain fundamental principles therefore exist in relation to the establishment of the GCC common market, one of which is the concept of Gulf economic nationality. In this regard, 'GCC citizens, either natural or legal, shall enjoy national treatment in each Member State'.[30] The intention of this ideology is for all GCC citizens to be afforded equal treatment with reference to all economic activity, including residence and free movement. This ideology also extends to assuring the ability of citizens within the GCC to seek employment and receive welfare benefits across Member States, as well as to be allowed access to economic opportunities in areas which are regarded generally as protected economic sectors, such as real estate, social services, healthcare, education and movement of capital.[31] Economic nationality in the context of the GCC therefore speaks to the right of an individual to equal treatment with regard to economic activity across the GCC states. Article 8 of the initial Economic Agreement of November 1981 considered only four aspects of this, namely the freedom of movement for residence and work, freedom of movement of capital, freedom to exercise economic activity and the right of ownership, inheritance and bequest. The idea of economic nationality further developed with the introduction of the December 2001 Economic Agreement which indicated a broader approach to the principle of national treatment, indicating 10 areas of protected economic activity, namely: movement and residence; the ability to work in private and public jobs; engagement in all professions and crafts; pensions and social security; participation in economic, investment and service activities; ownership of real estate; movement of capital; equal treatment for tax purposes; access to stock ownership and formation of companies and access to education, health and social services. As will be examined, the unilateral sanctions imposed on Qatar has hindered the free trade agreements and economic integration process of the GCC and has created scenarios which have given rise to claims of human rights violations.

[28] B El Din A Ibrahim, *Economic Co-Operation in the Gulf: Issues in the economies of the Arab Gulf co-operation council states* (Routledge, 2007) 8.

[29] ibid.

[30] Puig and Al-Haddab (n 15) 317.

[31] ibid.

IV. The 'Riyadh Agreements' and Subsequent Sanctions on Qatar

The premise of the 2017 Gulf Crisis is the alleged non-compliance by Qatar with three security agreements between the GCC states, signed in 2013 and 2014, referred to as the 'Riyadh Agreements'.[32] No public record of these agreements are held by the GCC, neither had they been discussed by the GCC Supreme Council or the Ministerial Council at their regular meetings in 2013 and 2014.[33] The alleged breaches of these agreements form the legal basis for the measures adopted by the sanctioning states. In what was described as an unprecedented regional power play at the time, 'in late-November 2013, King Abdullah of Saudi Arabia had pressured Qatar's young new Emir, Sheikh Tamim bin Hamad Al Thani, to sign a document pledging "non-interference" in neighbouring countries' affairs and to "change Qatar's ways"'.[34] Arising from this meeting was the conclusion of the first Riyadh Agreement, also known as the 2013 'handwritten agreement',[35] and the second Riyadh Agreement which essentially was the implementing mechanism for the first agreement.[36]

The first Riyadh Agreement contained the following provisions:

(a) No interference in the internal affairs of the GCC states, whether directly or indirectly.
(b) Not to give asylum/refuge or give nationality to any citizen of the Council states that has an activity opposing his country's regimes, except with the approval of his country; no support to deviant groups that oppose their States; and no support for antagonistic media.
(c) No support to the Muslim Brotherhood or any of the organizations, groups or individuals that threaten the security and stability of the GCC States through direct security work or through political influence.
(d) Not to give any support to any faction in Yemen that could pose a threat to countries neighbouring Yemen.[37]

The implementation mechanism addressed areas agreed to be monitored, which included: media outlets to ensure that they did not discuss topics harmful to the GCC states; persons involved in opposition activity against their government to not be given citizenship; support, whether financially or through the media, for individuals or external organisations hostile to the GCC and shutting down all academies and centres that train and rehabilitate GCC citizens to work against their own governments.[38]

[32] Altamimi, 'An Appraisal of the Gulf Cooperation Council's Mechanisms' (2020) 14.
[33] ibid.
[34] K Ulrichsen, 'Perceptions and Divisions' in A Krieg (ed), *Security and Defense Structures in Arab Gulf States: The Anatomy of a Crisis* (Palgrave Macmillan, 2019) 33.
[35] Riyadh Agreement, UN Treaty Registration No 55378, available at treaties.un.org/Pages/showDetails.aspx?objid=0800000280527ea2.
[36] Mechanism Implementing the Riyadh Agreement, UN Treaty Registration No 55378, available at treaties.un.org/Pages/showDetails.aspx?objid=0800000280527eaf.
[37] Riyadh Agreement (n 35) 5.
[38] Mechanism Implementing the Riyadh Agreement (n 36) 10, 11.

The Third Riyadh Agreement of November 2014, also known as the Supplementary Riyadh Agreement,[39] stressed that not committing to any of the articles agreed on, as well as its executive measures, amounted to a violation of the entirety of the agreement. Further commitments in the supplementary agreement included:

(a) Every state is committed to taking all the regulatory, legal and judicial measures against anyone who commits any encroachment against Gulf Cooperation Council states, including putting him on trial and announcing it in the media.
(b) All countries would be committed to the GCC discourse to support the Arab Republic of Egypt, and contribute to this security, stability and its financial support; cease all media activity directed against the Arab Republic of Egypt in all media platforms, whether directly or indirectly, including all the offenses broadcasted on Al-Jazeera, Al-Jazeera, Mubashir Masr, and to work to stop all offenses in Egyptian media.[40]

The supplementary Riyadh Agreement was concluded as a result of a conflict in March 2014 when Saudi Arabia and the UAE declared the Muslim Brotherhood to be a terrorist organisation and, accompanied by Bahrain, withdrew their Ambassadors from Qatar. The trio alleged Qatari support for Muslim Brotherhood associates in Syria and North Africa without providing evidence to substantiate their assertions, and claimed that they appealed to Doha not to support any party which aimed to threaten security and stability in the Gulf. The 2014 diplomatic conflict lasted nine months until its resolution by an agreement in late November, whereby Qatar made several concessions and the three GCC states agreed to return their Ambassadors to Doha in time for the annual GCC Summit which was scheduled to take place at that location in December. These concessions by Qatar included:

> [T]he relocation of several Egyptian members of the Muslim Brotherhood to Turkey and the removal of two Emirati dissidents who had been given refuge in Doha after the UAE's crackdown on domestic Islamists in 2012, the closure of the Egyptian branch station of Al Jazeera, the enforcement of the GCC Internal Security Pact … the dispatch in September 2015 of 1000 members of the Qatar Armed Forces to join the Saudi-led coalition in Yemen and defend the Saudi border against rebel Houthi attacks, and close cooperation with GCC partners on matters of intelligence and policing.[41]

Although these concessions by Qatar indicated a meaningful act by its new leadership which sought to indicate an effort to address perceived grievances of its regional counterparts within the GCC, they still proved to be insufficient to Qatar's adversaries.

Following Qatar's alleged refusal to accept the demands placed on it, the foreign ministers of the UAE, Saudi Arabia, Egypt and Bahrain met in Cairo on 5 July 2017, and adopted six principles which superseded the original demands and did not have a deadline attached to it. These included:

(a) commitment to combat extremism and terrorism in all its forms and to prevent their financing or the provision of safe havens;

[39] Supplementary Riyadh Agreement, UN Treaty Registration No. 55378, available at treaties.un.org/Pages/showDetails.aspx?objid=0800000280527ec6.
[40] ibid, 5.
[41] K Ulrichsen, 'Perceptions and Divisions' in A Krieg (ed), *Security and Defense Structures in Arab Gulf States: The Anatomy of a Crisis* (Palgrave Macmillan, 2019) 33.

(b) prohibiting all acts of incitement and all forms of expression which spread, incite, promote or justify hatred and violence;
(c) full commitment to Riyadh Agreement 2013 and the supplementary agreement and its executive mechanism for 2014 within the framework of the Gulf Cooperation Council (GCC) for Arab States;
(d) commitment to all the outcomes of the Arab–Islamic–US Summit held in Riyadh in May 2017;
(e) to refrain from interfering in the internal affairs of states and from supporting illegal entities and
(f) the responsibility of all states of the international community to confront all forms of extremism and terrorism as a threat to international peace and security.[42]

Consequently, the 2017 manifestation of the conflict began with another withdrawal of the three countries' ambassadors from Doha in June, this time also accompanied by their Egyptian counterparts, as well as an economic and trade blockade imposed on Qatar. At this point, 'the so-called "Anti-Terror Quartet" accused the Qatari leadership of violating both the spirit and the letter of the Riyadh Agreement that ended the 2014 dispute'.[43] Qatar, however, contended that the Riyadh Agreements fell outside of the scope of the GCC Charter. Furthermore, in 2017, Bahrain, Saudi Arabia and the UAE began to consider Qatar as a hostile state which posed a direct threat to their ideologies regarding how national and regional security should be pursued. Together with Egypt, they proceeded to severe all diplomatic relations with Qatar. This involved placing a requirement on all Qatari nationals to leave the jurisdictions of those countries, while also closing air, land and sea travel routes with Qatar. The following 13 demands were placed on Qatar:

(a) Curb diplomatic ties with Iran and close its diplomatic missions there. Expel members of Iran's Revolutionary Guards and cut off any joint military cooperation with Iran. Only trade and commerce with Iran that complies with US and international sanctions will be permitted.
(b) Sever all ties to 'terrorist organizations', specifically the Muslim Brotherhood, Islamic State, al-Qaida and Lebanon's Hezbollah. Formally declare those entities as terrorist groups.
(c) Shut down Al-Jazeera and its affiliate stations.
(d) Shut down news outlets that Qatar funds, directly and indirectly, including Arabi21, Rassd, Al-Araby Al-Jadeed and Middle East Eye.
(e) Immediately terminate the Turkish military presence in Qatar and end any joint military cooperation with Turkey inside Qatar.
(f) Stop all means of funding for individuals, groups or organisations that have been designated as terrorists by Saudi Arabia, the UAE, Egypt, Bahrain, the US and other countries.

[42] 'Arab countries' six principles for Qatar "a measure to restart the negotiation process"' *The National*, 19 July 2017, available at www.thenational.ae/world/gcc/arab-countries-six-principles-for-qatar-a-measure-to-restart-the-negotiation-process-1.610314.

[43] Ulrichsen, 'Perceptions and Divisions' (2019) 33.

(g) Hand over 'terrorist figures' and wanted individuals from Saudi Arabia, the UAE, Egypt and Bahrain to their countries of origin. Freeze their assets, and provide any desired information about their residency, movements and finances.
(h) End interference in sovereign countries' internal affairs. Stop granting citizenship to wanted nationals from Saudi Arabia, the UAE, Egypt and Bahrain. Revoke Qatari citizenship for existing nationals where such citizenship violates those countries' laws.
(i) Stop all contact with the political opposition in Saudi Arabia, the UAE, Egypt and Bahrain. Hand over all files detailing Qatar's prior contacts with and support for those opposition groups.
(j) Pay reparations and compensation for loss of life and other, financial losses caused by Qatar's policies in recent years. The sum will be determined in coordination with Qatar.
(k) Consent to monthly audits for the first year after agreeing to the demands, then once per quarter during the second year. For the following 10 years, Qatar would be monitored annually for compliance.
(l) Align itself with the other Gulf and Arab countries militarily, politically, socially and economically, as well as on economic matters, in line with an agreement reached with Saudi Arabia in 2014.
(m) Agree to all the demands within 10 days of it being submitted to Qatar, or the list becomes invalid.[44]

The move by Bahrain, Egypt, Saudi Arabia and the UAE which resulted in the imposition of the blockade on Qatar as well as the severance of diplomatic relations on 5 June 2017 has been described as a 'watershed moment in regional relations',[45] having constituted to a 'fundamental rupture of the regional order'.[46] Wright contends that disagreement extended beyond manageable state friction over autonomy, to a situation where the stability of monarchy and national security was considered as being threatened. He suggests that in situations where the GCC states had suffered from rivalry or actions which challenged the autonomy and security of fellow member states, there existed a common understanding and outlook for a regional order which largely prevailed, thereby allowing for practical cooperation and reconciliation. These aspects of practical cooperation and reconciliation would have been facilitated within the GCC framework. The progressive consensus for cooperation between GCC countries had been the practice since it was founded in 1981, but the 2017 blockade sought to reflect 'a fundamental difference in outlook between Qatar and the blockading states on regional order, in addition to the ideals of gradualist regional integration through the GCC as an organization'.[47] Although historical grievances certainly existed between the GCC states, Wright suggests that the 2011 region-wide uprisings had been decisive in reshaping the geopolitical landscape of the wider region, 'the legacy of which is still

[44] 'What are the 13 Demands Given to Qatar?' *The Gulf News* 23 June 2019, available at gulfnews.com/world/gulf/qatar/what-are-the-13-demands-given-to-qatar-1.2048118.
[45] S Wright, 'The Political Economy of the Gulf Divide' in A Krieg (ed), *Security and Defense Structures in Arab Gulf States: The Anatomy of a Crisis* (Palgrave Macmillan, 2019) 145.
[46] ibid.
[47] ibid, 146.

being felt in the contemporary age through the way it challenged the GCC consensus on regional order'.[48] As Ulrichsen explains, rather than the presence of any particular trigger, several factors combined which had the effect of altering the geopolitical climate in the Gulf, with the new Trump administration appearing

> willing to pursue regional policies that aligned closely with the interests of its declared partners in Riyadh and Abu Dhabi, due in no small part to a concerted outreach campaign by Saudi and Emirati leaders and their surrogates to shape the thinking of key members of the White House team as they took office.[49]

In terms of legality of the measures adopted, the states imposing the sanctions have alleged that Qatar's breach of the Riyadh Agreements provided legal justification for their decision to implement such measures. This would, as a consequence, affect the progress of GCC economic integration, particularly in relation to the nature of the allegations.

The fallout from the Riyadh Agreements serves as a useful platform for discussion of the legality of the unilateral sanctions against Qatar, within the framework of international law, as well as that of the GCC. As Jazairy, explains, the 'contemporary trend has generally been toward the centralization of the authority to use economic sanctions'.[50] The basis for this assertion is founded on Chapter V of the UN Charter designating the UN Security Council as the principal mechanism responsible for maintaining international peace and security, while Chapter VII gives the Security Council unfettered power to adopt economic sanctions in circumstances where international peace and security is threatened. Jazairy further explains however that 'some thirty states, mainly advanced Western ones, challenge this position and advocate that unilateral economic sanctions are legitimate tools with which to pursue certain foreign policy objectives'.[51] Despite this, he maintains that there exists an emergent, if not already established, rule of customary international law that unilateral coercive measures which affect the sovereignty of other states, the lawful interests of entities or persons under their jurisdiction, and the freedom of trade and navigation are illegitimate since they are almost universally seen by the international community in such a manner.[52] In 2013, the Group of 77 (G77), at the time comprising 134 UN developing nations, and China adopted a Ministerial Declaration firmly rejecting the imposition of laws and regulations with extraterritorial impact and all other forms of coercive economic measures, including unilateral sanctions against developing countries, while reiterating the urgent need for their non-recognition by the international community, as well as for immediate removal.[53] In terms of the effect on economic integration, the declaration recognised that 'such actions not only undermine the principles enshrined in the Charter of the United Nations and international law, but also severely threaten the freedom of trade

[48] ibid.

[49] Ulrichsen (n 41) 34.

[50] I Jazairy, 'Unilateral Economic Sanctions, International Law, and Human Rights' (2019) 22 *Ethics & International Affairs* 291, 292.

[51] ibid, 293.

[52] ibid, 294.

[53] Ministerial Declaration, Foreign Affairs Ministers, Member States of the Group of 77 and China, 26 September 2013, para 52, available at www.g77.org/doc/Declaration2013.htm.

and investment'.[54] However, as mentioned, the Riyadh Agreements have been used as justification for the sanctions by Qatar's GCC counterparts. The legal basis for this will now be considered.

It is noteworthy that the conflict has presented differing legal approaches in determining whether or not the sanctions can be justified, and what ought to be the appropriate forum for settlement of the dispute. Such matters are important in the context of providing clarity for how future relationships would evolve, particularly in terms of maintaining and building on the existing framework for integration within the GCC. On this point, the outcome of the pending contentious proceedings before the International Court of Justice (ICJ) in the case of the application of the International Convention on the Elimination of All Forms of Racial Discrimination (ICERD) *(Qatar v UAE)*, as well as two appeals relating to the jurisdiction of the International Civil Aviation (IACAO) Council (*Bahrain, Egypt, Saudi Arabia and the UAE v Qatar*) and (*Bahrain, Egypt and the UAE v Qatar*) could provide important guidance on the most appropriate forum by which conflict resolution which would impact on economic integration may be achieved. With reference to the ICERD proceedings, the ICJ will consider whether the sanctions are compliant with that Convention, and under what conditions. As Jazairy explains,

> If the court concludes they are not, this could in turn give new life to the possibility for individual victims, or entire states, to bring claims before the Committee on the Elimination of Racial Discrimination or for an affected state party to the ICERD to initiate contentious proceedings.[55]

The ICAO will also be in a position to provide guidance on whether a defence of countermeasures within the scope of agreements such as the Riyadh Agreements would render the dispute non-justiciable and outside of its ambit.

The states imposing the sanctions on Qatar adopted the position that Qatar manifestly failed to use the opportunity provided by the Riyadh Agreements to negotiate a solution to the dispute, particularly in light of it being used to discuss disagreements throughout 2014. The UAE has contended that by virtue of the Riyadh Agreements, Qatar made undertakings which had not been adhered to, and amounted to violations of international law.[56] These include allegations of support for rebel factions in conflict with the Government of Yemen, and the use of Al Jazeera and other media outlets to support and promote terrorist organisations and incite extremism. The UAE further alleged that the actions of Qatar has threatened not only the stability and security of the GCC states, but also other parts of the world, including vulnerable individuals and communities.[57] These allegations placed Qatar as being responsible for state-sponsored terrorism and extremism, and as a result the Riyadh Agreements became necessary as a response to address threats posed by extremist groups and their support from Qatar. The UAE also argued that it did not impose a travel ban on Qatari citizens, but implemented

[54] ibid.
[55] Jazairy, 'Unilateral Economic Sanctions' (2019) 297.
[56] *Qatar v UAE*, Request for the indication of provisional measures by the UAE, 2–3, available at www.icj-cij.org/files/case-related/172/172-20190322-REQ-01-00-EN.pdf.
[57] ibid, 4.

a system whereby prior permission to travel needed to be obtained. According to the UAE, no prohibition of such measures exists under customary international law, and this was a basic and legitimate exercise of sovereignty used by governments worldwide.[58] The UAE further claimed that it took steps to mitigate inconveniences to Qatari citizens in order to comply with its legal obligations, such as setting up a hotline to assist persons with the procedure to apply for a permit to enter the UAE. According to the UAE, Qatar 'signalled that it was seeking to resile from the Riyadh Agreements in a letter to the Secretary-General to the GCC on 19 February 2017'.[59] This was based on Qatar's claim that 'the subject of this agreement has been exhausted' while calling on its GCC counterparts to 'agree to terminate the Riyadh agreement which has been overtaken by events at the international and regional levels'.[60] It also highlighted Qatar's claim that the Riyadh Agreements constituted an abandonment of the GCC Charter and did not serve the interests and objectives of the GCC, while calling for a return to GCC principles.[61] Qatar has, however, claimed that the measures adopted against it were inconsistent with the Riyadh Agreements. As such, it followed that the states responsible for imposing coercive measures were purposefully and systematically seeking to intervene in the internal affairs of Qatar, in breach of the Riyadh Agreements and international law.[62] In essence, this would allow Qatar recourse to present its grievances to international tribunals for breach of treaty obligations.

V. Effects of the Blockade on Qatar and Legality of the Sanctions within the GCC Framework

Puig and Al-Haddab, in explaining the idea of Gulf economic nationality and its relationship with the notion of free trade within the GCC, note that:

> The norm of free trade within the GCC common market relies on the constitutional principle of Gulf economic nationality: GCC citizens, natural persons and legal persons, have the right to national treatment in each Member State with respect to all economic activities, a right that includes the freedom of movement and residence. GCC citizens anywhere in the region can work in either the private or public sector, exercise any profession or occupation, and engage in traditionally protectionist industries such as investment, real estate, and the provision of social and health services. GCC citizens can also receive welfare benefits such as pension and social security payments anywhere in the region.[63]

However, the constitutional principle of Gulf economic nationality was severely undermined with the imposition of unilateral sanctions on Qatar. The sanctions appear to

[58] ibid, 5.
[59] ibid, 4.
[60] ibid, fn 9.
[61] ibid.
[62] Verbatim Record of the Appeal Relating to the Jurisdiction of the ICAO Council under Article 84 of the Convention on International Civil Aviation (*Bahrain, Egypt, Saudi Arabia and UAE v Qatar*) and the Appeal Relating to the Jurisdiction of the ICAO Council under Article II, Section 2, of the 1944 International Air Services Transit Agreement (*Bahrain, Egypt and UAE v Qatar*) 19, available at www.icj-cij.org/files/case-related/173/173-20191205-ORA-01-00-BI.pdf.
[63] Puig and Al-Haddab (n 11) 324.

violate several aspects of the GCC agreements, including economic and human rights provisions. The nature of these sanctions and its effects on the GCC rule-based regime will now be examined in light of the conditions imposed on Qatar. Indeed, the sanctions imposed on Qatar since 2017 significantly bring into focus the issue of how lawful unilateral sanctions and coercive measures in international law and international relations among sovereign states are.

The Qatari economy experienced a significant economic impact particularly at the beginning of the siege as a result of Bahrain, Saudi Arabia and the UAE closing air, sea, and land transport channels with Qatar, especially since it was dependent on Saudi Arabia and the UAE for imports of goods. Qatari customs authorities have reported that 76 per cent of its sugar, 67 per cent of oil, 59 per cent of dairy products, 93 per cent of construction material, 47 per cent of timber and gravel, and 51 per cent of cables for construction had been imported from Saudi Arabia, the UAE and Bahrain.[64] Furthermore, as a result of the GCC crisis and the flow of goods being suspended, the costs associated with goods and transport increased, with the price of commodities in Qatar increasing by 83 per cent and the Government having to intervene to stabilise prices.[65] Most of the trade flow relating to Qatar's goods took place through Saudi Arabia and the UAE through land, air and sea and consequently the blockade severely restricted the ability of people in Qatar to access and afford items of necessity such as food and clothing. The time and costs associated with travel, and the transportation of goods was also affected due to the closure of airspace, with flights arriving and departing from Qatar having to be rerouted through a narrow flight-path around Saudi Arabia. The ongoing economic impact of the measures imposed on Qatar has yet proven to be as extreme in severity as initially anticipated as a result of its relations with states in Europe and Asia, as well as Turkey and Iran. Nonetheless, the demands placed on Qatar was indicative of an attempt to force a sovereign state to surrender aspects of its sovereignty in terms of both its domestic and foreign policy, especially in relation to the blockading countries asserting that sanctions would be lifted when proof of implementation was provided.

According to a report by the Office of the United Nations Commissioner for Human Rights (OHCHR), instrumentalisation of the media has been a key feature of the crisis, especially in Saudi Arabia and the UAE.[66] The blockading countries implemented measures which sought to criminalise expression of sympathy with Qatar on social media and elsewhere; Saudi Arabia classified sympathy with Qatar as a cybercrime, imposing a five-year prison sentence and a fine of three million riyals, with the UAE imposing sentences ranging from three to 15 years in detention and a fine up to 500,000 dirhams, and Bahrain imposing five-year prison sentences.[67] These three countries also prohibited broadcasting from media outlets funded by Qatar, including Qatar TV, Al Jazeera Network, and beIN Sports. Hotels were also prohibited from offering access to these

[64] Office of the United Nations High Commissioner for Human Rights (OHCHR), Technical Mission to the State of Qatar, 'Report on the impact of the Gulf Crisis on human rights' (December 2017), 11.

[65] ibid.

[66] ibid, 5–6.

[67] T Kharroub, 'Understanding the Humanitarian Costs of the Blockade' in The GCC Crisis at One Year – Stalemate Becomes Reality (Arab Center Washington DC, 2018) 93.

channels, thereby restricting the availability of information and freedom of the press.[68] According to Kharroub, the right to freedom of expression had also been hindered as a result of the blockading countries instilling 'fear among individuals regarding contact with family members in Qatar, thus depriving them of the right to communicate with family and conduct business and daily transactions'.[69] The OHCHR Report considered that both media and social media campaigns by blockading countries were premeditated and organised with the intended effect of generating a 'general feeling of hostility and hatred towards Qatar'.[70] These included at least 1,120 press articles and 600 anti-Qatar caricatures which purported accusations of 'Qatar's support to terrorism, calls for a regime change or a *coup d'etat*, attacks against leading figures and symbols of Qatar, as well as appeals for attacks on, and murder of Qataris'.[71] These measures are particularly alarming, considering that according to the United Nations Human Rights Committee (UNHRC), a 'free, uncensored and unhindered press or other media is essential in any society to ensure freedom of opinion and expression and the enjoyment of other Covenant rights. It constitutes one of the cornerstones of a democratic society'.[72]

Following the severance of ties and the imposition of the blockade on Qatar, the countries comprising the quartet, but for Egypt, who kept a small number of staff under protection, removed their diplomats from Qatar, ordered their citizens to leave Qatar, and imposed a travel ban to, and from Qatar. Qatari nationals residing in, or visiting the quartet countries were given 14 days to leave, while Qatari diplomats were instructed to vacate within 48 hours, while the quartet threatened their citizens with punishment if they chose to remain in Qatar. According to the OHCHR, although the Government of Egypt did not issue a formal directive for Qatari citizens to leave the country, students from Qatar who tried to return to Egypt in August 2017 after their summer break were either not issued visas or were told to apply for security clearance upon obtaining a visa.[73] According to the NHRC, Qatari nationals working in Bahrain, Saudi Arabia and the UAE, and/or with business interests in these countries, were forced to return to Qatar, reportedly with no access to their companies and other sources of business activity and income.[74] In explaining the consequences on the right to property, the OHRC reported:

> While the authorities could not determine the number of individuals affected with certainty, a national compensation claims commission established following the 5 June decision had documented at least 1,900 cases related to the right to property by the end of November 2017, with claims pertaining to private residences, stockshares, financial assets and livestock. The team conducted interviews with some of the claimants, mostly Qatari nationals who have property in KSA and UAE, particularly commercial entities. They confirmed that financial transactions between Qatar and KSA, UAE and Bahrain had been suspended, preventing

[68] ibid.

[69] ibid.

[70] OHCHR Qatar Technical Mission Report (2017) 6.

[71] ibid.

[72] General comment No 34 Article 19: Freedoms of opinion and expression, UN Doc CCPR/C/GC/34, para 13.

[73] OHCHR Qatar Technical Mission Report (n 64) 8.

[74] National Human Rights Committee (NHRC), Fifth General Report – Continuation of human rights violations: A year of the blockade imposed on Qatar (2018) 15.

> people from receiving salaries or pensions, perceiving rents, paying bills, or supporting relatives. They also highlighted the absence of any formal and available litigation mechanism to claim and/or manage their assets. Indeed, legal cooperation has been suspended, including power of attorney. Furthermore, lawyers in these countries are unlikely to defend Qataris as this would likely be interpreted as an expression of sympathy towards Qatar.[75]

The aforementioned violations of economic rights and the right to property appear to be in breach of GCC rules. Article 27 of the GCC Human Rights Declaration provides that private property is inviolable and no one shall be prevented from the disposition of his property except by the regulation (law), and it may not be expropriated unless for public interest with fair compensation.[76] Furthermore, Article 24 states that

> every person, who has the capacity of doing so, has the right to work and has the right to free choice of employment according to the requirements of dignity and public interest, while just and favourable employment conditions, as well as employees' and employers' rights, are ensured.[77]

Indeed, violations of the right to property arising from the sanctions as quoted in the OHRC Report have gone against GCC declarations which have been geared towards economic integration through harmonising access to property. For instance, Article 8 of the 1981 Economic Agreement provided for ownership of real estate property, while Article 3 of the 2001 Economic Agreement allows for the equal national treatment in ownership right of real estate. In addition, the Supreme Council's resolution (23rd session, December 2002) provided for equal tax treatment of GCC nationals in the field of stock ownership and formation of corporations, as well as the elimination of all the restrictions that would prevent this. This suggests that the sanctions pertaining to access to property are incompatible with the intentions of the GCC.

Article 14 of the GCC Human Rights Declaration states that the family is the natural and fundamental group unit of society, originally composed of a man and a woman, governed by religion, morals and patriotism; its entity and bonds are maintained and reinforced by religion, while motherhood, childhood and members of the family are protected by religion as well as the State and society against all forms of abuse and domestic violence. The NHRC recorded 646 cases of family separation due to the GCC crisis and blockade.[78] According to OHCHR, the official data from Qatar indicated 6,474 cases of mixed marriages involving citizens of Qatar, Bahrain, Saudi Arabia and the UAE.[79] From this, it can be ascertained that the decision by authorities in Bahrain, Saudi Arabia and the UAE to order their citizens to leave Qatar as well as expel Qatari nationals residing in their countries, resulted in thousands of individuals being deprived of the ability to be present with their children and families, thereby causing psychological distress and financial difficulty. The OHCHR Report noted that the crisis has

[75] OHCHR Qatar Technical Mission Report (n 64) 10–11.
[76] Human Rights Declaration for the Member States of the Cooperation Council for the Arab States of the Gulf (GCC) adopted by the high council in its Thirty-Fifth Session in Doha 9 December 2014, Article 27, available at www.gcc-sg.org/en-us/CognitiveSources/DigitalLibrary/Lists/DigitalLibrary/Human%20Rights/1453192982.pdf.
[77] ibid, Art 24.
[78] NHRC Fifth General Report (n 74), 13, 14.
[79] OHCHR Qatar Technical Mission Report (n 64), 9.

highlighted the need to address ongoing issues surrounding nationality and residence within the region, commenting that 'non-Qatari spouses and children of Qataris have faced acute uncertainties, even if the majority have reportedly remained in Qatar'.[80] It also cites NHRC reports documenting a high incidence of calls from women who feared applying to renew their national passport and Qatar residence identification, with women also deeply concerned about being expelled from Qatar, or compelled to return to their country of origin, thereby being separated from their spouse and children.[81] The right of individuals to access education has also been severely limited as a result of the restrictions on movement and residency. The NHRC recorded 513 violations of the right to education (66 by Saudi Arabia, 148 by the UAE, 28 by Bahrain, and 271 by the Arab Republic of Egypt).[82] The expulsion of Qatari students from the three Gulf countries meant that they were arbitrarily denied access to education, thereby denying them of a basic human right. The course registrations of Qatari students attending universities in the UAE were withdrawn, with students being told to return to Qatar. This process resulted in unanticipated financial costs for students, and those attempting to transfer to other universities faced difficulties in obtaining academic transcripts and with the transfer of credits.[83] In certain instances, the specialised area of studies that was being pursued abroad was not available in Qatar, and as a result some students were unable to continue their university education.[84]

The Supreme Council's resolution (9th Session, December 1988) resolved that GCC nationals, who are residents or visitors in any Member State, shall be given the same treatment accorded to the nationals of the host Member State concerning the services of the health centres, clinics and public hospitals, with this resolution being effective from 1 March 1989. All Member States have issued implementing directives to give effect to this. The 2001 Economic Agreement also stresses on the right to healthcare in Articles 12 and 13. Contrary to the nature of these provisions as a result of the imposition of sanctions on Qatar, the right to health had been severely violated. Qatar experienced a restriction in its access to medicines, including life-saving medicines, and medical supplies as a result in the cessation of trade. According to the NHRC, 50–60 per cent of its pharmaceutical stocks are obtained from 20 GCC-based suppliers.[85] The blockade also caused delays in the opening of new hospitals in Qatar and the suspension of medical care, with Qatari citizens, as well as individuals from other GCC countries and expatriates, being negatively affected.[86]

The decision to sanction Qatar also appear to breach certain aspects of the GCC Charter. For one, the violations discussed go against the spirit of Article 4 of the Charter which outlines the basic objectives of the Charter. These are:

(a) To effect coordination, integration and inter-connection between Member States in all fields in order to achieve unity between them.

[80] ibid.
[81] ibid.
[82] NHRC Fifth General Report (2018) 13, 18.
[83] ibid, 18.
[84] ibid.
[85] ibid, 51.
[86] ibid.

(b) To deepen and strengthen relations, links and areas of cooperation now prevailing between their peoples in various fields.
(c) To formulate similar regulations in various fields including the following: economic and financial affairs, commerce, customs and communications, education and culture.
(d) To stimulate scientific and technological progress in the fields of industry, mining, agriculture, water and animal resources; to establish scientific research; to establish joint ventures and encourage cooperation by the private sector for the good of their peoples.[87]

In conflict with Article 4, the actions of the blockading GCC countries have had the effect of weakening GCC relations, restricting economic cooperation, threatening freedom of movement and family life, and placing limitations on access to educational opportunities across the GCC countries. Furthermore, the measures imposed on Qatar were undertaken outside the scope of the GCC Supreme Council. Article 7 of the GCC Charter establishes the Supreme Council as the highest authority of the GCC.[88] According to Article 8 of the GCC Charter, the Supreme Council 'shall endeavour to realize the objectives of the Cooperation Council' particularly in relation to matters such as reviewing matters of interests to the Member States, establishing policy for the GCC and approving the rules of procedure of the Commission for the Settlement of Disputes.[89]

The Commission for the Settlement of Disputes is attached to the Supreme Council as provided for by Article 6(1)[90] and Article 10[91] of the GCC Charter. It should be considered that the dispute resolution mechanism as provided for by Article 10 was never invoked by the blockading GCC countries. According to Article 10, if a dispute arises over interpretation or implementation of the Charter and such dispute is not resolved within the Ministerial Council or the Supreme Council, the Supreme Council may refer the dispute to the Commission for the Settlement of Disputes. Pursuant to this, the Commission submits its recommendations or opinion, as applicable, to the Supreme Council for that body to take action which it deems appropriate. Article 10 also provides that the Commission for the Settlement of Disputes is to be established on an ad hoc basis, in accordance with the nature of the dispute. The GCC Charter therefore provided an avenue for the conflict to be arbitrated within the organisation itself. However, the blockading countries did not see it fit to have their grievances resolved within the structure of the GCC. The three GCC Member States involved in the blockade had effectively disregarded the organisation's conflict resolution mechanisms as provided for within the GCC Charter to address their disapproval with Qatari policy, and this, according to Baabood, 'demonstrates that the trust in the organization appears to have vanished'.[92]

[87] GCC Charter (n 9), Art 4.
[88] ibid, Art 7.
[89] ibid, Art 8.
[90] ibid, Art 6(1).
[91] ibid, Art (10).
[92] Baabood, 'The Future of the GCC' (2019) 162.

Where states take the decision to impose unilateral sanctions against another state within the same economic bloc without having regard to initially attempting to resolve their grievances within the framework of regional integration agreements, there is the possibility that this can bring the foundations of the entire agreement into jeopardy. In the case of the GCC, the failure to resolve the dispute within the provisions of the dispute resolution mechanism provided for by the GCC Charter suggests a lack of trust in the process set out under the Charter. Arguably, this also significantly undermines certain procedural aspects of the charter which ideally ought to be invoked where there is the occurrence of a dispute. An example of this is Qatar choosing to seek recourse at the World Trade Organization (WTO) in raising the question of the legality of trade embargoes imposed by the UAE based on an allegation that Qatar had been taking steps to support terrorism and destabilise the region. Qatar has maintained that such actions are baseless and unjustified, while suggesting that coercive attempts at economic isolation against Qatar affects trade in goods, trade in services and trade related aspects of intellectual property rights.[93] Raising such concerns for resolution outside of internal dispute resolution mechanisms in the first instance, as provided for by already existing regional agreements presents a myriad of complex issues, including issues of jurisdiction, and creates the possibility of the dispute being prolonged while there is attempt to determine such matters. For example, the UAE has contended that the WTO dispute system was not the proper forum to hear the dispute, as it could not be considered a trade dispute, but instead one which concerned national security, while the USA has also suggested that 'national security issues were political and not appropriate for the WTO dispute system, and that if the parties are unable to resolve the issue bilaterally … ask for assistance from the Director-General or another WTO member'.[94]

The question should also be asked as to whether the states imposing sanctions had a proper understanding of the socio-economic and human rights consequences of their actions within the context of the GCC FTAs and the damage their actions would have imposed in relation to the spirit of these agreements. Arguably, human rights-based approaches to the conflict would have allowed for a more analytical approach to dispute resolution. Furthermore, this issue highlights the possible need for human rights impact assessments prior to the commencement of FTAs. With regard to the human rights violations discussed, it should be considered that the GCC Charter and other agreements facilitating regional cooperation would have been constructed in a way so as to avoid the possibility of its provisions giving rise to situations of human rights violations. The human rights violations arising from the blockade are therefore contrary to the intentions of these documents. At the international level, the OHCHR has called for human rights impact assessments to be carried out prior to the conclusion of trade agreements.[95] In 2001, Oliver De Schutter, who was at the time the UN SR

[93] Request for Consultations by Qatar, 'United Arab Emirates – Measures Relating to Trade in Goods, Services and Trade Related Aspects of Intellectual Property Rights' 4, WTO Doc WT/DS526/1 (4 August 2017).

[94] RV Anuradha, 'Petrificus Totalus: The Spell of National Security' (2018) 13 *Asian Journal of WTO & International Health Law & Policy* 311, 316.

[95] OHCHR,' Report of the High Commissioner for Human Rights on Human Rights, Trade and Investment' (2003) UN Doc E/CN.4/Sub.2/2003/9, para 63.

on the right to food, issued certain guiding principles on human rights impact assessments for trade and investment agreements in a report to the UNHRC.[96] In addition, the International Labour Organization (ILO) has issued guidance which focuses on the relationship between labour and trade,[97] while the UNHRC has also explored whether human rights impact assessments of trade agreements should form part of a future treaty regime in the area of business and human rights.[98]

VI. Conclusion

The unilateral sanctions imposed on Qatar have damaged the economic integration process within the GCC, as demonstrated by the measures taken by the blockading countries being in conflict with the GCC Charter, the 2001 Economic Agreement, and the 1981 Economic Agreement which essentially represents the foundation attempts by the GCC towards economic integration. It can be said that the Qatar blockade 'seriously undermines the letter and the spirit of the regional organization, its agreements and achievements'.[99] The blockade is also contrary to the spirit of much publicised GCC achievement of its Common Market agreement of 2007, which created a common free trade area, facilitating the free movement of people, goods and capital between GCC Member States. In practice the blockade has negatively affected the operation of the GCC Common Market as evidenced by the abrupt closure of Qatar's only land boundary, effectively putting to a halt the flow of people, goods and capital, with the blockade restricting 'the freedom of movement enjoyed by GCC citizens, preventing families of different member states with marriage and tribal ties from visiting one another'.[100] Furthermore, the lives of nationals from the countries of Bahrain, Egypt, Saudi Arabia and the UAE living in Qatar have been disrupted as a result of them having to leave the country, thereby affecting their employment and education of their children. Arguably, the current crisis has shed light on the limitations of the GCC and exposed its vulnerabilities as the organisation was completely set aside and absent from every stage of the dispute, thereby rendering the GCC to be almost irrelevant. Essentially, the GCC had been completely ignored during the conflict, and the decision to impose a blockade which would have affected the common agreements was determined outside of the scope of the GCC and its dispute resolution mechanisms. As Baabood ascertains, the 'GCC was excluded as the mechanism to discuss the dispute, communicate the initial grievances against Qatar and was not chosen as a facilitator of dialogue or mediator between the disputing members'.[101]

[96] UN General Assembly (2011), 'Report of the Special Rapporteur on the right to food, Olivier De Schutter: Guiding principles on human rights impact assessments of trade and investment agreements', UN Doc A/HRC/19/59/Add.5.

[97] ILO, *Handbook on Assessment of Labour Provisions in Trade and Investment Arrangements* (ILO, 2017).

[98] United Nations Human Rights Council (2018), 'Open-ended intergovernmental working group on transnational corporations and other business enterprises with respect to human rights', available at www.ohchr.org/en/hrbodies/hrc/wgtranscorp/pages/igwgontnc.aspx.

[99] Baabood (n 11) 168.

[100] ibid, 169.

[101] ibid.

The GCC was also unable to prevent any potential military escalation, which was a real possibility, as stated by Kuwaiti Emir Sabah al-Ahmad al-Jaber Al Sabah during a September 2017 press conference with US President Donald Trump at the White House.[102] Also compromising the standing of the GCC was the fact that Kuwait and Oman were not consulted and did not take part in the blockade. Instead of choosing to support any particular side, Kuwait, with the support of Oman, persisted with efforts to advocate mediation and reconciliation, albeit with limited success. As a result of the blockade, the investment climate has been severely affected, with GCC nationals, especially the business community and non-nationals residing in GCC countries finding it difficult in terms of travel and conducting business.[103] As such, the blockade has not only rigorously diminished the GCC's agenda of pursuing common projects geared towards cooperation and integration, but it has also 'reflected negatively on its credibility in international cooperation with other regional and international countries and organizations'.[104] The blockade brings to the forefront the vulnerability and volatility of the GCC as a regional organisation, and has created serious questions and concerns in terms of the GCC's future role as a collective group. At present, the case can be made that the GCC as an organisation remains in name only, being restricted by the refusal of blockading countries to respect their commitments under the Charter to regional unity and conflict resolution. From the developments discussed, it may be argued that the GCC has emerged as the primary victim of the crisis, with the organisation being weak and divided at an unprecedented level when considering its history of over the past three decades. Indeed, the GCC can be used as a valid case study to demonstrate the damaging effects of unilateral sanctions, especially in relation to how such sanctions go against the spirit, nature and intentions of regional agreements which focus on economic integration.

The blockading states, by resorting to unilateral sanctions outside the scope of the GCC Charter and ignoring the dispute resolution mechanisms of the GCC, based their actions on unilateral assessment, thereby incurring responsibility for their wrongful conduct in the event of an incorrect assessment. It is clear that GCC Charter respects the obligation of each Member State in the exercise of its sovereignty and in having due regard for the sovereign rights of other Member States. The sanctions therefore appear to undermine principle of sovereign equality of states, peaceful coexistence and non-interference in the internal affairs of Qatar. They have exceeded the limits of the law and constitute a violation of principles of international law such as the prohibition on interference in the affairs of other states. They have also encouraged the rise of nationalism, which will weaken the common international system. The measures have also resulted in the violation of human rights of the people of Qatar. Furthermore, they were not genuinely designed to uphold the rules of international law or to promote the common good, but were imposed as a tool for foreign policy objectives to be achieved, both economic and political, as well as to promote and protect the narrow national interest of the states concerned. As a result, they had the effect of violating the regional

[102] ibid.
[103] ibid.
[104] ibid, 170.

norms of cooperation, peaceful existence and integration. Neither have the blockading states been able to substantiate their allegations of wrongful acts purportedly carried out by Qatar. The conflict suggests that the regional legal rules governing recourse to sanctions remain fundamentally incomplete. The blockading states resorted to the use of sanctions without being subject to of any regional framework which prescribe the rules and conditions for such actions. In this regard, the unilateral sanctions imposed on Qatar could not fit within the legal framework of the GCC, especially in terms of establishing a legal basis for carrying out such measures.

6

The Effect of Unilateral Sanctions on Foreign Investors and the Foreign Investment Regime

NICOLETTE BUTLER

I. Introduction

Sanctions were defined by Oppenheim as 'injurious and otherwise internationally illegal acts of a state against another as are exceptionally permitted for the purpose of compelling the latter to consent to a satisfactory settlement of a difference created by its own international delinquency'.[1] Sanctions are said to be collective when carried out in the setting of an international institution, eg the United Nations. On the other hand, they are said to be unilateral when carried out outside of an international institutionalised setting.[2] Sanctions can involve different types of actions, eg political or economic. This chapter will focus specifically on economic sanctions imposed outside of an institutional setting (unilateral economic sanctions). Recently, there has been a marked increase in the imposition of such unilateral economic sanctions by some states, eg US sanctions on Iran and Saudi coalition led sanctions on Qatar.

The imposition of unilateral economic sanctions can potentially affect many aspects of the targeted state's international activities, including foreign investment. International (or foreign) investment takes place when a national of one state invests in or begins a business in a different state. International investors are entitled to various protections under international law. The most basic protections available to investors and their property are collectively recognised as customary international law principles. In addition to this, individual investors may also enjoy further protections by virtue of an extensive network of almost 3,000[3] bilateral investment treaties (BITs) and treaties with investment provisions (TIPs). BITs and TIPs are agreements between two (bilateral)

[1] L Oppenheim, *International Law*, Volume 2 (Longmans, Green, and Co, 1905) 34.

[2] M Paparinskis, 'Investment arbitration and the law of countermeasures' (2008) 79 *British Yearbook of International Law* 264.

[3] See UNCTAD, International Investment Agreements Navigator, available at www.investmentpolicyhubold.unctad.org/IIA accessed 1 April 2020.

or more (plurilateral or multilateral) states that set out the terms and conditions that a national of one of the signatory states can expect to enjoy when investing in the other (or another) signatory state.[4]

The central aim of this chapter is to examine the potential effects of the imposition of unilateral economic sanctions on foreign investors and the international investment regime generally. In order to achieve this aim, the chapter is structured in five parts. This section has provided an introduction to the topic and an overview of the work. Section II examines how the imposition of unilateral economic sanctions might theoretically affect individual foreign investors. The answer to this question is quite complex, as it depends on the categorisation of any given foreign investor. Depending on their individual circumstances, foreign investors may derive investment protections from customary international law, as well as a particular BIT/TIP. Accordingly, section II analyses the effects of unilateral economic sanctions on foreign investors according to the level of protection to which they are entitled. It also examines the potential remedies available to aggrieved foreign investors that may have been negatively affected by the imposition of the unilateral economic sanctions in the investment host (targeted) state. Section III moves on to consider the effects of the imposition of unilateral economic sanctions from the perspective of another category of key actors in the regime of international investment, namely, states. It considers, firstly, the position of the sanctioning state, examining any exceptions that may be invoked by the sanctioning state to justify its actions as regards the international investment regime. It then moves on to consider the investment host (targeted) state response to the sanctions in terms of international investment obligations; in particular whether the targeted state might be able to raise any defence(s) to potential breaches of investment obligations. Finally, it considers any remedies available to the investment host (targeted) state. In recognition that the preceding sections' analyses of the potential effects of unilateral economic sanctions on the international investment regime are largely theoretical, section IV comprises a case study of two states that have been targeted by unilateral economic sanctions, namely Iran and Qatar. It evaluates whether any of the theoretical effects on the international investment regime have been borne out in practice. Section V offers brief concluding remarks on the topic.

A comprehensive analysis of the potential effects of the imposition of unilateral economic sanctions on foreign investors and the international investment regime itself is critical, given the significant levels of foreign investment taking place across the globe annually,[5] and in light of the fact that international investment is widely accepted as an important catalyst of economic growth and development (and all of the benefits that brings).[6] Anything that potentially undermines foreign investment and its associated economic benefits warrants careful examination. Further, the severity (eg complete embargoes) of many unilaterally imposed economic sanctions can exacerbate the

[4] R Dolzer and C Schreuer, *Principles of International Investment Law* (Oxford University Press, 2012).

[5] In 2018 (the latest year for which full statistics are available), investment flows declined for the third consecutive year. However, globally, foreign investment still amounted to $1.3 trillion in 2018, which is a staggering figure. Statistics can be found in UNCTAD's World Investment Report (2019) 1, available at www.unctad.org/en/PublicationsLibrary/wir2019_en.pdf.

[6] R Robinson, *Direct Foreign Investment: Costs and Benefits* (Praeger, 1987).

effects of those sanctions on foreign investment. Additionally, in light of the apparent recent increases in the imposition of unilateral economic sanctions by some states, a comprehensive analysis of their effect on the investment regime is very timely. Finally, the topic has not historically attracted a great deal of scholarly attention; consequently, this chapter endeavours to fill a critical gap in the literature.

II. The Potential Effects of Unilateral Economic Sanctions on Foreign Investors

The potential effects that the imposition of unilateral economic sanctions might have on any given single foreign investor in the targeted state is quite difficult to determine with certainty, as it is typically dependent on a number of factors, including the severity/type of sanction(s) imposed and length of time the sanction(s) remain in place. Another such factor is the existence (or absence of) a BIT/TIP between the home state of the particular investor concerned and the host (target) state; this will determine the level of protection that the investor can expect to receive in the targeted host state. Accordingly, this section does not seek to give a definitive answer to the question of how any given single investor might be affected by the imposition of unilateral economic sanctions (because that is impossible to achieve, given the variability of the factors described above), but rather, it seeks to give an overview of the theoretical potential impacts of the imposition of such sanctions on foreign investors and the regime of international investment more generally.

In order to provide such an overview, it is necessary to categorise foreign investors according to their nationality as well as according to the existence of an operational BIT/TIP between their home state and the investment host state. In terms of an investor from the sanctioning state with an investment in the host (targeted) state, if there is a valid BIT/TIP in force between the two states, the imposition of any sanction and the effects of that sanction are very likely to cause the investment host state (the target state) to breach the obligations contained therein. On the other hand, if there is no BIT/TIP, the imposition and effects of the sanction may cause the investment host state (the targeted state) to breach customary international law and the international minimum standard of treatment (IMST) protections in any case. These two hypothetical situations deal with investments between the sanctioning and target states.

Investments made by investors from third states in the host state (targeted state) may also have been affected by the sanctions. Again, their rights might be affected by the existence (or absence) of a BIT or TIP between their home (third) state and the targeted state. If there is a BIT or TIP, the host state may have breached the obligations contained therein. If there is no BIT or TIP, customary international law protections (including the IMST) may have been breached anyway.

In light of this, when examining the potential effects of unilateral economic sanctions on foreign investors, it is necessary to categorise foreign investors as follows:

(a) Investors from the sanctioning state with an investment in the host (targeted) state where there is no BIT or TIP (*customary international law governs*).

(b) Investors from the sanctioning state with an investment in the host (targeted) state where there is a *valid BIT or TIP in force* between the two states.
(c) Investors from a third state with an investment in the host (targeted) state where there is no BIT or TIP (*customary international law governs*).
(d) Investors from a third state with an investment in the host (targeted) state where there is a *valid BIT or TIP in force* between the investor's home state and the host (target) state.

These four different scenarios essentially give rise to two investment situations: investments protected by customary international law; and investments protected by BITs and TIPs. All foreign investors are entitled to a basic level of protection by virtue of customary international law. Notwithstanding this, investors may be entitled to additional protections contained in BITs and TIPs. Investors typically receive higher levels of protection through BITs and TIPs than that offered by customary international law.[7] The following subsections will outline the protections that investors can expect to receive under customary international law as well as those that they can expect to receive under BITs and TIPs.

A. Under Customary International Law

The protections available to foreign investors under customary international law are largely based upon the concepts of state responsibility, diplomatic protection and human rights. These concepts all involve the idea of a state (ie the investment host state) harming the interests of an alien (ie the citizen of the home state), and being responsible for that harm. The central protection offered to aliens by customary international law became known as the IMST. The notion of the IMST is not 'native to the field of international investment law per se; it is the sum of rules that developed from various fields of international law out of disputes on the status of aliens'.[8] However, the general concept has found specific application in the field of international investment. The exact content of the IMST (as applicable to the law of foreign investment) is not completely settled;[9] however, the core of the concept is widely accepted to be the entitlement of the foreign investment to fair and equitable treatment (FET) on the part of the host state.[10]

FET, rather unsurprisingly (given its name), is based on the principles of fairness and equity. The problem with this is that these principles are extremely difficult to define precisely and the fact that they may be interpreted differently by different people.

[7] S Subedi, *International Investment Law: Reconciling Policy and Principle* (Hart Publishing, 2016) 111.

[8] H Taychayev, 'Developing a coherent basis for international minimum standard of treatment' Kluwer Arbitration Blog (9 May 2018), available at www.arbitrationblog.kluwerarbitration.com/2018/05/09/developing-coherent-basis-international-minimum-standard-treatment, citing Dolzer and Schreuer, *Principles* (2012) 3.

[9] See Subedi, *International Investment Law* (2016) 80, K Leite, 'The fair and equitable treatment standard: a search for a better balance in international investment agreements' (2016) 32 *American University International Law Review* 363, 372 and M Sornarajah, *The International Law on Foreign Investment*, 4th ed (Cambridge University Press, 2017) 55.

[10] Subedi (n 7) 86.

Indeed, the tribunal in *Noble Ventures*[11] noted that FET was 'notoriously difficult to define'. However, case law[12] appears to suggest that

> the principle of fair and equitable treatment seems to be concerned mainly with the obligation not to deny justice in criminal, civil or administrative adjudicatory proceedings in accordance with the principle of due process embodied in the principal legal systems in use worldwide.[13]

Aside from a guarantee of treatment that is fair and equitable, another protection afforded by the customary international law and the IMST is compensation for expropriation. The so-called *Hull formula* is widely regarded as having been incorporated into the IMST.[14] The Hull formula essentially requires prompt, adequate and effective compensation when a host state expropriates the assets of a foreign investor.[15] 'Prompt' means that compensation should be paid as soon as possible after the harmful action, with the assumption being that any delay will cause further damage to the investor.[16] 'Adequate' is 'the most important and controversial'[17] aspect of the formula because it pertains to the amount or level of compensation that should be paid to the investor. It is widely accepted as being defined with reference to the market value of the asset.[18] Effective compensation requires that the payment be made in a usable currency, ie one that is transferable to the investor's native currency.[19]

It has also been suggested that the settlement of investment disputes by a tribunal that 'sits outside the host state' may also form part of the IMST.[20] However, this is to some extent controversial, given that jurisdiction is usually established by international tribunals by virtue of advance consent on the part of states when they sign BITs and TIPs (such agreements usually contain a dispute resolution provision which grants the investor direct access to arbitration, eg administered under the auspices of ICSID). Additionally, the local remedies rule (which is a widely recognised international legal rule) requires that the investor exhaust local remedies before moving to international dispute resolution options. Thus, the argument that the settlement of investment disputes via arbitration is part of the IMST and customary international law is not particularly convincing. Aggrieved investors with no BIT or TIP to rely on will likely have to fall back on the investment host state national courts and diplomatic protection options in the event of a dispute with the host state government.

The imposition of unilateral economic sanctions on the investment host (targeted) state may cause that state to breach one or more of the protections that form part of the IMST. This may happen, for example, because the severity of the sanctions causes the host state to expropriate the assets of foreign investors without payment of compensation

[11] *Noble Ventures v Romania* (ICSID Case No ARB/01/11).

[12] ibid. See also, eg, *Rumeli Telekom AS and Telsim Mobil Telekommunikasyon Hizmetleri AS v Republic of Kazakhstan* (ICSID Case No ARB/05/16) and *Waste Management Inc v Mexico* (ICSID Case No ARB/(AF)/00/3).

[13] Subedi (n 7) 90.

[14] ibid, 34.

[15] D Collins, *An Introduction to International Investment Law* (Cambridge University Press, 2017) 188–91.

[16] ibid.

[17] ibid.

[18] ibid.

[19] ibid.

[20] Sornarajah, *Foreign Investment* (2017) 155.

(perhaps because of a serious economic downturn due to the imposition of the sanctions, the host state literally cannot afford to compensate the investor).

B. Protections available in BITs and TIPs

The first BIT, between Germany and Pakistan, was signed in 1959.[21] Since then, almost 3,000 BITs and TIPs have been signed by 234 economies.[22] BITs and TIPs are individually negotiated agreements, and therefore are theoretically unique in terms of exact content. However, such agreements tend to be structured in a similar manner, and contain broadly similar provisions and investor protections.[23] For example, BITs and TIPs tend to provide: (i) a definition of investor and investment; (ii) conditions concerning the admission of foreign investors; (iii) for the fair and equitable treatment of foreign investors (FET); (iv) compensation for expropriation of foreign investors' assets; (v) most-favoured-nation (MFN) treatment; and (vi) dispute settlement provisions.[24]

i. Definition of 'Investor' and 'Investment'

The significance of the definition of the terms 'investor' and 'investment' cannot be overstated; it will determine the scope of the application of rights and obligations contained in investment agreements, and will ultimately determine the establishment of the jurisdiction of the arbitral tribunal.[25] BITs and TIPs do not provide a universally accepted definition of these terms; instead, each BIT/TIP includes its own definition to be applied for the purposes of the application of the treaty. That said, there is some convergence as to the meaning of these terms, with many treaties employing a similar approach to their definition. Most treaties take a broad definition of the terms, presumably in order to place more activity within their remit. That is not to say that anybody can be deemed an investor and any activity be deemed investment, and so high levels of protection are automatically granted. Rather, it simply means that many persons and activities can be considered under the terms of the treaty. It does not mean that everyone and everything will be accorded the protections contained therein, but it puts the onus on the tribunal to decide if the host state's behaviour amounts to a breach of the treaty obligations.

Typically, treaties define an investor as either a natural person or an entity which has legal personality (eg a company). Additionally, in order to be covered under the particular BIT/TIP, the investor must have the requisite nationality. For natural persons, nationality is based exclusively on the law of the state of the claimed nationality (ie according to the claimed nationality's national law, would the person qualify for

[21] Germany–Pakistan BIT (1959), available at investmentpolicy.unctad.org/international-investment-agreements/treaty-files/1387/download.

[22] UNCTAD Investment Policy Hub, 'Investment agreements by economy', available at www.investmentpolicyhubold.unctad.org/IIA/IiasByCountry#iiaInnerMenu.

[23] Subedi (n 7) 109.

[24] ibid, 108–09.

[25] OECD, 'International Investment Law: Understanding Concepts and Tracking Innovations' (2008) available at www.oecd.org/investment/internationalinvestmentagreements/40471468.pdf.

that nationality?). Some treaties also enable nationality to be based on other criteria, eg residency or domicile. For legal entities, the situation is less clear-cut; globalisation has meant that determining a company's nationality is increasingly complicated. Often, the treaty itself will define what will be accepted as a legal entity's nationality for the purposes of that treaty, and it can be based on, eg, place of incorporation.[26]

Similarly, there is no singular universal definition of the term 'investment', though, once again, BITs and TIPs do tend to include a broad definition of the term.[27] Often, treaties define investment as 'every kind of asset',[28] before proceeding to include a (usually non-exhaustive) list of assets that will be deemed as investment for the purposes of the particular treaty. Such lists often include enterprises/businesses, shares, stocks or other forms of equity participation, bonds, debentures, loans and other forms of debt, futures, options and other derivatives, rights under contracts, intellectual property rights, rights conferred pursuant to laws and regulations or contracts such as concessions, licences, authorisations and permits, and any other tangible and intangible, movable and immovable property, and any related property rights, such as leases, mortgages, liens and pledges.[29]

Therefore, if foreign investors' home states (whether that be the sanctioning state or otherwise) have an operational BIT or TIP with the targeted (host) state, the investor will need to demonstrate their status as an investor and the eligibility of their investment under the particular treaty. If the investor can demonstrate that they are indeed an investor with a covered investment, then they will benefit from the protections contained therein. This does not necessarily mean that the investment host (targeted) state will be liable for any damages; the investor will need to go on to demonstrate that the host state has breached one of the investment protection obligations below.

ii. *Admission of Foreign Investment*

In addition to the basic definitions of the terms 'investor' and 'investment', investment treaties typically deal with the conditions of admission and establishment of foreign investors in the contracting states. Whilst it is accepted that the issues relating to admission of investors and investment should be regulated by investment treaties, policies and practice tend to vary quite a bit from investment agreement to investment agreements. Some states take a liberal approach to investors, whilst at the other end of the spectrum, some states are far less welcoming.[30]

Regardless of which approach is followed, if under the terms and provisions of any given investment treaty an investor would ordinarily be permitted to enter the investment host state in order to establish a business, yet the imposed unilateral economic

[26] ibid.

[27] B Legum, 'Defining investor and investment: who is entitled to claim?' (2005) presented at a symposium organised by the OECD, ICSID and UNCTAD, and available at www.oecd.org/investment/internationalinvestmentagreements/36370461.pdf.

[28] OECD, 'International Investment Law' (2008) 25.

[29] Taken from the recently signed Japan–Jordan BIT (2018) available at www.investmentpolicy.unctad.org/international-investment-agreements/treaty-files/5808/download.

[30] Categorisation as it appears in UNCTAD, 'UNCTAD series on issues in international investment agreements (admission and establishment)' 3–4, available at unctad.org/en/Docs/iteiit10v2_en.pdf.

sanctions prohibit the admission and establishment by the investor, the targeted state would likely be in breach of the obligations of the treaty.

iii. Fair and Equitable Treatment

As has been observed above, the FET standard places an obligation on the investment host state to accord treatment that is 'fair and equitable' to the investor. This standard is widely accepted as forming part of the IMST of treatment under customary international law. Additionally, FET is routinely included explicitly as a provision in BITs and TIPs.

As discussed above, the major and most obvious problem with this standard lies in the inherent difficulties in interpreting what is 'fair and equitable', which may vary according to different peoples' perceptions, ie what one person finds to be fair and equitable, another person may not. Despite this interpretative complexity, the FET standard usually appears in most investment treaties. Moreover, it is the single most relied upon investment protection provision in investment disputes, and it is a provision with which investors have had much success in those disputes.[31] One of the reasons that FET provisions have been viewed as so powerful (from an investor's point of view) is that they have traditionally been interpreted in a very broad manner by many investment tribunals.[32] Accordingly, the FET provisions of applicable BITs/TIPs could be a significant weapon for foreign investors against the investment host (targeted state). If the host state takes any action which could undermine the FET standard, given the liberal interpretation of that standard demonstrated by numerous investment tribunals, investors would likely have a good shot at bringing successful arbitral proceedings.

iv. Compensation for Expropriation

Protection from and compensation for expropriation of assets is a right that foreign investors enjoy that is typically enshrined in BITs and TIPs. However, such agreements often simply codify and formalise the protection available under customary international law. Accordingly, the most common formulation for compensation for expropriation is the Hull formula, which requires prompt, adequate and effective compensation (as detailed above).

The protection from expropriation provision of a treaty creates an obligation to refrain from the adoption of any measures which directly or indirectly affect the ownership of the investor's capital or investment such as the deprivation of basic rights on ownership, possession or utilisation of capital and control or enjoyment over investment. Therefore, unilateral economic sanctions that undermine such protection would contravene the treaties concerned and cause compensation to become payable to the aggrieved foreign investor.

[31] Pink Series II FET (2012), see 'Executive summary', available at www.unctad.org/en/Docs/unctaddiaeia2011d5_en.pdf.

[32] G van Harten, 'Leaders in the Expansive and Restrictive Interpretation of Investment Treaties: A Descriptive Study of ISDS Awards to 2010' (2018) 29 *European Journal of International Law* 507, 518.

v. Most-Favoured-Nation Treatment

The most-favoured-nation (MFN) standard provided under BITs and TIPs potentially enables investors to benefit from other international investment treaties (including other BITs and TIPs) by importing more favourable terms from them into the original treaty itself. A key case on the MFN obligation is *Maffezzini v Spain*[33] in which the tribunal held that the MFN provision in the Argentina–Spain BIT could be used by the claimant to circumvent the 18-month waiting period before recourse to international arbitration became available. The claimant argued that a third-party treaty between Spain and Chile did not include such a waiting period, and that therefore the ISDS clause in that third-party treaty was less restrictive. The claimant argued that it could then be imported using the MFN provision contained in the original Argentina–Spain BIT. The tribunal accepted the claimant's arguments. This decision was highly criticised as providing overly generous investor protections (it was the first time a tribunal had allowed the MFN provision to be utilised in order to import a procedural right ie dispute settlement, rather than an uncontroversial substantive one).[34] This route and mechanism have also been utilised to import and rely on the FET standard under more favourable investment protection treaties than the one between the investor's home state and the investment host state.[35]

In terms of the application of MFN provisions to situations involving unilateral economic sanctions, such provisions could be applied to import more favourable protections into an existing BIT between the investor's home state (whether that be the sanctioning state or a third state) and the investment host (targeted) state, thereby widening the scope of protection that the investor enjoys as regards his or her investment in the host state. This could be a significant advantage if the original BIT or TIP is worded quite restrictively, as it could make available much more advantageous provisions, and increase the potential likelihood of success in the event of the investor bringing a claim against the host (targeted) state.

vi. Investor–State Dispute Settlement (ISDS)

BITs usually grant foreign investors direct access to independent, international tribunals in the case of a dispute between themselves and the investment host state. Investment treaty arbitration is the most popular form of investment dispute settlement nowadays, which is reflected by its routine inclusion in BITs and the proliferation

[33] *Emilio Agustín Maffezini v The Kingdom of Spain* (2000), ICSID Case No ARB/97/7.

[34] The expansive interpretation of MFN clauses has been criticised by commentators. See, eg, B Stern, 'ICSID arbitration and the state's increasingly remote consent: a propos the Maffezini case' in S Charnovitz et al (eds), *Law in the Service of Human Dignity. Essays in Honour of Florentino Feliciano* (Cambridge University Press, 2005) 247–60. Additionally, the broad approach to interpretation was also criticised in a number of subsequent cases, with a number of later ICSID tribunals taking a much narrower view of MFN provisions. See, eg, *Salini Costruttori SpA and Italstrade SpA v Hashemite Kingdom of Jordan* (2005) ICSID Case No ARB/02/13, *Plama Consortium Limited v Republic of Bulgaria* (2005) ICSID Case No ARB/03/24 and *Telenor Mobile Communications AS v Republic of Hungary* (2006) ICSID Case No ARB/04/15.

[35] See, eg, *Bayindir Insaat Turizm Ticaret Ve Sanayi A.S. v Islamic Republic of Pakistan* (2003), ICSID Case No ARB/03/29.

of these agreements. For example, the US Model BIT (2012) gives investors a range of options, enabling the foreign investor to submit a claim:

(a) under the ICSID Convention and the ICSID Rules of Procedure for Arbitration Proceedings, provided that both the respondent and the non-disputing party are parties to the ICSID Convention;
(b) under the ICSID Additional Facility Rules, provided that either the respondent or the non-disputing party is a party to the ICSID Convention;
(c) under the UNCITRAL Arbitration Rules; or
(d) if the claimant and respondent agree, to any other arbitration institution or under any other arbitration rules.[36]

This article is a fairly typical example of dispute settlement provisions contained in BITs. The precise details of the arbitration mechanism will be discussed in section II.c.ii below. Suffice it to say at this point that such dispute settlement provisions potentially serve to provide foreign investors whose investments have been affected by unilateral economic sanctions a direct action against the investment host (targeted) state.

C. Remedies available to Investors

The preceding sub-sections have set out the investment protections that investors can typically expect to receive under both customary international law and under any applicable BITs and TIPs, and examined how they might be applicable to foreign investors whose investments may have been detrimentally affected by the imposition of unilateral economic sanctions on the host state. This section will now consider what remedies (or dispute settlement options) might be available to those aggrieved investors whose investment has been negatively impacted by the imposition of unilateral economic sanctions.

i. Under National or International Law Generally

a. Traditional Methods of Dispute Settlement

If there is no BIT or TIP in operation between the investor's home state and the investment host state, the aggrieved investor will need to rely on traditional methods of dispute settlement, ie those available under national or international law generally. It would be wise for aggrieved investors to exhaust any remedies that might be available to them under the domestic law of the investment host state. This will often involve bringing a case in the national courts of the host state (if the host state has potentially breached any provisions of domestic legislation). This is not a particularly desirable

[36] Art 24, para 3, US Model BIT (2012), available at www.ustr.gov/sites/default/files/BIT%20text%20for%20ACIEP%20Meeting.pdf.

option for foreign investors who will likely worry that the national courts may demonstrate bias towards the host state government, and that the judiciary may not be fully independent. Additionally, foreign investors are likely to be linguistically and procedurally put at a disadvantage.

In terms of international dispute resolution in the absence of a treaty, the most obvious option available to an investor who believes the investment host state's actions may amount to a breach of the customary international law would be diplomatic protection. This basically entails the investor's home state intervening on behalf of its citizen abroad (ie the foreign investor) to demand protection and compensation from the host state which is alleged to have breached the international minimum standard of protection available under customary international law. From the investor's perspective, the downside of this is that they lose control over the dispute, and in turn, the investor will have to accept whatever outcome their home state can negotiate with the host state. The desirability of the negotiated outcome will very often depend on the balance of power and state of international relations between the home and host state.

b. Human Rights Remedies

Another option for investors who are not able to rely on a BIT/TIP is to pursue human rights remedies; aggrieved investors may simultaneously be victims of a human rights abuse which is attributable to the investment host state. Accordingly, investors may also be able to pursue a claim under a human rights treaty (provided that the host state is a party to a suitable human rights treaty, eg European Convention on Human Rights or the African Charter on Human and Peoples Rights). Such a claim would be based on an interference with the property rights of the investor; such rights are typically protected in human rights treaties. If the investment host state has interfered with the property rights of foreign investors, eg by expropriating such property, then the foreign investor could pursue a human rights claim. If investors have a choice between pursuance of a human rights claim or initiating an investment arbitration, investors will usually opt for investment arbitration; this is due to the many benefits of such a mechanism (eg party autonomy) and the fact that higher standards of protection are usually available for the protection of foreign property under BITs and TIPs than is available under human rights treaties (which typically contain a vague provision providing citizens' with a qualified right to own and enjoy property, subject to certain provisos). Therefore, cases where investors pursue human rights remedies, are few and far between. Nonetheless, this option is theoretically available to aggrieved foreign investors, but is likely only taken if there are literally no other options available.

ii. *By Virtue of BITs and TIPs*

Where there is a BIT or TIP in operation between the investor's home state and the investment host state, in the event of a breach of investor protection provisions contained therein, the treaty will more than likely grant the investor direct access to international investment arbitration. International investment arbitration can be carried out in an ad hoc manner (often under the UNCITRAL Rules), or it can be administered by an institution (eg the International Centre for the Settlement of Investment Disputes[37]). Whether it is ad hoc or institutional, it enables aggrieved investors to sue host state governments for alleged breaches of investment protections contained in BITs. There is a high degree of party autonomy in investment arbitration, meaning that the parties themselves usually select the arbitrators (usually one arbitrator is selected by the investor, one is selected by the host state, and the third, often presiding arbitrator, is selected by mutual agreement of the parties or by mutual agreement of the two already selected arbitrators). Proceedings are often held in camera, and case documents are not automatically published. In recent times, international investment arbitration has been the subject of a serious backlash, with critics asserting that it lacks legitimacy and transparency as a dispute resolution mechanism.[38] Despite the backlash, currently, it remains standard practice to include investment arbitration provisions in BITs and TIPs, meaning that aggrieved investors have a direct right of action against investment host states (providing there is a valid BIT/TIP between the home and host state in question).

The right to bring a case directly against the investment host (targeted) state is a considerable advantage accorded to foreign investors accorded under applicable BITs and TIPs. Settlement of an investment dispute by a neutral, independent international tribunal is certainly more desirable to aggrieved foreign investors than exhausting local remedies, utilisation of diplomatic protection and resort to human rights remedies. In terms of investors affected by the imposition of unilateral economic sanctions, ISDS would therefore represent the most desirable option for dispute settlement.

III. Consequences for the States Involved where there is a Valid Investment Treaty in Place

Thus far, this chapter has primarily concerned itself with the potential consequences of the imposition of unilateral economic sanctions on foreign investors. It has demonstrated that, theoretically, the imposition of unilateral economic sanctions can cause targeted states to breach investor protection obligations (whether those protections are contained in customary international law, or additional protections contained in BITs and TIPs). This section will now examine the potential consequences of the imposition of unilateral economic sanctions on the other important stakeholders in the investment relationship ie states.

[37] For more information on institutional arbitration under the auspices of ICSID, see www.icsid.worldbank.org/en.

[38] There is much literature on the backlash in investment arbitration. See, eg, M Waibel et al (eds), *The Backlash Against Investment Arbitration: Perceptions and Reality* (Walters Kluwer, 2010); S Franck, 'The legitimacy crisis in investment treaty arbitration: privatizing public international law through inconsistent decisions' (2005) 73 *Fordham Law Review* 1521; T Dietz, 'The legitimacy crisis of investor-state arbitration and the new EU investment court system' (2019) 26 *Review of International Political Economy* 749; and O Svoboda, 'Current State of Transparency in Investment Arbitration: Progress Made But Not Enough' (2017) COFOLA International Conference Proceedings, available at www.researchgate.net/publication/329595989_Current_State_of_Transparency_in_Investment_Arbitration_Progress_Made_But_Not_Enough.

A. Exceptions that may be Invoked by the Sanctioning State

The state that imposes and enforces unilateral economic sanctions will immediately breach the typical obligations contained in the BIT/TIP (as discussed above) between the sanctioning state and the targeted state. However, the sanctioning state may try to invoke certain exceptions in relation to the investment treaty regime, so as to justify its actions.

Typically, when negotiating international agreements and treaties, states try to leave themselves some flexibility to conditionally disapply the commitments within the treaty. In BITs and TIPs this typically manifests itself in an 'essential security' provision. For example, Article 18 of the US Model BIT 2012 states:

> Nothing in this Treaty shall be construed:
>
> 1. to require a Party to furnish or allow access to any information the disclosure of which it determines to be contrary to its essential security interests; or
> 2. to preclude a Party from applying measures that it considers necessary for the fulfilment of its obligations with respect to the maintenance or restoration of international peace or security, or the protection of its own essential security interests.[39]

This provision (specifically paragraph 2) allows the signatory states to apply any measures that they feel are necessary to maintain either international peace or security, or to maintain their own national security interests. Such provisions are commonly included in BITs and TIPs.[40] These types of provisions could clearly be invoked by sanctioning states to justify their actions when applying unilateral economic sanctions to effectively suspend the application of the BIT or TIP.

Typically, BITs and TIPs do not define what is meant by maintenance of international peace or security, nor do they define what will be construed as a state's essential security interests. Therefore, these terms are potentially open to a wide interpretation which may be used to cover or justify the actions of the sanctioning state in imposing the unilateral economic sanctions. The sanctioning state could argue that the sanctions are necessary in order to protect the economic security of the state.

B. Defences that may be Invoked by the Targeted State

Moving away from the potential justifications for the imposition of the unilateral economic sanctions by the sanctioning state, this sub-section will consider whether any defences might be successfully raised by the investment host (targeted) state for the likely breach of international investment obligations that will ensue. In this vein, the target state may try to argue that any breaches were unavoidable and try to

[39] Art 18 of the US Model BIT (n 36).

[40] See, eg, Art 18 of the Canada Model BIT (2014), available at www.italaw.com/sites/default/files/files/italaw8236.pdf; or Art 21 of the Japan–Morocco BIT (2019), available at www.investmentpolicy.unctad.org/international-investment-agreements/treaty-files/5908/download; and Art 13 of the Ethiopia–Qatar BIT (2017), available at www.investmentpolicy.unctad.org/international-investment-agreements/treaty-files/5982/download.

raise a number of defences including necessity, and general, as well as specific treaty exceptions.

i. Necessity

Necessity is one of the six widely accepted general defences to state responsibility which would otherwise arise from a breach of a legal obligation.[41] Article 25 of the ILC Articles on State Responsibility are generally accepted as codifying the doctrine of necessity.[42] According to Article 25, the defence can only be invoked in limited circumstances. Accordingly, the following cumulative requirements to successfully raise the defence of necessity are:

- Safeguarding of an essential interest;
- Grave and imminent peril;
- The only way; and,
- Does not seriously impair an essential interest of the State or States towards which the obligation exists, or of the international community as a whole.[43]

Additionally, the international obligation in question must not exclude the possibility of invoking necessity, and the state must not have contributed to the situation of necessity.[44] If successfully invoked, the necessity defence completely absolves a state under customary law for actions that would otherwise have breached the said international obligation, eg investment obligations. Necessity has been raised (with varying degrees of success) as a defence by breaching investment host states in a number of high-profile investment arbitration cases.

The most widely recognised line of investment cases to deal with the defence of necessity are those involving Argentina. Argentina went through a serious economic crisis in the 1990s. As a result of the crisis, the Argentine Government enacted a series of measures[45] that seriously adversely affected foreign investors and their property. Understandably, foreign investors were dismayed at the Government's actions, and a stream of investment claims were brought by injured investors, alleging violations of various Argentine BITs and TIPs. Five[46] such claims were brought to ICSID by US investors alleging that the Government had breached the provisions of the US–Argentina BIT. Argentina denied any wrongdoing or breach of treaty provisions. Argentina also proceeded to defend its actions under the customary international law doctrine of necessity and by making reference to Article 11 of the BIT, which states:

> This Treaty shall not preclude the application by either Party of measures necessary for the maintenance of public order, the fulfilment of its obligations with respect to the maintenance

[41] The others are: consent, self-defence, countermeasures, force majeure and distress.

[42] ILC Articles on State Responsibility (2001) Commentary, available at www.legal.un.org/ilc/texts/instruments/english/commentaries/9_6_2001.pdf.

[43] ibid.

[44] ibid.

[45] Measures included bank account and asset freezes, prohibition of sending money abroad, changing currency valuations and much more.

[46] *CMS Gas Transmission Company v Argentina*, ICSID ARB/01/8; *LG&E Energy Corp., LG&E Capital Corp, LG&E International Inc v Argentina*, ICSID ARB/02/1; *Enron Corporation and Ponderosa Assets, LP v Argentina*, ICSID ARB/01/3; *Sempra Energy International v Argentina*, ICSID ARB/02/16; and *Continental Casualty Company v Argentine Republic*, ICSID ARB/03/9.

or restoration of international peace or security, or the Protection of its own essential security interests.[47]

Article 11 essentially contains a general treaty exception (this is discussed in the next section), however, it is relevant to the doctrine of necessity in these cases, as the respondent argued that the actions were necessary to protect essential interests.

In *CMS*, the tribunal rejected Argentina's argument that its actions could be justified on the grounds of necessity. In *Enron* and *Sempra*, the tribunals followed suit, rejecting the necessity argument. In all three cases, the claimants were awarded large sums in compensation/damages. In *LG&E*, however, the tribunal accepted the necessity plea, on the grounds that the economic situation in Argentina at the time was so grave relating to measures taken within a certain time period. Outside that time period, though, Argentina was found to have breached its BIT obligations, and the defence of necessity was not applicable. A lesser amount of compensation was awarded than in the previous three cases. In *Continental*, the tribunal accepted all of the Argentine Government's actions could be excused by necessity (except one action relating to Treasury Bills); accordingly, a small amount was awarded in damages. All five cases were subject to annulment proceedings, but it is submitted that the results of the annulments are to a great extent irrelevant, given that the five grounds for annulment contained in Article 52 of the ICSID Convention are related only to defects with procedurals aspects of the arbitration (eg tribunal not properly constituted or manifest excess of powers), rather than being concerned with the correctness of the decisions themselves. What is most important for the purposes of this work, is that the five original ICSID tribunals came to varying conclusions regarding the defence of necessity. This demonstrates that when it comes to investment, the defence of necessity is not applied particularly coherently by investment tribunals.

In terms of the application of the defence of necessity by an investment host state to justify its potential breach of investment obligations as a result of the imposition of unilateral economic sanctions, it seems it would be down to an individual investment tribunal to decide whether necessity would be accepted as a defence. It is almost impossible to say whether such a defence would be accepted in this situation, given that there is no doctrine of precedent in investment arbitration, therefore each and every tribunal can decide to do as it pleases. However, it would be advisable for the targeted host state to attempt to raise the defence when faced with potential breaches of investment obligations due to the sanctions imposed.

ii. *General Treaty Exceptions*

BITs and TIPs can include provisions containing general treaty exceptions. General exceptions state a limited number of situations where the obligations contained in the treaty are suspended or do not apply. Suspension or non-application is conditional on the existence of a set of prescribed circumstances. General exceptions are included in order to relieve investment host states from possible treaty liability for measures taken in good faith to pursue a number of limited public welfare objectives. Such public welfare

[47] US–Argentina BIT (1991), available at www.investmentpolicy.unctad.org/international-investment-agreements/treaty-files/127/download.

objectives often include: security interests; promotion of animal and plant health; protection of the environment; regulation of the economy; preservation of diverse cultures; and preservation of public order.[48]

General exceptions now increasingly appear in BITs and TIPs negotiated by many states; of 29 new treaties reviewed by UNCTAD in its World Investment Report 2019, 19 include general exceptions.[49] In 2007 the trend towards including general exceptions was only just emerging.[50] States including Canada,[51] Japan,[52] Turkey[53] and Australia[54] now routinely include general exceptions in their BITs and TIPs.

Targeted states could try to invoke general treaty exceptions when faced with possible investment treaty breaches due to the imposition of unilateral economic sanctions. Exceptions relating to security could be particularly useful in this regard. Such exceptions have already been discussed above in the context of their invocation by the sanctioning state, but their application from the perspective of the investment (targeted) state merits further discussion. In this situation, such exceptions are essentially invoked as a defence. This is interesting, because investment tribunals have pronounced on a number of cases where security interests have been invoked as a defence in this way. Indeed, by raising defence of necessity in the five cases above where Argentina appeared as a respondent, the Argentine Government invoked Article 11 of the US–Argentina BIT, which contains a general treaty exception.

One important aspect of the general treaty exception is the so-called 'self-judging' character of the provision. Essentially, the question is who should judge whether conditions required for the provision to be invoked have been triggered? For example, who decides whether the essential security interests of the investment host state are at stake; is it the host state itself that is competent to judge its position? The *CMS* tribunal pondered this very question when it asked if the state adopting the measures is the only judge of the legality of the invocation of essential security interests, or if the invocation is 'subject to some form of judicial review'.[55]

The investment host (targeted) state will likely argue that the imposition of the unilateral economic sanctions set in motion a chain of events that led to the breaching of investor protection obligations contained in any given BIT/TIP, and that the breaches should be excepted or excused due to the fact that they were unavoidable in order to protect the interests of the investment host (targeted) state.

[48] These are some of the most common grounds for general exceptions, there may be of course others in individual treaties.

[49] UNCTAD, World Investment Report (2019) 105.

[50] UNCTAD, 'Note on International Investment Rulemaking', available at www.unctad.org/en/docs/c2em21d2_en.pdf at 11.

[51] Art 18 Canada Model BIT (2014).

[52] Art 15 Argentina–Japan BIT (2018), available at www.investmentpolicy.unctad.org/international-investment-agreements/treaty-files/5799/download.

[53] Art 4 Cambodia–Turkey BIT (2018), available at www.investmentpolicy.unctad.org/international-investment-agreements/treaty-files/5833/download.

[54] Art 15 Australia–Uruguay BIT (2019), available at www.investmentpolicy.unctad.org/international-investment-agreements/treaty-files/5853/download.

[55] *CMS Gas Transmission Company v Argentina*, ICSID ARB/01/8 Final award 12 May 2005, para 366 available at www.italaw.com/sites/default/files/case-documents/ita0184.pdf.

iii. Exceptions within Specific Obligations

Some investment treaty provisions themselves may include self-contained exceptions; this means that in a limited set of circumstances, the specific obligation contained in that provision might not be applicable. One example of this is related to MFN provisions. Many exceptions to MFN treatment reflect the reality that such treatment will not be extended to privileges given to third states by virtue of free trade agreements, customs unions or other mechanisms to foster regional integration. This is then duplicated in terms of double taxation treaties:

> This treatment does not extend, however, to the privileges that one Contracting Party grants to the nationals or companies of a third State, by virtue of its participation in or association with a free trade area, customs union, common market or any other form of regional economic organization. Treatment granted under this article is not applied to taxes and fiscal deductions and exemptions granted by one of the Contracting Parties to the investors of a third State under a double taxation or other tax-related agreement. [Unofficial translation][56]

What this essentially means is that investors protected by the BIT/TIP cannot use the MFN clause contained therein to claim treatment that is more favourable than that granted by the host state to investors of a third state under an FTA or taxation treaty. This therefore avoids a de facto multilateralisation of the most favourable FTAs/taxation treaties granted by virtue of an economic integration scheme.

Additionally, some treaties exclude certain sectors or industries from the scope of operation of MFN provisions, eg 'aviation, fisheries, maritime matters, including salvage'.[57] In this way, signatory states can utilise specific exceptions to protect certain sectors of their economy that may be viewed as special or sensitive for some reason. These types of specific exceptions may be utilised by the investment host (targeted) state to justify removal of investment protections due to the imposition of the unilateral economic sanctions.

C. Remedies available for Targeted State

This section will discuss situations in which there is a valid BIT/TIP in place between the state imposing the unilateral economic sanctions and the target state.

By imposing and enforcing the sanctions, the imposing state will undoubtedly be undermining the BIT/TIP provisions agreed between the two countries. The question, then, is what the target state can do about this. Ultimately the target state always has the option to unilaterally terminate the BIT/TIP. Usually BITs and TIPs include a

[56] See France–Libya BIT (2004), Art 4, available at www.investmentpolicy.unctad.org/international-investment-agreements/treaty-files/3491/download and as cited in S Nikièma, 'The Most-Favoured-Nation Clause in Investment Treaties' (IISD, 2017) available at www.iisd.org/sites/default/files/publications/mfn-most-favoured-nation-clause-best-practices-en.pdf accessed 9 March 2020.

[57] See Art 3.3.c of the China–Benin BIT (2004) available at www.investmentpolicy.unctad.org/international-investment-agreements/treaty-files/440/download.

termination clause which often provides that either contracting state can terminate the agreement unilaterally. For example, Article 16 of the Qatar–Singapore BIT[58] states that the agreement shall be valid, initially for a period of 10 years, and then automatically extended. However, either contracting party can give written notice through diplomatic channels that they wish to terminate the agreement. The agreement shall be duly terminated 12 months after receipt of the written notice. This is very typical of the sorts of termination clauses included in BITs and TIPs. Presumably, the target state would look to exercise its right to terminate the agreement with the sanctioning state. However, it should be noted that any unilateral termination is usually subject to the operation of a 'sunset clause'. Article 16 (paragraph 2) of the Qatar–Singapore BIT[59] goes on to state that the termination after receipt of written notice after one year is subject to a continuation of the protections contained in the agreement for a further period of 10 years (only for investments that were established before the date of written termination). Therefore, for the target state, although this is an option, it is not necessarily that desirable as it will not serve to cut ties with the sanctioning state immediately.

A more preferable option for the target state could be to rely on Article 60 of the Vienna Convention on the Law of Treaties 1969,[60] which deals with the termination or suspension of a treaty as a consequence of its breach. Article 60 (paragraph 1) states that 'A material breach of a bilateral treaty by one of the parties entitles the other to invoke the breach as a ground for terminating the treaty or suspending its operation in whole or in part'.[61] Article 60 goes on to define a material breach as '(a) A repudiation of the treaty not sanctioned by the present Convention; or (b) The violation of a provision essential to the accomplishment of the object or purpose of the treaty'.[62] The imposition of unilateral sanctions by one of the contracting partners to the BIT/TIP would undoubtedly qualify as a 'material breach' of the obligations contained therein. Therefore, the target state could utilise the imposition of the sanctions to terminate the BIT/TIP, arguably with immediate effect. Article 60 makes no mention of a transition period or sunset clause. Indeed, to operate a sunset clause would seem to be at odds with what Article 60 is trying to achieve (termination due to breach). Therefore, reliance on Article 60 of the Vienna Convention would appear to be a better option than termination of the BIT/TIP in accordance with the BIT/TIP's own termination provision, at least from the perspective of the targeted state because arguably the obligations of the BIT/TIP would cease to exist immediately. For foreign investors in the target state from the imposing home state, this would mean that they would fall back on human rights law remedies or customary international investment law immediately.

[58] Agreement Between the Government of the State of Qatar and the Government of the Republic of Singapore for the Reciprocal Promotion and Protection of Investments (2017), available at www.investmentpolicy.unctad.org/international-investment-agreements/treaty-files/5852/download.

[59] ibid.

[60] Vienna Convention on the Law of Treaties (1969), available at www.treaties.un.org/doc/Publication/UNTS/Volume%201155/volume-1155-I-18232-English.pdf.

[61] ibid.

[62] ibid.

IV. Case Studies: Iran and Qatar

The preceding sections of this chapter have set out the potential consequences of the imposition of unilateral economic sanctions on various categories of foreign investors, as well as the potential consequences of such sanctions for state parties (namely the state imposing the unilateral sanctions as well as the target state). This section will build on the analysis above by applying it to two case studies: Iran and Qatar.

Iran and Qatar have both recently been targeted by unilateral economic sanctions: the US has imposed a fresh round of sanctions on Iran,[63] whist a group of Arab nations (led by Saudi Arabia) has also imposed sanctions on Qatar.[64] Whereas the preceding sections of this work have set out the theoretical impacts of unilateral economic sanctions on investors and their investments, the aim of this section is to conduct a short case study analysis of the actual effects of unilateral economic sanctions on foreign investors in these two investment host states.

A. Iran

The US imposed its first sanctions on Iran in November 1979 in response to local students seizing the US embassy in Tehran, where around 50 hostages were detained for over a year.[65] The first sanctions included the freezing of approximately $12 billion of Iranian assets (including bank deposits, gold and other property), as well as a complete trade and investment embargo.[66] Additional sanctions were imposed by the US in 1984 and 1992. In 1996, the US intensified the effect of its sanctions by introducing measures to promote extraterritoriality of its sanctions by threatening to fine third-party states that breached its sanction, eg by investing in Iran's petroleum sector. It is interesting to note that these threats were not enforced for a number of years. However, in 2010, the US began to take the enforcement of these secondary sanctions more seriously. At the same time (between 2006 and 2010) collective sanctions were also imposed on Iran by the UN Security Council. The collective sanctions aimed to restrain Iranian development of nuclear weapons. Nonetheless, in 2015, a Joint Comprehensive Plan of Action was reached which would see US sanctions on Iran lifted, in return for the scaling back of Iran's nuclear capabilities. However, after the 2016 election, the US later withdrew from the deal, reimposing old sanctions and introducing some new sanctions on Iran (which would take effect in either August or November 2018).[67] The three-month gap

[63] For a comprehensive list of sanctions imposed by the US on Iran, see www.treasury.gov/resource-center/sanctions/programs/pages/iran.aspx.

[64] Allen & Overy, 'GCC sanctions in relation to Qatar', available at www.allenovery.com/en-gb/global/news-and-insights/legal-and-regulatory-risks-for-the-finance-sector/middle-east/gcc-sanctions-in-relation-to-qatar.

[65] Encyclopaedia Britannica, 'Iran Hostage Crisis', available at www.britannica.com/event/Iran-hostage-crisis.

[66] J Levs (CNN), 'A summary of sanctions against Iran', available at www.edition.cnn.com/2012/01/23/world/meast/iran-sanctions-facts/index.html.

[67] R Gladstone, 'Iran sanctions explained: US goals, and the view from Tehran' *New York Times*, 5 November 2018, available at www.nytimes.com/2018/11/05/world/middleeast/iran-sanctions-explained.html.

was to enable business owners to divest from Iran. The current sanctions imposed by the US on Iran include: targeting Iran's acquisition of US bank notes; Iranian trade in gold/precious metals; prohibiting the sale of graphite, aluminum, steel, coal and software used in industrial processes to Iran; disrupting transactions relating to the Iranian currency (rial); activities relating to Iran's issuance of sovereign debt; activities related to Iran's automotive sector; and punitive measures seeking to prevent third-party involvement in Iran's energy, shipping, insurance and financial sectors.[68]

Since 1979, the various unilateral economic sanctions imposed by the US have clearly had a devastating effect on the Iranian economy.[69] Specifically, the 2018 sanctions have 'driven Iran's economy into recession as major companies exit the Iranian economy rather than risk being penalized by the United States. Iran's oil exports have decreased significantly, the value of Iran's currency has declined sharply'.[70] However, the extent to which they can be considered effective or successful in terms of affecting the Iranian regime or its policies is less obvious: 'unrest has continued, [though] not to the point where the regime is threatened'.[71]

With regard to the effect of US sanctions on Iran on foreign investors, it is pertinent to note that US does not currently have (and indeed never has had) a BIT with Iran.[72] However, Iran has signed a total of 72 BITs/TIPs with countries other than the US, 59 of which are currently in force.[73]

In terms of Iran facing arbitration claims from aggrieved investors, there is only one known case where the Iranian Republic was the respondent,[74] but this was unconnected to the economic sanctions, having been decided in favour of the state (tribunal jurisdiction declined) under the auspices of the Permanent Court of Arbitration in 2014.[75]

The most obvious effect that the sanctions have had on all foreign investors (those from the US and third-party states alike) is to discourage them from investing in Iran in the first place, or requiring them to divest from Iran; this is evidenced by investment statistics. In 2015, Iran's inwards investment was around $2 billion. After the Joint Comprehensive Plan was negotiated, in 2016, investment levels jumped to $3.3 billion, and in 2017 peaked at over $5 billion. After sanctions were reimposed in 2018, inward investment fell back to $3.4 billion.[76]

[68] International Institute for Strategic Studies, 'The impact of renewed sanctions on Iran' (2019) 25 *Strategic Communications*, Comment, 3.

[69] See, eg, S Kerr, A England and N Bozorgmehr, 'Iran's economy slumps as US sanctions pile on the pain' *Financial Times*, 29 April 2019, available at www.ft.com/content/ac599cf4-6a72-11e9-80c7-60ee53e6681d. See also BBC News, '6 charts that show how hard US sanctions have hit Iran' (2 May 2019), available at www.bbc.co.uk/news/world-middle-east-48119109.

[70] US Congressional Report Service, 'Iran Sanctions' (12 July 2019), available at www.fas.org/sgp/crs/mideast/RS20871.pdf, first page summary.

[71] ibid.

[72] IIA Navigator, 'Iran', available at investmentpolicy.unctad.org/country-navigator/100/iran-islamic-republic-of.

[73] ibid.

[74] *Turkcell v Iran* (2014); see www.italaw.com/cases/2735.

[75] UNCTAD Investment Dispute Navigator, 'Turkcell v Iran' (2014), available at www.investmentpolicy.unctad.org/investment-dispute-settlement/cases/288/turkcell-v-iran.

[76] All investment statistics can be found in the UNCTAD (n 5), Iran Country Fact Sheet, available at www.unctad.org/sections/dite_dir/docs/wir2019/wir19_fs_ir_en.pdf.

B. Qatar

A Saudi Arabia led coalition (including Bahrain, Egypt and the UAE) imposed sanctions on Qatar in June 2017 in response to alleged Qatari support for terrorist activities.[77] Qatar vehemently rejected this claim, maintaining that there was no legitimate justification for the action, and that the actions amounted to a violation of its sovereignty.[78] The sanctions imposed a blockade of land, sea and air from the all of the coalition states to Qatar.[79] In terms of the effects of the diplomatic crisis and the sanctions on the Qatari economy, the IMF states that 'Economic performance improved in 2018. Qatar's economy has successfully absorbed the shocks from the 2014–16 drop in hydrocarbon prices and the 2017 diplomatic rift. Real GDP growth is estimated at 2.2 percent, up from 1.6 percent in 2017'.[80]

In terms of FDI statistics specifically, prior to the imposition of the sanctions, FDI inflows to Qatar had been steadily increasing,[81] having peaked at $986 million in 2017.[82] However, the year after the imposition of the sanctions, in 2018, investment inflows to Qatar moved into negative figures, at –$2.1 billion.[83] This represents a huge loss within the time span of just one year. The official UNCTAD statistics only cover up to 2018, therefore it is not known what may have happened to investment inflows from 2019 onwards at present. Up to 2018, though, it is reasonable to assume from the drop in FDI inflows that foreign investors have lost confidence and are significantly less willing to invest in Qatar as a result of the sanctions imposed.

In 2019 Qatar also introduced new domestic legislation regulating foreign investment in the country.[84] The new law introduced a number of important changes, eg allowing 100 per cent foreign ownership of companies, as well as a higher percentage of ownership of Qatari companies by foreign investors and the introduction of various investment incentives.[85] One of the central aims of the law is to attract more foreign investment into Qatar. Once more up-to-date FDI statistics detailing inflows from 2019 onwards become available, it will be possible to see what, if any effect, the new law might have had on FDI and whether it achieved its central aim of attracting higher levels of investment.

In terms of the specifics of the international investment regime, Qatar has signed 71 BITs and TIPs, 32 of which are currently in force.[86] In terms of BITs and TIPs with the

[77] 'The Gulf states reconsider their feud with Qatar' The Economist, 18 December 2019, available at www.economist.com/middle-east-and-africa/2019/12/18/the-gulf-states-reconsider-their-feud-with-qatar.

[78] Aljazeera News, 'Qatar blockade: five things to know about the Gulf crisis' (5 June 2019), available at www.aljazeera.com/news/2019/06/qatar-blockade-gulf-crisis-190604220901644.html.

[79] ibid.

[80] IMF Country Report Qatar, available at www.imf.org/en/Publications/CR/Issues/2019/06/02/Qatar-2019-Article-IV-Consultation-Press-Release-Staff-Report-46956.

[81] UNCTAD (n 5), Qatar Country Factsheet, available at www.unctad.org/sections/dite_dir/docs/wir2019/wir19_fs_qa_en.pdf.

[82] ibid.

[83] ibid.

[84] Qatar Foreign Investment Law, Law No 1 (2019).

[85] Investment Policy Hub, Investment Policy Monitor, available at www.investmentpolicy.unctad.org/investment-policy-monitor/measures/3360/new-law-regulating-foreign-investment-allows-up-to-100-percent-foreign-ownership.

[86] IIA Navigator, 'Qatar', available at www.investmentpolicy.unctad.org/international-investment-agreements/countries/171/qatar?type=bits.

members of the sanctioning coalition, Qatar entered into a BIT with Egypt in 1999,[87] which remains in force. Additionally, Qatar is a signatory state of the Arab Investment Agreement 1970,[88] Arab Investment Agreement 1980,[89] the Organisation of Islamic Co-operation 1981[90] and the GCC Economic Agreement 1981.[91] Qatar is a signatory to all of these agreements with one, some or all of the sanctioning coalition states.[92] This means that in theory the sanctioning coalition and Qatar are likely already breaching the terms of these various investment agreements in the manner set out above in this chapter. Some (in fact, most) of these agreements also contain dispute settlement provisions whereby the aggrieved investor can initiate a case against the investment host state using either the Arab Investment Court or international arbitration. Therefore, investors from the coalition sanctioning states could utilise these procedures to bring cases against Qatar for potential breach of investment protection obligations. However, according to publicly available information regarding known investment treaty disputes, investors from the coalition states have not sued the Qatari Government *en masse*.

In fact, in terms of investment disputes, there has been one known ICSID case[93] initiated against Qatar (in 2018), but it was discontinued quite promptly after the constitution of the tribunal and there is very little information about it in the public sphere. The case concerned a Jordanian TV and film producer who alleged that the Qatari Government did not pay him for creating television shows, and that it had seized his assets.[94] It is unknown whether the claim initiated had anything to do with the circumstances of the sanctions imposed.

C. Case Study Conclusions

The Iranian and the Qatari experiences demonstrate that relatively high intensity unilateral economic sanctions might be ineffective in procuring change by attempting to damage the targeted state's economy; according to the IMF, the Qatari economy has generally coped quite well with the imposition of the sanctions. Meanwhile, the Iranian economy has not held up quite as well, but despite this, the Government has not bent to the political will of the US. Therefore, in both states, the sanctions could be

[87] Qatar–Egypt BIT (1999), available at www.investmentpolicy.unctad.org/international-investment-agreements/treaty-files/1103/download.

[88] Arab Investment Agreement (1970) (Qatar and Egypt are signatories), available at https://investmentpolicy.unctad.org/international-investment-agreements/treaties/treaties-with-investment-provisions/3080/arab-league-investment-agreement-1970-.

[89] Arab Investment Agreement (1980) (Qatar and all the sanctioning coalition are signatory states), available at www.investmentpolicy.unctad.org/international-investment-agreements/treaty-files/2394/download.

[90] Organisation of Islamic Co-operation Agreement (1981) (Qatar and all the sanctioning coalition are signatory states), available at www.investmentpolicy.unctad.org/international-investment-agreements/treaty-files/2399/download.

[91] GCC Economic Agreement (1981) (Qatar, Saudi Arabia, Bahrain and the UAE are signatory states), available at www.investmentpolicy.unctad.org/international-investment-agreements/treaty-files/3105/download.

[92] See above nn 87, 88, 89, 90 and 91.

[93] *Al Awamleh and others v Qatar* (ICSID Case No ARB/18/38).

[94] UNCTAD Case Information, *Al Awamleh and others v Qatar* (ICSID Case No ARB/18/38), available at www.investmentpolicy.unctad.org/investment-dispute-settlement/cases/923/al-awamleh-and-others-v-qatar.

considered ineffective as they have not catalysed change. Additionally, we can see that specific sectors of targeted states' economies may be damaged significantly; in the cases of Iran and Qatar, severe decreases in inflows of investment can be observed. This is bad for both the targeted state and foreign investors. It is potentially also bad for the citizens of Iran and Qatar who will lose out on the benefits that foreign investment brings to the economy and to wider society.

The Iranian and Qatari experience also demonstrates that such sanctions do have the capacity to affect foreign investors in the ways demonstrated by the preceding sections of this chapter (through breaches of investor protection obligations in customary international law as well as BITs and TIPs). However, practically, there is often little concrete evidence of these effects, eg investment disputes. However, this does not mean that investors are not affected; rather, that they may choose not to bring disputes for some reason. Small and medium-sized enterprises can be dissuaded from bringing disputes due to the high costs involved, for example. Linked to this, as there have been no investment disputes brought as a consequence of the imposition of unilateral economic sanctions, there has been no concrete consideration by investment tribunals of the potential exceptions that may be invoked by sanctioning states or the potential defences that may be invoked by the targeted state or potential remedies.

V. Conclusion

This chapter has demonstrated that the imposition of unilateral economic sanctions, especially those of high intensity (eg complete embargoes/blockades) can, in theory, severely restrict the rights of investors and states within the context of the regime of international investment. Indeed, it could be argued that the application of such sanctions is, in effect, incompatible with the international investment regime itself, and therefore such sanctions should be considered unlawful in this regard. The imposition of such draconian measures in this highly globalised and interdependent world is very difficult to rationalise; the global economic and legal regulatory framework is governed by a network of international treaties (including BITs and TIPs) that make the imposition of unilateral economic sanctions inherently unlawful.

7

The World Trade Organisation and Unilateral Sanctions: Prohibited or Possible?

JAMES WATSON

I. Introduction

The use of unilateral economic sanctions has long been pursued by many nations as a tool to influence the behaviour of other nations. Such behaviour is sometimes considered justified by an enacting country, on grounds of national security or to express displeasure with internal policies of a third country. Usually the enactment of such unilateral sanctions is purely based on political imperatives and has very little to do with economic realities. It is a stick as opposed to a carrot, aimed at influencing the behaviour of another country. While such measures may seem to be more commonplace today, they have been used and resisted for decades. From unilateral measures against Cuba, to South Africa, Russia and Iran, it is often trade measures that are used for political means. The question that arises is how legitimate is it to use such measures in international law?

This practice is indeed questionable in the context of international trade law and the governing framework of the World Trade Organization (WTO), which does not necessarily seek to comment on the political choices of its members – only their adherence to global trade rules. Unilateral actions are not generally considered to be part of the normal framework of international trade law. Article XXI of the General Agreement on Tariffs and Trade (GATT) deals with security exemptions from the general principles,[1] but by reading the words of this Article in themselves a layperson might find it difficult to see where such unilateral sanctions could be justified. Often such economic sanctions are also tied together with other more diplomatic and policy measures and as such it is not always easy to understand if an economic sanction is effective.

[1] Article XXI, WTO, legal texts, XXX.

The practice of imposing economic sanctions has evolved with time and countries now consider themselves able to invoke 'smart' sanctions that target financial transactions, business interests and affect freedom of movement. This is an idea that has grown with sanctions on Russia, for the invasion of the Crimea, Iran over its nuclear ambitions and earlier in Iraq with the Oil-for-Food programme. These smart sanctions are meant to target the government that is cast as pariah, but not hurt the poorer citizens of a country – as trade measures so often do harm the welfare of people. There is much debate over whether an economic sanction can ever be smart, or if they are even useful in destabilising political opponents.[2]

It would seem, however, that these measures have no place in WTO law, as it relates to the free movement of goods and services between its members.[3] Whether the measures are designed to be smart or blunt, the WTO does not have a system of tolerance for trade measures with political aims. There are some commentators who suggest that the WTO exemptions under Articles XX and XXI could be used to justify unilateral trade measures.[4] It is highly questionable that unilateral measures are effective, and while that is not the main focus of this chapter to assess their success, indeed many papers have reviewed the value of such sanctions, it is important to understand what these tools are and how they relate to international economic law. The following sections assess this hypothesis and explores some of the current applications of unilateral trade measures for political ends.

This chapter will, therefore, examine the use of unilateral economic sanctions, in the context of the WTO obligations of its members, on trade in services and goods. It will also examine the role of the dispute settlement body in dealing with such sanctions as they arise. It will also consider the current and future role of the WTO in dealing with these phenomena, as such sanctions my become less reported to the WTO, as the global trading system comes under increasing pressure from its core founding members, who may increasingly seek to avoid the rules they created.

II. Unilateral Economic Sanctions

It is first important to understand what is being considered when we speak about unilateral economic sanctions. The term generally refers to trade measures that are imposed by one country on another without a basis in economic terms, ie they are not retaliatory nor necessarily as a consequence of economic activities of the parties. This does not exclude unilateral measures that are a consequence of economic activities.

[2] See inter alia D Cortright and GA Lopez, *Smart Sanctions: Targeting Economic Statecraft* (Rowman & Littlefield Publishers, 2002); E Shagabutdinova and J Berejikian, 'Deploying Sanctions while Protecting Human Rights: Are Humanitarian "Smart" Sanctions Effective?' (2007) 6 *Journal of Human Rights* 59; J Gordon, 'Smart Sanctions Revisited' (2011) 25 *Ethics & International Affairs* 315.

[3] See n 1.

[4] See inter alia RL Howse and JM Genser, 'Are EU Trade Sanctions on Burma Compatible with WTO Law?' (2008) 29 *Michigan Journal of International Law* 165; DW Drezner, 'Sanctions Sometimes Smart: Targeted Sanctions in Theory and Practice' (2011) 13 *International Studies Review* 96.

Economic sanctions can be defined as the withdrawal of common and customary trade relations for political ends – such as foreign policy, security policy or human rights policy.[5] The trade tools that are often wielded by governments as unilateral sanctions can include embargos, boycotts or quotas, but can also include non-tariff barriers, such as licensing and packaging requirements or asset seizures.[6] Given the inherent political nature of such measures, it is often the more visible tools that are preferred by governments wishing to make a public statement on the activities of the target country.

An embargo is usually a prohibition of exporting specific goods and services to a country, generally the idea is to cut the supply of critical goods and services to create as much disruption as possible in the target country.[7] The idea of starving an opponent state into submission is far from new. Trade embargoes are perhaps most familiar in relation to US–Cuba relations, when in 1962 the then President Kennedy announced a full trade embargo covering all goods and services, some of which still remain in place today.[8] Nevertheless, it is not common to find many full embargoes between countries, instead embargoes have tended to focus on one or two specific sectors – such as the embargo on trading uranium and military equipment with Iran in the early 2000s.[9] There are, indeed, many embargoes in place between different countries today across the world, which suggests that governments do see the political value of such measures even if their economic effectiveness is a secondary consideration.

A boycott, on the other hand, usually implies that a country will not take goods or services from the target country.[10] This should deny the target country of a source of income and wealth. The term 'boycott' has origins in the nineteenth century when a certain Captain Boycott, acting as a land agent, was in 1880 subject to social ostracism organised by the Irish Land League.[11] The definition of the means to influence his behaviour as 'social ostracism' is a perfect way to describe the intention of states prosecuting boycotts today. The measures are a form of censure for actions that a country takes. The boycott applied to apartheid-era South African goods and sports teams is a good example. The aim was to weaken the economy and cause hardship for the citizens and thus government of the target country, as a means to change its ways. However, boycotts are also increasingly being driven by citizens and not governments, for example, 'flight shame' in Scandinavia,[12] which saw people boycotting flying and, in Asia, South Koreans have boycotted Japanese beer and products due to differences

[5] J. Masters, 'What are Economic Sanctions?' Council on Foreign Relations (12 August 2019), available at www.cfr.org/backgrounder/what-are-economic-sanctions.

[6] See B. Radcliffe, 'How Economic Sanctions Work', Investopedia (25 June 2019), available at www.investopedia.com/articles/economics/10/economic-sanctions.asp.

[7] M Smeets, 'Can Economic Sanctions be Effective?' Staff Working Paper ERSD-2018-03, WTO (15 March 2018).

[8] C Leung, '10 Examples of Trade Embargoes, The Borgen Project' (23 July 2018), available at borgenproject.org/examples-of-trade-embargoes.

[9] ibid.

[10] Smeets, 'Can Economic Sanctions be Effective?' (2018).

[11] Encyclopaedia Britannica, 'Boycott' (August 2019), available at www.britannica.com/topic/boycott.

[12] M Goldstein, 'Does Flight-Shaming Over Climate Change Pose An Existential Threat To Airlines?', Forbes (4 June 2019), available at www.forbes.com/sites/michaelgoldstein/2019/06/04/does-flight-shaming-over-climate-change-pose-an-existential-threat-to-airlines/#5912d5183cfc.

going back to World War II.[13] These movements are more difficult to assess in terms of impacts on world trading rules and as such the focus here will be on boycotts enacted by governments.

Quotas are designed to limit the amount of a critical good that can be exported or imported to and from a target country, with the aim of not necessarily creating critical shortages of medicines or fuel.[14] This is designed so that populations do not suffer too much under the economic sanctions, while conversely allowing governments to still benefit from trade in sectors it needs from the targeted state. Quotas have been used by the EU in its revised trade sanctions with Belarus, to allow processing of textiles in Belarus and reimport without penalty.[15] This clearly allows EU-based companies to benefit from trade relations with Belarus while targeting the broader economy with removal of non-preferential tariff rates. This shows that quotas can be used to target specific sectors to punish, but also to benefit states that are seeking to punish. This makes their use rather ambiguous from a global trade rules perspective.

It could be argued that quotas may have been the blueprint for unilateral actions that came to be declared smart sanctions in time. For example, the Oil-for-Food programme of the United Nations (UN) was set up to provide food and medicine for Iraqi civilians, while allowing the world to receive Iraqi oil at a time when the regime was widely given pariah status.[16] Unfortunately, that particular scheme resulted in massive corruption and brought negligible benefit to the Iraqi citizens.[17] Nevertheless, quotas remain a common tool for economic unilateral sanctions carried out by states.

As mentioned earlier, there are also non-tariff barriers that can be used as a means to deliver unilateral economic sanctions. These will not be explored in detail here, given that the majority of open unilateral sanctions are of the form of quotas, embargoes and boycotts. The next section will examine the position of these measures in the WTO legal context.

III. Unilateral Sanctions in WTO law

The WTO has set up a quite comprehensive international legal system for governing global trade in goods and services. Underpinning this are the treaties that make up the acquis of international trade law – the General Agreement on Tariffs and Trade (GATT) 1994, the General Agreement on Trade in Services (GATS) and, also of importance for unilateral sanctions, the Dispute Settlement Understanding (DSU). These are the key elements that will be examined in this section and a view will be developed of the application of unilateral economic sanctions and their viability in international trade law.

[13] K Sohelli, 'South Koreans are cancelling vacations to Japan and boycotting its beer in a trade war more bitter than Trump's feud with China', Business Insider (27 September 2019), available at www.businessinsider.com/south-koreans-boycott-japan-products-cancel-vacations-over-trade-war-2019-9?r=US&IR=T.

[14] M Gocmez, 'An Overview of Other Economic Sanctions Besides Tariffs' (14 January 2019), available at www.morethanshipping.com/an-overview-of-other-economic-sanctions-besides-tariffs.

[15] EU, Trade with Belarus website: ec.europa.eu/trade/policy/countries-and-regions/countries/belarus.

[16] S Otterman, 'Iraq: Oil for Food Scandal, Council on Foreign Relations' (28 October 2005), available at www.cfr.org/backgrounder/iraq-oil-food-scandal.

[17] ibid.

The GATT was founded in 1947 in the ashes of World War II and had at its centre the notion of building peace through international norms, to create peace and harmony at a global level. This means that unilateral economic sanctions are inherently in conflict with the multilateral cooperative nature of the organisation that the WTO has become. It has been argued that unilateral economic sanctions are designed to undermine the nature of the international treaties set up to govern global trade.[18]

Of great importance to understanding the legality of unilateral sanctions is the undertaking of the members of the WTO to refrain from using unilateral measures; indeed, Article 23 of the DSU strengthens the members' resolve to always solve trade disputes through the multilateral system provided for in the DSU.[19] The members of the WTO have essentially agreed to not act outside of the conventions of the DSU, which implies that no WTO member should bring a unilateral trade measure into play against another WTO member. The WTO itself cautions strongly against the use of unilateral trade measures and the danger to develop and create a spiral of measures resulting in a fully blown trade war.[20]

Instead the DSU insists that members use its provisions to address trade measures that a party believes impair their rights under the WTO Agreements. Any member who believes that they have been targeted by a unilateral measure must invoke the DSU and not resort to actions in retaliation themselves.[21] Some commentators have suggested that this not a strength of the system, but a weakness, as it effectively allows unilateral actions by the parties, as it takes at least 18 months for a case to be heard under the DSU.[22] Thus a unilateral action has about a year and a half of life before it could be declared illegal under the DSU system. The real weakness of the system here is identified as the redress – there is none, so if a party is found to have applied a unilateral measure that was unjustified they must simply remove it and no compensation is given to the injured party.[23] The DSU insists that members should comply with the rules at all times, so acting ahead of a ruling is also a violation. It might stop trade wars, but it will not make the injured party feel any better.

A good example of this was the behaviour of the US on steel in the early 2000s. The Government applied raised tariffs claiming this was in line with the WTO rules. When challenged, the US lost the case in the Dispute Settlement Body of the WTO and subsequently removed the measures – some two years later. Thus, the US was behaving outside the WTO rules, but the injured parties had no right to redress even after legal victory.[24]

Having established that legally there is no room for unilateral economic sanctions in the WTO's DSU it is also necessary to assess the room for such measures in the GATT 1994. Unilateral measures could appear to violate several provisions of the GATT 1994: Article I (the Most Favoured Nation Treatment); Article II (Schedules of Concessions); Article III (National Treatment), Article V (Freedom of Transit), Article IX (General

[18] Smeets (n 7).

[19] WTO, 'Introduction to the WTO dispute settlement system', available at www.wto.org/english/tratop_e/dispu_e/disp_settlement_cbt_e/c1s3p3_e.htm.

[20] ibid.

[21] ibid.

[22] R Brewster, 'Shadow Unilateralism: Enforcing International Trade Law at the WTO' (2009) 30 *University of Pennsylvania Journal of International Economic Law* 1133.

[23] ibid.

[24] ibid.

Elimination of Quantitative Restrictions) and Article XIII (Non-discriminatory Administration of Quantitative Restrictions).[25] These are serious breaches of the expected code of conduct of WTO members, and the list applies not just to trade in goods, but also trade in services. It is thus hard to see how the use of unilateral trade measures for policy ends could ever be justified under international trade law.

Non-discrimination is a key concept in WTO law, which is well reflected in the Articles mentioned above. It rests on two pillars of GATT/WTO law: the most-favoured-nation treatment obligation and the national treatment obligation. Under both of these principles, countries cannot normally discriminate between their trading partners. Both Articles I and III of GATT incorporate the principle of non-discrimination in international trade. Article I(1) on General Most-Favoured-Nation Treatment provides equality of treatment with respect to like products originating in or destined for the territories of all other contracting parties. It reads as follows:

> [A]ny advantage, favour, privilege or immunity granted by any contracting party to any product originating in or destined for any other country shall be accorded immediately and unconditionally to the like product originating in or destined for the territories of all other contracting parties.[26]

Likewise, Article III on National Treatment on Internal Taxation and Regulation provides equality of treatment with respect to domestic and like products from WTO member countries. Paragraphs (1) and (2) of Article III provide that:

> 1. The contracting parties recognize that internal taxes and other internal charges, and laws, regulations and requirements affecting the internal sale, offering for sale, purchase, transportation, distribution or use of products, and internal quantitative regulations requiring the mixture, processing or use of products in specified amounts or proportions, should not be applied to imported or domestic products so as to afford protection to domestic production.
>
> 2. The products of the territory of any contracting party imported into the territory of any other contracting party shall not be subject, directly or indirectly, to internal taxes or other internal charges of any kind in excess of those applied, directly or indirectly, to like domestic products. Moreover, no contracting party shall otherwise apply internal taxes or other internal charges to imported or domestic products in a manner contrary to the principles set forth in paragraph 1.[27]

GATT Article V on Freedom of Transit also guarantees freedom of transit through the territory of each contracting party, via the routes most convenient for international transit, for traffic in transit to or from the territory of other contracting parties without any distinction which is based on the flag of vessels, the place of origin, departure, entry, exit or destination, or on any circumstances relating to the ownership of goods, of vessels or of other means of transport. Article V(2) reads as follows:

> There shall be freedom of transit through the territory of each contracting party, via the routes most convenient for international transit, for traffic in transit to or from the territory of other contracting parties. No distinction shall be made which is based on the flag of vessels, the place of origin, departure, entry, exit or destination, or on any circumstances relating to the ownership of goods, of vessels or of other means of transport.

[25] METI, 'Report on Unilateral Economic Sanctions' (2014) 629.
[26] www.wto.org/english/docs_e/legal_e/gatt47.pdf (footnotes omitted).
[27] www.wto.org/english/docs_e/legal_e/gatt47.pdf (footnotes omitted).

There are similar provisions in other WTO agreements such as the General Agreement on Trade in Services (GATS).

IV. Unilateral Economic Sanctions and International Trade Law: Exemptions?

The WTO Agreements include Articles that allow for exemptions to the basic rules of free trade and economic liberalism. As mentioned earlier, Article XXI covers general security exemptions and Article XX covers all general exemptions. Article XX lists 10 clauses that would allow members to resort to non-GATT compatible activities, which would be justified to satisfy a specific need in relation to policy goals. One of the most interesting exemptions for the purposes of assessing unilateral economic sanctions with policy goals comes under GATT Article XX(a):

> **Article XX**
>
> **General Exceptions**
>
> Subject to the requirement that such measures are not applied in a manner which would constitute a means of arbitrary or unjustifiable discrimination between countries where the same conditions prevail, or a disguised restriction on international trade, nothing in this Agreement shall be construed to prevent the adoption or enforcement by any contracting party of measures:
>
> (a) necessary to protect public morals;[28]

The first exemption listed in the Article is that based on the necessity to protect public morals. Many countries would argue that they enact unilateral economic measures to protect people and ergo public morals from outrages committed by hostile governments. In spite of this there are only a limited number of cases in the WTO that have assessed the use of the public morals exemption.[29] Article XX (a) is also undefined – the determination of what constitute public morals has been left to the interpretation of the panellists and appellate body delegates.

In the *US – Gambling* case the panel assessed the term 'public morals' in the following way 'standards of right and wrong conduct maintained by or on behalf of a community or nation'.[30] The panel also noted that 'the content of these concepts for Members can vary in time and space, depending upon a range of factors, including prevailing social, cultural, ethical and religious values'.[31] This seems to leave a wide interpretation as to what could be considered acceptable to a social or societal value distinguishing itself from the international trade regime. The definition of public morals in the *US – Gambling* case is all the more important as it was relied upon in

[28] WTO, Legal Texts of the WTO Agreements, available at www.wto.org/english/res_e/publications_e/ai17_e/gatt1994_art20_jur.pdf.

[29] BBM Al Modarra, 'Defining the Contours of the Public Morals Exception under Article XX of the GATT 1994' (2017) 18 *Estey Journal of International Law and Trade Policy* 142.

[30] Panel Report, 'United States – Measures Affecting the Cross-Border Supply of Gambling and Betting Services' (WTO, 2004), para 6.465.

[31] ibid.

the subsequent *China – Publications and Audiovisual Products* case.[32] The width of definition is entirely necessary when the global context is considered; what is allowed in one country can be considered prohibited in another for religious or cultural reasons. There is no one-size-fits-all global culture and the WTO panel in the *US – Gambling* case succinctly expressed this: 'Members should be given some scope to define and apply for themselves the concepts of "public morals" … in their respective territories, according to their own systems and scales of values'.[33]

This broad definition could give concern to those states that would see the possibilities for abuse of such a wide interpretation of how to read 'public morals'. In this regard the panel and the subsequent WTO Dispute Settlement Board did provide more guidance on the term: 'we must nonetheless give meaning to these terms in order to apply them to the facts of this case'.[34] The meaning for these terms was taken from the *Oxford English Dictionary* by the panel, which concluded that the term 'public morals' are the standards relating to actions that are right or wrong according to a community or nation.[35] Even with this clarification it seems that there is a good opportunity for Member States of the WTO to find justification for unilateral economic sanctions in relation to policy objectives against other states – as long as the measures are 'necessary'.

The second part of the reliance on an exemption under Article XX(a) is that it must be considered 'necessary' to protect public morals. This makes the analysis slightly more complicated, as one party may see a unilateral measure as 'necessary' while the injured party will surely disagree. The use of the term 'necessary' is quite consistent throughout the various clauses of Article XX,[36] and indeed a panel had already made a ruling on the means to assess 'necessary – the *US–Gasoline* case.[37] This was in the context of an Article XX(b) case rather than Article XX(a), but the panel and Appellate Body made use of the work in the *US – Gasoline* case in the *China – Publications and Audiovisuals* case. Thus, the WTO dispute system also demonstrated that it could rely on the precedent behaviour of earlier panels and appellate bodies decisions.

A three-tier test has been developed to assess the term 'necessary' in the WTO in the *US – Gasoline* case. These three tests are:

(a) that the policy in respect of the measures for which the provision was invoked fell within the range of policies designed to protect human, animal or plant life or health;
(b) that the inconsistent measures for which the exception was being invoked were necessary to fulfil the policy objective; and
(c) that the measures were applied in conformity with the requirements of the introductory clause of Article XX.[38]

[32] Panel Report, 'China – Measures Affecting Trading Rights and Distribution Services for Certain Publications and Audiovisual Entertainment Products' (WTO, 2009).
[33] Panel Report, 'United States-Measures Affecting the Cross-Border Supply of Gambling and Betting Services', 16.461, WT/DS285/R (2004).
[34] ibid.
[35] ibid. 465.
[36] Art XX(a), (b) and (d) use 'necessary'.
[37] Panel Report, 'United States – Standards for Reformulated and Conventional Gasoline' (1996) para 6.20.
[38] ibid.

In the *China – Publications and Audiovisuals Products* case the Chinese Government had enacted a defence of a number of trade restricting measures on the basis of Article XX(a). The panel and the Appellate Body made use of the test varying the terms to assess public morals as opposed to protection of human, animal or plant life or health. In relation to the first test, the Appellate Body essentially declined to determine the public morals of China, preferring to give the broader type of definition identified above in the *US – Gambling* case.[39] On the second test, a further assessment of necessity is made, this time in the context that public morals are accepted, but is the measure necessary to protect this moral right?

This is a complex question, and the panel assessed three further questions to assess this aspect of necessity: (i) how the measures contributed to meeting the protection of public morals; (ii) how trade restrictive the measures are; and (iii) weighing and balancing the first two points.[40] In this case the panel decided that the measures did not meet the necessity requirement in Article XX(a), as there were less restrictive measures that could have been utilised that the Chinese had not deployed.[41] China appealed the verdict and the WTO Appellate Body upheld the methodology and the outcome of the panel verdict, noting that:

> The less restrictive the effects of the measure, the more likely it is to be characterized as 'necessary'. Consequently, if a Member chooses to adopt a very restrictive measure, it will have to ensure that the measure is carefully designed so that the other elements to be taken into account in weighing and balancing the factors relevant to an assessment of the 'necessity' of the measure will 'outweigh' such restrictive effect.[42]

This outcome once again throws doubt on the ease with which WTO Member States can enact unilateral economic measures, against other WTO members. The decision is, however, entirely in line with the reasoning of WTO panels and Appellate Bodies, who traditionally have assessed the proportionality of a measure to achieving an objective. As commentators have acknowledged, the WTO tries to balance the moral gain achieved by breaching the rules of the GATT 1994 against the moral loss of delivering the freedom to trade.[43]

The final test of the overall assessment of necessity, is the so-called eye of the needle test.[44] Does the measure pass the requirements of Article XX's chapeau? This was outlined in the *US – Gasoline* case and has drawn criticism from some commentators as it has seen to be interpreted too severely and used to deny the effect of the exemptions.[45] The purpose of the chapeau test is to determine whether, even if an exemption may be invoked, it has been applied in a way that is consistent with the GATT, thus its application

[39] Panel Report, 'China – Measures Affecting Trading Rights and Distribution Services' (2009) para 7.759.

[40] ibid. para 7.819.

[41] ibid.

[42] Appellate Body Report, 'China – Measures Affecting Trading Rights and Distribution Services for Certain Publications and Audiovisual Entertainment Products' (2009) para 310.

[43] See S Charnovitz, 'The Moral Exception in Trade Policy' (1998) 38 *Virginia Journal of International Law* 689.

[44] See S Gaines, 'The WTO's Reading of the GATT Article XX Chapeau: A Disguised Restriction on Environmental Measures' (2001) 22 *University of Pennsylvania Journal of International Law* 784.

[45] ibid.

rather than the content of the measure is what is at stake.[46] This is an important test; a type of proportionality so that measures applied in exemption of the GATT are the ones that are the most consistent with the GATT requirements. This avoids abuse of the use of exemptions, while balancing the rights of members to protect their public morals.

Essentially, the *US – Gasoline* case sets out that a member has rights under the Article XX exemptions, but these should not be abused to the extent that the legal requirements of the WTO Agreements are thwarted.[47] As ever in an international organisation, the test revolves around balancing rights – the right to employ a measure to protect your nation's public morals, and the right of the injured party to enjoy free trade.

The chapeau test was enshrined in the environmentally contentious *US – Shrimp* case, which considered the prohibition of selling shrimp on the US market if fishermen had not used a turtle-excluding device.[48] The Appellate Body saw the assessment of whether a measure breached the general rules of the GATT as a fundamental question as to whether the measure could be allowed on the basis of any of the exemptions. It stated 'An abusive exercise by a Member of its own treaty rights thus results in a breach of the treaty rights of the other Members, and, as well, a violation of the treaty obligation of the Member so acting'.[49]

The chapeau as outlined above contains two further tests: '(measures) constitute a means of arbitrary or unjustifiable discrimination between countries where the same conditions prevail, or a disguised restriction on international trade'; these two elements must be assessed if the measure is to be seen as a legitimate exemption.

In the *US – Shrimp* case the Appellate Body found that the measures applied by the US were indeed an example of unjustified discrimination, based on the fact that the US had not undertaken any serious attempt to negotiate a deal with the shrimp importing countries in Asia – whereas it had in the Caribbean.[50] The Appellate Body also found that the measures failed the unjustifiable discrimination test as they were rigid and applied in an extraterritorial manner, without due regard to the conditions prevailing in other countries.[51] The Appellate Body went on to state that other measures were available in this case to achieve the US's objective, but were not explored.[52] This makes it clear that when applying unilateral economic measures a WTO member should have exhausted all means of finding an alternative approach.

In relation to the second test in the chapeau – a disguised restriction on international trade – the *US – Gasoline* case Appellate Body ruled that the interpretation of disguised restrictions are 'restrictions amounting to arbitrary or unjustifiable discrimination in international trade taken under the guise of a measure formally within the terms of an exception listed in Article XX'.[53] This suggests that the second test is similar to the first, but that there is a degree of deception over the intention of the measure.

[46] Appellate Body Report, 'United States – Standards for Reformulated and Conventional Gasoline' (1996) 22.
[47] ibid.
[48] WTO, 'United States – Import Prohibition of Certain Shrimp and Shrimp Products' (1998).
[49] ibid, 158.
[50] R Howse, 'The Appellate Body Rulings in the Shrimp/Turtle Case: A New Legal Baseline for the Trade and Environment Debate' (2002) 27 *Columbia Journal of Environmental Law* 491.
[51] ibid, 10.
[52] ibid.
[53] Appellate Body Report, 'United States – Standards for Reformulated and Conventional Gasoline' (1996) 25.

Understanding the background to the application of Article XX and, importantly, its chapeau, provides a good indication as to what measures could be accepted as a justified unilateral economic sanction exemption under WTO law with the stated aim of protecting public morals. The tests established offer clear guidance as to the format that a nation would need to pursue to be able to succeed in elaborating economic sanctions on the basis of Article XX(a).

Another recent panel decision has upheld this line of reasoning, *United States – Tariff Measures on Certain Goods from China* assessed the claim that tariffs on industrial sectors imposed by the US could be justified under the XX(a) public morals exception.[54] The US had conducted a trade review which found that China's policies relating to technology transfer, technology licensing, acquisition of US technology, and trade secrets were unreasonable or discriminatory, and negatively impacted US commerce.[55] This resulted in a set of tariffs being imposed on the relevant sector on Chinese goods imported into the US, the Chinese launched a complaint at the WTO and the US sought to defend the measures utilising Article XX(a).

The US based this reasoning on the fact that some of the practices are subject to criminal proceedings in the US, and that such behaviour was a threat to the social fabric of the US, such as democracy and political institutions.[56] The Chinese counterargument recalled that criminal conduct is not the bar to assess public morals by, given different cultural norms across the world, and that public morals should only be considered if the content of a product is offensive. The panel in its reasoning followed the methodology in the *US – Gasoline* and *China – Measures Affecting Trading Rights and Distribution Services for Certain Publications and Audiovisual Entertainment Products* cases, and concluded that indeed public morals do include a standard of 'right and wrong' which was up to the WTO member to define; economic concerns could be included in this.[57]

However, the panel decided that the US had failed to demonstrate the link between the tariff measures taken and the public morals objective pursued. This was due to a non-linkage between the products covered by the tariffs and the products identified in the US trade review, and thus the measures were considered not to be directly based on the public morals objective.[58] The panel upheld the reasoning that unilateral tariffs based on public morals cannot simply be wielded as a member would choose and that a strong linkage must be demonstrated between the measures and a public moral outrage.[59]

Article XXI of the GATT also provides opportunities for countries enacting unilateral economic sanctions to argue their defence on the basis of security exemptions. Article XXI recognises the importance of national security in applying measures that

[54] Panel Report, 'United States – Tariff Measures on Certain Goods from China', WTO Doc WT/DS543/R (adopted 15 September 2020), available at docs.wto.org/dol2fe/Pages/SS/directdoc.aspx?filename=q:/WT/DS/543R.pdf&Open=True.

[55] J Zhou, 'No Unilateral Action – WTO Panel Ruled U.S. Section 301 Tariffs on Chinese Imports Inconsistent with WTO Obligations' (2020) 24 *American Society of International Law*, available at www.asil.org/insights/volume/24/issue/26/no-unilateral-action-wto-panel-ruled-us-section-301-tariffs-chinese#_edn1.

[56] ibid.

[57] Panel Report, 'United States Zhou, 'No Unilateral Action Tariff Measures' (2020).

[58] ibid.

[59] Zhou, 'No Unilateral Action' (2020).

are not in line with the general WTO rules.[60] A more detailed of analysis of Article XXI is contained below in section VII. It is important here to note that Article XXI may offer a route for countries to apply unilateral economic sanctions, as long as the measures are enacted during a state of emergency and in good faith.[61] It is imperative that a nation can demonstrate these elements, otherwise the veracity of the measures would struggle to be accepted by WTO panels and Appellate Bodies.

V. Unilateral Economic Sanctions in Practice

Having reviewed the relevant sections of the WTO agreements in relation to unilateral economic sanctions it is useful to assess existing sanction regimes to determine the likelihood that they are WTO compatible, and to also assess the arguments that are made to justify the potentiality of legality or otherwise under WTO law.

An interesting case study to consider is that of the EU's economic sanctions on the Myanmar regime of the early 2000s. These were not tested at the WTO, but were contentious in that EU officials chose to have more lenient sanctions than counterparts in the rest of the world, based on the assessment that they may not be WTO-compatible.[62] As a background to the assessment of the sanctions, it is worth recalling that the Myanmar regime was considered to be one of the most brutal regimes in the world. Political repression, destruction of villages and forced labour were just some of the human rights abuses levelled against the military government (which had been in power since 1962, following a coup and the ousting of a democratically elected government).[63]

The EU had enacted a regime, known as the Common Position, against the Myanmar Government, which included unilateral economic sanctions.[64] These sanctions appeared to have little effect on the functioning of the military Government in Myanmar.[65] In 2007 the measures against Myanmar were upgraded to include the prohibition of imports of textiles, precious metals, gems and timber. This had been introduced despite some concerns from EU trade officials to the WTO compatibility of the measures. A concern that was based on an earlier situation where the US state of Massachusetts had tried to create a state law that would limit public finance ending up in the Myanmar Government's budget – which the EU itself had threatened to take action against in the WTO.[66]

The question of whether these measures would be WTO-compatible is largely academic as the Myanmar Government never challenged the measures for many

[60] WTO, Analytical Index of the GATT, available at www.wto.org/english/res_e/booksp_e/gatt_ai_e/art21_e.pdf.

[61] See Panel Body Report, 'Russia – Measures Concerning Traffic in Transit' WT DS512/R (5 April 2019).

[62] RL Howse and JM Genser, 'Are EU Trade Sanctions on Burma Compatible with WTO Law?' (2008) 29 *Michigan Journal of International Law* 178.

[63] ibid.

[64] Commission Regulation 481/2007, OJ L 111/50.

[65] Howse and Genser, 'Burma' (2008).

[66] R Strumberg and MC Porterfield, 'Who Pre-empted the Massachusetts Burma Law? Federalism and Political Accountability Under Global Trade Rules' (2001) 31 *Publius: The Journal of Federalism* 173.

reasons. In any case, there is much literature devoted to the issue given the concerns of the EU regarding their unilateral economic sanction regime.[67] Nevertheless, it is worth examining the arguments put forward to express whether such sanctions would have passed the Article XX tests. Scholars have examined the application of the unilateral economic sanctions in great detail and assessed the tests of Article XX against the EU's measures.[68]

The first question would be to assess whether the EU measures were directed at protecting public morals in line with the *US – Gambling* case. Given the outrageous ethical behaviour of the Myanmar military Government, including the human rights abuses and political repression, it is fair to assume that a WTO panel and Appellate Body would have indeed seen these activities as an outrage to public morals and importantly UN laws. Howse and Genser argue that 'any formal association with an abusive foreign government can violate a Member's public morals: this is the underlying rationale behind many government decisions to sever diplomatic relations with abusive regimes'. However, the EU maintained diplomatic presentation to Myanmar throughout the application of the unilateral economic sanctions and thus it would seem that the EU had not lived to this standard of behaviour.

The other possibility Howse and Genser raise is that trading with a regime which conducts regular violations of labour law would indicate complicity for the trade partners in endorsing such violations. On these grounds it may be more realistic to envisage the panel or Appellate Body supporting the notion that an exemption could be valid on the grounds of public moral protection, given that the EU has some of the best labour laws in the world. All the members of the EU are signatories to the European Convention on Human Rights, which outlaws political repression and forced labour.[69] Thus, there is room for agreement that on this ground the measures enacted could be seen as contrary to the EU's public morals.

Even if the unilateral economic sanctions imposed by the EU on Myanmar were concluded to be in line with the exemption of public morals, it has been demonstrated earlier in the chapter that the measures would still be subject to the Article XX chapeau test. Here the panel or Appellate Body would have to determine whether the measures were applied in a manner that was not arbitrary or unjustifiable, particularly considering if the same measures were applied in a country where the same conditions prevail, or if the measures were a disguised restriction on trade.[70]

It is here that the assessment of the measures opens serious questions, were the EU measures applied in the same way to other countries where human rights abuses took place. Or would these be seen as arbitrary discrimination as the EU did not apply the same measures to countries who also did not meet the standards of the European

[67] See inter alia G Andreasson, 'Evaluating the effects of economic sanctions against Burma' (Lunds University, 2008); C Portela and J Orbie, 'Sanctions under the EU Generalised System of Preferences and foreign policy: Coherence by accident? In the trade-development nexus in the European Union: Differentiation, coherence and norms' (London, 2016) 63–76; M Ewing-Chow, 'First Do No Harm: Myanmar Trade Sanctions and Human Rights' (2007) 5 *Northwestern Journal of Human Rights* 153.

[68] ibid.

[69] Convention for the Protection of Human Rights and Fundamental Freedoms, 4 November 1950, ETS No 5, 213 UNTS 222.

[70] See n 26.

Convention on Human Rights? The Appellate Body in the *United States – Shrimp/Turtle* case took the view that the US had failed to take into account different conditions in different Member States among other failures in the application of the law to protect turtles.[71]

Howse and Genser argue that the door has been left open by the Appellate Body in the *United States – Shrimp/Turtle* case for future measures as the Appellate Body stated it was not against bilateral, plurilateral or multilateral actions to protect the environment. They recognise that unilateral economic sanctions even for human rights abuses would contravene the chapeau if they do not treat like countries alike, but hold that this would not be an issue for the measures on Myanmar as although the measures are clearly discrimination they are not unjustified or arbitrary: 'This is because Member States have good reason to single out Burma'.[72]

To understand the meaning of this statement it is asserted that while WTO Member States have various track records on human rights, the situation was so bad in Myanmar that it warranted special differentiation. The fact is raised that Myanmar is the only country to have been targeted by the International Labour Organization (ILO) under its Article 33 resolution procedure, which requires members to adhere to the obligations of the Forced Labour Convention.[73] Also, the volume of the number of UN General Assembly Human Rights Council resolutions is cited as another reason to distinguish Myanmar.[74] These elements, it is contested, would be sufficient to determine that the unilateral economic sanctions would not be discrimination between countries in which the same conditions prevail nor would they be determined to be unjustified or arbitrary. Recognising that other WTO members may also have human rights abuses as serious as those in Myanmar, Howse and Genser go on to dismiss concerns that these could be considered 'like' countries as 'the chapeau does not prohibit selectivity as such with respect to countries targeted by sanctions, but only selectivity that is inherently unreasonable, i.e., arbitrary or unjustifiable'.[75]

The crux of the argument is that Myanmar's breach of universally recognised human rights sets these unilateral economic measures aside from those used by the US in the *United States – Shrimp/Turtle* case. The fact that this is well recognised across international institutions reinforces this argument. From a purely objective point of view it is clear to see the aim of the EU to try and change the Myanmar Government's ways through trade sanctions, it nevertheless remains questionable as to whether these measures would stand the chapeau test.

In relation to the consideration of sea turtles, they are also protected under other international treaties – such as the lists in the Convention on the International Trade in Endangered Species.[76] As are human rights, with at least seven recognised international

[71] Appellate Body Report, 'United States – Import Prohibition of Certain Shrimp and Shrimp Products', WT/DSF8/AB/R, 12 October 1998, fn 109, p 65.

[72] Howse and Genser (n 62) 192.

[73] Art 33 of the ILO Constitution, Declaration Concerning the Aims and Purposes of the International Labour Organisation, 10 May 1944, 49 Stat 2712, 15 UNTS 35.

[74] Howse and Genser (n 62) 192.

[75] ibid, 193.

[76] CITES Identification Guide – Turtles and Tortoises, An initiative of Environment Canada and PROFEPA (SEMARNAP), Minister of Supply and Services Canada, 1999.

treaties relating to the protection of human rights.[77] Which means that the action of other international bodies is not incontestable in itself. It is also not clear if volumes of resolutions from other international organisations count in the determination of Appellate Body decisions, and as such the application of Article XX exemptions in the Myanmar case remains an open question.

Given that the WTO Appellate Body has not shied away from making controversial decisions, while upholding GATT law, notably on cases like *United States – Shrimp/Turtle*, it is hard to share the optimism of Howse and Genser. This is not to say that their argumentation is flawed, merely that it could be possible to argue that all countries who breach human rights law are surely not treated the same by the EU. Hence the understandable concern of the EU officials at the time of the approval of the enhanced economic sanctions. There is a risk that such measures could have fallen foul of the WTO rules.

VI. Are American Unilateral Economic Sanctions on Russia WTO-Compatible?

There has been a historical long-standing tradition of economic sanctions being deployed by the US against Russia, not least through the Cold War, but also since the end of that conflict.[78] Most notably in recent times the US has enacted specific unilateral economic sanctions against Russia following its annexation of Crimea and continued political repression of opposition groups.[79] This has been of greater interest to international economic legal commentators since the accession of Russia to the WTO in 2012. The question of the legality of the unilateral economic sanctions is also an academic one, as Russia has not chosen to challenge the measures in the WTO dispute settlement system.

It is important to place the context of the economic sanctions examined here in the light of the accession of Russia to the WTO. The US Congress debated the extension of the US policy of permanent normal trade relations (PNTR) to Russia in 2012, and while the principle was agreed, a compromise for those concerned Congressmen and women was to also enact economic sanctions on persons in Russia identified for corruption and human rights violations.[80] These sanctions mainly focused on individuals and included travel bans and asset freezes.[81]

In 2014 these sanctions were extended in the context of the flare-up of conflict in the Ukraine and enhanced in the Support for the Sovereignty, Integrity, Democracy, and

[77] United Nations, 'Core International Human Rights Instruments' (2004), available at www.unfpa.org/resources/core-international-human-rights-instruments.

[78] M Doraev, 'The Memory Effect of Economic Sanctions Against Russia: Opposing Approaches to the Legality of Unilateral Sanctions Clash Again, Legal Scholarship Repository' (Penn Law, 2015).

[79] United States Government, Exec Order No 13660 3 CFR, 2014.

[80] A Baskin and B Zagaris, 'U.S. Blacklists Russian Officials Linked to Human Rights Violations' (2012) 27 *International Enforcement Law Reporter* 918.

[81] Russia and Moldova Jackson-Vanik Repeal and Sergei Magnitsky Rule of Law Accountability Act of 2012, 404–06.

Economic Stability of Ukraine Act of 2014.[82] The number of individuals targeted was extended considerably and also to Russia's largest banks, defence and energy companies. This was accompanied by an economic embargo on the Crimea, which covered most trade activities between the US and the Crimea.[83] The purpose of these increased sanctions is stated as 'to promote a diplomatic solution that provides a lasting resolution to the conflict and helps to promote growth and stability in Ukraine and regionally, including in Russia'.[84] The US clearly states its willingness to roll back the sanctions if Russia makes progress.

Again, this case would need to be considered in the context of Article XX, as the main reasons for the invocation of the unilateral trade measures are related to the annexation of Crimea, human rights abuses and political repression. This particular case could be considered wider than simply applying to Article XX(a) as Article XX(b) which seeks to protect human life or health could also come into play.[85] In any case, the US would still be left needing to prove that the measures are compatible with the chapeau, which remains the biggest challenge to gaining an exemption from the GATT.

In this case, Russia has enacted an annexation of part of the territory of another state and as such there are not many instances where such a blatant act contrary to international law could be considered as 'where similar conditions prevail'. This act alone could be a sufficient variability to allow the panels and the Appellate Body to view the application of unilateral economic sanctions as justified and non-discriminatory. The chapeau of Article XX is the key to the use of the exemptions to the GATT and, unless there is a very solid case, covering international legal norms, extensive negotiations, like treatment to all members with similar conditions, it is hard to see when members would easily be able to invoke Article XX and win a case in defence of unilateral economic sanctions.

Of course, there is more than Article XX GATT in play here, as the US could also have recourse to GATT Article XXI and claim that the unilateral measures were targeting the protection of essential security interests. The vagary of this provision has caused much academic and political comment, with Neuwirth and Svetlicinii arguing that the ambiguity of Article XXI is beneficial due to its opaqueness.[86] Considering that its vagueness is a virtue allowing the provision to cater for an ongoing redefinition of what constitute security interests in an ever-changing world.[87] If their line of argumentation were to be followed it would be imaginable that such US sanctions could be deemed WTO-compatible at a moment in time by a panel. However, the case law is evolving in the WTO and more light has been shed on Article XXI in recent panel decisions.

The application of Article XXI to defend unilateral economic sanctions is considered below in the context of the panel decision relating to Ukraine and Russia. Indeed,

[82] Support for the Sovereignty Integrity Democracy and Economic Stability of Ukraine Act of 2014 ss 8–9, Pub L No 113-95, 128 Stat 1088, 2014.

[83] Executive Order No 13685, 79 Fed Reg 77357, 19 December 2014.

[84] The Ukraine Freedom Support Act of 2014, Pub L No 113-272, 128 Stat 2952, 2014.

[85] WTO, General Legal Texts, Article XX, available at www.wto.org/english/docs_e/legal_e/06-gatt_e.htm (5 October 2019).

[86] RJ Neuwirth and A Svetlicini, 'The Economic Sanctions over the Ukraine Conflict and the WTO: "Catch-XXI" and the Revival of the Debate on the Security Exceptions' (2015) 49 *Journal of World Trade* 891.

[87] ibid.

we will now examine some recent case law to assess the actual practice of the WTO Dispute Settlement Body.

VII. Recent WTO Case Law: the Consideration of Unilateral Economic Sanctions Placed on Qatar and Russia

Two recent cases in the WTO have considered the use of unilateral economic sanctions. In 2017 Qatar resorted to the WTO Dispute Settlement Body[88] due to the actions of four states – Bahrain, Egypt, Saudi Arabia and the United Arab Emirates (UAE) – claiming that the economic coercive measures taken by these states against Qatar amounted to a violation of the WTO rules. Qatar claimed that the measures adopted by the UAE were discriminatory, prevented freedom of transit and frustrated the majority of trade between Qatar and the UAE. The UAE argued that the measures had been taken to protect the UAE's essential security interests in full conformity with WTO rules.

The UAE sought to rely on 'essential security interests' to justify their trade sanctions, as per Article XXI of the GATT 1994 which states:

> Security Exceptions
>
> Nothing in this Agreement shall be construed
>
> (a) to require any contracting party to furnish any information the disclosure of which it considers contrary to its essential security interests; or
>
> (b) to prevent any contracting party from taking any action which it considers necessary for the protection of its essential security interests
>
> (i) relating to fissionable materials or the materials from which they are derived;
>
> (ii) relating to the traffic in arms, ammunition and implements of war and to such traffic in other goods and materials as is carried on directly or indirectly for the purpose of supplying a military establishment;
>
> (iii) taken in time of war or other emergency in international relations; or
>
> (c) to prevent any contracting party from taking any action in pursuance of its obligations under the United Nations Charter for the maintenance of international peace and security.[89]

This Article aims to allow members to apply measures that would be exempt from the general WTO measures in relation to their national security. As of today, the *Qatar – UAE* case remains in consideration with a report due at the end of 2020.[90] However, the case encourages us to consider what are 'essential security interests'?

[88] Qatar requested on 4 August 2017 WTO dispute consultations with the UAE, Bahrain and Saudi Arabia concerning measures adopted by the three countries which allegedly restrict trade in goods and services from Qatar, and trade-related intellectual property rights: 'Qatar files WTO complaints against the United Arab Emirates, Bahrain and Saudi Arabia', WTO News and Events, available at www.wto.org/english/news_e/news17_e/ds526_7_8rfc_04aug17_e.htm. See WT/DS526/1, WT/DS527/1.

[89] WTO (n 60).

[90] WTO, 'United Arab Emirates – Measures Relating to Trade in Goods and Services, and Trade Related Aspects of Intellectual Property Rights', available at www.wto.org/english/tratop_e/dispu_e/cases_e/ds526_e.htm.

An earlier case between Ukraine and Russia, which opened in 2016, resulted in a panel decision in 2019. This panel ruling provides an interpretation of the security exception under Article XXI. The case concerned a complaint from Ukraine following Russia's alleged restrictions on transit by road and rail from Ukraine through the Russian Federation to third countries.[91]

Russia responded to Ukraine's complaint by invoking a reliance on Article XXI, arguing that the dispute with Ukraine involved 'obvious and serious national security matters that Members have acknowledged should be kept out of the WTO, an organization which is not designed or equipped to handle such matters', and cautioned 'that involving the WTO in political and security matters will upset the very delicate balance of rights and obligations under the WTO Agreements and endanger the multilateral trading system'.[92] Russia also requested that the panel decline jurisdiction to examine Russia's invocation of the security exception under Article XXI as Russia claimed that the provision was 'self-judging' in nature and therefore not reviewable by the panel.[93]

The panel considered Ukraine's complaint and Russia's position, and determined that the DSU did not contain 'any special or additional rules of procedure applying to disputes involving Article XXI of the GATT 1994', and therefore Russia's invocation of Article XXI(b)(iii) was 'within the panel's terms of reference for the purposes of the DSU'.[94] In reaching this conclusion, the panel noted that Article XXI was to be interpreted as any other treaty provision in accordance with Articles 31 and 32 of the Vienna Convention on the Law of Treaties (VCLT).[95]

The panel also found that

> the existence of an emergency in international relations is an objective state of affairs, the determination of whether the action was 'taken in time of' an 'emergency in international relations' under subparagraph (iii) of Article XXI(b) is that of an objective fact, subject to objective determination.[96]

In analysing the negotiating history of Article XXI(b), the panel noted that:

> [T]he 'balance' that was struck by the security exceptions was that Members would have 'some latitude' to determine what their essential security interests are, and the necessity of action to protect those interests, while potential abuse of the exceptions would be curtailed by limiting the circumstances in which the exceptions could be invoked to those specified in the subparagraphs of Article XXI(b).[97]

The panel then assessed whether the measures taken by Russia were covered by the exceptions under Article XXI. The panel noted that Article XXI(b) acknowledges that

[91] Panel Body Report, 'Russia – Measures Concerning Traffic in Transit' (2019) 1.3, 2.1, 3.1.

[92] ibid, 7.22.

[93] ibid, 7.26, 7.57.

[94] ibid, 7.56.

[95] ibid, 7.59.

[96] ibid, 7.77. The Panel went on to say 'the ordinary meaning of Article XXI(b)(iii), in its context and in light of the object and purpose of the GATT 1994 and the WTO Agreement more generally, is that the adjectival clause 'which it considers' in the chapeau of Article XXI(b) does not qualify the determination of the circumstances in subparagraph (iii). Rather, for action to fall within the scope of Article XXI(b), it must objectively be found to meet the requirements in one of the enumerated subparagraphs of that provision'. 7.81–7.82.

[97] ibid, 7.98.

'a war or other emergency in international relations involves a fundamental change of circumstances which radically alters the factual matrix in which the WTO-consistency of the measures at issue are to be evaluated'.[98] In the panel's view, there was

> no need to determine the extent of the deviation of the challenged measure from the prescribed norm in order to evaluate the necessity of the measure, i.e. that there is no reasonably available alternative measure to achieve the protection of the legitimate interests covered by the exception which is not violative, or is less violative, of the prescribed norm.[99]

In assessing whether the security exception applied to the measures taken by Russia, the panel considered Russia's position that the following factors were to be taken into account to determine whether the situation was an emergency in international relations:

(a) the time period in which it arose and continues to exist,
(b) that the situation involves Ukraine,
(c) that it affects the security of Russia's border with Ukraine in various ways,
(d) that it has resulted in other countries imposing sanctions against Russia, and
(e) that the situation in question is publicly known.[100]

It accepted that there was evidence before the panel that 'relations between Ukraine and Russia had deteriorated to such a degree that they were a matter of concern to the international community'. The panel took into account that the situation between Ukraine and Russia was 'recognized by the UN General Assembly as involving armed conflict'[101] and that 'a number of countries have imposed sanctions against Russia in connection with [the] situation'.[102]

Consequently, the panel was satisfied that the situation between Ukraine and Russia since 2014 constituted an emergency in international relations, within the meaning of Article XXI(b)(iii) of the GATT 1994.[103] The panel also considered the relevance of the phrase 'which it considers' in the chapeau of Article XXI(b) and whether that adjectival clause qualified only the requirement of 'necessity' of

> the measures for the protection of the invoking Member's essential security interests, or also the determination of these 'essential security interests', or finally and maximally, to qualify as well the determination of the sets of circumstances described in each of the subparagraphs of Article XXI(b).[104]

The panel concluded that it was for Russia to determine 'the "necessity" of the measures for the protection of its essential security interests',[105] ie there is a 'self-judging' element to the application of Article XXI(b) of the GATT. However, as discussed below, this is tempered by the panel's power to review whether a state has acted in good faith.

[98] ibid, 7.109.
[99] ibid, 7.108.
[100] ibid, 7.119.
[101] ibid, 7.122.
[102] ibid, 7.122.
[103] ibid, 7.123.
[104] ibid, 7.127.
[105] ibid, 7.146.

In its analysis, the panel clarified that

> essential security interests … may generally be understood to refer to those interests relating to the quintessential functions of the state, namely, the protection of its territory and its population from external threats, and the maintenance of law and public order internally.[106]

It then made the following analysis in relation to the power of each member to define for itself what it considers to be its essential security interest.

In general, it is left to every member to define what their essential security interests in that state are.[107] However, a member is not free to elevate any concern to that of an 'essential security interest': 'Rather, the discretion of a Member to designate particular concerns as "essential security interests" is limited by its obligation to interpret and apply Article XXI(b)(iii) of the GATT 1994 in good faith'.[108]

'The obligation of good faith requires that Members do not use the exceptions in Article XXI as a means to circumvent their obligations under the GATT 1994'.[109] 'It is therefore incumbent on the invoking Member to articulate the essential security interests said to arise from the emergency in international relations sufficiently to demonstrate their veracity'.[110] The obligation of good faith applies not only to the member's definition of the essential security interest, but also to their connection with the measure at issue, meaning that the measures at issue must 'meet a minimum requirement of plausibility in relation to the proffered essential security interest, i.e., that they are not implausible as measures protective of these interests'.[111]

The panel concluded that Russia, in light of its discretion to determine the necessity of the measures for the protection of its essential security interest, had satisfied the conditions of the chapeau of Article XXI(b) of the GATT and met all the requirements for invoking the national security provision.[112]

As the WTO panel clarified, an 'emergency in international relations' is intended in the context of a

> situation of armed conflict, or of latent armed conflict, or of heightened tension or crisis, or of general instability engulfing or surrounding a state. Such situations give rise to particular types of interests for the Member in question, i.e. defence or military interests, or maintenance of law and public order interests.[113]

The existence of an 'emergency in international relations' is an objective state of affairs, the determination of which is subject to objective determination.[114]

According to this WTO panel, even if the situation is considered as an 'emergency in international relations', the next question which must be answered is whether the measures which were adopted were taken in 'good faith' to protect interests 'relating to the quintessential functions of the state, namely, the protection of its territory and

[106] ibid, 7.130.
[107] ibid, 7.131.
[108] ibid, 7.131–7.132.
[109] ibid, 7.133.
[110] ibid, 7.134.
[111] ibid, 7.138.
[112] ibid, 7.145–7.149.
[113] ibid, 7.76.
[114] ibid, 7.77.

its population from external threats, and the maintenance of law and public order internally'.[115]

The obligation to act in good faith applies not only to the State's definition of the essential security interests said to arise from the particular emergency in international relations, but also to adoption of the measure(s) at issue.[116] The concept of 'good faith' is enshrined in Article 26 of the VCLT,[117] and also applies to Article XXI of the GATT.[118] As the panel in the Russia WTO Case explained, the 'good faith' obligation requires that Members not use the exceptions in Article XXI as a means to circumvent their obligations under the GATT 1994. Whether a measure has been taken in 'good faith' is to be assessed by a WTO panel[119] and it is not open to a WTO Member unilaterally to elevate any concern to that of an 'essential security interest'.[120]

The panel thus concluded that Russia could rely on Article XXI for the measures taken as they had passed the tests laid down. The decision was not appealed, but the panel made it clear that had the measures been taken in 'normal times' then Ukraine would have made a prima facie case that the measures were inconsistent with Article V of the GATT.[121]

To return to the case of Qatar in its dispute with third countries, such as the UAE, which sought to rely on the nature of the trade measures targeting Qatar as being essential security interests, it is possible to speculate whether this defence would hold up to panel scrutiny. The UAE and others would need to demonstrate that there was an emergency in international relations, meaning demonstrating that there is armed conflict, latent armed conflict, heightened tension or crisis, or general instability surrounding a state. This would be a trickier situation than in the case of Russia–Ukraine as no specific armed conflict or sense of international concern resulting in sanctions being imposed against the UAE and others would be able to be demonstrated. The second test of applying the measures in 'good faith' may also pose a challenge to those countries seeking to rely on Article XXI in their treatment of Qatar. Are the measures being applied against Qatar being done so in good faith? Or are these measures simply designed to circumnavigate the parties' obligations under the GATT 1994? The outcome of this case will surely rest on these two points.

VIII. Conclusion

This chapter has examined the use of unilateral economic sanctions and the WTO legal norms that apply to their use in the context of WTO members relations. It has been

[115] ibid, 7.130.
[116] ibid, 7.138.
[117] VCLT, Art 26: 'Every treaty in force is binding upon the parties to it and must be performed by them in good faith'.
[118] See Panel Body Report (n 61) 7.132. See also S Peng, 'Cybersecurity Threats and the WTO National Security Exceptions' (2015) 18 *Journal of International Economic Law* 477. See also Appellate Body Report, 'United States – Import Prohibition of Certain Shrimp and Shrimp Products' (1998) 158.
[119] Panel Body Report (n 61) 7.43, 7.132-7.139.
[120] ibid, 7.131–7.132.
[121] ibid, 7.166–7.184, 7.189–7.196 and 7.239–7.240.

demonstrated that unilateral economic sanctions are relatively widely used today, but that their application is far from certain to be tolerable under WTO law. It is certain that unilateral economic sanctions are in themselves non-permissible in the WTO according to the DSU, but that the Article XX exemptions offer some hope to some commentators that they could be legal under the right set of circumstances.

In practice, it appears to be difficult to assume that even human rights abuses could be considered worthy of passing the chapeau test, which may seem extremely controversial, but the WTO Appellate Body and panels are simply tasked with assessing the legality of the trade aspect of the measures. Thus, the outcomes should not surprise anyone if such measures were to be struck down, as has happened in the past in relation to measures enacted on the premise of protecting the environment.

In Article XXI there may be more room to manoeuvre, as long as the situation is not 'normal'. If an objective test demonstrates that there is indeed an emergency in international relations and that the measures have been taken in good faith, at least the panel believes there are grounds for exempting unilateral economic sanctions from WTO legal principles. However, the requirement would seem to be that the states are at war, or something akin to war. In this case it would not be surprising that exemptions would be allowed.

The panel was also very clear that if the emergency and good faith tests were not passed, there would be no grounds for unilateral economic sanctions. This reinforces the notion that unilateral economic sanctions are a rare exception and far from the norm in international economic relations.

The jurisprudence in this area is largely untested; few cases have been through all the way to appeal in the WTO. This is evolving, and jurisprudence continues to evolve in line with international law norms. In this era of political use of economic sanctions for policy results, it seems likely that the WTO will become busier in dealing with unilateral economic sanctions.

8

Unilateral Sanctions, Universal Postal Union and State Responsibility

TRISHA RAJPUT[1]

I. Introduction

Postal services make it possible for any person to send a letter, packet or parcel to a domestic or international addressee, according to certain established standards of regularity, speed and security. The importance of correspondence has been recognised in Article 12 of the Universal declaration of Human Rights, which states that 'no one shall be subjected to arbitrary interference with his privacy, family, home or correspondence, not to attack upon his honour and reputation'.[2] Postal service as a medium of communication and information exchange remains especially relevant for areas that are remote and are not yet on the digital map. For regions and areas that are not connected with modern technology, the postal service has important role in the cultural and social life of the people living there.[3] In addition, there is an enormous economic value of postal exchange that has been instrumental in the emergence and entrenchment of e-commerce.[4]

[1] School of Business, Economics and Law, University of Gothenburg. The author would like to thank Carolina Dackö, Partner at Manheimmer Swartling, Gothenburg for her valuable insight into US sanctions on Iran.

[2] UN General Assembly, Universal Declaration of Human Rights, 10 December 1948, 217 A(III).

[3] Constitution of the Universal Postal Union (Berne 2018). Art 1.1 provides: 'Postal service: all international postal services, whose scope is determined and regulated by the Acts of the Union. The main obligations of postal services are to satisfy certain social and economic objectives of member countries, by ensuring the collection, processing, transmission and delivery of postal items.'

[4] For more details on how postal service has facilitated e-commerce refer to HB Okholm, MH Thelle, A Möller, B Basalisco and S Rølmer, 'E-commerce and Delivery: A study of the state of play of EU parcel markets with particular emphasis on e-commerce, 2015', available at www.copenhageneconomics.com/dyn/resources/Publication/publicationPDF/8/238/0/E-commerce-and-delivery.pdf. The 25th UPU Congress decided to enhance the focus on e-commerce through resolutions C 31 /2012 (Development of e-commerce) and C 33/2012 (Promoting cross-border e-commerce). The UPU E-Commerce Forum, held on 26 and 27 March 2014 in Berne, also emphasised on the relationship between e-commerce and postal industry.

The first documented record of the earliest postal service is from Egypt in 2000 BC, followed by China under the Chou dynasty in 1,000 BC.[5] Physical evidence from the ancient times of the postal service from China, Egypt, Persia and the Roman Empire has been recovered in the form of cuneiform tablets, wax tablets, parchment papers and also wooden sheets.[6] The nature and scope of postal service that existed historically was much different to what is available to us today. In ancient times such service was only for official purposes and mainly confined to imperial court circles or merchants,[7] but today it is considered a public good and is available to all. The benefits of postal service extend to all countries, people and generations,[8] is transnational[9] in nature, requires international cooperation and collective action.[10] The ability to correspond/communicate is of collective and common interest to the international community, so an international postal service can be characterised as a global good.[11] The postal service is facilitated by the Universal Postal Union (UPU), which has 192 countries as its members.[12] UPU is a truly universal forum for cooperation between various postal sector players. Article 1(2) of the UPU Constitution provides that the UPU aims 'to secure the organization and improvement of the postal services and to promote in this sphere the development of international collaboration'.[13]

The purpose of this chapter is to consider the interplay of sanctions with rules of the UPU that guarantees postal communication and State responsibility. Sanctions that target postal communication may affect both letters and parcels. Economic sanctions also have the consequence of limiting meaningful exchange of post, in particular parcel exchange between countries in a widespread manner. Academic discussion on the interplay of sanction and postal communication is limited, but its consideration is both timely and important given the reimposition of economic sanctions on Iran by the Trump administration[14] and the arbitration action initiated by Qatar against United

[5] AC Brix, 'Postal system', available at www.britannica.com/topic/postal-system; YA Chen, 'Exhibiting Postal Stationery of the Imperial China', available at www.postalstationery.org/pdf/ExhibitingPostalStationery ImperialChina.pdf.

[6] J Muir, *Life and Letters in the Ancient Greek World* (Routledge. 2008).

[7] In ancient China, the postal service was mainly for imperial communication and in Europe of the Middle Ages, postal communication was mainly for mercantile usage. See n 5 above.

[8] I Kaul, P Conceição and KL Goulven, 'How to Improve the Provision of Global Public Goods' in I Kaul (ed), *Providing Global Public Goods: Managing Globalization* (Oxford University Press, 2003).

[9] JP Touffut, *Advancing Public Goods* (Edward Elgar, 2006).

[10] The World Bank defines global public goods as commodities, resources and services, regulations and policy institutions that have strong cross-border externalities and can be supplied only through international cooperation and collective action. For more discussion on the issue refer to V Bhargava, *Global Issues for Global Citizens: An Introduction to Key Development Challenges* (World Bank, 2006).

[11] ILC, Commentary to the Draft Articles on Responsibility of States for Internationally Wrongful Acts, Art 48, paras 6–7, II Yearbook of the ILC, (Part II) (2001) 126 discusses 'collective interests' and 'common interests'. G Shaffer, 'International Law and Global Public Goods in A Legal Pluralist World' (2012) 23 *European Journal of International Law* 669–93.

[12] Any member country of the UN may become a member of the UPU. Any non-member country of the UN may become a UPU member provided that its request is approved by at least two-thirds of UPU members.

[13] UPU Constitution (n 3).

[14] Sanctions have been imposed by the US on Iran through the Presidential Documents, Executive Order 13846 of 6 August 2018; Re-imposing Certain Sanctions with Respect to Iran, Federal Register, Vol 83, No 152, 7 August 2018.

Arab Emirates (UAE), Saudi Arabia, Bahrain and Egypt under the UPU framework. Unilateral sanctions raise various international legal issues with regard to the right of postal communications, and this chapter will explore selected issues with reference to two case studies and then present a conclusion informed by the analysis presented.

Section II of the chapter presents the legal framework offered by UPU rules[15] that guarantees postal communication in a comprehensive manner. More specifically, it considers the question whether a unilateral sanction that takes the form of suspension of postal communication inconsistent with the UPU rules can be justified. It should be noted that the UPU rules provide for exceptions which may be utilised by its members to employ measures that restrict postal communication. This section evaluates the nature and scope of the exception available under the UPU rules. Section III presents a case study on US sanctions on Iran. The US sanctions are briefly reviewed to highlight how they interrupt postal communication. This section assesses the prospect of seeking recourse through arbitration under UPU rules and ICJ. In this context, exception under the UPU rules, necessity and countermeasures under the Articles on the Responsibility of States for Internationally Wrongful Acts (ARISWA) is considered as a justification for imposing sanctions on postal communication. This analysis is useful for drawing guidance on whether the exception under the UPU and widely discussed necessity and countermeasures operates to limit the possibility of a state to use it as a justification for non-performance of its obligation under the UPU rules. Section IV focuses on express restrictions on postal communication through the case study on Qatar. This case study highlights the difficultly in pursuing arbitration under the UPU framework and exemplifies how member countries give way to their security concerns over their obligation under the UPU rules. Section V concludes by offering some broad observation about the challenges associated with available remedies to the states subjected to the sanctions and suggests deepening of the role of UPU as a forum for consultation.

II. Universal Postal Union

In the sixteenth century Franz von Taxis proposed a postal service for the European states. Initially, the postal relations between countries were based on bilateral agreements, tailormade to suit the requirements of individual countries. However, the variety of rates calculated in different currencies caused great operational inconvenience. Countries utilised different units of weight and different scales, which made the delivery of the postal service complicated. An attempt was made in Paris on 11 May 1863 to harmonise the different bilateral agreements; a number of general principles were adopted to guide the state administrations when concluding postal conventions. Despite the adoption of uniform principles, international postal services by and large remained inefficient. To address the inefficiencies of international postal transactions, a proposal for establishing a postal union was put forward. In 1868, Heinrich von Stephan, a senior

[15] The term 'rules' has been used generally in this chapter to refer to the Constitution, Convention and Regulations of the UPU combinedly.

official in the postal administration of the North German Confederation proposed a postal union of civilised countries. The Plenipotentiary Conference of 1874 resulted in signing of the Treaty of Berne, which established the Universal Postal Union (UPU) and the collective Convention governing the international postal service.

A. Purpose and Function of UPU

The UPU comprises four bodies – namely Congress, Council of Administration (CA), Postal Operations Council (POC) and the International Bureau – and its mission is to 'facilitate communication between the inhabitants of the world'.[16] The Treaty Concerning the Creation of a General Postal Union and the Detailed and Administrative Regulations were the two first Acts concluded in 1874. The former became the Convention, which evolved until the 1964 Vienna Congress together with its Detailed and Administrative Regulations. The 1964 Vienna Congress changed the structure and content of the Acts of the Union, approving the separation into different parts of the Convention and adopting the new structure of the Acts of the UPU comprising:

(a) the UPU Constitution;
(b) the General Regulations;
(c) the Universal Postal Convention; and
(d) the Universal Postal Convention's Detailed Regulations.

The General Regulations of the UPU contain the provisions which relates to the application of the Constitution and the operation of the Union. They are binding on all member countries and are not subject to reservations. The Universal Postal Convention contains the basic and essential obligations of governments concerning the common rules applicable to the international postal service for letter-post and parcel-post items. The Convention standardises postal rates, guarantees freedom of transit, establishes the principle that postage will be retained by the sender country, and sets out general rules for all postal services and the specific rules for letter services. The Regulations, previously known as the Detailed Regulations of the Universal Postal Convention, contains the operational and commercial rules applied by the postal services, and include provisions relating to the execution of the letter-post service. The Constitution, the General Regulations, the Convention and the two sets of Regulations are binding on all member countries.[17]

The Preamble of the Constitution of the UPU states its mission clearly, as follows:

> With a view to developing communications between peoples by the efficient operation of the postal services, and to contributing to the attainment of the noble aims of international collaboration in the cultural, social and economic fields, the plenipotentiaries of the governments of the contracting countries have, subject to ratification, adopted this Constitution.

The Preamble highlights the importance of communication between the inhabitants of the world through postal services and conceives the role of the UPU as a facilitator.

[16] The UPU was founded in 1874 when delegates from 28 countries attended the Plenipotentiary Conference in Berne on 15 September 1874. As of December 2017, 192 states were members of the UPU.

[17] All UPU Acts, available at www.upu.int/en/Universal-Postal-Union/About-UPU/Acts.

In fact, the opening phrase, 'with a view to developing communications between peoples', suggests UPU's role as a guarantor of communication through medium of postal items. The Preamble also recognises that communication is important from a social, cultural and economic perspective. In this respect Article 3 of the Universal Postal Convention and Regulations, entitled 'Universal Postal Service', is particularly important. It requires that the members of the UPU must ensure that the users/customers enjoy quality basic postal services in their territory.[18] For that, member countries must establish, within the framework of their national postal legislation or by customary means, the scope of the postal services offered and the requirement for quality and affordable prices. In addition, the postal services offered must consider the national conditions as well as the requirement of the population.[19]

B. Rights under the UPU

Article 1 of the Constitution, entitled 'Scope and the Objectives of the Union', highlights two main principles of the Union, namely the 'Creation of Single Postal Territory' and 'Guaranteeing Freedom of Transit'.

Article 1 states:

> The countries adopting this Constitution shall comprise, under the title of the Universal Postal Union, a single postal territory for the reciprocal exchange of postal items.
>
> Freedom of transit shall be guaranteed throughout the entire territory of the Union, subject to the conditions specified in the Acts of the Union.[20]

To create 'A Single Postal Territory' as defined under Article 1bis there is an obligation upon contracting parties to the UPU Acts to guarantee:

(a) the free circulation of postal items over a single postal territory;
(b) the freedom of transit, national treatment and non-discrimination of postal items in transit from other countries; and
(c) the freedom of transit and national treatment of postal items for other countries.

Firstly, the UPU guarantees 'the free circulation of postal items over a single postal territory composed of interconnected network'. UPU member countries comprise a single postal territory for the reciprocal exchange of letter-post items. The concept of a single postal territory allows for the facilitation and improvement of international mail exchanges through the established common rules and standards within it, ranging from the definition of a postage stamp to customs matters and the prohibition of exchanging certain substances and items.

Article 1bis of the Constitution entails that the contracting parties of the union must offer reciprocal exchange of postal items. The use of the word 'reciprocal' lays emphasis on reciprocity. Keohane remarks that 'reciprocity refers to exchanges of

[18] Universal Postal Convention and Regulations, Vol I, S I, Art 3.1 Universal Postal Convention and Regulations, Vol I, S I.

[19] Art 3.2.

[20] Art 3.2.

roughly equivalent values in which the actions of each party are contingent on the prior actions of the others in such a way that good is returned for good, and bad for bad'.[21] In the context of this provision, reciprocity may be best understood as equivalence of action, which allows for the exchange of postal items thereby enabling free circulation of mail across borders. In summary, the UPU facilitates this single global postal territory through multilateral agreements, some of which are updated and signed by all member countries every four years. However, the exchange of postal items is not absolute as the Convention allows exception from this obligation to members that do not participate in exchange of postal items containing infectious or radioactive substances.[22]

Article 1 of the Constitution provides that 'freedom of transit is to be guaranteed throughout the entire territory of the Union". Article 1bis (3) and (4) are instructive in this regard.

Article 1bis (3) of the Constitution imposes an obligation on members to guarantee free transit of letter-post items from other members. Article 1bis (3) of the Constitution mandates that the member countries:

> [P]rovide for the reciprocal exchange of letter-post items, including freedom of transit, and to treat postal items in transit from other countries like their own items, without discrimination subject to the conditions specified in the Acts of the Union.[23]

In contrast, Article 1bis (4) of the Constitution guarantees free transit of postal items destined for another member. Article 1bis (4) of the Constitution provides:

> Freedom of transit: obligation for an intermediate member country to ensure the transport of postal items passed on to it in transit for another member country, providing similar treatment to that given to domestic items, subject to the conditions specified in the Acts of the Union.[24]

In addition, Article 1bis (3) and (4) also indicates the treatment of postal items for/from other countries. Article 1bis (3) of the Constitution includes an obligation of national treatment and the prohibition of non-discrimination with regard to letter-post items in transit from other countries while Article 1bis (4) of the Constitution mandates a member country to provide 'similar treatment to postal items in transit for other members countries as given to domestic goods'. On important point is that Article 1bis (3) explicitly sets forth an obligation of non-discrimination which is not clearly expressed in Article 1bis (4).

Further, Article 4 of the Constitution specifies that the freedom of transit carries with it the obligation for each member country to ensure that its designated operators forward closed mail which is passed to them by another designated operator always through securest and the quickest routes. Article 4 of the Constitution states:

> The principle of the freedom of transit is set forth in article 1 of the Constitution. It shall carry with it the obligation for each member country to ensure that its designated operators forward, always by the quickest routes and the most secure means which they use for their own items, closed mails and à découvert letter-post items which are passed to them by another designated operator. This principle shall also apply to missent items and misrouted mails.

[21] RO Keohane, 'Reciprocity in International Relations' (1986) 40 *International Organization* 1–27.
[22] UPU, Convention, Vol I, S V Prohibitions and customs matters. 19 Items not admitted. Prohibitions (n 18).
[23] See n 3.
[24] See n 3.

The 1964 Vienna Congress Resolution C 23 resolution further emphasises on the importance of freedom of transit:

> Congress, considering that freedom of transit is one of the essential and fundamental principles of the Universal Postal Union, appeals to the good faith and solidarity of all the member countries of the Union to ensure, in all circumstances, strict respect for the application of this principle, without which the Universal Postal Union cannot completely fulfil its mission and thus contribute as much as could be wished to the strengthening of the bonds of international friendship.[25]

It should be noted that both the above-mentioned two principles are relevant for all postal items that include both documents[26] and goods.[27] Article 1.6 bis of the Constitution defines postal items to include letter post, parcel post, money orders, etc.[28]

C. Exception under the UPU

The current state of international affairs is witnessing a rise in unilateral sanctions. The sanctions in the area of trade have been subject of much awe and discussion over the last two years.[29] One important point to note is that in some cases even though no measures may be taken to interrupt postal communication directly, the fact that the economic relations are interrupted have an impact on postal exchange. Currently there are several instances of restrictions on circulation of mail; for example, the US imposes restrictions on the circulation of mail to and from Iran[30] and Syria,[31] and there are sanctions on Qatar by Egypt, Saudi Arabia, United Arab Emirates (UAE) and Bahrain.

[25] Art 4.1, Commentary (n 18).

[26] UPU, Universal Postal Convention and Regulations, Vol I, S I, Art 1.4, which defines a document as a 'letter-post, parcel-post or EMS item consisting of any piece of written, drawn, printed or digital information, excluding objects of merchandise, whose physical specifications lie within the limits specified in the Regulations'.

[27] UPU, Universal Postal Convention and Regulations, Vol I, Sec I, Art 1.5 defines goods as 'a letter-post, parcel-post or EMS item consisting of any tangible and movable object other than money, including objects of merchandise, which does not fall under the definition of "documents" as provided in paragraph 1.4 above and whose physical specifications lie within the limits specified in the Regulations'.

[28] See n 3 above.

[29] This statement is asserted on the basis of duties imposed by the US on imports from China etc. Currently US has approximately over 25 anti-dumping and countervailing duty orders on China. For comprehensive insight into the GATT disputes involving security exception refer to T Voon, 'The Security Exception in WTO Law: Entering a New Era' (2019) 113 *American Journal of International Law Unbound* 45 and RV Anuradha, 'Petrificus Totalus: The Spell of National Security' (2018) 13 *Asian Journal of WTO and International Health Law and Policy* 311.

[30] The USPS is the designated authorised operator in the US; its website provides details of the restrictions on mail, as follows: 'The Office of Foreign Assets Control (OFAC) of the U.S. Department of the Treasury and the Bureau of Industry and Security (BIS) of the U.S. Department of Commerce administer sanctions that restrict the mailing of items to certain destinations and recipients, including a broad embargo on items to and from Iran. Many shipments to Iran also require the filing of information with the U.S. Census Bureau. Before mailing any items to Iran, mailers should refer to IMM 510, 520, and 530 and to Publication 699, *Special Requirements for Shipping Internationally*, for additional information'; available at pe.usps.com/text/imm/il_004.htm. 'Designated operator' is defined as any governmental or non-governmental entity officially designated by the member country to operate postal services and to fulfil the related obligations arising out of the Acts of the Union on its territory.

[31] The USPS is the designated operator is the US; its website provides details of the restrictions on mail, as follows: 'The Office of Foreign Assets Control (OFAC) of the U.S. Department of the Treasury and the Bureau

The social and cultural cost associated with the restriction of mail is incontestable but there is also a substantial economic cost associated with it. For instance, business-to-consumer and consumer-to-consumer e-commerce both domestically and internationally[32] materialises through delivery of post.[33] Sanctions that target postal communication also effect e-commerce[34] which translates into economic costs. However, political outcries over such restrictions have remained limited for reasons unknown. One reason could be the economic costs associated with the restriction of mail does not measure close to the costs associated with the type of restrictions against activities that fall within the scope of Agreements of the WTO.

Members of the UPU may be compelled politically and economically to adopt measures that are inconsistent with the rules of the UPU, in particular with rules of reciprocal exchange of post and freedom of transit that are pertinent for the right of communication. Generally, the various rationales of coercive measures have been a subject of much discussion and debate in international law.[35] It is well documented that coercive measures are used as tools to force states to make the relevant changes to their political, economic and social system. However, it has been argued that all 'coercive measures' are unlawful as it requires the target state to change social, economic or political policies which are well within its domestic jurisdiction.[36] This argument finds support from the idea of sovereign equality found in 1970 General Assembly Resolution 2625 Declaration on Principles of International Law concerning Friendly Relations and Cooperation among States in Accordance with the Charter of the United Nations, which provides that one element of sovereign equality is the state's freedom to choose and develop its political, social, economic and cultural systems.

of Industry and Security (BIS) of the U.S. Department of Commerce administer sanctions that restrict the mailing of items to certain destinations and recipients, including a broad embargo on items to and from Syria. Many shipments to Syria also require the filing of information with the U.S. Census Bureau. Before mailing any items to Syria, mailers should refer to IMM 510, 520, and 530 and to Publication 699, *Special Requirements for Shipping Internationally*, for additional information', available at pe.usps.com/text/imm/ps_041.htm.

[32] See n 4. The 25th UPU Congress decided to enhance the focus on e-commerce through resolutions C 31 /2012 (Development of e-commerce) and C 33/2012 (Promoting cross-border e-commerce). The UPU E-Commerce Forum, held on 26 and 27 March 2014 in Berne, also emphasised on the relationship between e-commerce and postal industry. According to UPU, in 2013, the number of international tracked postal items monitored in the postal networks reached 397 million, and in 2014 the total number of international tracked postal shipments was 460 million, corresponding to a year-on-year growth of 15.9%. The growth further accelerated in 2015 with a total number of 568 million international postal shipments, or a 23.3% year-on-year growth rate. Package delivery firms are particularly keen about cross-border e-commerce given the higher margins with international shipping.

[33] Most of the items that are shopped online are in the lightweight category and may be delivered through international parcel service, letter-post services including small packets up to 2kg, and express mail services (EMS). In fact, the national designated operators such as Royal Mail, Post Nord, La Poste, DPD and GLS are key players in this category as they have an extensive network and are much cheaper than the logistic service providers such as DHL, TNT, etc. See www.upu.int/uploads/tx_sbdownloader/researchOnPostalMarketsTrendsAndDriversForInternationalLetterMailParcelsAndExpressMailServicesEn.pdf.pdf.

[34] It should be noted that the e-commerce dynamics are uneven. For instance, it is more dominant in Asia compared to Africa.

[35] M Happold, 'Economic Sanctions and International Law: An Introduction' in M Happold and P Eden (eds), *Economic Sanctions and International Law* (Hart, 2016).

[36] This line of argument has been advanced by Pierre-Emmanuel Dupont, 'Unilateral European Sanctions as Countermeasures: The Case of the EU Measures Against Iran' in M Happold and P Eden (eds), *Economic Sanctions and International Law* (Hart, 2016).

The question that arises at this juncture is whether a unilateral sanction that takes the form of suspension of postal communication inconsistent with the UPU rules can be justified.

Under the UPU rules, restrictions on postal communication may be justified only if they are taken to comply with Security Council decisions. The exception to deviate from UPU rules is provided under paragraph 2 of Article VI of the Rules of Procedure of the Postal Operations Council entitled 'Assistance to the United Nations'. This states:

> 2. As regards the members of the United Nations, the Union agrees that in accordance with article 103 of the Charter no provision in the Universal Postal Convention or related Agreements shall be construed as preventing or limiting any State in complying with its obligations to the United Nations.[37]

One aspect that emerges from the above discussion, especially in context of conflict of laws, is the fact that Article VI of the Rules of Procedure of the Postal Operations Council gives priority to the obligations arising from the UN Charter. In the absence of a definite hierarchical relationship or *indifferenciation hierarchique des normes hierarchial* (non-differentiation of hierarchical norms),[38] it becomes increasingly complicated to clearly determine the priority and extent of application of the rules of the regimes when instances of interconnection arise. But Article VI settles the position. When the obligations under the UN Charter conflict with UPU rules, the obligation under the Charter trumps the obligation under the UPU rules. This means that if the right of communication is suspended by a UN Member State that is also a member of the UPU, and such suspension is based on a Security Council Resolution, such suspension is permissible. One may argue that Article VI favours the more stringent obligation by permitting the interruption of postal communication facilitated by the UPU. In addition, Article 25 of the UN Charter also has a conflict-resolving role as it categorically indicates that the 'Members of the United Nations agree to accept and carry out the decisions of the Security Council in accordance with the present Charter'.

III. US Sanction on Iran: Case Study

A. Facts, Context Surrounding the US Sanctions and its Impact on Postal Communication

The purpose of this section is to briefly present the sanctions imposed by US on Iran and examine its consequences for postal communication. It should be noted that it is not the intention here to delve deep into the nature and legality of the US sanctions, but to pursue the argument that the current sanctions regime that the US pursues contradicts the right of communication facilitated through the UPU. Since the US is a part of

[37] UN–UPU Agreements, Part V Relations with the UN and legal status Agreement between the United Nations and the Universal Postal Union.

[38] J Combacau, '*Le Droit International: Bric-à-Brac ou Système?*' (1986) 31 *Archives De Philosophie Du Droit* 85; B Simma and D Pulkowski, 'Of Planets and The Universe: Self Contained Regimes in International Law' (2006) 17 *European Journal of International Law* 484.

the UPU, its existing regime on sanctions leads us to a discussion on interference with the right of communication facilitated by the UPU rules. The US–Iran situation is an excellent example of how postal communication may be restricted as a result of sanctions that do not directly target postal exchange.

The US framework on sanction on Iran has two categories: primary and secondary. The primary (or direct) sanctions prohibit US persons (which includes citizens, residents and companies incorporated in the US) to engage in any dealing with the Government of Iran, individuals located or residing in Iran, and companies located or organised in Iran. This means that in reality there is total embargo on any kind of business, trade and commercial transactions between the US and Iran. Communication via postal exchange between the US and Iran is restricted and regulated.[39] Simple letter exchange between Iran and US is not hindered, but any other postal service to Iran is complicated as the handlers are often unclear of the rules and regulations.

The other dimension of US sanction regime is penalisation of non-US companies that engage in specified activities (sectorial sanctions) or significant dealings with certain designated persons (SDNs), referred to as secondary sanctions. To explain further, a company registered in the EU which, for example, sells cars to Iran or equipment for Iran's automotive sector, will be in breach of US secondary sectoral sanctions. This also means that the EU company, in principle, would be subject of the extraterritorial jurisdiction of the US law. In reality, the secondary sanctions act a deterrent for companies to engage with Iran as they do not want to lose access to the significant US market.[40] The secondary sanctions were relaxed after the Joint Comprehensive Plan of Action (JCPOA) was implemented on 16 January 2016. The JCPOA was signed between Iran, the EU, China, France, Germany, Russia, the UK and the US. Under the JCOPA, Iran committed to limit its nuclear programme and in exchange the other participants agreed to lift certain economic and trade sanctions. The Congressional Research Service highlights in a recent report that the JCPOA sanctions relief

> enabled Iran to increase its oil exports to nearly pre-sanctions levels, regain access to foreign exchange reserve funds and reintegrate into the international financial system, achieve about 7% yearly economic growth, attract foreign investments in key sectors, and buy new passenger aircraft.[41]

[39] The following items are some of the limited types of shipments that may be allowed under US law without the need for an export licence: personal gifts up to $100 in value; humanitarian donations to relieve human suffering; informational materials in any medium, including publications, films, photographs, music, and artwork; commercial sales of eligible agricultural commodities, including food for people or animals, seeds, vitamins, food additives, nutritional supplements, natural fibers (eg, cotton, wool, linen, silk, hemp, sisal) and fibre products, wood and wood products, and other plant or animal products (for a list of eligible agricultural commodities, see www.fas.usda.gov/sites/default/files/2014-04/schedulebeligiblecommodities06-28-06.pdf); commercial sales of many medicines and eligible medical supplies; computers, mobile phones, smart phones, modems, peripherals, radio equipment, home satellite equipment, anti-virus software, and other personal communications hardware and software (for additional information regarding eligible shipments of personal communications hardware and software, see www.treasury.gov/resource-center/faqs/Sanctions/Pages/faq_iran.aspx#gld1); commercial sales of replacement parts for medical devices sent on a one-to-one basis (ie, one replacement part for one defective part) (replacement parts must be in limited quantities consistent with the intent to repair specific broken equipment (and not for resale or inventory; this does not cover shipments of medical devices themselves, see about.usps.com/publications/pub699/pub699_online_021.htm).

[40] BR Early, 'Confronting the Implementation and Enforcement Challenges Involved in Imposing Economic Sanctions' in N Ronzitti (ed), *Coercive Diplomacy, Sanctions and International Law* (Brill, 2016) 67.

[41] Congressional Research Service, Iran sanctions, RS20871 (2019), available at fas.org/sgp/crs/mideast/RS20871.pdf.

However, on 8 May 2018, the US announced its withdrawal from the JCOPA[42] and indicated that all sanctions that were lifted or waived would be reimposed no later than 180 days. After the secondary sanctions were imposed companies had a 90- or180-day period to wind down their Iranian business. The 90-day wind-down period applied to activities related to: the purchase or acquisition of US dollar banknotes or precious metals by the Government of Iran; transactions related to the purchase and sale of Iranian Rials; the Iranian automotive sector; purchase, subscription to the Iranian sovereign fund; the facilitation of the issuance of the Iranian sovereign fund; and the direct or indirect sale, supply, or transfer of graphite, raw or semi-finished metals such as aluminium, steel, coal and software for integrating industrial processes.[43] The 180-day wind-down period applied to activities related to: Iran's port operators, and shipping and shipbuilding sectors; petroleum-related transactions including the purchase of petroleum, petroleum products, or petrochemical products from Iran; transactions by foreign financial institutions with the Central Bank of Iran and designated Iranian financial institutions under Section 1245 of the National Defence Authorization Act for Fiscal Year 2012 (NDAA); and financial messaging services to the Central Bank of Iran and Iranian financial institutions.[44] The US has also added over 700 persons to the US List of Specially Designated Nationals and Blocked Persons, which includes several major Iranian banks.[45] Postal services as such remain excluded from the specified activities that are penalised through secondary sanctions. The practical implications of the secondary sanctions in context of postal communication is not easy to assess or gauge because of the lack of statistics. However, it is clear that the secondary sanction has a chilling effect on companies by discouraging them to engage in any business with Iran especially when they want to continue to access the US market.

The secondary sanctions dimension brings to fore an interesting difference in approach between the US and EU, which also generates consequences for postal communication. Europe disagrees in a limited sense with the US approach and remains committed to the agreement under JCOPA. In fact, the EU has undertaken steps to protect EU companies from secondary sanctions by updating the Council Regulation (EC)2271/96, referred to as the Blocking Statute. The Blocking Statute shields EU persons and companies from the effects of the US secondary sanctions. For example, it would nullify the effects of court orders or administrative decisions that are based on the secondary sanctions. In effect, the Blocking Statute makes it illegal for EU companies to comply with the US secondary sanctions.[46] This means any person who suffers damage because someone else follows the US secondary sanctions would, under the

[42] Memorandum, the President of the United States indicated that 'Iranian or Iran-backed forces have gone on the march in Syria, Iraq, and Yemen, and continue to control parts of Lebanon and Gaza'. Iran had publicly declared that it would deny the IAEA access to military sites and that, in 2016, Iran had twice violated the JCPOA's heavy-water stockpile limits.

[43] Presidential Documents, Executive order 13 846 of 6 August 2018 Re-imposing Certain Sanctions with Respect to Iran, Federal Register, Vol 83, No 152, 7 August 2018.

[44] ibid.

[45] ibid.

[46] It is interesting to note that on some occasions third-party countries may encourage economic and commercial relations with sanctioned state. For this view refer to BR Early, 'Sleeping with Your Friends' Enemies: An Explanation of Sanctions-Busting Trade' (2009) 53 *International Studies Quarterly* 49.

Blocking Statute, have the right to claim damages from that person/entity. For example, if a postal carrier or express carrier (eg DHL) denies services to Iran, by reference to US sanctions, the denied entity could sue the carrier for damages. However, what remains unclear is the how damage will be assessed. It seems this is more a question of politics because in reality it seems unlikely that any EU country intends to punish its companies or persons for not engaging in trade with Iran.

B. Questions of Legality

i. Challenging US Restrictions in the UPU

As discussed above, even though the US sanctions on Iran do not expressly target postal communication, in reality they have disrupted postal exchange between the countries. Thus, the US acts inconsistently with its obligations under the UPU rules. Iran as a Member of the UPU has the option of challenging the sanctions through arbitration under Article 32 of the UPU constitution to restore direct postal relations with them, and to obtain reparation for the harm incurred. Article 32 of the UPU constitution provides:

> In the event of a dispute between two or more postal administrations of the Member countries concerning the interpretation of the Acts of the Union or the responsibility imposed on the Postal administration by the application of those Acts, the question at issue shall be settled by arbitration.

In the event that Iran challenges the sanctions through the arbitration, there is limited possibility for the US to justify its action under the UPU rule. As discussed in section II above, restriction on postal communication may be justified only if there is an existence to the threat to peace or breach of peace, or an act of aggression under Article 39 of the UN Charter as set out in Article VI of the Rules of Procedure of the Postal Operations Council of the UPU. This means the nature and scope of the exception is narrow and relies completely on the actions taken specifically under the UN Charter. Since the restrictions imposed by the US are not authorised by the Security Council they cannot be justified through the exceptions crafted under the UPU rules. It is important to note that the exception provided under Article VI of the Rules of Procedure of the Postal Operations Council is a contrast to well-developed provisions under the treaties of economic nature, which provide exceptions from the interruption of commercial relations. For instance, Article XX of the General Agreement on Tariff and Trade (GATT), entitled 'General Exceptions', provides a basis for deviation from any of the commitments under the GATT when it is necessary for: the protection of public morals; the protection of human, animal or plant life or health; securing compliance with laws or regulations which are not inconsistent with the provisions of the GATT Agreement; and securing the conservation of exhaustible natural resources.[47] Article XXI of the GATT also allows members to adopt trade-restrictive measures against other members for the purpose of security.[48] Article XXI(a) and (b) is particularly notable as it provides the possibility for the WTO members to maintain

[47] General Agreement on Tariffs and Trade 1994, 15 April 1994.

[48] ibid.

trade measures that they may consider necessary to protect their 'essential security interests'. Interestingly, this phrase has not been defined under the GATT agreement and arguably remains a matter of interpretation. A broad interpretation of the phrase may potentially allow for an array of circumstances that have a bearing on or connection with a security interest to be the basis for imposing trade restrictive measures. The US advocates for a broad interpretation of 'essential security interests', which means that the security exception may be utilised for commercial purposes, for instance, protection of industries that are threatened by imports.[49]

Since the scope of exception under the UPU rules is narrow, the question that arises at this juncture is whether inconsistency of the UPU rules may be justified by seeking recourse to rules outside the framework of UPU rules? In this context, rules of customary international law on state responsibility (ARISWA), and in particular the defence of necessity, which is one of the many circumstances to preclude wrongfulness, may be of particular interest. It is worth mentioning that the UPU is a specialist technical regime.[50] It has its own sector-specific laws comprising of tailor-made substantive rules on the legal consequences of breach, dispute settlement and remedies, but nevertheless it is a part of contemporary public international law system. Does this mean that the option of relying on rules of customary international law as a basis for defence against a violation of UPU rules is available?

The discussion on the possibility of utilising necessity to justify the breach of commitments under the UPU rules is an interesting one. Article 25(2)(a) of ARISWA provides that the necessity may not be invoked as a defence if the international obligation in question excludes its use explicitly or impliedly. There is nothing in the UPU rules that suggest that members cannot invoke necessity as a defence. Therefore, in principle necessity may be utilised to justify deviation from the UPU rules provided the important elements set by Article 25 of ARISWA are present in the plea of necessity.

Article 25 provides that:

> 1. Necessity may not be invoked by a State as a ground for precluding the wrongfulness of an act not in conformity with an international obligation of that State unless the act:
>
> (a) is the only way for the State to safeguard an essential interest against a grave and imminent peril; and
>
> (b) does not seriously impair an essential interest of the State or States towards which the obligation exists, or of the international community as a whole.

[49] The US approach reflects a strong commercial focus. In fact, perusal of its legislative development regarding national security-related measures in the US displays that economic welfare of the domestic industries has been linked with national security. 19 USC 1862(c) (2012) Section 232 (c) of the Trade Expansion Act of 1962 provides that: 'In the administration of this section, the Secretary and the President shall further recognise the close relation of the economic welfare of the Nation to our national security and shall take into consideration the impact of foreign competition on the economic welfare of individual domestic industries: and any substantial unemployment, decrease in revenues of government, loss of skills or investment, or other serious effects resulting from the displacement of any domestic products by excessive imports shall be considered without excluding other factors, in determining whether such weakening of our internal economy may impair the national security'.

[50] It should be noted that the term 'regime' is conceived broadly to refer to a particular governance framework which consists of norms with some degree of binding authority over actors. JW Meyer, 'Reflections on Institutional Theories of Organizations' in R Greenwood, C Oliver, K Sahlin and R Suddaby (eds), *The Sage Handbook of Organizational Institutionalism* (Sage, 2008) 792, which indicates that 'regime' is a term

> 2. In any case, necessity may not be invoked by a State as a ground for precluding wrongfulness if:
>
> (a) the international obligation in question excludes the possibility of invoking necessity; or
> (b) the State has contributed to the situation of necessity.'

In the *Gabčíkovo-Nagimaros* case, the International Court of Justice (ICJ) held that 'the state of necessity is a ground recognized by customary international law' that:

> [C]an only be accepted on an exceptional basis ... can only be invoked under certain strictly defined conditions which must be cumulatively satisfied; and the State concerned is not the sole judge of whether those conditions have been met.[51]

The following elements must be present for a plea of necessity to be valid.

a. An Essential Interest

Necessity may be invoked as a basis for defence if it is to safeguard an 'essential interest'. This raises the question whether the US sanctions are in place to safeguard an 'essential interest'. The term 'essential interest' is not specifically defined. In fact, the ARISWA commentaries do not set any limit either by way of definition or a list, and as a matter of fact explains that 'the extent to which a given interest is "essential" depends on all the circumstances, and cannot be prejudged'.[52] It is the inherent right of the state to determine what it considers as an 'essential interest'. Ago has emphasised that 'essential interest' is not limited to interests in preserving the existence of the state.[53] This line of reasoning is also expressed in *Impregilo*, where the tribunal indicated that 'essential interest' includes other subsidiary interests.[54] In addition to interests such as political or economic survival, the maintenance of conditions in which essential services can function, the keeping of internal peace, the survival of part of its population and ecological preservation are all essential interests that may be justified through necessity.[55] For example, in the *Gabčíkovo* case, Hungary's argument that its natural environment in the region affected by the Gabčíkovo-Nagymaros Project related to an essential interest of that state was accepted by the ICJ.[56] It is interesting to note that essential interest is not only confined to the 'State and its people' but also extends to international community as a whole.[57]

employed in political science for the idea – organizational packages infused with cultural meaning (often from professions as 'epistemic communities'). On another occasion 'international regimes' has been referred to as institutions entirely composed of norms: See SD Krasner, 'Structural Causes and Regime Consequences: Regimes as Intervening Variables' (1982) 36 *International Organization* 185.

[51] *Gabčíkovo-Nagimaros Project (Hungary v Slovakia)*, ICJ, Judgment, ICJ Reports 1997, para 40.

[52] ILC, 'The International Law Commission's Articles on State Responsibility: Introduction, Text and Commentaries' (Cambridge University Press, 2002) 183.

[53] R Ago, 'Addendum – Eight Report on State Responsibility' (29 February, 10 and 19 June 1980) UN Doc A/CN.4/318/Add.5–7 in Yearbook of the ILC (1980) II(1)19.

[54] *Impregilo v Argentina* (Award) ICSID Case no ARB/07/17, 21 June 2011, [346]; *Suez v Argentina* (Decision on Liability) ICSID Case no ARB/03/17, 30 July 2010, [260]: 'The provision of water and sewage services to the metropolitan area of Buenos Aires certainly was vital to the health and well-being of nearly ten million people and was therefore an essential interest of the Argentine State'.

[55] Report of the ILC (1980) UN Doc A/35/10, 71.

[56] *Gabčíkovo-Nagymaros Project (Hungary v Slovakia)* (Judgment) [1997] ICJ Rep 7, para 51.

[57] ARISWA Art 25 1(b).

Two important points emerge from the above discussion. First, the scope of 'essential interest' is broad and second the interest pursued may extend beyond the territorial jurisdiction of the state imposing the sanction. US has indicated that the sanctions on Iran is in place to advance the goal of applying financial pressure on Iranian regime to seek a long-lasting solution in light of the threats posed by its nuclear weapon programme and its support for terrorist groups. Further the sanctions are pursued in the interest of international community and for the peace of the region.[58] In principle, US sanctions may be able justify the 'essential interest' requirement for pursuing a matter of international peace and security.

b. Grave and Imminent Peril

The requirement of 'grave and imminent peril' acts as a check against states invoking the plea of necessity. The ICJ in the *Gabčíkovo* case distinguished 'peril' from material damage[59] and observed that it invokes the idea of risk. The ILC commentary indicates that the danger to the essential interest of the state must be 'extremely grave.[60] This is the same formulation proposed by Ago[61] and by Grotius. Grotius proposed that 'under the plea of necessity nothing short of extreme exigency can give one power a right over what belongs to another no way involved in the war'.[62] The *Torrey Canyon* incident in 1967 is a good example of what constitutes grave peril. The Liberian oil tanker with a cargo of 117,000 tons of crude oil went aground off the coast of Cornwall. The collision resulted in a hole in the hull, and the leakage of 30,000 tons of oil. The ship was bombed to burn the remaining oil. The ILC considered Britain's destruction of the ship as necessary to address a situation of extreme danger that qualified as a state of necessity.[63] The ICJ has explained that 'imminent' is synonymous with 'immediacy' or 'proximity' and goes far beyond 'possibility'.[64] The Caroline test, which is instructive in this regard, states that danger must be instant, overwhelming and leaving no moment for deliberation.[65]

Fulfilling this requirement in context of the US and Iran case study would imply that the sanctions imposed are to safeguard international peace and security against grave and imminent peril. The situation as it stands today is that the US highlights Iran's failure to comply with the obligations under JCPOA. The US argues that Iran's engagement with enrichment and reprocessing-related activities, ballistic missile testing and development poses a peril in its own right to world peace and security. This line of

[58] MR Pompeo, Secretary Of State, The Return of UN Sanctions on the Islamic Republic of Iran, 19 September 2020, available at www.state.gov/the-return-of-un-sanctions-on-the-islamic-republic-of-iran.

[59] *Gabčíkovo-Nagymaros Project (Hungary v Slovakia)* (Judgment) [1997] ICJ Rep 7, para 54.

[60] Report of the ILC on the work of its Thirst-Second Session, UN Doc A/35/10 (1980).

[61] Addendum to the Eighth Report on State Responsibility, by Mr Roberto Ago, UN Doc A/CN.4/318/ADD.5–7.

[62] H Grotius, *On the Law of War and Peace* 80 (1901; AC Campbell trans 2001).

[63] Report of the ILC (1980), UN Doc A/35/10, 83. cf the *Gabčíkovo-Nagymaros Project* case, ICJ Rep 1997, 7.

[64] *Gabčíkovo-Nagymaros Project (Hungary v Slovakia)* (Judgment) [1997] ICJ Rep 7, para 54.

[65] J Crawford, *The International Law Commission's Articles on State Responsibility – Introduction, Text and Commentaries* (Cambridge University Press, 2002) 179; cf Report of the ILC (1980), UN Doc A/35/10, 93.

argumentation is also the basis for the call to reimpose sanctions on Iran pursuant to the snapback process under UN Security Council resolution (UNSCR) 2231.[66] The problematic part is that the US has argued Iran's conduct of non-compliance with JCOPA since 2018 without any major instance, incident or occurrence that establishes grave peril. Therefore, it may be difficult for the US to successfully defend its avoidance of its obligation under the UPU. Also, there is currently no indication in the present context through Iran's actions or inaction that establishes the realisation of peril, however far off it might be.

c. That the Act be the 'Only Means'

Another requirement set by Article 25(1)(a) of ARISWA is that the inconsistent act can only be justified by seeking a recourse to the plea of necessity if the act was the 'only means to safeguard an essential interest against grave and imminent peril'. This requirement simply entails that the act should be the only available option for the state to purse its essential interest. This means that the act may fall short of the demands of 'only means' requirement if there is an alternative available. Simply stated, the plea of necessity is excluded if there are other lawful means available in order to pursue an essential interest of the state that is under grave and imminent peril (rather than by breaching an international obligation), even if they may be more costly or less convenient. The ILC has articulated that the necessity plea 'is excluded if there are (otherwise lawful) means available, even if they may be more costly or less convenient'.[67] According to the thirty-second session of the ILC,

> the adoption by the State of a conduct not in conformity with an international obligation binding it to another State must definitely have been its only means of warding off the extremely grave and imminent peril which is apprehended; in other words, the perils must have been escapable by any other means, even a more costly one, that could be adopted in compliance with international obligations.[68]

More recently, in its *Israeli Wall Advisory Opinion*, the ICJ held that it was 'not convinced that the construction of the wall along the route chosen was the only means to safeguard the interests of Israel against the peril, which it has invoked as justification for that construction'.[69]

[66] See n 58. The US bid to reimpose the sanctions was not supported by Britain, France, and Germany simply because the US is no longer a party to JCPOA and thus has no legal right to challenge Iran's breach of the agreement.

[67] Report of the ILC, fifty-third session, 2001, 203.

[68] *Gabčíkovo-Nagymaros Project (Hungary v Slovakia)* (Judgment) [1997] ICJ Rep 7, paras 44–45. The contrasting approach is that an alternative only exists if it is both feasible and effective. This sound approach was expressed clearly in the Oscar Chin case where Judge Anzilotti in a sperate opinion: 'No one can, or does, dispute that it rested with the Belgian Government to say what were the measures best adapted to overcome the crisis: provided always that the measures selected were not inconsistent with its international obligations, for the Government's freedom of choice was indisputably limited by the duty of observing those obligations'. *Oscar Chinn (United Kingdom v Belgium)* [1934] PCIJ Ser A/B No 63, Separate Opinion of Judge Anzilotti para 107, 114.

[69] *Legal Consequences of the Construction of a Wall in the Occupied Palestinian Territory*, ICJ, Advisory Opinion, ICJ Reports 2004, para 140.

Following the above discussion, the question that arises is whether the imposition of US sanctions that impact postal communication is the only option to safeguard the interest. This question requires a brief consideration of the purpose and achievement of JCPOA. This consideration is important because the US exited the platform of JCPOA and imposed unilateral sanctions on Iran, disrupting postal communication. This suggests that the sanctions offer better leverage compared to JCPOA's ability to block both Iran's uranium and plutonium paths to a nuclear weapon through constructive engagement. The JCPOA is a key element of the global nuclear non-proliferation architecture endorsed by UN Security Council Resolution 2231(2015). The most important achievement of the agreement is a robust verification regime, implemented by the International Atomic Energy Agency. The JCPOA has reduced Iran's enrichment capacity by approximately 75 per cent and the stockpile of enriched uranium by approximately 90 per cent[70] It has also limited the level of uranium enrichment and the stockpile of enriched uranium Iran can possess.[71] A procurement channel, which is a significant transparency and non-proliferation mechanism, was created to review transfers of sensitive nuclear-related items to Iran that require an approval by the UN Security Council. JCPOA is critical for the security of the region and world, and instead of pursing negotiations under its framework the US exited the Agreement in 2018. Iran's nuclear policy demands concerted and constructive engagement efforts on the part of US and Iran, which was problematic to the US. In the given situation, the existence of JCPOA presented an alternative course of action that was available for the US. In my opinion, US exiting the JCPOA and its subsequent imposition of sanctions has had a negative impact on the efforts and progress made under the JCPOA, and the regional and world security that it upholds. It should be noted the following the imposition of US sanctions Iran has taken steps that undermine the objective JCPOA.

d. Balancing Requirement

The claim of necessity can only succeed if it also 'does not seriously impair an essential interest of the State or States towards which the obligation exists, or of the international community as a whole'.[72] This requirement inheres balancing of competing interests: on one hand, the interest of the state that has invoked the plea of necessity, and on the other the interest of the state that has been prejudiced by breach of international law. The ILC codified the rule on necessity restrictively by phrasing it in the negative. Necessity arises where there is an irreconcilable conflict between essential interests on the one hand and an obligation of the state invoking necessity on the other. One may argue that the interest of postal communication is one that is important for the entire international community as discussed above. However, the position of postal communication as an essential interest within the meaning of Article 25 of ARISWA is debatable.

[70] eeas.europa.eu/delegations/iran/2281/iran-and-eu_en.
[71] ibid.
[72] Commentaries to the draft articles on Responsibility of States for internationally wrongful act adopted by the ILC at its fifty-third session (2001).

e. Contribution to the Situation

Article 25(2)(b) of the ARISWA provides that a state cannot invoke necessity if it has contributed to the situation of necessity. The ARISWA commentary states that the state's contribution must be 'sufficiently substantial and not merely incidental or peripheral'.[73] This part of the requirement is not problematic for the sanctions considered here since the US actions have not contributed to the situation of necessity.

From the above discussion, it is clear that international practice, case law and scholars support the view that the legal operation of necessity should be confined only to exceptional circumstances and the US sanctions fall short of the requirements under the necessity defence. Therefore, in practice, for a UPU member to justify that suspension of postal communication on the basis of necessity would be a difficult exercise given the high threshold set forth by Article 25 of the ARISWA.

It should be recapitulated that the defence of necessity is considered before the arbitration panel instituted under the UPU framework. The jurisdiction of the arbitration proceeding instituted under Article 153 of the General Rules of the UPU[74] is mainly confined to matters relating to the rules under the UPU.[75] Although, jurisdiction has not been considered analogous or restrictive to applicable law,[76] it determines the competence of the dispute settlement body in question.[77] Moreover, the consideration of defence of necessity as a circumstance precluding wrongfulness would be beyond the competence of the arbitration proceedings under Article 153 of the General Rules of the UPU[78] as it would have to address questions regarding the nature and validity of US sanctions. In this respect, the ICJ may be a more appropriate forum available to resolve the question on the validity of the sanctions imposed by the US as it has a broad jurisdictional competence by virtue of Article 38 of the ICJ, compared to Article 32 of the UPU Constitution. Article 38 of the ICJ statute identifies a much broader jurisdictional scope relating to all matters specially provided for in the Charter of the United Nations or in treaties and conventions in force, in all legal disputes concerning the interpretation of a treaty; any question of international law; existence of any fact which, if established, would constitute a breach of an international obligation; and the nature or extent of the

[73] ILC, fifty-third session, 2001.

[74] Article 153 Arbitration Procedure: '1. If a dispute has to be settled by arbitration between member countries, each member country must advise the other party in writing of the subject of the dispute and inform it, by means of a notice to initiate arbitration, that it wishes to initiate arbitration. 2. If the dispute concerns questions of an operational or technical nature, each member country may ask its designated operator to act in accordance with the procedure provided for in the following paragraphs and delegate such power to its operator. The member country concerned shall be informed of the progress of the proceedings and of the result. The respective member countries or designated operators shall hereafter be referred to as "parties to the arbitration"'.

[75] UPU, Constitution, Ch IV Settlement of disputes, Art 32 provides that: 'In the event of a dispute between two or more member countries concerning the interpretation of the Acts of the Union or the responsibility imposed on a member country by the application of those Acts, the question at issue shall be settled by arbitration'.

[76] ILC, Report of the Study Group on Fragmentation of International Law: Difficulties arising from the Diversification and Expansion of International Law, 55th Session of the International Law Commission, Geneva, 5 May–6 June and 7 July–8 August 2003, A/CN.4/L.644. para 45.

[77] The functions of a court cited by Shapiro are conflict resolution, social control or regime enforcement. M Shapiro and AS Sweet, *On Law, Politics & Judicialization* (Oxford University Press, 2002).

[78] See n 74.

reparation to be made for the breach of an international obligation. Further, Article 36 complements the broad jurisdiction of the ICJ and generously 'opens a full range of international law',[79] such as general or particular international conventions, customs, judicial decisions, and teaching of qualified publicists within its ambit.

In fact, not so long ago, Iran instituted proceedings before the ICJ against the US arguing that the sanctions violated the of Treaty of Amity, Economic Relations and Consular Rights between Iran and the US which was entered into force on 16 June 1957.[80] The ICJ indicated that the US must remove impediments on the free exportation to the territory of Iran goods required for humanitarian needs such as medicines and medical devices, and foodstuff and agricultural commodities, as well as goods and services required for the safety of civil aviation, such as spare parts, equipment and associated services (including warranty, maintenance, repair services and safety-related inspections) necessary for civil aircraft. To this end, the US must ensure that licences and necessary authorisations are granted and that payments and other transfers of funds are not subject to any restriction in so far as they relate to the goods and services referred to above.[81] However, in reality, the ICJ ruling did not secure the outcome that Iran would have desired because soon after this provisional ruling the US repudiated the Treaty of Amity, Economic Relations and Consular Rights with Iran.[82]

ii. Challenging the US Sanctions as a Countermeasure

Another alternative for challenging the US sanction is to seek redressal through the ICJ. If US sanctions are challenged, one option that the US may have would be to justify them as countermeasures. Generally, non-performance of an obligation owed to the target state may be justified as a countermeasure within the meaning of Article 49 of the ARISWA.[83] Alland succinctly defines 'countermeasures' as unilateral sanctions which are intrinsically unlawful, adopted by one or more states against another state when the former considers that the latter has committed an internationally wrongful act which could justify such a reaction.[84] Countermeasures are subject to both procedural and substantial conditions. The first is that, before imposing countermeasures, the injured state should call upon the responsible state to fulfil its obligations.[85] The ICJ in *Gabčíkovo* has clarified that this requirement also applies to non-armed countermeasures.[86] The second procedural requirement is that the state must notify

[79] T Broude, *International Governance in the WTO: Judicial Boundaries and Political Capitulations* (Cameron May 2004) 259.

[80] International Court of Justice, Alleged Violations of the 1955 Treaty of Amity, Economic Relations, And Consular Rights (*Islamic Republic of Iran v United States of America*) Request for The Indication of Provisional Measures, 2018, 3 October General List No 175.

[81] ibid, para 98.

[82] 'US to end Treaty of Amity with Iran after ICJ ruling' BBC, available at www.bbc.com/news/world-middle-east-45741270.

[83] ARSIWA Art 49.

[84] D Alland, 'The Definition of Countermeasures' in J Crawford, A Pellet, S Olleson (eds), *The Law of International Responsibility* (Oxford University Press 2010) 1135.

[85] ARSIWA Art 52(1)(a).

[86] *Gabčíkovo-Nagymaros Project (Hungary v Slovakia)* [1997] ICJ Rep 7, 56 (para 84).

of any decision to take countermeasures and offer to negotiate with the responsible state.[87] ARISWA Article 52 also provides that countermeasures may be suspended if the international wrong has ceased and when the underlying dispute is pending before a court or tribunal.[88]

The first essential element of countermeasure to be lawful is the existence of an internationally wrongful act (either action or omission)[89] which injured the state taking the countermeasure. Article 49(1) prescribes that a countermeasure may be taken by an injured state against a state which is responsible for an internationally wrongful act in order to induce that state to comply with its obligations under Part Two.[90] Although the rules on ARISWA set out clear criteria of what constitutes a wrongful act, ultimately it is the state adopting the unilateral sanction that is exercising its judgement if the wrong is committed without the requirement of seeking a recourse to an international tribunal with competence to evaluate it. The argument has been made that the determination on the existence of wrongful act must be made exclusively by an international tribunal or judicial body competent to consider the issue, but the reality is that the reacting state often remains *judex in re sua*.[91] However, a state runs the risk of incurring responsibility for its wrongful act in the event of an adverse assessment by a competent international judicial body.[92] The second essential element of the countermeasure is that it must be directed against the state which has committed the internationally wrongful act and must not be directed to the third states.[93] The third element requires that countermeasures be discontinued when the responsible state resumes the performance of its obligations.[94] The fourth element requires that the countermeasures be proportional to the commensurate with the injury suffered, taking into account the gravity of the internationally wrongful act and the rights in question.[95]

In reality, the countermeasure argument may not stand its ground because Article 50 states that countermeasures should not affect the protection of human rights.[96] Postal communication or correspondence may be argued as an essential human right

[87] ARSIWA Art 52(1)(b).

[88] ARSIWA Art 52(3)(b).

[89] Art 2 of ARISWA. In addition, Art 12 of the ILC states that breach of an international obligation by a state is when an act of that state is not in conformity with what is required of it by that obligation, regardless of its origin or character.

[90] ARSIWA Art 49.

[91] PE Dupont, 'Countermeasures and Collective Security: The Case of the EU Sanctions against Iran' (2012) 17 *Journal of Conflict and Security Law* 301; T Gazzini, 'The Normative Element Inherent in Economic Collective Enforcement Measures: United Nations and European Union Practice' in LA Sicilianos and LP Forlati (eds), *Economic sanctions in international law* (Brill, 2004) 279–308. This position may be contrasted with how countermeasures are imposed in the WTO system. A countermeasure is only imposed after the Appellate Body or the panel has presented the finding that the measure in question inconsistent. If the defaulting member fails to implement the recommendations by removing or modifying the measure inconsistent with WTO law then the complainant member can request for authorisation from the dispute settlement body (DSB) to impose countermeasures. This means that the inconsistency of the measure is first determined by the quasi-judicial bodies of the WTO and then the countermeasures are authorised by the political body namely the DSB.

[92] P Okowa, 'Admissibility and The Law on International Responsibility' in MD Evans (ed), *International Law* (Oxford University Press, 2018) 477.

[93] *Gabčíkovo-Nagymaros Project*, ICJ Reports 1997, 7, 55–56, para 83.

[94] ARISWA Art 52(3)(a).

[95] ARISWA Art 51.

[96] ARISWA Art 50.

and thus may not be a subject of sanctions. It is stressed that postal services are a critical medium of communication and information exchange between individual and communities. The postal service occupies an important role in the cultural and social life of people. Such a line of argumentation finds support from Article 12 of the Universal Declaration of Human Rights, which states that 'no one shall be subjected to arbitrary interference with his privacy, family, home or correspondence, not to attacks upon his honour and reputation'.[97] Similar reasoning may also be found in Article 7 of the Charter of Fundamental Rights of the European Union, which states that 'everyone has the right to respect for his or her private and family life, home and communications'.[98] In addition, it is widely accepted that states have human rights obligations to persons who may not be in their territory or under their effective control but who may be directly affected by their actions.[99] Further, *Naulilaa* clearly indicates that 'a lawful countermeasure must be limited by the requirements of humanity and the rules of good faith applicable in relations between States'.[100]

IV. Sanctions Targeting Postal Communication with Qatar: Case Study

The case of Qatar presents a contrast to the US–Iran situation discussed above as express restrictions have been placed on postal communications to and from Qatar. In 2013, after two years of intense diplomatic negotiations, member countries of the Gulf Cooperation Council (GCC) finalised the Riyadh Agreement. The Agreement mainly focuses on maintaining the region's security and stability. The first Riyadh Agreement specifically provides that a member of the GCC must not support any faction in Yemen, the Muslim Brotherhood or any of the organisations, groups or individuals that threaten the security and stability of the Council States through direct security work or through political influence.[101] The mechanism implementing the Riyadh Agreement 2014 under the section of foreign policy also provides that the members shall not support any entities or currents that pose threats to the GCC countries, including:

(a) Not to support Muslim Brotherhood with money or via media in the GCC countries or outside.
(b) Approve the exit of Muslim Brotherhood figures, who are not citizens. within a time limit to be agreed upon. The GCC countries; shall coordinate with each other on the lists of those figures.
(c) Not to support external gatherings or groups in Yemen. Syria or any destabilized area. which pose a threat to the security and stability of GCC countries.

[97] UN General Assembly, Universal Declaration of Human Rights, 10 December 1948, 217 A(III).
[98] OJC 326, 26.10.2012, 391–407.
[99] M Milanovic, *Extraterritorial Applications of Human Rights Treaties: Law, Principles and Policy* (Oxford University Press, 2011); N Melzer, *Targeted Killings in International Law* (Oxford University Press, 2008).
[100] *Naulilaa* (Responsibility of Germany for damage caused in the Portuguese colonies in the south of Africa), UNRIAA, vol II, 1013 (1928) 1026.
[101] First Riyadh Agreement, On Saturday, 19/ I /1435 (Hijri Calendar. November 2013).

(d) Not to support or shelter whoever perform opposition activities against any ace country. being current officials, former officials or others; and shall not give them any foothold inside their countries or allow then, to act against any of the GCC countries.
(e) Close any academies, establishments or centers that train and qualify individuals from GCC citizens lo work against their governments.

Saudi Arabia, the UAE and Bahrain (hereafter combinedly referred to as the sanctioning GCC states) severed diplomatic ties and imposed restrictions on trade, transport and travel through air, land and maritime routes with Qatar on 5 June 2017. Postal communication to and from Qatar is also suspended by the sanctioning GCC countries (UAE has only recently allowed indirect post).[102] Currently, Egypt has also suspended postal communication with Qatar. The sanctioning states allege that the above-mentioned sanctions are in place because Qatar supports entities such as Muslim Brotherhood, which threatens national and regional security and thus violates the Riyadh Agreements.[103]

The three sanctioning GCC States and Egypt (combinedly referred to as the defaulting countries) are all members of the UPU and are obligated to comply with the UPU rules. It is important to note that on 20 September 2018, soon after the suspension of postal communication, Qatar negotiated with the defaulting member countries to resolve the postal restrictions within the frame of the UPU. In October 2017 the Council of Administrators (COA)[104] also urged the defaulting countries to re-establish direct postal services with the State of Qatar. Despite the indication from COA, the defaulting countries did not reinstate postal communication failing, so Qatar through recourse to Article 32 of the UPU Constitution sought to initiate arbitration proceedings to restore direct postal relations with them, and to obtain reparation for all harm incurred since June 2017.

It has been reported by the Qatar's Ministry of Transport and Communication that the defaulting members have on more than one occasion thwarted the initiation of arbitration proceedings.[105] More specifically, the defaulting member countries have blocked the appointment of a third arbitrator for the proceedings. In this context,

[102] The UPU said in a technical notice to postal operators seen by *Agence France-Presse* that 'effective Feb 9, 2020, Emirates Post will resume the sending of mails to the State of Qatar, using open and closed transit options via Oman'. 'UAE restores mail services with Qatar after 2.5 years', available at www.dailysabah.com/mideast/2020/02/11/uae-restores-mail-services-with-qatar-after-25-years. This was an outcome of diplomatic negotiations at the UPU headquarters.

[103] The security agreements between the GCC states, signed in 2013 and 2014, and combinedly called the Riyadh Agreements. The GCC has no public record of these agreements, and neither the GCC Supreme Council nor the Ministerial Council discussed them in their regular meetings in 2013/14. The Riyadh Agreements are only publicly available in an annex to a 2018 ICJ pending case concerning the quartet's appeal regarding the scope of the ICAO Council's jurisdiction. Appeal Relating to the Jurisdiction of the ICAO Council under Article 84 of the Convention on International Civil Aviation (*Bahrain, Egypt, Saudi Arabia, and United Arab Emirates v Qatar*), online: www.icj-cij.org/files/case-related/173/173-20180704-APP-01-01-EN.pdf.

[104] The Council of Administration (CA) consists of 41 member countries and meets annually at the UPU headquarters in Berne. The Council ensures the continuity of the UPU's work between Congresses, supervises its activities and studies regulatory, administrative, legislative and legal issues. See www.upu.int/en/the-upu/council-of-administration/about-ca.html.

[105] Ministry of Transport and Communication, 'UPU Council of Admin. Endorses Qatar Resolution Calling on Int'l Bureau to Appoint 3rd Arbitrator as per General Regulations', 27 February 2020, available at www.motc.gov.qa/en/news-events/news/upu-council-admin-endorses-qatar-resolution-calling-int%E2%80%99l-bureau-appoint-3rd.

Article 153 of the General Regulation of the UPU is of relevance as it provides that parties can choose between one of three arbitrators.[106] Where the parties have agreed to have three arbitrators for an arbitration proceeding, the third arbitrator is to be jointly agreed upon by the parties and need not be a member country or a designated operator. The conduct of defaulting members to stall the initiation of arbitration proceedings by not cooperating for the appointment of the third arbitrator did not reflect good faith with respect to their commitment to resolve the dispute at hand. Good faith is recognised as a general principle of law and it also applies to the process of arbitration, the arbitrators or arbitration institutions and also parties to the dispute.[107] The Declaration of the Principles of International Law on Amicable Relations and Cooperation among States stipulates that 'every state has the duty to fulfill in good faith its obligations under international agreements valid under the generally recognized principles and rules of international law'.[108] In the Nuclear Tests Case the ICJ stated that one of the basic principles governing the creation and performance of legal obligations, whatever their source, is the principle of good faith.[109]

The question that arises is what options did Qatar have to resolve the situation at hand and get the arbitration proceedings on course? Article 153(8) of the UPU rules is instructive in this regard:

> If one or both parties to the arbitration do not, within a period of three months from the date of the notice to initiate arbitration, appoint an arbitrator or arbitrators the International Bureau shall, if so requested, itself call upon the defaulting member country to appoint an arbitrator, or shall itself appoint one automatically. The International Bureau will not be involved in the deliberations unless otherwise mutually requested by the parties.

Article 153 (8) presents a fall-back solution in case the defaulting member countries refuse to cooperate for the appointment of the third arbitrator and use this technicality as a strategy to frustrate the arbitration proceedings by refusing to cooperate in the appointment of the third arbitrator. Based on this provision, Qatar proposed a resolution to the COA urging the UPU's International Bureau to appoint the third arbitrator in the proceeding against the four defaulting members. On 28 February 2020, the resolution proposed by Qatar to the COA was adopted. The COA resolution has important ramification for Qatar's right to seek redress of violation of the rights guaranteed under the UPU rules. At this stage, one may only speculate the outcome of the arbitral proceedings.[110] The postal restrictions are inconsistent with the rules of the UPU, but what remains to be seen is the arguments that the defaulting members may raise to justify their action. Since the restrictions are utilised to coerce Qatar into

[106] An arbitrator may be a member country or a designated operator not directly involved in the dispute.

[107] BM Cremades, 'Good Faith in International Arbitration' (2012) 27 *American University International Law Review* 761.

[108] Declaration on Principles of International Law Concerning Friendly Relations and Co-operation Among States in Accordance with the Charter of the United Nations, GA Res 2625 (XXV), UN GAOR, 25th Sess, Supp No 18, UN Doc A/8018, at 124 (24 October 1970).

[109] *Nuclear Tests Case (Austl v Fr)*, 1974 ICJ 253, 268 (December 2020).

[110] [2020–28] Arbitration pursuant to Article 32 of the Constitution of the Universal Postal Union (*The State of Qatar v The United Arab Emirates*); [2020–27] Arbitration pursuant to Article 32 of the Constitution of the Universal Postal Union (*The State of Qatar v The Kingdom of Saudi Arabia*); [2020–26] Arbitration pursuant to Article 32 of the Constitution of the Universal Postal Union (*The State of Qatar v The Arab Republic of Egypt*).

complying with the Riyadh Agreements it may be that defence could be couched as a matter of security. The discussion in sections II and III highlighted the narrowness of the exception available under the rules of the UPU, which means that the justification that relies on security reasons may not stand unless authorised by the UN. Currently, there is no sanction on postal communication to and from Qatar authorised by the UN. More specifically, if one was to take the example of Yemen, which is the subject of the Riyadh Agreements, the UN General Assembly has only authorised freezing of assets,[111] a travel ban[112] and a targeted arms embargo[113] of designated individuals and entities.[114] These measures are in place to ensure political transition in Yemen. While the UN commends the engagement of the GCC in assisting the political transition in Yemen, it does not authorise any restrictions on Qatar.

V. Conclusion

This chapter has considered the implications for the postal communication under international law when a state or a group of states imposes unilateral sanctions against another state. An interesting dimension that is revealed through the US–Iran case study is that sometimes states may not actively pursue total cessation of postal communication, but lack of clarity regarding what is permissible renders to some extent the effect of a total ban. In addition, to ensure that there is no physical movement of goods, commercial sanctions also target services providers such as carriers and freight-forwarders. While postal communication has been recognised an essential public good that connects people and contributes to the sense of community, its

[111] Set out in paras 12–14 of Resolution 2140 (2014):and para 3 of Resolution 2511 (2020): 'Obligation to freeze all funds, other financial assets and economic resources that are owned or controlled, directly or indirectly, by the individuals or entities designated by the Committee, or by individuals or entities acting on their behalf or at their direction, or by entities owned or controlled by them; no funds, financial assets or economic resources to be made available to or for the benefit of such individuals or entities'.

[112] Set out in para 16 of resolution 2140 (2014):and para 3 of resolution 2511 (2020): 'Prohibits the entry into or transit through States' territories of individuals designated by the Committee'.

[113] Set out in para 13 of Resolution 2511(2020): 'All Member States shall take the necessary measures to prevent the direct or indirect supply, sale or transfer to, or for the benefit of designated individuals and entities and those acting on their behalf or at their direction in Yemen, from or through their territories or by their nationals, or using their flag vessels or aircraft, of arms and related materiel of all types, including weapons and ammunition, military vehicles and equipment, paramilitary equipment, and spare parts for the aforementioned, and technical assistance, training, financial or other assistance, related to military activities or the provision, maintenance or use of any arms and related materiel, including the provision of armed mercenary personnel whether or not originating in their territories'.

[114] The Designation Criteria has been identified in the Resolution 2140 (2014, Adopted by the Security Council at its 7119th meeting, on 26 February 2014) as: '17. Decides that the provisions of paragraphs 11 and 15 shall apply to individuals or entities designated by the Committee as engaging in or providing support for acts that threaten the peace, security or stability of Yemen; 18. Underscores that such acts as described in paragraph 17 above may include, but are not limited to: (a) Obstructing or undermining the successful completion of the political transition, as outlined in the GCC Initiative and Implementation Mechanism Agreement; (b) Impeding the implementation of the outcomes of the final report of the comprehensive National Dialogue Conference through violence, or attacks on essential infrastructure; or (c) Planning, directing, or committing acts that violate applicable international human rights law or international humanitarian law, or acts that constitute human rights abuses, in Yemen'.

economic contribution remains undervalued and thus not actively pursued independently. The cessation of postal communication is viewed as collateral damage and is not usually challenged independent of the commercial and financial sanctions, but pursued diplomatically. The UPU rules offers arbitration for settling disputes under Article 153, however, by and large the implementation of arbitration award is dependent on the respondent member country's good faith. The lack of enforcement mechanism or process in the UPU system which ensures implementation is a limiting factor for the protection and preservation of rights associated with postal communication. The position may be contrasted with, for instance, the WTO system where compensation or retaliation is available to pressure the respondent to withdraw the WTO-inconsistent measure. However, in the UPU system realisation of both compensation and retaliation to pressure the respondent to act does not seem politically viable. Moreover, the case study on Qatar has revealed that the defaulting member/s can delay the initiation of arbitration by blocking the appointment of the arbitrator. While Article 153 provides that the Bureau will call upon the defaulting member country to appoint an arbitrator, or shall itself appoint one automatically, the fact of the matter is that the possibility of blocking the appointment by the defaulting member adds to the complexity of addressing the situation of postal restrictions under the UPU framework. Qatar had to invest considerable effort in seeking a resolution for the appointment of the arbitrators. Obtaining a resolution in their favour for appointment of the third arbitrator is only a small victory for Qatar; the outcome of the arbitration proceeding still remains to be seen. In fact, it would come as no surprise if the defaulting members use the tactic to block the appointment of the arbitrators again in the future on other occasions. This can be contrasted with the WTO dispute settlement system where the panel member may be appointed by the director general if there is no agreement between the disputing parties within 10 days. Appointment of the panel member by the WTO director general has become usual practice and thus it does not pose a challenge to the initiation of the panel proceedings for resolution of the dispute.

The impact of sanctions that pursue businesses located outside the jurisdiction of the sanctioning country may have a huge bearing for postal communication. The third-party actors provide services that the sanctions restrict and, in some cases, they serve as intermediaries by facilitating indirect contact with sanctioned customers. The EU through the Blocking Statute has tried to limit the exterritoriality of the US sanctions, but in practice this may not work out because the fear of losing out the US market will discourage businesses from indulging in actions that are sanctioned. The unsuccessful attempt of the Blocking Statute to counter the effect of secondary sanction highlights the inefficiency of the legislative action. Other tools such as non-recognition of foreign orders, judicial decisions, etc, are also available and assist in blocking the extraterritorial effect, but may have a limited impact. It seems political condemnation can also work fruitfully to coerce against restrictive measures that do not have the support of the international community. Political condemnation relies on power-based tactics and hinges on the balance of power between states. Recently, UAE discontinued sanctions on postal communication that it had imposed on Qatar.[115] This was an outcome

[115] 'UAE restores mail services with Qatar after 2.5 years' *Daily Sabar*, available at www.dailysabah.com/mideast/2020/02/11/uae-restores-mail-services-with-qatar-after-25-years.

of diplomatic negotiations at the UPU headquarters. In light of this, it is submitted that the UPU's role as a forum for consultation to resolve disruption of postal services in a limited way (indirect postal communication is allowed) between disputing parties may become more relevant in addressing sanctions directed towards postal communication. The partial resolution of postal relations between Qatar and UAE highlight the fact that the role of diplomatic negotiations within the framework of the UPU should not be undermined to resolve the issue of postal communication despite the fact that the postal issue is just a part of a much broader political rift between the relevant members.

To sum up, the legal position on disruption of postal communication to comply with sanctions authorised by the Security Council is crystal clear under the UPU rules. However, determining the legality of unilateral sanctions and availing a suitable remedy under the UPU rules is not a straightforward exercise. Finally, existing literature has extensively explored the economic impact of unilateral sanctions, but relatively limited work has considered its socio-cultural impact. The discussion on the disruption of postal communication carried out in this chapter makes it abundantly clear that this deserves more attention.

9

Unilateral Coercive Measures: Towards International Humanitarian Law and International Human Rights

LOUISA ASHLEY

I. Introduction

The use of coercive measures including economic sanctions has been favoured by certain, predominantly Western, states as an alternative to the use of armed force, asserting pressure to effect change at arm's length via an apparently non-lethal use of force. Yet the assumption that the use of economic sanctions presents 'non-lethal' and 'non-destructive' solutions is a misapprehension.[1] For the target state, the impact of multilateral and unilateral coercive measures (UCMs) on its humanitarian capacity can be long-term and devastating, and can be the cause, directly and indirectly, of the collateral damage of gross human rights and humanitarian violations.

Concerns about the humanitarian implications of comprehensive sanctions (both multilateral and unilateral) have been well rehearsed, for example, in the wake of the consequences suffered by the general population of Iraq and Haiti in the 1990s.[2] The public and political outcry that followed prompted a move by the Security Council away from comprehensive measures to those designed to be 'smart' by targeting named individuals, groups, governments and organisations.[3] Yet, somewhat ironically, compared to comprehensive measures, the humanitarian impact of smart sanctions has been said to be more difficult for the target state to circumvent because they are more difficult to 'cheat'.[4]

[1] WM Reisman and DL Stevick, 'The Applicability of International Law Standards to United Nations Economic Sanctions Programmes' (1998) 9 *European Journal of International Law* 86, 95.

[2] See, eg, DW Drezner, 'Sanctions Sometimes Smart: Targeted Sanctions in Theory and Practice' (2011) 13 *International Studies Review* 96, 97–99; ME O'Connell, 'Debating the Law of Sanctions' (2002) 13 *European Journal of International Law*, 59; and WM Reisman, 'Assessing the Lawfulness of Non-military Enforcement: The Case of Economic Sanctions' (1995) 89 *American Society of International Law Proceedings* 350.

[3] UNSC 'Speakers for Clearer Definition, Tighter Targeting of UN Sanctions as Council Draws on 'lessons learned' to Refine Sanctions' (17 April 2000) Press release SC/6845.

[4] O'Connell, 'Debating the Law of Sanctions' (2002) 79, citing 'US Plan for Smart Sanctions must be "Nipped in the Bud", Iraq', Agence Fr Press (14 May 2001) 2001 WL 2405528.

Contemporary use of UCMs has followed the Security Council's move away from comprehensive sanctions to targeted measures. UCMs are a source of controversy for a number of reasons, for example: they fall outside of the scope of the United Nations Charter; they are not authorised by relevant UN bodies; and they contravene 'the basic principles of the multilateral trading system'.[5] Concerns persist about the legality of such unilateral measures and that they negatively impact the socioeconomic development of developing countries.[6] Whilst ostensibly designed to 'apply pressure to bring about a change in the conduct of the target',[7] their impact can result in significant collateral damage to the socioeconomic status and basic human rights of the broader population.[8] Direct and indirect effects include disrupting and destabilising supply chains for the provision of essential services and supplies, including power, medical supplies and foodstuffs, and limiting access to healthcare and education, as well as threatening the right to life and breaching the individual human rights of named subjects.[9]

UCMs are taken in this chapter to be sanctions imposed by one state, or by a regional body of states (such as the EU), against another in response to an alleged breach by the target state of its obligations under international law.[10] The primary focus is upon economic UCMs, defined as:

> measures of an economic – as contrasted with diplomatic or military – character taken by states to express disapproval of the acts of the target state or to induce that state to change some policy or practice or even its governmental structure.[11]

The use of economic sanctions is not new. Woodrow Wilson was a proponent of them as a powerful weapon causing no injury beyond the target state; he claimed a century ago that:

> A nation that is boycotted is a nation that is in sight of surrender. Apply this economic, peaceful, silent deadly remedy and there will be no need for force. It is a terrible remedy. It does not cost a life outside the nation boycotted.[12]

[5] UNGA Report of the Secretary-General, 'Unilateral economic sanctions as a means of political and economic coercion against developing countries' (2017) UN Doc A/72/307, para 1.

[6] ibid. Although, as Surya Subedi notes in this collection, the argument that the use of UCMs is by developed nations against developing is weakened by the imposition of measures against Qatar and Syria by other developing Arab states.

[7] V Lowe and A Tzanakopoulos, 'Economic Warfare' in R Wolfrum (ed), *Max Planck Encyclopedia of Public International Law* (Oxford University Press, 2012) 10.

[8] For a review of the broader impact of US economic sanctions requiring the disclosure by companies of certain minerals in their supply chain originating from the Democratic Republic of Congo or neighbouring countries, M Owen, 'The Limits of Economic Sanctions under International Humanitarian Law: The Case of the Congo' (2012) 48 *Texas International Law Journal* 103, 112.

[9] OHCHR, 'Thematic study of the Office of the United Nations High Commissioner for Human Rights on the impact of unilateral coercive measures on the enjoyment of human rights, including recommendations on actions aimed at ending such measures', (2012) A/HRC/19/33, para 27, citing European Court of Justice, Kadi Case, Joined Cases C-402/05 P and C-415/05 P, *Yassin Abdullah Kadi and Al Barakaat International Foundation v Council and Commission*, European Court of Justice, 3 September 2008, 47 ILM 923 (2008), paras 348 and 349, where the Court held that the applicants' rights of defence as well as their right to an effective legal remedy had in fact been infringed.

[10] A more detailed assessment of the definition and legality of unilateral economic sanctions and retorsion is provided elsewhere in this collection, in particular see chs 1 and 2 by Profs Surya Subedi and Nigel White respectively. For this reason, only brief consideration of these matters offered here.

[11] AF Lowenfeld, *International Economic Law* (Oxford University Press 2002) 698.

[12] Reisman and Stevick, 'The Applicability of International Law Standards' (1998) 89, citing SK Padover (ed), *Wilson's Ideals* (American Council on Public Affairs, 1942).

Whilst the use of UCMs may be a popular domestic solution for the imposing state, those at the mercy of the 'terrible remedy' include the broader population of the target state, despite the 'smart' nature of the sanctions imposed. In particular, 'the right to life, the rights to health and medical care, the right to freedom from hunger and the right to an adequate standard of living, food, education, work and housing' have been cited as coming under threat.[13] Scholars, state representatives, and the Human Rights Council have referred to the use of UCMs as 'economic warfare'.[14] The impact of certain UCM regimes has been discussed in terms of collective punishment by creating conditions of starvation amongst the civilian population, prompting accusations of the commission of a war crime under international humanitarian law (IHL).[15] However, obtaining quantitative data to evidence that human rights and humanitarian law violations are a direct consequence of sanctions and not due to other factors, for example domestic mismanagement, is problematic.[16]

The UN Charter provides authority for the use of multilateral sanctions via the Security Council;[17] however, UCMs employed by one state, or a regional group of states, are not subject to a specific and designated legal framework. In the context of this absence, scholarship on the humanitarian and human rights implications of UCMs has generally addressed fundamental principles of international humanitarian law (IHL) and international human rights law (IHR) and, to a lesser degree, the law of countermeasures as encapsulated by ARSIWA (draft Articles on the Responsibility of States for Internationally Wrongful Acts).[18] As White and Abass observe, the concept of countermeasures under ARISWA 'is a fairly narrow one at one end of a spectrum of non-forcible measures' whilst 'at the other end of the spectrum are sanctions undertaken by international organizations', between which 'there is something of a grey area where regulation is rudimentary, indeed, arguably, non-existent'.[19] It is in this in-between 'grey area' that UCMs are situated.

This chapter does not set out to debate the comparative nature of the regulatory frameworks (or lack thereof) governing multilateral sanctions imposed by international organisations, such as the Security Council, countermeasures and UCMs.

[13] UNHRC Res 27/21 (2014), 'Human rights and unilateral coercive measures' (03 October 2014) A/HRC/RES/27/21.

[14] Lowe and Tzanakopoulos, 'Economic Warfare' (2012); ICESCR – General comment No. 8, paras 12–14; OHCHR 'Civilians Caught in Sanctions Crossfire Need Geneva Convention Protection, Says UN Expert' (8 November 2018) Press Release.

[15] OHCHR, 'Thematic study' (2012) para 10, citing Protocol Additional to the Geneva Conventions of 12 August 1949, and relating to the Protection of Victims of International Armed Conflicts (Protocol I), Art 54; Protocol Additional to the Geneva Conventions of 12 August 1949, and relating to the Protection of Victims of Non-International Armed Conflicts (Protocol II), Art 14.

[16] R Garfield and S Santana, 'The Impact of the Economic Crisis and the US Embargo on Health in Cuba' (1997) 87 *American Journal of Public Health* 15, 15.

[17] Pursuant to Art 39 of the United Nations Charter (the Charter), there is the power for the Security Council to pass resolutions imposing 'measures not involving the use of armed force' to maintain or restore international peace and security. Those measures may, under Art 41, 'include complete or partial interruption of economic relations'.

[18] See, eg: A Hofer, 'The Developed/Developing Divide on Unilateral Coercive Measures: Legitimate Enforcement or Illegitimate Intervention?' (2017) 16 *Chinese Journal of International Law* 175; Lowe and Tzanakopoulos (n 7); O'Connell (n 2); ND White and A Abass, 'Countermeasures and sanctions' in M Evans, *International Law*, 5th edn (Oxford University Press, 2018).

[19] White and Abass (ibid) 524.

This is addressed elsewhere in this collection. Rather, it provides some analysis of state practice in the use of UCMs and explores the proposition that failing their abolition, IHL principles could be applied to correct the negative effect of unilateral sanctions on the enjoyment of human rights by, for example, examining the application of principles of IHL to both the decision to impose high-intensity economic UCMs, and to their impact and consequences.

Section II briefly outlines an emerging consensus of concern as to the use of UCMs, as reflected by the Human Rights Council and related mechanisms. Section III takes particular sanctions regimes as case studies to specifically address and explore the relevance and application of IHL principles. The focus is primarily on Venezuela and Iran, with illustrative reference to Cuba. Consideration is also given in this section to alternative legal recourse via the International Court of Justice (ICJ) and under the Charter of the Organization of American States (OAS). Despite the inclusion of humanitarian exceptions to the application of UCMs these are, as this section illustrates, largely ineffective.

The chapter concludes that whilst arguments against the legality of UCMs are strong, the likelihood of a move away from their use is less so. As such, the humanitarian and human rights consequences of UCMs must be governed by a legal framework that has key IHL principles at its heart and that accommodates the concept of decentralised economic warfare. Such a framework should also include the requirement for a human rights / humanitarian impact assessment to be conducted before the deployment of UCMs. Without the creation of such a framework, there remains the option for the use of economic UCMs to be outlawed entirely.

II. The Position of the Human Rights Council

The Human Rights Council has become increasingly vocal in respect of the use of UCMs, indicating disquiet and sharing the concerns held by numerous states as to the motivations for their use and impact. This reflects a change in the focus of scholarship in respect of UCMs. As Mary Ellen O'Connell explains, the latter part of the 1960s was characterised by discussion of the lawfulness or otherwise of economic sanctions imposed by the UN. In the 1990s, the debate moved to the effectiveness of economic sanctions as a means to promote human rights and democracy. More recently, the focus has been upon an assessment of the human rights and humanitarian implications of the use of such measures.[20]

The Human Rights Council defines UCMs as including, but not limited to, 'economic or political measures, to coerce another State in order to obtain from it the subordination of the exercise of its sovereign rights and to secure from it advantages of any kind'.[21] In 2012, the High Commissioner for Human Rights reminded states that their actions 'in the international arena must be consistent with customary

[20] O'Connell (n 2).

[21] UNHRC Res 27/21 (2014) (n 13). This approach echoes Art 20 of the OAS Charter, which requires that 'No State may use or encourage the use of coercive measures of an economic or political character in order to force the sovereign will of another State and obtain from it advantages of any kind'.

international law principles and the Charter of the United Nations as also interpreted by the International Court of Justice' and that states must refrain 'from adopting unilateral coercive measures that breach their human rights obligations under treaty or customary international law'.[22] Furthermore, states 'should avoid the application of any coercive measures having negative effects on human rights, particularly on the most vulnerable' and that 'essential supplies, such as medicines and food, are not used as tools for political pressure, and that under no circumstances should people be deprived of their basic means of survival'.[23]

Building upon these recommendations, two years later the Council unequivocally called for states to stop using UCMs, stressing that 'unilateral coercive measures and legislation are contrary to international law, international humanitarian law, the Charter and the norms and principles governing peaceful relations among States'.[24] The wording of the 2014 resolution follows much of the wording in a draft resolution proposed the year before by Iran (on behalf of the non-aligned movement) and the State of Palestine (on behalf of the Group of Arab States).[25] That such a draft resolution would be sponsored by Iran and Palestine is not surprising – each has a vested interest being targets of sanctions by the US and others.[26]

The final resolution (in tandem with the draft) states that economic UCMs 'can have far-reaching implications for the human rights of the general population of targeted States, disproportionately affecting the poor and the most vulnerable classes', and that long-term measures 'may result in social problems and raise humanitarian concerns'. It calls for states to stop 'adopting, maintaining or implementing unilateral coercive measures' that are not 'in accordance with international law, international humanitarian law, the Charter of the United Nations and the norms and principles governing peaceful relations among States'.[27] It proceeds to state the negative impact upon a variety of rights including 'the right to life, the rights to health and medical care, the right to freedom from hunger and the right to an adequate standard of living, food, education, work and housing'.

The growing concern of the impact of UCMs is further illustrated by the creation of the position of Special Rapporteur on the Negative Impact of Unilateral Coercive Measures on the Enjoyment of Human Rights.[28] The first appointee to this role (in May 2015), Idris Jazairy, called for the international community to give this 'form of warfare that relies on starvation and disease' the same concern as any other conflict would warrant.[29] Subsequent Human Rights Council resolutions and endorsed reports reflect

[22] OHCHR (n 9) paras 39–40.
[23] OHCHR (n 9) paras 41–42.
[24] UNHRC Res 27/21 (2014) (n 13) preamble.
[25] UNHRC Draft Res 'Human rights and unilateral coercive measures' (24 September 2013) A/HRC/24/L.5/Rev.1.
[26] See US Treasury Department: sanctions against Palestine, available at home.treasury.gov/policy-issues/financial-sanctions/sanctions-programs-and-country-information/counter-terrorism-sanctions/palestinian-authority; and sanctions against Iran, available at home.treasury.gov/policy-issues/financial-sanctions/sanctions-programs-and-country-information/iran-sanctions.
[27] UNHRC Res 27/21 (2014) (13) para 1.
[28] This position was initially held by Mr Idriss Jazairy (Algeria). Ms Alena Douhan (Belarus) was appointed in March 2020; see www.ohchr.org/EN/Issues/UCM/Pages/SRCoerciveMeasures.aspx.
[29] OHCHR, 'Civilians Caught in Sanctions Crossfire' (2018).

the mounting concern for the impact of UCMs on human rights. In a joint communique in 2016, Russia, China and India came together to denounce the far-reaching and negative impact of unilateral sanctions:

> [T]he imposition of unilateral sanctions, which exceed the ones agreed by the United Nations Security Council, is inconsistent with principles of international law, undermines the prerogatives of the United Nations Security Council as set forth in the UN Charter, reduces effectiveness of its sanctions regimes, disproportionally affects States against which they are imposed, as well as, when applied extra-territorially, has a negative impact upon third States and international trade and economic relations at large. Good-faith implementation of principles of sovereign equality of States, non-intervention in the internal affairs of States and cooperation excludes imposition of unilateral coercive measures *not based on international law*.[30] (emphasis added)

The final words of this statement – 'not based on international law' – are central to the determination of the lawfulness of measures taken. In the CJEU case of *Centro-Com*, the Court ruled that Member States were permitted to only take measures contrary to EU law when seeking to comply with mandatory Security Council resolutions.[31] This of itself casts doubt upon the legality of measures adopted by individual EU Member States on an autonomous basis. This is notwithstanding the arguments pursued below that the lawfulness of UCMs should be determined by developing a regulatory / governance regime that incorporates key IHL principles to mitigate the detrimental and often severe impact upon fundamental rights and freedoms.

Under Article 49 ARSIWA, countermeasures must be proportionate and taken as a means of inducement, not punishment.[32] Furthermore, 'if they are effective in inducing the responsible State to comply with its obligations of cessation and reparation, they should be discontinued and performance of the obligation resumed'.[33] As section III illustrates, principles of proportionality and inducement are apt for application to the governance and regulation of UCMs. They ought also to be considered in tandem with two further pertinent questions. Firstly, what of those measures that are not effective at inducing compliance? Secondly, what of those UCMs whereby the impact is disproportionate and indiscriminate vis-a-vis the (alleged) actions / omissions of the targeted state? These questions assist with determining how key principles of IHL can be engaged and relied upon when addressing the lawfulness or otherwise of the impact of UCMs upon the civilian population.

III. Applying IHL Principles to UCM Regimes: Case Studies

This section considers the current use of UCMs against two states, Venezuela and Iran, with illustrative reference to Cuba to assess how legal principles in respect of human

[30] Joint Communiqué of the 14th Meeting of the Foreign Ministers of the Russian Federation, the Republic of India and the People's Republic of China (19 April 2016), para 6, available at www.fmprc.gov.cn/mfa_eng/wjdt_665385/2649_665393/t1356652.shtml.

[31] ECR I-00081 *The Queen, ex parte Centro-Com Srl v HM Treasury and Bank of England* (1997).

[32] ARSIWA, Commentary to Art 49, para 6.

[33] ibid, para 7.

rights and humanitarian law might be engaged. Two factors have determined these states as appropriate. At the time of writing, each state is subject to a series of UCMs imposed primarily by the US. By and large, the sanctions are framed as being in response to breaches by the target state of rights obligations towards its people.

The IHL framework under The Hague Conventions, Geneva Conventions and Additional Protocols was conceived with the conditions of armed conflict in mind. As such, those frameworks are not directly applicable to UCMs that are invoked as a peace-time measure. However, the use of UCMs has been said to amount to 'decentralised' economic warfare.[34] There may be grounds to argue that imposing UCMs amounts to a form of war, albeit economic rather than military, so that the laws of war are, or ought to be, engaged. Even without pursuing this line of argument (there is not the scope to do so here[35]), there are strong arguments that IHL principles of necessity, distinction and proportionality can be aptly incorporated to the governance of UCMs. Indeed, according to Owen, these are principles that apply to economic sanctions in times of peace as well as times of war.[36] For Reisman and Stevick, economic instruments 'should be tested rigorously' against IHL criteria before a decision to use or continue with their use is taken.[37] They also point to the problematic use of UCMs because of 'their relative incapacity to discriminate between licit targets and … their durable resultant collateral injuries, which persist long after the conclusion of the campaign'.[38]

Principles of distinction and proportionality are at the heart of customary international law,[39] and various international instruments address distinction and proportionality in armed conflict. Under the Geneva Conventions Additional Protocol I, it is a grave breach to launch 'an indiscriminate attack affecting the civilian population or civilian objects in the knowledge that such attack will cause excessive loss of life, injury to civilians or damage to civilian objects'. It is a war crime to intentionally launch an attack during international armed conflict 'in the knowledge that such attack will cause incidental loss of life or injury to civilians or damage to civilian objects' (ICC Rome Statute (1998), Article 8(2)(b)(iv).

The principle of proportionality has attracted significant attention as an appropriate means of monitoring the use and impact of UCMs.[40] Proportionality is also at the heart of the law of countermeasures, although it has a separate meaning within that framework, whereby 'the potential effectiveness of the measure is not a fundamental criterion', but rather whether the measure is 'proportional to the original wrong',[41] and adopted as a means of inducement, not punishment.[42] The focus in this chapter is

[34] Lowe and Tzanakopoulos (n 7) 10.

[35] See chs 1–3 for a full discussion of the arguments.

[36] Owen, 'The Limits of Economic Sanctions' (2012).

[37] Reisman and Stevick (n 1) 95.

[38] ibid.

[39] 'IHL Database: Customary IHL', referring to Rule 14 Proportionality in Attack as a customary rule of IHL, and its presence in the Geneva Conventions as well as, eg, ICC Statute and the Convention on Certain Conventional Weapons, available at https://ihl-databases.icrc.org/customary-ihl/eng/docs/v2_rul_rule14.

[40] See, eg, J Gutmann, M Neuenkirch, F Neumeier and A Steinbach, 'Economic Sanctions and Human Rights: Quantifying the Legal Proportionality Principle', Research Papers in Economics 2/18 (2018) Universitat Trier, Fachbereich IV – Volkswirtschaftslehre, and O'Connell (n 2) 65–79.

[41] O'Connell (n 2) 65–79, 78 and 77 respectively.

[42] ARSIWA (n 32) para 6.

upon the meaning under IHL rather than the law of countermeasures. The principle of necessity under the Geneva and Hague Conventions has been described as permitting the lawful use of force 'to overpower an enemy',[43] but in a manner that is 'the least destructive measure capable of achieving its desired outcome'.[44] Any losses, namely collateral damage, 'should not exceed the expected military advantage'.[45] There now follows some consideration of how these fundamental IHL principles might be adopted and adapted to a governance regime for UCMs.

A. Venezuela

As noted above, the principles of necessity, proportionality and distinction require that action taken is necessary and proportionate to achieving the objective and distinguishes between the target and the civilian population. Satisfying these principles in relation to the imposition of UCMs against Venezuela is fraught with difficulty. There may be apparent grounds for coercive action to change state behaviour in response to significant state-sponsored human rights violations and government mismanagement. However, even though there may have been convincing arguments in favour of the principles of necessity, distinction and proportionality having been met at the outset, when coercive action risks contributing to and/or causing a humanitarian crisis, this may come into doubt as the duration and intensity of the measures taken extends.

The US has had a series of UCMs in force against Venezuela for over a decade. Sanctions in the mid-to-late 2000s related to anti-terrorism and drug trafficking measures, whilst measures in response to anti-democratic actions, human rights violations and corruption followed in 2014, under Barack Obama's administration.[46] More recent sanctions imposed by Canada and the EU, as well as the US, have been presented as a response to human rights abuses under Nicolás Maduro's rule and his government's mismanagement.[47] Maduro and his government are no longer recognised by the internal community at large, and the country finds itself in an intractable position. It is heavily in debt to mainly US creditors; unable to restructure debt due to sanctions preventing dealing by US nationals with the Maduro regime;[48] struggling to access its gold

[43] N Tsagourias and A Morrison, *International Humanitarian Law: Cases, Materials and Commentary* (Cambridge University Press, 2018) 39.

[44] Owen (n 8) 118.

[45] R Kolb and R Hyde, *An Introduction to the International Law of Armed Conflicts* (Hart Publishing, 2008) 132, cited by Owen (n 8) 118.

[46] Congressional Research Service, 'Venezuela: Overview of U.S. Sanctions' 22 January 2020, available at fas.org/sgp/crs/row/IF10715.pdf.

[47] EU Sanctions Map: Venezuela, available at www.sanctionsmap.eu/#/main/details/44/?search=%7B%22value%22:%22%22,%22searchType%22:%7B%7D%7D. The Government of Canada imposed targeted asset freezes and prohibitions on dealing against named individuals within the Maduro regime in response to the Maduro Government's 'systemic erosion of Venezuela's democratic institutions and its grave human rights abuses' and pursuant to a 2017 Association between the US and Canada, 'Canadian Sanctions Related to Venezuela' Government of Canada, available at www.international.gc.ca/world-monde/international_relations-relations_internationales/sanctions/venezuela.aspx?lang=eng.

[48] Jo Gordon, 'Off Target: How US Sanctions are crippling Venezuela' (2018) 145 *Commonwealth Foundation* 12.

reserves in the UK;[49] and there is a burgeoning humanitarian catastrophe exacerbated by an inability to trade with and import food and medical supplies from numerous countries,[50] and further worsened by the COVID-19 pandemic.[51]

The cause of Venezuela's socioeconomic crisis is complex. Whilst the imposition of UCMs and their consequences may have played a significant role, other domestic and global factors have been instrumental. As an oil-producing and oil-exporting country, the Venezuelan economy suffered due to the global fall in oil prices in 2008, and recession followed.[52] By 2014, the Venezuelan economy was in a 'free fall' crisis and burdened by significant debt.[53] Following democratic elections in December 2015, a coalition of opposition parties won a majority in the National Assembly.[54] President Maduro responded in January 2016 by declaring a national emergency and began to rule by decree, dismantling the powers of the National Assembly along the way.[55] As a result, over the course of the next 18 months a number of countries refused to recognise the legitimacy of Venezuela's National Constituent Assembly and its decisions.[56] Part of the response of those countries was to impose sanctions in the form of targeted economic UCMs to bring Maduro and his government to heel.

i. Determining Necessity

Alleged human rights violations committed by the Maduro-led Venezuelan Government and those in public office are the subject of a number of matters under investigation by various bodies including the International Labor Organization (ILO), the ICC and the Human Rights Council. The global focus on the human rights situation in Venezuela may well be used as evidence of the necessity for intervention by the international community, but whether UCMs are the appropriate and necessary form of intervention would require balance against principles of proportionality and distinction. Furthermore, UCMs should be used to effect change in state practice. Resorting to UCMs before and/or during formal investigations by bodies such as the ILO, the ICC and the Human Rights Council has the potential to undermine the purpose of those bodies and amount to arbitrary unilateral action without the consent of the international community,

[49] *The 'Maduro Board' of The Central Bank of Venezuela (Appellant) v The 'Guaidó Board' of The Central Bank of Venezuela (Respondent)* [2020] EWCA Civ 1249 (permission to appeal was granted by the UK Supreme Court to the Respondent in December 2020).

[50] M Weisbrot and J Sachs, 'Economic Sanctions as Collective Punishment: The Case of Venezuela' (Center for Economic and Policy Research 2019), available at cepr.net/images/stories/reports/venezuela-sanctions-2019-04.pdf.

[51] Human Rights Watch, 'Venezuela: Urgent aid needed to combat Covid-19' (26 May 2020), available at www.hrw.org/news/2020/05/26/venezuela-urgent-aid-needed-combat-covid-19.

[52] M Weisbrot and R Ray, 'Update on the Venezuelan Economy' (Center for Economic and Policy Research, 2010) 4, available at cepr.net/documents/publications/venezuela-2010-09.pdf.

[53] Gordon, 'Off Target' (2018).

[54] Government of Canada, 'Canadian Sanctions related to Venezuela', available at www.international.gc.ca/world-monde/international_relations-relations_internationales/sanctions/venezuela.aspx?lang=eng.

[55] ibid.

[56] S Brodzinksy and D Boffey, '40 countries protest Venezuela's new assembly amid fraud accusations' *The Guardian* (2 August 2017), available at www.theguardian.com/world/2017/aug/02/venezuela-voting-fraud-corruption-allegations-protests.

perceived as a form of punishment and/or as a tool to promote regime change. With the principle of necessity in mind, this section briefly summarises those matters before the ILO, ICC and Human Rights Council.

Following submission of a complaint by workers unions to the ILO in 2015 and a lack of response from the Government of Venezuela, an ILO Commission of Inquiry (CoI) was convened in March 2018 to progress the matter further.[57] The CoI reported in September 2019, finding the Government to be in breach of its ILO convention obligations. It cited institutions and practices that were prejudicial to 'the existence and action of free and independent employers' and workers' organizations and the development of social dialogue in good faith in a climate of trust and mutual respect'.[58] Allegations included murder and acts of physical aggression against trade union leaders and members and employer representatives, arbitrary detention, interference, control and favouritism.[59] Following its investigations, the CoI recommended an 'immediate cessation of all acts of violence, threats, persecution, stigmatization, intimidation or other forms of aggression' against relevant persons and organisations, and 'the adoption of measures to ensure that such acts do not recur in future'.

The CoI's findings were reported in October 2019 with an implementation deadline for recommendations being no later than 1 September 2020.[60] By this time, UCMs had been in full force against Venezuela for some years. Just prior to the CoI's findings, in September 2019, the Human Rights Council resolved to establish an independent international fact-finding mission to 'investigate extrajudicial executions, enforced disappearances, arbitrary detentions and torture and other cruel, inhumane or degrading treatment since 2014, with a view to ensuring full accountability for perpetrators and justice for victims'.[61] This decision followed a report by the High Commissioner for Human Rights based upon 558 interviews, 159 meetings and documentary analysis.[62]

Arguably, the Human Rights Council has been slow to take action in response to the human rights situation in Venezuela. This might, in part, be due to the presence of Venezuela on the Human Rights Council's membership since 2015.[63] Before the Human Rights Council's decision to establish an independent fact-finding mission,[64] reports

[57] ILO, 'For national reconciliation and social justice in the Bolivarian Republic of Venezuela', Report of the Commission of Inquiry appointed under Art 26 of the Constitution of the International Labour Organization to examine the observance by the Government of the Bolivarian Republic of Venezuela of the Minimum Wage-Fixing Machinery Convention, 1928 (No 26), the Freedom of Association and Protection of the Right to Organise Convention, 1948 (No 87), and the Tripartite Consultation (International Labour Standards) Convention, 1976 (No 144) (ILO, 2019).

[58] ibid, ch 7.

[59] ibid, ch 7, para 365.

[60] ibid, Summary.

[61] UNHRC, 'Human rights situations that require the Council's attention' (24 September 2019) A/HRC/42/L.4/Rev.1, para 24.

[62] OHCHR Report, 'Human rights in the Bolivarian Republic of Venezuela' (05 July 2019) A/HRC/41/18, paras 6–7.

[63] Venezuela has been a member of the Human Rights Council since January 2013. Its membership was renewed for the period 2015–18 and the country was then re-elected in 2019, with its current membership coming to an end in 2022; see www.ohchr.org/EN/HRBodies/HRC/Pages/PastMembers.aspx and www.ohchr.org/EN/HRBodies/HRC/Pages/CurrentMembers.aspx respectively.

[64] UNHRC Res 45/L.43/Rev.1 (2020) 'Situation of human rights in the Bolivarian Republic of Venezuela' (1 October 2020) A/HRC/45/L.43/Rev.1, the mandate of the mission was extended for a further two years.

and evidence of state repression caused the ICC Prosecutor in February 2018 to open a preliminary investigation into crimes allegedly committed in Venezuela 'since at least April 2017 in the context of demonstrations and related political unrest'.[65] Later that year, in September 2018, a referral was made to the ICC by a number of states parties (Argentina, Canada, Colombia, Chile, Paraguay and Peru) against Maduro and his government, requesting an investigation into crimes against humanity.[66]

Those states parties, save for Canada and Paraguay, are arrival and/or destination countries for Venezuelan refugees.[67] The refugee crisis has brought its own pressures to bear on those states and challenges in respect of the resurgence of paramilitary activity and the presence of organised crime and trafficking through and along Venezuela's porous border.[68] The Latin-American states making the referral are also in receipt of US development aid, and may have geopolitical and diplomatic reasons for making a referral to the ICC that would appease the US, although for most of these states aid was reduced in 2019, sometimes significantly so.[69] Indeed, it would seem that recourse to the ICC is highly politicised with the Maduro Government making its own request in early 2020 for the ICC to investigate US sanctions as crimes against humanity.[70]

The matter is further complicated when reviewing the political rhetoric that was employed by Trump and his administration, which calls into question the motivation for imposing UCMs and casts doubt upon their necessity. The US based Center for Economic Policy and Research (CEPR) highlights comments by Mike Pompeo, the then US Secretary of State, in March 2019 that give cause to question the motivation for US involvement in Venezuela and the use of UCMs. Pompeo is reported as saying:

> Well, we wish things could go faster, but I'm very confident that the tide is moving in the direction of the Venezuelan people and will continue to do so. It doesn't take much for you to see what's really going on there. *The circle is tightening, the humanitarian crisis is increasing by the hour*. I talked with our senior person on the ground there in Venezuela last night … You can see the increasing pain and suffering that the Venezuelan people are suffering from. [emphasis added][71]

CEPR's analysis is that these comments demonstrate the humanitarian crisis is not solely the result of the economic policies of the Venezuelan Government over a prolonged period of time, nor simply collateral damage, but is 'part of the strategy to topple the government'.[72] Furthermore, CEPR refers to comments made by the US

[65] International Criminal Court, 'Statement of the Prosecutor of the International Criminal Court, Fatou Bensouda, on opening Preliminary Examinations into the situations in the Philippines and in Venezuela' (8 February 2018), available at www.icc-cpi.int/Pages/item.aspx?name=180208-otp-stat.

[66] International Criminal Court Preliminary examination: Venezuela I, available at www.icc-cpi.int/venezuela.

[67] ACAPS Thematic Report, 'Venezuela Humanitarian Crisis' (23 May 2018) 3–6, available at reliefweb.int/sites/reliefweb.int/files/resources/20180523_acaps_thematic_report_humanitarian_crisis_in_venezuela.pdf.

[68] ibid, 11.

[69] Congressional Research Service 'U.S. Foreign Assistance to Latin America and the Caribbean: FY2019 Appropriations' (1 March 2019), available at fas.org/sgp/crs/row/R45547.pdf.

[70] A Rizvi, 'Venezuela Foreign Minister asks ICC to investigate US sanctions as crimes against humanity' *Jurist* (14 February 2020), available at www.jurist.org/news/2020/02/venezuela-foreign-minister-asks-icc-to-investigate-us-sanctions-as-crimes-against-humanity.

[71] Weisbrot and Sachs, 'Economic Sanctions as Collective Punishment' (2019) 5.

[72] ibid, 5.

administration that betray a broader strategy of appropriating Venezuela's oil.[73] For CEPR, there are grounds to argue a breach of Articles 19 and 20 of the Organization of American States (OAS) Charter. Article 19 enshrines the principle of non-interference, prohibiting 'not only armed force but also any other form of interference or attempted threat against the personality of the State or against its political, economic, and cultural elements'. Article 20 refers to coercive measures, whereby: 'No State may use or encourage the use of coercive measures of an economic or political character in order to force the sovereign will of another State and obtain from it advantages of any kind'.

Venezuela remains a member of the OAS, despite reports in April 2017 of its proposed withdrawal.[74] However, its membership relates to the interim government of Juan Guaidó, which is supported by the US and others, rather than the presidential government of Maduro.[75] The US is also a long-standing member of the OAS. Given that Venezuela's membership is recognised by a government led by Guaidó, a close ally to the US, it is unlikely that any action would be sought under the OAS Charter against the US, unless it was possible for Maduro's government to secure standing. Even so, statements made by Trump, Pompeo and others could well be used as evidence to undermine claims by the US that the use of far reaching UCMs was necessary and proportionate.

ii. Determining Proportionality and Distinction

There is a lack of consensus that economic sanctions, whether unilateral or multilateral, succeed in reducing the human rights abuses by governments in the target state. Indeed, the indication is that such measures intensify and worsen the human rights situation.[76] This of itself might be sufficient to cast doubt upon imposing UCMs in compliance with the principles of proportionality and distinction. Nonetheless, in 2019 the US imposed additional steps to block property of the Government of Venezuela and US persons purchasing or using Venezuelan government debt as collateral due to human rights abuses and 'ongoing attempts to undermine Interim President Juan Guaido and the Venezuelan National Assembly's exercise of legitimate authority in Venezuela'.[77] The US has firmly placed responsibility for 'the deepening humanitarian crisis in Venezuela' with Maduro's regime.[78] Elsewhere, UCMs are said to be the cause of the 'inability of the government to function'.[79]

[73] ibid, 18.

[74] ACAPS (2018) 7, citing BBC News, 'Venezuela to withdraw from OAS as deadly protests continue' (27 April 2017), available at www.bbc.co.uk/news/world-latin-america-39726605.

[75] OAS Member States: www.oas.org/en/member_states/member_state.asp?sCode=VEN.

[76] D Peksen, 'Better or Worse? The Effect of Economic Sanctions on Human Rights' (2009) 46 *Journal of Peace Research* 59, 68, 73–74.

[77] US Treasury, 'Blocking Property of the Government of Venezuela', Executive Order 13884 (5 August 2019), available at home.treasury.gov/policy-issues/financial-sanctions/sanctions-programs-and-country-information/venezuela-related-sanctions.

[78] US Treasury, 'Imposing Additional Sanctions With Respect to the Situation in Venezuela', Executive Order 13808 (24 August 2017), available at home.treasury.gov/policy-issues/financial-sanctions/sanctions-programs-and-country-information/venezuela-related-sanctions.

[79] Gordon (n 48).

Unsurprisingly, US motives have attracted scrutiny, suggesting an underlying agenda of regime change rather than purported protection for the people of Venezuela.[80] There is a danger, as noted by Livingstone Sewanyana, Independent Expert on the Promotion of a Democratic and Equitable International Order (appointed as part of the Human Rights Council's Special Procedures), that 'In order to discredit selected governments, failures in the field of human rights are maximized so as to make violent overthrow more palatable. Human rights are being "weaponized" against rivals'.[81] Weaponising rights and causing injury beyond the named targets of the measures calls into question proportionality and distinction.

Whilst EU and Canadian measures against Venezuela are narrow in focus,[82] the broad and far-reaching impact of US UCMs against Venezuela suggests a failure to adhere to principles of proportionality and distinction. There are reports of large numbers of the population being denied access to medical, fuel and food essentials, prompting mass migration out of the country.[83] This indicates violation of the principle of distinctiveness – whilst the UCMs are supposedly targeted against named companies and individuals, the impact is on the most vulnerable populations without access to financial reserves and at the mercy of alternative unregulated markets to secure medical and other essential supplies.[84]

In addition, there are concerns that civilian populations are suffering from starvation. One report estimates that between 2017 and 2018 there were 40,000 deaths and widespread starvation due to UCMs, prompting allegations of collective punishment.[85] In August 2018, following his visit earlier that year to Venezuela, Sewanyana found that UCMs by the US, Canada and the EU had 'directly and indirectly aggravated the shortages in medicines such as insulin and anti-retroviral drugs'.[86] That sanctions had caused delays in distribution had, according to Sewanyana, contributed 'to many deaths' and should be investigated as a crime against humanity by the ICC (under Article 7 of the Rome Statute), but that 'the geopolitical submissiveness of the Court may prevent this'.[87] Interestingly, the Venezuelan Government, as led by Maduro, rebutted the contents of a report by the High Commissioner for Human Rights that found the supplies in hospitals and their capacity seriously wanting, a response that could be used to undermine the

[80] P Torres, J Borger, J Parkin Daniels and T Phillips, 'The plot that failed: how Venezuela's "uprising" fizzled', *The Guardian* (3 May 2019); see also comments made by Mike Pompeo, above in this chapter.

[81] UNHRC, 'Report of the Independent Expert on the promotion of a democratic and equitable international order on his mission to the Bolivarian Republic of Venezuela and Ecuador' (3 August 2018) A/HRC/39/47/Add.1, para 29, available at https://documents-dds-ny.un.org/doc/UNDOC/GEN/G18/239/31/PDF/G1823931.pdf?OpenElement.

[82] EU measures include an embargo on the sale of arms and equipment for internal repression and asset freezes for 25 named individuals: Council of the European Union, 'Venezuela: Council renews sanctions until 14 November 2020', Press Release (11 November 2019), available at www.consilium.europa.eu/en/press/press-releases/2019/11/11/venezuela-council-renews-sanctions-until-14-november-2020. Canadian measures include asset freezes and dealings prohibitions with listed persons / persons acting on their behalf in accordance with an agreement it has with the US; see www.international.gc.ca/world-monde/international_relations-relations_internationales/sanctions/venezuela.aspx?lang=eng.

[83] Weisbrot and Sachs (n 50) 2.

[84] UNHRC Report (n 81) para 36.

[85] Weisbrot and Sachs (n 50) 2.

[86] UNHRC Report (n 81).

[87] ibid, para 36.

strength of arguments that the impact of UCMs on the Venezuelan healthcare system is in breach of IHL principles.[88]

The UN World Food Programme reported in 2019 that approximately one-third of the population in Venezuela was either moderately or severely food-insecure, with a lack of dietary diversity being 'of major concern'.[89] The report refers to depleting coping mechanisms amongst families that have used savings to buy food and to a deterioration in basic services (water, sanitation, housing, electricity, cooking facilities).[90] Yet food insecurity has plagued the people of Venezuela for some time.[91] Attributing food and other insecurities to UCMs would be subject to further investigation. If it was found that UCMs increased food, energy and/or medical insecurity there would be grounds upon which to suggest that both proportionality and distinction were in breach.

Compliance with the principles of proportionality and distinction are also called into question by the extraterritorial scope of the US's UCMs, which significantly interferes with world trade and inter-state trading relationships. The US has specifically threatened sanctions against India if it continues to purchase oil from Venezuela.[92] By seriously limiting access to trade, extraterritoriality has been cited as contributing to Venezuela's move from high inflation to hyper-inflation, and putting vulnerable populations at greater risk by exacerbating the lack of access to essential services and supplies such as food, medicine and energy.[93]

The issues raised in this section are not peculiar to Venezuela. The US sanctions regime against Cuba has been running in some form or another since 1960.[94] Alleged consequences of the UCMs against Venezuela mirror, for example, reports of the severe and detrimental impact of US unilateral sanctions against Cuba and its public health infrastructure, supplies and outcomes.[95] The effects of sanctions have also been described in terms of gross violations of humanitarian principles. Following the US's escalation in UCM pressure against Cuba, the Cuban Foreign Minister stated in 2019 that, 'the blockade has caused incalculable humanitarian damages. It is a flagrant, massive and systematic violation of human rights'. He described the blockade as an act of genocide pursuant to Articles II(b) and (c) of the Convention on the Prevention and Punishment of the Crime of Genocide (1948), stating 'there is not one single Cuban family that has not suffered the consequences of this'.[96]

[88] The response describes a well-resourced healthcare system with medical supplies being well stocked and available, 'Venezuela comments on UN's 'human rights' report' *The Communists* (19 July 2019), available at thecommunists.org/2019/07/19/news/venezuela-comments-un-human-rights-report.

[89] OHCHA World Food Programme, 'WFP Venezuela Food Security Assessment Main Findings: Data Collected between July and September 2019' (23 February 2020), available at reliefweb.int/report/venezuela-bolivarian-republic/wfp-venezuela-food-security-assessment-main-findings-data.

[90] ibid.

[91] Associated Press in Caracas, 'One in three Venezuelans not getting enough to eat, UN finds', *The Guardian* (24 February 2020), available at www.theguardian.com/world/2020/feb/24/venezuela-hungry-food-insecure-un-world-food-program.

[92] Weisbrot and Sachs (n 50) 2.

[93] ibid, 19–21.

[94] CM DeMelfi, 'Nothing but the Facts: An In-Depth Analysis of the Effects of Economic Sanctions Against Cuba' (2006) 5 *Journal of International Business Law* 146.

[95] Garfield and Santana, 'The Impact of the Economic Crisis' (1997).

[96] UNGA, 'General Assembly Adopts Annual Resolution Calling on United States to End Embargo against Cuba, as Brazil Rejects Text for First Time' (7 November 2019) Press Release.

In contrast, there is scholarship that celebrates the relative success of Cuba's response to US sanctions. Cuba has succeeded, despite the crippling effect of the sanctions on its trade with the US, to function and manage its public services, albeit at times at reduced capacity, and by taking measures to fight corruption in public office,[97] as well as diversifying its trading relations.[98] Even so, it remains that despite having been imposed for over five decades, US sanctions have failed to achieve the US's ultimate objective of regime change,[99] and the duration and intensity of the UCMs surely calls into question their necessity, proportionality and distinction.

B. Iran

The US sanctions regime against Iran first began in 1979 in the form of a blocking order against all property and interests in property of the Iranian Government.[100] UCMs were used to impose further pressure in the early 2010s by the UN and the EU as well as the US in response to Iran's nuclear ambitions and human rights violations.[101] The primary objective of EU measures was couched in human rights terms. Asset freezes and travel restrictions were introduced against those involved in 'grave human rights violations in the repression of peaceful demonstrators, journalists, human rights defenders, students or other persons who speak up in defense [*sic*] of their legitimate rights'.[102] In addition, sanctions prohibiting access to equipment used for internal repression and telecommunications equipment were imposed. Restrictions could be extended to those:

> [C]omplicit in or responsible for directing or implementing grave violations of the right to due process, torture, cruel, inhuman and degrading treatment, or the indiscriminate, excessive and increasing application of the death penalty, including public executions, stoning, hangings or executions of juvenile offenders in contravention of Iran's international human rights obligations.[103]

i. Determining Necessity and Proportionality

The impact of sanctions is said to have played a part in prompting Iran to enter the Joint Comprehensive Plan of Action (JCPOA),[104] which led to the lifting of the

[97] M Hove, E Ndawana and MA Nhemachena, 'How Cuba survived sanctions and the lessons for Zimbabwe' (2020) 24 *Jadavpur Journal of International Relations* 1, 8.

[98] UNGA Res 73/8 (2018), 'Necessity of ending the economic, commercial and financial embargo imposed by the United States of America against Cuba' (1 November 2018) UN Doc A/RES/73/8, see statement by Equatorial Guinea.

[99] Hove, Ndawana and Nhemachena, 'How Cuba survived sanctions' (2020) 8.

[100] US Treasury, 'Blocking Iranian Government Property', Executive Order 12170 (14 November 1979), available at home.treasury.gov/system/files/126/12170.pdf. For current and historical details of US sanctions against Iran, see US Department of the Treasury Resource Centre at treasury.gov/resource-center/sanctions/Programs/Pages/iran.aspx.

[101] For an overview of the history of US sanctions against Iran, see Congressional Research Service, Iran Sanction (updated July 2020), at fas.org/sgp/crs/mideast/RS20871.pdf.

[102] EU Sanctions map: Iran, www.sanctionsmap.eu/#/main/details/17/?search=%7B%22value%22:%22%22,%22searchType%22:%7B%7D%7D.

[103] ibid.

[104] See UNSC Res 2231 (25 July 2015) UN Doc S/RES/2231/2015, Joint Comprehensive Plan of Action (JCPOA), the nuclear agreement between Iran, and the permanent five members of the UNSC, plus Germany

majority of the UCMs (and UN sanctions) that had been imposed in the early 2010s.[105] This change in Iranian state practice could indicate that the imposition of UCMs in the early 2010s was a necessary and proportionate means of affecting a change in the actions of Iran's ruling regime. However, in May 2018 the US withdrew from the JCPOA and reimposed UCMs against Iran. This was in response to Iran publicly stating it would deny the International Atomic Energy Agency access to military sites and, two years earlier, having twice violated the JCPOA's heavy-water stockpile limits. The US declared the reimposed sanctions to be the 'toughest U.S. sanctions ever imposed on Iran', designed to 'target critical sectors of Iran's economy, such as the energy, shipping and shipbuilding, and financial sectors', with the US promising to engage 'in a campaign of maximum financial pressure on the Iranian regime … to enforce aggressively these sanctions that have come back into effect'.[106]

Reimposed UCMs included blocking sanctions: to prevent Iran from purchasing US bank notes or precious metals; against certain Iranian persons, for example, to prohibit any transactions in foreign exchange and transfers of credit or payments between financial institutions or by, through, or to, any financial institution subject to the jurisdiction of the US and in which the sanctioned person has any interest; against Iran's energy, shipping, and shipbuilding sectors and port operators, measures to prevent trade with the automotive and petroleum sector, and more.[107] In addition, sanctions were imposed against both US and non-US persons dealing with Iran's civil aviation industry.[108]

The EU has expressed its view of the extraterritorial aspect of the UCMs by amending its Blocking Regulation to circumvent the extraterritorial scope of US sanctions.[109] This response calls into question the proportionality of the UCMs imposed by the US and is consistent with the EU's position on this in the past. In 1996, the EU filed a complaint with the World Trade Organization (WTO) against the extraterritorial reach of US sanctions against Cuba, Iran and Libya contained in the US's Helms-Burton and D'Amato-Kennedy Acts.[110] It withdrew the complaint for further consideration, proceeding instead to pass the Blocking Regulation to prohibit EU Member State compliance

(P5+1), see European Council, 'Joint Comprehensive Plan of Action and restrictive measures', available at www.consilium.europa.eu/en/policies/sanctions/iran/jcpoa-restrictive-measures.

[105] M Nesbitt, 'Canada's Unilateral Sanctions Regime Under Review: Extraterritoriality Human Rights Due Process and Enforcement in Canada's Special Economic Measures Act' (2016) 48 *Ottawa Law Review* 507, 517.

[106] US Treasury, 'Re-imposition of the sanctions on Iran that had been lifted or waived under the JCPOA', (Resource Centre, 4 November 2018), available at home.treasury.gov/policy-issues/financial-sanctions/sanctions-programs-and-country-information/iran-sanctions/re-imposition-of-the-sanctions-on-iran-that-had-been-lifted-or-waived-under-the-jcpoa.

[107] US Treasury, 'Re-imposing certain sanctions with respect to Iran', Executive Order 13846 (6 August 2018), available at home.treasury.gov/policy-issues/financial-sanctions/sanctions-programs-and-country-information/iran-sanctions.

[108] US Treasury, 'Deceptive Practices by Iran with respect to the Civil Aviation Industry' Iran-Related Civil Aviation Industry Advisory (23 July 2019), available at home.treasury.gov/policy-issues/financial-sanctions/recent-actions/20190723.

[109] Commission Delegated Regulation (EU) 2018/1100 (7 August 2018) and Guidance Note, 'Questions and Answers: adoption of update of the Blocking Statute' (2018/C 277 I/03), available at eur-lex.europa.eu/legal-content/EN/TXT/?uri=uriserv:OJ.CI.2018.277.01.0004.01.ENG&toc=OJ:C:2018:277I:TOC#ntr1-CI2018277EN.01000401-E0001.

[110] PK Chudzicki, 'The European Union's Response to the Libertad Act and the Iran-Libya Act: Extraterritoriality without Boundaries' (1997) 28 *Loyola University Chicago Law Journal* 505, 506.

with the extraterritorial sanctions, and to protect the interests of EU Member States that suffered loss as a result.[111] The EU has yet, however, to enforce the Blocking Regulation, and so whilst it is 'symbolically important', it is 'largely seen as toothless'.[112]

The EU has, however, reiterated its position in respect of the secondary aspects of the sanctions against Cuba.[113] This reflects the almost universal position of the international community as illustrated by the voting on a General Assembly resolution in 2018 on ending US sanctions against Cuba, where 189 states voted in favour of the resolution with only the US and Israel voting against (and with no abstentions).[114] Furthermore, France, Germany and the UK have taken direct action to bypass extraterritorial constraints to establish the Instrument in Support of Trade Exchanges (INSTEX) to allow EU economic entities to trade legitimately with Iran.[115] The first transaction via this mechanism took place in April 2020, enabling the sale of medical supplies from the EU to Iran.[116]

In defiance of the US's imposition of extraterritorial UCMs, this is a bold step taken to demonstrate EU commitment to the JCPOA with Iran.[117] It indicates a refusal to comply with US secondary measures, suggesting those measures are unnecessary, disproportionate and unlawful. Indeed, it has been said that it is 'an emergent (if not already established) rule of customary international law' that UCMs 'with secondary or extraterritorial effects, "which affect the sovereignty of other States, the legitimate interests of entities or persons under their jurisdiction and the freedom of trade and navigation"' are almost universally seen by the international community as unlawful.[118]

There would appear to be a growing consensus that 'sanctions that extend beyond national borders, and which seek to block a country's trade altogether, amount to economic warfare against civilians' where people 'die, but from lack of food and medicine, rather than from explosive devices'.[119] However, and despite the signal the amendment of the EU Blocking regulation (a regulation that also

[111] EC Council Regulation (EC) No 2271/96, 'Protecting against the effects of the extra-territorial application of legislation adopted by a third country, and actions based thereon or resulting therefrom' (22 November 1996).

[112] IJazairy, 'Unilateral economic sanctions, International Law and Human Rights' (2019) 33 *Ethics and International Affairs*, 291, 299.

[113] Europa 'The European Union and Cuba held Dialogue on Unilateral Coercive Measures', Press Release (30 November 2019), available at eeas.europa.eu/headquarters/headquarters-homepage/71260/european-union-and-cuba-held-dialogue-unilateral-coercive-measures_en.

[114] UNGA Res 73/8 'Necessity of ending the economic, commercial and financial embargo imposed by the United States of America against Cuba' A/73/L.3 (1 November 2018) 19, available at undocs.org/en/A/73/PV.30.

[115] UKFCO 'Iran and INSTEX: E3 statement', Press Release (20 November 2019), available at www.gov.uk/government/news/e3-statement-on-iran-and-instex.

[116] A Brzozowski, 'EU's INSTEX mechanism facilitates first transaction with pandemic-hit Iran' *Euractiv* (1 April 2020), available at www.euractiv.com/section/global-europe/news/eus-instex-mechanism-facilitates-first-transaction-with-pandemic-hit-iran, and 'EU sells medical goods via INSTEX' *Financial Tribune* (3 April 2020), available at financialtribune.com/articles/business-and-markets/102669/eu-sells-medical-goods-via-instex.

[117] E Geranmayeh and E Batmanghelidj, 'Trading with Iran via the special purpose vehicle: How it can work' *European Council on Foreign Relations* (7 February 2019), available at www.ecfr.eu/article/commentary_trading_with_iran_special_purpose_vehicle_how_it_can_work.

[118] Jazairy, 'Unilateral economic sanctions' (2019) 294, citing UNGA Res 73/8 (2018), 'Necessity of ending the economic, commercial and financial embargo imposed by the United States of America against Cuba' 01 November 2018) UN Doc A/RES/73/8.

[119] OHCHR (n 14).

applies to Cuba) and establishment of INSTEX sends, as Joy Gordon comments, 'for banks, shipping companies, insurers, technology companies, or the energy industry, the bottom line is that no one can risk losing access to U.S. markets, regardless of whether U.S. sanctions accord with international law'.[120] The continued dominance of the US in terms of global trade means that private entities are likely to comply with the extra-territorial scope of sanctions, deepening the negative human rights and humanitarian effects of UCMs.

ii. Determining Distinction

In the midst of the sanctions against Iran in the first half of the 2010s, concerns were raised of another pending humanitarian disaster due to a lack of medical and laboratory supplies. As Ali Gorji explains, whilst the sanctions did not make direct reference to medical supplies, the flow into the country of medical supplies was interrupted due to 'difficulties in holding license [*sic*] for export of medicine, financial transaction, and shipment as well as fear of possible U.S. sanction by pharmaceutical companies and international banks'.[121] Studies indicate that during that period, the significant negative impact upon health and medical supplies affected the treatment of numerous conditions, including diabetes, cancer, asthma and pulmonary disease as well as anti-viral, anti-depressant drugs and medication and those related to transplants and more.[122] In addition, one study concludes that indirect effects of UCMs include an increased presence of carcinogenic air pollution.[123] These studies highlight detrimental consequences of UCMs beyond their named targets to the broader population, in breach of the principle of distinction.

Following the reintroduction by the US of UCMs in 2018, concerns were raised that although sanctions contained humanitarian exemptions, issues relating to international interbank transfers 'may make such exemptions inoperative'.[124] Iran was swift to act in submitting an application to the ICJ in July 2018, alleging violations by the US of the Treaty of Amity, Economic Relations and Consular Rights (agreed between the two states in 1955).[125] Iran included a request for 'provisional measures' to preserve its rights under the 1955 Treaty, pending the Court's final decision in the case. Finding that the US's obligations under the bilateral treaty were engaged, the ICJ unanimously ordered

[120] Gordon (n 48).

[121] A Gorji, 'Sanctions against Iran: The Impact on Health Services' (2014) 43 *Iranian Journal of Public Health* 381, 381.

[122] S Setayesh and TK Mackey, 'Addressing the impact of economic sanctions on Iranian drug shortages in the joint comprehensive plan of action: promoting access to medicines and health diplomacy' (2016) 12 *Global Health*, available at doi.org/10.1186/s12992-016-0168-6.

[123] S Shahabi, H Fazlalizadeh, J Stedman, L Chuang, A Shariftabrizi and R Ram, 'The Impact of International Economic Sanctions on Iranian Cancer Healthcare' (2015) 119 *Health Policy*, 1309 refers to reduced access to refined oil due to the extraterritoriality of US sanctions led to Iran using outdated equipment and producing lower grade petroleum with an increased rate of benzine, a carcinogenic air pollutant, said to create a higher risk of cancer in Tehran in particular.

[124] OHCHR (n 14).

[125] Alleged Violations of the 1955 Treaty of Amity, Economic Relations, and Consular Rights (*Islamic Republic of Iran v United States of America*), Request for the Indication of Provisional Measures, Order of 3 October 2018, available at ICJ, www.icj-cij.org/public/files/case-related/175/175-20181003-ORD-01-00-EN.pdf.

a number of provisional measures. These included that the US 'remove any impediments' to the free exportation to Iran of supplies for medicine and medical equipment, foodstuffs and agricultural commodity, and equipment and services necessary for the safety of civil aviation that were otherwise interrupted as a result of the reimposed sanctions.[126] In doing so, the ICJ acknowledged the potential of economic sanctions to cause 'irreparable prejudice'.

The ICJ's court order and its recognition of the potential negative impact of US sanctions against Iran could well be used as evidence of a violation of both the principle of proportionality – whether such measures were proportionate in response to Iran's disengagement at that stage with the JCPOA, and the principle of distinction – because the effect of the measures would appear to go well beyond the named targets to impact a significant proportion of the civilian population. Action by the US since the ICJ's order suggests it is in breach of the Court Order, having implemented additional sanctions and having been slow to make changes with 'uncertain benefit' in respect of access to medical supplies and equipment.[127]

IV. Conclusion

> Sanctions are silent killing, especially for those who are dealing with chronic diseases or emergency disorders; the needful are left abandoned.[128]

The arguments against the legality of UCMs are significant. Whilst their design has followed the Security Council's approach of using targeted sanctions, UCMs are unlawful being beyond the scope of the UN Charter, and as such are not subject to the authority of the Security Council. They undermine and contravene the principles of the multilateral trading system; studies indicate that UCMs are highly disruptive to supply chains of essential services and supplies and the capacity of the target state to trade. Consequently, their socioeconomic impact directly and indirectly causes gross human rights abuses and humanitarian suffering whilst, paradoxically, there is little evidence that UCMs succeed in meeting their stated objective.

There is not universal condemnation of the use and/or impact of UCMs. There is, unsurprisingly, a divide between those that situate the cause of the human rights and humanitarian suffering with the government of those people, and those that attribute humanitarian crisis to states imposing UCMs. Both positions risk being politicised and polarised, failing to take account of complex historical, systemic and geopolitical factors. However, evidence from various studies and sources cited in this chapter indicates that the consequences of UCMs all too often adversely affect those suffering from the human rights abuses that sanctions are purportedly imposed to address. Furthermore, such

[126] ibid, para 102. At the time of writing, proceedings on the merits of the case are suspended pending the outcome of preliminary objections by the US, ICJ Press Release No 2020/28, 21 September 2020, available at www.icj-cij.org/public/files/case-related/175/175-20200921-PRE-01-00-EN.pdf.

[127] J Klingler, B Barnes and T Sepheri, 'Is the US in Breach of the ICJ's Provisional Measures Order in Alleged Violations of the 1955 Treaty of Amity?' (2020) 24 *American Society of International Law*.

[128] Gorji, 'Sanctions against Iran' (2014) 381.

evidence indicates that the sanctions often fail to be effective at securing their stated objective: a change in state behaviour.

Described as 'economic terrorism'[129] and 'economic asphyxiation',[130] the deployment of UCMs has been compared to 'medieval sieges of towns with the intention of forcing them to surrender'.[131] The citing of human rights abuses by the target state as grounds for intervention by the imposing state has been portrayed as a veil for action driven by political ideology often to support regime change.[132] Jorge Arreaza Montserrat, Venezuela's Minister for Foreign Affairs, has referred to the US's action against Cuba as 'imperial arrogance' amounting to collective punishment.[133] In a similar vein, Iran's delegate before the UN said the US 'has been addicted to imposing unilateral sanctions when it comes to States that do not submit to, or follow, its contradictory and expansionist policies'.[134]

Former Special Rapporteur on UCMs, Idriss Jazairy, has called for the international community to give the 'form of warfare' meted through unilateral sanctions 'that relies on starvation and disease', the same concern as an armed conflict would warrant.[135] As this contribution has demonstrated, the laws of war in relation to the principles of necessity, proportionality and distinction, and the prohibition of collective punishment, are apt for application to the decision to impose and the continued use of UCMs. Yet, in taking this approach, there is an implicit acceptance of UCMs as a legitimate means of resolving inter-state issues, which of itself is contrary to the position of certain states (see reference to China, India and Russia above, for example) and the Human Rights Council. Furthermore, just because those principles might be applied, it does not mean they can be easily satisfied.

Pursuant to the principle of distinction, attacks must not be directed against the civilian population.[136] UCMs present a particular difficulty in satisfying this principle because there is an 'incapacity to discriminate between licit targets and because of their durable resultant collateral injuries, which persist long after the conclusion of the campaign in which they were deployed'.[137] Humanitarian and human rights protection is ostensibly incorporated into sanctions regimes via humanitarian exceptions designed

[129] Javad Zarif, Iranian Foreign Minister, quoted with reference to US sanctions against Iran, 'Trump orders tougher sanctions on Iran' *The Financial Times* (19 September 2019).

[130] UNHRC Report (n8 1) para 39 and 37 respectively.

[131] ibid.

[132] S Lee, 'Law and Development of Cuba under US-led Sanctions and its Implications for HR757' (2017) 24 *Journal of International and US* Committee *of Foreign Relations* 77; 'Understanding The Impact Of U.S. Policy Changes On Human Rights And Democracy In Cuba And U.S. Cuban Relations – The Way Forward', Hearings Before the US Senate Subcommittee on Western Hemisphere Transnational Crime, Civilian Security, Democracy, Human Rights, and Global Women's Issues, and The Committee On Foreign Relations United States Senate, 3 February 2015 and 20 May 2015, 3, available at www.govinfo.gov/content/pkg/CHRG-114shrg96108/pdf/CHRG-114shrg96108.pdf.

[133] UNGA, 'General Assembly Adopts Annual Resolution Calling on United States to End Embargo against Cuba, as Brazil Rejects Text for First Time', Press Release (7 November 2019), available at www.un.org/press/en/2019/ga12212.doc.htm.

[134] ibid.

[135] OHCHR (n 14).

[136] See, especially: Art 8(2)(e)(i), ICC Statute and Art 13, Additional Protocol II, Geneva Conventions, both applicable to non-international armed conflicts, and Art 48, Additional Protocol I, Geneva Conventions.

[137] Reisman and Stevick (n 1) 95.

to permit the safe passage of essential medical supplies, health services and food, etc into the target state. However, as noted, the lack of access to international interbank transfers and the extraterritorial reach of US sanctions has been cited as compromising access and capacity to trade in these supplies.

In addition, the prohibition of collective punishment broadly requires that a population should not be punished for acts of individuals that the population cannot be regarded as jointly and severally responsible for.[138] Targeted UCMs are aimed at specific people and entities yet the failure to distinguish between the target and the general populace has been described at its most extreme as causing starvation and suffering tantamount to collective punishment.[139] If UCMs are to be used as a means to effect change in state practice in compliance with IHL, their focus should be proportionate and distinctive in relation to that objective. One compelling recommendation is for a human rights impact assessment test to be conducted before implementing sanctions unilaterally, and to monitor on a regular basis the effects of the measures, including their adverse effect on human rights.[140] This could include a 'contextual inquiry' where the impact of potential UCMs is measured 'against the criteria of the international law of armed conflict and other relevant norms of contemporary international law before a decision is made to initiate or to continue to apply them'.[141] Without such an assessment being undertaken, the use of UCMs would be unlawful.[142]

In the meantime, the US maintains a robust approach seeking to undermine its adversaries using unilateral sanctions to full effect as demonstrated by the recent passing of the Ceasar Syrian Civil Protection Act 2019, although much of what is contained in this Act has been subject to sanctions for some time under Executive Orders introduced by the Obama administration.[143] The 2019 Act encompasses regimes supporting Assad in Syria by citing human rights abuses in Syria as the basis for action so that, 'Instead of Iranian and Hezbollah actors looking like they are being targeted on political grounds, they now could be targeted on the basis that they are supporting the unprecedented human rights abuses in Syria'.[144]

Although there is evidence of a groundswell against the unilateral actions of the US with states taking action to defy the extraterritoriality of certain US economic sanctions (see the reference to INSTEX, the amended European Blocking Regulation, and recent Human Rights Council Resolutions, above), more decisive geopolitical action

[138] Art 50 of the Hague Convention IV: 'No general penalty, pecuniary or otherwise, shall be inflicted upon the population on account of the acts of individuals for which they cannot be regarded as jointly and severally responsible'. Similar provisions apply under the Geneva Conventions, eg dealing with the protection of prisoners of war.

[139] Weisbrot and Sachs (n 50).

[140] Jazairy (n112) 296.

[141] Reisman and Stevick (n 1) 132 and 95, respectively.

[142] Reisman and Stevick (n 1) 132.

[143] D Stroul and K Bauer, 'The Caesar Act Comes Into Force (Part 1): Increasing the Assad Regime's Isolation', The Washington Institute (11 June 2020), available at www.washingtoninstitute.org/policy-analysis/caesar-act-comes-force-part-1-increasing-assad-regimes-isolation.

[144] Ibrahim Olabi, of the Syrian Legal Development Programme, quoted in M Chulov, 'US "Caesar Act" sanctions could devastate Syria's flatlining economy' *The Guardian* (12 June 2020), available at www.theguardian.com/world/2020/jun/12/us-caesar-act-sanctions-and-could-devastate-syrias-flatlining-economy.

at an international level would be needed to police the use of UCMs. Despite growing calls by states, the Human Rights Council and Special Rapporteurs to refrain from imposing UCMs, it is unlikely that the US, and others, would desist. The US is the main champion of high intensity UCMs and under Donald Trump the US's exceptionalism approach to geopolitics arguably expanded, whilst engagement with international organisations such as the Human Rights Council and the World Health Organization contracted. It remains to be seen what strategy the US will adopt under a fresh, Joe Biden-led, administration.

10

Maritime Lawfare: The Impact of Unilateral Sanctions on Law and Practice on Navigation and Seaborne Trade

ABHINAYAN BASU BAL

I. Introduction

In recent years, statutes and regulations emanating from unilateral sanctions have become increasingly complex and numerous. They have had a significant impact not only on the shippers and shipowners involved in shipping operations, but also on financial institutions and insurance companies serving the maritime transport industry worldwide. Although unilateral sanctions as a phenomenon has been in existence for some time, it still remains a subject of contemporary interest which cuts across multiple disciplines and various branches of law. Recently, the detention of an oil tanker by Gibraltar in order to enforce EU sanctions on Syria has raised serious doubts about the legality of the action under international maritime law and induced the international maritime community to assess the legal and practical impacts of such action on navigation and seaborne trade.

Maritime law evolved from the customs and practices of merchants and seafarers, as seaborne trade has been one of the important uses of the oceans to humankind. Initially, this specialised branch of law was created by and for private interests, making it largely private in character.[1] However, during the sixteenth century, there was much strife and conflict among the European maritime powers for control of the oceans, which resulted in the development of the public international law of the sea. In 1609, the celebrated Dutch jurist Hugo Grotius published an extensive treatise

[1] Freedom of the seas had already become established custom in the interest of trade and commerce in the 13th century, as shown in the Maritime Codes of Macassar and Malacca compiled during those times. RP Anand, *Origin and Development of the Law of the Sea* (Nijhoff, 1982) 30–31.

entitled *Mare Liberum* in which he stated that 'The vagrant waters of the seas are … necessarily free'; and that:

> [T]he right of occupation … rests upon the fact that most things become exhausted by promiscuous use and that appropriation, consequently, is the condition of their utility to human beings. But this is not the case with the sea; it can be exhausted neither by navigation nor by fishing, that is to say, in neither of the two ways in which it can be used.[2]

Since then, the doctrine of freedom of the seas has been consolidated through state practice and has remained a cornerstone of public international law of the sea.[3] The right of innocent passage is an outcrop of freedom of navigation, the latter being one of the elements of freedom of the seas.[4] The right of innocent passage allows foreign ships to pass through the territorial sea of another state.[5] However, on 4 July 2019, Gibraltar police with support from the UK Royal Marines seized the Panama-flagged and Singapore-owned/managed oil tanker *Grace 1* in the Strait of Gibraltar,[6] which it claimed was heading for Syria in breach of EU sanctions.[7] Gibraltar justified the seizure of *Grace 1* stating that the ship carrying 2.1 million barrels of Iranian crude oil was bound for the Baniyas Oil Refinery, which is subject to EU sanctions pursuant to a list publicised by the EU in July 2014.[8] Interestingly, *Grace 1* was seized pursuant to the Sanctions Regulations 2019 enacted by Gibraltar on 3 July, just one day before the seizure. The ship was subsequently ordered to be released by the Gibraltar Supreme

[2] H Grotius, *Mare Liberum* (Leiden, 1609). For the English translation along with Latin text on the basis of the Elzevir edition of 1633, see H Grotius, *The Freedom of the Seas; Or, The Right which Belongs to the Dutch to Take Part in the East Indian Trade* (trans R Van Deman Magoffin) (originally published by the Carnegie Endowment for International Peace, Oxford University Press, 1916; reprint, Lawbook Exchange, 2001).

[3] At present, the dominant cornerstone of law of the sea is the doctrine of 'common heritage of mankind', enunciated by Ambassador Arvid Pardo of Malta in his 1967 speech in the United Nations General Assembly, which is now entrenched in the United Nations Convention on the Law of the Sea, 1982 (UNCLOS). The doctrine of common heritage of mankind is a restatement of 'freedom of the seas' or *mare liberum*, and also the much older Roman law doctrines of *res communis* and *res publico* that were applied within the confines of the Roman Empire. See 'Address By Ambassador Arvid Pardo' (1968) *Proceedings of the American Society of International Law at Its Annual Meeting (1921–1969)*, 62, 216–29.

[4] At present, freedom of the seas refers to 'freedom of the high seas'. Part VII of UNCLOS deals with 'high seas', which is not a maritime zone of a coastal state but is of crucial significance in respect of the coastal state's rights and jurisdiction. There are six freedoms of the high seas which are set out in Art 87; they comprise navigation, overflight, laying of submarine cables or pipelines, construction of artificial islands and installations, fishing and scientific research.

[5] Previously, there was only land and sea; there were no 'high seas' and no concept of innocent passage. The right of innocent passage only evolved in the 19th century and was predicated and premised on whether the territorial sea was viewed as an extension of coastal state sovereignty or only as jurisdiction comprising a 'bundle of servitudes' as pointed out by Churchill and Lowe. See RR Churchill and AV Lowe, *The Law of the Sea*, 3rd edn (Manchester University Press, 1984) 92.

[6] Gibraltar, located at the southern tip of the Iberian Peninsula, is of great strategic importance to international shipping and trade. It is a British Overseas Territory and is the subject of an irredentist territorial claim by Spain. Any maritime issue involving Gibraltar engenders a view from Spain, but there was not much discussion on jurisdiction after the seizure of *Grace 1*. Any detailed discussion on the issue is beyond the scope of this chapter.

[7] Council Regulation (EU) No 36/2012 of 18 January 2012 concerning restrictive measures in view of the situation in Syria. On 17 May 2019, the Council extended EU restrictive measures against the Syrian regime until 1 June 2020.

[8] Pursuant to Council Regulation (EU) No 36/2012, provision of 'economic resources' of any kind to a listed person or entity is prohibited.

Court after 43 days in detention upon receiving written assurances from Iran[9] that the tanker would not sail to countries 'subject to EU sanctions'.[10]

Against this backdrop, this chapter examines whether Gibraltar's act to detain *Grace 1* may be construed as 'maritime lawfare', an expression introduced by the present author to depict a strategy of using law to substitute traditional military action and build economic pressure on an adversary by disrupting navigation of ships and seaborne trade. The *Grace I* incident is used as a case study to critically examine Gibraltar's conduct as a coastal state by questioning whether the detention of the ship is legally tenable from the vantage point of international maritime law. The chapter addresses some of the wider law of the sea issues arising from the imposition of unilateral sanctions leading to legal outcomes and certain maritime actions, such as blockade and interdiction to enforce such sanctions on passing ships.

Following this introduction, section II examines the situation when the right of innocent passage and possibly transit passage could be suspended, even temporarily, by the state imposing unilateral sanctions for ships trading with the targeted state. Section III elucidates the notion of maritime lawfare and investigates what is permissible and what is not and what are the possible grey areas that could be exploited by the state imposing sanctions. Section IV concludes the chapter.

II. Maritime Sovereignty and Jurisdiction

The current public international law related to the sea is mainly contained in the United Nations Convention on the Law of the Sea, 1982 (UNCLOS).[11] It represents, in addition to some newly created law, a codification of customary law and state practices,[12] as well as a revision of the 1958 Geneva Conventions on the Law of the Sea.[13] The regimes

[9] On 12 July, Panama announced its decision to withdraw its flag from any ship violating 'sanctions and international legislation'. This decision resulted in the removal of *Grace 1* from the Panamanian ship register due to the link with Iran and Syria. However, according to the *Autoridad Marítima de Panamá*, *Grace 1* was removed from the Panamanian ship register on 29 May 2019, ie, before its detention at Gibraltar. While *Grace 1* was at detention in Gibraltar, it was entered into the Iranian ship register and was renamed as *Adrian Darya 1*. See J Saul, P Hafezi and M Parraga, 'Flags of inconvenience: noose tightens around Iranian shipping' *Reuters* (26 July 2019), available at www.reuters.com/article/us-mideast-iran-tanker-flags-insight/flags-of-inconvenience-noose-tightens-around-iranian-shipping-idUSKCN1UL0M8.

[10] Notice of revocation of specification of ship, LN 2019/164 commenced on 15 August 2019 during the release of *Grace 1*; available at www.gibraltarlaws.gov.gi/legislations/notice-of-revocation-of-specification-of-ship-4663/download.

[11] United Nations Convention on the Law of the Sea (UNCLOS), Montego Bay, 10 December 1982, entered into force on 1 November 1994, 1833 UNTS 397.

[12] M Dixon, *Textbook on International law*, 7th edn (Oxford University Press, 2013) 219.

[13] On 29 April 1958, as recorded in the Final Act (A/CONF.13/L.58, 1958, UNCLOS, Off. Rec. vol. 2, 146), the United Nations Conference on the Law of the Sea opened for signature four conventions and an optional protocol: the Convention on the Territorial Sea and the Contiguous Zone (CTS); the Convention on the High Seas (CHS); the Convention on Fishing and Conservation of the Living Resources of the High Seas (CFCLR); the Convention on the Continental Shelf (CCS); and the Optional Protocol of Signature concerning the Compulsory Settlement of Disputes (OPSD). There was some success with the 1958 Geneva Conventions before UNCLOS, particularly CTS, in the area of jurisdiction and sea territory. While UNCLOS have replaced most (but not all) of this Convention, not all signatories of this convention have signed UNCLOS, most notably the US.

referred to in the ensuing discussion are those of UNCLOS and they are also applicable to the *Grace 1* incident during its passage through the Strait of Gibraltar.[14] In addition, it is first necessary to acquire a grasp of the legal notions of sovereignty and jurisdiction within the context of UNCLOS. In international law, the notion of sovereignty emanates from the status of independent, autonomous statehood.[15] It can be asserted only by virtue of being a state. It represents the absolute, supreme manifestation of ownership and power over territory comprising *terra firma* and waterbodies. Jurisdiction, in a strictly legal sense, is the authority of a judicial body such as a court of law to apply and interpret the law and thereby administer justice. In a broader sense, jurisdiction is the legal competence of a lawmaking body such as a legislature to legislate.[16] In the context of UNCLOS, jurisdiction is the authority of a coastal state to legislate and regulate activities within certain defined limits. Also, jurisdiction is the competence of a coastal state to enforce laws administratively or in practice, or judicially through court action, or through diplomatic process. Thus, in the territorial sea, a coastal state enjoys a combination of both legislative as well as enforcement jurisdictions.[17] Finally, it should be noted that a coastal state's sovereign authority including jurisdiction diminishes seawards until it reaches a vanishing point where universality prevails.[18]

UNCLOS, often referred to as the 'constitution for the oceans',[19] codified the customary rules related to innocent passage and transit passage as part of freedom of navigation, propounded under the freedom of the seas.[20] UNCLOS establishes, inter alia, a comprehensive set of rules reconciling the rights of territorial sovereignty exercised by a coastal state in relation to its internal waters and territorial sea, and international straits, and the navigational rights of third-party states through those waters. Although states have sovereign rights over their territorial seas, the sovereignty of the coastal state is, however, not unlimited and is subject to the entitlement of the ships of a third-party state to innocent unimpeded passage through the coastal state's territorial sea. It is because the

[14] The UK is a party to UNCLOS by accession, and as of 2005, all EU members are parties to UNCLOS. Iran has signed the Convention but did not ratify. Syria has not signed the Convention. Gibraltar as an overseas territory of the UK does not have the authority to become party to treaties in its own right. The UK extends the territorial scope of its ratification of treaties to include Gibraltar. See 'Extension of treaties to overseas territories, available at assets.publishing.service.gov.uk/government/uploads/system/uploads/attachment_data/file/308103/Extension_to_OTs_guidance.pdf. The current status of UNLCOS is available at treaties.un.org/pages/ViewDetailsIII.aspx?src=TREATY&mtdsg_no=XXI-6&chapter=21&Temp=mtdsg3&clang=_en.

[15] PK Mukherjee, *Maritime Zones and Boundaries* (WMU Publications, 2001) 5.

[16] ibid.

[17] According to Churchill and Lowe, *The Law of the Sea* (1984), 'State practice and doctrine on the question of the extent of a coastal State's rights to enact legislation – its legislative, as opposed to its enforcement, jurisdiction – varied according to whether the territorial sea was regarded as a mere "bundle of servitudes" or as a belt of maritime territory under the plenary jurisdiction of the State. The aim in all cases was to reconcile the right of innocent passage with the legitimate interests of the coastal States in the enforcement of their laws in the territorial sea'. It is to be noted that plenary jurisdiction implies comprehensive jurisdiction to make and enforce laws. There are no limitations where plenary jurisdiction is claimed in applying sovereignty.

[18] For a detailed discussion on sovereignty and jurisdiction, see Dixon, *International law* (2013) 148–49; and H Yang, *Jurisdiction of the Coastal State over Foreign Merchant Ships in Internal Waters and the Territorial Sea* (Springer, 2006) 30–36.

[19] See TB (Tommy) Koh, 'A Constitution for the Oceans', Remarks made as President of the Third United Nations Conference on the Law of the Sea, adapted from the statements made on 6 and 11 December 1982 at the final session of the Conference at Montego Bay, available at www.un.org/depts/los/convention_agreements/texts/koh_english.pdf.

[20] See n 4.

freedom of navigation is of such great importance to all states that the right of innocent passage through the territorial sea has been generally recognised. While this right, at first glance, may appear to be straightforward, to prevent a coastal state from seeking to exercise its own discretion in interpreting 'innocent passage', UNCLOS sets out rules as to the precise manner in which the permitted encroachment into sovereign territorial seas may be employed. A brief discussion on the regimes of both innocent passage and transit passage under UNCLOS is made below.

A. Territorial Sea and Innocent Passage

The territorial sea regime comprises a 12-nautical-mile belt of water measured seaward from the baselines.[21] Article 2 provides that the sovereignty of a coastal state extends beyond its land territory into the territorial sea. This sovereignty is exercised subject to the right of innocent passage of a foreign ship.[22] The focus is on the 'manner' in which the passage is carried out, not the type of ship. In the *Corfu Channel case* (1949), the International Court of Justice (ICJ) relied on the criterion of 'whether the manner in which the passage was carried out was consistent with the principle of innocent passage'.[23] If a ship is engaging in innocent passage, the coastal state has no legal right to impede its passage, nor is it entitled to impose any requirements on foreign ships which have the practical effect of denying or infringing upon the right of innocent passage or to discriminate in form or in fact against the ships of any state. Although a coastal state is entitled to suspend innocent passage of third-party states' ships in its territorial sea, such right is, however, subject to express conditions laid down in Article 25(3).[24]

B. International Straits and Transit Passage

UNCLOS also affords various rights to a third-party state's ships to pass freely through straits used for international navigation.[25] The sovereignty of states bordering these

[21] Baselines are defined in Arts 5 and 7 of UNCLOS.

[22] Passage is defined in Art 18 and innocent passage in Art 19(1). Passage is innocent so long as it is not prejudicial to the peace, good order or security of the coastal state. In Art 19(2), 12 activities are identified as not constituting innocent passage. Under Art 19(2)(j) reference is made to 'research or survey activities' in one breath as an item of non-innocent passage. In Art 40, similarly, 'marine scientific research and hydrographic survey ships, may not carry out any research or survey activities' during transit passage through international straits without prior approval of the states bordering the relevant strait. Art 21(1) lists eight items in respect of which the coastal state may adopt laws and regulations in relation to innocent passage through the territorial sea.

[23] *Corfu Channel (United Kingdom of Great Britain and Northern Ireland v Albania)*, Judgment, ICJ Reports 1949, 30.

[24] Art 25(3) requires the suspension to be: temporary; applicable only to specified areas of the territorial sea (ie, it is not possible to suspend innocent passage throughout the entirety of the coastal state's territorial sea at one time); necessary for the protection of the coastal state's security, including weapons exercises; non-discriminatory in form or fact between foreign ships (ie, the suspension must not apply to only a specific state's ships); and published in advance to have effect.

[25] As background, it is important to note that in the pre-UNCLOS era, straits used for international navigation such as the Gibraltar fell within the high seas because of the customary prevalence of a three-nautical-mile territorial sea. With the expansion of the territorial sea to 12 nautical miles under UNCLOS,

straits is exercised within them subject to the right of 'transit passage' of foreign ships.[26] A definition of 'international strait' is conspicuous by its absence.[27] Article 38(2) defines 'transit passage' as 'the exercise ... of the freedom of navigation and overflight solely for the purpose of continuous and expeditious transit of the strait between one part of the high seas or an exclusive economic zone'. The requirement for continuous and expeditious transit does not, however, prevent a ship or aircraft from manoeuvring or conducting other necessary navigational activities in the strait for the purpose of entering or leaving the coastal state's territory. The normal rules on innocent passage through the territorial sea do not apply to passage through international straits as they differ in four different ways: first, all ships and aircrafts have a right of passage, including warships;[28] second, the right of transit passage includes overflight by all aircraft, including military aircraft;[29] third, it can only stop due to '*force majeure* and distress';[30] and finally, 'there shall be no suspension of transit passage'.[31] Also, it is important to strike the right balance between the navigational interest of third states and the interest of the coastal state bordering the strait.[32] Thus, contrary to the right of suspension of innocent passage through the territorial sea, there exists no entitlement to a coastal state to suspend transit passage by ships or aircraft through international straits.

C. The Conceivable Erosion of Freedom of Navigation

As mentioned above, in the context of UNCLOS, jurisdiction is the authority of a coastal state to legislate and regulate activities within certain defined limits. The modern interpretation of jurisdiction is based on the *Lotus case* (1927) that makes a clear distinction between legislative and enforcement jurisdictions.[33] While jurisdiction on land has no

these straits would have been subject to the sovereignty of the states bordering the strait. A new regime was thus created whereby foreign ships are given the right of 'transit passage' through these straits. This regime is dealt with in Part III, Arts 34–44.

[26] UNCLOS, Art 36 provides that the regime is not applicable 'to a strait used for international navigation if there exists through the strait a route through the high seas or through an exclusive economic zone of similar convenience with respect to navigational and hydrographical characteristics'. Art 37 provides that the regime of 'transit passage' applies to straits used for international navigation between one part of the high seas or an exclusive economic zone (EEZ) and another part of the high seas or an EEZ.

[27] Thus, whether a strait is used for international navigation is largely a question of fact, presumably left to the courts to decide in the event of a dispute. For example, in the *Corfu Channel* case (n 23), the ICJ concluded that there was a right of innocent passage in international straits, that this right was non-suspendable, and that it included warships; see Y Tanaka, *The International Law of the Sea*, 3rd edn (Cambridge University Press, 2019) 96–98.

[28] UNCLOS, Art 38(1).

[29] ibid.

[30] UNCLOS, Art 39(1)(c).

[31] UNCLOS, Art 44.

[32] See discussion on *Case Concerning Passage Through the Great Belt* in Tanaka, *International Law of the Sea* (2019) 130.

[33] In *the Case of the S.S. Lotus (France v Turkey)* Séries A No 10 PCIJ (1927) (the *Lotus Case*), the Permanent Court of International Justice (PCIJ) laid the two competing general rules of jurisdiction. It involved collision between a French mail steamer and a Turkish collier, named *Lotus* and *Boz-Kourt*, respectively. The collision resulted in the *Boz-Kourt* sinking and eight Turkish crew members lost their lives. The *Lotus* arrived in Constantinople and the French responsible officer for the *Lotus* and the captain for *Boz-Kourt* was tried in court. The officer of the *Lotus* claimed that the Turkish court lacked jurisdiction, a claim that prompted France and Turkey to send the question to the PCIJ, if the Turkish court had authority to judge the French officer. See Dixon (n 12) 148.

restrictions, jurisdiction at sea has certain limitations. Jurisdiction at sea exists between two competing principles, namely freedom of navigation and sovereignty, which grapple with each other for dominance. The right of innocent passage plays a pivotal role in this competition in the territorial sea.[34] However, subsequent developments, such as the 9/11 attacks,[35] and the rise in concerns related to protection and preservation of the marine environment,[36] have led to the gradual erosion of the principle of the freedom of navigation in favour of the principle of sovereignty.

UNCLOS, which has received 168 ratifications so far, is widely accepted because its provisions are broad and all-encompassing. However, as a treaty that seeks to be more all-encompassing, it eventually ends up becoming less specific. Although this does not mean that the right of innocent passage is not sufficiently covered in UNCLOS, it does suggest that in certain cases the answer cannot simply be derived from the provisions on innocent passage without examining the context. Some answers may also have to be gleaned from the development of customary law on the subject and the recognition of innocent passage as part of freedom of navigation. The right of innocent passage is an important principle that seeks to reconcile territorial sovereignty and the freedom of navigation.[37] The detention of *Grace 1* is a matter of concern as UNCLOS does not restrict freedom of navigation to safeguard national security, beyond the limited exception, as discussed in some detail in the next section of this chapter.

III. Maritime Lawfare

The international character and intertwined relationships in the shipping business makes maritime lawfare seem like a cat-and-mouse game for both sanctions imposing and evading states. The detention of *Grace 1* in Gibraltar reveals two sides of modern maritime lawfare: on one side are states that impose unilateral sanctions, ie use legal measures based on satellite imagery, information technology and behavioural analytics to expose contraventions; while on the other side are states that attempt to avoid sanctions, ie use legal structures to own and register ships in third countries to make it difficult to identify and trace the true beneficial interests.[38]

[34] It is to be noted that in the EEZ a coastal state only enjoys 'sovereign rights', a concept created by UNCLOS and consciously cast at a level lower than that of 'sovereignty'. Therefore, under UNCLOS 'sovereign rights' is not to be construed in the general sense of public international law as an element of the sovereignty per se. See UNCLOS, Art 56(1).

[35] See, eg, DR Rothwell and T Stephens, *The international law of the sea*, 2nd edn (Hart Publishing, 2016) 76; S Kaye, 'Freedom of Navigation in a Post 9/11 World: Security and Creeping Jurisdiction' in D Freestone, R Barnes and D Ong (eds), *The Law of the Sea: Progress and Prospects* (Oxford University Press, 2006) 348–51.

[36] Rothwell and Stephens (ibid) 76–77.

[37] Tanaka (n 27) 141.

[38] It is to be noted that Art 91 of UNCLOS allows states to fix conditions for the grant of ships' nationality. Pursuant to that, many developing states have established ship registries that permit the registration of ships in their jurisdictions without any or all of the strictures of the traditional closed registry system. These open registries currently account for 60% of the world's merchant fleet and many of them offers greater flexibility in certain aspects of the corporate structure. For example, a state with an open registry system may provide anonymity, through permitting greater use of bearer shares whereby the identity of the ultimate owner of the ship may be hidden. For a detailed discussion on nationality and registration of ships, see PK Mukherjee and M Brownrigg, *Farthing on International Shipping*, 4th edn (Springer, 2013) 199–222.

The states that impose sanctions use legal hurdles as a financial weaponry to mandate shipowners, managers, charterers, brokers, flag registries, oil companies, port operators, classification societies, insurance companies and banks to implement appropriate controls to hit carefully chosen targets linked to an adversary to restrict trade and transportation of goods.[39] Reports and advisories issued by the US, for example, have announced heightened compliance expectations that, if not recognised, would present significantly increased risk of adverse regulatory action for all actors involved in the maritime industry, including support players such as banks and insurers.[40] By making the expectations explicit, the advisories significantly increase enforcement exposure and reduce available mitigation for parties that fail to enhance their compliance programmes accordingly.[41] Conversely, the states that attempt to avoid sanctions use various tactics to escape detection, such as establishing shell companies, transhipment, dark operations by switching off automatic identification system (AIS), and frequent name changes to ships.[42]

Given the above, the remainder of this section first analyses the nature of the sanctions that Gibraltar applied to detain *Grace 1*, as well as the legality and acceptance of such sanctions under international law. Then, blockade and interdiction, which are the two predominant maritime actions to enforce sanctions against target states, are discussed briefly. The circumstances surrounding the *Grace 1* incident is then discussed in contextual detail to examine the legal issues related to innocent passage. Finally, lessons learnt on maritime lawfare from the *Grace 1* incident is briefly presented.

A. Unilateral Sanctions as a Tool for Peaceful Coercion

States have long resorted to unilateral sanctions to further their political and economic objectives, but their legality in customary international law is contested.[43] In recent years, unilateral sanctions have been the subject of severe criticism based on the

[39] For example, in 2019, the US Department of Treasury's Office of Foreign Assets Control (OFAC) issued a series of stern warnings for maritime stakeholders to comply with maritime sanctions against Iran, Syria and North Korea.

[40] For example, see OFAC advisory to the maritime petroleum shipping community on the subject, 'Sanctions Risks Related to Shipping Petroleum and Petroleum Products from Iran', issued on 4 September 2019, available at home.treasury.gov/system/files/126/iran_advisory_09032019.pdf.

[41] For example, in January 2019, OFAC reached a million-dollar settlement with elf Cosmetics Inc arising from the company's failure to identify North Korean content in false eyelash kits sourced from suppliers in China. That settlement came on the heels of a strongly worded July 2018 advisory to the manufacturing sector, urging adoption of due diligence intended to eliminate North Korean forced labour and North Korean content from US supply chains.

[42] For example, reports suggest that the beneficial ownership of *Grace 1* remains unclear from the records held in Singapore. Ownership databases also show connection between the registered owner and manager where both are listed under the same address in Singapore. Before the seizure of the ship in July 2019, the last registered port call was in 2017, at Qingdao, China. Other port calls it may have made during the two-year period has been masked by turning off its AIS from time to time. See O Primor, 'The Multinational Story Behind the *Grace 1*' *Windward* (5 July 2019), available at wnwd.com/blog/the-multinational-story-behind-the-grace-1. See also C Baraniuk, 'Tracking sanctions-busting ships on the high seas' *BBC News* (1 February 2019), available at www.bbc.com/news/business-47046979.

[43] CE Cameron, 'Developing a Standard for Politically Related State Economic Sanction' (1991) 13 *Michigan Journal of International Law* 218–54.

negative impact that such coercive measures have on human rights.[44] While the term 'sanctions' is used in common parlance, the UN Charter[45] uses the term 'measures',[46] and the EU uses the term 'restrictive measures'.[47] The EU, as a supranational organisation comprised of several Member States, imposes sanctions against non-Member States.[48] EU sanctions are usually embedded in larger contexts of overlapping policy instruments and other sanctions regimes. There are three main types of EU sanctions applied in combination with other sanctions regimes: first, the EU implements UN sanctions; second, EU autonomous sanctions are available that go beyond UN sanctions, sometimes described as 'supplementary' measures; and third, EU autonomous sanctions applied in the absence of UN sanctions.[49] The EU sanctions on Syria, as related to the *Grace 1* incident, can be classified under this third category. These autonomous sanctions are generally applied in conjunction with unilateral sanctions by the US or by other countries or regional organisations. They are employed in instances where the UN Security Council is unable to reach an agreement due to opposition by a permanent member. They also serve as an instrument of EU foreign policy, with a view to expressing concern about what is believed to be unacceptable behaviour and to reaffirming EU values on the international scene. For the purposes of this chapter, EU autonomous sanctions against Syria would therefore be considered as unilateral sanctions.

Economic sanctions are targeted towards a state, legal body, or individual by restricting exports and imports, and disrupting financial transactions.[50] The first two are pure trade-related restrictions and are relatively easy to comprehend.[51] Disrupting financial transactions may include the freezing of bank accounts or other assets of the targeted state or entities, or even withholding aid.[52] Economic sanctions, which is often referred to as 'economic warfare',[53] has emerged as a standard foreign policy tool used in both unilateral and multilateral context.[54]

[44] For example, on 26 September 2014, the Human Rights Council adopted resolution 27/21 and Corr.1 on human rights and unilateral coercive measures. The resolution stresses that unilateral coercive measures and legislation are contrary to international law, international humanitarian law, the Charter and the norms and principles governing peaceful relations among states, and highlights that in the long term, these measures may result in social problems and raise humanitarian concerns in the states targeted. The resolution is available at digitallibrary.un.org/record/781801?ln=en.

[45] United Nations, *Charter of the United Nations*, 24 October 1945, 1 UNTS XVI, available at www.un.org/en/sections/un-charter/un-charter-full-text.

[46] N Ronzitti, 'Sanctions as Instrument of Coercive Diplomacy: An International Law Perspective' in N Ronzitti (ed), *Coercive Diplomacy, Sanctions and International Law* (Brill Nijhoff, 2016) 9; UN Charter, Art 41.

[47] Ronzitti (ibid) 11.

[48] PL Lindseth, 'Supranational Organizations' in JK Cogan, I Hurd and I Johnstone (eds), *The Oxford Handbook of International Organizations* (Oxford University Press, 2016) 152.

[49] T Biersteker, and C Portela, 'EU sanctions in context: three types', EU Institute for Security Studies, July 2015, available at www.iss.europa.eu/sites/default/files/EUISSFiles/Brief_26_EU_sanctions.pdf.

[50] GC Hufbauer, JJ Schott, and KA Elliott, *Economic Sanctions Reconsidered*, Vol 1, 2nd edn (Institute for International Economics, 1990) 36; T Guay, 'Economic Sanctions' in R Kolb (ed), *The SAGE encyclopedia of business ethics and society* Vol 1 (SAGE Publications, 2018) 1026–28.

[51] Hufbauer, Schott, and Elliott (ibid) 36.

[52] ibid.

[53] M Happold, 'Economic sanctions and international law' in M Happold, and P Eden (eds), *Economic Sanctions and International Law* (Oxford, Hart Publishing, 2016) 1.

[54] ibid.

The legality of unilateral economic sanctions is a complex subject.[55] While the Security Council pursuant to the UN Charter can make recommendations or decide on sanctions that are binding on all Member States,[56] but non-UN sanctions do not have such international legal basis.

> Consistent with the Lotus Principle of international law,[57] as a general proposition and in the absence of positive legal obligations to the contrary, it is certainly correct that a State has the legal discretion to choose with which other States it pleases to have, and to allow the legal and natural persons subject to its jurisdiction to have, economic/financial dealings.[58]

Therefore, the question of legality does not arise in the context of the decision of a state to impose sanctions, but on the intention of such an action. If the action is taken during peacetime and is coercive towards another state, then such action may be deemed as unlawful.[59] It is so because there exists the general principle of 'non-intervention' in customary international law, which has also been incorporated in various UN resolutions.[60] The principle of non-intervention makes it unlawful for one state to attempt to influence another state's sovereignty.[61] Some scholars consider economic sanctions imposed outside the Security Council as 'economic warfare' and have termed them unlawful based on *jus in bello*, which is applicable to 'normal' warfare.[62] In general, most scholars criticise economic sanctions as they cause suffering for innocent civilian population.

B. Maritime Methods to Enforce Unilateral Sanctions

Maritime methods which are generally used to physically restrict ships to transport goods to a target state are of two types, namely blockade and interdiction.[63] The classic maritime blockade is a method of warfare by which a belligerent party(ies) to an armed conflict seek to prevent all ships and aircraft (enemy, neutral and friendly) from

[55] D Joyner, 'International Legal Limits on the Ability of States to Lawfully Impose International Economic/Financial Sanctions' in AZ Marossi and MR Bassett, *Economic Sanctions under International Law: Unilateralism, Multilateralism, Legitimacy, and Consequences* (Springer, 2015) 85.

[56] UN Charter, Arts 25, 39–51. For a detailed discussion see M Bothe, 'Compatibility and Legitimacy of Sanctions Regimes' in N Ronzitti (ed), *Coercive Diplomacy, Sanctions and International Law* (Brill Nijhoff, 2016) 34.

[57] This principle provides that 'restrictions upon the independence of States cannot … be presumed' and that international law recognizes that states possess 'a wide measure of discretion which is only limited in certain cases by prohibitive rules.' *Lotus case* (*France v Turkey*) (n 33).

[58] Joyner, 'International Legal Limits' (2015) 86.

[59] ibid, 86–87.

[60] For example, the General Assembly adopted resolution 3281 (XXIX) containing the 'Charter of Economic Rights and Duties of States' on 12 December 1974, and article 32 states that 'no State may use or encourage the use of economic, political or any other type of measures to coerce another State in order to obtain from it the subordination of the exercise of its sovereign rights'.

[61] Joyner (n 55) 88–89.

[62] ibid, 86–87; Happold, 'Economic sanctions' (2016); see also V Lowe and A Tzanakopoulos, 'Economic Warfare' in *Max Planck Encyclopedia of Public International Law* (Oxford University Press, 2012) section 1.

[63] LE Fielding, 'Maritime Interception: Counterpiece of Economic sanction in the New world order' (1993) 53 *Louisiana Law Review* 1191, 1204; H Heinegg, 'Blockades and Interdictions' in M Weller (ed), *The Oxford Handbook of the Use of Force in International Law* (Oxford University Press, 2015) 927, 934.

entering or exiting specified ports, or coastal areas belonging to, occupied by, or under the control of an opposing force(s).[64] Blockade is expressly referred to in Article 42 of the UN Charter, the long-standing Paris Declaration,[65] and military manuals of several countries.[66] The Declaration of London[67] lays down the basic accepted concepts of blockade.[68] Blockade by its very nature has to be blocking off the affected state's coastline in some way.[69] Therefore, the so-called British 'long distance blockade' of World Wars I and II, where large swathes of sea were patrolled by surface vessels and submarines, has been declared unlawful and does not constitute as blockade.[70] Also, barring of passage through an international strait is not blockade in the strict sense of the concept.[71] The action against *Grace 1* by Gibraltar happened far off from the coast of Syria and therefore does not constitute as blockade.

Interdiction, on the other hand, could be 'stopping, boarding, inspecting, searching, and potentially seizing the cargo or the vessel'.[72] What these various interventions share in common are 'that they have an impact on the freedom of navigation enjoyed by foreign vessels'.[73] Each of the above interventions have different 'legal bases' and 'constitutes an infringement of the sovereignty of the flag State or the State of registry'.[74] The practice of the Security Council, state practice, and the progressive development of international treaty law provide evidence of the legality of interdiction operations if they serve a recognised purpose.[75] Since interdiction is a legal action that involves use of force, therefore, such use of force must be legal.[76]

Although interdiction is different from blockade in several ways, the most important distinction between the two methods is that if a blockade is done without the support of the UN, then it is an act of aggression.[77] In contrast, an interdiction, if not supported by a suitable legal basis, would constitute as an unlawful intervention, but not an act of aggression.[78]

The legal bases for interdiction can be gleaned from the provisions of UNCLOS and the Suppression of Unlawful Acts (SUA) Convention, as amended by the 2005

[64] P Drew, *The Law of Maritime Blockade: Past, Present, and Future*, 1st edn (Oxford University Press, 2017) 113. Also, Fielding (ibid) 1207.

[65] Declaration Respecting Maritime Law, Paris, 30 March 1856.

[66] Heinegg (n 63), 926

[67] London Declaration Concerning the Laws of Naval Warfare, 1909 (not entered into force).

[68] It is based on four rules: 1) It 'must be established by the government of the belligerent nation', together with a declaration which have the minimum requirement of 'the date the blockade is to begin, its geographical limits, and the grace period granted neutral vessels and aircraft to leave the area'; 2) The State must 'notify all affected nations of its imposition'; 3) The blockade 'must be effective'; and 4) It 'must not bar access to or departure from neutral ports and coasts'. Fielding, 'Maritime Interception' 1195–96.

[69] Heinegg, 'Blockades' (2015) 927.

[70] Fielding (n 63) 1205–07.

[71] Heinegg (n 63) 927.

[72] ibid 934–36.

[73] ibid 936–38.

[74] ibid.

[75] ibid 926.

[76] ibid 936–38.

[77] United Nations General Assembly Resolution 3314, XXIX, Art 3(c); Fielding (n 63) 1198–99.

[78] Fielding (n 63) 1199.

Protocol.[79] Article 27 of UNCLOS does not give a coastal state criminal jurisdiction over foreign ships passing through its territorial sea, except in specified cases.[80] Also, a violation of the domestic criminal law of the coastal state will justify the exercise of its criminal jurisdiction only in cases where the crime has been committed on board a ship passing through the territorial sea after having left the coastal state's internal waters.[81] If the ship concerned has not left a port of the coastal state, the exercise of criminal jurisdiction is limited.[82] If the offence giving rise to interdiction measures has been committed before entry into the territorial sea and if the ship, proceeding from a foreign port, is only passing through the territorial sea without entering internal waters, the coastal state may not take any steps on board the ship.[83] A coastal state 'may take the necessary steps in its territorial sea to prevent passage which is not innocent'.[84] On the high seas, interdiction is justified if a ship is engaged in piracy, slave trade, unauthorised broadcasting, missing nationality, or the same nationality as a state's warship.[85] The SUA Convention also allows for interdiction on the high seas if the flag state of a ship authorises for boarding and searching on suspicion of offences as listed in article 3.[86] Finally, a state can prevent a ship from entering a zone where a rescue operation is underway.[87]

For interdiction, the rules for use of force is of particular interest. The UN Charter[88] stipulates a general ban on the use of force in international relations, with certain specific exceptions.[89] These exceptions can be divided into three broad categories: Charter exceptions; implicit Charter exceptions; and exceptions outside the Charter based on customary international law.[90]

[79] Convention for the Suppression of Unlawful Acts Against the Safety of Maritime Navigation (SUA Convention), Rome, 10 March 1988, 1678 UNTS 221; reprinted in (1988) 27 ILM 668. Protocol for the Suppression of Unlawful Acts against the Safety of Fixed Platforms Located on the Continental Shelf, Rome, 10 March 1988, 1678 UNTS 304; Protocol of 2005 to the Convention for the Suppression of Unlawful Acts Against the Safety of Maritime Navigation, London, 14 October 2005, IMO Doc LEG/CONF. 15/21; Protocol of 2005 to the Protocol for the Suppression of Unlawful Acts against the Safety of Fixed Platforms Located on the Continental Shelf, London, 14 October 2005, IMO Doc LEG/CONF. 15/22.

[80] Article 27 provides that a state should not intervene unless the criminal act done by an individual is related to the coastal state, disturbs the coastal state, the ship asks for assistance or if it is necessary for the suppression of illicit traffic in narcotic drugs or psychotropic substances.

[81] UNCLOS, Art 27(2).

[82] UNCLOS, Art 27(1).

[83] UNCLOS, Art 27(5). Note, however, that this restriction does not apply to cases provided for in UNCLOS Part XII on the protection of the marine environment or with respect to violations of laws and regulations adopted in accordance with Part V which deals with exclusive economic zone.

[84] UNCLOS, Art 25(1). Activities identified as not constituting innocent passage is listed in UNCLOS, Art 19(2), which is discussed in more details in section III.C of this chapter.

[85] UNLCOS, Art 110. D Guilfoyle, *Shipping interdiction and the law of the Sea* (Cambridge University Press, 2011) 23–24.

[86] Heinegg (n63) 939.

[87] Here interdiction is implied when assistance is rendered at sea pursuant to UNCLOS, Art 98; see Heinegg (n 63) 938–39.

[88] UN Charter, Art 2(4) stipulates that 'All Members shall refrain in their international relations from the threat or use of force against the territorial integrity or political independence of any State, or in any other manner inconsistent with the Purposes of the United Nations'.

[89] N Schrijver, 'The Ban on the Use of Force in the UN Charter' in M Weller (ed), *The Oxford Handbook of the Use of Force in International Law* (Oxford University Press, 2015) 465–70.

[90] ibid.

Charter exceptions are of three types: those based on Articles 53(1), 77 and 107, which are 'measures against former enemy states from the Second World War'; those based on Article 24, which gives power to the Security Council via Articles 39 and 42 to authorise the use of force to maintain or restore international peace and security; and the right of self-defence, which is set out in Article 51.[91] The first type of Charter exception is rendered obsolete and lacks any current legal relevance. The second type of Charter exception when applied in the absence of UN sanctions do not have the recommendation or command of the Security Council to initiate military enforcement action to mitigate a threat to peace, breach of peace, or an act of aggression. Hence, use of force based on unilateral sanctions is not permissible. Under the third type, states have the right to both individual and collective self-defence through use of force in case of an 'armed attack' or an 'imminent armed attack'.

Implicit Charter exceptions are of two types: those 'uniting for peace' based on UN General Assembly Resolution 377, which gives power to the General Assembly to make the same recommendation as the Security Council, should the latter fail in its objective; and those based on the UN General Assembly Resolution 3070 (1973), which allows 'the right of National Liberation Movements to employ all necessary means and seek international assistance in their legitimate struggle against colonialism, racist regimes, or alien occupation'.[92]

Finally, there are two non-Charter exceptions to protect life, founded on customary international law. The first exception recognise that a state can take military action to rescue its own nationals from life-threatening situations, such as, upon being held hostage, or stuck in an armed conflict in another state.[93] This exception has been controversial ever since the adoption of the recourse to war provisions of the UN Charter.[94] There is significant disagreement among legal scholars as to whether the protection of nationals abroad can be looked upon as protecting the state and the discussion has not produced universal agreement on the legal basis for or even the lawfulness of such action.[95] The second exception is regarding protection of non-nationals through use of force in another state's territory, which is allowed 'in the event of flagrant and mass violations of human rights'.[96] With respect to this exception, limited state practice[97] and the absence of a widely accepted *opinio juris* regarding the legitimacy of the use of force for humanitarian purposes not authorised by the Security Council has led scholars to conclude that humanitarian intervention without the authorisation of the Security Council cannot be regarded as a customary international law exception to the prohibition on the use of force.[98]

[91] ibid, 473.

[92] ibid, 474.

[93] K Watkin, *Fighting at the Legal Boundaries: Controlling the Use of Force in Contemporary Conflict* (Oxford University Press, 2016) 383.

[94] ibid, 386.

[95] For a comprehensive discussion on the issue, see ibid, 386–87.

[96] Schrijver, 'The Ban on the Use of Force' (2015) 474–75.

[97] Examples relating to this exception are Operation Provide Comfort in 1991, aimed at the protection of Kurds in northern Iraq, and the Shi'ites in the south, and the North Atlantic Treaty Organization (NATO) action in Kosovo in 1999 under the name Operation Allied Force in response to the suppression of the Albanians in Kosovo by the Serbs. See ibid, 475.

[98] Schrijver (n 89) 476.

Another possible argument to justify the use of force through an interdiction could be a third-party countermeasure.[99] The state practice on third-party countermeasure is fast evolving and its use in contemporary international relations to respond to breaches of norms expressing community interests, particularly in the fields of human rights and humanitarian law, is becoming increasingly common.[100] However, it is also hotly debated within the international legal community as to whether the instances where the third-party countermeasures have been exercised did 'contribute to the generality and consistency of practice necessary for the existence of customary international law'.[101] While the aforesaid proposition could be an interesting inquiry in its own right, a detailed discussion is beyond the scope of this chapter.

Be that as it may, Gibraltar did not invoke any of the above exceptions or make an argument for a third-party countermeasure to justify its maritime action on *Grace 1*.[102] Therefore, it is relevant to consider whether there existed a connection between the use of force and the activities not constituting innocent passage, as stipulated in Article 19 of UNCLOS.

C. The Detention of *Grace 1* and its Right of Innocent Passage

Grace 1 was detained pursuant to the Sanctions Regulations 2019 made under the Sanctions Act 2019.[103] The Sanctions Regulations give the Chief Minister of Gibraltar powers to designate a ship as a 'specified ship' if he 'has reasonable grounds to suspect that the ship … has been, or is likely to be, involved in a breach of the EU Regulation'. A 'specified ship notice' was issued by Gibraltar on 3 July 2019 naming the *Grace 1*.[104] Under the Sanctions Regulations a specified ship 'must be detained if it is in British Gibraltar Territorial Waters (BGTW)'[105] and 'may not leave BGTW unless permitted to do so by an order of the court or where the notice designating the ship as a specified ship has been revoked'.[106] Gibraltar confirmed that the ship was well inside its territorial sea when boarded and *Grace 1* was detained under an order of the Chief Justice of the Supreme Court of Gibraltar.

[99] A third-party countermeasure is defined as an otherwise unlawful act of a peaceful character taken by a state other than an injured state in response to a breach of a communitarian norm (obligations owed to the international community as a whole (*erga omnes*), such as the prohibitions of genocide, slavery and torture; and those that are owed to a group of states, such as under a multilateral treaty regime (*erga omnes partes*)) owed to it (as defined in Art 48 of the Articles on Responsibility of States for Internationally Wrongful Acts (ARSIWA), adopted by the ILC in 2001) in order to obtain cessation and reparation. See M Dawidowicz, *Third-Party Countermeasures in International Law* (Cambridge University Press, 2017) 34.

[100] Dawidowicz, ibid 282–284.

[101] F Paddeu, 'Book Review of Third-Party Countermeasures in International Law' (2018) 77 *Cambridge Law Journal* 427, 428.

[102] See Notice of revocation of specification of ship (n 10).

[103] The Sanctions Act 2019, Act No 2019-06, available at www.gibraltarlaws.gov.gi/uploads/legislations/sanctions/2019-06o.pdf#viewer.action=download.

[104] Specified ship notice (LN. 2019/132), available at www.gibraltarlaws.gov.gi/legislations/specified-ship-notice-2019-4641/download. This notice was subsequently revoked by the Notice of revocation of specification of ship (n 10).

[105] It is to be noted that UNCLOS only uses the term territorial 'sea', although in some national legislation, such as in the UK and its Overseas Territories including Gibraltar, territorial 'water' is used.

[106] Sanctions Regulation 2019, Reg 6(1).

The legal bases for the detention of *Grace 1* by Gibraltar may be gleaned from the notice of revocation of specification of ship.[107] This notice states that the detention 'was required for the purposes of complying with Council Regulation (EU) No. 36/2012 concerning restrictive measures in view of the situation in Syria'.[108] Article 14(2) of the EU Regulation No 36/2012 stipulates that 'no funds or economic resources shall be made available, directly or indirectly, to or for the benefit of the natural or legal persons, entities or bodies listed in Annex II and IIa'.[109] The oil transported by *Grace 1* qualified as provision of 'economic resources' to the Baniyas Oil Refinery, which is subject to EU sanctions pursuant to a list publicised by the EU in July 2014.[110] The Sanctions Regulation 2019 of Gibraltar was therefore made in compliance with the international obligation mentioned in section 16(1)(b) of the Sanctions Act 2019.

Be that as it may, from the point of view of international maritime law, Article 2 of UNCLOS stipulates that a coastal state has sovereignty over its territorial sea, which is exercised 'subject' to the Convention and to other rules of international law. As mentioned earlier, in the context of UNCLOS, jurisdiction is the authority of a state to legislate and regulate activities within certain defined limits. A coastal state can take action against passing foreign ships in its territorial sea under its domestic law. However, such domestic law has to comply with UNCLOS when the coastal state is a party to that Convention. When *Grace 1* made its passage through the Strait of Gibraltar, the ship was stopped and detained in BGTW. Gibraltar could have exercised enforcement jurisdiction over *Grace 1*, if the passage was non-innocent.[111] Gibraltar's newly drafted regulations forced the detention, as the ship 'must be detained if it is in BGTW'.[112] But, such regulations are part of Gibraltar's enforcement jurisdiction, which as a coastal state, Gibraltar is not allowed to exercise unless it is within the limits prescribed under UNCLOS.

Grace 1 was seized in BGTW when it entered by prior arrangement with a Gibraltar ship agent for spares and provisions.[113] Gibraltar and the UK both consider that BGTW extend three nautical miles from the territory in accordance with UNCLOS.[114] When *Grace 1* sailed through the Strait of Gibraltar, the regime of 'transit passage' was

[107] ibid.

[108] ibid, s 2.

[109] Notice of revocation of specification of ship (n 10) para 3. Annex II and IIa of Council Regulation (EU) No 36/2012 refers to an exhaustive list of natural or legal entities that are included in the restrictive measures.

[110] Notice of revocation of specification of ship (n 10) para 4. The list is made pursuant to Council Regulation (EU) No 36/2012, Annex IV via Article 1(e).

[111] UNCLOS, Arts 19 and 25, which is discussed in detail below.

[112] Sanctions Regulation 2019, Reg 6(1)(a).

[113] Notice of revocation of specification of ship (n 10) para 1.

[114] Spain insists that the Treaty of Utrecht did not cede any coastal waters to Gibraltar. However, UK's claim to territorial waters around Gibraltar extend to a limit of three nautical miles around Gibraltar. The limit is restricted to two nautical miles on the west side, in the Bay of Algeciras, where a median line exists between British and Spanish waters. The Territorial Sea Act, 1987 of the UK extended its waters up to the 12 nautical miles, the maximum permitted by Art 3 of UNCLOS. However, the provisions of the above Act were not extended to the British Overseas Territories, so the UK's claim to territorial waters remains up to three nautical miles from Gibraltar. See 'Gibraltar: Territorial Waters', Question for Foreign and Commonwealth Office, available at questions-statements.parliament.uk/written-questions/detail/2016-09-14/46430. A map showing the territorial waters around Gibraltar provided by the Foreign & Commonwealth Office of UK is available at publications.parliament.uk/pa/cm201415/cmselect/cmfaff/461/46107.htm.

applicable pursuant to Article 37. However, when the ship entered BGTW for spares and provisions, it interrupted its transit passage. Such interruption was not due to '*force majeure* and distress', as allowed under Article 39(1)(c). Based on the chain of events mentioned above, the passage of *Grace 1* through BGTW is therefore examined under the regime of 'innocent passage' and not that of 'transit passage'.

Article 25(1) permits a coastal state to take the necessary steps in its territorial sea to prevent passage which is not innocent, while Article 19(2) lists 12 activities that are identified as not constituting innocent passage. In the US–USSR joint statement on the interpretation of innocent passage, the activities listed in Article 19(2) has been set out as exhaustive.[115] However, in view of one scholar, the list in Article 19(2) is non-exhaustive,[116] as it pertains to something that is considered 'prejudicial to the peace, good order or security of the coastal State' under Article 19(1).[117] The scholar argues that the interpretation of Article 19(2) should not be taken too far, without considering Article 19(1), as the focus should be on whether a breach has occurred in accordance with the stipulation in Article 19(1).[118] The scholar also extends an additional viewpoint according to which a breach of Article 19(2) is not a breach at all if it is not done with the intent to breach Article 19(1).[119] With respect to this viewpoint, he argues that the challenge is that even if one considers the list in Article 19(2) as exhaustive, it may be difficult to determine in a uniform manner when a breach has occurred. For example, instruments used for ordinary navigation can also be used for marine scientific research and hydrographic surveys, and UNCLOS does not prescribe any specific kind of evaluation to determine whether or not a ship is 'carrying out … research or survey activities' under UNCLOS Article 19(2)(j)).[120] Also, it is to be noted in this context that even if an action is deemed as non-innocent, that action must have occurred in the territorial sea for the ship to lose its innocence. An action taken outside the territorial sea cannot result in a breach of Article 19.[121] Thus, it is clear from the above discussion that the interpretation of Article 19 can differ based on law and practice of a coastal state.

The notice of revocation does not specify what breach under Article 19 could have possibly resulted in the passage of the *Grace 1* through BGTW to become non-innocent. One possible line of argumentation may be that Gibraltar considered the list of activities under Article 19(2) as non-exhaustive and also interpreted the violation of the EU

[115] The US–USSR Joint Statement on the Uniform Interpretation of Rules of International Law Governing Innocent Passage (1989), s 3, states: 'Article 19 of the Convention of 1982 sets out in paragraph 2 an exhaustive list of activities that would render passage not innocent. A ship passing through the territorial sea that does not engage in any of those activities is in innocent passage.'

[116] Yang, *Jurisdiction of the Coastal State* (2006) 167–69.

[117] UNCLOS, Art 19(1).

[118] Yang (n 18) 168.

[119] ibid.

[120] See ibid, 169. However, it is submitted that shore stations may observe from the movement of a ship whether it is carrying out, for example, hydrographic survey. Hydrography consists of two dimensions; one is primarily the determination of water depth at sea or bathymetry; and the other is the physical location or position where that depth is to be found expressed in geographical coordinates of latitude and longitude. The practical methodology employed for obtaining hydrographic data through hydrographic survey comprise of two parameters, namely, depth sounding and corresponding, co-relative positioning of the depth. For this, a ship needs to move in parallel lines in grids, a movement which could be easily identified from a shore station.

[121] This requirement is spelled out in Art 19(2) of UNCLOS, which states that 'passage of a foreign ship shall be considered to be prejudicial to the peace, good order or security of the coastal State if *in the territorial sea it engages* in any of the following activities'; see Yang (n 18) 164.

sanctions against Syria as 'prejudicial' to its 'peace, good order or security', under Article 19(1).[122] However, such reasoning is problematic for several reasons. First, the UK is not directly involved with the war in Syria. Second, the sanctions do not relate to any specific security threat on the UK; instead the sanctions are intended to create economic and political pressure on the Syrian Government to end the civil war. Finally, detaining *Grace 1* simply because it is sailing to Syria is contrary to UNCLOS. Gibraltar is bound by Article 24(1)(b) of UNCLOS to not 'discriminate in form or in fact against the ships of any State or against ships carrying cargoes to, from or on behalf of any State'. Moreover, UNCLOS does not restrict freedom of navigation to safeguard national security, beyond the limited exception in Article 25(3). As such, any blanket closure of the territorial seas to ships connected to a target state would be a violation of the right of innocent passage under Article 17. The state imposing unilateral sanctions may claim that restrictions placed on the ships of the target state are necessary for the purposes of national security and, therefore, it may seek to rely on the right of temporary suspension under Article 25(3). Such suspension to the territorial seas is, however, not permissible under UNCLOS if there is no indication that they are temporary suspensions; they apply to the entirety of the states' territorial seas; and they apply not only to the ships of the target state, but also to all ships traversing the waters. If the restrictions are placed only to the ships of the target state, they would be considered discriminatory.

More importantly, if Article 19(1) is applied independently of Article 19(2), it may result in change in state practice and lead to undesirable transformation of the doctrine of freedom of navigation. As discussed above, theoretically it is possible to interpret the list in Article 19(2) in several different ways, but a narrow interpretation of Article 19 is in the best interests of the international community. States have been careful in applying the rules of Article 19, and so far, there is limited state practice related to independent use of paragraph 1. Gibraltar's attempt to apply EU unilateral sanctions may seem as a plausible interpretation of Article 19(1), but applying that as established state practice is currently not tenable. However, a repeat of the *Grace 1* incident to enforce unilateral sanctions through independent use of paragraph 1 may establish new state practice and change the interpretation of Article 19. Such a development must be avoided as it would be detrimental to well-established principles of international maritime law developed over hundreds of years.

D. Lessons Learnt on Maritime Lawfare from the *Grace 1* Incident

The *Grace 1* incident illustrates both the potential and pitfalls of maritime lawfare. Diplomats have argued that 'a decision to impose sanctions may be taken less on its intrinsic merits than because of its attractions in relation to the alternatives'.[123] When the choice is between no action at all or military action, then using unilateral sanctions seems to be a reasonable intermediate position. In that respect, maritime

[122] Notice of revocation of specification of ship (n 10) para 2 mentions that 'the detention of the Vessel was required for the purposes of complying with Council Regulation (EU) No 36/2012 of 18 January 2012 concerning restrictive measures in view of the situation in Syria'.
[123] R Renwick, *Economic Sanctions* (Hamilton Printing Company, 1981) 1.

lawfare may seem to have the potential to be exceptionally powerful in peacefully and inexpensively achieving real-time military objectives traditionally achieved by force of arms.

However, states might wish to avoid instigating a maritime lawfare against adversaries that can escalate the situation. Iran called the seizure of *Grace 1* an 'illegal interception' and a diplomatic crisis began between the UK and Iran. On 19 July 2019, Iran responded by seizure of the UK-flagged and Sweden-owned oil tanker, the *Stena Impero*, in the Strait of Hormuz claiming that the tanker had violated 'international maritime rules'.[124] The tanker was en route to a port in Saudi Arabia when Iran's Islamic Revolutionary Guard Corps (IRGC) seized it and directed it to the nearby Iranian port of Bandar Abbas. The Iranian authorities gave scant detail of what unlawful actions caused them to detain the tanker and the information seems contradictory: one set of reports claims that the tanker collided with a fishing vessel and subsequently failed to respond to calls from the smaller craft; another claims that the tanker violated navigation rules; and a third qualified the detention as a countermeasure.[125]

The tit-for-tat seizures led to political debates across the world and increased diplomatic activities to resolve the situation without resorting to military action.[126] The co-chair of the EU's foreign relations committee and former Swedish Prime Minister, Carl Bildt, pinpointed the ambiguities of the UK's action in Gibraltar, saying:

> The legality of the UK seizure of a tanker heading for Syria with oil from Iran intrigues me. One refers to EU sanctions against Syria, but Iran is not a member of the EU. And the EU as a principle doesn't impose its sanctions on others. That's what the US does.[127]

While *Grace 1* was at detention in Gibraltar, it was entered into the Iranian ship register and was renamed as *Adrian Darya 1*.[128] On 15 August 2019, *Grace 1* (*Adrian Darya 1*) was ordered to be released by the Gibraltar Supreme Court upon receiving written assurances from Iran that the tanker would not sail to countries 'subject to European Union sanctions'.[129] During the release Gibraltar's Chief Minister stated:

> [T]his assurance has the effect of ensuring that we have deprived the Assad regime in Syria of more than one hundred and forty million dollars of valuable crude oil. … In light of the

[124] Mindful of the scope of this chapter, no analytical discussion is made on the *Stena Impero* incident.

[125] See D Osler, 'When can a State seize a vessel?' *Lloyd's List, Maritime Intelligence* (23 July 2019), available at lloydslist.maritimeintelligence.informa.com/LL1128496/When-can-a-state-seize-a-vessel. See also, M Hartwig, 'Tanker Games – The Law Behind the Action', *EJIL:Talk! Blog of the European Journal of International Law* (20 August 2019), available at www.ejiltalk.org/tanker-games-the-law-behind-the-action.

[126] The UK Government insisted that *Grace 1* was seized due to its suspected destination to a port in Syria and not due to the fact that the ship was carrying Iranian oil. UK asserted that *Grace 1* circumnavigated Africa before being stopped at the Mediterranean's western entrance in the strait of Gibraltar, which left little doubt that the ship was bound for Syria. UK argued that EU sanctions against Syria were there to be enforced and international law to be upheld. Critics found UK's decision odd as few previous shipments of oil to Syria have been impounded. The Spanish claimed that the UK acted under the instruction of the US as the Trump administration continues to make attempts to freeze all Iranian oil exports as part of its policy of maximum economic sanctions designed to force the Iranians to reopen talks on the nuclear deal signed in 2015.

[127] P Wintour, 'Gulf crisis: story began with UK's seizure of Iranian-flagged ship in Gibraltar' *The Guardian* (20 Jul 2019), available at www.theguardian.com/world/2019/jul/20/gulf-crisis-tanker-retaliation-iran-hormuz.

[128] Panama removed *Grace 1* from its ship register due to links with Iran and Syria; see n 9.

[129] Notice of revocation of specification of ship (n 10) para 13.

> assurances we have received, there are no longer any reasonable grounds for the continued legal detention of the Grace 1 in order to ensure compliance with the EU Sanctions Regulation. … The net effect is that this operation has become the most successful implementation of the European sanctions regime to date. It also amounts to a demonstration that Gibraltar is a jurisdiction that acts in keeping with the law and is committed to the rules based, international legal order. Gibraltar can be proud of the role it has discharged in guarding the entrance to the Mediterranean and enforcing EU sanctions.[130]

After the release of *Adrian Darya 1* by Gibraltar, on 16 August 2019, a US court issued a warrant to seize the ship alleging unlawful use of the American financial system to support and finance the sale of crude oil to Syria by IRGC, which Washington has designated as a 'terrorist' organisation.[131] On 26 August the ship's master was offered several million dollars to pilot the ship to a country that would impound the ship on behalf of the US.[132] On 30 August, the US Treasury specifically designated *Adrian Darya 1* as a 'blocked property' using anti-terrorism rules and blacklisted the ship's master using measures targeting 'those providing support to terrorism or acts of terrorism'.[133] In the beginning of September, satellite imagery revealed that *Adrian Darya 1* was skirting the Syrian coast with its AIS offline, awaiting imminent ship-to-ship transfer. On 3 October, satellite imagery showed that *Adrian Darya 1* was tethered to another Iranian-flagged ship called *Jasmine*, to possibly discharge part of its cargo via a ship-to-ship transfer.[134] The Iranian Ambassador to the UK commented that Iran had made no commitment to secure the destination of the oil, only that it would not sell the oil to parties which are under EU sanctions.[135] A little more than a month after the *Grace 1* was released, on 27 September 2019, the Iranian authorities allowed *Stena Impero* to leave Bandar Abbas.[136]

[130] 'Chief Minister's Statement on the release of The Grace 1–595/2019' *HM Government of Gibraltar* (15 August 2019), available at www.gibraltar.gov.gi/press-releases/chief-ministers-statement-on-the-release-of-the-grace-1-5952019-5187.

[131] K Shubber, and A Williams, 'US reveals seizure warrant for Iranian tanker' *Financial Times* (17 August 2019), available at www.ft.com/content/0488b60e-c076-11e9-b350-db00d509634e.

[132] D Sevastopulo, 'US offers cash to tanker captains in bid to seize Iranian ships' *Financial Times* (4 September 2019), available at www.ft.com/content/20188064-cefb-11e9-99a4-b5ded7a7fe3f.

[133] The *Adrian Darya 1* and its master were identified as blocked property pursuant to Executive Order (EO) 13224 of the US, which targets terrorists and those providing support to terrorism or acts of terrorism. This EO expressly created extraterritorial sanctions through section 1(d), which gives the authority to designate foreign persons who 'assist in, sponsor, or provide financial, material, or technological support for, or financial or other services to or in support of, such acts of terrorism or those persons listed'. See 'Treasury Targets Oil Tanker Adrian Darya 1 and its Captain', US Department of the Treasury Press Release (30 August 2019), available at home.treasury.gov/news/press-releases/sm765.

[134] A Clark, and S Cheong, 'Iran Tanker the U.K. Detained May Be About to Offload Its Oil' *Bloomberg* (3 October 2019), available at www.bloomberg.com/news/articles/2019-10-03/iran-tanker-the-u-k-detained-may-be-about-to-offload-its-oil.

[135] 'Enemies misinterpret Iran's commitment on Adrian Darya super tanker' *IRNA* (14 September 2019), available at en.irna.ir/news/83475208/Enemies-misinterpret-Iran-s-commitment-on-Adrian-Darya-super.

[136] M Safi, 'UK-flagged tanker seized by Iran released and heading for Dubai' *The Guardian* (27 September 2019), available at www.theguardian.com/world/2019/sep/27/uk-flagged-tanker-seized-by-iran-in-july-released-leaves-bandar-abbas-port.

IV. Concluding Remarks

As the *Grace 1* saga reached its epilogue with few embarrassments and last laughs, maritime stakeholders feel pushed to continually monitor and comply with various sanctions regimes. They fear that non-compliance would result in severe consequences, including financial penalties and even criminal liability for business representatives. Gibraltar's unique position, both geographically and politically, made it possible to enforce the EU's unilateral sanctions on *Grace 1*, but there are serious doubts as to whether such actions are tenable under international law. The intentions behind the imposition of the unilateral sanctions may be admirable, but the enforcement mechanism devised by Gibraltar would lead to unintended legal and economic consequences.

The legal issues surrounding maritime lawfare are complex and pertain to various specialised branches of law. From the point of view of international humanitarian law, the author submits that Gibraltar could have attempted to justify the interdiction of *Grace 1* based on the customary international law exception of protection of non-nationals through use of force in another state's territory. Gibraltar could have asserted that the EU has maintained its unilateral sanctions for over a decade due to continuous 'repression of the civilian population' in Syria.[137] While highlighting the spirit and intent of the EU sanctions on Syria, Gibraltar could have drawn further support from the UN inspectors' reports on Syria[138] and the former UN Secretary-General's statement that accused the Syrian Government of war crimes.[139] By doing so, Gibraltar could have built a case for applying the 'universal jurisdiction' principle[140] on *Grace 1*.[141] Although it cannot be said with certainty that this line of

[137] 'Syria: EU renews sanctions against the regime by one year' Council of the EU (17 May 2019), available at www.consilium.europa.eu/en/press/press-releases/2019/05/17/syria-eu-renews-sanctions-against-the-regime-by-one-year.

[138] 'Syrian air force used deadly chemical weapons in 2017 attacks, global watchdog finds' *UN News* (8 April 2020), available at news.un.org/en/story/2020/04/1061402.

[139] 'Ban Ki-moon accuses Syrian regime of potential crimes against humanity' *The Guardian* (16 February 2012), available at www.theguardian.com/world/2012/feb/16/united-nations-syria-crimes-against-humanity.

[140] The universal jurisdiction principle is applied where a crime is considered so heinous (eg piracy) that all states have jurisdiction in principle to try a person or entity accused of it. When universal jurisdiction is applied, the nationality of the ship, the shipowner, the cargo owner and the crew become irrelevant. Therefore, the nationality of *Grace 1* would not have mattered. *Grace 1* would have been considered the perpetrator by virtue of making available the 'economic resource', ie, oil, to Baniyas Oil Refinery, which is subject to sanctions.

[141] In earlier instances, EU sanctions have required its Member States to adopt the the universal principle in order to prohibit or criminalise certain acts effectively. For example, in *Ebony Maritime SA and Loten Navigation Co Ltd v Prefetto della Provincia di Brindisi and others* (Case C-177/95 [1997] ECR I-1111), the Court of Justice effectively treated breaches of EU economic sanctions as offences with universal jurisdiction, because the offence of entering Yugoslav waters imposed to implement to EC legislation could only be committed outside Member States' territory. Therefore, all it took for a violator to fall within the criminal jurisdiction of a Member State was entry into a Member State's territory after an alleged breach of the sanctions. The nationality of the ship, the shipowner, the cargo owner and the crew was irrelevant. However, in the *Ebony Maritime*, the Court of Justice did not suggest that all EU legislation should receive such wide interpretation; instead, it appears that its interpretation was based upon the Security Council Resolution which the EU was implementing. S Peers, *EU Justice and Home Affairs Law: Volume II: EU Criminal Law, Policing, and Civil Law* (Oxford University Press, 2016) 225.

argumentation would have made the interdiction legal in the eyes of all,[142] Gibraltar's action would have then exhibited as its intention to protect the UN's interest and its attempt to attract support from the wider international community. It could have also added to the state practice on legitimacy of use of force for humanitarian purposes not authorised by the Security Council and attached further recognition to the above customary international law exception.[143]

Additionally, Gibraltar could have attempted to justify the interdiction of *Grace 1* based on the emerging state practice related to third-party countermeasures.[144] While UNCLOS does not include a derogation for EU sanctions,[145] a possible circumstance precluding wrongfulness of the interdiction of *Grace 1* could have been a third-party countermeasure claim to redress the massive violations of human rights and humanitarian law in Syria.[146] This could have then appeared as an interesting test case and may have added to the emerging state practice on third-party countermeasure for breach of a communitarian norm.[147]

From the point of view of international maritime law, the possible loss of the right of innocent passage to unilateral sanctions is particularly worrying as the question is not just about the legality of the action, but about the possibility that such action becomes standard practice. The principle of freedom of navigation has seemingly eroded already in favour of the principle of sovereignty due to security and environmental concerns of coastal states. If a handful of coastal states choose to repeatedly apply unilateral sanctions on neutral ships passing through their territorial seas, new state practice may be established which may seriously undermine the right of innocent passage. Such new practice would further erode the principle of freedom of navigation without any systematic deliberation within the international maritime community.

Maritime lawfare on shipping lanes would not only create legal uncertainty for shipowners but pose new risks for all the other maritime stakeholders. The increase in scrutiny from multiple government agencies globally and technological advances that allow contraventions to be exposed in real-time have pushed maritime stakeholders to develop elaborate due diligence techniques. However, to categorically prove no links with third parties and avoid breach of sanctions regulations comes at a cost, which has

[142] It could be argued that the use of this non-Charter exception is an attempt to circumvent the Security Council and decide on an action that would normally be done at the direction of the Council. It could be further argued that such action is heavily motivated by intent, is subjective, and relies on the assessment of regional entities instead of a collective international group such as the Security Council.

[143] See n 97.

[144] See n 99.

[145] See the discussion in section III.C of this chapter.

[146] Individual states have taken third-party countermeasures in the absence of effective enforcement by the Security Council. See Dawidowicz (n 99) 417–18. For example, in 2012, following the lack of an effective response to the then unfolding situation in Syria, the US Secretary of State, Hilary Clinton, called for the states that were part of the Friends of Democratic Syria group to take measures against Syrian President Al-Assad, explaining that '[when f]aced with a neutered Security Council, we have to redouble our efforts outside of the United Nations with those allies and partners who support the Syrian people's right to have a better future'. See 'Clinton Calls for "Friends of Democratic Syria" to Unite Against Bashar al-Assad' *The Guardian* (5 February 2012), available at www.theguardian.com/world/2012/feb/05/hillary-clinton-syria-assad-un.

[147] As mentioned earlier in section III.B above, the author simply touches on the issue of third-party countermeasure and avoids any detailed discussion as it is beyond the scope of this chapter.

to be borne by businesses and consumers globally.[148] In maritime lawfare, the affected group is much wider than the targeted adversary, and therefore there are doubts on its effectiveness in accomplishing its policy goals.[149] More importantly, scholars have repeatedly termed unilateral sanctions as unlawful. So, any attempt to implement such sanctions by misinterpreting well-established principles of international maritime law must be vehemently resisted.

[148] Z Fang, H You, F Lu and M Feng, 'Maritime network dynamics before and after international events' (2018) 28 *Journal of Geographical Sciences* 937 used AIS data before and after implementation of economic sanctions to show effect on maritime network dynamics, which has important connections with maritime transport efficiency, maritime safety, and optimisation of the global maritime logistics network.

[149] For a discussion on the fallacies of unilateral sanctions see, H Hakimian, 'Seven key misconceptions about economic sanctions' *World Economic Forum* (9 May 2019), available at www.weforum.org/agenda/2019/05/seven-fallacies-of-economic-sanctions.

11

Can Unilateral Sanctions and International Environmental Obligations of States Coexist?

AMRISHA PANDEY

I. Introduction

Respect for the rule of law enables the UN Charter to achieve its aim and objectives. Chapter VII of the Charter authorises the Council to undertake certain measures for the protection of the aims and objects of the Charter.[1] Article 39 of the Charter permits the Council to intervene in certain conditions; and in accordance with the provisions of Articles 41 and 42, the Council is allowed to intervene only after determining the existence of any threat to the peace, breach of peace or act of aggression which disrupts international peace and security.[2] These sanctions are multilateral in nature and one of the peaceful means offered to the Security Council for the preservation of its object and purpose.[3]

Similarly, in the recent past, a growing number of states have opted to impose unilateral sanctions for the protection of international peace and security. Although the legality of unilateral sanction is contested, states like the US find this measure attractive and use it frequently. Other Member States and regional organisations such as the EU and groups of African countries started using this provision outside the authority of the Council. This investigation confines itself to the impact of sanctions on the environment and the possible means offered by international law to contain that threat. Further, it analyses the manner in which unilateral sanctions are perceived in international law, the impact they cause directly or indirectly on the environment of the sanctioned country; the manner in which they interfere with the international obligation arising from the environmental treaties/conventions, and determines the consequences of such actions.

[1] Chapter VII of the Charter of the United Nations and Statute of the International Court of Justice, 193 Members, 49 Original Members and 144 Members having been admitted in accordance with Art 4, San Francisco, 26 June 1945.

[2] ibid, Art 39.

[3] ibid, Art 41.

This study consists of five parts. Section I introduces the content and structure of the chapter. Section II investigates the connection between the sanctions and the impact they have on the environment of sanctioned and non-sanctioned states. Section III compares and evaluates the common denominators of both regimes: unilateral sanctions and environmental concerns. Based on this comparison, section IV determines whether the two can exist simultaneously or whether they demand intervention by the international community of states aiming for an equitable future. The main object of this analysis is not the legality of the regime of unilateral sanctions, but the potential remedies to the harmful impacts it casts on the environment.

II. International Law and the Environment

Unilateral sanctions are becoming the preferred tool of choice for shaping foreign policy in the post-Cold War era. They are employed as alternative and peaceful means to force a country to alter its behaviour while creating economic pressure on the sanctioned government.[4] Since unilateral sanctions are enacted and imposed by a single state or a group of states collectively, they require international support to be effective. That support primarily depends on the cause and nature of the sanctions. Otherwise, the states comply with the sanctions to avoid the repercussions of non-compliance. Although the success of the regime or the fulfilment of the object of the regime remains a matter for discussion, the economy of the sanctioned state will be damaged, creating hardships for civilians. Here, the author intends to explore the difficulties faced by the environment, whilst acknowledging that not all environmental issues can be blamed on the impact of unilateral sanctions. This chapter investigates the possible reasons that directly and indirectly adversely affect the environment of the sanctioned state and the extraterritorial impacts it has on other states.[5]

The issue of environmental protection, sustainable development, growing freshwater security, and changes in climatic conditions are of global concern.[6] They were driven by the mantra of cooperation by states at every possible level, and to the best of their abilities. Due to the dynamic and transboundary nature of the environmental concern, states are repeatedly advised to exercise their sovereign right responsibly and with respect to the rights of others.[7] Environmental concerns in a legal discipline are wide-ranging, from human rights issues to the right to development; from environmental law to the secondary responsibility of the state; from the concern of equity to inter and intra-generational equity; and through the spectra of social, economic and environmental justice. To tackle the emergent crisis, this chapter examines the competence of the principles of environmental law to tackle the environmental problems of this

[4] MP Malloy, 'United States Economic Sanctions: Theory and Practice' (2002) 16 *Ethics and International Affairs* 177, 180.

[5] Z Fotourehchi, 'Are UN and US Sanctions a Cause or Cure for the Environment: Empirical Evidence from Iran' (2020) 22 *Environment, Development and Sustainability* 5483.

[6] L Jianping, L Minrong, W Jinnan, L Jianjian, S Hongwen and H Maoxing, 'Global Environmental Issues and Human Wellbeing' in L Jianping, L Minrong, W Jinnan, L Jianjian, S Hongwen and H Maoxing (eds), *Report on Global Environmental Competitiveness* (Springer, 2013/14).

[7] P Penz, 'Environmental Victims and State Sovereignty: A Normative Analysis' (1996) 23 *Social Justice* 41.

century, as well as the slow and steady progression of the notion of the *environmental rule of law*, to subsume the adverse impact of unilateral sanctions on the environment. The investigation advances with the issue of water security.

A. Water Security/Crisis

States are struggling to ensure water security for all and, if the projections are to be believed, the situation is expected to be much worse in the future. UN-Water proposes the following definition of water security:

> The capacity of a population to safeguard sustainable access to adequate quantities of and acceptable quality water for sustaining livelihoods, human wellbeing, and socio-economic development, for ensuring protection against water-borne pollution and water-related disasters, and for preserving ecosystems in a climate of peace and political stability.[8]

This definition pulls together human rights, environmental protection and development needs, all rooted in sustainability. It is for this reason that international law and its relevance for water regulation needs to develop and align itself within a broader spectrum of sustainability.[9] Since the definition adopted by the UN-Water and the Sustainable Development Goals (SDGs) 2030[10] both embrace the holistic management of water resources, the combined study is believed to reconceptualise how to achieve water security for all. The synergy between the two is also visible from the acts of the states working independently and in collaboration with other states. The issue of water security is the subject of repeated dialogue that highlights different perspectives and the interdependence of the goals set by the UN.[11]

Most states share freshwater resources with their neighbours in the form of rivers, lakes and glaciers, and some share underground aquifers located beneath territorial borders.[12] Due to the transboundary nature of the resource and the relevance of the hydrological cycle, it is imperative to regulate, manage and use the shared resource conjointly and with regard to shared rights.[13] This understanding is inherent in the development of international legal and governance mechanisms dedicated to deal with the regulation of shared watercourses. Additionally, international water resource management (IWRM) is found by experts working in the field to be the most efficient model. IWRM proposes to determine the ecological unit of the watercourse and to address it holistically. Thus, the unit chosen is a geographical, not a political one and

[8] UN-Water, 'Water Security & the Global Water Agenda: A UN-Water Analytical Brief' United Nations University, Institute for Water, Environment & Health (UNU-INWEH) (2013).

[9] EB Weiss, 'The Coming Water Crisis: A Common Concern of Mankind' (2012) *Georgetown Law Faculty Publications and Other Works* 1671.

[10] UN, Transforming Our World: the 2030 Agenda for Sustainable Development, A/RES/70/1, Resolution adopted by the General Assembly on 25 September 2015.

[11] ibid.

[12] UNDESA, 'International decade for Action "Water for Life" 2005–2015: Transboundary Waters' available at www.un.org/waterforlifedecade/transboundary_waters.shtml. See also PH Gleick, 'Water and Conflict: Fresh Water Resources and International Security' (1993) 18 *International Security* 79.

[13] E Benvenisti, 'Collective Action in the Utilization of Shared Freshwater: The Challenges of International Water Resources Law' (1996) 90 *The American Journal of International Law* 384.

its management is done holistically by taking into account all over-arching issues.[14] This requires cooperation and transparency at every possible level by the states and stakeholders involved.

Cooperation is the key mantra, a cardinal principle of international law and governance for ensuring water security for all. From the international law perspective, the duty to cooperate in the management of water resources is the foundation upon which the UN Watercourse Convention is built.[15] The Watercourse Convention dictates that the cooperation between the states sharing the freshwater resource is indispensable for achieving the *equitable and reasonable utilisation* and *preventing significant harm* to the shared resource and its ecosystem.[16] Both principles acknowledge the transboundary nature of the resource and conjointly limit the sovereign right of the state to decide the nature and extent of the resource present within their physical territory (emphasis added). The need for cooperative development and management of shared water resources was further emphasised in 2013's call for *International Year of Water Cooperation*, followed by several joint declarations from governments, international and regional organisations and civil society.[17] The requirement for the shared and cooperative management of the watercourse is crystallised into a hard law principle of international law and one of the necessities for achieving equitable utilisation of the shared resource.[18] The principles enumerated in Articles 5 and 7 of the Watercourse Convention are regarded as the customary principles of water law; moreover, a necessity to cooperate is a legal requirement for the state to participate in the management of shared watercourses.

Similarly, the Convention on the Protection and Use of Transboundary Watercourses and International Lakes (Water Convention) was adopted in Helsinki in 1992 and entered into force in 1996. Almost all countries sharing transboundary waters in the region of the United Nations Economic Commission for Europe (UNECE) are Parties to the Convention.[19] This Convention is the living embodiment of the cooperation of the European states in managing and regulating shared freshwater resources, as well as achieving their joint commitment in achieving the SDGs 2030.[20]

[14] UNDESA (n 12).

[15] UN, Convention on the Law of the Non-Navigational Uses of International Watercourses, 1997, Registration Number: 52106; Adopted by the General Assembly of the United Nations on 21 May 1997, Entered into force on 17 August 2014, See General Assembly Resolution 51/229, annex, Official Records of the General Assembly, Fifty-first Session, Supplement No 49 (A/51/49).

[16] C Leb, 'The UN Convention: The *Eminence Grise* Behind Cooperation on Transboundary Water Resources' (2013) 38 *Water International* 146.

[17] UN, International Year of Water Cooperation, 2013, A/RES/65/154, Distr: General 11 February 2011 (Resolution adopted by the General Assembly on 20 December 2010 on the report of the Second Committee (A/65/436/Add.1)) 65/154.

[18] C Leb, 'One Step at a Time: International law and the Duty to Cooperate in the Management of Shared Water Resources' (2015) 40 *Water International* 21.

[19] UN, UNECE, Convention on the Protection and Use of Transboundary Watercourses and International Lakes, Helsinki, 17 March 1992, UNTS, Vol 1936, 269, Signatories: 26 and Parties: 43, Registration No 33207, 6 October 1996. (The Convention was adopted by the Senior Advisers to the Economic Commission for Europe Governments on Environmental and Water Problems at their Resumed Fifth Session held at Helsinki from 17 to 18 March 1992. The Convention was opened for signature at Helsinki from 17 to 18 March 1992 and was open for signature at UN Headquarters in New York until 18 September 1992. Amendments to Arts 25 and 26 of the Convention entered into force on 6 February 2013).

[20] UN, 'Report of the Meeting of the Parties on its Eighth session – Programme of work for 2019–2021' ECE/MP.WAT/54/Add.1, (Economic Commission for Europe Meeting of the Parties to the Convention on the Protection and Use of Transboundary Watercourses and International Lakes, 30 January 2019.

The principle of 'no harm' dictates that the states must use their resources in a manner that does not cause significant harm to other states; the principle of reasonable and equitable utilisation urges the states sharing a resource to determine their right over the resource equitably and reasonably. Both principles have developed and gained acceptance from academic writing[21] and judicial pronouncements in national and international jurisdictions. The ICJ in the *Gabčíkovo-Nagymaros* case[22] affirmed the relevance of the principles advocated by the Watercourse Convention long before it came into force and, since 1997, the judgment and the reasoning for the judgment have been sources of research, inspiration and reference for academic and judicial purposes.[23]

In the twentieth century, upstream states advocated the *theory of absolute sovereignty* and the downstream states the *theory of absolute territorial integrity*. Interpretation is mainly driven by the geopolitical concerns or the personal interests of the upstream and downstream states. The conflict was eventually settled by the emergence of the *theory of limited sovereignty* in light of the understanding of the transboundary nature of the issue for regulating the international watercourses.[24] Building on this, the Watercourse Convention embraced the principle of *equitable and reasonable utilisation principle* and the *principle of no significant harm*. Together, they aim to establish equity among the state parties sharing the resource.[25] Sovereignty as a concept does not limit, but frees the state to decide for itself what rights it wishes to give away, and to what extent, for the sake of common and shared objectives. Concerning shared watercourses, the sovereignty debate emphasises imposing similar restrictions for all states, or a commitment from the states to exercise their sovereign right only with respect to the similar right for others.[26]

To ensure water security for all and to manage the world's shared water resources peacefully, the contested notion of sovereignty needs to embrace new meaning.[27] Perhaps it is time to reconfigure sovereign rights of the state over the resources within their territory in a positive sense, thus preventing them from making unilateral decisions without taking into consideration the similar rights of others.[28] Wouters and Tarlock's suggestion highlights the emergence of the universal lawmaking trend in favour of the duty to cooperate as an *erga omnes* obligation for the peaceful management of the world's water resources.[29]

[21] S Deets, 'Constituting Interests and Identities in a Two-Level Game: Understanding the Gabčíkovo-Nagymaros Dam Conflict' (January 2009) 5 *Foreign Policy Analysis* 37.

[22] ICJ, *Gabčíkovo-Nagymaros Project (Hungary/Slovakia)* Judgment of 25 September 1997, ICJ Reports 1997.

[23] EN Ward, 'Report on the Activities of the International Court of Justice During 1997' (1998) 6 *African Yearbook of International Law Online* 245, 52.

[24] SC McCaffrey, *The Law of International Watercourses*, 3rd edn (Oxford University Press, 2019) 98.

[25] O McIntrye, *Environmental Protection of International Watercourses under International Law*, 1st edn (Ashgate Publishing Limited. 2007) 132–51.

[26] SC Mccaffery and KJ Neville, 'The Politics of Sharing Water: International Law, Sovereignty and Transboundary Rivers and Aquifer' in K Wegerich and J Warner (eds), *The Politics of Water* (Routledge, 2010) 18, 37.

[27] G Fitzmaurice, 'The Future of Public International Law and of the International Legal System in the Circumstances of Today' (1973) 55 *Annuaire de l'Institut de Droit International* 197, 249.

[28] M Ragazzi, 'International Obligations Erga Omnes: Their Moral Foundation and Criteria of Identification in Light of Two Japanese Contributions' in GS Goodwin-Gill and S Talmon, *The Reality of International Law: Essays in Honour of Ian Brownlie* (Oxford University Press, 1999) 455.

[29] P Wouters and AD Tarlock, 'The Third Wave of Normativity in Global Water Law: The Duty to Cooperate in the Peaceful Management of the Worlds Water Resources: An Emerging Erga Omnes? (2013) 23 *Journal of Water Law* 51.

The principle of sovereignty is the bedrock of international law. A transformation from the 'notion of sovereignty as control, to the sovereignty as responsibility'[30] is the result of the gradual transformation of the concept to accommodate the needs of the contemporary world. This was a well-intentioned transformation clearly reflected by the development of the responsibility to protect (R2P), which focuses primarily on prevention and protection with an emphasis on peaceful means of conflict resolution.[31] Therefore, the manner in which we use and interpret 'sovereignty' is significant for the matters requiring state cooperation, because the issue of national sovereignty is often linked to issues of national security and geopolitics.

The advancement in international water law creates a legal obligation on the state to cooperate in ensuring water security for all. Water security intercepts human rights law, environmental law and development law in many ways, as evidenced in the human right to water and sanitation,[32] to a healthy environment[33] and to development.[34] It is the impact on the application of these environmental obligations, together with the obligations owed to the international community of states, and the correlative obligations arising from the human rights discourse and other legal instruments, that are investigated under the influence of the unilateral sanctions.

When using a unilateral sanction, the sanctioning state dominates the sovereign right of the sanctioned state, and also dictates or restricts the ways in which non-sanctioned states relate to the sanctioned state. This dynamic can lead to the domination of the state imposing sanctions over the rights of other states. It is precisely this scenario that predominantly calls for the reconceptualisation of the notion of sovereignty.[35] The obligations arising from the water law, the human rights discourse and the right to development, along with the obligations arising from the SDGs, rest broadly upon the 'duty to cooperate' among the states at every possible level. The 'duty to cooperate' is a crucial requirement for ensuring water security for all and for the peaceful management of the resource, which is hindered by the overbearing impacts of unilateral sanctions.

For instance, under the influence of unilateral sanctions imposed by the USA, Iran's water crisis incorporates various other factors, creating a vicious cycle; the impacts are often felt across generations and are transboundary.[36] Iran, like most countries,

[30] G Nolte, 'Sovereignty as Responsibility' (2005) 99 *American Society of International Law Proceeding* 389, 92.

[31] G Evans and M Sahnoun (eds), The Responsibility to Protect: Report of the International Commission on Intervention and State Sovereignty (International Development Research Centre, Ottawa, 2001) 17.

[32] UN, The Human Right to Water and Sanitation, A/RES/64/292, 64th Session, Agenda item 48, Resolution adopted by the General Assembly on 28 July 2010; See also United Nations, 15/9 Human Rights and Access to Safe Drinking Water and Sanitation, A/HRC/RES/15/9, Human Rights Council Fifteenth session, Agenda item 3, Promotion and protection of all human rights, civil political, economic, social and cultural rights, including the right to development on 6 October 2010.

[33] UN, Human Rights and the Environment, A/HRC/RES/37/8, Human Rights Council, 37th Session 26 February–23 March 2018, Agenda item 3 – Resolution adopted by the Human Rights Council on 22 March 2018.

[34] UN, A/HRC/RES/15/9 (n 32).

[35] Mccaffery and Neville, 'The Politics of Sharing Water' (2010) 18, 37.

[36] HJ Nkuepo, 'Natural Resources, Intergenerational Injustice, Environmental Degradation, Water Pollution and the Right to Healthcare' (28 February 2019), available at ssrn.com/abstract=2012920 and dx.doi.org/10.2139/ssrn.2012920.

happens to share natural water resources with its bordering state, Afghanistan.[37] The boundary conflict over the Hirmand (Helmand) River is one of the main reasons behind the drying of Lake Hamoun in eastern Iran: the drying of the lake increases the intensity of dust storms and the arid climate makes farming impossible. The Hamouns are transboundary wetlands on the Iran–Afghan border made up of three lakes: Hamoun-e Helmand, which is entirely in Iran; Hamoun-e Sabari on the border; and Hamoun-e Puzak, almost entirely inside Afghanistan.[38] The three lakes are linked and fed by water from the Helmand River. Although the 1973 Hirmand Water Treaty exists between the two states, the Treaty lacks the competence to resolve the crises as it is said to have been designed on misunderstandings and non-reliable data.[39] It is evident from the above-mentioned examples that the water crisis of Iran ranges from within the state territory to transboundary issues with extraterritorial impact.

Although the water crisis of Iran and its geographical region could not be blamed entirely on sanctions, they certainly are responsible for creating situations which are discouraging the cooperation and joint management of the shared resource between the states.[40] For instance, at the time the Hirmand Water Treaty of 1973 was drafted, not much was known in terms of water management or the hydrological cycle.[41] Nevertheless, the situation changed with the advancement in water law and the means to manage shared watercourses. If the available tools discussed above had been utilised wisely, not only could the dispute between the countries have been resolved, but the initiative could have improved the acrimonious relationship between the neighbouring countries. Additionally, by collectively using the human right treaties along with the duties arising from the SDG's commitment to the state, the fate of the environment in Iran could be altered. The next section investigates the issue of climate change and the rising temperature of the planet due to global warming.

B. Greenhouse Gas Emissions, Air Pollution and Human Health

To tackle climatic change and curtail greenhouse gas emissions, the UN finalised an agreement in 1992, declaring the climate change and its adverse effects to be a common concern of humankind.[42] The United Nations Framework Convention on Climate Change (UNFCCC; Paris Agreement) was signed in 2015 to support the objectives of the UNFCCC in a more discreet manner. This meant assisting developing countries and

[37] F Man, 'Water Dispute Escalating between Iran and Afghanistan' (Atlantic Council: South Asia Centre, August 2016).

[38] ibid.

[39] V Thomas and MM Varzi, 'A Legal Licence for an Ecological Disaster: The Inadequacies of the 1973 Helmand/Hirmand Water Treaty for Sustainable Transboundary Water Resources Development' (2015) 31 *International Journal of Water Resource Development* 499.

[40] 'Water Reservoirs in Some Parts of the Country are Completely Salty' (Mehr News Agency, 2016), available at http://goo.gl/BdoAog.

[41] Thomas and Varzi, 'A Legal Licence for an Ecological' (2015) 31.

[42] UN, The United Nations Framework Convention on Climate Change, 1992, UNTS Vol 1771, 107; Signatories: 165. Parties: 197.

other vulnerable countries through appropriate financial and technological support.[43] An enhanced transparency mechanism was put in place to ensure accountability and monitor the progress of the commitments, alongside the activities of the states in that regard.

Simultaneously, the impact of climate change on health gained prominence. As the connection between the two became better understood, the WHO took the lead in developing a large country-based dataset.[44] This helps us better understand and identify the threats to environmental changes and therefore plan the means to mitigate or adapt well in advance. By working in close partnership with heads of states and other ministries involved, the quality and credibility of the data gathered is ensured.[45] The health of peoples remains a critical element for the achievement of the SDGs. It is often said that a country aspiring to economic growth cannot base its aspirations on an unhealthy workforce. Health is an inherent human right, and environmental health is a precondition of this.[46] This is evident in the call for 'the right to a healthy environment', which clearly states that the sustainable health of the environment and our surroundings is essential for humans to enjoy most of their civil and political, as well as the socio-economic and cultural, rights.[47] Similarly, the SDGs stipulate that only by committing to progress across the four dimensions of social inclusion, environmental sustainability, good governance and economic development can the eradication of poverty be achieved.[48]

Burning of fossil fuels is one of the biggest contributors to the increasing concentration of greenhouse gas emissions. The share of petroleum products alone accounts for half of the carbon emissions in the US and almost one-third of all the carbon emissions globally.[49] Emissions drive climate change and cause air pollution. Subsequent research supports the claim made by the WHO of a link between human health and pollution due to the combustion of petroleum products, suggesting that in particular this harms the young and even unborn children, with a potential to cause immediate damage over

[43] UN, The Paris Agreement, 2015. The Paris Agreement was adopted on 12 December 2015 at the 21st session of the Conference of the Parties to the United Nations Framework Convention on Climate Change (UNFCCC) held in Paris from 30 November to 13 December 2015. In accordance with its Art 20, the Agreement was open for signature at the UN Headquarters in New York from 22 April 2016 until 21 April 2017 by states and regional economic integration organisations that were parties to the UNFCCC.

[44] WHO, 'Climate Change and Human Health – WHO UNFCCC Health and Climate Change Country Profile Project: Monitoring health impacts of climate change and progress in building climate resilient health systems', available at www.who.int/globalchange/resources/countries/en.

[45] WHO, 'WHO Health and Climate Change Survey Report: Tracking Global Progress' (2019) WHO-CED-PHE-EPE-19.11.

[46] D Briggs, 'Environmental Pollution and the Global Burden of Disease' (2003) 68 *British Medical Bulletin* 1.

[47] UN, 'Report of the Special Rapporteur: Issue of human rights obligations relating to the enjoyment of a safe, clean, healthy and sustainable environment' A/HRC/40/55, 8 January 2019; Human Rights Council, 40th Session 25 February–22 March 2019, Agenda item 3: Promotion and protection of all human rights, civil, political, economic, social and cultural rights, including the right to development.

[48] NA Roshan, S Mehrbod and M Abbassi, 'The Impacts of Sanctions on Sustainable Development: Focusing on Lobor' (2015) 36 *Science Journal* 3458, 459.

[49] C Nunez, 'What Are Fossil Fuels? Fossil fuels, explained: Much of the world's energy comes from material formed hundreds of millions of years ago, and there are environmental consequences for it' *National Geographic* (2 April 2019), available at www.nationalgeographic.com/environment/energy/reference/fossil-fuels.

the course of an individual's lifetime.[50] Since the impacts are transnational and range across generations, it broadly raises the question of equity.

States pledged to reduce greenhouse gas emissions (GHG) within a very tight timeframe in the Paris Agreement, which entered into force on 4 November 2016.[51] They were expected to maintain a balance between anthropogenic emissions by sources and its removal by sinks of CO_2 to produce net zero emissions in the atmosphere by their progressive effort and strategy, based on the best available science and technological advancements in the field.[52] The ability to honour such a commitment largely depends on the limited capacity of the state and the appropriate assistance they could gather as per the requirements of the Paris Agreement. The multilateral agreement creates international obligations on the state parties arising from the commitments made by the states and, on the other hand, raises the collective responsibility of others to honour the commitment to deliver the necessary assistance, thus, giving rise to the international obligations from both ends.[53] The country often needs cooperation with other countries, eg for the transfer of technological know-how and the best technology available in the sector, to address the issue of GHG-based climate change.

The current regional practice of the MENA region and North Africa witnesses the introduction of new local content requirements (LCRs) into their legal frameworks through legislation, regulations, guidelines, industry contracts and other bidding practices to facilitate domestic production and enhance the standard of technological advancement for oil and gas exploration.[54] One of the goals set by the authorities is technological advancement by enhancing national technical capacity. As per the guidelines, they emphasise strengthening local capacity by producing the machines and equipment domestically. Following international precedents, they brought in the best available research and development facilities to develop and allow access to local state-of-the-art technology,[55] thus promoting technology transfer. The intention was to enhance the quality of products produced locally by making it mandatory for international oil companies (IOC) and service providers to invest in technological advancement, and to enhance quality and reduce the harm caused by the use and

[50] F Perera, 'Pollution from Fossil-Fuel Combustion is the Leading Environmental Threat to Global Paediatric Health and Equity: Solutions Exist' (2018) 15 *International Journal of Environmental Research and Public Health* 16.

[51] Paris Agreement (n 43).

[52] UN, 'Nationally Determined Contributions (NDCs): The Paris Agreement and NDCs' United Nations Climate Change, available at www.unfccc.int/process-and-meetings/the-paris-agreement/nationally-determined-contributions-ndcs#eq-2.

[53] 'Article 27. Violation of Treaty Obligations' (1935) 29 *The American Journal of International Law* 1077; See also K Joseph, P Yuri and S Constantinos (eds), *Between the lines of the Vienna Convention? Canons and other Principles of Interpretation in Public International Law* (Kluwer Law International BV, 2018).

[54] DS Olawuyi, 'Local Content and Procurement Requirements in Oil and Gas Contracts: Regional Trends in the Middle East and North Africa' (Oxford Institute for Energy Studies, November 2017) Abstract.

[55] ibid, at 6. See also See Trade Arabia, 'Big boost to Saudi industries as Aramco to double local market sourcing' (1 December 2015), available at www.tradearabia.net/news/IND_295936.html. See also S Tordo, M Warner, O Manzano, and Y Anouti, *Local Content Policies in the Oil and Gas Sector* (World Bank, 2013); and R Darling, 'Beyond Taxation: How Countries Can Benefit from the Extractive Industries Through Local Content (New York: Revenue Watch Institute, 2011) 1–10; also Shared Value Initiative, 'Extracting with Purpose Creating Shared Value in the Oil and Gas and Mining Sectors' Companies and Communities' 27, available at www.sharedvalue.org/sites/default/files/resourcefiles/Extracting%20with%20Purpose_FINAL_Full%20Report_Single%20Pages.pdf.

combustion of petroleum products, thus lessening the burden of greenhouse gases in the Earth's atmosphere.

Iran, however, is restrained from participating in this initiative because it is subject to unilateral sanctions. As far as the regional initiative is concerned, Iran belongs to the same group of countries. This situation is resulting in a breach of the international obligation for the State of Iran against its regional counterparts, in addition to the violation of various environmental obligations arising from the multilateral agreements.

Another set of problems arises from the financial restraints and restrictions imposed on the importing of technology, making it rather challenging to access the required apparatus for the production of the petroleum products of standard quality. Due to limited financial power and curtailed access to the world market to purchase the best-quality petroleum products, Iran was pushed to produce the petroleum products domestically to fulfil state demands. As Roshan suggests, the production and use of sub-standard local petroleum products or 'sort of petrol' increased to about 79 per cent of total gasoline production in 2012.[56] Further, in 2017, the reported refining capacity of Iran had increased from 1.55 or 2.15 million barrels per day, and this is projected to increase from 2.15 to 2.40 million barrels per day in 2019/20.[57] Petroleum produced at the local refinery was sub-standard, resulting in rising air pollution and increased concentration of greenhouse gases due to the burning of fossil fuel, etc, thus, causing environmental degradation and adversely affecting human health.[58] The official data suggests that almost 70 per cent of deaths in Iran are caused by respiratory illness and heart failure which can be linked, either directly or as a critical factor, to air pollution.

The repercussions of not complying with sanctions are often felt in the form of fines and prosecutions. The states fear possible boycott, limited access to the global market and funds, a risk of being blacklisted or excluded from the global financial systems, etc.[59] This encourages them to comply with the sanctions. It also restricts non-sanctioned states and other international and regional organisations to work with or invest in the sanctioned country during the time sanctions are in place, thereby multiplying the hardships.

Nevertheless, the question remains as to what extent it is justifiable for a country to decide unilaterally, and coerce other states to act in breach of the international obligations arising from the environmental agreements. In the example under investigation, the obligations arising from the UNFCCC, the Paris Agreement, various human rights treaties and the SDGs are all at stake. By failing to comply with these, the foundation for the realisation of various sets of rights stands on a questionable ground. It is for these reasons that reconceptualisation of the regime of unilateral sanction is desirable. The following section discusses the SDGs and rising environmental concerns.

[56] Roshan, Mehrbod and Abbassi, 'The Impacts of Sanctions on Sustainable Development' (2015) *Cumhuriyet Science Journal* 473.

[57] 'Iran's Refining Capacity Grows Nearly 40% since March 2017' *Teheran Time* (20 July 2019), available at www.tehrantimes.com/news/438341/Iran-s-refining-capacity-grows-nearly-40-since-March-2017.

[58] 'Quality of Iran petrol below global standards' Reuters (14 December 2010), available at www.reuters.com/article/iran-gasoline-quality-idAFHOS45321820101214.

[59] J Erickson, 'Punishing the violators? Arms Embargoes and Economic Sanctions as Tools of Norm Enforcement' (2020) 46 *Review of International Studies* 96.

C. Sustainable Development Goals

The SDGs of 2030 lay down the parameters to be achieved by countries within the given timeframe.[60] The set goals are holistic and ambitious at the same time. Given the changing climatic conditions and the accompanying uncertainty, the importance of sustainable finance, data and technology sharing, and easy access to the cooperation of neighbouring countries becomes essential.

Sustainable development as a principle revolutionised environmental lawmaking and governance at the end of the twentieth century. As a concept, it requires a holistic and simultaneous progression of various interdependent aspects to ensure that the development is sustainable, thus making it extremely difficult to confine within strict jurisdictional boundaries in terms of territory as well as authorities, institutions or the ministries involved. By 2015, sustainable development had made its mark and gained massive acceptance universally,[61] evident from the enactment of SDGs 2030.[62] It is believed that adherence to the rules of environmental law will benefit the initiative and, therefore, this marks the inception of the evolving concept of the *environmental rule of law* and its importance for the attainment of the SDGs.

The first ever mention of the environmental rule of law can be traced back to the World Summit 2002, where a majority member of the summit was of the opinion that the summit must focus on the implementation of existing commitments rather than making new commitments.[63] This diverted the focus of the summit, but the theme was set by the discussion predominantly focussing on 'the public–private partnerships by viewing them as not providing a substitute for the effective environmental rule of law'.[64] Since 1990, most of the countries have enacted environmental legislation, and several multilateral agreements regulating different aspects of the environment have come into force. These agreements received considerable support and membership from states. However, the compliance was not high, mainly due to the dynamic and ever-evolving environmental issue, and a lack of capacity to understand and deal with the emerging crisis, etc.[65] Thus, through a global initiative, the UNEP aimed to develop guidelines and enhance understanding by fostering innovation and research for improving compliance with multilateral environmental agreements.[66]

A decade later, the outcome of the Rio 20+ conference emphasised environmental governance.[67] The outcome report of the conference, 'The Future We Want',[68] stressed

[60] UN, A/RES/70/1 (n 10).

[61] V Barral, 'Sustainable Development in International Law: Nature and Operation of an Evolutive Legal Norm' (2012) 23 *The European Journal of International Law* 377.

[62] UN, A/RES/70/1 (n 10).

[63] UN, Plan of Implementation of the World Summit on Sustainable Development (2002).

[64] UNEP, 'Environmental Rule of Law: First Global Report' (2009) 27.

[65] ICJ, *Gabčíkovo-Nagymaros Project (Hungary/Slovakia)* Judgment on 25 September 1997, ICJ Reports 1997.

[66] UNEP, 'Manual on Compliance with and Enforcement of Multilateral Environmental Agreements' (2006).

[67] UN 'Report of the United Nations Conference on Sustainable Development Rio de Janeiro', A/CONF.216/16 (20–22 June 2012).

[68] UN, 'The Future We Want: Outcome document of the United Nations Conference on Sustainable Development Rio de Janeiro, Brazil, 20–22 June 2012' A/RES/66/288, Resolution adopted by the General Assembly on 27 July 2012.

the need for states to have strong institutions, the capacity to access and disseminate information, strong political will and concrete enforceable environmental laws. The World Congress on Justice, Governance and Law for Environmental Sustainability confirmed and aligned with the report and its outcome in tandem, together highlighting the need to shape 'the environmental rule of law' for enhancing compliance with the obligations arising from the legal agreements and political commitments. Ever since then the UNEP has been working tirelessly to turn this into reality. The first international instrument to use the term 'the environmental rule of law' officially was crafted in 2013:[69]

> Where the UNEP calls for the United Nations system to take the lead and support national Governments upon their request in the development and implementation of environmental rule of law with attention at all levels to mutually supporting governance features, including information disclosure, public participation, implementable and enforceable laws, and implementation and accountability mechanisms including coordination of roles as well as environmental auditing and criminal, civil and administrative enforcement with timely, impartial and independent dispute resolution.[70]

To further the initiative, the IUCN and the UN Environment corresponded with the first World Environmental Congress in 2016 and adapted the IUCN World Declaration on Environmental Rule of Law.[71] The declaration consists of 13 principles to facilitate and deliver the solutions for ecologically sustainable development. The environmental rule of law focuses on ensuring compliance with, and enforcement of, environmental regulations, and it aims to address the implementation gap developed between environmental laws and their implementation and enforcement.[72] It integrates and identifies the critical needs of the environment and links this with elements of the rule of law, thus laying the foundation for the establishment of the rule of law governing the vital link between humans and the environment, and its link with the life on the planet, thus reaffirming that without the environmental rule of law development cannot be sustainable.[73]

Simultaneous enactment of SDGs made clear to the world community the importance of the environmental rule of law for the realisation of the SDGs. As such, Goal 16 cross-cuts most of the goals while emphasising the promotion of peaceful and inclusive societies for sustainable development, providing access to justice for all and building effective, accountable and inclusive institutions at all levels.[74] The importance of the rule of law in advancing the three pillars of the UN – peace and security, human rights and development – and for the attainment of the SDG 2030 to ensure the access to

[69] UNEP, 'Advancing Justice, Governance and Law for Environmental Sustainability' 27th Session of UNEP Governing Council/Global Ministerial Environment Forum, para 5(a), available at www.informea.org/es/node/19107.

[70] ibid.

[71] IUCN, IUCN World Declaration on the Environmental Rule of Law (IUCN World Congress on Environmental Law, having met in Rio de Janeiro (Brazil) from 26 to 29 April 2016).

[72] ibid, Overview 1.

[73] LA Avilés, 'Sustainable Development and the Legal Protection of the Environment in Europe' (2012) 12 *Sustainable Development Law & Policy* 29–34, 56–57; see also TY Soon, 'Environmental Planning for Sustainable Development' (World Scientific Connecting Great Minds), available at www.worldscientific.com/page/9653.

[74] UN, A/RES/70/1 (n 10) Goal 16.

justice for all were highlighted by members of the UN in a resolution adopted by the General Assembly in 2019.[75] In this resolution, the need for enhanced cooperation among the states, stakeholders and organisations, along with the need for greater coordination between the donors and recipients, is requested. Again, the importance of the rule of environmental law in sustainable development is recognised, thus for ensuring compliance, the environmental rule of law is preferred and appreciated as a step in the right direction.[76]

In addition to the existing hurdle in achieving SDGs and the discrepancies in the implementation of the current environmental law, the recent report from the UN General Assembly suggests that unilateral sanctions impede sustainable development. Namsuk Kim from the Development Policy Analysis Division of the Department of Economic and Social Affairs introduced the Secretary-General's report on unilateral economic measures as a means of political and economic coercion against developing countries.[77] The report highlights the negative impact of sanctions that were felt and reported by Member States on the socio-economic development of the affected country. In the report, international institutions state that the unilateral sanctions adversely affect the population in affected countries and impede international trade.[78] Most of the countries register their disagreements, stating that they view such measures as inconsistent with the principles of the Charter, the norms of international law and the multilateral trading system.[79] Other members, international organisations and international institutions share the view that such measures violate the legal principles of freedom of trade and navigation, and the norms of international law and the rule of law.[80]

Other Member States and the EU registered their displeasure with the regime of unilateral sanctions and characterise those measures as being an obstacle to the realisation of the right to development, detrimental to sustainable development, disruptive of the transport and communication link between two or more countries, a deterrent to the prospects of receiving investments in the sanctioned country and other financial aid from international or regional institutions, etc.[81] Other Member States and the EU further report that third countries other than the one sanctioned, as well as other sectors and companies could also suffer losses due to restrictive measures. In other words, the regime of unilateral sanctions disrupts cooperation amongst states in every possible manner. This observation raises an exciting finding indicating that states

[75] UN, The Rule of Law at the National and International levels – Sixth Committee (legal) 74th Session, A/RES/73/207 (14 October and 20 November 2019).

[76] ibid. See also UNEP, 'Advancing Justice, Governance and Law for Environmental Suatainability: Rio+20 and the World Congress of Chief Justices, Attorneys General and Auditors General' (UNEP Nairobi, 2012).

[77] UN, 'Unilateral Sanctions Impede Sustainable Development, Speakers Say, as Second Committee Debates Macroeconomic Policy', Meetings Coverage: General Assembly Second Committee Seventy-Second Session, 6th and 7th Meetings (AM & PM) GA/EF/3474 5 October 2017), available at www.un.org/press/en/2017/gaef3474.doc.htm.

[78] UN, 'Unilateral Economic Measures as a means of Political and Economic Coercion Against Developing Countries: Report to the Secretary-General' A/72/307, 9 August 2017, 72nd Session, Item 18(a) of the provisional agenda: Macroeconomic Policy Questions: International Trade and Development.

[79] ibid, Summary.

[80] ibid, Annex.

[81] UN, 'Replies Received from Member States and the European Union' in 'Report to the Secretary-General A/72/307' (9 August 2017).

and international organisations have not only registered their concern regarding the legality of the regime of unilateral sanctions, but on several occasions have registered their dissatisfaction with the regime because it restricts non-sanctioned states' ability to enjoy fundamental freedoms and rights recognised and guaranteed by international law.

For the achievement of the SDGs, it is considered important to develop the international trading mechanism in a holistic fashion, to improve not only the system in terms of delivering economic growth, but also to improvise the means to achieve inclusive and sustainable growth, poverty reduction and welfare enhancement.[82] To devise the system of international trade and development on every possible front, the allocation of stable and long-term public and private resources for sustainable development from the global financial system is a must.[83] As far as the SDGs are concerned, they represent global commitment to overcome some of the most significant challenges the international community of states are exposed to, whereas the economic isolation or lockdown of a sanctioned state may in many ways deter such efforts and commitment. Additionally, the SDGs commit themselves to abide by the principles of the Charter, human rights treaties[84] and various other environmental conventions,[85] and to reaffirm the principles of the Rio Declaration on Environment and Development, including the principle of common but differentiated liability, for the advancement of the set goal.[86] Therefore, when an effort of such a scale and potential is restricted due to a regime decided unilaterally by a state, the justifiability of the regime becomes questionable.

Therefore, the author believes that the establishment of the environmental rule of law could act as the answer to fight the overbearing impact of unilateral sanctions on sustainable development. It is worth noting that the environmental rule of law is the result of the collection of state practices and the best practices for achieving development sustainably.[87] It represents the bottom-up approach of universal lawmaking as it aims to design the laws, implement them using capable government institutions that can be held accountable by the informed public, together leading to the culture of compliance by embracing environmental and social values.[88]

D. Biological Diversity

Protection and conservation of biological diversity have innumerable benefits to human wellbeing and health. A large majority of the population thrives on biological diversity as a means of sustenance. Unfortunately, unsustainable and rapid development

[82] UN, International Trade and Development: Report of the Secretary-General, A/72/274, 2 August 2017, 72nd Session, Item 18(a) of the provisional agenda Macroeconomic policy question: International trade and development, para 1.

[83] UN, International Financial System and Development: Report of the Secretary-General, A/72/306, 9 August 2017, 72nd Session, Item 18(b) of the provisional agenda: Macroeconomic policy questions.

[84] UN, A/RES/70/1 (n 10) para 11.

[85] ibid, para 12

[86] ibid, para 13.

[87] IUCN, 'IUCN World Declaration on the Environmental Rule of Law' (n 71) 1.

[88] ibid.

over the last century has resulted in extensive degradation of the Earth's ecological and biogeochemical systems.[89] The result of the transformation of these systems is felt by the life on the planet. With a rapidly changing climate and the rising of greenhouse gas emissions, the Earth's temperature is on the rise, leading to fluctuations within ecosystems and biodiversity, along with regional climates, and that could harm many species.[90]

It is this realisation that led to the signing of the multilateral agreement for the protection of biological diversity in 1992. The protection and conservation of biological diversity are recognised as the 'common concern' by the Convention on Biological Diversity (CBD).[91] Like most of the conventions or the treaties within environmental law, the CBD was drafted based on the cardinal principles of conservation and protection of the biological diversity using inter-state cooperation. It is a landmark Convention in the history of environmental law as it not only acquired nearly universal membership, but has, alongside the UNFCCC, 1992,[92] formally affirmed 'that it is not the biological diversity but the loss of biological diversity which is of common concern to the humankind'.[93] The Convention raises specific obligations on the state for the conservation of biological diversity, which are to be read with general principles of international law, thus raising several obligations for the state to perform internally as well as in collaboration with others.

Similarly, and with a more niche objective, the Convention on Trade in Endangered Species (CITES), a convention on international trade in endangered species in wild fauna and flora, was drafted.[94] The notion of the emerging environmental rule of law (as discussed above) is of particular importance in this context. The findings of the global report on the environmental rule of law demonstrate the link between the weak presence of environmental law and its compliance mechanisms, and the manner in which it relates to the illegal trade in endangered species.[95] It argues that the institutional weakness of the Government to inspect, prosecute and punish the violators encourages the

[89] WHO, 'Connecting Global Priorities: Biodiversity and Human Health: A State of Knowledge Review' (World Health Organization and Secretariat of the Convention on Biological Diversity, 2015) XI.

[90] L Harper, 'What is Biodiversity and How Does Climate Change Affect It?', State of the Planet Earth Institute and Columbia University (15 January 2018), available at blogs.ei.columbia.edu/2018/01/15/biodiversity-climate-change.

[91] UN, Convention on Biological Diversity, 1992 (Signatories: 168, Parties: 196) UNTS Vol 1760, 79; the Convention was open for signature at Rio de Janeiro by all states and regional economic integration organisations from 5 June 1992 until 14 June 1992 and remained open at the UN Headquarters in New York until 4 June 1993).

[92] UN, United Nations Framework Convention on Climate Change, 1992 (Signatories: 165, Parties: 197) UNTS Vol 1771, 107; The Convention was agreed upon and adopted by the Intergovernmental Negotiating Committee for a Framework Convention on Climate Change, during its 5th Session, second part, held at New York from 30 April to 9 May 1992. In accordance with its Art 20, the Convention was open for signature by States Members of the UN or of any of its specialised agencies or that are parties to the Statute of the International Court of Justice and by regional economic integration organisations, at Rio de Janeiro during the UN Conference on Environment and Development, from 4 to 14 June 1992, and remained thereafter open at the UN Headquarters in New York until 19 June 1993.

[93] UN, Convention on Biological Diversity (n 91) Preamble.

[94] UN, Convention on International Trade in Endangered Species of Wild Fauna and Flora, 1973, signed in Washington, DC on 3 March 1973; 183 Parties (as of 24 September 2019), 993 UNTS 243, 27 UST 1087, 12 ILM 1085 (1973) [1976] ATS 29.

[95] IUCN (n 71) 31.

trend for non-compliance, thus resulting in corrupt practices.[96] This environment is lucrative for the illicit trafficking of flora and fauna, resulting in the decline of natural resources and the growth of organised crime.[97] Illegal trade in environmental contraband is fourth in line after drugs, counterfeiting and human trafficking. The UN has conclusively correlated the link between illicit wildlife trafficking and corruption.[98]

In the case of Iran, the alarming increase in the smuggling of wild cats over the last few decades is notable, as the country suffered political instability and the impact of strict and coercive unilateral sanctions. Iran has been a signatory to the Convention since 1976 and is under international legal obligation to comply with the provisions of the Convention.[99] The Standing Committee of CITES (SC65) concluded on 14 July 2014 that to undertake steps for better implementation of the Convention and to give effect to the resolutions it is crucial to translate the decisions of the Convention into national law.[100] However, it is difficult for a state to comply with such initiatives under the influence of sanctions. The recommendation, however, seems to be in line with the emerging notion of the environmental rule of law. The Committee also expressed its concern about the global trade in cheetahs, providing evidence of the smuggling of live cheetahs for the pet trade. East Africa was recorded as having the highest recorded level of illegal trade in live cheetahs. The International Union for Conservation of Nature's (IUCN) Red List of Threatened Species – the global authority on the status of biological diversity[101] also classified the Asiatic cheetah at significant risk of extinction.[102] Therefore, the Committee requested countries to monitor strictly and provide credible data concerning wild cats, and to report and contain the threat of their extinction. This required complying with the Convention and working in collaboration with neighbouring states in every possible manner.

This section has explored some of the environmental concerns resulting from the impact of unilateral sanctions by further demonstrating the relationship between unilateral sanctions and the violation of international obligations of the state/s arising from the multilateral/international environmental agreements. The following section evaluates the concerns arising from both regimes.

[96] J Friedberg and B Zaimov, 'Politics, Environment, and the Rule of Law in Bulgaria' (1994) 4 *Duke Journal of Comparative & International Law* 225.

[97] A Goyenechea and RA Indenbaum, 'Combating Wildlife Trafficking from Latin America to the United States: The Illegal Trade from Mexico, the Caribbean, Central America and South America and What We Can Do to Address It' (Defenders of Wildlife, 2015).

[98] Government of the UK, Declaration of the London Conference on the Illegal Wildlife Trade (London, 2014).

[99] ibid; CITES, 'List of Contracting Parties with Status of Iran (Islamic Republic of)', available at www.cites.org/eng/disc/parties/chronolo.php.

[100] CITES, 'CITES Standing Committee (SC65) Conclusions: A Focus on the Front Lines: Roll out of wildlife targeted actions to strengthen enforcement and conservation starts to show results' Press Release, available at www.cites.org/eng/news/pr/2014/SC65_focus_on_the_front_lines.

[101] IUCN, 'IUCN 2019: West Asia Regional Office Annual Report 2019' (2020), available at portals.iucn.org/library/dir/publications-list?field_pub_ca ll_number_tid=%22IUCN-2020-005%2C%20En%22.

[102] K Walker, 'Hitting Nature Where It Hurts: Iran Feels the Pernicious Effects of US sanctions on biodiversity conservation' *Equal Times: Environment*, 27 February 2019, available at www.equaltimes.org/hitting-nature-where-it-hurts-iran?lang=en#.Xin7M2gzauW.

III. Variance in Law and Environmental Security

To preserve the object and purpose of the multilateral agreements discussed above, the establishment of a robust system of environmental law seems a necessity. It requires a country to undergo a reformative change at every possible level, along with expertise, human resources and a vast sum of investments, because a culture of compliance, reporting and monitoring is at the heart of the environmental rule of law.[103] For a country undergoing political instability or armed conflict, this may be somewhat challenging.

Under the impact of coercive unilateral sanctions, the country suffers instability, financial restraints, inflation and the devaluation of the local currency. These further reduce the spending power of the state, making options such as poaching and unsustainable and illegal exploitation of resources much more attractive. This study reveals that these options usually flourish amid sanctions, giving rise to the vast social and political cost of smuggling as well as unprecedented health hazards.[104] Consider Cambodia's attempts to protect its natural resources. Cambodia enacted the environmental legislation, but the country's legislation and the supporting institutions did not support the initiative whilst the country was at war.[105] However, right after Cambodia gained stability, it reassessed its environmental law and implementation strategies to realise the environmental rule of law for attaining sustainable development.[106]

The above analysis implies that in a country with a weak environmental rule of law corrupt practices and non-compliance of the provisions of environmental law are encouraged. In other words, the presence of the environmental rule of law and its strict compliance creates the situation favourable for honouring the objectives of CITIES, CBD and other multilateral environmental treaties/conventions, both within and beyond national boundaries. The regime of sanctions has most definitely increased the hardship of the nation. Major environmental problems, such as increased air pollution, biodiversity losses, diminishing water resources, non-compliance with SDG 2030 and others, are transboundary and determined to cross all geographical and political boundaries. The transboundary issue is most severely impacted because the political isolation of the sanctioned state not only reduces considerably the coordination between neighbouring states, but creates distrust among the states by posing a threat to international peace and security,[107] thus affecting both sanctioned and non-sanctioned states.

Sovereignty and cooperation are the cardinal principles underpinning the success of the regime of unilateral sanctions and environmental concerns. However, the manner in which these notions are construed creates all the difference – absolute sovereignty of the sanctioning state and limited cooperation guide the sanctions regime, whereas

[103] IUCN (n 71) 17–31.

[104] E Batmanghelidj and G Heydari, 'Sanctions, Smuggling, and the Cigarette: The Granting of Iran Office of Foreign Asset Control's Licenses to Big Tobacco' (2014) 5 *International Journal of Preventive Medicine* 138.

[105] Y Sokphea, 'Practices and Challenges Towards Sustainability' in K Brickell and S Springer (eds) (Routledge Handbook Online, September 2016).

[106] WJ Schulte and A Stetser, 'On the Path to Sustainable Development: An Assessment of Cambodia's Draft Environmental Impact Assessment Law' (2014) 3 *Cambodian Law and Policy Journal* 1.

[107] MS Bonetti, 'The Analysis and Interpretation of Economic Sanctions' (1997) 25 *Journal of Economic Studies* 324.

environmental concerns advocate the use of limited sovereignty and demand excessive cooperation. As far as sanctions are concerned, the unilateral sanctions regime exhibits absolute sovereign authority without taking into account similar rights for others. Moreover, during the time sanctions are in place, they limit cooperation between the states concerned as well as between the targeted state and other international and regional entities. Thus, unilateral sanctions produce an extraterritorial impact for the sanctioned and sanctioning states as well as for third parties.[108]

For instance, under international environmental law, states are expected to conduct themselves in a manner that is respectful of similar rights of others. Yet cooperation is demanded at every possible level and in the form of various specific and general obligations rooted in national and international legal documents. These principles together form the soul and philosophy of most, if not all, multilateral environmental agreements. If we compare the intent and the manner in which these principles are used in the above-mentioned regimes, it is relatively easy to deduce the state practice, *opinio juris*, and the emerging legal obligation from various multilateral agreements in favour of such interpretation for the environmental concern.

An increasing volume of state practice has the principles of environmental law and sustainability at its heart,[109] whereas unilateral sanctions are contested in law and academic circles;[110] more so, strong dissatisfaction of the regime is registered by most of the states and regional organisations using the UN as a platform.[111] Some academics were suspicious that the growing state practice might lead to formal recognition of the practice of imposition of unilateral sanctions and develop it into customary law if the practice continues to reflect *opinio juris*.[112] Contrary to speculation, this evolving state practice has gained strong opposition from the states and international organisations, and this resentment has risen because it works against the principles of the Charter, principles of international law and the principle of the rule of law. Additionally, some non-sanctioned states, like India, have gone on record making statements refusing the sanctions imposed by a state unilaterally, both in the case of US-imposed sanctions on Russia[113] and Iran,[114] as they were propagated by creating direct and indirect pressure on the sanctioned and non-sanctioned states using coercive or other means.[115]

[108] R Mohamad, 'Unilateral Sanctions in International Law: A Quest for Legality' in AZ Marossi and MR Bassett (eds), *Economic Sanctions Under International Law: Unilateralism, Multilateralism, Legitimacy, and Consequences* (TMC Asser Press, 2015) 71.

[109] UN, 'Implementation of Agenda' 21, The programme for the Further Implementation of Agenda 21 and the Outcomes of the World Summit on Sustainable Development', A/RES/64/236 (64th Session, Agenda item 53(a) – Resolution adopted by the General Assembly, 31 March 2010).

[110] J Ilieva, A Dashtevski and F Kokotovic, 'Economic Sanctions in International Law' (2018) 9 *UTMS Journal of Economics* 201; see also Marossi and Bassett, *Economic Sanctions under International Law* (2015) 71.

[111] UN, A/72/307 (n 78).

[112] M Hakimi and JK Cogan, 'The Two Codes on the Use of Force' (2016) 27 *European Journal of International Law* 257.

[113] R Chauhan, 'Decoding India's Stand on International Sanctions', Centre for the Advance Study of India (15 December 2014), available at www.casi.sas.upenn.edu/iit/chauhan.

[114] N Verma, 'India Says It Only Follows UN Sanctions, Not US Sanctions on Iran', Reuters New Delhi (28 May 2018), available at in.reuters.com/article/india-iran/india-says-it-only-follows-u-n-sanctions-not-u-s-sanctions-on-iran-idINKCN1IT0W5.

[115] I Jazairy, 'Unilateral Economic Sanctions, International Law, and Human Rights' (2019) 33 *Ethics & International Affairs* 291.

Former foreign minister Mrs Sushma Swaraj emphasised this, saying that India is sworn to comply with sanctions imposed by the UN and not by one country unilaterally.[116] It is this contestation which demands further research in this field.

Against this backdrop, the work of the Asian African Legal Consultative Organisation (AALCO) shows the consistent practice of developing nations towards the unilateral sanctions and their extraterritorial impacts on states.[117] They consider the extraterritorial implications and the impact of sanctions on third parties as restrictive and in violation of some of the basic freedoms guaranteed by international law and its general principles. Similar to the reasoning mentioned above, the findings reaffirmed that these sanctions work against the spirit of the multilateral sanction guaranteed by the Charter, as they promote self-interest and are against the rule of law.[118]

The central bank of a developing country plays a pivotal role in its development and in facilitating the realisation of the basic human rights of the people.[119] Upon closer scrutiny, the sanctions were regarded as causing damage to the banking sector and the economy, thus inflicting suffering among civilians by causing deprivation of their basic human rights.[120] Therefore, by emphasising the role of the central banks, AALCO proposed as a remedy that they must be granted immunity, and the assets and property under their possession must not be attached amid sanctions.[121] The AALCO registered its vexation towards a unilateral sanction regime using the UN as a platform, and has been unvarying ever since. It not only registered its dissatisfaction with the regime of sanctions, but also recommended certain changes to accommodate or subside the negative impact of sanctions.

Furthermore, the trends dictate that unilateral sanctions are often imposed upon smaller countries by larger and economically powerful countries. This is because enforcing sanctions requires a huge economic and political arm which is more likely to be mobilised by a larger and powerful country.[122] Perhaps the more fundamental question here is why a foreign policy tool that is wielded much more by the rich countries than by the poorer is gaining significance – although the means and instruments of economic coercion are categorised as a grey area in international law,[123] and environmental concerns have gained authority in terms of law, morale and the necessity in the Anthropocene.

[116] D Maheshwari, Sushma refuses to back US sanctions on Iran as Zarif visits India' *National Herald* (28 May 2018), available at www.nationalheraldindia.com/international/sushma-swaraj-refuses-to-back-us-sanctions-on-iran-as-zarif-foreign-minister-visits-india.

[117] AALCO, 'Extraterritorial Applications of National Legislation: Sanctions Imposed Against Third Parties'. AALCO/53/TEHRAN/2014/SD/26, prepared by AALCO New Delhi, India, 2014.

[118] ibid, para 15.

[119] G Epstein, 'Central Banks as Agents of Economic Development – Working Paper Series 104', University of Massachusetts Amherst, Political Economy Research Institute (September 2005).

[120] R Mohamad, 'Unilateral Sanctions in International Law' keynote speech at TMC Asser Institute, The Hague (11 July 2013) 3.

[121] AALCO, *Unilateral and Secondary Sanctions: An International Law Perspective* (AALCO Secretariat, 2013) ch 3.

[122] L Davis and S Engerman, 'History Lessons: Sanctions: Neither War nor Peace' (2003) 17 *Journal of Economic Perspective* 96.

[123] A Hofer, 'The Developed/Developing Divide on Unilateral Coercive Measures: Legitimate Enforcement or Illegitimate Intervention?' (2017) 16 *Chinese Journal of International Law* 175.

The enumerated principles of environmental law govern the environmental legislation of the state as well as multilateral environmental agreements.[124] They have attained validity, conformation and consistent support by states over the past few decades, and later gained confirmation by academic writings and jurists' opinions, along with decisions of the courts of law and arbitral decisions, both nationally and internationally.[125] They have survived the test of time and varying circumstances. The variance between the two regimes discussed above is clear and they are, at times, in contradiction to one another; therefore, a legitimate space must be identified or created so they can coexist.

IV. Sanctions and the Environmental Security: Can they Coexist?

In addition to the fact that unilateral sanctions stand on shaky legal and moral ground, they are often blamed for not achieving what they intended originally, which undermines the regime itself. In Iran, sanctions did gain some traction by causing damage to the Iranian economy, but failed to achieve a similar level of success politically. As Hakim suggests, sanctions most definitely weaken the economy, destabilise state welfare programmes and force the state instead to shift to survival mode.[126] Sanctions cripple the economic and political ties of the sanctioned state with the rest for the world. Under sanction, the government is pressurised, and its capabilities are impacted by economic restraints and political isolation. The regime of the sanctioned state often tends to overlook the real problem and concentrate on treating the symptoms of the issues superficially for short-term gain,[127] to be dealt with in detail once the state attains normalcy. However, in the case of Iran, sanctions have been imposed for more than four decades, and over such an extended period, economic stagnation and disintegrated planning could easily result in environmental disaster. The environment-related challenges are currently considered as an evolving threat for the rule of law and the protection of human rights, posing a constant and direct threat to inter- and intra-generational equity, and peace and security.[128]

[124] P Sands and J Peel, *Principles of International Environmental Law*, 4th edn (Cambridge University Press, 2018).

[125] S Kravchenko, TMR Chowdhury and MJH Bhuiyan, *Routledge Handbook of International Environmental Law* (Routledge, 2012).

[126] K Walker, 'Hitting Nature Where It Hurts: Iran Feels the Pernicious Effects of US Sanctions on Biodiversity Conservation' *EqualTimes* (27 February 2019), available at www.equaltimes.org/hitting-nature-where-it-hurts-iran?lang=en#.XkBMgWgzauX; see also S Hakim, 'The Impact of Economic Sanctions on The Environment: The Iranian Example' (poster explaining the 'Survival Mode' at Imperial College London, Centre for Environmental Policy).

[127] K Madani, 'Water Management in Iran: What is Causing the Looming Crisis?' (2014) 4 *Journal of Environmental Studies and Sciences* 315.

[128] UNDP, 'Capacity4dev: Environmental Crime Threatening Peace and Security, INTERPOL-UN Environment Report', UN Environment Programme – Environment for Development, EU (8 December 2016), available at europa.eu/capacity4dev/unep/blog/environmental-crime-threatening-peace-and-security-finds-new-interpol-un-environment-report.

In order to minimise the harmful impact of sanctions on the civilian population and to reduce their suffering, the regime focuses on targeting specific individuals or entities. This tactic is applied equally by the UN's regional and unilateral sanctions regimes. Additionally, exceptions to the sanction regime on humanitarian grounds (to reduce the hardships of civilians) is permissible and despite sanctions, the sanctioning authority provides for an exemption on humanitarian grounds. For instance, the US sanctions regime of 2019 did not prevent the US from donating a large sum of money to help earthquake victims of Iran (February and May 1997).[129]

After acknowledging the difficulty of, and learning from the experience of the impact of sanction regimes on humanitarian action and after noting the exceptions granted on humanitarian grounds, this chapter now seeks to weigh the available options to sketch a future course of action.

Interestingly, one of the most potent tools used amid economic sanctions is financial restriction. Financial restrictions imposed on banks, financial systems, donors, etc create an additional burden for the environmental concerns discussed above, mainly because these require huge investments and cooperation. This restriction legally binds the banks to *the principle of due diligence* and *know your customer or customers' customer*, such that they have to be specific regarding the client and the money they operate with. This obligation stretches to monitoring activities to assure that they are in no way violating the sanctioned regime.[130] This is a resource-intensive and high-risk job for the bank. Therefore, they often choose not to deal with such organisations amid sanctions; this phenomenon is termed 'derisking'.

Moreover, hefty fines, civil and criminal prosecutions and reputational loss in the international market prevent financial institutions from participating in transactions which might fall within the ambit of the sanctioned regime.[131] The same applies to the donor institutions or donors. They are reluctant to provide funds due to robust compliance mechanisms and risk of fine and persecution, thus making it very difficult for a sanctioned state to move finances and to acquire foreign funding.

Despite the upgraded sanctions regime with the provision of exceptions on humanitarian grounds, the situation demands exacting standards from the state to ensure strict implementation responding to the humanitarian out-cry.[132] Serious hardship can be experienced by the sanctioned state due to financial restrictions applied by an organisation acting within the framework of exceptions for humanitarian action. The level of difficulty expected for the exception granted for environmental concerns would be higher, which could cause harm to the global environment due to the difficulty in

[129] ICRS Report, 'Iran Sanctions', RS20871 (updated 24 January 2020) 5: 'Exception for U.S. Humanitarian Aid The terrorism list designation, and other U.S. sanctions laws barring assistance to Iran, do not bar U.S. disaster aid. The United States donated $125,000, through relief agencies, to help victims of two earthquakes in Iran (February and May 1997); $350,000 worth of aid to the victims of a June 22, 2002 earthquake; and $5.7 million in assistance for victims of the December 2003 earthquake in Bam, Iran, which killed 40,000. The U.S. military flew 68,000 kilograms of supplies to Bam'.

[130] T Keatinge, '"Counter-terrorist regulation restricts charity banking worldwide …": Uncharitable Behaviour' (Demos, 2014).

[131] 'Major Settlements/Fines Paid by banks for Violations' (Iran Sanctions (n 129), updated 15 November 2019) 33.

[132] A Debarre, 'Issue Brief: Safeguarding Humanitarian Action in Sanctions Regimes' (International Peace Institute, June 2019) 1.

establishing the causal link between the developing environmental crisis and its relation to the direct and indirect impact caused to the state subjected to a unilateral sanctions regime.[133] A multi-layer and multi-sectoral collaboration is required at every possible level to address the environmental crisis, making state involvement mandatory for the task. Due to the nature of the environmental issue, it is challenging to keep a close tab on the chain of events, the money trail and the sharing of expertise and technology. Therefore, in their existing form it seems improbable that unilateral sanctions and environmental security might coexist. A legal apparatus is thus required to rethink and accommodate the changing needs of the modern world.

V. Conclusion

This study confirms the harmful impact of unilateral sanctions on the environment. Sanctions do not directly cause environmental degradation, but they certainly aggravate the crisis by limiting the ability of the state in so many ways. The limitations imposed on the sanctioned state create a situation of political and financial isolation, thus discouraging the compliance with international obligations arising from environmental treaties and the Conventions for the sanctioned and non-sanctioned state.

International law generally lacks a mechanism for the enforcement of international obligations[134] and this is more so in the case of environmental law treaties.[135] But environmental treaties stand on a strong legal foundation. If states decide to override the international obligations under such treaties, they would be labelled as states in violation of international obligations arising from international law and would suffer reputational loss among the community of states. Additionally, states possess the option of using secondary means of state responsibility to compensate for the lack of a robust primary compliance mechanism.[136] Therefore, it is strongly recommended to contain the impacts of unilateral sanctions in a way that does not conflict with international obligations arising from environmental treaties.

The author proposes to explore the possibility of the establishment of the emerging notion of *the environmental rule of law*,[137] which is equally applicable for all; and to modify the existing practice of granting an exception to the regime in the way it accommodates the environmental concerns and respects the environmental rule of law. This issue is worth exploring for two reasons: primarily, these mechanisms will enhance the accountability of the states involved; and secondly, it might place an additional financial and administrative restraint upon the state imposing the sanction.

[133] T Crawford, 'The Problems of Causation in Private Legal Remedies for Damage from Acid Rain' (1984) 17 *Natural Resources Lawyer* 413.

[134] AT Guzman, 'A Compliance-Based Theory of International Law' (2002) 90 *California Law Review* 1823.

[135] AE Boyle, 'Saving the World? Implementation and Enforcement of International Environmental Law Through International Institutions' (1991) 3 *Journal of Environmental Law* 229.

[136] Draft Articles on Responsibility of States for Internationally Wrongful Acts, with commentaries 2001 (Text adopted by the International Law Commission at its 53rd session, in 2001, and submitted to the General Assembly as a part of the Commission's report covering the work of that session (A/56/10); See also: *Yearbook of the International Law Commission* (2001) II, Part Two.

[137] IUCN (n 71).

Finally, the notion of the environmental rule of law could provide a platform for comparing various international obligations that are owed to the international community with the obligations arising from the sanctions and owed to the sanctioning state. This comparison could inspire focused research into the negative impact of unilateral sanctions and into the means to contain those threats. Therefore, it is expected that international law will advance itself in a manner that strictly restricts the survival of any regime if it is violative of *the rule of law* or *the environmental rule of law*.[138]

A sharp and consistent rise in the practice of states to use unilateral sanctions as a tool of foreign policy is indicative of the need for a set of rules to govern unilateral sanctions. In the absence of such rules, the sanctions imposed by one state on another would undermine the fundamental principles of international environmental law and contribute to the degradation of the environment, both nationally and internationally.[139]

Respect for the rule of law enables the UN Charter to achieve its aims and objectives. Chapter VII of the Charter authorises the Security Council to undertake certain measures for the fulfilment of the aims and objects of the Charter.[140] It is evident that transnational crimes pose an imminent threat to international peace and security, which deepens when the prospects to contain that threat are underexplored, and the threat can transcend national borders.[141] The consequences of environmental challenges could affect the entire international community by aggravating the causes that can induce a change in climatic conditions and loss of biological diversity, etc. Thus, environmental threats discussed in section II above qualify on all those parameters. It is well established that environmental concerns are transboundary, can easily transcend national borders and possess the potential to cause imminent threat to international peace and security.[142] Additionally, to this author's knowledge, the issue of the detrimental impact of unilateral sanctions on the environment is underexplored (or not extensively written about), mainly because of the difficulty in establishing a causal link between the two. Therefore, the prospects to contain that threat are underexplored too. Perhaps by emphasising these aspects of environmental issues as being a consequence of unilateral sanction, the UN can actively engage in the exploration of the subject under the powers and duties vested in its Charter.

[138] ibid.

[139] Davis and Engerman,'History Lessons' (2003) 96.

[140] UN, Charter of the United Nations and Statute of the International Court of Justice, 1948 (193 Members, 49 Original Members and 144 Members having been admitted in accordance with Article 4) Ch VII.

[141] UN, 'Transnational Threats' (United Nations and the Rule of Law), available at www.un.org/ruleoflaw/thematic-areas/transnational-threats.

[142] G Pleuger, 'Climate Change as a Threat to International Peace – The Role of the UN Security Council' in SV Schorlemer and S Maus (eds), *Climate Change as a Threat to Peace: Impacts on Cultural Heritage and Cultural Diversity*, new edn (Peter Lang AG, 2014) 33.

12

Use of Cyber Means to Enforce Unilateral Coercive Measures in International Law

ALI ABUSEDRA, ABU BAKAR MUNIR AND MD TORIQUL ISLAM

I. Introduction

The objective of this chapter is to examine the use of cyber means to enforce unilateral coercive measures in international law. In doing so it will consider the relationship between sanction regimes and cyberwarfare, and what might influence the effectiveness of such measures. It will begin by discussing the concept of 'cyber warfare' and the threats that cyberattacks pose to States, organizations and the international legal order. It will then consider sanctions as a response to cyberwarfare, and whether there exists any basis in international law to support the imposition of sanctions as a consequence of cyberattacks. It will also examine existing unilateral legal and institutional frameworks to address the threat of cyberwarfare and the need for cross-border law enforcement co-operation in confronting cyberattacks.

While the twentieth century was marked by conventional military aggressions, the twenty-first century has witnessed the emergence of sophisticated, non-conventional security threats in the form of cyberattacks. The Internet has also experienced a substantial increase in the global use of various modes of electronic behaviour, particularly with advances in information and communications technologies (ICTs) and their widespread dispersal. Consequently, societies are becoming more dependent on ICTs, with aspects of governance being migrated to digital platforms. The cyber domain now constitutes an important component of a state's activities in various spheres, including aspects of its social, economic and political as well as defence undertakings. Although cyberspace presents opportunities to individuals and national security, so too does it pose threats to both of these actors.

The interaction between cyberspace and the 'real' world presents various complex issues from a legal, technical and operational perspective. The emergence of new technologies provides opportunities for cybercriminals to try to avoid detection, but also for states to mitigate the effects of cybercrime. The 'war on terror' which began in the 1990s is also witnessing a gradual paradigm shift into the realm of cyber warfare. Leon Panetta, in his capacity as a former US Secretary of Defense, warned for instance that foreign cyber actors were probing America's critical infrastructure networks, targeting computer control systems which operate chemical, water and electricity plants, as well as transport systems.[1] The United Nations Group of Governmental Experts has also identified cyberwar as one of the most urgent dilemmas of the twenty-first century.[2]

In the context of Clausewitz's 'Principles of War', it can be said that cyberwarfare is not less than a conventional war, since 'war is the continuation of politics by other means'.[3] The legal regulatory frameworks on the imposition of unilateral sanctions are the most ambiguous areas of international relations.[4] As Holland remarks, international law is a vanishing point of jurisprudence because it lacks a lawmaking body, interpreting agency and enforcement mechanisms.[5] Such an outlook gives rise to the perspective that sanctions are a 'grey area' of international law,[6] and this is likely to be greyer in the near future when considering current trends of extreme nationalism, protectionism and unilateralism. Unilateral sanctions denote a middle ground in foreign diplomacy, being comparatively harsher than oral condemnation, but less robust than the use of force.[7] However, sanctions may lead to wars rather than preventing them, while some scholars are of the views that economic sanctions result in the loss of more lives than all other means of war.[8]

II. Defining 'Cyberwarfare'

'Cyberwarfare' refers to warfare whose means and methods are conducted in cyberspace. As Melzer explains, while 'warfare' is commonly understood in reference to the conduct of military hostilities during armed conflict, 'cyberspace' can be described as 'a globally interconnected network of digital information and communications infrastructures, including the Internet, telecommunications networks, computer systems and the information resident therein'.[9] This would mean, for example, that infecting the computer network of an adversary with a malicious virus would amount to an act of cyberwarfare, whereas an aerial attack on a military cyber command facility

[1] US Department of Defense: Remarks by Secretary Panetta on Cybersecurity to the Business Executives for National Security, New York City (11 October 2012), available at archive.defense.gov/Transcripts/Transcript.aspx?TranscriptID=5136.

[2] N Tsagourias, 'The Law of Cyber Warfare: Restrictions, Opportunities and Loopholes' (2017) 15 *Canadian Journal of Law and Technology* 27.

[3] C Von Clausewitz, *On War, ed. and trans* (1976) M Howard and Paret (Princeton University Press, 1976) 75.

[4] CE Cameron, 'Developing a Standard for Politically Related State Economic Action' (1991) 13 *Michigan Journal of International Law* 218.

[5] TE Holland, *The elements of jurisprudence* (Oxford University Press, 1917); RD Sloane, 'Law at the Vanishing Point: A Philosophical Analysis of International Law. By Aaron Fichtelberg' (2010) 104 *American Journal of International Law* 549.

[6] A Hofer, 'The Developed/Developing Divide On Unilateral Coercive Measures: Legitimate Enforcement or Illegitimate Intervention?' (2017) 16 *Chinese Journal of International Law* 175.

[7] B Early, 'Statecraft and the Limitations of Economic Sanctions' *E-International Relations* (21 August 2016), available at www.e-ir.info/2016/08/21/statecraft-and-the-limitations-of-economic-sanctions.

[8] AM. Codevilla, 'Do Economic Sanctions Work?' *Hoover Institution* (29 March 2018), available at www.hoover.org/research/do-economic-sanctions-work.

[9] N Melzer, *Cyberwarfare and International* Law (UNIDIR Resources Paper, 2011) 4.

would not.[10] Nonetheless, although cyberwarfare is conducted in cyberspace, it may produce effects outside the cyber domain, and in some situations, this could be the outcome desired by the attacker. Targets might therefore include persons or industries which are dependent on computer networks for their operation and functionality, for example, transport networks, power grids or persons who are connected to medical or military computer systems.

While 'cyberwar' has been popularised by the media in news headlines, the international cyber defence community is yet to ratify a single universal definition. Eugene Kaspersky, the founder of Kaspersky Lab, which is a multinational cybersecurity and anti-virus provider, considers the term 'cyberwar' a misnomer, and instead suggests the label 'cyberterrorism'.[11] According to Kaspersky, in order to refer to a 'war' an individual would need to know who is behind the attack, when it took place and when the perpetrator would act again. In a similar regard, Howard Schmidt, who served as the White House Cyber-Security Coordinator during the Obama administration, remarked that 'cyberwarfare' is 'terrible metaphor' and a 'terrible concept' as there 'are no winners in that environment'.[12] There are also variations in how countries interpret the term 'cyberwar', for example, with Russia preferring the description of 'information warfare', while China favours 'networked operations' or 'information operations'. In considering the definitional conundrum and the nature of Internet-based attacks, Barnett coins the term metaphorically as 'A Different Kettle of Fish'.[13]

Due to the specific characteristics of cyberspace, cyberwarfare is very unique in the context of how international law may be interpreted and applied to cyberattacks. In this regard, Melzer further explains that 'cyberspace is the only domain which is entirely man-made. It is created, maintained, owned and operated collectively by public and private stakeholders across the globe and changes constantly in response to technological innovation'.[14] As such, cyberspace is not confined to geopolitical or natural boundaries. Instead, it involves the travel of data 'in the form of multiple digitalized fragments through unpredictable routings before being reconstituted at their destination'.[15] During this process, cybercriminals are able to render identification and designation difficult as their activities can be disguised through means such as employing Internet Protocol (IP) address 'spoofing' or setting up 'botnets' which can be used for malicious activities such as stealing data, spamming users of the network and carrying out Distributed Denial of Service (DDOS) attacks. Member States within the United Nations System 'confer on the Security Council primary responsibility for the maintenance of international peace and security'.[16] Should it be determined by the Security Council that there exists a 'breach of the peace', an 'act of aggression' or a 'threat to the peace', it can proceed to undertake or authorise such measures deemed necessary to

[10] ibid.

[11] D Shamah, 'Latest Viruses could Mean "End of World as We Know It" Says Man who Discovered Flame' *The Times of Israel* (6 June 2012), available at www.timesofisrael.com/experts-we-lost-the-cyber-war-now-were-in-the-era-of-cyber-terrorIbi.

[12] R Singel, 'White House Cyber Czar: 'There Is No Cyberwar'' *Wired* (4 March 2010), available at www.wired.com/2010/03/schmidt-cyberwar.

[13] RW Barnett, 'A different Kettle of Fish: Computer Network Attack' (2002) 76 *International Law Studies* 22.

[14] Melzer, *Cyberwarfare* (2011) 5.

[15] ibid.

[16] Art 24, UN Charter.

maintain or restore international peace and security.[17] In considering this framework, it can be suggested that the Security Council's responsibilities also encompasses maintaining international peace and security in cyberspace, since cyberwarfare can have a detrimental impact on international relations between states. The Security Council can take measures such as making recommendations to Member States,[18] and requesting that Member States comply with provisional measures,[19] as well as making determinations on enforcement, whether armed or unarmed.[20]

The UN Charter provides for the 'complete or partial interruption of … telegraphic, radio, and other means of communication'[21] as an example of unarmed enforcement. This provision may be interpreted as outlining an express basis for UN-backed cyber sanctions and cyber blockades, despite the fact that the nature of the attack not being territorial, but instead existing in cyberspace. The Security Council may also deem that actions not involving force would be inadequate, and therefore proceed to 'take such action by air, sea or land forces as may be necessary to maintain or restore international peace and security'[22] as provided for under Article 42 of the UN Charter. Since this Article appears to provide a basis for actions of armed enforcement only 'by air, sea or land forces' from a textual interpretation, the question arises as to whether there is an exclusion against forces operating in cyberspace. However, Melzer contends that 'article 42 of the UN Charter cannot reasonably be interpreted as depriving the Security Council of the possibility to authorize the use of armed force in cyberspace'[23] since the purpose of this Article was not meant to restrict the means of enforcement accessible to the Security Council, but rather to extend them. A 'threat to the peace' is more of a political concept which enables the Security Council to act with broad discretion.[24] Unlike an 'armed attack', a threat to the peace does not presuppose an act which is wrongful against the international community. Therefore, in principle, the Security Council ought to be able to 'authorize enforcement action, including military force, against cyber threats far below the threshold required for self-defensive action or even for a qualification as interstate force'.[25] The Security Council's discretion when determining whether a threat to the peace arises as a result of a cyber operation is not overall unfettered, as it is required to conform to the purposes and principles of the Charter[26] as well as in accordance with the 'principles of justice and international law'.[27]

Peters suggests that current financial sanction practices require immediate updates in order to have adequate impact in resolving modern crises, and as such, cyber-based

[17] Ch VII, UN Charter.
[18] Art 39, UN Charter.
[19] Art 40, UN Charter.
[20] Arts 41 and 42, UN Charter.
[21] Art 41, UN Charter.
[22] Art 42, UN Charter.
[23] Melzer (n 9) 19.
[24] ibid.
[25] ibid.
[26] ibid.
[27] Art 1(1), UN Charter.

strategies should be considered.[28] He contends that overall economic sanctions have existed for decades without any achievement or significant progress towards their desired effects, and that cyber sanctions 'could enhance sanction strategies to more effectively achieve national ends'.[29] It should be considered whether any possible recourse to solutions in international law for cybercrimes can actually have the effect of punishing and deterring hackers. Supporters of expansive cybercrime laws emphasise a state's need to counter online threats, which continue to grow in terms of their sophistication, frequency and damage caused. On a national level, sanctions which are supported by local political, diplomatic and economic influences tend to be the traditional response by a state in relation to a foreign incident or crisis. These may be targeted towards another state or against individual actors. Some sanctions, for instance those imposed on Iran by the US, took many years before 'any actions were realized, implemented, and resolved, and even longer before any results could possibly be tracked to those effects'.[30] As an illustration, from the period 1979 to 2017, 11 distinct legislative acts outlining economic sanctions as well as 17 different Executive Orders have been implemented against Iran as a result of US suspicions regarding their behaviour towards weapons of mass destruction proliferation and alleged terrorist support.[31] If traditional sanctions fail, there are limited choices available to states, and this can lead to costly military action, which has a 'perceived national ineffectiveness'.[32] In this regard, Peters contends that cyber sanctions offer 'an approach to augment U.S. economic sanction effectiveness without a boots on the ground commitment'.[33]

The vast majority of international law norms, be it treaty law or customary international law, were developed many years before the invention of computers. As Delerue explains,

> most of the legal questions relating to cyber operations depend on norms contained in the UN Charter adopted in 1945, the Geneva Conventions of 1949 and their Protocol Additionals, and, most importantly, in the customary international law of responsibility of States for internationally wrongful acts codified by the International Law Commission of the United Nations.[34]

These norms, however, do not only apply to those state activities conducted at the time of their codification or adoption, but to state activities in general. It would therefore follow that international law in general would be applicable to cyber activities. While this conclusion 'has been confirmed by both academic literature and State practice',[35] it is not indicative of the application of the norms of international law in this area being a simple process. While states are increasingly attributing cyber operations to other states publicly, they 'are not assessing the lawfulness of the

[28] M Peters, 'Cyber Enhanced Sanction Strategies: Do Options Exist?' (2016) 6 *Journal of Law & Cyber Warfare*, 95, 95.
[29] ibid.
[30] ibid, 96.
[31] DE. Remmack, 'Iran: U.S. Economic Sanctions and the Authority to Lift Restrictions', Congressional Research Service (15 July 2016).
[32] Peters, 'Cyber Enhanced Sanction Strategies' (2016) 96.
[33] ibid, 97.
[34] F Delerue, *Cyber Operations and International Law* (Cambridge University Press, 2020) 13.
[35] ibid, 13.

cyber operations concerned nor invoking the legal responsibility of the perpetrating States'.[36] This has been the case, for instance, with the hack of Sony Pictures Entertainment in addition to the WannaCry and NotPetya malware occurrences. As Delerue comments:

> Interestingly, since they [States] are not qualifying the cyber operations concerned as internationally wrongful acts, they also seem to be adopting only responses taking the form of lawful measures, at least publicly. These responses take, notably, the form of new sanctions against individuals or entities related to the perpetration of the cyber operations, or deportation of diplomats.[37]

In fact, to date, 'no State has ever publicly framed its response within the international legal mechanism of countermeasures or invoked the right of self-defence in response to cyber operations'.[38] In further consideration of the relationship between international law and cyberattacks, the next section will consider the issue of cyberwarfare in the context of the law of self-defence and international humanitarian law.

III. Cyberwarfare in the Context of *Jus ad Bellum* and *Jus in Bello*

Jus ad bellum refers to a set of criteria which need to be considered before engaging in war, with the effect being to determine whether entering into the war is permissible, in the sense of it being a 'just war'. The UN Charter is the most important source regarding *jus ad bellum* rules. However, other aspects of law, such as the precise framework governing the use of force in instances of self-defence, are derived from customary law developed by state practice and *opinion juris*, as recognised in international law jurisprudence. From this perspective, it should be considered whether circumstances might exist which could classify cyber warfare as amounting to either (i) an internationally wrongful threat or use of force; (ii) an armed attack which justifies recourse to the use necessary and proportionate force in self-defence; and (iii) a threat to the peace, breach of the peace or act of aggression, thereby making such attack subject to the intervention of the UN Security Council. Article 2(4) of the UN Charter incorporates the legal basis for the *jus ad bellum* and Article 51 approves the use of force for self-defence. It states that in their foreign relations, the member nations shall refrain from exercising threats or use of force against the political independence and territorial integrity of any nation or treat some other manner incompatible to the goals of the UN. Furthermore, Article 51 of the UN Charter allows a state to exercise its intrinsic right to individual and collective self-defence as a response to armed conflict.

The restrictions as prescribed for economic sanctions have also been suggested to apply against cyberwar. For example, the UN General Assembly Governmental Group of Experts Report in 2013[39] affirms that customary international law and in particular,

[36] ibid, 431.
[37] ibid.
[38] ibid.
[39] A/RES/68/243.

the UN Charter are applicable against cyber warfare for maintaining peace, security and solidarity worldwide and securing a free, safer, peaceful and easily accessible ICT infrastructure. Likewise, NATO considers the cyber defence as one of its indivisible part of the joint defence tasks as it believes that cyberattacks could have the same impacts as of traditional armed conflict, and accordingly, they might lead to the application of Article 5 of the North Atlantic Treaty, which provides that if a NATO ally is subject to an armed attack, each and every other member of NATO will consider this act of violence as an armed attack against all members and will take the actions it deems necessary to assist the ally attacked.

The phrase *Jus in bello* is a Latin term which means 'law in waging war'. It also refers to International Humanitarian Law (IHL), which governs the way in which warfare is conducted, while military experts refer to it as the law of armed conflict (LOAC). The non-binding handbook, Tallinn Manual on the International Law Applicable to Cyber Warfare,[40] which was created by an independent International Group of Experts (IGE) at the request of NATO, applies *jus in bello* norms to cyberspace. Generally speaking, IHL seeks to minimise unnecessary harm during an armed conflict by establishing rules of proper conduct of hostilities. In order for IHL to govern a cyberattack, it must constitute an 'armed conflict'. The International Committee of the Red Cross (ICRC) addresses only two types of armed conflicts which exist in IHL, namely international armed conflicts, opposing two or more states, and non-international armed conflicts between governmental forces and non-governmental armed groups, or between such groups only.[41] In light of these provisions, it should be considered whether the scope of the LOAC extends to arm conflict. In its Legality of the Threat or Use of Nuclear Weapons advisory opinion, the International Court of Justice (ICJ) invoked 'the Martens Clause' in the Preamble to the Hague Convention IV of 1907, which states that:

> Even in cases not explicitly covered by specific agreements, civilians and combatants remain under the protection and authority of principles of international law derived from established custom, principles of humanity, and from the dictates of public conscience.

This provision may be interpreted as confirmation that even without being mentioned explicitly, IHL extends to the sphere of cyberspace. From this perspective, cyber warfare as a modern concept ought to be considered through the prism of the long-standing principles that form the foundations of *jus in bello*.

There is also the possibility that cyberattacks can transform into one of an indiscriminate nature. Precision in cyberattacks tends to be reserved for those which have highly sophisticated characteristics. However, because of determinants such as human error or deliberate human actions, a cyberattack can easily go rogue, and become transformed into an indiscriminate attack with widespread devastating consequences. Therefore, where a cyberattack in the form of a virus, for example, is able to replicate itself with the effect of widespread cross-border infection, then it will be unlikely for the actors employing the virus to justify its usage under LOAC. To give an example of how

[40] MN Schmitt, *Tallinn Manual on the International Law Applicable to Cyber Warfare* (Cambridge University Press, 2013).

[41] International Committee of the Red Cross (ICRC) Opinion Paper, 'How is the Term "Armed Conflict" Defined in International Humanitarian Law?' Opinion Paper (March 2008) 2.

widespread computer exploits can be, Conficker, which was a worm discovered in 2008, exploited a vulnerability in the Windows Operation System resulting in the infection of millions of computers in over 190 countries, including government, enterprise and home computers, for the purpose of establishing a botnet infrastructure. Conficker was able to spreads by several means while taking the form of three variants, one of which exploits peer-to-peer networking capabilities, thereby providing a fitting example of how malware mutates and evolves in time.

Military necessity as a legal concept is often used in IHL as part of the legal justification criteria when evaluating potential legitimate military targets. In terms of cyberattacks, assessing their *in bello* necessity does not necessarily pose advanced new challenges. It also plays an important role in that it displays precedence over other IHL principles seeking to balance the need to take up arms with the need for victory a military struggle. It could therefore be suggested that hostile cyberattacks arising from military necessity ought to be compliant with other IHL principles of humanity, proportionality, distinction/discrimination, neutrality, and perfidy. To satisfy military necessity, a cyberwar must therefore constitute an attack as required by the law of armed conflict. The concept of military necessity essentially approves the use of force needed to accomplish a mission. In his work entitled 'Cyber Operations and the *Jus in Bello*: Key Issues', Schmitt asserts that violent action is essential to constitute an attack.[42] The principle of distinction requires that cyberattacks must be directed to specific military personnel and objectives, or against any dual structures used for both the military and civilian purposes. Article 23 of the Hague Convention,[43] for example, prohibits the combatants to demolish or confiscate any enemy property, unless required for achieving the goals of the war. Article 36 of the 1977 additional Protocol I to the Geneva Convention[44] requires each state party to make sure that any new weapons it deploys or considers deploying are compliant with the rules of IHL.

Although possible to determine, attribution remains a vital problem in the issue of cyberwar. To fulfil the requirements of the principle of distinction, the proposed cyberwar must be carried on by any state or non-state entity. A fitting example of the problem of attribution can be observed in the 2007 cyberattacks on Estonia. These were manifest in sophisticated DDOS attacks by way of botnets employed for spamming and 'ping floods' against both public and private entities in Estonia, including the Estonian Parliament, government ministries, banks, broadcasters and newspapers. The attacks took place at a time when Estonia and Russia had a disagreement concerning the relocation of the Bronze Soldier of Tallinn, a controversial Soviet World War II memorial, built on the site of several graves. With regards to the difficulty of attribution, the Russian Government denied any involvement in the attacks, claiming that certain patriotic 'hacktivists' of Russia could have independently launched the cyberattacks.

[42] MN Schmitt, 'Cyber Operations and the *Jus in Bello*: Key Issues' (2011) 87 *International Law Studies* 92.

[43] Hague Convention (IV) Respecting the Laws and Customs of War on Land and Its Annex: Regulations Concerning the Laws and Customs of War on Land (adopted 18 October 1907, entered into force 26 January 1910) 36 Stat 2277; UNTS 539 (Hague Convention).

[44] Protocol Additional to the Geneva Conventions of 12 August 1949, and Relating to the Protection of Victims of International Armed Conflicts (Protocol I), (adopted 8 June 1977, entered into force 7 December 1978).

The principle of proportionality entails that the use of force employed in self-defence must be in connection with an immediate and actual armed conflict and must not exceed the threats itself. Attacks which result in substantial losses to the lives of civilians or their assets, or the excessive use of force than essential are completely prohibited. This principle becomes much more critical while applying to any dual-use infrastructure. The theory postulates that the predictable loss incurred by the civilians must not exceed the actual and direct military gain presumed. The last requirement for the imposition of the law of armed conflict against cyberwar is the unnecessary suffering caused by civilians. Cyberattacks on a national power grid, water dam, radio transmission systems, or banking systems for example may cause widespread unnecessary suffering to the civilian lives. In this regard, according to Article 27 of the Hague Convention,

> In sieges and bombardments all necessary steps should be taken to spare as far as possible edifices devoted to religion, art, science, and charity, hospitals, and places where the sick and wounded are collected, provided they are not used at the same time for military purposes.[45]

The existence of threats in the form of cyberattacks therefore causes tremendous security dilemmas and threats to world peace including cybercrimes, technological volatility and other subversive activities. These background realities produce earnest scholarly attention in the legal arena encompassing cyberwar. While initial presumptions were that the internet was not subject to legal regulation, today's assumption is that international law governing the use of force applies to military-like cyberattacks, which is now also considered as the 'fifth domain' of conventional war (after land, sea, air and space). Thus, many nation states are adopting strategies for securing cyberspace. Various international organisations and military alliances, for example, NATO have undertaken programs to raise awareness, including supporting the development on the Tallinn Manual, which is discussed in section IV. Moreover, recent dialogue among current and former government officials from the US, China and Russia at Moscow on guidelines for conflicts within and among computer networks appears to suggest that cyberwarfare is a present-day topic of concern. Nevertheless, it continues to be a long-debated issue as to whether *jus ad bellum* (international law governing the use of force) and *jus in bello* (law of armed conflict) apply to cyberwar. There evidently exists a myriad of differences between traditional warfare and cyberwarfare in terms of the nature, consequences, targets, and initiator of the attacks, for example.

IV. The Tallinn Manuals and Draft Articles on State Responsibility

Both the Tallinn Manual and Draft Articles on Responsibility of States for Internationally Wrongful Acts (Draft Articles)[46] are attempts to codify customary international law in the subjects they address, namely the international law applicable to cyber warfare and

[45] Hague Convention (n 43).

[46] The International Law Commission's Draft Articles on Responsibility of States for Internationally Wrongful Acts, in Report of the International Law Commission, 53rd session (23 April–1 June; 2 July–10 August 2001), General Assembly Official Records, 56th Session, supp no 10, UN Doc A/56/10.

state responsibility. The first Tallinn Manual,[47] which was initially titled the 'Tallinn Manual on the International Law Applicable to Cyber Warfare', essentially provides academic, non-binding approaches to the interpretation of international law in relation to cyber operations and cyberwarfare. The manual was authored between 2009 and 2012 by an international group of experts on the invitation of the Tallinn-based NATO Cooperative Cyber Defence Centre of Excellence, and published in 2013. It focuses mainly on those cyber operations which are most disruptive and destructive, such as those which may occur during armed conflict, or those that qualify as an 'armed attack', thereby allowing states to respond in self-defence. It does so by advocating that existing international law (*jus ad bellum*) and international humanitarian law (*jus in bello*) apply to cyber warfare. The document contains a total of 95 rules, rule 43 of which addresses the issue of indiscriminate means or methods. It suggests that to employ means and methods of cyber-warfare in an indiscriminate manner is prohibited. Giving consideration to Article 51(4)(b) and (c) of the Additional Protocol I of the Geneva Conventions relating to the Protection of Victims of International Armed Conflict, the manual considers acts which can be indiscriminate in nature are those not aimed towards any specific military objectives, nor restricted in their consequences as expected by the law of armed conflict. In this context, the manual explains a piece of malware would violate the rule if it cannot be restrained, but expands harmfully beyond its targeted objects.

Following publication of the Tallinn Manual, the NATO Cooperative Cyber Defence Centre of Excellence released Tallinn 2.0[48] in February 2017. The intention of Tallinn 2.0 was to expand the scope of the Tallinn Manual with emphasis being placed on 'cyber operations' as opposed to 'cyber conflict', as discussed in the first manual. The essence of the analysis contained in Tallinn 2.0 rests on the notion that cyber operations cannot exist in a legal vacuum, but instead, already existing international law obligations may be equally applied to the cyber domain. Tallinn 2.0 is divided into four parts with a total of 20 chapters, each of which examines distinct fields of international law as may be applied to cyber operations, while referring to a wide range of century-long case law and international treaties whose scope may be extended to focus on the cyber realm.

Tallinn 2.0 concedes that some cyber operations, similar to actions of a state, are not always actionable per se, with a wide range of cyber activities being generally unregulated. It also affirms that 'a State may not intervene, including by cyber means, in the internal or external affairs of another State'.[49] The manual thus emphasises the role of state sovereignty, and that the principles of international law apply to cyberspace in this area. For instance, Rule 4 of the Manual stresses that 'a State must not conduct cyber operations that violate the sovereignty of another State'. The essence of the perspective contained in Rule 4 lies within the notion that sovereignty is a precondition of international peace and solidarity, therefore encroachment on sovereignty could

[47] Tallinn Manual (n 40).

[48] MN Schmitt, *Tallinn Manual 2.0 on the International Law Applicable to Cyber Warfare* (Cambridge University Press, 2017).

[49] ibid, Rule 32.

be harmful to international relations. Rule 6 of Tallinn 2.0 also declares 'a State must exercise due diligence in not allowing its territory, or territory or cyberinfrastructure under its governmental control, to be used for cyber operations that affect the rights of, and produce serious adverse consequences for, other States'.

Tallinn 2.0 also gives detailed focus on the topic of jurisdiction, with the manual containing six rules and extensive annotation on the issue. According to the manual, subject to limitations outlined in international law, a state may exercise territorial and extraterritorial jurisdiction over cyber activities. This implies that, in principle, cyber activities and the individuals who engage in them are subject to the same jurisdictional prerogatives and limitations as any other form of activity. Rule 9 further asserts that a state can exercise its territorial jurisdiction over (a) cyberinfrastructure and persons engaged in cyber activities on its territory; (b) cyber activities originating in, or completed on, its territory; or (c) cyber activities having a substantial effect on its territory. The manual also considers cyber operations in the context of state responsibility, particularly in relation to the International Law Commission's (ILC) Articles on State Responsibility. For example, Rule 14 of the manual suggests that 'a State bears international responsibility for a cyber-related act that is attributable to the State and that constitutes a breach of an international legal obligation'. The IGE also considered the United Nations Convention on the Law of the Sea, and extended its applicability to cyber operations, Rule 45 of the Manual suggests that 'cyber operations on the high seas may be conducted only for peaceful purposes, except as otherwise provided for under international law'. The experts concluded that 'of particular note in the cyber context is the high seas freedoms of navigation, overflight, and the laying of submarine cables'.

Version 2.0 of the Tallinn Manual also suggests that international human rights law applies to the domain of cyber operations. While Rule 35 affirms that private individuals may enjoy the same protection of international human rights, including the freedom of expression, and the right to privacy in respect of cyber-related affairs, Rule 36 states that 'with respect to cyber activities, a state must: (a) respect the international human rights of individuals, and (b) protect the human rights of individuals from abuse by third parties'. From the perspective of the Vienna Convention on Diplomatic Relations, 1961 and the Vienna Convention on Consular Relations 1963, the IGE suggested in Rule 40 that 'a receiving State must take all appropriate steps to protect cyber infrastructure on the premises of a sending State's diplomatic mission or consular post against intrusion or damage'. Also, addressing diplomatic and consular relations is Rule 41, which advises that the protection granted for diplomatic and consular documents, archives and official correspondence should also apply to electronic versions of the same.

In terms of telecommunications, where there is a lack of customary international law, the IGE, through Rule 64 of the manual asserts that 'a State retains its entire freedom under international telecommunication law with regard to military radio installations'. Furthermore, Rule 63 states that 'a State's use of radio stations may not harmfully interfere with other States' protected use of radio frequencies for wireless cyber communications or services'. The IGE advised that the rule 'applies exclusively to interference caused by one State with another's use of frequencies that enable cyber communications or services, wherever those communications or services take place, including in outer space'.

The rules encompassing countermeasures are governed by the ILC's Articles on the Responsibility of States for Internationally Wrongful Acts. Countermeasures are generally available to states subject to internationally wrongful act, although this is not an unfettered privilege. As influenced by the ILC Articles, Rule 20 of the Tallinn Manual, provides that states are entitled the right to employ cyber or non-cyber countermeasures proportionally and with other limitations of international law. In the context of cyber operations, the IGE advised that the victim nation should consider many issues, including the extent of the injury; the consequence of the infringed principles of international law; the rights of the victim nation, and the holistic need for compliance with international obligations by the responsible state.

Article 2(4) of UN Charter states that 'All Members shall refrain in their international relations from the threat or use of force against the territorial integrity or political independence of any state, or in any other manner inconsistent with the Purposes of the United Nations'. As a customary rule of *jus cogens*, this prohibition is applicable to all states, whether or not they are members of the UN. Whether a specific cyber-attack amounts to a 'threat' of force, thereby violating Article 2(4) of the UN Charter depends upon whether the

> particular use of force envisaged would be directed against the territorial integrity or political independence of a State, or against the Purposes of the United Nations or whether, in the event that it were intended as a means of defence, it would necessarily violate the principles of necessity and proportionality.[50]

If this guidance is applied to cyberwarfare, it is likely that the threat of using cyberwarfare would violate Article 2(4) only in instances where it amounts to an unlawful use of force under the same circumstances. This approach is supported by Rule 12 of the Tallinn Manual, although it has been contended that a demonstration of cyber force could constitute to a 'threat of force' within the meaning of Article 2(4).[51] The IGE was also divided as to whether a state manifestly lacking any capability to make good its threat would be in violation of Article 2(4). Similarly, no consensus could be achieved with regard to a state possessing the capability to carry out the threat but which clearly has no intention of doing so.

There exists at least two areas of uncertainty concerning the law of self-defence in the context of cyber-attacks. Firstly, there is ambiguity as to whether a cyber operation which does not result in physical injury or damage can nonetheless amount to an armed attack in situations where it results in severe non-destructive or non-injurious consequences. Some members of the IGE preferred a narrow approach which restricted the existing law to physical effects whereas others advocated interpretation focusing on the nature of the physical consequences rather than their severity. In the absence of conclusive state practice, however, it is arguable the law of self-defence has not evolved in terms of addressing a situation where non-destructive or non-injurious cyber operations could be regarded as armed attacks. However, it is

[50] Legality of Threat or Use of Nuclear Weapons, Advisory Opinion, 1996, ICJ 226, 48 (8 July).

[51] See, eg, F Delerue, 'Emerging Voices: Cyber Operations and the Prohibition of the Threat of Force', Opinio Juris, available at opiniojuris.org/2014/07/21/emerging-voices-cyber-operations-prohibitionthreat-force (noting that a demonstration of force can constitute a 'second form of threat of force').

possible that while understandings of 'armed conflict' might be severity based in the future, the measurement mechanism to determine the severity remains open to determination. The 'norm' could therefore possibly evolve based on defined categories of targets, such as critical infrastructure which give rise to risks which can lead to harm, or based on various essential activities, such as cybersecurity. Severity might alternatively be measured in terms of degree of harm, such as in the context of its economic impact. The second area of uncertainty is the relationship between the use of force and armed attack thresholds. Whereas the IGE has adopted the position that there exists a difference between the two, the USA has rejected any such notion. It is the US's view that the inherent right of self-defence is applicable to any illegal use of force. Nonetheless, there has been no international cybercrime incidents where the international community has come to common consensus of regarding such incidents as meeting the threshold of an armed attack.

In considering the law of state responsibility, a state bears responsibility for an act if three criteria are met, namely: the attribution of the conduct to the state; the conduct amounts to an internationally wrongful act; and there is an absence of circumstances precluding wrongfulness.[52] Where assumed that a cyberattack can reach the threshold of an armed attack, resulting in the inherent right of self-defence to be triggered, it then becomes necessary to attribute the cyberattack in order to determine to whom the act of self-defence should be directed. The Draft Articles on Responsibility of States for Internationally Wrongful Acts (Draft Articles),[53] like the Tallinn Manual, attempts to codify customary international law in terms of its applicability to cyber warfare and state responsibility. It is a non-binding report produced by the ILC, established in 1948 by the United Nations General Assembly (UNGA) for the promotion of the progressive development of international law, including its codification. The Draft Articles establishes that in order to give rise to state responsibility,[54] internationally wrongful acts have to be attributable to a state and constitute a breach of an international obligation.[55]

Acts can also be attributed to a state where a person or group is acting under the state's direct and effective control,[56] which is the threshold established in the *Nicaragua* case.[57] In accordance with the commentary to the Draft Articles of the ILC, the effective criteria control should be interpreted extensively, with some level of control being enough to attribute the acts to a state.[58] However, as explained by the ICJ in the *Nicaragua* case, 'even the general control … over a force with a high degree of dependency on it' in the absence of further evidence, would not amount to effective control.[59] Another view of required control was presented by the International Criminal Tribunal for the former Yugoslavia (ICTY) in the *Tadić* case regarding the lower threshold of overall control.

52 Delerue, *Cyber Operations* (2020) 112.
53 UN Doc A/56/10 (n 46).
54 ibid, Art 1.
55 ibid, Art 2.
56 ibid, Art 4.
57 *Military and Paramilitary Activities in and against Nicaragua (Nicaragua v United States of America) (Merits)*, Judgement of 27 June 1986, ICJ Reports 1986.
58 Draft Articles on State Responsibility, Commentary accompanying Article 8, paras 3–9.
59 *Nicaragua* case (n 57), para 115.

In this case, the ICTY established the overall control threshold in distinguishing whether or not the armed conflict at hand was international, in stating 'an armed conflict exists whenever there is a resort to armed force between States'.[60] Later, the ICJ addressed the differing thresholds of required control in the *Bosnia Genocide* case, where it concluded that the effective control threshold was the accurate one for the purpose of attribution under the law of state responsibility.[61] The IGE has also considered when state responsibility may occur under Article 11 of the Draft Articles. According to the IGE, attribution could be made to a supporting state. If non-state actors would engage in cyber operations against a state and then another state would support and with its cyber capabilities protect the non-state actors against counter cyber operations, attribution could be made to the supporting state.[62]

In the Tallinn Manual, the IGE expands on the way of attributing cyberattacks in order to establish state responsibility. The IGE found Article 8 of the Draft Articles particularly important in the context of cyber activities. Following Article 8 of the Draft Articles, the Tallinn Manual explains that for a state to be considered responsible for a cyberattack, the attack needs to be attributable to the state and constitute a breach of an international obligation.[63] In its commentary, the IGE largely conforms to the existing framework of state responsibility with prohibited activities by state and non-state organs in their exercise of governmental authority being attributed to the state.[64] As such, the activities of private corporations endorsed by a government to conduct offensive cyber operations against another state, or with the purpose of participating in cyber intelligence gathering maybe attributed to the authorising state.[65] When the Government contracts with a private company to conduct cyber operations, such conduct will be attributable to the state.[66] The IGE, however, appears not to agree upon the requisite control needed of non-state actors in order to establish attribution. While the effective control test in *Nicaragua* applies, the IGE did not rule out the possibility of the less strict overall control requirement from the *Tadić* case being adopted in the cyber context.[67] Furthermore, the IGE has stressed when state responsibility may occur under Article 11 of the Draft Articles. From this context, 'if non-state actors would engage in cyber operations against a State and then another State would support and with its cyber capabilities protect the non-state actors against counter cyber operations'[68] attribution could therefore be made to the supporting state.

[60] ICTY, *The Prosecutor v Dusko Tadic*, Decision on the Defence Motion for Interlocutory Appeal on Jurisdiction, IT-94-1-A, 2 October 1995, para 70.

[61] Case Concerning the Application of the Convention on the Prevention and Punishment of the Crime of Genocide (*Bosnia and Herzegovina v Serbia and Montenegro*), Judgement of 26 February 2007, ICJ Reports 2007, paras 402–07.

[62] Tallinn Manual on the International Law Applicable to Cyber Warfare, Commentary accompanying Rule 6, para 14.

[63] ibid Rule 6.

[64] Draft Articles on State Responsibility, Arts 4 and 5.

[65] Tallinn Manual, Commentary accompanying Rule 6 (n 62) para 8.

[66] ibid, para 9,

[67] *Prosecutor v Duško Tadić*, A Ch, ICTY, Judgement of 15 July 1999, para 131.

[68] Tallinn Manual, Commentary accompanying Rule 6 (n 62) para 14.

While it is not disputed that the rules on state responsibility which govern attribution apply to cyber conduct, 'cyber operations, and more generally the ubiquitous character of the Internet appear to be particularly challenging'[69] for the existing rules. According to Delerue, 'in some cases, the degree of control required by the ICJ might amount to too high a threshold to be applicable and relevant to the use of new technology'.[70] Therefore, reflection is needed to define an appropriate threshold to cater for attribution in instances of cyber operations, while also being cognisant of lowering the threshold too significantly.[71]

Although the Tallinn Manual and Draft Articles serve as a codification of customary international law to a great extent, they ought not to be treated in absolute terms since they are produced by experts. Nonetheless, because of its complex nature, it is generally challenging to treat customary international law as completely absolute. As explained by Ago, 'it is one thing to define a rule and the content of the obligation it imposes, and another to determine whether that obligation has been violated and what should be the consequences of the violation'.[72]

V. Unilateral Approaches to Cybersecurity Sanctions

To date, the US and the EU are the only major international actors to have developed a framework for sanctions based on cyber activities. In the US, the main source of authority for cyber-related sanctions is Executive Order 13694, 'Blocking the Property of Certain Persons Engaging in Significant Malicious Cyber-Enabled Activities' (EO 13694) which was signed into effect by President Barack Obama on 1 April 12015.[73] EO 13694 provides for the authorisation of economic sanctions as a response to malicious cyber activities by establishing a flexible and broad mandate in order to deter future cyberattacks against the private sector as well as critical infrastructure through measures such as blocking access to assets and property. It authorises the imposition of sanctions on those individuals and entities determined to be responsible for, or complicit in malicious cyber activities which result in enumerated harms that are reasonably likely to cause, or have materially contributed to a significant threat to the national security, foreign policy, or economic health or financial stability of the US. This particular EO has been amended to further allow for the imposition of sanctions on individuals and entities determined to be responsible for tampering, altering, or causing the misappropriation of information with the purpose or effect of interfering with or undermining election processes or institutions by EO 13757.[74] This EO, which was issued on 28 December 2016, focuses on specific harms caused

[69] Delerue (n 34) 144.
[70] ibid.
[71] ibid.
[72] Draft Articles on State Responsibility, General Commentary, para 2.
[73] Executive Order No 13694, 80 Fed Reg 18 (2 April, 2015). For analysis of this executive order, see J Lee, 'Cybersecurity Sanctions: A Powerful New Tool', LAW 360 (2 April 2015), available at www.gibsondunn.com/wp-content/uploads/documents/publications/Lee-Cybersecurity-Sanctions-A-Powerful-New-Tool-Law360.pdf.
[74] Executive Order No 13757, 82 Fed Reg 1 (28 Dec 2016).

by significant malicious cyber activities, while directing the Secretary of the Treasury, in consultation with the Attorney-General and the Secretary of State, to impose sanctions on those persons he determines to be responsible for, or complicit in malicious cyber activities. The US Department of State and other US government agencies work to identify individuals and entities whose conduct meets the criteria set forth in EO 13694, as amended, and assign them to be sanctioned under the delegated authority of the Treasury's Office of Foreign Assets Control (OFAC). Persons designated under this authority are added to OFACS's list of Specially Designated Nationals and Blocked Persons (SDN List). Additionally, in 2018, EO 13848 on 'Imposing Certain Sanctions in the Event of Foreign Interference in a United States Election' signed by President Donald Trump, addresses threats by means election interference through cyber means.[75]

Other than the US, the EU is the only major international actor to propose a concrete policy regime to deal with attacks originating from cyberspace. According to Pawlak and Biersteker, the EU's framework of autonomous sanctions 'is one of the tools designed to strengthen the rule-based international order and ensure broader global adherence to the internationally agreed norms of responsible behaviour in cyberspace'.[76] In June 2017, the EU scaled up its response to cyber threats and malicious cyber activities by establishing a Framework for a Joint EU Diplomatic Response to Malicious Cyber Activities (the 'Cyber Diplomacy Toolbox').[77] This framework enables the EU and its Member States to use all Common Foreign and Security Policy (CFSP) measures, including restrictive measures should they be deemed necessary, to 'prevent, discourage, deter and respond to malicious cyber activities targeting the integrity and security of the EU and its Member States'.[78] Following the establishment of the Cyber Diplomacy Toolbox, in April 2019 the Council adopted a regulation entitled the Cybersecurity Act, which introduced a system of EU-wide certification schemes in addition to the EU Agency for Cyber Security to replace the existing European Union Agency for Network and Information Security.[79]

The legal framework which founded the cyber sanctions regime in the EU was adopted in May 2019, thereby establishing a basis by which the EU would be able to impose targeted restrictive measures as a response to cyberattacks. On 17 May 2019, the EU established a sanctions framework which included targeted restrictive measures as a mechanism deter and respond to cyberattacks deemed as constituting an external threat to the EU or its Member States.[80] The new framework established by the European Council represents a unilateral effort by the EU to strengthen its response to cyberattacks and has resulted in the broadening of EU sanctions both in scope and substance.

[75] Executive Order No 13848, 83 Fed Reg 46 (12 September 2018).

[76] P Pawlak and T Biersteker, *Guardian of the Galaxy: EU Cyber Sanctions and Norms in Cyberspace*, European Union Institute for Security Studies (2019) 9.

[77] Council of the European Union, 'EU imposes the first ever sanctions against cyber-attacks' Press Release 294/20 (14 May, 2020), available at www.consilium.europa.eu/en/press/press-releases/2020/05/14/cyber-security-council-extends-sanctions-regime-until-18-may-2021.

[78] ibid.

[79] ibid.

[80] Council of the European Union, 'Cyber-attacks: Council is now able to impose sanctions' Press Release 367/19, (Brussels, 17 May, 2019) www.consilium.europa.eu/en/press/press-releases/2019/05/17/cyber-attacks-council-is-now-able-to-impose-sanctions

The framework is outlined in two documents, being Council Decision (CFSP) 2019/797 and Council Regulation 2019/796. This recently introduced EU framework is significant for two reasons. Firstly, it allows the EU to implement unilateral cyber sanctions. This is noteworthy as it allows for the expansion of the EU's sanctions toolkit from traditional areas of sanctions, such as those imposed as a result of terrorism or based on conflicts in international relations.[81] Secondly, it signals a substantial stride arising from the EU's continued interest in developing an open and secured cyberspace in light of concerns surrounding the operation of malicious actors, particularly in relation misuse of information and communications technologies at state and non-state levels. Considering allegations of a plot by Russia to hack the Organization for the Prevention of Chemical Weapons in the Hague[82] as well as the cyberattack on the German Parliament,[83] European leaders have expressed concern regarding the potential for future cyber-attacks on EU Member States. In this regard, the framework equips the EU with economic recourse to punish cyber-attacks more directly, efficiently and unified.

In accordance with the new EU framework, persons, entities and bodies subject to sanctions will be listed in the Annex to the Council Decision (CFSP) 2019/797 ('Annex I'). With the intention to ensure greater consistency in how sanctioned parties are listed, the European Council has the sole authority to establish and amend Annex I as needed, and would review Annex I 'at regular intervals and at least every 12 months'.[84] The Council has the option of reviewing its decision in light of observations or the presentation of substantial new evidence. The framework includes cyberattacks 'with significant effect, including attempted cyber-attacks with a potentially significant effect, which constitutes an external threat to the Union or its Member States'.[85] To be considered as an external threat, it would mean that the attack originates from outside the EU, uses infrastructure outside the EU, or is with the support, at the direction of or under the control of a person outside the EU.[86] The types of conduct considered as cyber-attacks include unauthorised access to as well as interference with IT systems, in addition to data interference and interception. The approach by the Council in assessing the '*significant effect*' is largely result-oriented, with focus being, inter alia, pursuant to Article 3 of the Council Regulation, on the scope, scale, impact or severity of disruption caused; the amount of economic loss caused; the economic benefit gained by the perpetrator or the amount or nature of data stolen or the scale of data breaches.[87]

[81] E Moret and P Pawlak, European Union Institute for Security Studies, Brief, 'The EU Cyber Diplomacy Toolbox: towards a cyber sanctions regime?' 2 (12 July 2017), available at www.iss.europa.eu/content/eu-cyber-diplomacy-toolbox-towards-cyber-sanctions-regime.

[82] J Barnes, 'UK Plays Pivotal Role in EU's New Cyber-Attack Sections Regime – 'This Is Decisive Action', *Express* (17 May 2019), available at www.express.co.uk/news/uk/1128512/UK-news-EU-cyber-attack-section-regime-European-Council-latest-update.

[83] T Severin and A Shalal, 'German Government under Cyber Attack, Shores Up Defenses', Reuters (1 March 2018), available at uk.reuters.com/article/uk-germany-cyber/german-government-under-cyber-attack-shores-up-defences-idUKKCN1GD4N9.

[84] Council Regulation 2019/796 of 17 May 2019, concerning restrictive measures against cyber-attacks threatening the Union or its Member States, preamble, Art 13, OJ. L 129I, 17.5.2019, 1–12.

[85] Council Decision (CFSP) 2019/797 of 17 May 2019, concerning restrictive measures against cyber-attacks threatening the Union or its Member States, Art 1(1), OJ. L 129I, 17.5.2019, 13–19.

[86] ibid, Art 1(2).

[87] ibid, Art 3.

Under the framework, sanctioned persons and entities include those actors responsible for the cyber-attack, and those who have attempted to, or who have provided 'financial, technical or material support' to, or otherwise involved in the cyber-attack, for example, by directing, encouraging, planning and facilitating the attack.[88] Although the framework primarily targets attacks against Member States and the Union itself, sanctions measures under the framework can also be applied to cyber-attacks with a significant effect against 'third States or international organisations', if sanctions measures are deemed 'necessary to achieve common foreign and security policy (CFSP) objectives'.[89] In establishing an initiative to combat cyberattacks in general, the framework provides an expansive range in terms of the subjects of cyberattacks covered including critical infrastructure, storage of classified information, essential services necessary for the maintenance and operation of essential social and economic activities, and government functions such as including elections.[90] The main restrictive measures under the framework are asset freezing and travel bans, with the provision that generally, all funds and economic resources 'belonging to, owned, held or controlled by' the sanctioned person or entity will be frozen.[91] Furthermore, 'no funds or economic resources shall be made available directly or indirectly to or for the benefit of' the sanctioned party.[92]

The EU sanctions framework bears resemblance to the US measures, both in terms of the conduct it addresses as well as and parties which may be subject to sanctions. Similar to the US sanctions regime, the EU framework considers a wide range of significant interferences while expressly highlighting interference with 'public elections or the voting process'.[93] In a similar regard to the focus of the US sanction regime on significant, malicious cyber-enabled activities, the focus of the EU framework on wilfully carried out cyberattacks with significant effect provides the European Council with significant discretion and flexibility when determining what ought to be classified as conduct which warrants the response of a sanction. In terms of parties covered by the US and EU sanction regimes, both EO 13694 and EO 13848 as well as the EU framework sanction persons and entities deemed responsible for the attack in addition to those who are agents, or are complicit through the provision of material assistance during the commission of the cyber-attack. The EU framework expressly allows for the placing of sanctions on parties whose conduct is against a third [non-Member] State or international organisations, to the extent that the EU satisfies itself that the sanctions are necessary to achieve CFSP objectives, particularly in relation to the EU's foreign policy objectives. In comparison, with US EO 13694, the likelihood of imposing sanctions for cyber-attacks against a third party seems to be limited. Considering the recent establishment of the EU framework, the extent by which rights under this provision would be exercised remains uncertain.

[88] ibid, Art 4.
[89] Council Regulation 2019/796 (n 84), Art 1(6).
[90] Council Regulation 2019/797 (n 85), Art 1(4).
[91] ibid, Art 5(1).
[92] ibid, Art 5(2).
[93] ibid, Art 1(4)(c).

On 14 May 2020 the European Council announced is decision to extend its cyber sanctions regime for a year, to 18 May 2021. By virtue of this extension the EU will retain its ability 'to impose targeted restrictive measures on persons or entities involved in cyber-attacks which cause a significant impact, and constitute an external threat to the EU or its Member States'.[94] Restrictive measures can also be imposed as a response to cyber-attacks against international organisations or third states, or in situations where they are considered necessary to achieve the objectives of the Common Foreign and Security Policy (CFSP).[95] According to the European Council, in terms of this extension, the underlying purpose of its restrictive measures framework against cyber-attacks 'remains that of deterring and responding to cyber activities directed against the EU or its Member States'.[96] Restrictive measures within the framework include a ban on persons travelling to the EU as well as an asset freeze on persons and entities. Furthermore, EU persons and entities are forbidden from making funds available to those sanctioned.[97]

On 30 July 2020, the Council of the European Union for the first time imposed restrictive measures against six individuals and three entities responsible for or involved in various cyberattacks, including the WannaCry, NotPetya and Operation Cloud Hopper'attacks as well as the attack against the Organization for the Prohibition of Chemical Weapons (OPCW).[98] The sanctions imposed by the Council include a travel ban, an asset freeze and a prohibition against making funds available to those individuals and entities sanctioned. Those sanctioned included North Korean organisation Chosun Expo, for facilitating and supporting the Wannacry attack; Chinese organisation Tianjin Huaying Haitai Science and Technology Development Co Ltd, for facilitating and supporting Cloud Hopper, which was a sustained cyber campaign targeting large-scale service providers in order to access to commercial secrets; and Unit 74455 of the GRU, the Russian military intelligence service, for the NotPetya cyberattack in June 2017 as well as four GRU officers who attempted a cyberattack against the OPCW in 2018.[99]

The UK Office of Financial Sanctions Implementation (OFSI) published a notice on 31 July 2020, confirming that the six individuals and three entities sanctioned by the EU have been added to the UK's consolidated list of asset freeze targets.[100] The UK has already set out the Cyber (Sanctions) (EU Exit) Regulations 2020 which will come into force at the end of the Brexit transition period, replacing the EU regime set out in the Regulation, and which will enable the UK to designate individuals and entities involved

[94] Press Release 294/20 (n 77).

[95] ibid.

[96] ibid.

[97] ibid.

[98] Council of the European Union, 'Council extends cyber sanctions regime until 18 May 2021' Press Release 294/20 (30 July 2020), available at www.consilium.europa.eu/en/press/press-releases/2020/07/30/eu-imposes-the-first-ever-sanctions-against-cyber-attacks.

[99] Council Decision (CFSP) 2020/1127 of 30 July 2020 amending Decision (CFSP) 2019/797 concerning restrictive measures against cyber-attacks threatening the Union or its Member States, available at eur-lex.europa.eu/legal-content/EN/TXT/HTML/?uri=CELEX:32020D1127&from=EN.

[100] Office of Financial Sanctions Implementation HM Treasury, 'Financial Sanctions Notice' (31 July 2020), available at assets.publishing.service.gov.uk/government/uploads/system/uploads/attachment_data/file/905891/Notice_Cyber-Attacks_2020_1125.pdf.

in malicious cyber activities, such as accessing or interfering with information systems or data, where such activity undermines (or is intended to undermine) the integrity, prosperity or security of the UK or another country; directly or indirectly causes (or is intended to cause) economic loss to, or prejudice to the commercial interests of, those affected by the activity; undermines (or is intended to undermine) the independence or effective functioning of: (i) an international organisation; or (ii) a non-governmental organisation or forum whose mandate or purposes relate to the governance of international sport or the Internet; or otherwise affects a significant number of persons in an indiscriminate manner.[101] In welcoming the implementation of the EU sanctions, the Foreign & Commonwealth Office (FCO) noted that 'the UK was at the forefront of efforts to establish the EU Cyber Sanctions regime and will continue to implement this regime at the end of the Transition Period, through our own autonomous UK Cyber Sanctions regime'.[102] It remains to be seen whether the UK now move towards the introduction of its own unilateral cyber sanctions framework arising from these regulations in the aftermath of Brexit.

VI. Need for Law Enforcement Cooperation

It should also be ensured that sanctions do not have the effect of hindering law enforcement operations. In situations where malicious cyber activities are conducted outside of a country's borders, law enforcement cooperation is undertaken through Mutual Legal Assistance Treaties (MLAT). By this process, an investigating police force which is unable to conduct cross-border operations are able to rely on their partners in other countries to assist in identifying perpetrators and take any enforcement action deemed necessary. This type of cooperation demands time for careful investigation and so that law enforcement agencies can operate according to due process and ensure a high standard of proof in order for cybercriminals to be successfully prosecuted. However, the reality that the criminal infrastructure and related evidence is often located across several jurisdictions often complicates the investigative process. An example of this was the 'Avalanche' network, which had been in operation since 2009, unlawfully conducting phishing scams, spamming and malware attacks. The network was only dismantled by law enforcement in 2016 following over four years of joint global investigation efforts involving the work of investigators and prosecutors from over 30 countries, including the US Federal Bureau of Investigation (FBI) and the European Agency for Law Enforcement Cooperation (Europol).[103]

However, problems arise in circumstances where cyber sanctions might have the effect of compromising political relations between states, as well as practical operational aspects of law enforcement cooperation. As a result of its international nature,

[101] The Cyber (Sanctions) (EU Exit) Regulations 2020, available at www.legislation.gov.uk/uksi/2020/597/regulation/4/made?view=plain.

[102] Foreign & Commonwealth Office, Press Releas,: 'Foreign Secretary welcomes first EU sanctions against malicious cyber actors', available at www.gov.uk/government/news/foreign-secretary-welcomes-first-eu-sanctions-against-malicious-cyber-actors.

[103] Pawlak and Biersteker, *Guardian of the Galaxy* (2019) 80.

it is possible to conduct cybercrime activities from countries which are already sanctioned, thereby allowing perpetrators to operate beyond the reach of law enforcement and making the investigative process more difficult. Non-cooperative regimes may be faced with targeted sanctions, or indictments, as is the case with the current US approach to Venezuela. However, it should be understood that 'sanctions regimes and criminal investigations operate on the basis of a different logic and timeframe'.[104] For instance, sanction regimes tend to be more driven by urgency due to political motivation, whereas law enforcement activities often require longer timeframes in order to respect the requirements of due process.[105] On this conflict, Pawlak and Biersteker comment:

> While some level of misalignment is unavoidable, especially when the specific crime does not rise to the level of national security significance (in contrast to many sanctions regimes), it is important to look at the whole picture of how specific listings can work in concert with law enforcement measures to punish and prevent criminal behaviour. The effectiveness of this cooperation will depend to a large extent on whether the cyber-criminal under scrutiny is acting in coordination with the government or not.[106]

In the event of minimal to non-existent law enforcement cooperation between countries, the investigating police have to rely on the perpetrator travelling outside of its country of residence in order for an arrest to be made. This can be done through the issuance of international arrest warrants or Red Notices. These mechanisms are often not accessible in the public domain, thereby giving criminals a false sense of security as they would be unaware of potential consequences should they decide to travel. Examples of such an occurrence include the Russian national Aleksandr Panin, who was accused of masterminding the SpyEye malware, and was apprehended on a visit to the Dominican Republic.[107] Similarly, Vladimir Drinkman, who suspected of the theft of credit card details from retailer TJ Maxx, was arrested while on a trip to the Netherlands.[108] In such circumstances, travel bans as a type of sanction may potentially have a negative impact on the police being able to arrest cyber attackers outside of their home jurisdiction. Where sanctions are to be imposed, it is therefore 'necessary to take into account potential adverse implications for the ongoing criminal investigations and take measures to deconflict both types of instruments'[109] so that both the effectiveness of law enforcement and cyber sanctions regimes are not compromised.

Since cyberwarfare is unlikely to be limited to a particular state, international cooperation is therefore important in order to facilitate adequate responses where there is a need for crisis management. Cyberattacks can easily spread across jurisdictions, with those targeting a particular state also having the ability to cause damage beyond the initial target area. For instance in 2017, NotPetya, which was a destructive malware attack, was spread through a malicious update for M.E.Doc, an accounting software primarily used in Ukraine. Many multinational companies such as the international

[104] ibid.
[105] ibid.
[106] ibid, 81.
[107] ibid, 80.
[108] ibid.
[109] ibid.

shipping company Maersk, who had offices situated in Ukraine, were either encouraged or required to use this software and, as a result, it was able to quickly spread to, and affect, computer systems located beyond the physical borders of that country.[110] In addition, Stuxnet, which was a malware targeting the Iranian nuclear programme, was able to be identified on over 200,000 computers across several countries, mainly in Iran, Indonesia and India, and also to a lesser extent in the US.[111]

States are also able to employ cyber methods such as the use of cryptocurrency payments in order to evade sanctions, although the scale of evasion is not well known at present. For instance, the US Treasury's Financial Crimes Enforcement Network (FinCEN) has declared that Iran could be using cryptocurrencies as a method to evade sanctions, considering that it has been involved in some $3.8 million worth of bitcoin transactions since 2013.[112] It is unclear to what degree this represents an Iranian sanctions evasion strategy and despite the cited figures not yet amounting to a significant sum of money, it has been predicted that the volume of funds representing these type of transactions are expected to increase over time.[113] Concerns also exist over states which face unilateral sanctions imposed on them by the US, such as Iran, Venezuela and Russia, being able to establish and implement blockchain technology platforms for their financial industries which would serve as resistance mechanisms against the sanctions.[114] Both Iran and Russia have conducted pilot tests on Hyperledger Fabric, which is a software platform for blockchain systems, often used to create permissioned ledgers for private firms. This software was used by in 2018 by Sberbank, Russia's largest bank, to settle purchases for a $12 million corporate bond transaction. Although sanctions exist which prohibit US companies from providing equity financing or debt to Sberbank, the software itself was not under any sanctions.[115]

Compliance with sanctions is therefore an important challenge when considering the use of crypto assets. As Pawlak and Biersteker explain, for financial transactions involving traditional currencies, 'a given bank will typically have a detailed understanding about the transaction, including the name and location of the bank and identities of other parties involved'.[116] However, in contrast to this practice, 'cryptocurrencies are sent between anonymous actors, typically operating under pseudonyms, whereby their locations and identities are often concealed'.[117] Furthermore, although certain transaction details may be available on public blockchains, other data such as names and geographical information tend to be widely unavailable. This means that there is a risk that these types of transactions may not be prevented by the financial institutions. As a result financial institutions are now resorting to technological solutions, such as anti-money laundering (AML) software which would enable them to scrutinise blockchain ledgers to determine whether any transactions took place in sanctioned jurisdictions.[118]

[110] ibid, 84.
[111] ibid.
[112] ibid, 82.
[113] ibid.
[114] ibid.
[115] ibid.
[116] ibid.
[117] ibid.
[118] ibid, 83.

The need to 'better mitigate risks linked to virtual asset transactions, particularly in connection with money laundering and terrorist financing' was identified in a 2019 statement issued by the Paris-based Financial Action Task Force (FATF), which sets global standards for countering illicit finance. In that same year, the FATF also issued and adopted an Interpretive Note to Recommendation 15 on New Technologies (INR 15) followed by the Guidance for a Risk-Based Approach to Virtual Assets and Virtual Asset Service Providers.[119]

Measures such as cryptocurrencies, ransomware attacks and cyber heists have therefore developed as mechanisms to generate funds in order to undermine country or sector-specific sanctions which have already taken effect. In the case of ransomware attacks and cyber heists, states are able to employ these activities in order to gain access to funds. States are also able to anonymise transactions through the use of cryptocurrencies, enabling the receiving party to remain unknown. A 2016 cyberattack on the Central Bank of Bangladesh resulted in hackers exploiting the SWIFT system in order to transfer funds to an account in the Philippines. This attack, as well as several others were linked to North Korea due to similarities in the code which was used for the exploit.[120] Another instance of a cyberattack being linked to North Korea was the 2017 WannaCry ransomware attack, where over £108,000 was taken from online bitcoin wallets. The following year, the US Department of Justice issued a criminal complaint which charged Park Jin Hyok, a North Korean citizen, for being involved in the attacks, as well as linking him with malicious cyber activities undertaken by the North Korean Government. In a similar regard, an Expert Panel reported to the Security Council on North Korean's evasion of financial sanctions through the use of cyberattacks 'to illegally force the transfer of funds from financial institutions and cryptocurrency exchanges'.[121]

As a result of the aforementioned developments, there has been an increase in attention by governments and the private sector in their focus on how crypto assets might be used to evade sanctions. To expand on this, Pawlak and Biersteker explain:

> Individual, companies and other entities engaged in cryptocurrency transactions are bound by the same sanctions compliance obligations as other traditional financial activities. For instance, on 19 March 2018, US President Trump signed Executive Order EO13827 banning US persons from using any digital currencies linked to the Venezuelan government.8 In the same month, the US Treasury's Office of Foreign Assets Control (OFAC) stated that all its existing sanctions regimes apply to all US cryptocurrency firms, including those based outside the country that supply cryptocurrency services to US persons. It added that OFAC might start to list cryptocurrency addresses pertaining to companies and individuals that are on US sanctions blacklists.[122]

Nonetheless, 'the decentralised, transnational and anonymous nature of cryptocurrency practices makes it possible for a sanctioned actor to access virtual assets from anywhere in the world without having to make use of the formal banking system'.[123]

[119] ibid.
[120] ibid, 81.
[121] ibid.
[122] ibid, 82.
[123] ibid.

Cryptocurrency firms are able to 'engage – knowingly or otherwise – in providing services within sanctioned regimes without such transactions being easily traceable by banks' compliance departments or regulatory authorities'.[124] Furthermore, companies and individuals may be located in a sanctioned regime, but can prevent disclosure of their location and identity through the use of mechanisms such as virtual private networks (VPNs), which allow them to anonymously engage in transactions which may be in breach of sanctions. In addition, companies and individuals may also act as virtual asset peer-to-peer (P2P) exchangers, enabling them 'to broker unlicensed transactions on behalf of third parties, which can open the door to money-laundering and other financial activities that might fall under sanctions'.[125]

Despite the challenges faced by law enforcement in defending against cyberattacks, there is indication that collaborative efforts in this area can lead to perpetrators being held accountable for their actions, as demonstrated by the high-profile indictment of the 'Evil Corp' organisation members responsible for the Dridex malware attacks in 2019.[126] Maksim Yakubets and Igor Turashev were indicted by the US Department of Justice in December 2019 following years of collaborative work between the US Federal Bureau of Investigation (FBI) and the UK National Crime Agency (NCA).[127] Another associate of the group, who was named in the indictment, although not indicted, is Denis Gusev, whose businesses are subject to US sanctions imposed by the US Treasury Department. Yakubets has also been faced with allegations of working with the Russian Federal Security Service since 2017, which has prompted questions as to whether this is an instance of a state actor either officially or unofficially conducting financially motivated attacks on behalf of a state.[128]

VII. Conclusion

According to paragraph 7 of the Preamble to the UN Charter, armed force shall not be resorted to, save in the common interest. Likewise, Article 2(4) of the UN Charter prohibits the threat or use of force and requests all Member States to respect the sovereignty, territorial integrity and political independence of other states. Separate from the use of force, one avenue to exert pressure on states breaching international law is that of sanctions, as it is difficult to quantify sanctions as 'force' within the context of Article 2(4). By conventional war, the sentiment is one which involves the use of force by a state through its military power on another state in order to challenge certain governance mechanisms. Moreover, a 'just war' can still involve acts of violence which result in the unfortunate loss of human lives and injury to both military and civilian infrastructure. The IGE has agreed that 'non-destructive cyber psychological operations intended solely to undermine confidence in a government or economy' does not equate

[124] ibid.
[125] ibid, 83.
[126] PwC, 'Cyber Threats 2019: A Year in Retrospect' (February 2020) 22, available at www.pwc.co.uk/cyber-security/assets/cyber-threats-2019-retrospect.pdf.
[127] ibid.
[128] ibid.

to the use of force.[129] In comparing the decision by the ICJ in the *Nicaragua* case where it was decided that funding of guerrilla groups engaging in activities against another state did not amount to use of force, the IGE concluded that undertaking cyber operations as a component of an insurgency would also not amount to the use of force. Such funding would however be considered as breaching the principle of non-intervention. Furthermore on the ICJ's reasoning in the *Nicaruagua* case,[130] providing the necessary training and malware tools for insurgent groups to conduct cyberattacks would qualify as use of force. Since Article 2(4) is not remedial in nature, but more so represents a prohibition, responses to such a breach may include sanctions and countermeasures as determined by the Security Council, as well as self-defence. In considering a 'consequence-based approach', the Stuxnet worm caused significant damage to property, and therefore prima facie may be regarded as an 'armed attack'. This view was supported by the IGE in the Tallin Manual.

Although international rules relating to cyber warfare is currently in its early development, this does not mean that the term 'cyber-war' is entirely a lawless frontier, nor the province of a small elite. If not even recognised in the customary and treaty-based international law, this area of legal scholarship is nevertheless regulated hypothetically by at least two old age doctrines of (i) *ubi jus ibi remedium*, in that no wrong can go unpunished, so where there is a wrong against rights, there exists a remedy too; and (ii) the Martens Clause, which stipulates that despite the existence of a legal vacuum, as is somewhat the case with cyberwarfare, neither the civilians nor the combatants would be deprived of legal protection completely, but instead be protected by principles of the law of the nations as derived from the practice of international law, laws of humanity, and the dictates of public conscience.

Considering the nature of the damage cyberattacks might cause, assessing them through the lens of proportionality may prove challenging. For example, an *ex ante jus in bello* analysis of DDoS attack's proportionality may carry a greater degree of uncertainty compared to a conventional strike. O'Donnell and Kraska writing in 2003 expressed the view that 'information warfare may prove to be an effective means of coercion that is more adept at insulating civilians from the dangerous kinetic effects of war'.[131] To date, no cyberattack has been considered to constitute an armed attack, but with technological evolution it is not inconceivable that in the future, cyberattacks will satisfy this threshold. At present, however, the law governing *jus ad bellum* does not satisfactorily address the unique characteristics of cyberattacks, while also being subject to varying interpretations. It might therefore be possible for states to manipulate interpretations of *jus ad bellum as* well as its application to cyberattacks where the intention is to satisfy national policy prerogatives. Consequently, states can potentially manipulate the interpretations of *jus ad bellum* and its application to cyberattacks to serve national interests.

[129] Tallinn Manual (n 40) 46.

[130] ICJ, *Military and Paramilitary Activities in and against Nicaragua (Nicaragua v United States of America)*, merits, 1986.

[131] BT O'Donnell and JC Kraska, 'Humanitarian Law: Developing International Rules for the Digital Battlefield' (2003) 8 *Journal of Conflict and Security Law* 133, 134.

13

Conclusions: The Current Law on Unilateral Sanctions, Remedies against Unlawful Use of such Sanctions and Recommendations

SURYA P SUBEDI

I. The Current Law on Unilateral Sanctions

As demonstrated in the chapters in this volume, unilateral sanctions are liable to undermine many well-established norms of international law, whether they are the rules of the law of the sea, human rights, freedom of aviation, the right of communications (including postal communications), international environmental law, WTO law, international investment law, or regional economic integration treaties. The state which imposes unilateral sanctions against another state beyond the limits prescribed in international law runs the risk of violating the latter's sovereignty and the provisions of bilateral, regional and international or multilateral treaties, and of undermining the cardinal principles of international law, including sovereign equality of states, peaceful coexistence and non-intervention or non-interference in the internal affairs of other states.

Although the lawfulness of the use of economic and financial force or other forms of unilateral coercive measures has been a contested issue in international law, limitations have been progressively imposed in both conventional and customary international law on the freedom of states to resort to unilateral sanctions. A set of norms governing the limits of unilateral sanctions has emerged through treaty law and state practice, according to which such sanctions cannot be taken if they involve the violation of a series of international norms such as the violation of human rights of the people in the target state. As our analysis has shown, recent state practice has crystallised into additional rules of customary international law which increase the limitations on the use of unilateral sanctions. Accordingly, there is now a positive prohibition in customary international law on coercive uses of economic and financial force or other forms of unilateral coercive measures by states, if such uses do not meet the requirements stipulated in the law. For instance, the 1970 Declaration on Principles of International Law concerning Friendly Relations and Co-operation among States (Resolution 2625 (XXV)), which is widely regarded as an authoritative interpretation of the Charter of the UN, affirms that the use of coercive economic and other measures in order to obtain from a state the subordination of the exercise of its sovereign rights and to secure from it advantages of any kind violates the principle of non-intervention.

Any unilateral sanctions that are not proportionate or violate the principles of *jus cogens* character, such as the right of self-determination of states, or the principles of the Charter of the UN, or the general principles of international law such as those on non-intervention, would also be unlawful. According to the ILC's Draft Articles on State Responsibility, the circumstances in which wrongfulness could be precluded are the following: consent, self-defence, countermeasures, *force majeure* distress and necessity. Unilateral sanctions do not figure in the circumstances that could preclude wrongfulness. Hence, the imposition of unilateral sanctions that do not fall within the scope of either retorsion or countermeasures would be unlawful in international law, if they do not meet the substantive and procedural prerequisites stipulated in customary international law.

Unilateral sanctions that do not fall into the category of retorsions or countermeasures under customary international law may constitute a violation of several provisions of the Charter of the United Nations, viz, Articles 2(1), 2(3), 2(7) and 33, the provisions in the 1970 Declaration on Principles of International Law concerning Friendly Relations and other well-established principles such as the Five Principles of Peaceful Coexistence (also known as the Principles of *Panchasheel)* and the general international law principle of non-intervention.

The status of unilateral sanctions in international law depends also on their possibility of violating many fundamental rights and freedoms of the people of the target state and of third countries doing business with the target state, for example by denying them their right to property in the state imposing the sanctions and the target state, by depriving them the right to family, and by unduly restricting their freedom of movement. Correspondingly, unilateral sanctions may constitute a violation of both the civil and political rights and the economic, social and cultural rights guaranteed through the 1948 Universal Declaration of Human Rights, which are universally accepted as legally binding, the 1966 Covenants on Civil and Political Rights and on Economic, Social and Cultural Rights, the International Convention on the Elimination of All Forms of Racial Discrimination of 1965 (which has near universal acceptance), the International Convention on the Protection of the Rights of all Migrant Workers and Members of their Families of 1990, and several of the ILO Conventions.

Unilateral sanctions may also contravene some other principles of international law, including: the principles of international trade and investment stipulated in the 1994 WTO agreements and in several bilateral and regional investment agreements to which both the state imposing sanctions and the target state are a party; the principle of non-discrimination embodied in several international treaties and recognised in customary international law; the freedom of navigation and overflight and peaceful maritime commerce; the right of innocent and transit passage as guaranteed in the 1982 UN Convention on the Law of the Sea; the freedom of aviation as stipulated in the 1944 Convention on International Civil Aviation (also known as the Chicago Convention); and the 1944 International Air Services Transit Agreement.

National legislation or measures aimed at extending the effects of unilateral sanctions to nationals, or entities of third countries, with the purpose of requiring or dissuading them from entertaining lawful commercial (or other) relations with the target country or its citizens, would also be unlawful under international law. This is especially so with regard to those unilateral sanctions that have extraterritorial reach in which the sanctions unduly harm the third states and undermine their economy and their freedom of action. Furthermore, unilateral sanctions that do not operate within the limits of international law may themselves constitute an internationally wrongful act, giving rise to state responsibility.

However, the legal status of any unilateral sanctions is determined by the nature of the measures taken by states. Not all unilateral sanctions of retorsive character, including those commonly known as 'smart' or targeted sanctions, would necessarily be unlawful. Furthermore, unilateral sanctions are permissible if they pertain to the areas not regulated or prohibited by international law. For instance, unfriendly measures such as withdrawal of voluntary aid programmes or severance of diplomatic relations would be permissible under international law.

Although there is as yet no treaty as such governing the use of unilateral sanctions, the analysis presented in this study demonstrates that a range of other treaties and various rules of customary international law do apply to unilateral sanctions. In accordance with the practice of states over the past several decades and the existence of an *opinio juris* in such practice as analysed throughout this study, it can be submitted that a rule of customary international law has now come into existence according to which unilateral sanctions that are not consistent with the Charter of the UN and other principles of international law, are unlawful. Thus, it can be submitted that the lawfulness of unilateral sanctions should be determined on the basis of the limitations imposed on the freedom of action of states by assessing: (i) the general international law principle of non-coercion and non-intervention; (ii) the customary international law rules on countermeasures; (iii) other rules of treaty law and customary intentional law applicable to human rights and humanitarian law; and (iv) other relevant multilateral treaties of law-making character.

Accordingly, what can be distilled from the analysis presented in this volume is that unilateral sanctions are a form of self-help. The current state of the law on the various measures of self-help not involving the use of armed force is as follows:

(1) In cases of minor breaches of international law or misdemeanours, states can, in exercise of their sovereign rights inherent in them as a state, take low-intensity measures of retorsive character against other states or against particular individuals or business organisations in other states.
(2) Countermeasures are permissible in response to a prior breach of international law, provided that such measures meet the substantive and procedural requirements stipulated in customary international law as outlined in the Draft Articles on State Responsibility of the ILC in 2001, as well as the other norms of customary international law which have developed through the subsequent state.
(3) Trade sanctions are permissible within the limitations prescribed in the WTO law.
(4) Low-intensity measures commonly known as 'smart' or targeted sanctions such as visa or banking restrictions, or freezing of assets of those individuals who have

violated human rights, or those who are associated with the government of a country that has violated human rights, or have contributed to such violations, would not necessarily be unlawful under international law. The same applies to 'cyber sanctions' against individuals or business organisations in other states who have carried out hostile cyber-attacks.

(5) Any other unilateral sanctions or coercive measures against the state as a whole would be unlawful, unless they meet the procedural and substantive requirements stipulated in international law as outlined below in this chapter.

(6) Apart from justifications for retorsions, or 'unfriendly acts' of states, or the measures of retorsive character such as the so-called 'smart' or targeted sanctions of limited scope under the principle of sovereignty of states, or justifications for countermeasures under the rules of customary international law on countermeasures, there is no other justification in international law for unilateral sanctions.

States have invoked the principle of state sovereignty to justify the sanctions that they impose on other states, but state sovereignty is not an unqualified attribute of states; rather, its exercise is conditioned by the rules of international law, including *jus cogens*, and treaty law, whether bilateral or multilateral. Therefore, unilateral sanctions can only be justified either as a retorsion or countermeasures. If they cannot be justified as the one or the other, unilateral sanctions are unlawful, unless they meet the procedural and substantive conditions outlined below in this chapter. If the lawfulness of retorsions is contested by the targeted state, then a reference will have to be made to the nature and scope of the principle of state sovereignty vis-à-vis that measure of retorsion. Ultimately, if contested, the lawfulness of any retorsion needs to be ascertained on a case-by-case basis.

Since the institution of unilateral sanctions is not recognised in international law, it has been argued that the rules on countermeasures are applicable to unilateral sanctions. If unilateral sanctions are regarded as countermeasures, they may be valid measures if the conditions for countermeasures prescribed in international law are fulfilled. Under the customary international law of state responsibility, countermeasures, which would otherwise constitute illegal measures, would be justified if taken by a state injured by an internationally wrongful act of another state, provided they complied with the principle of proportionality, respect for obligations for the protection of fundamental human rights and respect for obligations of a humanitarian character, as well as peremptory norms of general international law. Therefore, to ascertain the rules applicable to unilateral sanctions, it is necessary to ascertain the rules applicable to countermeasures themselves. This is because, in the absence of a clear recognition of the institution of unilateral sanctions in international law, some states have invoked the right to countermeasures when imposing unilateral sanctions against another state. For instance, the UAE invoked countermeasures when justifying its use of unilateral economic sanctions against Qatar in a case before the ICJ.[1] Together with the UAE, Bahrain, Egypt and Saudi Arabia did the same in another case before the ICJ.[2]

[1] 'The State of Qatar institutes proceedings against the United Arab Emirates and request the Court to indicate provisional measures' Press Release No 2018/26, ICJ (11 June 2018).

[2] 'Appeal Relating to the Jurisdiction of the ICAO Council under Article 84 of the Convention on International Civil Aviation (*Bahrain, Egypt, Saudi Arabia and United Arab Emirates v Qatar*)', Press Release No 2018/26, ICJ (5 July 2018).

The main legal justification for countermeasures under customary international law is outlined in the Draft Articles on State Responsibility of the International Law Commission. But if states invoke the notion of countermeasures to justify unilateral sanctions, such states will have to meet a series of requirements prior to resorting to such a measure and these conditions include: (i) it must have been established that the targeted state has committed an internationally wrongful act; (ii) the sanctioning or targeting state must establish that it is an 'injured state'; (iii) the measures must aim to induce the targeted state to comply with its obligations; (iv) the measures must be proportionate to the injury suffered; (v) the measures may not affect human rights, or *jus cogens* norms; and (vi) the measures must be terminated when the wrongful act has ceased.

However, the difficulty with unilateral sanctions is that many of them go beyond the scope of permissible levels of countermeasures. An example are the US sanctions imposed on states under the so-called the Helms-Burton Act. As stated by Ruys,

> it is clear that sanctions adopted by individual States – such as the notorious US sanctions imposed on Cuba pursuant to the Helms-Burton Act – often serve foreign-policy purposes of the State(s) concerned, without necessarily constituting a reaction to a prior breach of international law.[3]

II. The International Legal Framework for Unilateral Sanctions

Based on the analysis presented in this study of both treaty law and the evolving and extant rules of customary international law, it can be submitted that to be lawful, any unilateral sanctions of non-retorsive character must operate within the following procedural and substantive framework of international law:

(1) Unilateral sanctions are measures of exercising pressures short of the threat or use of military force directed against a target state or entity, which are taken by an individual state or a group of states, and which are not authorised by the UN, and which seek to limit or deprive altogether the freedom that other states enjoy. Such measures include economic and financial sanctions, asset freezes, trade sanctions, commodity interdictions, and restrictions on banking and transfer of funds, the freedom of navigation, aviation and transit and on the right to communications.

(2) States must refrain in their international relations from using or encouraging the use of unilateral sanctions to coerce another state in order to obtain from it the subordination of the exercise of its sovereign rights and to secure from it advantages of any kind.

[3] T Ruys, 'Sanctions, retorsions and countermeasures: concepts and international legal framework' in L van den Herik (ed), *Research Handbook on UN Sanctions and International Law* (Edward Elgar, 2017) 23. See the Cuban Liberty and Democratic Solidarity (LIBERTAD) Act 1996, 22 USC §§ 6021–6091.

(3) The act of adopting, maintaining or implementing unilateral sanctions not in accordance with international law, including the provisions in the Charter of the UN and the principles of human rights and humanitarian law, constitute an internationally wrongful act giving rise to State responsibility.
(4) Unilateral sanctions must be regarded as exceptional measures to be taken in response to an extraordinary situation when no other alternative measures are available or adequate to address the situation.
(5) When adopting national legislation or measures aimed at extending their effects to nationals or entities of third countries, with the purpose of dissuading them from entertaining lawful commercial or other relations with the target country or its citizens, states have an obligation to ensure that such extraterritorial reach of the measures do not unduly harm the third states and undermine their economy and their freedom of action and do not have detrimental impact on their citizens.
(6) Unilateral sanctions that undermine the sovereignty of third states are not permissible under international law.
(7) National legislations concerning unilateral sanctions that affect the rights of the people in third countries are contrary to international law.
(8) Third states should not be required to recognise the extraterritorial nature of unilateral sanctions nor to apply them, since such measures run counter to the fundamental principles of international law, including human rights norms, and other rules of customary international law.
(9) The state imposing unilateral sanctions must specify what exact obligations under international law were violated by the targeted state and with what obligations that state is required to comply.
(10) Unilateral sanctions must be accompanied by an offer to negotiate, and they should not be taken before the responsible or targeted state is given a notice of claim and a reasonable opportunity to present a response.
(11) The injured state which decides to take unilateral sanctions must notify the target state of the decision to take such measures. In case of urgency, states can take provisional measures to preserve their rights within the limits of international law.
(12) Unilateral sanctions must be preceded by a demand by the injured state that the responsible state comply with its obligations under international law.
(13) Unilateral sanctions may be taken only when redress by other means has been exhausted or is unavailable, and the target state has unduly refused reparation against its internationally wrongful act or compliance with its international obligations.
(14) Unilateral sanctions must be aimed at inducing the target state's compliance of its international obligations, and at obtaining cessation and a satisfactory reparation for a wrongful act.
(15) The international law rules on countermeasures developed by the ILC in 2001 in its Draft Articles on State Responsibility apply also to unilateral sanctions.
(16) Unilateral sanctions taken must be proportionate to the injury suffered from the internationally wrongful act committed by the state concerned.
(17) Unilateral sanctions should be reversible and should not be for punitive purposes.
(18) Unilateral sanctions must be terminated when the alleged internationally wrongful act has ceased to exist.

(19) Unilateral sanctions must not be imposed in breach of the peremptory norms of international law and must not result in the violation of human rights and humanitarian law principles.
(20) Any serious violations of human rights by a state should be referred either to a human rights treaty body or to the UN Human Rights Council or to the UN Security Council.
(21) States that are not themselves injured by the internationally wrongful act of another state are not entitled to impose unilateral sanctions.
(22) Unilateral sanctions must not be taken in such a way as to impair diplomatic or consular inviolability.
(23) Unilateral sanctions should not be taken when there are treaty means between the targeting and target states for the peaceful settlement of a dispute on the subject matter.
(24) Unilateral sanctions should not affect any dispute settlement procedure which is in force between the two states and applicable to the dispute.
(25) If there is an international dispute resolution mechanism available for the settlement of disputes between the targeting and targeted states, then that mechanism should be resorted to over the imposition of unilateral sanctions.
(26) When there is a provision, or the possibility, to request provisional measures from an international dispute settlement body, that should be availed before imposing unilateral sanctions.
(27) Unilateral sanctions must be suspended if the dispute is submitted in good faith to a court or tribunal with the authority to make decisions binding on the parties.
(28) The state affected by unlawful unilateral sanctions is entitled to counteract with reciprocal and non-reciprocal measures within the limits of international law.
(29) States which take unilateral sanctions against another state for allegedly committing an internationally wrongful act should inform the UN Security Council of the measures taken and the reasons for it.
(30) Unilateral sanctions should be suspended if the matter has been addressed by the UN Security Council or another competent international or regional organisation of states.

These conclusions have been reached on the basis of the interpretation of several fundamental principles of international law; the Charter of the UN; several other treaty provisions concerning human rights, freedom of aviation, freedom of navigation, right to postal and other forms of communications, trade and investment, regional economic integration and environmental protection; the rules of customary international law on countermeasure expressed in the ILC's Draft Articles on State Responsibility of 2001; the principle of non-intervention articulated in the 1965 UN General Assembly resolution on non-intervention; the 1970 Declaration on the Friendly Relations Among States[4]

[4] The UN Declaration on Principles of International Law concerning Friendly Relations and Co-operation among States, UNGA Res 2625 (XXV), 24 October 1970. The provision on economic coercion reads as follows: 'No State may use or encourage the use of economic … measures to coerce another State in order to obtain from it the subordination of the exercise of its sovereign rights and to secure from it advantages of any kind. Also, no State shall [seek to overthrow the regime] or interfere in civil strife in another State. The use of force to deprive peoples of their national identity constitutes a violation of their inalienable rights and of the

and several other General Assembly resolutions; the resolutions of the UN Human Rights Council; and the more recent practice of a vast majority of states and the additional norms of customary international law crystallised by more recent state practice.

What has been outlined above is essentially a restatement of the law that is in existence today. Consequently, any use of unilateral sanctions not consistent with the rules of international law outlined above would constitute a wrongful act, entailing the responsibility of that state and thereby opening the door to the possibility of compensation or reparation for the victims subjected to such unilateral sanctions. This position may have been a *de lege ferenda* until the end of the twentieth century, but the world has moved on since then, and the new evidence of state practice that has crystallised into new norms of international law has made the above-mentioned rules part of *lex lata*.

Given its organic nature, customary international law is subject to modification by more recent practice in this rapidly changing world. The era of valuing the practice of major powers over the practice of the majority consisting of medium and smaller powers is over. The practice of all states in all continents has to be taken into account to establish the contemporary rules of customary international law today. Accordingly, this state practice has given rise to the formation of additional rules of customary international law applicable to unilateral sanctions and countermeasures. Consequently, some new qualifications have been added to the use of such measures under the Draft Articles of the ILC of 2001 on State Responsibility.

The rulings of the ICJ in several cases also support the list of procedural and substantive requirements for unilateral sanction outlined above. For instance, the Court held in the *Nicaragua* case that:

> In view of the generally accepted formulations, the principle [of non-intervention] forbids all States or groups of States to intervene directly or indirectly in internal or external affairs of other States. A prohibited intervention must accordingly be one bearing on matters in which each State is permitted, by the principle of State sovereignty, to decide freely. One of these is the choice of a political, economic, social and cultural system, and the formulation of foreign policy. Intervention is wrongful when it uses methods of coercion in regard to such choices, which must remain free ones. The element of coercion, which defines, and indeed forms the very essence of, prohibited intervention, is particularly obvious in the case of an intervention which uses force, either in the direct form of military action, or in the indirect form of support for subversive or terrorist armed activities within another State.[5]

The ICJ also held that states that are not themselves injured by the internationally wrongful act of another state should not impose unilateral sanctions, in the following pronouncement:

> The acts of which Nicaragua is accused, even assuming them to have been established and imputable to that State, could only have justified proportionate countermeasures on the part of the State which had been the victim of these acts, namely El Salvador, Honduras

principle of non-intervention. Every State has an inalienable right to choose its political, economic, social and cultural systems, without interference in any form by another State'.

[5] *Case Concerning Military and Paramilitary Activities In and Against Nicaragua (Nicaragua v United States of America)*, ICJ Reports, 1986, para 205.

> or Costa Rica. They could not justify counter-measures taken by a third State, the United States, and particularly could not justify intervention involving the use of force.[6]

With regard to the rights of states to impose unilateral sanctions to uphold the integrity of international law or to protect human rights, the ILC observes that

> the current state of international law on countermeasures taken in the general or collective interest is uncertain. State practice is sparse and involves a limited number of States. At present, there appears to be no clearly recognized entitlement of States referred to in article 48 to take countermeasures in the collective interest.[7]

Since the Commission left the matter open to be determined by the further development of international law, reliance could be made on the subsequent state practice on this issue. As analysed throughout this study, more recent practice suggests that states that are not themselves injured by the internationally wrongful act of another state are not entitled to impose unilateral sanctions or adopt countermeasures.

Those states which seek to justify the use of unilateral sanctions based on their freedom of action under the principle of sovereignty of states have shown inconsistency in their approach. Hence, their inconsistent practice of using unilateral sanctions cannot be invoked in defence of the legality of such sanctions. But the practice of an overwhelming majority of states that opposes the use of unilateral sanctions has been consistent. This consistency has been crystallising into the rules of customary international law. The fact that the use of unlawful sanctions is commonplace in the contemporary world does not mean that the practice of states against the principles of international law can be regarded as lawful. Nor can it give rise to the formation of customary international law or modify an existing rule of international law. An unlawful activity remains unlawful whether the unlawfulness persists or remains unchallenged before a court of law.

III. Remedies available to States Subjected to Unlawful Unilateral Sanctions

As stated by the ILC in its commentary to the Draft Articles on State Responsibility, 'International obligations may be established by a customary rule of international law, by a treaty or by a general principle applicable within the international legal order'.[8] Therefore, an international obligation may arise from the violation of a rule of customary international law on unilateral sanctions outlined above. However, the difficulty with the reliance on customary international law in holding a state responsible for an internationally wrongful act is that the injured state would not be able to seek legal remedy against the wrongdoer. There is no international adjudicatory body with compulsory jurisdiction to entertain such cases and a matter can be referred to international courts and tribunals only if the state concerned has consented to it either by virtue of an existing treaty or by virtue of the conclusion of a special agreement to do so.

[6] ibid, para 249.

[7] ILC, 'Draft articles on Responsibility of States for Internationally Wrongful Acts, with commentaries (2001) 139, available at legal.un.org/ilc/texts/instruments/english/commentaries/9_6_2001.pdf.

[8] ibid, 55.

Nevertheless, unilateral sanctions that are not consistent with the Charter of the UN and other principles of international law would remain unlawful whether or not there is an effective legal remedy against this unlawfulness.

Although there is no proper mechanism in international law for the resolution of disputes arising out of the imposition of unilateral sanctions, a number of mechanisms could be utilised by the affected state to seek some form of remedy against such sanctions. The first one is of course the ICJ. Although it has no compulsory jurisdiction, it can entertain cases by consent of the states concerned. It also can entertain cases alleging violation of the provisions of certain treaties, whether bilateral or multilateral, to which the state imposing sanctions, and the target state, are a party, if the violation is due to the imposition of such sanctions. An example of the utilisation of a human rights treaty is the legal proceedings before the ICJ instituted by Qatar against the UAE in 2018 alleging violation of the provisions of the Convention on the Elimination of All Forms of Racial Discrimination (CERD) due to the economic blockade against Qatar by the UAE together with three other Arab countries.[9] The cases referred to the ICJ by Iran against the US alleging violation of the 1955 Treaty of Amity between the two countries due to the unilateral sanctions imposed by the US against Iran, is an example of the use of a bilateral treaty against unilateral sanctions. The first case involving issues of unilateral sanctions was the *Oil Platforms* case[10] decided by the ICJ in 2003, and the second was the proceedings instituted by Iran against the US sanctions in 2018.[11]

Although the UN General Assembly, or another international organisation authorised by or in accordance with the Charter of the UN, can seek an advisory opinion of the ICJ on the legality of an individual case of unilateral sanctions, or the legality of unilateral sanctions as an institution itself in international law, the Advisory Opinion is not binding and would not necessarily result in an effective remedy for the target state injured by the sanctions even if they are pronounced unlawful.

In cases of trade sanctions that are inconsistent with the provisions in WTO agreements, states can refer the matter to the Dispute Settlement Body of the WTO. For instance, Qatar has resorted to it against the blockading states of Saudi Arabia and the UAE, alleging that the unilateral coercive economic measures taken by these states in June 2017 against Qatar violated the GATT/WTO agreements.[12] The targeting states

[9] The State of Qatar instituted proceedings against the UAE at the ICJ with regard to alleged violations of the International Convention on the Elimination of All Forms of Racial Discrimination (CERD) of 21 December 1965. The alleged violations were part of a package of economic and other measures taken by the UAE together with Bahrain, Egypt and Saudi Arabia against Qatar on 5 June 2017. Qatar complained that some of these measures taken by the UAE against Qatar and the Qatari people violated UAE's obligations under the CERD. Press Release No 2018/26, ICJ (11 June 2018).

[10] *Oil Platforms (Islamic Republic of Iran v United States of America)*, Judgments, ICJ Reports (2003) 161.

[11] Iran instituted proceedings at the International Court of Justice on 16 July 2018 under a bilateral treaty against the US challenging its unilateral economic sanctions against Iran: Iran institutes proceedings against the United States with regard to a dispute concerning alleged violations of the Treaty of Amity, Economic Relations, and Consular Rights between Iran and the United States, and requests the Court to indicate provisional measures. Press Release No 2018/34, ICJ (17 July 2018).

[12] Qatar requested on 4 August 2017 WTO dispute consultations with the UAE, Bahrain and Saudi Arabia concerning measures adopted by the three countries which allegedly restrict trade in goods and services from Qatar, and trade-related intellectual property rights: 'Qatar files WTO complaints against the United Arab Emirates, Bahrain and Saudi Arabia', WTO News and Events, available at www.wto.org/english/news_e/news17_e/ds526_7_8rfc_04aug17_e.htm. See WT/DS526/1, WT/DS527/1.

may invoke the so-called security exception provisions in defence of their measures, but the WTO Dispute Settlement Body may not agree with their strategy, illustrated for instance in the case against the Russian Federation by Ukraine.[13] The target state can also refer the matter relating to the violation of the freedom of navigation and other maritime rights guaranteed under the 1982 Convention on the Law of the Sea to the International Tribunal for the Law of the Sea based in Hamburg, if both the targeting and target states are party to the Convention.

Moreover, inter-state investment arbitration is available for the target state, or legal entities within that state, if there is a bilateral investment treaty between the states concerned. States can always resort to a flexible international arbitration to resolve their differences, if both parties consent. If unilateral sanctions result in the violation of a treaty, whether bilateral or multilateral, the target state could avail itself of the dispute settlement mechanism stipulated in the treaty concerned. As mentioned earlier, this is the course of action Iran took against the US sanctions, by invoking a bilateral treaty and referring the matter to the ICJ against the US sanctions. Qatar adopted the same strategy against the UAE by invoking violation of the provisions of a multilateral treaty, the CERD and also referred the matter to the ICJ against the UAE. If unilateral sanctions result in the violation of a bilateral treaty, the target state could also avail itself of other options stipulated in the treaty, such as the termination or suspension of the treaty in whole or in part, in accordance with Article 60 of the Vienna Convention on the Law of Treaties of 1969.[14]

Individuals residing in the target state suffering from unilateral measures also have several remedy options at their disposal. One option would be to apply for a judicial review of the measures taken by the government of the targeting state, to the national courts in the targeting state itself. A judicial review would however depend on meeting a number of conditions pertaining to the jurisdiction of the courts in the targeting state. Another option would be to petition to various UN human rights committees. In regions where there is a regional human rights court and/or commission, a case can be filed against the targeting state for violating the rights of the individuals in the target state, if the rights in question are protected by the regional human right treaty concerned;[15] *Kadi*[16] is an example.

Another option for private entities, whether natural or juridical, in the target state would be to resort to international investment arbitration against the targeting state, if there is a bilateral or regional investment agreement between the two states, and if the

[13] 'Russia – Measures Concerning Traffic in Transit', Panel Body Report, WT/DS512/R (5 April 2019) 1.3, 2.1, 3.1.

[14] Art 60(1) and (3) of the Vienna Convention on the Law of Treaties of 1969 reads as follows: '1. A material breach of a bilateral treaty by one of the parties entitles the other to invoke the breach as a ground for terminating the treaty or suspending its operation in whole or in part … 3. A material breach of a treaty, for the purposes of this article, consists in: (a) A repudiation of the treaty not sanctioned by the present Convention; or (b) The violation of a provision essential to the accomplishment of the object or purpose of the treaty'. The Convention Came into force on 27 January 1980. It has been ratified by 116 states as of January 2018.

[15] See for a more detailed analysis of such options of remedy: 'Report of the Special Rapporteur on the negative impact of unilateral coercive measures on the enjoyment of human rights', UN Doc A/HRC/33/48 of 2 August 2016.

[16] *Kadi v Council and Commission*, Court of First Instance, Case T-315/01, 21 September 2005.

coercive economic measures have undermined the rights of investors.[17] For instance, Qatar Airways has taken this course of action by instituting proceedings under various investment treaties against[18] four Arab States – Bahrain, Egypt, Saudi Arabia, and the UAE – which imposed coercive economic measures against Qatar in June 2017.

Further, there is a mechanism for inter-state complaints under various human rights treaties, which allow the state whose citizens have suffered from human rights violations resulting from unilateral sanctions, to refer the matter to the UN human rights committees.[19] Indeed, Qatar not only instituted proceedings before the ICJ against the UAE, but also made an inter-state complaint against the UAE and Saudi Arabia before the Committee on the Elimination of Racial Discrimination under the Convention on the Elimination of All Forms of Racial Discrimination after the four Arab states, including Bahrain, Egypt, Saudi Arabia and the UAE, imposed a series of coercive measures against Qatar in June 2017.

IV. Human Rights Violations and Unilateral Sanctions

It has been argued that unilateral sanctions can be used against those states that violate human rights. Yet the question remains as to whether the states imposing such sanctions are entitled to act as judge and jury, decide who has violated human rights and impose unilateral sanctions on those they found to be at fault. If the targeted state is a party to a human rights treaty, then the mechanisms stipulated in the treaty, ie the interstate complaint mechanism, should be used against the delinquent state. Even if the targeted state is not a party to a human rights treaty, it would still have violated the rights enshrined in the Universal Declaration of Human Rights, if the rights guaranteed in them have been violated. As there is no explicit mechanism for enforcement of the rights recognised in the general international law of human rights, including the Universal Declaration of Human Rights, other states could bring the matter to the attention of the UN Security Council or the Human Rights Council. The Universal Periodic Review mechanism of the Human Rights Council mechanism is a means of holding the delinquent state to account for violations of human rights guaranteed under both human rights treaties and the UDHR.

Under the UN system of human rights[20] any violations of human rights by a state could be referred either to a human rights treaty body, or to the Human Rights Council if the country concerned is not a party to the treaty in question. The Security Council too could take an action of its choice or refer the matters relating to the commission of

[17] See A Van Aaken, 'International Investment Law and decentralised targeted actions: An uneasy relationship', *Columbia FDI Perspectives*, No 164 (2 January 2015).

[18] V Djanic, 'Qatar Airways Lodges Treaty-based Arbitration Cases against Four Middle Eastern Countries,' *Investment Arbitration Reporter* (22 July 2020), available at www.iareporter.com/articles/qatar-airways-lodges-treaty-based-arbitration-cases-against-four-middle-eastern-states. See also 'Qatar Airways seeks $5bn in compensation' *Gulf Times* (23 July 2020) 1.

[19] See SP Subedi, *The Effectiveness of the UN Human Rights System: Reform and the Judicialization of Human Rights* (Routledge, 2017).

[20] See generally, ibid.

the crimes against humanity to the International Criminal Court. Although the Human Rights Council has no powers of enforcement, it is in a position to recommend the Security Council to take non-forcible measures against the state found to have violated human rights, or recommend that the matters concerning the crimes against humanity be referred to the International Criminal Court.

The UN system of human rights does not envisage the application of unilateral sanctions by individual states or a group of states against a target state for alleged violations of human rights. Only if neither the Security Council nor the Human Rights Council is able to take or recommend any measures can unilateral sanctions be taken against the delinquent state, provided that the decision as to whether violation of human rights has taken place is based on the reports of independent human rights institutions such as the UN special rapporteurs for human rights, or the independent commissions of enquiry established by the UN Security Council, or the Human Rights Council or the Office of the UN High Commissioner for Human Rights.[21] This is because, by violating human rights, the state in question would have committed an internationally wrongful act against all states. The states members of the UN have agreed, individually and collectively, to protect human rights globally. Thus, any human rights violation becomes a matter of global concern and an internationally wrongful act against all states, giving rise to state responsibility and the right to take countermeasures or impose sanctions under narrowly defined conditions (outlined above) against the delinquent state. But this does not mean that states are entitled to act as judge and jury, decide who has violated human rights and impose unilateral sanctions on those they find to be at fault. They have to follow the norms and the procedures stipulated in the Charter of the UN, human rights treaties and the resolutions of the General Assembly and the Human Rights Council.

Importantly, however, the states taking unilateral sanctions are under an obligation themselves to ensure that their measures do not result in the violation of the human rights of the people in their target state. If their sanctions result in the violation of human rights, then the states employing countermeasures or unilateral sanctions will themselves have committed an internationally wrongful act, giving rise to their own state responsibility and the right of the target state to take its own retaliatory countermeasures or sanctions. Therefore, a balancing act between the right of states imposing sanctions and the rights of the people in the target state is needed when invoking the right to protect human rights globally to justify unilateral sanctions.

States have a collective as well as an individual obligation to protect the human rights of anybody anywhere under the Charter of the UN, the Universal Declaration of Human Rights of 1948, and the World Outcome Document of 2005 of the UN General Assembly, and other international human rights instruments. Consequently, the notion of human rights has been recognised as an integral part of international

[21] This indeed was the case for the targeted EU sanctions against the Maduro Regime of Venezuela. A UN report on human rights in Venezuela, published in July 2019, had described the appalling scale of violations, from extrajudicial killings to grave disregard of fundamental rights in the country. For these reasons the UK was also in support of the proposal for the referral of the situation in Venezuela to the International Criminal Court. See 'UK welcomes new sanctions against Maduro regime', Press Release of the British Foreign & Commonwealth Office (27 September 201910, available at www.gov.uk/government/news/uk-welcomes-new-sanctions-against-maduro-regime.

law, determining that the way citizens within a given state are being treated by the government of that state does not remain an exclusively domestic matter, but is a matter of international regulation and concern. The surrender of certain sovereign rights is an inevitable side effect of UN membership. Membership of the UN involves accepting the exception to the principle of non-interference in the internal affairs of States contained in Article 2(7) of the UN Charter, in favour of human rights.[22] For instance, the Vienna World Conference on Human Rights of 1993 unequivocally states that 'the promotion and protection of all human rights and fundamental freedoms … is a *legitimate concern* of the international community' (emphasis added).[23]

States can discharge their collective and individual obligation to protect human rights anywhere and anytime by exercising their sovereign rights and take measures which could fall into the category of 'retorsions' or 'smart' or targeted sanctions of limited scope against foreign governments, individuals, political leaders and those associated with power, in cases of violations of human rights. However, any unilateral sanctions more comprehensive than the 'smart' or targeted sanctions of limited scope, taken in response to alleged violations of human rights, would be difficult to justify because such measures themselves may result in the violation of human rights of the people in the target state and violation of other substantive and procedural requirements for unilateral sanctions outlined above. Therefore, except for retorsions or 'smart' or targeted sanctions of limited scope, the decision to impose unilateral sanctions of more comprehensive nature for violations of human rights should be taken only when authorised by the UN or in compliance with the substantive and procedural requirements stipulated in international law.

States members of the UN have created various UN human rights mechanisms and human rights treaty bodies to be employed in response to human rights violations. Having created such mechanisms and having transferred the powers to respond to human rights violations to the UN Charter-based bodies such as the Human Rights Council and human rights treaty bodies, individual states should not undermine these bodies by taking their own actions, including imposing unilateral sanctions on states for alleged violations of human rights. If the UN human rights bodies or other treaty bodies are not effective in protecting human rights, they need to be strengthened by further enabling and empowering them.[24] International rule of law is promoted by strengthening the existing mechanisms and the discipline in the conduct of international relations.

It should be borne in mind that most of the international interventions invoking the principle of the Responsibility to Protect (commonly known as 'R2P') ostensibly to protect human rights in conflict-ridden countries have been a disaster, causing more

[22] Art 2(7) of the UN Charter 'Nothing contained in the present Charter shall authorize the United Nations to intervene in matters which are essentially within the domestic jurisdiction of any state or shall require the Members to submit such matters to settlement under the present Charter; but this principle shall not prejudice the application of enforcement measures under Chapter VII'.

[23] Declaration and Programme of Action, World Conference on Human Rights, A/CONF/157/24, para 4.

[24] See generally on the powers and functions of various UN human rights mechanisms, including the Human Rights Council, and the treaty bodies, and a set of proposals to reform these UN human rights mechanisms: Subedi, *The Effectiveness of the UN Human Rights System* (2017) ch VIII.

harm than good; the international intervention in Libya is an example.[25] Likewise, no unilateral sanctions have averted an impending human rights crisis or led to the change in government in a country ruled by autocratic regimes or reduced the suffering of the ordinary people in the country concerned. As demonstrated in many of the chapters in this study, most unilateral sanctions have actually exacerbated human rights violations in the target countries. The real victims of such measures become the ordinary citizens of the targeted country, who already suffer from the oppression of the authoritarian regime in the country. The sanctions victimise theses citizens all over again. Therefore, the need is to bring clarity to the law and strengthen the UN human rights bodies to tackle human rights violations rather than seek to address the situation by resorting to instruments of dubious character such as unilateral sanctions.

V. The Way Forward

The state or group of states imposing unilateral sanctions against another state are presupposing a prior determination that the alleged act in question was illegal. But if that presupposition turns out to be wrong, the targeting states are risking committing an international wrongful act themselves against the target state, and are risking undermining the integrity of the international legal order founded on the various cardinal principles of international law such as the sovereign equality of states, the right to economic self-determination or economic sovereignty of states, the principle of non-intervention and peaceful resolution of disputes between States. Therefore, the states imposing such sanctions should not be the ones determining whether the target state has committed an internationally wrongful act.

Since an unlawful unilateral sanction would undermine the rules-based international legal order, the time has come to bring some order and discipline to this area of state activity. The first option would be to conclude an international treaty under the auspices of the UN to regulate unilateral sanctions which could include provisions for judicial settlement of disputes arising out of the use of unilateral sanctions. Such a treaty could provide for a dispute settlement mechanism with compulsory jurisdiction, or empower some existing dispute settlement mechanisms such as the ICJ, or the Dispute Settlement Body of the WTO, and include provisions for a summary or speedy procedure needed to resolve disputes related to unilateral sanctions. The second option would be to require states to resort to a speedy international arbitration on matters associated with the use of unilateral sanctions.

The third option would be to empower political bodies such as the UN Human Rights Council to authorise the imposition of sanctions against those states that violate human rights. The fourth option would be to require states that have resorted to or feel the need to resort to unilateral sanctions to refer the matter either to the Human Rights Council or to the Security Council of the UN which could then establish a committee

[25] See H Teimouri and SP Subedi, 'Responsibility to Protect and the International Military Intervention in Libya in International Law: What Went Wrong and What Lessons could be Learnt from It?' (2018) 23 *Journal of Conflict & Security Law* 1.

to entertain the cases for imposition of sanctions in a speedy manner. Although the Human Rights Council has no powers of enforcement, there is nothing to prevent it from recommending to the Security Council to take non-forcible measures against the state found to have violated human rights. Both the Security Council and the Human Rights Council could agree a formal mechanism whereby the latter could recommend to the former that it imposes sanctions on states that have violated human rights.

However, when speaking of mechanisms for a legal remedy against any unlawful unilateral sanctions, or for resolutions of disputes between states on issues that give or may give rise to unilateral sanctions, the law on unilateral sanctions, and particularly the limitations of such sanctions, have to be made clear. In the absence of such codification, the instrument of unilateral sanctions will remain open to abuse. Time has come for the UN General Assembly to adopt a Declaration on the nature and scope of unilateral sanctions with a view eventually to concluding a treaty on the subject matter, or with a view of the ILC to taking up this topic for study to come up with a more elaborate set of draft Articles, or the draft of an international convention, to fill the gap in the law or to bring clarity to the law to regulate such an important area of state activity. Offering to contribute to the debate on this topic, a draft resolution to be adopted by the UN General Assembly on the subject matter is presented in Appendix 1 below. The content of the draft resolution is based on the current rules of international treaty law and customary international law on unilateral sanctions, as examined in the various chapters of this study.

Adopting a resolution or a declaration alone would not suffice to bring discipline to this area of state activity. Therefore, the Security Council of the UN should establish a committee to whom all states imposing unilateral sanctions against other states should be required to report. The committee should have the powers to examine the human rights implications of the sanctions employed, as well as the implications of the sanctions for the freedom of trade, navigation and aviation and environmental protection. Furthermore, the committee should be able to track the impact of the sanctions and should report back to the Security Council.

In the absence of codification or progressive development of the law pertaining to unilateral sanctions, this area of the law will remain unruly and will continue to undermine the integrity of the rules-based international order. As observed by Ruys,

> The international legal framework governing recourse to sanctions – however that term is understood – will nonetheless remain fundamentally incomplete as long as no greater clarity is shed on this outstanding issue, leaving the recourse to economic sanctions at least partly to the mercy of political considerations and power games.[26]

Tomuschat is also of the view that 'the international community would make a great step forward if it succeeded in bringing unilateral responses by States to encroachments upon their rights under stricter discipline'.[27] It is hoped that this study serves as a scholarly endeavour to this effect and the draft Declaration on the Rules of International Law on Unilateral Sanctions by the UN General Assembly appended to this volume provides guidance in this direction.

[26] Ruys, 'Sanctions, retorsions and countermeasures' (2017) 50.

[27] C Tomuschat, 'Are Counter-Measures Subject to Prior Recourse to Dispute Settlement Procedures (1994) 5 *European Journal of International Law* 77, 78.

APPENDIX

Draft Declaration on the Rules of International Law on Unilateral Sanctions

The General Assembly,

Recalling,

The principles of the Charter of the United Nations, including the sovereign equality of states, prohibition on the use of force, non-interference in the internal affairs of other states and the obligation of states to settle their disputes by peaceful means;

Resolution 2131 (XX) entitled Declaration on the Inadmissibility of Intervention in the Domestic Affairs of States and the Protection of their Independence and Sovereignty, which was adopted by the General Assembly a vote of 109 votes to none;

The Declaration on Principles of International Law concerning Friendly Relations and Co-operation among States in accordance with the Charter of the United Nations adopted by the General Assembly on 24 October 1970 (resolution 26/25 (XXV)), during a commemorative session to celebrate the twenty-fifth anniversary of the United Nations, which has widely been regarded as an authoritative interpretation of the Charter of the United Nations;

The relevant principles and provisions contained in the Charter of Economic Rights and Duties of States, proclaimed by the General Assembly in its resolution 3281 (XXIX) of 12 December 1974, in particular Article 32 thereof;

The call of the World Conference on Human Rights, held in Vienna from 14 to 25 June 1993, which urged states to refrain from any unilateral measure not in accordance with international law;

Resolution 37/21 on Human Rights and Unilateral Coercive Measures adopted by the Human Rights Council on 23 March 2018;

International treaties concerning the protection of human rights;

Various conventions concerning the freedom of trade and commerce, transit, navigation and aviation of states;

The Draft Articles on Responsibility of States for Internationally Wrongful Acts of 2001, recommended by the International Law Commission; and

The relevant rules of customary international law that have come into existence through state practice,

Declares that:

(1) Unilateral sanctions are measures of exercising pressures short of the threat or use of military force directed against a target state or entity, which are taken by an individual state or a group of states, and which are not authorised by the UN, and which seek to limit or deprive altogether the freedom that other states enjoy. Such measures include economic and financial sanctions, asset freezes, trade sanctions, commodity interdictions, and restrictions on banking and transfer of funds, the freedom of navigation, aviation and transit and on the right to communications.

(2) States must refrain in their international relations from using or encouraging the use of unilateral sanctions to coerce another state in order to obtain from it the subordination of the exercise of its sovereign rights and to secure from it advantages of any kind.

(3) The act of adopting, maintaining or implementing unilateral sanctions not in accordance with international law, including the provisions in the Charter of the UN and the principles of human rights and humanitarian law, constitute an internationally wrongful act giving rise to State responsibility.

(4) Unilateral sanctions must be regarded as exceptional measures to be taken in response to an extraordinary situation when no other alternative measures are available or adequate to address the situation.

(5) When adopting national legislation or measures aimed at extending their effects to nationals or entities of third countries, with the purpose of dissuading them from entertaining lawful commercial or other relations with the target country or its citizens, states have an obligation to ensure that such extraterritorial reach of the measures do not unduly harm the third states and undermine their economy and their freedom of action and do not have detrimental impact on their citizens.

(6) Unilateral sanctions that undermine the sovereignty of third states are not permissible under international law.

(7) National legislations concerning unilateral sanctions that affect the rights of the people in third countries are contrary to international law.

(8) Third states should not be required to recognise the extraterritorial nature of unilateral sanctions nor to apply them, since such measures run counter to the fundamental principles of international law, including human rights norms, and other rules of customary international law.

(9) The state imposing unilateral sanctions must specify what exact obligations under international law were violated by the targeted state and with what obligations that state is required to comply.

(10) Unilateral sanctions must be accompanied by an offer to negotiate, and they should not be taken before the responsible or targeted state is given a notice of claim and a reasonable opportunity to present a response.

(11) The injured state which decides to take unilateral sanctions must notify the target state of the decision to take such measures. In case of urgency, states can take provisional measures to preserve their rights within the limits of international law.

(12) Unilateral sanctions must be preceded by a demand by the injured state that the responsible state comply with its obligations under international law.

(13) Unilateral sanctions may be taken only when redress by other means has been exhausted or is unavailable, and the target state has unduly refused reparation against its internationally wrongful act or compliance with its international obligations.
(14) Unilateral sanctions must be aimed at inducing the target state's compliance of its international obligations, and at obtaining cessation and a satisfactory reparation for a wrongful act.
(15) The international law rules on countermeasures developed by the International Law Commission in 2001 in its Draft Articles on State Responsibility apply also to unilateral sanctions.
(16) Unilateral sanctions taken must be proportionate to the injury suffered from the internationally wrongful act committed by the state concerned.
(17) Unilateral sanctions should be reversible and should not be for punitive purposes.
(18) Unilateral sanctions must be terminated when the alleged internationally wrongful act has ceased to exist.
(19) Unilateral sanctions must not be imposed in breach of the peremptory norms of international law and must not result in the violation of human rights and humanitarian law principles.
(20) Any serious violations of human rights by a state should be referred either to a human rights treaty body or to the UN Human Rights Council or to the UN Security Council.
(21) States that are not themselves injured by the internationally wrongful act of another state are not entitled to impose unilateral sanctions.
(22) Unilateral sanctions must not be taken in such a way as to impair diplomatic or consular inviolability.
(23) Unilateral sanctions should not be taken when there are treaty means between the targeting and target states for the peaceful settlement of a dispute on the subject matter.
(24) Unilateral sanctions should not affect any dispute settlement procedure which is in force between the two states and applicable to the dispute.
(25) If there is an international dispute resolution mechanism available for the settlement of disputes between the targeting and targeted states, then that mechanism should be resorted to over the imposition of unilateral sanctions.
(26) When there is a provision, or the possibility, to request provisional measures from an international dispute settlement body, that should be availed before imposing unilateral sanctions.
(27) Unilateral sanctions must be suspended if the dispute is submitted in good faith to a court or tribunal with the authority to make decisions binding on the parties.
(28) The state affected by unlawful unilateral sanctions is entitled to counteract with reciprocal and non-reciprocal measures within the limits of international law.
(29) States which take unilateral sanctions against another state for allegedly committing an internationally wrongful act should inform the UN Security Council of the measures taken and the reasons for it.
(30) Unilateral sanctions should be suspended if the matter has been addressed by the UN Security Council or another competent international or regional organisation of states.

Calls upon Member States to refrain from promulgating and applying laws and measures that contravene the substantive principles and procedural rules of international law on the use of unilateral sanctions included in this Declaration.

Requests the Security Council to require all states imposing unilateral sanctions against other states to report to the Council and establish a new Unilateral Sanctions Committee with the powers to examine the human rights implications of such sanctions as well as the implications for the freedom of trade, navigation and aviation and report to the Council.

INDEX

www.ingramcontent.com/pod-product-compliance
Ingram Content Group UK Ltd.
Pitfield, Milton Keynes, MK11 3LW, UK
UKHW020233290926
15470UKWH00002B/524

9 781509 948383